Java SOA Cookbook

Java SOA Cookbook

Eben Hewitt

O'REILLY®

Beijing • Cambridge • Farnham • Köln • Sebastopol • Tokyo

Java SOA Cookbook
by Eben Hewitt

Printed in the United States of America.

Published by O'Reilly Media, Inc., 1005 Gravenstein Highway North, Sebastopol, CA 95472.

O'Reilly books may be purchased for educational, business, or sales promotional use. Online editions are also available for most titles (*http://safari.oreilly.com*). For more information, contact our corporate/institutional sales department: (800) 998-9938 or *corporate@oreilly.com*.

Editor: Simon St.Laurent
Production Editor: Loranah Dimant
Copyeditor: Emily Quill
Proofreader: Loranah Dimant
Indexer: Lucie Haskins
Cover Designer: Karen Montgomery
Interior Designer: David Futato
Illustrator: Robert Romano

Printing History:
March 2009: First Edition.

ISBN: 978-0-596-52072-4

[LSI] [2011-03-18]

1300201169

Table of Contents

Part III. Business Processes

Part IV. Interoperability and Quality of Service

Preface

Overview

I have heard it said that SOAs are like snowflakes—no two are alike. That is the case because a primary purpose of a service-oriented architecture is to offer a loosely coupled architecture for enterprise integration, and the internal landscapes differ so widely from one enterprise to the next. Additionally, SOA is about designing interfaces from a business perspective, which has historically been left up to developers.

This presents certain challenges for an author attempting to illustrate implementation choices and best practices. Many books have surfaced in the last few years that cover the general idea of SOA from an architect's or manager's perspective. These offer a conceptual picture of SOA, but not an in-the-trenches view.

Books that address SOA from an architect's perspective frequently offer little more than laundry lists of important and upcoming WS-* specifications. These books, while successful in sorting out the abstract ways in which an SOA can be built, do not tell a programmer/architect what to actually type to make things work. That is, many SOA books might tell you *what* you're supposed to do, but not *how* to do it.

They might, for example, indicate that you should make a composite service. It all sounds very convincing and important. But then you get back to your desk, fire up your IDE, and realize that you don't know what to type. Some books may go further, offering a syntax overview of XML-based languages such as BPEL, but then exit stage left before telling you how to really use it. It's hard to fault these books because the very nature of SOA means that you can build it with such a wide variety of tools.

My goal with this book is to show you how to really use some of the basic building blocks of SOA: web services, orchestrations, policies, and more. It is intended to fill in the gaps for developers in the real world. But to do this, I had to get concrete. And to keep the book to a manageable length, I had to focus the spotlight on what matters most, and leave some things out.

The focus of this book is on the following:

SOAP-based web services

A SOAP web service in .NET or Java EE 5 is a component whose annotations generate an XML description of the services it offers (called a WSDL). This description is not specific to the platform your component is written in, so a client written in another language can invoke your service.

This makes SOAP-based services an important part of SOA, and much of this book is devoted to using XML and SOAP web services and the Java APIs that support them.

It can be complex to use SOAP initially (as opposed to something like POX over HTTP), which gives SOAP its detractors. Vendors implement the SOAP standards for a variety of decorating features (including reliability, security, location transparency, and so forth); there's a lot of value in getting these features in a standard, interoperable way.

And while you may recall a number of web services books published some years ago, things have changed considerably. Creating SOAP web services in Java SE 6 and EE 5 is an entirely different animal. This book covers the very latest material, and doesn't stop at creating web services. It shows you how to bring them together in a real-world way.

RESTful web services

REST (REpresentational State Transfer) is a way of building on the architecture of the World Wide Web that is opposed to SOAP, at least in the popular mind. We examine this argument in the REST chapter, and I then offer fairly complete coverage of how to create RESTful services in a variety of ways, including using the new JAX-RS specification, JSR 311 (the Java API for RESTful web services). I also cover how to use popular APIs that have become de facto standards for REST, such as the Atom Publishing Protocol.

Java EE 5

While I show examples of consuming web services from languages other than Java, the overwhelming bias is toward implementing SOA with Java. The reason for that is simple: my background and area of expertise are in Java.

I do not address how to write web services with anything earlier than Java EE 5 and Java SE 6, as there are a number of books that cover how to do that. There have been considerable changes in web services in the latest version of Java. Annotations, new APIs, and burgeoning implementations of various WS-* specifications mean real changes for web services in just the last year or so. This book sticks with the latest stuff.

SOA

This cookbook is unusual among O'Reilly cookbooks in one respect: the solutions are not always code examples because SOA problems are not always code problems. The predominant focus of the book is how to implement Java EE 5 web services and work with related technologies such as BPEL orchestrations and WS-* specifications. The chapters covering these topics offer concrete, real-world code examples that indicate what to type to make something work. In that respect, this book is like other O'Reilly cookbooks. But, where possible, the book also offers solutions to the "people problems" of SOA, such as organization and ROI. These chapters do not involve code solutions because they are not code problems. I have tried to restrict these topics to those that have a clear solution, recommendation, or best practice in order to honor the general cookbook format. I have not always succeeded, and many such topics are hotly debated. Beyond that, I must leave such items to the many competent books in the category of general SOA. If you want a really good book on such SOA matters, I recommend *SOA in Practice* by Nicolai M. Josuttis (O'Reilly) (*http://www.oreilly.com/catalog/9780596529550*).

Glassfish and WebLogic
: While there are a number of excellent application servers that provide web service functionality, Glassfish is the first project to support Java SE 6 and fully implement the new Java web services standards in an interoperable way. There is no leftover disposition toward RPC, as remains in some vendors. While many examples have been tested and are shown in other containers, such as Oracle's WebLogic 10gR3 or Axis 2, Glassfish v2 is the default for these examples.

  I really tried to focus on portability, and you should be able to make these examples work in your engine without much trouble.

BPEL orchestrations
: The WS-BPEL standard is an important development in recent years as companies look for ways to organize, streamline, and represent their business processes in ways that are available to developers, systems analysts, and architects. BPEL allows you to create composite services by sewing multiple web services together in a flow, presenting a single view of the orchestration to the world. Because you can combine multiple web services in a very loosely coupled manner, orchestrations also help promote reuse of your services.

  BPEL is supported by a few open source implementations, such as Apache ODE, as well as a variety of commercial products; each flavor is examined here.

Enterprise Service Bus (ESB)
: The ESB is not strictly necessary for SOA, but it frequently is an important part of mature SOAs. An ESB acts as a mediator, router, and layer of indirection between service integration points. Early EAI (Enterprise Application Integration) efforts soon found themselves laden with many point-to-point integrations that required creating a specific interface for each connected node's route to any other node. The ESB reduces such complexity. Instead of connecting every service to every other service, you can just connect them to the ESB. In this way, the ESB serves the same function as any computer bus, and is responsible for mediation and routing messages to appropriate services.

Unlike most other topics in the book, there is no standard for ESB; as a consequence, vendors implement them very differently. The terminology is not always the same (what one vendor calls a pipeline, another might refer to as a channel, though the concepts are similar). The features in some cases overlap with other elements of an SOA suite of tools. For example, some ESBs do light repository work, or maintain an internal rules engine.

In 2005, Sun began promoting the Java Business Integration (JBI) specification, and ultimately created a reference implementation in OpenESB. Many vendors, however, view this as a Java-centric, bloated spec. Moreover, a Sun specification doesn't take advantage of whatever vendor tools might already exist. As a result, JBI doesn't rule the SOA marketplace in any way.

This book therefore offers an overview of the ESB landscape to help you understand the features offered by a variety of popular vendors, to outline the role that ESBs play within SOA, and to help you make an informed decision about what to look for in a vendor.

Intended Audience

This book is intended for experienced Java developers and architects. The world of web services is enormous, complex, and rapidly changing. I assume that you have a background writing, deploying, and maintaining enterprise applications in Java. You need to be familiar with Java SE 5 or 6; servlets and JSP; Enterprise Edition containers such as Glassfish, WebLogic, or Tomcat; and Internet protocols such as HTTP. You should be comfortable using Enterprise JavaBeans, and be familiar with all of the standard enterprise stuff, including JDBC, JNDI, EARs and WARs, and the basic principles and concerns of modern enterprise development. If you have used web services with earlier versions of Java, this book will be handy in learning the updated APIs. They have radically changed, and this cookbook should help you get underway quickly.

Daily Java enterprise developers will get the most out of this book. But SOA is a special kind of architecture and an organizational strategy, not a development style or methodology, so some of the recipes address architectural matters such as governance and patterns, with the expectation that it is useful for developers to understand the larger context in which their work will operate. On the other side of the coin, architects will find that the APIs and capabilities may augment their work. Finally, there are more hands-on architects today than ever before, those who are responsible for both designing and writing applications that must advance the architectural agenda of the overall enterprise. This book attempts to address these audiences. I only touch on business matters, such as SOA ROI. While such topics may seem out of place in a development book, I believe it is important for you as a developer to take a comprehensive and global view of SOA to keep your activities in line with what SOA requires not just in code, but in perspective.

It is assumed that if you are doing web services development that you have a basic understanding of XML, XML schema, and the Java APIs that deal with them. In some cases, you might have been working with a technology for years, but haven't used the latest APIs. So the chapter on XML addresses how to use the StAX APIs for working with XML streams, but it doesn't cover SAX and DOM. It also includes a variety of tools that can aid in SOA development. DTD is left out entirely in preference of Schema.

To maintain a solutions-based focus, I left out a lot of basic web services overview material and assumed that you are an SOA implementer-to-be and therefore have at least heard of SOAP and WSDL. Introductory sections within different chapters offer a good overview of each topic and situate them within the ongoing debates regarding SOA implementations. Then we'll quickly get down to business.

I have tried to balance the book so that you have everything you need, and nothing you don't. It's impossible to please everyone, of course, but I hope the balance works for you.

Because SOA outlines a way for getting different platforms to interoperate, there are recipes dealing with languages other than Java, such as Ruby, Python, and .NET. It is not required that you have a background in these languages, as the recipes are fairly simple and limited, shown only to express how you can get different platforms to communicate.

What This Book Covers

While Java is known for its portability, and many web services artifacts are portable, vendors frequently offer considerable extras in an attempt to make things more convenient for you (or lock you in, depending on your level of cynicism). Given the fact that we're covering such a wide array of material already, it is simply not possible to cover the minor changes in how to do everything on specific platforms. Given products such as WebLogic, Tomcat, WebSphere, Glassfish, ServiceMix, CXF, Mule, Active Endpoints, OpenESB, and dozens of other vendor offerings that address different aspects of SOA, there is problem of multiplication in a book such as this one. So I've chosen a middle-of-the-road stance for the most part, and kept mostly focused on what tools will be available to the most people. Here's the lineup:

Part I, SOA Fundamentals

Chapter 1, *Introduction to SOA*
: This chapter defines relevant terms and introduces architectural topics that will guide the growth of your SOA. The items covered in this chapter are not exhaustive, nor are they intended to be followed in a specific order; it is an orientation to SOA concepts.

Chapter 2, *XML Schema and the SOA Data Model*
: Because SOA and web services rely so heavily on XML, this chapter covers how to use XML, XPath, and Schema in ways that specifically support your service-oriented effort. Some useful tools are highlighted, as well as how to use JAXB to convert between Java and XML. We'll cover key SOA topics such as canonical data models and schema-based validation.

Chapter 3, *Working with XML and Java*
: Whereas Chapter 2 focuses largely on XML schema, design, and validation topics, this chapter extends the discussion of Java and XML into document instance processing. It addresses the new StAX API, JAXB, and XML catalogs.

Part II, Web Services

Chapter 4, *Getting Started*
: As Java programmers, we're used to a variety of convenience methods and classes; this chapter is a bit of a "convenience chapter." That is, you'll just set up shop with some different containers so that you are ready to execute clients and services in a few different popular environments. You'll do a "Hello World" service, and I'll introduce WSDL, discuss service clients, and show you tools for monitoring and debugging your services during development. Then we can move on to more specific API work in the coming chapters.

Chapter 5, *Web Services with SAAJ*
: The SOAP with Attachments API for Java (SAAJ) is introduced in this chapter, which deals largely with how to build SOAP messages programmatically. SAAJ is a low-level API that works directly with the XML in your services and clients.

Chapter 6, *Creating Web Service Applications with JAX-WS*
: The Java API for XML Web Services (JAX-WS) builds on the older JAX-RPC API to make creating and invoking web services much easier than it is with SAAJ. This chapter covers how to do many of the same kinds of things you do with SAAJ, but in a slimmer, more abstract manner. But beware: if you're used to the JAX-RPC API, things have changed considerably.

Chapter 7, *Providing SOAP-Based Web Services*
: Now that we've seen how to consume SOAP-based web services, this chapter covers how to provide them with a variety of advanced features, including binary content, headers, and more.

Chapter 8, *RESTful Web Services*
: REpresentational State Transfer, popularly known as REST, does not use SOAP. As a consequence, you don't use the SAAJ or JAX-WS APIs to work with a REST-based SOA. This chapter covers REST, discusses why it's popular, and explores how to create meaningful web services that take advantage of the native protocols of the Web, without some of the overhead that SOAP-based services can create.

Part III, Business Processes

Chapter 9, *Service Orchestrations with BPEL*
: This chapter introduces using the WS-BPEL (Business Process Execution Language) 2.0 standard to create business processes or workflows. BPEL allows you to orchestrate invocations of multiple web services and perform a variety of powerful activities on the inputs and outputs, including XSL transformations and other common elements of structured programming.

Chapter 10, *Advanced Orchestrations with BPEL*
: BPEL is a large and complicated beast, and this chapter dives into some of the more advanced aspects of using orchestrations, including dealing with faults, parallel activities, delays, and correlations.

Chapter 11, *SOA Governance*
: Your SOA needs some measurement, some standards, and some tools in place to watch over it. Without these, you could spend considerable time and effort inadvertently creating a monstrous mash of rogue and duplicate services and unknown clients. Add to the mix the potential for poor documentation, low visibility, and inconsistency, and you've got a very expensive art project on your hands. SOA governance, an extension of IT governance, can provide some structure, visibility, consistency, and even policy enforcement to your SOA.

Part IV, Interoperability and Quality of Service

Chapter 12, *Web Service Interoperability*
: Integration has been a thorn in the side of architects and developers for decades, and web services valiantly aim to overcome many of the issues surrounding it. And while very simple web services may readily interoperate out of the box, in the real world things can be trickier. This chapter introduces standard ways to enhance the ability of your web services to interoperate with services and clients on other platforms. The WS-Addressing specification is examined, along with implementing clients in a variety of languages, such as Ruby and .NET. You'll also find tips and tricks for working around gray areas in the specifications.

Chapter 13, *Quality of Service*
: This chapter examines concrete, standard ways that SOAP-based services can improve their reliability, with specifications such as WS-ReliableMessaging.

Chapter 14, *Enterprise Service Bus*
: Here we step away from the recipe format to provide an overview of the enterprise service bus (ESB), which frequently serves as the backbone of an agile SOA. Because ESBs are typically implemented as a collection of patterns and there is no standard specification for what an ESB is, I offer an overview of some of the leading ESBs. Despite the fact that they generally serve as message mediators and provide routing, security, and rules, they all work very differently. There is no single, clear market leader in this area, but we'll take a look at some of the most popular, including the

Oracle Service Bus, TIBCO's ActiveMatrix ESB, OpenESB, and Apache ServiceMix.

Unfortunately, there wasn't time to cover more topics relevant to SOA, such as security with WS-Security. Although related topics such as authentication are addressed in a few recipes, web services security is not given a full treatment here.

How to Read This Book

This is a cookbook, which means that (for the most part) topics are presented in a consistent problem/solution format, each succinctly stated. As necessary, solutions are elaborated upon within a discussion section. You could read the book cover to cover, though you probably won't use it that way. Generally, the chapters build on the knowledge gained in the previous chapters, but it is also structured as a useful reference that you can turn to during the different stages of building out your SOA, or use as a jumping-off point for your work.

Using Code Examples

This book is here to help you get your job done. In general, you may use the code in this book in your programs and documentation. You do not need to contact us for permission unless you're reproducing a significant portion of the code. For example, writing a program that uses several chunks of code from this book does not require permission. Selling or distributing a CD-ROM of examples from O'Reilly books does require permission. Answering a question by citing this book and quoting example code does not require permission. Incorporating a significant amount of example code from this book into your product's documentation does require permission.

We appreciate, but do not require, attribution. An attribution usually includes the title, author, publisher, and ISBN. For example: "*Java SOA Cookbook*, by Eben Hewitt. Copyright 2009 Eben Hewitt, 978-0-596-52072-4."

If you feel your use of code examples falls outside fair use or the permission given above, feel free to contact us at *permissions@oreilly.com*.

The examples are intended to be as self-contained as much as is reasonable. I find it frustrating when I read a computer book that contains small snippets of toy code with lots of //... throughout where stuff you need to know happens, or admonishments to refer to the downloadable code elsewhere that leaves out any pertinent code from the discussion.

There is arguably nothing that takes as much raw code as web services. Even a simple WSDL can span multiple pages. Add to that any schemas it references and you've got 10 or 20 pages of raw code on your hands before you even start talking, most of which doesn't apply to the topic at hand. That is hard to read in a book. I have tried to balance this appropriately so that you have what you need when you need it.

It's also tough when every example makes such liberal use of the author's environment scripts and utilities that a newcomer can't distinguish the API ostensibly being illustrated from the author's own convenience classes. That makes it difficult to follow and understand. Such examples might make life easier for the author, but not for the reader. So I try not to do that.

Another way of approaching code examples is the single book-length "case study" that all examples refer back to. Some readers like these, but I find that the story of the case study begins inevitably to take over after a certain point, and it contorts the examples trying to fit every item into an artificial environment. Some systems just won't need to pass basic authentication data in headers; why strain your example or add reams of useless storyline to your fictional case study? This book takes a simpler approach.

For examples to be effective, I think that they must generally be complete, self-contained, and as easy as possible to replicate in the reader's own environment. Finally, they must be free of "toy code" and reflect real-world usage. These goals are admittedly hard to achieve when covering a topic with so many moving parts. Building web services is all about layers of indirection, which means even a simple example can involve a lot of different files and setup. As you can see, I've thought a lot about how to achieve all of these goals for the solutions outlined here, and I hope I've found a good working balance.

You can find the code examples at *http://examples.oreilly.com/9780596520724*.

Hang in There!

Finally, don't be discouraged. This stuff is hard. Really hard. The existing specs are sprawling, and loads of new specs are being cranked out faster than the industry can keep up. Vendors are behind, and developers are further behind them. It's an incredibly complex undertaking. There is also a lot of hype out there around SOA, which doesn't make it any easier to sort out. In such a setting, it can be tough to figure out what's real, what's fried air, and what's real but still two years away.

Happily, recent advances in the Java APIs have made doing web services much easier than it has been in the past. But as the world gets used to what's out there and gains an appetite for more sophisticated software, web services alone won't be enough. They have to orbit in a solar system with BPEL orchestrations, brokered ESBs, Business Activity Monitoring tools, SCA, and all manners of new layers. But SOA is real, and this stuff works. While the ideas on which SOA is based have their roots in technologies that are decades old, SOA truly represents a shift in how enterprises can do business.

Thank you very much for picking up this book. I hope it gives you some of the answers you need to make your stuff work. It is impossible to cover everything that an SOA practitioner needs in a single book, but I've done my best to hit the big targets and give you a solid foundation on which to build. I really hope you enjoy it.

Conventions Used in This Book

The following typographical conventions are used in this book:

Italic
: Indicates new terms, URLs, email addresses, filenames, and file extensions.

`Constant width`
: Used for program listings, as well as within paragraphs to refer to program elements such as variable or function names, databases, data types, environment variables, statements, and keywords.

`Constant width bold`
: Used for emphasis in code listings.

This icon signifies a tip, suggestion, or general note.

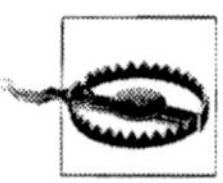

This icon indicates a warning or caution.

Safari® Books Online

When you see a Safari® Books Online icon on the cover of your favorite technology book, that means the book is available online through the O'Reilly Network Safari Bookshelf.

Safari offers a solution that's better than e-books. It's a virtual library that lets you easily search thousands of top tech books, cut and paste code samples, download chapters, and find quick answers when you need the most accurate, current information. Try it for free at *http://mysafaribooksonline.com*.

How to Contact Us

Please address comments and questions concerning this book to the publisher:

O'Reilly Media, Inc.
1005 Gravenstein Highway North
Sebastopol, CA 95472
800-998-9938 (in the United States or Canada)
707-829-0515 (international or local)
707-829-0104 (fax)

We have a web page for this book, where we list errata, examples, and any additional information. You can access this page at:

http://www.oreilly.com/catalog/9780596520724

To comment or ask technical questions about this book, send email to:

bookquestions@oreilly.com

For more information about our books, conferences, Resource Centers, and the O'Reilly Network, see our website at:

http://www.oreilly.com

Dedication

This book is dedicated to all of my friends and colleagues at DTC, especially the Architecture and Programming groups. Barney Marispini, Bob LaChapelle, Bob Lemm, Brian Lee, Brian Mericle, Chris Servis, Deryl Heitman, John O'Brien, Kevin Williams, Mike Moore, Phillip Rower, Scott Ramsey, Steve Miller, Tom Schaeffer—this is for you. Thank you for being such a terrific team to work with, and for always pushing each other to be the best. It is a luxury to work with such a fantastic, dedicated set of people.

Acknowledgments

Special thanks go to Steve Miller, Deryl Heitman, John O'Brien, and Rich Kuipers for being so unbelievably supportive of this project. This book would not exist without your unmitigated generosity, understanding, patience, and raw vision. Thank you for believing so strongly in this project. I'm so grateful to work for the best company in the world.

Thank you to my tech reviewers, Jason Brittain and Nicolai Josuttis. You caught me in occasional flights of fancy and helped me to clarify important aspects of the topics.

Big thanks go to Barney Marispini, who painstakingly read complete early drafts, offered numerous helpful corrections and input, and really improved the quality of the book.

Thank you to Simon St.Laurent, with whom it has been a consummate pleasure to work, for his editorial guidance on this project. A huge thanks is due to my production editor, Loranah Dimant, my indexer, Lucie Haskins, and to all of the staff at O'Reilly, for their professionalism, dedication, and attention to detail. It's been a real pleasure to work with you all.

Thank you to Alison Brown, for being perfect. This, as with so many things in my happy life, could not have happened without you.

PART I

SOA Fundamentals

CHAPTER 1

Introduction to SOA

1.0 Introduction

This chapter briefly introduces the landscape of service-oriented architecture (SOA) and illustrates some organizational challenges that SOA can precipitate. While you are likely familiar with a variety of SOA definitions, the solutions outlined in this book—and indeed, the construction of the book itself—are in some part predicated on a specific understanding of how we define the various constituent parts of SOA.

Heterogeneity is a fact of life in the modern IT landscape. There are hundreds of programming languages in the world, all used to write applications that populate the modern enterprise. Sometimes you need these applications to talk to each other, which can become a tricky proposition very quickly.

Aging systems written in languages with waning platform support must work in conjunction with applications written in disparate modern languages. These systems may have many apparent warts and wrinkles, and it may be tempting to simply rip out the systems and replace them. This can be prohibitively expensive, however, and rarely goes as smoothly as originally envisioned. It can also make you very vulnerable from an operational standpoint. These applications have stood the test of time. They have been vetted in the battlefield of daily use. And while we would like for our systems to look as neat and tidy as possible, many times what naive developers see as code sprawl is simply the reality of handling the many twists and turns and exceptional cases that the real world demands our applications account for.

There certainly is plenty of bad code in the world that isn't worth saving. Many legacy applications were written with principles in mind that have since changed dramatically. Sometimes well-intentioned programs are written in such a snaky way that it can be very difficult to reuse them in other applications. But for those legacy applications that are mission-critical, that serve as the backbone of an organization, there is a way to modernize, reuse, and enhance their power.

By wrapping legacy systems with web services that operate within the supporting framework of a service-oriented architecture, you buy yourself time. This extension of time comes in the form of vendor neutrality, which allows you to defer migration decisions, or simply extend the life of aging but otherwise solid software.

Mergers and acquisitions can very quickly create integration problems. Heterogeneous platforms with potentially redundant or overlapping functionality can undermine the agility, responsiveness, and service delivery capability of an organization. In the web-based world of global commerce, no opportunity remains for stop-the-world migrations, and the "Sunday at 3 a.m." cut-over opportunity is more costly than ever.

SOA represents a way to seize new business opportunities and reduce time to market by embracing, rather than denying, differences in your organization. Perhaps it is not necessary to rip out and replace these legacy applications, or throw yourself at the mercy of a vendor, signing up in desperation for their entire unified stack in the hopes that you will never again have this kind of problem. A service-oriented architecture allows you to address your integration needs in an evolutionary, rather than revolutionary, way.

An evolution toward services seeks to align the work of IT more closely with business goals and ensure that the enterprise is responsive to change and ready to tackle new opportunities.

The problems and solutions presented in this chapter offer some prescriptive solutions with the intention of starting you down a good road; they are subject to modification as appropriate within your environment. The scenarios are more general and subjective than you are probably used to seeing in a cookbook. Because SOA represents a kind of architecture, it is useful for developers to understand the larger business context in which the services they create will operate. In order to realize the benefits of SOA, and to code meaningful services that offer real business value, any given service implementation needs to work harmoniously with defined overarching business goals.

The recipes in this chapter do not have code-based solutions. They are presented as conceptual challenges that apply across implementations. While it is possible for a Java developer to skip this chapter altogether and jump into code with the next chapter, within an SOA it's very useful for developers to think like architects, and vice versa. In fact, depending on the size and structure of an organization, these roles are sometimes even collapsed altogether. Whether or not this is the case for your organization, it is advantageous to use the recipes in this chapter to define common terms as a foundation for the remainder of the work in this book.

1.1 Defining a Service

Problem

What is a service?

Solution

A service is a software component with the following properties:

- It is defined by an interface that may be platform-independent.
- It is available across a network.
- The operations defined in the interface carry out business functions by operating on business objects.
- Its interface and its implementation can be decorated with extensions that come into effect at runtime.

A service can mean other things as well. Sometimes the definition is broader, to include, for example, a distributed component whose interface is designed by the business. Sometimes the definition is more narrow, such as a SOAP-based web service.

Discussion

One initial difficulty in approaching SOA is that people don't always agree on what is meant by its fundamental building block, the service. Many definitions of a service refer to slippery or very abstract concepts, such as "adaptability" and "agility," that are too vague to be useful to the developer. Presumably, given the choice, no one wants to make unadaptable, leaden software that doesn't meet business needs. But the fact of the matter is that, despite best efforts, this happens all too often. Knowing that SOAs should be "adaptable" and "agile" may be laudable, but that alone doesn't help make a state change. Let's unpack these terms a bit.

Other definitions are too narrow for the real world. It is tempting, for example, to indicate that a service must be a software component that talks SOAP. But this limitation is artificial; there are many practitioners using REST who believe, quite reasonably, that they are doing services. Perhaps our definition should include something about messages being XML-based, as this is a common denominator between RESTful web services and SOAP-based services. But this is also too limiting for a general definition.

So how do you arrive at a definition that is specific enough to be useful and yet general enough to admit the wide variety of approaches that people take in the real world?

Let's examine each aspect of the service definition before proceeding.

Platform-independent interface

The work a service can do must be described with an external interface. Some architects allow that such an interface can actually be tied to a specific platform, as in the case of a Java interface describing the operations on a remote session EJB. Services can certainly be approached in this manner, and such an approach may be justified within a given business context. Dictating that consumers must use a certain platform, such as Java or .NET, to consume a service can save valuable time and money and drastically simplify your implementation.

Many SOAs operate within a company, behind a firewall, in a known environment that is relatively static. I have talked with architects in such circumstances whose entire SOA is defined on EJB. That's a very specific platform, and they think they are doing SOA, and they are smart and experienced people.

Their view is that it would introduce unwarranted developer effort, offer more complexity than benefit, and garner unnecessary runtime overhead to use SOAP and its many attendant specifications *given their business context*. So while many authors are tempted to indicate that a service must be defined in a manner that does not dictate platform, and while that sort of service is the chief topic of this book, my definition does allow for platform-specific implementations.

However, a service is generally created to address a systems integration problem, or at least has an eye toward integration issues. A WSDL is one way to describe functionality in a way that does not dictate implementation. While WSDLs may commonly use SOAP over HTTP, this is not a requirement; other protocols can be used for bindings, and the same abstract WSDL can address a variety of bindings, offering even greater flexibility.

HTTP is perhaps not the ideal transport layer for web-based services, but its simplicity and pervasiveness have made it the default choice. Consequently, there is considerable support for such service implementations.

RESTful web services use XML and native HTTP methods to define their interfaces, and this approach has many proponents who cite the complexity and "bloat" of SOAP-based services. I want to avoid this argument for now, and just indicate that REST sufficiently satisfies the condition of platform independence. It is less clear that it satisfies an emphatic interface that can operate as part of a service contract, however.

Because a service is not merely a piece of functionality, but something describable by a contract that constrains consumers, it is important that a clearly defined interface work within contract automation. Without a clear interface, service reusability opportunities shrink. Without platform independence, possible consumers go down and service components become more tightly coupled.

Of course, nothing is free, and you pay for platform independence with performance and complexity.

Available across a network

The world is filled with very useful programs whose functions can be invoked only from within the same virtual machine or within the same physical machines. These programs simply do not qualify as services. Just as in the real world, your customers have to be able to contact your business to contract for your cleaning or consulting or catering services. If you're the only one who knows your phone number, or if you don't have a phone, then there's no show. If your function is not available remotely, it is simply not a service.

Operates on business objects

My third criterion for a service is that it generally carries out business functions, and generally does so by operating on business documents. What does this mean? A calculator that adds two numbers together may not be a good candidate for a service because integers are not business objects. They can never be defined in a particular way for your organization.

A "business object" means an instance of an entity in your business domain, such as a Customer, a Product, an Invoice, a Student, or an Application for Employment. You can decide for yourself what these will mean, as they are the entities that differentiate your business from others. Further examination of your `add` operation must question whether the idea of adding is particular to your business. It is not. Anyone in the world can add all day long, and will do so (presupposing any basic mastery of the task) in a manner identical to everyone else. Moreover, you have no opportunity for innovation in the method in which you add; you cannot conceive of and employ some custom scheme for adding within your operation's implementation to gain a competitive advantage in the market. Unless you have a very creative accounting department, you don't decide for yourself what integers and adding mean.

There is certainly a wide array of popular services publicly available that operate on *facts*. These include determining the distance from one location to another, or performing calculations such as shipping costs based on weight, or finding the location of the nearest store. While a zip code or a weight in ounces may not in themselves appear to be business objects, such services do perform a business operation that is distinguishable from something absolutely generic such as adding two numbers together.

This is just a general guideline. Consider a service that converts currency. There are many such publicly available web services, and a euro is the same for everyone, so these don't appear to be business objects. But there is always the matter of perspective. At a bank, the idea of currency might be considerably more detailed in its definition than it is at a pet food store, making it a kind of business object to the bank.

There are always exceptions to the rule. The idea here is to think in terms of services exchanging business documents, rather than accepting lists of simple values.

You probably don't need an SOA if you don't have a business of some size, or at least of some length of history. While programmers might enjoy writing a video game for their own personal use, no one builds an SOA out in the garage on Saturday afternoons. If you're talking about an SOA, you're talking about a business of some measure. And your SOA will realize its potential ROI (return on investment) if its constituent services operate at the appropriate level of granularity in order to maximize their reuse. Of course, this begs the question what is meant by "appropriate level." That will depend on the business processes that define your services, and what related processes might be able to reuse them.

I must stress that this guideline is open to a wide variety of interpretations, and is presented as a starting point so that you can make some distinctions. You want to avoid being so vague that you do not have enough to work with. Indeed, there are utility or functional services that operate in the realm of technology alone; these are described in Recipe 1.3.

Decoratable

This refers to the idea that you must be able to decorate the service operation in some way in order to provide for functional and non-functional requirements. It is this aspect that elevates the service to something meaningful with an SOA.

If you are using SOAP, a variety of WS-* specifications (such as WS-ReliableMessaging or WS-SecureConversation) add capabilities to your service that do not impact the core business functionality, but make your service adaptable for use within an SOA. The ability to add HTTP headers, for example, is one way of decorating a REST-based service implementation. EJBs make the cut because, while the mechanism is not based on WS-* standards, interceptors do allow for decoration of like functionality.

The point here is that you want to be able to provision your SOA, and by necessity its constituent services, with technical means of governance (which we will discuss later). You want to be able to include policies at runtime that augment how the service can be used. The ability to interact securely, to allow for transactional operations, and, in some cases, to accept monitoring instrumentation are non-functional requirements that bridge the gap between a theoretically pure implementation of your Invoice Processing service and the real world that involves this particular network with these external constraints that must be accounted for. Baking such items into your service can severely curtail or obliterate its possibilities for reuse, especially in federated environments. But the need to deal with them remains; when possible, move such requirements into decorators.

This requirement may guide your choice of platform or implementation. The fact that there are so many non-functional requirements that so often come into play in software components (and the fact that so many of them are recognized by WS-* specifications) is a leading reason why I have chosen to focus on SOAP-based services in this book (and in building a real-world SOA). To have such common requirements dealt with in a standard way within these specs offers a boost to interoperability and maintainability, and allows developers to focus on their business problem.

Other considerations

What else might be true of the operation if it is to qualify as a service? It seems that a service is worth all the trouble to define and create only if it will be reused. A chief aim of SOA is that its components are self-contained and do not represent overlapping functionality. Its components should provide a degree of reusability. That is, they must not be limited to a narrowly defined business context that has little or no relevance elsewhere in the enterprise. It is possible that you will write a service that does not get reused. It is possible that your business will change directions, or that a service is too poorly defined, either too granular or too broad in scope, to ever fit into another use case. Sniffing out such matters is where architects are valuable.

Some architects will add the requirement that a service must be stateless. I agree that in general it is a good idea to ensure that your service operations are stateless, but I would not require it as a defining feature of services. If they must maintain state, they can do so externally through a database or other temporary serialization mechanism. Conversational state is often best avoided if possible, but when it must be maintained within the service composition, it can be handled through a specification such as WS-SecureConversation and WS-Conversation. This is a spec that has been around for a few years now, and is implemented in containers like WebLogic 10gR3.

1.2 Defining SOA

Problem

The term "SOA" is surrounded by hype, hyperbole, and generality. You want a definition that you can work with.

Solution

You must define SOA with some modicum of care before proceeding in order to set expectations appropriately. This is made somewhat difficult given the avalanche of hype surrounding SOA in recent years. But it can be done. There are many possible definitions of SOA. Here is my offering:

> SOA is a kind of architecture that uses services as building blocks to facilitate enterprise integration and component reuse through loose coupling.

Let's unpack that a little bit, shall we?

SOA is a kind of architecture

While this is perhaps overstating the obvious, there is a small lesson here. Simply creating a set of services does not automatically render an architecture. Architecture, while it should guide the creation of services, is a diverse matter separate from the implementation of the services themselves.

In the term "SOA," "service-oriented" modifies "architecture" as an adjective. That is, an SOA describes a sort of architecture one can undertake. It is not a development mode. You cannot simply annotate an EJB to indicate that it's a web service and decide that because you now have a web service, you must have the felicitous beginnings of an SOA. If you are not very careful with your approach, you could indeed have the beginnings of a very elaborate, very expensive mess.

One point that must be made is that you cannot simply buy an SOA. You cannot expect a single vendor to hand over an SOA once your CIO writes a check. Building an SOA involves considerable analysis and integration.

SOA is built with services

This is the "service" part of "service-oriented architecture" and I rely here on my definition in Recipe 1.1. It's not an SOA if it's not an architecture, or if that architecture doesn't use the service as the common unit of measure (just as an object-oriented system uses the object or class as its common unit).

Without services, there is nothing to build on, monitor, or govern, and nothing to execute to provide your business value. But at the other extreme, one can labor long and hard, producing a perfectly lovely set of architectural diagrams with little relation to the real world. If you focus narrowly on cranking out a set of service implementations and forget the architecture—or, more likely, leave it out on purpose while dismissing the "astronaut architects" with their heads in the clouds—you will not only have no SOA, but you'll have something even worse. You will have spent considerable time and money over-engineering a solution to the wrong problem. There is actually a name for this sort of furious work: the anti-pattern known colloquially as Just a Bunch of Web Services (JaBoWS). In addition, cowboy developers operating without architectural guides can inadvertently cause the business to fall prey to another SOA anti-pattern: Rogue Service, wherein there are services operating on the network that are not part of the known, governed set of services in the catalog. So a bunch of services without architecture or governance does not an SOA make.

In my view, it is debatable whether a "service" that is wholly outside the context of an architecture is actually a service at all. It is in part the contextual role within a supporting architecture that elevates an operation to the level of a service. This status is afforded, but not directly stated, by the last criterion in my definition of a service: it can be decorated with runtime extensions that handle certain technical non-functional requirements.

SOA facilitates integration

SOA represents a way of thinking about systems integration. An SOA serves to offer increased or new business functionality or opportunities by connecting multiple systems together. In its most straightforward form, this means that you can do B2B work more quickly.

CORBA, connector architecture, EDI, and point-to-point EAI efforts over decades have all demonstrated the ability to integrate diverse systems. But such efforts can be costly and brittle. They can distract developers and IT departments from addressing their real business problems, as they work for months getting systems to talk. These solutions all define their own formats for message exchange. SOA, in general, reuses XML as a standard means of message format, allowing integration efforts to leap into action more readily.

Some CIOs, in frustration with previous EAI projects and in an honest attempt to address their problems quickly and decisively, have thrown in the towel, called up their favorite vendor, and signed up for their entire stack in an attempt to avoid the integration problem altogether. But this can be a very expensive proposition indeed and it has the drawback of tying your organization to that vendor, locking you into operating on their time tables, and you'll be able to provide only the functionality they expose.

So while integration happens, SOA attempts to address the pain points of integration efforts.

SOA facilitates reuse through loose coupling

The idea that SOA facilitates reuse through loose coupling is a key modification of the point that it simply supports enterprise integration efforts. SOA suggests two distinct ideas: it facilitates reuse in the first place, and it does so by creating loosely coupled components.

Early enterprise integration or primitive service provider efforts have not focused quite so specifically on the idea of reuse. But it is now possible, given the new standards and the employment of a generic format such as XML in message exchanges, to realize enterprise services in a sufficiently general way that services can be reused.

This reuse can come in the form of general interoperability. If two software components can interoperate, that in no way means they are loosely coupled. But loosely coupled components have a greater chance of interoperating.

One of the foundational aspects of SOA is that services are created from the ground up with the intention of having them interoperate with unforeseen or unknown components. This makes a sharp distinction from typical integration efforts, which likely target a single set of known interfaces.

While reuse can be achieved as a side effect of ensuring that your services are loosely coupled, it is not a necessary aim for every service. It is possible that you have certain services that you know have little likelihood of being reused in a composition or within an unforeseen business context. Such services may have been created as pilot projects; or it may have made sense given the circumstances to create some functionality as a service in order to tap into a larger architectural infrastructure to make it more visible, for example, through a service inventory; or to take advantage of centralized schemas; or to quickly gain runtime metrics afforded by SOA monitoring tools.

Reuse is not strictly necessary within any given service. However, an SOA entirely populated by non-reusable components is likely not an SOA at all, but rather a fancy, bloated, over-engineered collection of point-to-point EAI dinosaur bones.

Invoking services

Be careful allowing a service to directly invoke another service (that is, to have itself be the client of that service), as this can strikingly reduce the business contexts available for reusing the service. Sometimes it seems necessary to make one service the client of another service within its implementation. But you are introducing a degree of coupling here that you might not want later. If you find yourself in this situation, consider using an orchestration technology such as BPEL (covered in Chapters 9 and 10).

Also, it can be difficult without service-level agreement (SLA) monitoring software and metrics in place to keep track of how much traffic a service is receiving from where. If your service crosses business domains, it becomes particularly important to consider that it could see sudden, unexpected explosions in traffic due to compositions external to your current subject. Another problem with direct invocation is that it adds complexity to your topography without allowing visibility through tools. There are tools by the big SOA suite vendors that show dependencies across the service-related resources stored in your enterprise repository, but they can be very expensive.

The architectural solution to this problem is that when you want to have one service directly invoke another, consider whether you can create an orchestration (or process service, as defined in Recipe 1.4) instead. As a service wraps a system or subsystem, an orchestration wraps a set of services that together make a flow. But the orchestration is itself exposed as a service, so it looks just like any other service to the client.

Other considerations

An SOA will mean something different to different organizations, and I encourage you to consider your specific definition and decide what elements to emphasize within your own business context and its attendant constraints.

1.3 Identifying Service Candidates

Problem

You need to identify whether or not a proposed software project makes a good candidate for a service. This process is sometimes called "service discovery" or "service elicitation."

Solution

Start from the top down or the bottom up to zero in on a set of possible candidates, and know that you will likely approach development from the middle out, according to business process requirements.

Recalling that the term "service" does not imply any specific implementation platform, a proposed piece of software might be a good service candidate if you can affirm at least some of the following criteria:

1. Could this functionality be appropriately designed to satisfy the definition of a service as stated in this chapter?
2. Is this service likely to be consumed across multiple platforms? Does it need to interoperate? Would external business partners have any use for this service? Does it need to cross functional barriers or firewalls? Can it use a popular protocol such as HTTP or SMTP?
3. Would implementing this functionality as a service help you break an integration barrier? Would it wrap or replace a proprietary point-to-point interface? Would it operate in front of ERP, CRM, financial applications, or other systems?
4. Does it clearly map to one or more business processes? Or is it simply a program? (It is generally accepted that services can map to a single process, but mapping to more than one process can offer more opportunities for reuse.)
5. Does the function that the proposed service represents cross business domains? This could point to a greater opportunity for reuse.
6. Does the service exchange business documents or fall readily into one of the three general service categories identified in Recipe 1.4.
7. Would a business person be interested in reports on the output of this service? Would IT be interested in monitoring its life cycle or runtime? Or perhaps it represents a functional or utility service that in the long term could increase general business agility. (If none of these, it may be too small an operation to merit a place in the service catalog.)
8. Does it offer business value? Is there an existing service commodity that already performs this function?
9. Is the proposed service the right level of granularity? (If it is very fine-grained, this will weaken the interface aspect of the contract, shrink the possibility of reuse, and promote undue chattiness. If it is very coarse-grained, it could be a candidate for a process service that decomposes into other entity or functional services.)
10. Would making this function a service allow it to be composable? That is, can it participate as a seamless blackbox with other services behind a unifying contract (like an orchestration)? Or does it represent just an isolated function, with little relation to other system components?

11. Does the candidate represent an idea with an identifiable life cycle? Can the business define the interface?
12. Is it advantageous if the software can be discovered dynamically (as from a registry/repository)?
13. Does it present an opportunity to aid in the goal of providing a "single version of the truth"?
14. Depending on the implementation, would the benefit derived from using XML to represent your data outweigh the performance hit for marshaling and unmarshaling to and from XML? Is human-readability of the documents exchanged a factor?
15. Would implementing this as a service lower the cost of future integration projects? Would it facilitate new products or business services?

Again, these are just points to consider. There are no hard-and-fast rules in this area. The idea is to make sure that you don't run out and make everything into a service. I know of companies that did this years ago; they now have more than 5,000 "services" and they're in a lot of pain. Just use this as a guideline.

Discussion

Not everything in your enterprise can or should be made a service. Do not fall into the "tool trap": if you have a hammer, everything looks like a nail. There are many real and important problems that services and SOA simply do not address. Once you have established SOA as a goal within your organization, it may be tempting to declare that every new project coming down the pike should be written as a service. This is not going to aid in the creation of a functioning SOA that gives you a real return on investment in the long run. It will, however, start the process of building out Just a Bunch of Web Services, the anti-pattern mentioned earlier.

But the fact of the matter is that you do have some services to build, and some SOA infrastructure to get in place, and so the question remains: "How will I know a service candidate when I see one?" As you start building out your service catalog, it is important to have solid criteria for determining what should and should not be a service.

It is important to conduct interviews with business segment leaders and use other information gathering techniques to understand the business models that you will use as the basis of your service elicitation analysis. Ultimately, such models will be the real key to deriving service candidates. It is this model that can be iteratively refactored in order to determine if the appropriate boundaries have been defined for the service, and that it meets an appropriate level of granularity.

As you begin to populate your service catalog, and through the life of your SOA, there are two basic approaches that you can use in analyzing and assessing your enterprise to discover service candidates.

While the checklist just shown features a number of useful questions, it should be viewed only as a guideline. When you as a developer/architect are asked to determine if some proposed software should be written as a service, refer back to this checklist, and you'll be well on your way. In time, you will likely start to tailor your own set of criteria.

Now let's turn to the matter of how to approach discovering service opportunities within your organization.

Top-down or bottom-up approach

A *top-down* approach starts from a high-level business view. Using this approach, you examine a road map laid out by the business that sets established business goals for a given time frame. You then evaluate the goals for potential service creation. This is not a process that simply maps a list of prioritized business projects directly to services. It requires instead that you use existing architectural documents and business process modeling techniques to determine what in your enterprise would make the most sense if written as a service.

The architects, CTO, CIO, or other responsible party in your organization should have an IT roadmap that is based directly on a business roadmap. That roadmap may exist at various levels of granularity or span a variety of timelines or departments within IT. But such documents can serve as the basis for identifying hot topics that can be examined as candidates for service creation. The roadmap itself, if it exists, will be too high level for service design. But once items on the roadmap are approved for work, start with identifying the business processes that are involved. Mapping the business processes required by a project will often point to an external system that you might be able to integrate via services, and will frequently point to internal systems that can be wrapped as services.

Many IT projects include a user-facing presentation layer. Often, only certain aspects of a project should be written as a service on the backend. Service-oriented architects need to communicate with project managers across projects or products to coordinate their efforts. This can be challenging in an environment used to dedicated project teams.

Businesses that are relatively young, have few disparate systems, or are generally very forward thinking might benefit most from this approach. It is easier for businesses to champion SOA efforts in such a scenario, as they get new products delivered that have been on their wish list.

A *bottom-up* approach starts from the view of a legacy technology. It takes existing functionality and wraps it in a service in order to achieve more general business goals such as increased agility, interoperability, or eased integration. This can sometimes be termed "service enablement": the basic functionality exists already, but you make it available as a first-class citizen within a service-oriented architecture.

This approach starts by identifying "pain points" within the enterprise that could be usefully addressed as a service. This is a common approach if you have had no architects doing forward planning work with your systems integration, and find yourself with an "accidental architecture" of rampant, undocumented, proprietary, or generally ugly point-to-point communications. If this is the case, you must approach such an effort with caution, taking care to understand the processes that are already using this tightly coupled functionality.

The business realizes value with this approach by freeing up previously complicated intersections of technology for greater agility and flexibility going forward. This can translate directly into shorter time to market.

This approach may work best for companies that have been in business for decades, have lots of legacy systems, use a wide range of disparate platforms (possibly as the result of many mergers or acquisitions), or have many existing point-to-point connections. But beware of simply taking the existing interfaces of these legacy systems and then making a web service out of them. A bad interface that runs with SOAP over HTTP is still a bad interface. Designing the interfaces so that they will be usable going forward often means that you have to do some overhaul within current state business models (that you might have defined using a top-down approach for something else).

A bottom-up approach rarely works. IT can end up being the driver, which you don't want. The business needs to be aware of SOA and assist in the governance and the definition of processes. The interfaces of the future are not likely to be found in legacy code. Legacy code can be wrapped with new interfaces. And this usually means that you start not at the top or the bottom, but in the middle, according to the requirements of your business processes. You can then find ways to reuse existing systems with a new facing appropriate for the process.

See Also

Recipe 1.5.

1.4 Identifying Different Kinds of Services

Problem

You need to identify the different kinds of services you can build in order to design them with appropriate levels of granularity and proper division of labor.

Solution

There are three basic kinds of services: entity, functional, and process services.

Discussion

The three basic categories into which your service candidates might fall are as follows:

Entity service
: An entity service represents one or more business entities. An entity is a noun that makes up the objects in an enterprise. Examples of entities include Customer, Invoice, Employee, Product, and so on. An entity service might feature CRUD (Create, Read, Update, Delete) operations for basic entities that are fundamentally decomposed. Just because something is a noun doesn't mean it is an entity service. For example, CustomerAccount might be created by a number of different systems interacting. In such a case, you may need to promote the creation of accounts to a workflow process service. Keep service autonomy as a goal, and that should help steer you to the appropriate service type.

  Because many entities are referred to throughout the enterprise, they can be easy to identify, and services based on them afford a good prospect for reuse. These can be employed as a "single source of the truth" strategy within a master data management scheme.

Functional service
: A functional service does not represent either a business process or a business entity, and it has no representation within a business model. It can be represented within a sequence diagram, however. A functional service is a technology-oriented service, not a business-oriented service. Its purpose is to provide reusable, centralized functionality that other services will rely on.

  A functional service may be required to perform a given function, such as sending an email, or handling exceptions in a standardized manner that supports them with logging or notification capability. A functional service might act as a centralized rules engine or security service.

  It is important for such services to be as autonomous as possible.

Process service
: A process service represents a series of related tasks. These tasks may be carried out within the boundaries of a single business domain, across multiple business domains, or across organizations. A process service can be represented as an orchestration invoked by an ESB, with a coarse-grained contract that causes the process service to appear as a unified whole to clients.

  One example is the processing of an invoice. Process compositions may become even more complex, composing other processes. An example of this might be a New Hire service that defines a process around intake of new employees, which is an entity service. But such a service might also call on an IT infrastructure provisioning service to light up a new workstation for the employee. Along the way, it could also use a functional service to send an email and another functional service that handles errors.

While such categories may not organize your physical service inventory or development project setup, it can be useful to understand what kind of service you are working on in order to help organize your approach and steer conversations with other developers and analysts. Architects may want to note such distinctions on their models.

1.5 Modeling Services

Problem

You have determined a service candidate and want to begin modeling the service.

Solution

Employ established architectural modeling techniques such as generalization, decomposition, and aggregation.

Discussion

Once you have determined a reasonable candidate service, model the service using a set of techniques, refactoring its definition until you know what kind of service it is, you feel comfortable with its definition and level of granularity, and you're sure it's still a service.

To aid in this effort, employ these information modeling techniques:

Generalization
: Analyze your service to determine what it *represents* conceptually, in general terms. In object-oriented (OO) programming, this is called finding IS-A relationships. You want to find the appropriate level of generalization for your service. You may determine that a Customer is a Person and an Employee is a Person too. This could be a useful degree of generalization within your enterprise. But the fact that a Person is a *Homo sapiens* may be the wrong degree of generality for your dot com. Perhaps the more common problem is that you do not get general enough in your design, failing to realize what aspects of different components truly align and differentiate them. Designing services at too specific a level can shrink their possibility for reuse, and make for very complicated interfaces and orchestrations, defeating the very purpose of your SOA efforts.

  It doesn't matter what kind of service you're working with. The Person example shown earlier regards an entity, but it's the same for a process service.

Decomposition
: Analyze your service to determine what other elements it *composes*. Such analysis can reveal functional or entity services that may be worthy of standing alone in their own right. In some cases, your process will be composed of other independent processes. Note that the finer grained your service is, the better chance of

composability and reuse it has. The coarser grained your service is, the more interoperable it is, and the more suitable it is for a client-facing endpoint.

Aggregation
: Analyze your service to determine what other elements it may be *a part of*. These elements may be existing processes, services, or service candidates themselves. In object-oriented programming, this is called finding HAS-A relationships. Employing this technique can help you discover composable services.

These are foundational techniques and will serve you well. But for service modeling, you need to look beyond these basic principles and consider these additional aspects:

Reusability
: This is often considered in object-oriented design, but not to the extent that it must be within a service model. To determine how to write the contract, you need to perform a systems analysis that gives you the best guess on how it will be reused throughout your enterprise. When it's not certain how the service will be reused, keep it sufficiently generic to promote the possibility of reuse.

Security
: This is typically dealt with at the application level for objects, but it must be modeled at the individual service level when you're creating services. You will have an overall security model for your SOA that might include SAML, a Policy Enforcement point, transport security, digital signatures, Kerberos, or other related measures. These are typically indicated in policies enforced by tools to support the contract.

Interoperability
: Java objects only have to work with other Java objects. But services are intended to interoperate. As you model a service, you must consider it from this viewpoint, identifying other platforms you'll be working with. Adhering to the Basic Profile (discussed later) helps here.

SLAs
: Services, like the systems they wrap, should have defined service-level agreements. The business process your service participates in might need to respond within 100 milliseconds, or a flag should be raised. This is particularly important in an SOA because eventually your well-designed service will be reused by many processes, and analysis at the process level will be important to helping the business understand what it can expect.

Granularity
: Your service will participate in an evolving landscape of many services. Getting the proper level of granularity is key to ensuring that you can reuse a service, that you can expose it successfully to your business partners, and that your security constraints will be appropriate.

Contract

Within your model, identify what elements you will need in your overall service contract. Some of these may be direct attributes of the service, and others may serve as metadata that you make available within the context of WS-MetadataExchange. Some elements will be non-functional, and some can be declared and enforced within the sorts of SOA runtime environments offered by commercial vendors.

Process

Process analysis is a discipline all its own, probably unfamiliar to many OO developers. Because business processes can be represented as services, and because business processes will make use of services, it's important to understand the IT world from this perspective. A real discussion is beyond the scope of this book, but if you have business analysts and Lean or Six Sigma professionals in your organization, they can be a very valuable resource.

Consider these things when you are modeling a new service, in addition to the object-oriented analysis skills you bring to bear.

I only touch on the subject of SOA modeling briefly here. As mentioned earlier, the ideas surrounding SOA, service modeling, process modeling, and so on fill entire books. This chapter is intended to give a grounding in some of the key concepts. If you are interested in SOA modeling, you might check out Michael Bell's book *Service-Oriented Modeling: Service Analysis, Design, and Architecture* (Wiley).

Service documentation

Document the service candidates you elicit with an enterprise view. Do this as an iterative process, using a standard format, in order to visualize your service-enabled enterprise. This documentation must ultimately be composable into a larger enterprise service catalog.

Be careful of attempting to model your entire business up-front. Circumstances are likely to change before you complete such an effort. It is reasonable to take a more modular approach here, working with a single business domain, system set, or problem, and model that using an iterative approach. Eventually your models will meet at domain or functional borders.

1.6 Making a Service Composable

Problem

You want to make sure that your service is designed in such a way that it can be reused within a composition.

Solution

Do not tie your service interface or implementation to any specific business process. Instead, move business process-specific code into an orchestration or new process service.

Discussion

A composed service is an aggregate of other existing services. While you can realize reuse for a service by invoking the same service from different applications, a service is composable if it is defined in such a way that it can be reused by inclusion within another service's implementation.

There are two matters here: the service interface must not negatively impact its composability, and its implementation must not inadvertently do so either. In order to provide business value, a service must perform work specific to some business use case. But you must consider the distinction between the execution of a specific unit of work (a service call), and the workflow around that operation that makes it available and valuable to the business in the form of some given business application.

The general idea of composability in software is not very different from its colloquial use. Because of their design, Lego bricks can be used to form a variety of exciting shapes. A Java Address class can be used to compose both an Employee object and a Company object. Likewise, the composability of services must be included as an initial consideration in the design process.

Consider a software company. There programmers type code on different, specific aspects of the system—one for user interface, one for database, and so on. These are roughly analogous to the member services. Then there are the programming managers. They don't type anything into an IDE, but they coordinate the activities of their employees to ensure that eventually all of the programmers' efforts are incorporated as features in the single software product that customers are interested in. Each programmer does important work on his own, but the addition of the manager presents an interface to the business that coordinates the activities, as a process service might. The process service doesn't do any independent work: its single function is to direct the activities of other services, and in so doing, creates something new.

In a more service-oriented example, imagine you are a retail company, and need to write a service that your point of sale application will invoke to perform pre-approvals of a customer's credit during checkout. If the customer is credit-worthy, your salesperson can offer her a discount for filling out your private label credit card application. Your requirements dictate that you must first check your customer database to determine if the customer already has your credit card, so the salesperson doesn't offer her something she already has.

If you already have a Customer lookup service that indicates, among other things, whether a customer has your private label card, that service can perhaps be reused by, and composed into, your CreditCheck service. That assumes that the Customer lookup service was designed for general purposes and includes all of the relevant data. Likewise, you want the service that performs the basic CreditCheck to do only the credit check, and nothing else. You don't want that service itself checking the local customer database, even if it is doing so by reusing the existing customer lookup service. Doing so would dilute the composability of the CreditCheck. In object-oriented programming, this idea is called "high cohesion"—the design restriction that dictates that the operations of a class must be very closely related.

It may seem that the customer lookup and the credit check are closely related, but that is debatable. Getting customer data is a simple operation, with no apparent business case other than the fact that you need to know stuff about your customers. Likewise, the act of performing a credit check says absolutely nothing about whether you must first check your local customer database to see if the customer already has your card. That is a requirement that a specific IT project must fulfill, but it is not relevant to the act of checking credit. To conflate these ideas is to make a category mistake, and limit the reusability and flexibility of your SOA.

So now you are left with three separate ideas and therefore three separate services:

- The Customer lookup service that you already had and which you designed to be free of any particular use case, so it is available for further composition.
- The basic credit check service that simply hits the credit bureau with a name and address and returns a result.
- The overall credit check process service as described by the business analyst, which does no work itself other than coordinating the activities of the worker (member) services.

It is the job of this third composing service to coordinate the activities in such a way that the business requirements are fulfilled. That is, it is the job of the workflow to know that you want to check if the customer already has a card before wasting cycles invoking the credit check service. In this workflow, this is the consumer-facing service, and consumers will be wholly unaware of how their result is delivered behind the scenes.

This is useful because it helps push the business requirements that are incidental to this particular use case up into a customer view that is specific to this use case, allowing the member services to retain their independence. It is possible, for example, that you want to reuse the CreditCheck service in some new way. Your business may want to perform credit checks of prospective new hires, who would not be in your customer database. This would be difficult to deal with had the customer check been baked in at the service level. A frequent goal in object-oriented programming is to isolate what might change; it's the same thing here.

The bottom line: the business process service must be defined outside the worker service, which can be other process services, or entity or functional services. Services are not always composable, but as you design your services, remember that composability is something to strive for; at the least, perform a check to see if your evolving design helps or hurts your possibility for composition, even if you don't see an immediate need.

Note that service composition is particularly hard on runtimes. It is important to ensure that your SLAs are always met, and this becomes somewhat tricky when you have a set of services composing a variety of basic services that also compose to varying degrees another set of services.

Chapter 9 covers how to define and create orchestrations technically.

1.7 Supporting Your SOA Efforts

Problem

You want to develop a set of guidelines and principles for designing and implementing your service-oriented architecture. It should not only record the decisions you make but also serve as an educational tool for others in your organization.

Solution

Create a reference architecture, which is a representation of your real-world implementation. Internally, you can build on this to include a collection of roadmaps, conceptual blueprints, guiding principles, and standards and conventions that will serve as the foundation of your service-oriented architecture. If you have established a Center of Excellence (CoE) or SOA Team (which is a very good idea), they will be the custodians of these resources, and will likely be responsible for sharing them with the larger development teams for educational purposes.

You could use your reference architecture documents as the cornerstone for an online resource to aid in the education of others. This could be an internal website, wiki, or portal that establishes a single entry point into your architectural blueprints and other supporting resources.

In April of 2008, OASIS published a document it called the "Reference Architecture for Service Oriented Architecture Version 1.0." You can read the PDF at *http://docs.oasis-open.org/soa-rm/soa-ra/v1.0/soa-ra-pr-01.pdf*. It is written for enterprise architects, and covers governance, social structures, service modeling and ownership, security, and more. It's very abstract, but worth a read. You will find many such documents online that you might want to screen and contextualize for your internal use.

Discussion

A *reference architecture* (RA), as defined within the Rational Unified Process, is a predefined set of architectural patterns, designed and proven for use in particular business and technical contexts, together with supporting documents that enable their use. These can grow organically from architectural documents, standards, and conventions you have in place already. But it is useful to tailor them for SOA as appropriate.

A reference architecture serves as a blueprint across multiple projects or within a single project. Architects and developers can verify that a subsequent implementation adheres to established guidelines and will have increased likelihood of meeting business goals.

You can think of the reference architecture as being analogous to the United States Constitution. It serves to establish a variety of abstract bodies, such as the three branches of government, each of which has different responsibilities, as well as a set of revisable guidelines that ensures that people operate according to principles that support the overarching goals of the republic. (Of course, all analogies have limited usefulness and can be misleading. Your mileage may vary!)

Aims of the reference architecture

The reference architecture can help ensure the success of your architectural efforts in a variety of ways:

Act as a blueprint

The reference architecture can capture the intersection between your IT infrastructure, your code, and your models. Because these different aspects are implemented by different teams, they can inadvertently act in isolation, rendering the enterprise unable to take advantage of a potential wealth of existing work.

The blueprint can assist solutions architects to view the SOA not only from a coding or system perspective, but rather to take the more holistic view required to ensure quality-of-service levels.

Your SOA reference architecture might link to other existing enterprise architecture documents, such as network and hardware IT infrastructure, and add to this the idea of service layers. For example, within Oracle/BEA, it defines an SOA RA containing the following service layers:

Data Services and Connectivity Services

These provide flexible access to underlying data tiers and enterprise applications.

Business-Oriented Services

A logical layer above Data Services where business processes are conducted.

Presentation Services

Package business capability services, repurposed for a variety of channels.

While Oracle/BEA's list may not be the one you choose (you might collapse Data and Connectivity Services and you might throw out Presentation Services altogether, or add another layer of your own), the point is that it is useful to conceptualize your services on this level, and not simply on the level of Entity, Process, or Functional, as these are complementary classifications.

Promote best practices
: The RA can declare that services and clients must be created and consumed following certain guidelines. Perhaps there are design patterns that you want consistently implemented in certain situations. Perhaps you want to require a set of acceptable methods for service creation, messaging, encoding, and so forth.

  By declaring guidelines, standards, and conventions, the RA will help to ensure consistency across the board in service implementation. Architects have an easier task in enforcing the guidelines when they are spelled out clearly in a living public document. Once everyone is used to consistently implementing services in a given manner, this will mean quicker time to market. Developers can create new assemblies with confidence that the services they are reusing will fit well together.

  The RA should address how to deal with cross-cutting concerns such as security and rules engines, which are sometimes themselves implemented as services.

Clarify trade-offs
: You cannot do everything. Certain requirements are always at odds with each other. Reconciling terrific performance with strong security is a continual struggle.

Enable governance
: The governance of your SOA is highly dependent on the creation of an RA. The RA serves as a constitution of sorts for your SOA Center of Excellence or governance board to follow.

Reference architecture site

Your SOA reference architecture can be a deliverable, a living set of resources that can be used for a variety of purposes, and not simply some documentation that accompanies your code. As a deliverable in its own right, it works well when implemented within a website that is easy to update, such as a wiki. Members of the SOA team or governance board or the architects involved at your organization can create a site that they populate with architectural models, standards and conventions documents, and resources for evangelizing and education, and that can perhaps serve as a gateway to runtime tools.

The size and shape of your RA site will be dictated by the size, organization, and distribution of your development teams.

As a suggestion, the items outlined in the following sections might be useful within a reference architecture.

Conventions. Conventions enable clearer communication. They are a matter of subjective taste initially, but once established, they must be followed to make things easier to find and understand. Here are some examples of conventions you might consider creating guidelines for:

- Document names, including schemas, WSDLs, and binding customization files
- File locations and physical project structure of service implementation projects

Standards. These are more strict than guidelines, and are less a matter of taste. They have a functional purpose, such that if the standards are not followed, degraded performance or functional side effects can occur.

If you are unfamiliar with WSDLs or Schema design patterns, consult Chapter 2.

It can be useful to standardize the following:

- Allowing use of binding customization files, such as for JAXB or JAX-WS (see Chapter 3)
- Whether customizations are allowed, inline or external (see Chapter 3)
- Importing WSDL bindings versus defining them inline
- Importing schema types in WSDL versus defining them inline
- Default protocol choice, and when other protocols are acceptable
- Choosing which "start from" method (see Chapter 2)
- Appropriate use of schema design patterns (see Chapter 2)
- Using interfaces
- Using optimization methods, such as FastInfoset and MTOM/XOP
- Using headers
- Using attachments
- If using SOAP, to dictate acceptable style, use, and parameter style values, such as document/literal wrapped
- Using one-way methods
- Using asynchronous clients
- Encoding for binary data
- Centralized schema

These guidelines should ideally include examples of correct and incorrect use of each item.

There are many more items to consider depending on your implementation choices, system maturity level, and environment. While the focus of this book is on Java, you might need to determine standards relating to service creation in RPG, .NET, or what have you. This list indicates the appropriate scope of guidelines for your service implementations and SOA. Failure to adhere to such guidelines can cause interoperability problems and severe performance degradation, and can waste development time.

Keep your standards up-to-date. Make sure to include your team members in determining guidelines. Receive their feedback openly and incorporate their suggestions as appropriate. Create new items, drop old or obvious ones, and make updates as necessary to ensure that the guidelines are fresh, relevant, and useful.

Specifications. There are dozens of specifications that can come into play very quickly in the world of SOA and Java-based web services. Linking to the specifications can help ensure that everyone can quickly find the definitive answer to a question, and it helps implicitly direct people to what they must understand to be productive within the SOA environment. Relevant Java specifications might include the following:

- JAX-WS
- JAXB
- SAAJ
- JAXR
- Web Services
- WS-Annotations
- DOM, SAX, StAX

These are only the Java-specific specs. Important SOAP and WS-* specs, some of which we will examine in detail later on, include the following:

- XML Schema
- XSLT
- SOAP
- WSDL
- OASIS UDDI
- WS-Policy
- BPEL
- WS-Security
- WS-Trust

- WS-ReliableMessaging
- WS-Transaction
- WS-MetadataExchange

Centralized bookmarks. Create a wiki page that encourages developers to bookmark web resources publicly so that it's easy for everyone to find and use them. Invite others to participate.

Industry standards. In addition to the various specifications you will be using, include links to a set of industry standards that everyone would benefit from knowing. These might include:

- Basic Profile 1.1
- OASIS XML Catalog
- W3C Web Services Architecture
- OASIS Web Services Implementation Methodology

This is where you should indicate what BP 1.1 guidelines you are following, or state your position on them. Define a set of best practices for your organization based on accepted industry best practices, and incorporate them into your design. Some of these can be elicited from standards such as the WS-I Basic Profile. For example, the BP 1.1 requires that WSDLs use a target namespace. Use this opportunity to explicitly state such conventions so that other developers in your organization can quickly adhere to them.

Security. Create one section of the site devoted to security. This is a large and complex topic in the world of web services, and there are many standards that make this work. Vendors are at different stages of implementation with respect to these standards, and it could be very useful to sort this out for your team. Finally, these guidelines can be important for ensuring interoperability, and can indicate items such as:

- Use of particular cipher suites
- Use of digital signatures
- Transport layer security
- Authentication methods

As your SOA grows, it will be useful to have an aggregate list of roles allowed within each service, as this will help organize process orchestration efforts.

Cookbook. Depending on your team's level of experience, you might include working examples of code that illustrate how to create services and the attendant assemblies.

Consider establishing your architecture concurrently alongside your pilot projects. Developing an architecture entirely up-front without really seeing how the tools work together and how the standards are implemented can have a devastating effect on your deadline and ultimately your product. This is particularly true when you're in a learning stage, such as during pilots. Make a general plan with the understanding that you probably won't stick to it. Do a little and then revise your plan. Architectures can be agile too, and don't have to be complete to get people working in the right direction. You can also, as Frederick Brooks wrote, "Make one to throw away."

Glossary. Consider creating a list of important terms and their agreed-upon definitions that you will go by so that they are clear in your team's mind. Some concepts within SOA are contentious, vague, or hype-laden, which can make it difficult to know that everyone is actually talking about the same thing. Using a glossary for terms, such as service, contract, governance, and so forth, can aid meaningful communication.

Documentation. Here you can link to JavaDoc, project documentation, vendor documentation, requirements, use case documents, modeling analysis documents, and other such items.

If you have IT or business roadmaps or other enterprise architecture documents that might play a role in building out your SOA, you can link to them here as well.

Artifacts. If your infrastructure allows it, you might consider having a view into the runtime artifacts within your SOA. These might include centralized schemas, business process modeling documents as derived from a modeling tool, visual representations of BPEL orchestrations, and other items. Offer appropriate users insight into monitoring tools so that they have the information necessary to make good decisions about new service candidates, SLAs, new compositions, or infrastructure changes.

News. You might consider establishing a feed that aggregates various SOA-related websites into your reference architecture portal. This helps to keep everyone abreast of industry trends and give your team the best chance to keep one another informed.

Conclusion

While some of the items indicated here may seem excessive, remember that the purpose of the reference architecture is manifold: it serves to instruct newcomers on the way that you want web services done in your organization; it helps experienced developers find and use web services that your organization has written or endorsed; and it helps the governance board or Center of Excellence make decisions regarding service candidates and future architectural directions.

1.8 Selecting a Pilot Project

Problem

You are ready to get started with SOA and therefore need to select a first project. You are not sure how to make your selection.

Solution

Use the following criteria to measure how viable a particular project might be as a pilot:

- Does the project create business value?
- Does the project have limited scope?
- Would the project make a good service?
- Do the team members have a good understanding of the problem domain the project addresses?
- Is the project useful but not mission critical?

Discussion

Considering these criteria should help you make a good decision about which project to use as a starting point. In this section, we'll examine each criterion in greater detail.

Does the project create business value?

SOA is in many ways about aligning IT with the business so that eventually there is a blurring of lines between the two. How this emerges will be very dependent on your organization and its culture. But SOA requires considerable support. It represents a new way of thinking about systems, and there are many APIs to learn. While there are free and open source tools to use as application servers, enterprise service buses, business process execution and more, many organizations will make expensive software purchases. That process can require lots of time and input from the business. The investment that the business must make in education of the team and evangelizing to the larger IT group means real time and money that initially are not spent getting something new. It is frequently viewed as a sunk cost in infrastructure that the business hopes will pay off in the long run.

For these reasons, it is important to win the business over; otherwise, the investment upon which an SOA team is dependent could dry up. The way to win the business over is to show them the money. Choose a project that will have some immediate return so that the business can remain supportive. Illustrate clearly that the real return on SOA is realized over the course of several years, as IT may be more responsive and ready to quickly address changing business needs.

Does the project have limited scope?

The project should have limited scope. It should represent functionality that is somewhat isolated from systems that are not well known. But you will get the most out of your pilot project if it does span multiple systems. It cannot be merely a proof of concept about web services, but must be a full-blown, real-world project. Otherwise, you run the risk of underestimating scalability requirements and overall complexity.

Some practitioners recommend starting with a basic service set, and introducing the ESB and orchestration services later. In my view, you want to choose a project of limited business scope so that you have the time and clarity to simultaneously introduce the ESB initially. You don't want to over-engineer your solution, but if you are planning to connect your work with an ESB at some point, you won't have to revisit this. Moreover, because ESB is not standardized, products offer very different features or different means of providing certain functionality. You want to understand this central piece of your architecture early on.

Introducing SOA can lead to a lot of new APIs for developers, new application servers, new languages, and new infrastructure. It represents a new way of thinking about development. Thinking in services is different from thinking in objects. Making a switch from functional or procedural programming to object-oriented programming can take time, and represents a dramatic change for developers. I have seen Java classes in excess of 15,000 lines of code, with a single method 700 or 800 lines long. Just because you're writing in Java and a program compiles and runs doesn't mean it's object-oriented, and doesn't magically make it good. Do not underestimate the difference that services can represent for OO developers too. You need to take the time to educate everyone on the team (though not necessarily at the same time). That takes development time away. If the project has a very large scope, it might never be completed when you have so many external considerations.

You want to be able to isolate unknowns so that you can more easily identify problems during the development and quality assurance phases of the project. Be careful of choosing a product that uses brand-new products. The team will already have a number of mysteries to deal with when working with new infrastructure and APIs. Isolate your changes so that the SOA enablement work can be a leading focus. Consultants can help here.

Consider the target consumers for your initial service. You mitigate your risk by choosing something that is internal to your business, rather than customer-facing. This gives you time to build out a little infrastructure before the external world gets involved, introducing new and unanticipated issues. Internally consumed services will help you focus on implementing your first services properly, and shield you, for a time, from more advanced and complex issues such as federated security. Internal services may also represent an opportunity to gauge traffic with greater confidence.

Would the project make a good service?

This may be obvious; consider whether the functionality really satisfies the criteria highlighted in Recipe 1.1. Be careful to not have external forces choose a pilot for you if the proposed project wouldn't actually make a good service. This happens—SOA teams get formed, and then the boss insists that the pilot must be whatever the next thing on the project list is, regardless of whether it is actually a useful service candidate. Writing services initially adds considerable complexity and expense to a project in the hopes that the benefits will outweigh such costs in the long run. If the service will never be reused or never be invoked from another platform, you might not have a very good service candidate on your hands, which means you might not realize much ROI.

Make sure that the service you choose will give you an opportunity to explore the full development life cycle. If you plan on utilizing a "start from schema" approach, for example, you want to address this head-on in your pilot, as it precipitates work surrounding the custodianship of the schemas, modifies the build process, and so forth.

It might be an overarching SOA goal of your organization to move your work in an architecturally neutral direction. This can be the case in companies with decades of legacy data tied to a specific platform. Finding a data service that wraps some central entity representations can help reduce ETL (Extract, Transform, Load) or data movement operations.

Do the team members have a good understanding of the problem domain?

If you have subject matter experts for the given problem domain available, you can mitigate considerable risk. Introducing new systems, new software, new processes, and new problem domains at the same time that you introduce services and SOA creates a dangerous concoction. If you are working with vendors or consultants, make sure they have a background in the vertical business area you're addressing (financial, retail, etc.).

Is the project useful but not mission critical?

While it is important to realize business value early in establishing an SOA, be careful not to bite off too much in the initial stages. SOA pilot projects often lose track of their deadlines, miss certain requirements, or fail altogether. Choose a project that won't undermine your business if it takes some extra work to get it up and running as a service.

This makes service enablement of existing pain points an attractive pilot project. There is already a process or functionality in place to fall back on should it prove necessary. Obviously I am not recommending that you plan to fail, but things happen, and it's smart to be realistic about it up-front.

The fact of the matter is that services are hard. They are hard conceptually, and they are hard practically. There is enormous complexity added to an environment to make your services portable, reusable, composable, and interoperable. They are difficult for both the business and IT to wrap their minds around.

Do some research on architectural frameworks, methodologies, and design patterns, and select some that will support you best given your environment.

The second pilot

Once you have completed the initial pilot, the second project, which should probably be considered a pilot extension, becomes very important. The chief goal of the pilot is to establish a foundation for SOA, understand the technical implications, and create something of value using new constraints and new strategies.

The second project provides a key opportunity to build out some of the organizational and cross-cutting concerns that SOA precipitates, such as governance (see Recipe 1.9). The second pilot will, for this reason, need to have a similarly limited business scope as the initial pilot. Don't leap into rewriting your payment infrastructure with your second SOA project. You need time to learn the behavioral patterns of your new tools and time for the education and daily reality of running the production services environment to set in.

You can also use the second project to build on your initial architecture. You may add functional or meta services, such as a rules service or security service. You may introduce BAM tools at this stage, or deepen your work with WS-Policy or security concerns in general. You might clarify and refine how you will handle service versioning, which may not have been a central focus of the pilot. You might take advantage of some more robust features of orchestration than you may not have had time or need to explore initially.

These things should have been laid out in your SOA roadmap. The roadmap will change, but keep it updated, and remember that SOA is a long-term investment. Plan big, but start small.

1.9 Establishing Governance

Problem

You need a reliable organizational mechanism to transfer knowledge, enforce standards, provide infrastructure for growth and change, and in general offer strategic leadership regarding your service-oriented architecture.

Solution

Establish a Center of Excellence, sometimes called a "Competency Center" or SOA governance board, comprised of stakeholders from the business and technology sides of the house, whose job it is to provide the enterprise this support.

Discussion

Depending on the maturity level and size of your company you may already have IT governance standards in place. SOA governance is an extension of IT governance, specialized for the particular needs of SOA. Because SOA represents a strategic initiative of which a set of tools and techniques is only a part, you need to have a way to gradually introduce the strategy into your organization.

This book does not address much of the organizational or business aspects of SOA. While they are very real and important parts of SOA, there are many good books that address SOA from that angle, and this book is intended to address the technical side. But it is important as a developer/architect to be clear that SOA is not merely a collection of web services.

SOA requires new processes. It must be clear to your organization how to design SOA-based solutions, elicit service candidates, and coordinate a new development cycle to support your incubating SOA.

You might include solutions and systems architects, as well as business stakeholders in the Center of Excellence. This helps ensure that IT acts in alignment with the business and has access to its current priorities and future plans.

Keep the governance team somewhat lean. As long as the SOA governance team has enough resources to remain aware of the activities of the enterprise and enforce and grow the reference architecture, that should be enough. Grow it responsibly. You don't want your SOA to die by committee.

The responsibilities you might assign to such a governing body are as follows:

Establish business case
: This may be performed early on during SOA adoption by the enterprise architect and others. The business case for SOA includes the vision, the goals that SOA will accomplish, and probably a plan to fund the initiative.

Outline roles
: SOA will introduce new roles within IT, and they should be clearly stated. You need people to be responsible for carrying out the governance work, make

architectural decisions, establish the reference architecture, vet services, process service candidates, and establish and grow new infrastructure such as the ESB. You may also decide who will support and maintain services after they are deployed, and ensure that your knowledge transfer plan accounts for this.

Assist in setting the roadmap
: The governance team has a special purview that may make them key elements in helping the enterprise architect or technical executives set the IT roadmap. The roadmap may go so far as to map defined activities to larger goals, and map those goals to a larger set of aspects of your business vision.

Maintain the reference architecture
: The CoE can also have the maintenance of the reference architecture under its purview, which will aid in building and linking process models into the larger enterprise.

Facilitate development at design time
: Architects in this context act as a guide to developers, enforcing the reference architecture and supporting their efforts. They might select tools, frameworks, and infrastructure applications, and adopt and adapt methodologies to support the service-oriented enterprise.

Facilitate services at runtime
: The subjects of SOA governance include developers and services too. Runtime monitoring tools should be in place to ensure that SLAs are being met. It is under the purview of the governance team to keep track of this and plot for future growth so needs are met just before they arise.

Facilitate services' life cycles
: The governance team can see when services may need to be versioned, and assess the impact of that versioning. Versioning is a more complex issue in SOA than in traditional development because of its distributed nature. The person or team who develops a given service may not have any clear view into the larger set of processes that now compose this service. It is the job of the governance team to understand and prepare for this and oversee its proper implementation.

Enable knowledge transfer
: The CoE can support the knowledge transfer effort. The learning curve on SOA and on web services APIs and infrastructure can be considerable. Even if some members of your team are not building services, they should be aware of the language and familiar with the ideas in order to work in a complementary manner. Eventually such developers may move on to create and consume services, and they need to be prepared to understand and follow the guidelines laid out in the reference architecture.

Common pitfalls governance helps you avoid

Organizations that attempt SOA without governance in place can fall victim to a variety of ailments, including total failure of the SOA initiative. There are a few common, avoidable pitfalls.

You can't govern what you don't know about. So, to ensure that all of your service-related code and documents are visible, implement a central repository that has the documents of record for each version of each service. This will help track these important documents during design and runtime.

Service redundancy. A common pitfall, particularly within large or decentralized organizations, is service redundancy or overlap. The same or similar service is repeatedly created throughout different groups in the enterprise. This is expensive, wasteful, and confusing. As a result you can find yourself with sharply increased maintenance costs. It is the job of the CoE to prevent this by monitoring what's getting developed, encouraging collaboration between implementation teams, and establishing and using a centralized repository for service discovery.

Sundry artifacts. On a practical level, ensure that governance is in place to manage the many new kinds of artifacts that SOA can introduce, such as WSDLs, schemas, SCA configurations, policies, and more. Left to their own devices, developers will view such documents as simply part of the code like everything else, and bake them directly into their project files. The artifiats will end up scattered across the enterprise, and versioning and client dependency management will quickly get out of control.

DBA (Death by Acronym). While Death by Acronym is a syndrome we see in IT and is not particular to SOA, SOA practitioners are among those most vulnerable to it. To die by acronym is to erroneously believe that one understands whatever the acronym represents. Because acronyms act as stand-ins for very complex concepts, they gain the status of sound bites and lead us to affirm to one another only the most bare, surface, and general meanings of the concepts at play. The result is strangled communication that undermines collaborative efforts. At its most insidious, companies looking to claim market share for a rising buzzword will rebrand a collection of only marginally related products with the buzzword. SOA is susceptible to both of these kinds of problems.

Education is the only known cure. In the case of SOA, it means not trusting any single source, and cross-checking with a variety of references.

Resume padding

This is a reality. Beware of developers and architects who seek to advance their careers at the cost of populating your SOA with frivolous functionality or over-engineered solutions. You can recognize these types by their endlessly new answers to problems that have already been solved.

Governance can handle this problem by making all service-related development efforts transparent, and by managing solution implementations.

Bunny services

One bunny is pleasant to find in your yard. Two bunnies are even better, chasing each other hither and yon. Fifty bunnies is a problem. Just because something is good doesn't mean that more is necessarily better. The cake you're baking might need half a teaspoon of salt; add a tablespoon and it's ruined.

Once you get good at services, it will be tempting to make lots of them. Review your landscape. Not everything should be a service. Allow services to proliferate in your organization in the manner of multiplying bunnies, and expect performance, maintenance, and management problems. Remember the old saw, "just because you can, doesn't mean you should."

Summary

In this chapter, we established working definitions of central terms such as service-oriented architecture and services themselves. We started from a very general level and addressed chiefly matters of organization, such as how to establish a reference architecture and choose a pilot project. But we also examined fairly specific criteria useful in determining worthy service candidates as well as specific guidelines to establish to support the goals of SOA within your organization.

While there are additional design considerations we will address, most of the rest of this book is very practical, and addresses coding problems with coding solutions. Even coding problems have more than one solution. But in the case of the topics in this chapter, there are many other legitimate points of view, and many people who might disagree with some of my conclusions in it.

There are many good books that cover these topics and others in greater detail. If you are interested in high-level service design and organizational considerations, you might read Thomas Erl's *SOA: Principles of Service Design* (Prentice Hall) and Nicolai M. Josuttis's *SOA in Practice* (O'Reilly) (*http://www.oreilly.com/catalog/9780596529550*).

CHAPTER 2

XML Schema and the SOA Data Model

2.0 Introduction

XML is the *lingua franca* of SOA. It is used for message payloads, application configuration, deployment, discovery, runtime policies, and increasingly for representing executable languages such as BPEL that are central to the SOA landscape. Web service interfaces are represented with XML in the form of WSDL, and XML is used as the chief data transport mechanism in SOA. Because XML is so inextricably linked with web services development, and because its inherent flexibility and expressiveness make it so powerful, it's a natural fit for designing your data model for use within a SOA.

Designing data models as XML provides you with a valuable implementation-independent foundation. It frees you to focus greater attention on ontology (the determination of what exists), and to be less subjected to vendor constraints. Because the libraries have at once become more sophisticated and easier to use, XML is more attractive than ever as a place to start working with data models for your SOA.

Pundits and artists alike have long pointed out that our use of new communications devices—whether cell phones, texting, IM, email, or PowerPoint—does not merely change *how* we communicate, but inevitably must augment or rearrange fundamentally *what* we communicate. Marshall McLuhan summarized this in 1967 as "the medium is the message," meaning that the form of a message will subsume the ostensible content of the message itself. As an architect, it's important to be aware of the subtle (or perhaps profound) shift in thinking that can arise from using XML as a foundational layer for SOA. Of course, how big that shift is typically depends entirely on your organization's environment.

One of the strengths of XML—indeed, its chief aim—is to be flexible. A lot of IT shops around the world find themselves in the position of maintaining dozens upon dozens of application silos, each one married to a rigid data model that must be accommodated with every new update or rollout. Many such shops are now looking to SOA for answers. Using XML for data exchange within your SOA encourages a more modal approach, offering contextual data views that can flow, be transformed, and interact meaningfully across a variety of services and tiers.

This chapter does not represent an introduction to XML, and is in no way intended to be comprehensive in its coverage of XML, schema, or data binding. I am assuming that you are *relieved* by this. You probably already have a basic understanding of XML and schema and know what data binding is, or you wouldn't be reading this book. If you don't, there are a lot of books and online tutorials to cover that for you.

We'll examine XML Schema through the specific lens of SOA, which demands a certain openness and flexibility. That means, in short, keeping things fairly simple. Now, if you want to go bananas writing super-complex polymorphic schemas, you're free to do so, but I don't recommend it. Keeping it simple maximizes interoperability. The more sophisticated your schema, the more you must buy into vendor- or tool-specific processing habits, which is not a good place for an SOA programmer/architect to be. But this can seem counterintuitive to us object-oriented programmers. For example, Martin Fowler has written about the "anemic model" anti-pattern, which is an object containing only data and no behavior, thereby giving up one of the chief benefits of employing an object-oriented language. Coming from an object-oriented world, your first impulse might be to attempt to use schemas to capture everything that you can capture in a Java model. And there are tools to help you do that. You can, for instance, find plug-ins to have JAXB generate hashcode and equals implementations for you, which it doesn't do by default. That sounds really neat at first, and is crucial in designing an object-oriented system. From a straight Java view, you want your stuff to be fully encapsulated, and you may think about rounding out your objects with serialVersionUID and so forth. But within the SOA landscape, these things have little place, as they are not general.

XML Schemas are very powerful, but they are not object-oriented, and are intended to capture a data model rather than an object model. Schemas do allow designers to create models that can be made to look very much like objects; JAXB, for example, lets you generate Java 5 enumeration types, and there is a degree of polymorphism that you can achieve through schemas. But ultimately the whole point is that your services must be general enough that they can communicate across languages. So I encourage you to be somewhat conservative in your approach.

Keeping your interface simple will help ensure you don't get painted into a corner later. It encourages you to consider your service design at the appropriate level of granularity. But there are different ways of designing schemas that can help you or hurt you in the long run, so we'll look at those in this chapter.

And despite the admonition to keep it simple, it is very difficult to read and debug a series of BPEL orchestrations that invoke multiple WSDLs that import multiple schemas without a solid understanding of namespaces and schema. XML has been with us now for more than 10 years, and its ubiquity may belie the real complexity that lurks below its simple surface.

The recipes in this chapter will provide you with practical tools for dealing with XML Schema. But because Schema allows you to represent the same data structure in a variety of ways, some of the recipes here also focus on design choices that will help ensure that not only is your data model structured in a way that represents the instances you need, but in a way that keeps your SOA flexible in the long run.

2.1 Designing Schema for SOA

Problem

You want to define your data types with XML Schema to use within your SOA, but Schema is so flexible that you aren't sure how to do it. You want to follow patterns and best practices for Schema that make the most sense specifically in an SOA context.

Solution

Follow one of the Schema design patterns discussed here: Russian Doll, Salami Slice, or Venetian Blind.

There are several generally accepted design patterns that apply when creating XML schemas. The inherent flexibility that XML Schema affords means that it can be difficult to figure out how to start writing them in a consistent, clear manner that will give you the perfect combination of expressiveness, flexibility, and strong-enough typing. This is all aggravated when your aim is to design them for an SOA in a way that allows you both to generate to Java code and to use as raw XML.

Schema defines basic building blocks for defining entities: simple types, complex types, elements, and attributes. Beyond these, there are many choices to make regarding global or local types, namespace qualification, and more. Making uninformed choices at this level can crush your SOA, inadvertently limiting its flexibility. Without careful schema design, you could work very hard to make loosely coupled services that are composed using orchestrations and brokered ESBs for different domains, only to suddenly find that in reality the services in your SOA are very tightly coupled at the root because of a poor choice in schema design. A simple schema change here could force you to redeploy whole sets of service compositions.

But XML is at the heart of your SOA, and you want to use the considerable power of Java while maintaining the flexibility that XML gives you. You can have it both ways, but you just need to think about the ramifications of your schema design choices. In this section, we'll look at three well-known design patterns for constructing schemas: Russian Doll, Salami Slice, and Venetian Blind. There are two others that people sometimes employ: Garden of Eden and Chameleon, which we'll have to discuss in the following recipe because of the attractive nuisance it makes.

The patterns here are generally differentiated by one thing: whether or not your elements and types are globally defined. A global element or type is one that is a child of the schema node. A local element or type is one that is nested within another element or type. A local element cannot be reused elsewhere.

Now let's look at the patterns.

Russian Doll

In real life, a Russian doll is a wooden shell that acts as a container for several other identical-looking dolls, each of which is also a shell containing the next smaller doll. Opening the top of the outermost doll reveals the next smaller doll.

This design pattern is perfectly named, and therefore easy to remember. The pattern is to create a single global root element that contains, like its namesake, all of its constituent types; all other elements beside this single global element are local. All element declarations are nested inside the root element, and can therefore only be used once, within that context. The root element is the only one that gets to use the global namespace.

Russian Doll has the following characteristics:

- It has a single global root element.
- All types are local, i.e., nested within the root element.
- It supports only schemas designed entirely in a single file.
- It has high cohesion with minimal coupling.
- Because types are not exposed, the schema is fully encapsulated.
- It is the easiest pattern to read and write.

Do not use Russian Doll if you need to reuse types.

Example 2-1 demonstrates the Russian Doll design pattern.

Example 2-1. Book.xsd using the Russian Doll schema design pattern

```
<xsd:schema xmlns:xsd="http://www.w3.org/2001/XMLSchema"
           targetNamespace="http://ns.soacookbook.com/russiandoll"
           xmlns:tns="http://ns.soacookbook.com/russiandoll"
           elementFormDefault="unqualified">
<xsd:annotation>
    <xsd:documentation>
      Book schema as Russian Doll design.
    </xsd:documentation>
</xsd:annotation>
<xsd:element name="book">
    <xsd:complexType>
        <xsd:sequence>
            <xsd:element name="title" type="xsd:string"/>
            <xsd:element name="price" type="xsd:decimal"/>
            <xsd:element name="category" type="xsd:NCName"/>
            <xsd:choice>
                <xsd:element name="author" type="xsd:string"/>
                <xsd:element name="authors">
                    <xsd:complexType>
                        <xsd:sequence>
                            <xsd:element name="author"
```

```
                                    type="xsd:string"
                                    maxOccurs="unbounded"/>
                            </xsd:sequence>
                        </xsd:complexType>
                    </xsd:element>
                </xsd:choice>
            </xsd:sequence>
        </xsd:complexType>
</xsd:element>
</xsd:schema>
```

As you can see, this schema defines a single global element, "book". The types required to create a book element are all nested within it. Elements and types cannot be referenced. Namespaces are localized. The "authors" element redefines its child "author" elements. This is potentially a maintenance issue.

Russian Doll has certain advantages. For simple schemas, it is easy to read and write because there is no mixing, no references, no hunting for type definitions. There is no flexibility built into this design, which makes it predictable. It is easy to understand the intentions of the author, and you know exactly what the resulting document instance will look like.

Because it is entirely self-contained, schemas that follow this pattern are decoupled from other schemas. Changing types will not affect other schemas.

The clear disadvantage to Russian Doll with respect to straight XML work is that the types you carefully define cannot be reused elsewhere. And it can become unwieldy for very large schemas.

Russian Doll is perhaps an appropriate design to use when wrapping legacy data from a source that is fairly static, say, a modified DB2 filesystem table on a midrange that holds isolated records. Within a master data management effort, this sort of definition can be reflected quickly by generative tools.

Salami Slice

Salami Slice represents the opposite end of the design spectrum from Russian Doll.

Using this pattern, you declare all elements as global, but declare all types locally. You set all elements into the global namespace, making the schema available for reuse by other schemas. Each element acts as a single definition "slice," which can be combined with others.

With Salami Slice, you have many components, all defined individually, which are then brought together under global elements. Russian Doll is absolutely rigid and inflexible in its design, giving you the closed definition of the single element it defines. Salami Slice is entirely open, allowing a wide variety of possible combinations. The physical structure of an actual Russian doll allows only one way to put the doll together; slices of salami offer no guidance for how they might be arranged on a sandwich.

Salami Slice has the following characteristics:

- All elements are global.
- All elements are defined within the global namespace.
- All types are local.
- Element declarations are never nested.
- Element declarations are reusable. Salami Slice offers the best possibility for reuse of all the schema design patterns.
- It is difficult to determine the intended root element, as there are many potential choices.

Example 2-2 shows your book schema redesigned with Salami Slice.

Example 2-2. Book.xsd using the Salami Slice schema design pattern

```
<xsd:schema xmlns:xsd="http://www.w3.org/2001/XMLSchema"
          targetNamespace="http://ns.soacookbook.com/salami"
          xmlns:tns="http://ns.soacookbook.com/salami"
          elementFormDefault="qualified">
    <xsd:annotation>
      <xsd:documentation>
          Book schema as Salami Slice design.
      </xsd:documentation>
    </xsd:annotation>
    <xsd:element name="book">
        <xsd:complexType>
            <xsd:sequence>
                <xsd:element ref="tns:title" />
                <xsd:element ref="tns:author" />
                <xsd:element ref="tns:category" />
                <xsd:element ref="tns:price" />
            </xsd:sequence>
        </xsd:complexType>
    </xsd:element>

    <xsd:element name="title"/>
    <xsd:element name="price"/>
    <xsd:element name="category"/>
    <xsd:element name="author"/>
</xsd:schema>
```

The advantage to this pattern is that because the elements are declared globally, the schema is reusable. But because changing an element affects the composing elements, Salami Slice schemas are considered tightly coupled.

Schemas that follow this pattern are verbose. Things are clearly arranged and flat.

Note too that schema reuse can often mean tight coupling for your services. See the discussion at the end of this recipe for more on that matter.

The Russian Doll and the Salami Slice operate at opposite ends of the spectrum. Because of their purity in insisting on either total rigidity or total flexibility, they have clear advantages and clear disadvantages. The next pattern, Venetian Blind, meets in the middle and offers the best of both worlds.

Venetian Blind

Venetian Blind is an extension of Russian Doll. It contains only one single global root element. It departs from Russian Doll in that it allows for reuse of all types as well as the global root element.

Using Venetian Blind means that you define a single global root element for instantiation, and compose it with externally defined types. This has the benefit of maximizing reuse.

Venetian Blind has the following characteristics:

- It has a single global root element.
- It mixes global and local declarations. Contrast this with Russian Doll, in which all types are local, and Salami Slice, in which all types are global.
- It has high cohesion but also high coupling. Because its components are coupled and not self-contained, it can occasion coupling with other schemas.
- It maximizes reuse. All types and the root element can be recombined.
- Because types are exposed, encapsulation is limited.
- It allows you to use multiple files to define your schema.
- It is verbose. Breaking apart each type in this way gives you very selective, granular control over each individual aspect or your element, but makes for a lot of typing.

In Example 2-3, there are five reusable types: `TitleType`, `AuthorType`, `CategoryType`, `PriceType`, and the book element itself.

Example 2-3. Book schema using the Venetian Blind design pattern

```
<xsd:schema xmlns:xsd="http://www.w3.org/2001/XMLSchema"
       targetNamespace="http://ns.soacookbook.com/venetianblind"
       xmlns:tns="http://ns.soacookbook.com/venetianblind"
       elementFormDefault="unqualified"
       attributeFormDefault="unqualified">
<xsd:annotation>
  <xsd:documentation>
     Book schema as Venetian Blind design.
  </xsd:documentation>
</xsd:annotation>

<!-- Single global root element exposed -->
<xsd:element name="book" type="tns:BookType" />

<!-- The root is given a type that is defined here,
     using all externally defined elements.-->
```

```
<xsd:complexType name="BookType">
    <xsd:sequence>
        <xsd:element name="title" type="tns:TitleType"/>
        <xsd:element name="author" type="tns:AuthorType"/>
        <xsd:element name="category" type="tns:CategoryType"/>
        <xsd:element name="price" type="tns:PriceType" />
    </xsd:sequence>
</xsd:complexType>

<!-- Each type used by the global root is defined below,
     and are potentially available for reuse depending on
     the value of the 'elementFormDefault' switch
     (use 'qualified' to expose, 'unqualified' to hide) -->
<xsd:simpleType name="TitleType">
    <xsd:restriction base="xsd:string">
        <xsd:minLength value="1"/>
    </xsd:restriction>
</xsd:simpleType>

<xsd:simpleType name="AuthorType">
    <xsd:restriction base="xsd:string">
        <xsd:minLength value="1"/>
    </xsd:restriction>
</xsd:simpleType>

<xsd:simpleType name="CategoryType">
    <xsd:restriction base="xsd:string">
        <xsd:enumeration value="LITERATURE"/>
        <xsd:enumeration value="PHILOSOPHY"/>
        <xsd:enumeration value="PROGRAMMING"/>
    </xsd:restriction>
</xsd:simpleType>

<xsd:simpleType name="PriceType">
    <xsd:restriction base="xsd:float" />
</xsd:simpleType>

</xsd:schema>
```

Choose Venetian Blind when you need to maximize reuse and flexibility, and take advantage of namespace exposure.

See Also

Recipe 2.2.

Garden of Eden

The Garden of Eden schema design pattern, identified by Sun Microsystems, is a combination of Salami Slice and Venetian Blind. To make a schema following this pattern, define all elements and types in the global namespace, and then reference elements as necessary.

With Garden of Eden, you get the maximum reuse of all the schema design patterns. You can freely reuse all elements and types. There is no encapsulation of elements in such a schema. There are many potential root elements, as they are all global. Documents following this pattern can be harder to read. Unlike Russian Doll, in which it is clear what the root element is, with Garden of Eden, the author's intentions are masked. The only intention you can gather is that the author intends to allow you the most flexibility when creating XML instance documents based on the schema. Of course, as the schema author, you can define elements out of the box that combine a variety of types your users might need, thereby illustrating to them the reason you're following this pattern.

The Book schema you've been working with is shown in Example 2-4, rearranged to use Garden of Eden.

Example 2-4. Book schema following the Garden of Eden design pattern

```
<xsd:schema xmlns:xsd="http://www.w3.org/2001/XMLSchema"
  targetNamespace="http://ns.soacookbook.com/eden"
  xmlns:tns="http://ns.soacookbook.com/eden"
  elementFormDefault="qualified">
    <xsd:annotation>
        <xsd:documentation>
        Book schema as Garden of Eden design.
        </xsd:documentation>
    </xsd:annotation>

    <xsd:element name="book" type="tns:bookType"/>
    <xsd:element name="title" type="xsd:string"/>
    <xsd:element name="author" type="xsd:string"/>
    <xsd:element name="category" type="xsd:string"/>
    <xsd:element name="price" type="xsd:double"/>

    <xsd:complexType name="bookType">
        <xsd:sequence>
            <xsd:element ref="tns:title"/>
            <xsd:element ref="tns:author"/>
            <xsd:element ref="tns:category"/>
            <xsd:element ref="tns:price"/>
        </xsd:sequence>
    </xsd:complexType>

</xsd:schema>
```

In this schema, instance documents can refer to and use the `Book` type directly, or they can use a combination of the elements. This pattern, which is loosely followed in a hybrid model by the OAGi industry schemas, can make it easier for you to maintain schemas in the long run within a SOA, as it allows you to recombine aspects of your existing schemas as required. This might be a good choice to consider for general or core types within SOA that you expect to be reused many times, or that don't fall within an obvious single business domain.

Of course, you need not limit yourself to a single pattern, but can use all of the different patterns just described, depending on the level of encapsulation and direction or flexibility you need for a given definition.

2.2 Creating Canonical Data Model

Problem

You want to create a canonical data model for your SOA, as discussed in Woolf and Hohpe's *Enterprise Integration Patterns* (Addison-Wesley Professional), but you aren't sure how to proceed.

Solution

Read the discussion below. You may choose not to do this. If you do choose to employ a canonical data model, you probably want to have a data architect create this up-front, following a detailed analysis of your organization's data from a master data management perspective, and before you have lots of services in place.

In short, your mileage may vary, but the solution is probably to define schemas local to services that reuse a separate layer of schemas, defined independently of services, at the enterprise level.

Discussion

Creating a canonical data model can be tough. You can do everything else right, but if you get this wrong, you will have painted yourself into a corner that can take considerable effort and restructuring to get out of. I know of one software company with dozens of interacting products that spent 10 months working on its schema definition of Product. Let's proceed with caution.

Perform your schema analysis and design in a separate, prior process from your service analysis. Your services will exchange business documents, and these business documents will be composed of cross-domain entities. For example, a variety of services across different business domains will potentially need to use certain core types, such as Customer or Product or Invoice. So far everything seems fine.

But on a practical level, this immediately drops the problem of schema reuse into your lap. You have the following choices:

- Maximize reuse of types and eliminate redundant type definitions. Define your Customer and Product and Invoice schemas using a schema pattern that allows for recomposition. Write schemas to represent core or general types that might be used in many places, such as Address, or SSN, or CreditCard. Write service-specific schemas that reuse those core types. You have a perfect, pristine design. All you have to do now is cross your fingers that no requirements ever change for just one service. If something happens to cause a schema change, you could find yourself needing to rebuild, retest, and redeploy lots of services. I know of one company with 2,500 web services. As Sponge Bob Square Pants says, good luck with that.

- Maximize service flexibility and minimize interdependence. Define Customer and Product and Invoice separately for each service. You have a contract totally customized for each service, with no compromises. This might mean a lot of redundancy (also known as "schema denormalization"), but it allows services to evolve independently. It also allows a more fully encapsulated service. For example, if you have defined a Customer service that is to serve as the gateway to all customer-related operations, it makes sense that the service is the owner of the schema, and that its dependencies do not leak outside of it. Of course, depending on the number of services you have or plan to have in your enterprise, this could mean a lot of redundancy. Just cross your fingers that no requirements ever change for a core type that's defined in lots of different schemas because you will then have a significant amount of error-prone, manual work ahead of you.

Neither of these choices is particularly attractive.

Perhaps there is a way that you can have the best of both worlds by using one of the fundamental principles of computer science, the layer of abstraction. You can apply it here as the canonical data model, sometimes called the canonical schema pattern.

Defining the canonical data model

Canonical data model refers to the practice of defining single schemas to represent types globally, and reusing those types by reference in the schemas locally designed for the service. In the way that an enterprise service bus acts as a mediator, allowing any number of web services to talk to one another without having to create a specific point-to-point relationship between each one, a canonical data model allows you to define gold copy schemas for the types in your enterprise; any service that needs to talk types can use the service bus or some like mechanism to translate its version into the canonical version.

The canonical schema is your gold standard. It is capable of representing everything about an entity. Every service that refers to an entity may need to customize it in some way to perform its local work. But those differences are specific to the schema for that service, and any specific schema can always get to the canonical schema. Because the entity service schema and the canonical schema are two distinct documents, you can maximize both freedom and reuse.

Of course, you don't want to have designed your schema as only a bunch of strings just so that it's flexible enough to accommodate any data. Your entity service is probably going to represent a real database that requires a field to be a certain length, for example. You want your service to reflect the actual constraints you're dealing with. The more specific you can be, the more schema-based validation you can do.

You also have defined a canonical schema, which represents the way that your company wants to represent Address and Name and such items. The canonical schema is more flexible and general than the local entity schema. It is more accommodating because not every address restriction for every application you need to integrate with will have been magically defined according to the same constraints. You can get to the canonical representation from any local entity schema. And from the canonical schema, you can get to any other representation. On the bus, you can use XSLT within an orchestration or an intercepting service to translate from one type to another as necessary, fill in any undefined fields with defaults, and so forth.

Now say, for example, that your company has just purchased another company. The two organizations will have a different Customer entity service, with different representations of things like Address and Name. With a canonical data model in place, you just need to have the two services map to the canonical model; they don't need to map to each other or be individually rewritten (which is antithetical to the purpose of integration). So now you have three customer schemas: your canonical customer schema, your service customer schema, and the schema that had been defined by the company you purchased.

Over time, you can use governance to migrate service schemas to match the canonical schema better in order to cut down on potentially expensive runtime transformations.

Recommendations

I advocate starting with schema design as one of the key tasks within an SOA. Here are my recommendations:

- As much as possible, design schemas for the canonical data model separately from service design, before creating your service contracts.
- Keep the types in the canonical schemas somewhat flexible and general, as they will potentially need to absorb a variety of service entity definitions. For example, it's probably fine to use an enumeration in a service schema, but use a string to represent that same type in a canonical schema. It is surprising how little we can actually agree on. Maybe your `USState` enumeration has 50 items, but maybe the enum in the schema of the service you need to integrate with includes Guam and Puerto Rico.
- Design entity service schemas as independent documents that are included within your WSDL. Do not define types locally within the WSDL.
- When you define a schema for a service, import from the canonical model as much as possible.
- Design schemas separately from service design.
- Apply enterprise standards to all schema design, and closely guard the governance surrounding the canonical model. Do not attempt to centralize core business entity

types such as Customer or Invoice unless you have a governance structure in place to manage schema changes.

- Keep canonical schemas in an enterprise repository. You can make this an LDAP server, or a web server to start if you're on a budget. You can graduate to document control software or, ideally, an SOA-specific product that accounts for all of your SOA artifacts. The schemas should be available at runtime on a network.
- Consider defining certain "fundamental" types that are centrally used in their own namespace, and in their own schema. For example, a U.S. phone number, a Social Security number, or other data structures that are not defined by your business make fine candidates for centralized types that are reused throughout many schemas.
- Do not require your canonical schemas to be a frontend to any database. They exist to define concepts and act as ideal mediators.
- Pattern restrictions are better to use in service schemas than canonical schemas. They can play an important role in validation.
- Avoid using certain advanced schema constructs such as polymporphism, choice, or unions. These will seriously damage interoperability. The tool support for generated code on many platforms is either non-existent or poor at best.

Be strict with yourself regarding the point about fundamental types, and do not allow yourself a wide definition of them. For example, while an address seems like something that is defined by the post office and is not specific to your business, this is not generally the case in actual practice. A new shipping service may need a different degree of granularity or type restriction from what your point of sale has used for the last 20 years. It is a non-trivial undertaking to get all of that legacy data into compliance just so you can define a single address type that both systems use, with little profit potential for the business.

In this book, I advocate starting from the data model and using that to compose the idea of the service contract as a facilitator of document exchange. Delay writing code as long as possible. After the schemas are clear, the contract can fall out from it, and both can be refined in an iterative process. Then you can generate Java code for your services to use, or give them to developers to implement. This helps ensure that you are not tightly bound to an implementation because it mimics what your clients will have to do.

Of course, you are now bound between your schema and your Java code, and a schema change requires new code generation. But there are two points here: any schema change means per force a contract change; they're part of the contract. So regeneration is the least of your problems. Generation should be part of your build. Don't commit generated objects to a repository, and don't grow to rely on implementation-specific features in your services. Starting from Java can tempt you with generics and other unnecessary language features that don't have a place in a service contract.

There's no silver bullet here, so don't get too hung up—you are going to have some redundancy or some coupling. Pick your poison and prefer a redundancy over a coupling. You can't know exactly how requirements and business relationships will evolve and change over time.

Updating the canonical data model

Canonical schema is a weird beast. Some SOA practitioners call it an anti-pattern, which is good to be aware of. But many others refer to it not only as a pattern in the positive sense but as one of the most important fundamental aspects of creating a solid SOA. Architects I've spoken with indicate that one of the first things they do when embarking on an SOA journey is define their canonical data model up-front. This is ontology and taxonomy work.

The canonical data model shouldn't be an anti-pattern if you do lots of analysis and clarification of the concepts. Make sure that you are including everything that an entity might need to be in your enterprise, and keep it general enough to account for this. Use a schema pattern that allows flexibility in your design.

Then, as you define your entity services, define a schema local to the service. Reuse types from the canonical model as much as possible, via import.

Any changes to the canonical model must go through SOA governance, and they must be rare. Services represent business entities. These things don't change every day. You will need to make changes to the canonical model eventually. But then you can version those schemas explicitly, and if you indicate the version in the namespace, you will not have to change all of the services at once. Create a new version of the schema, indicate the version in the namespace, and then you are free to change only the service that you want to change to use the new version of the canonical model. Update remaining services as you have time, but be sure to do it soon. If you have more than two versions of the canonical schema, it isn't canonical anymore: it's just another messy layer on what is sure to be a doomed SOA. Govern this process, and you'll be fine.

See Also

Recipe 2.4.

2.3 Using Chameleon Namespace Design

Problem

You want to design a clever workaround for namespace dependencies within your schemas and think that using a Chameleon pattern will work within an SOA.

Solution

Don't do this. The Chameleon pattern is very clever. Its approach is to have you design your common types in a schema with no namespace, called the Chameleon. You then define a "master" schema that does have a namespace that `<include>`s the first schema. The common types from the Chameleon get namespace-coerced and assume the namespace defined in the master. Examples 2-5 and 2-6 show how this works.

Example 2-5. Chameleon customer

```
<xsd:schema xmlns:xsd="http://www.w3.org/2001/XMLSchema"
            elementFormDefault="qualified">

<!-- Defined without namespace -->
<xsd:complexType name="CustomerType">
    <xsd:sequence>
       <xsd:element name="name" type="xsd:string"/>
    </xsd:sequence>
</xsd:complexType>

</xsd:schema>
```

Example 2-6. Master invoice schema namespace-coerces the Chameleon

```
<xsd:schema xmlns:xsd="http://www.w3.org/2001/XMLSchema"
            targetNamespace="urn:Invoice"
            xmlns="urn:Invoice"
            elementFormDefault="qualified">

<xsd:include schemaLocation="CustomerChameleon.xsd"/>

<!-- Invoice has a Product and a Customer -->
<xsd:element name="Invoice">
    <xsd:complexType>
        <xsd:sequence>

            <!-- Define product here -->
            <xsd:element name="product">
             <xsd:complexType>
                <xsd:sequence>
                   <xsd:element name="name" type="xsd:string"/>
                   <xsd:element name="sku" type="xsd:string"/>
                </xsd:sequence>
            </xsd:complexType>
            </xsd:element>

            <!-- Pull from Chameleon -->
            <xsd:element name="customer" type="CustomerType"
               minOccurs="1" maxOccurs="1" />
        </xsd:sequence>
    </xsd:complexType>
</xsd:element>

</xsd:schema>
```

The master schema here defines an Invoice type that includes the Product defined in the Chameleon schema. This is a powerful leveraging of the ways that namespaces work in XML schema, and makes it seem very attractive initially. It appears that you may be able to get around some of the dependency problems introduced in the last recipe on schema design. If you declare no namespace and use Chameleons for common types wherever possible, clients are not broken if you later substitute types.

But you should know that the use of the Chameleon design pattern is heavily debated. Chameleon depends on certain areas of the schema specification whose interpretation is not strictly agreed upon by vendors. As a primary purpose of SOA is to achieve interoperable generic services, be careful signing yourself up for something that is only sometimes supported.

Also, Chameleon will generally degrade performance during validation, even from vendors who do support it. That's because the delay in namespace resolution prevents parsers from caching components of the schema based on their namespaces.

Chameleons also limit the ability to use XPath identity constraints. XPaths do not use the default namespace, so their use must be prefixed, which undermines the point of Chameleon in the first place.

Chameleons increase the likelihood of component name collisions because types are not bound by their namespaces.

Ultimately, namespaces, like packages, are there for a reason, which is to logically group a set of types and set them off as being constituent of a given general idea. If you can't put your types in a namespace, you may need to reconsider your design. If you could put your types in a namespace, but choose not to in the hopes of gaining flexibility, expect interoperability and collision problems sooner or later.

2.4 Versioning Schemas

Problem

There are lots of different ways to indicate versions for schemas, and you're not sure which, if any, is most appropriate in an SOA context.

Solution

Strongly consider using some part of the namespace to indicate the schema version. This supports the canonical data model pattern. You must do so in a way that does not disrupt tools that perform code generation, however.

Discussion

Your XML schemas will evolve over time, even those in your canonical model that you hope to change only infrequently, so you need a strategy for versioning your schemas that will support your work on a practical level within an SOA. There are a few options, which we'll discuss here.

Use the version attribute

The most straightforward way to version a schema is to use the built-in attribute that exists just for this purpose. It looks like this:

```
<xs:schema xmlns:xs="http://www.w3.org/2001/XMLSchema"
  version="1.0.0">
```

The chief benefit of versioning this way is that it's easy and doesn't require any additional work. It is also advantageous because if the existing schema or WSDL that imports the versioned schema is compatible with the new version, it doesn't need to change.

But, as with so many easy things, it doesn't really get us what we want. The downside is that it is not enforceable by tools. Moreover, it is not clear from an importing artifact (such as a WSDL or another schema) what version you are using unless you also represent the version in the location of the physical document. This becomes a maintenance issue,because it violates the DRY (Don't Repeat Yourself) rule. It also begs the question why you'd bother asserting the version in this attribute if it alone is not sufficient.

Hack the root element

You could define the root element in your schema to carry a version attribute of its own. This would allow validation to be enforceable with tools, but this is not really a solution. The enforced validation requires additional and custom preprocessing. You do not want to pollute your data model with implementation-specific items (such as a schema version number). This is altogether inappropriate within web service usage.

Change the name or URI of the schema document

You could simply change the name of the file or its location. This would allow importing schema documents or WSDLs to clearly represent what version they are using, as shown below:

```
<customer
  xmlns="http://www.soacookbook.com/Customer"
  xmlns:xsi="http://www.w3.org/2001/XMLSchema-instance"
  xsi:schemaLocation="http://www.soacookbook.com/Customer
  http://www.soacookbook.com/Customer-v1.0.0.xsd">
```

This is similar to the previous choice. The `schemaLocation` attribute is not authoritative, meaning that it is a hint to processors, and can be ignored. This would work for WSDL documents because they do explicitly import based on physical location. However, this could create considerable inconsistencies and difficulties with tools because the namespace has not changed, though the version has. That advertises to consumers that the

WSDL is compatible with the namespace in general, and not simply this specific version. Generated code used by clients out in the world will be out of sync.

Use the namespace and document name

The best solution is to use the namespace itself to indicate the version of the schema. This is familiar from many of the specifications we work with in web services. Consider the following namespaces:

- The namespace for SOAP 1.2 is `http://www.w3.org/2003/05/soap-envelope`.
- The namespace for WS-Addressing 1.0 is `http://www.w3.org/2005/08/addressing`.
- The namespace for XML Schema 1.0 is `http://www.w3.org/2001/XMLSchema`, and it uses the namespace for instances of `http://www.w3.org/2001/XMLSchema-instance`.

These namespaces, all of which are central to web services, indicate their version by including the year and month of their publication in the namespace itself. There is no confusion as to whether you are looking at a SOAP 1.1 or SOAP 1.2 envelope. However, you are not free to simply replicate this structure directly in the schemas you define for use in a WSDL. That's because web services rely on code generated by tools. Tools such as `wsimport` and `WSDL2Java` generate package names for the client artifacts they create from a WSDL using the namespace. And in Java, it is illegal to begin a package name with a number.

This is easily remedied. You could do something like this:

```
<definitions name="MyService"
   targetNamespace="http://ns.soacookbook.com/sales/v2009Q1"
   xmlns="http://schemas.xmlsoap.org/wsdl/"
   xmlns:soap="http://schemas.xmlsoap.org/wsdl/soap/"
   xmlns:tns="http://www.soacookbook.com/sales/v2009Q1"
   xmlns:xsd="http://www.w3.org/2001/XMLSchema">
```

Using a prefix such as "v" to indicate "version" takes care of the client-side generation problem. You don't have to use a date, of course, and can use a more standard version number.

This has the advantage of making clear in WSDLs, in importing schemas, and in generated client code what exactly is being used. It also allows these items to continue using the version they're compatible with until they're ready to take the update.

Because you have changed the namespace, you should create a new document based on the new version, and keep both versions until you can update everybody. Not everything can or should be migrated to the new schema at once.

Make sure that you decide on a single convention up-front, publish it in your developer documentation and governance guidelines, and enforce the structure you've chosen.

2.5 Reference Schemas

Problem

You have a sneaking suspicion that someone, somewhere, has already designed an XML schema for a basic entity like Address. You want to build off of the work of a standards body or working group comprising smart people who have had lots of time to consider this sort of thing, and you don't want to reinvent the wheel.

Solution

Check out the many industry schemas that have been defined by the Open Applications Group (OAGi) at *http://www.openapplications.org*. They define XML schemas for a variety of verticals. Registration basically means giving them your email address, and then you can download for free the wide variety of schemas they have written. You can use them outright, which will simplify integration with other companies that also use them outright, or you can use them as a starting point and incorporate what you can from them into your own designs.

The Open Applications Group has done a lot of work over many years creating schemas according to best practices, and specifically for the purpose of supporting B2B integration efforts. It has published whitepapers, which you can also download, on how it has defined its schemas. These whitepapers are interesting in their own right, but they also should encourage you to do the same within your enterprise.

As part of your governance plan, create a set of standards, best practices, and requirements that you publish internally as part of your reference architecture. Reviewing the OAGi documents will help guide you on how to do this.

I warn you that OAGi's schemas and whitepapers can be long and involved, so you may benefit from condensing them a bit for your own purposes.

2.6 Common Schema Types

Problem

You want to define some typical regular expression type constraints for use in your schema and you don't want to reinvent the wheel.

Solution

Try one of the following commonly used regular expressions. While regular expression usage can vary from platform to platform, these have all been tested with Java, and will work on validation of a SOAP payload.

Person's name

This type would be used for two separate elements for first name and last name. Names must be at least 2 characters and no more than 30 characters; must consist of alphabetic characters; and may contain hyphens, single quotes, periods and spaces. Yes, I do know someone whose legal name contains a "." (hi, J.!). And, I have a cousin with the legal name "M'Lee":

```
<xs:element name="name">
<xs:simpleType>
    <xs:restriction base="xs:string">
       <xs:minLength value="2" />
       <xs:maxLength value="30" />
       <xs:pattern value="[A-Za-z\-. ']{2,30}" />
    </xs:restriction>
</xs:simpleType>
</xs:element>
```

This is not necessarily the best way to restrict a name, but at least it's something to work with. The airline industry does not allow for any special characters, including the very common hyphen, for example. Just do what works for you.

U.S. phone number

This handles the common hyphenated field separation as well as using dots or spaces for field separators:

```
<xs:element name="usPhone">
<xs:simpleType>
    <xs:restriction base="xs:string">
        <xs:pattern value="\(?\d{3}\)?[ \-\.]?\d{3}[ \-\.]?\d{4}" />
        <xs:minLength value="10" />
        <xs:maxLength value="16" />
    </xs:restriction>
</xs:simpleType>
</xs:element>
```

Note that there is one shortcoming to this regex. I have heard that neither the area code nor the prefix is allowed to start with a zero or a one for valid U.S. numbers, and this regex does not capture that idea. However, while I have never seen such a phone number, I also cannot find that telephonic rule. Moreover, I have found the stricter version of this expression to be unworkable in the real world, given the millions of records of test data generated by people who did not know that rule.

Email address

This regex allows typical email addresses that start with an alphanumeric character. It can also contain hyphens and periods followed by the @ sign and the domain name meeting the same criteria followed by an alpha suffix between two and nine characters long:

```
<xs:element name="email">
<xs:simpleType>
    <xs:restriction base="xs:string">
        <xs:pattern value="(\w+\.)*\w+@(\w+\.)+[A-Za-z]{2,9}" />
        <xs:minLength value="6" />
        <xs:maxLength value="255" />
    </xs:restriction>
</xs:simpleType>
</xs:element>
```

U.S. postal code

This allows zip (5 digit), or zip+4 in the format 85266-1234:

```
<xs:element name="usZip">
<xs:simpleType>
    <xs:restriction base="xs:string">
        <xs:pattern value="\d{5}(-\d{4})?" />
        <xs:minLength value="5" />
        <xs:maxLength value="10" />
    </xs:restriction>
</xs:simpleType>
</xs:element>
```

Social Security number

This is the standard structure. It does allow for leaving the hyphens off, as they might get entered by a user with hyphens, but be stored in a database without them:

```
<xsd:simpleType name="SSN">
    <xsd:restriction base="xsd:string">
        <xsd:pattern value="\d{3}(-)?\d{2}(-)?\d{4}" />
        <xsd:minLength value="9" />
        <xsd:maxLength value="11" />
    </xsd:restriction>
</xsd:simpleType>
```

Note that this is a very simple and straightforward representation, but it is not perfect. It is a rule that none of the three fields in a Social Security number is allowed to be all zeros, and this regex does not account for that.

Canadian postal code

Canadian postal codes contain six characters of alternating letters and numbers. The first three identify the Forward Sortation Area and the second three identify the Local Delivery Unit. The following are valid example codes: M1A 1A1, H9Z 9Z9.

```
<xs:element name="caPostalCode">
<xs:simpleType>
    <xs:restriction base="xs:string">
        <xs:pattern value="[ABCDEGHJKLMNPRSTVXY]\d[A-Z] \d[A-Z]\d" />
        <xs:minLength value="7" />
        <xs:maxLength value="7" />
    </xs:restriction>
```

```
</xs:simpleType>
</xs:element>
```

Canadian provinces

There are 14 Canadian provinces. Like the U.S. states, they use two-character abbreviations:

```
<xsd:simpleType name="CAProvince">
    <xsd:restriction base="xsd:string">
        <xsd:length value="2" />
        <xsd:enumeration value="AB" />
        <xsd:enumeration value="BC" />
        <xsd:enumeration value="MB" />
        <xsd:enumeration value="NB" />
        <xsd:enumeration value="NL" />
        <xsd:enumeration value="NS" />
        <xsd:enumeration value="NT" />
        <xsd:enumeration value="NU" />
        <xsd:enumeration value="ON" />
        <xsd:enumeration value="PE" />
        <xsd:enumeration value="QC" />
        <xsd:enumeration value="SK" />
        <xsd:enumeration value="YT" />
    </xsd:restriction>
</xsd:simpleType>
```

URL

This matches a URL with the `http://` optional. `https://` is allowable too, as is leaving off the protocol altogether and just going with something like www.domain.com. Port numbers are optional too, but if specified they must be between two and five digits in length:

```
<xs:element name="url">
<xs:simpleType>
    <xs:restriction base="xs:string">
        <xs:pattern value="(https?://)?[-\w.]+(:\d{2,5})?(/([\w/_.]*)?)?" />
    </xs:restriction>
</xs:simpleType>
</xs:element>
```

So these are all valid examples:

- `http://www.domain.com`
- `https://www.domain.com`
- `http://www.domain.com:8080`
- `http://www.domain.com:8080/some.xsd`
- `http://www.domain.com:80/path/doc.xml`

IP address

For an IP address, you need to represent values 0–255 across four octets:

```
<xs:element name="ip">
<xs:simpleType>
    <xs:restriction base="xs:string">
        <xs:pattern value="(((\d{0,2})|(1(\d){0,2})|(2[0-4]\d)|(25[0-5]))\.){3}
         ((\d{0,2})|(1(\d){0,2})|(2[0-4]\d)|(25[0-5]))" />
    </xs:restriction>
</xs:simpleType>
</xs:element>
```

This pattern allows 127.0.0.1, 192.168.1.1, 10.0.134.147, and so on.

There are surely many other common types of regular expressions that it would be convenient to have defined for you, but these should be enough to get you started.

2.7 Validating an XML Document Against a Schema

Problem

You have an XML document instance and you want to make sure it is valid against an XML schema.

Solution

Extend `org.xml.sax.helpers.DefaultHandler` and set it as the error handler on your DOM `DocumentBuilder`.

Note that the `DefaultHandler` class is provided for convenience so you don't have to implement methods you aren't interested in. But all of its methods are no-op, so you need to rethrow exceptions, log, or print a stack if you want to make the error known.

Example 2-7 shows a useful example.

Example 2-7. DomValidator.java

```
package com.sc.ch02.schema;

import static java.lang.System.out;

import java.io.IOException;
import javax.xml.parsers.DocumentBuilder;
import javax.xml.parsers.DocumentBuilderFactory;
import javax.xml.parsers.ParserConfigurationException;
import org.xml.sax.SAXException;
import org.xml.sax.SAXParseException;
import org.xml.sax.helpers.DefaultHandler;

/**
 * Validates an XML document according to a schema.
 */
```

```
public class DomValidator {

    private static final String SCHEMA_LANG_PROP =
        "http://java.sun.com/xml/jaxp/properties/schemaLanguage";
    private static final String XML_SCHEMA =
        "http://www.w3.org/2001/XMLSchema";

    private static final String SCHEMA_SOURCE_PROP =
        "http://java.sun.com/xml/jaxp/properties/schemaSource";

    //run the example
    public static void main(String[] args) {

        String schema = "C:/repository/books/SOACookbook/code/" +
                "soacookbook/bin/ch02/Catalog.xsd";
        String xmlDoc = "bin/ch02/Catalog.xml";

        boolean valid = validate(schema, xmlDoc);

        out.print("Valid? " + valid);
    }

    //do the work
    private static boolean validate(String schema, String xmlDoc) {
        DocumentBuilder builder = createDocumentBuilder(schema);

        ValidationHandler handler = new ValidationHandler();
        builder.setErrorHandler(handler);

        try {
            builder.parse(xmlDoc);

        } catch (SAXException se) {
            out.println("Validation Error: " + se.getMessage());
        } catch (IOException ioe) {
            ioe.printStackTrace();
        }

        return handler.isValid();
    }

    /**
     * Convenience method sets up the validating factory and
     * creates the builder.
     */
    private static DocumentBuilder createDocumentBuilder(
            String schema) {

        DocumentBuilderFactory factory =
            DocumentBuilderFactory.newInstance();

        factory.setNamespaceAware(true);
        factory.setValidating(true);
        factory.setAttribute(SCHEMA_LANG_PROP, XML_SCHEMA);
        factory.setAttribute(SCHEMA_SOURCE_PROP, schema);
```

```
        DocumentBuilder builder = null;
        try {
            builder = factory.newDocumentBuilder();
        } catch (ParserConfigurationException pce) {
            pce.printStackTrace();
        }

        return builder;
    }
}

/**
 * This class gets notified by the parser in the event of a
 * problem.
 */
class ValidationHandler extends DefaultHandler {
    private boolean valid = true;
    private SAXException se;

    /**
     * The default implementation does nothing.
     */
    @Override
    public void error(SAXParseException se) throws SAXException {
        this.se = se;
        valid = false;
        throw se;
    }

    /**
     * The default implementation does nothing.
     */
    @Override
    public void fatalError(SAXParseException se)
        throws SAXException {

        this.se = se;
        valid = false;
        throw se;
    }

    public boolean isValid() {
        return valid;
    }
}
```

Under normal circumstances, the program should give the following output:

```
Valid? true
```

If you rearrange either your schema or your XML document so that it is invalid, you will see a message similar to this one:

```
Validation Error: cvc-elt.1: Cannot find the declaration of element 'dude'.
Valid? false
```

The DOM parser built-in to Java SE 6 is not namespace-aware by default, so you must set that property on the `DocumentBuilderFactory`. If you forget to set that, there's no show; any errors in validation will be blissfully overlooked, even if the handler is set.

For documents to be validated correctly, the schema for elements in the default namespace must be declared.

2.8 Validating an XML Document Against Multiple Schemas

Problem

You have an XML document instance that uses elements from more than one namespace and you need to validate it.

Solution

Using the code from the last recipe, simply create a string array of the names of the schemas you need, and pass that to your `DocumentBuilderFactory`.

Say you have the following XML document that is defined by multiple schemas:

```
<c:customer cid="99" xmlns:c="urn:ns:soacookbook:customer">
  <gen:name xmlns:gen="urn:ns:soacookbook:general">
    Indiana Jones
  </gen:name>
  <a:address xmlns:a="urn:ns:soacookbook:address">
    <a:street>1212 Some Street</a:street>
    <a:city>Washington,DC</a:city>
    <a:state>VA</a:state>
  </a:address>
</c:customer>
```

This is more what we're accustomed to in the real world. Validating such a document is almost exactly the same as validating a document with a single schema. But in this case, you pass the `DocumentBuilderFactory` an array of strings representing the names of the schemas you need:

```
...

//create a string path to each schema needed for Customer.xml

String schemaAddress = ROOT + "a.xsd";
String schemaGeneral = ROOT + "gen.xsd";
String schemaCustomer = ROOT + "Customer.xsd";

String[] schemas =
    {schemaAddress, schemaGeneral, schemaCustomer};

//change this method to accept vararg schema
private static DocumentBuilder createDocumentBuilder(
            String...schemas) {
```

```
...

//business as usual
factory.setAttribute(SCHEMA_SOURCE_PROP, schemas);
```

It is important to note that I have been using strings to refer to the paths of schema documents, but that is not your only option. You can use any of the following to specify the value you pass to `factory.setAttribute`:

- A string pointing to the schema URI
- An `InputStream` you have previously used to capture the schema contents
- A SAX `InputSource`
- A `File` object
- An array containing elements of any of these types

2.9 Restricting Schema Types with Regular Expressions

Problem

You need to represent some basic simple types in your schema, such as a phone number or a Social Security number, and you want a stronger constraint than `xs:string` gives.

Solution

Use a regular expression inside a pattern to define your constraint, and enforce it with `<xs:restriction>`.

In XML Schema, your elements can be expressed by simple types that are defined as strings, but wrapped with a restriction element that defines a pattern. The pattern is a regular expression indicating the range of acceptable values. You can also get help from Schema with other built-in restriction elements, such as `<minLength>` and `<maxLength>`.

Here is an example:

```
<?xml version="1.0" encoding="UTF-8"?>
<xs:schema xmlns:xs="http://www.w3.org/2001/XMLSchema"
    targetNamespace="http://ns.soacookbook.com/cart"
    xmlns:tns="http://ns.soacookbook.com/cart"
    elementFormDefault="qualified">

    <xs:element name="usPhone" type="tns:USPhoneType" />

    <xs:simpleType name="USPhoneType">
        <xs:restriction base="xs:string">
            <xs:pattern value="\(?\d{3}\)?[ \-\.]?\d{3}[ \-\.]?\d{4}"/>
        </xs:restriction>
    </xs:simpleType>

</xs:schema>
```

Upon validation of an XML document instance, this will reject values for the domain element that do not conform to the regular expression.

Here is an XML document instance that passes validation for this constraint:

```
<?xml version="1.0" encoding="UTF-8"?>
<cart:usPhone xmlns:cart="http://ns.soacookbook.com/cart"
   xmlns:xsi="http://www.w3.org/2001/XMLSchema-instance"
   xsi:schemaLocation="http://ns.soacookbook.com/cart
   Cart.xsd">(888) 999-0101</cart:usPhone>
```

While not part of a regular expression, you can add other schema constraints regarding the length of acceptable values:

```
...
<xs:restriction base="xs:string">
    <xs:pattern value="..."/>
    <xs:minLength value="10"/>
    <xs:maxLength value="16"/>
</xs:restriction>
...
```

Table 2-1 offers an overview of some of the most commonly used regular expression constructs.

Table 2-1. Common regular expression constructs

`\d`	Any digit 0–9
`\D`	The disjoint of `\d`
`\s`	Space or tab character
`\S`	The disjoint of `\s`
`\w`	A word: upper- or lowercase letter, number, or underscore
`\W`	The disjoint of `\w`
`.`	Any single character
`?`	Zero or one occurrence
`*`	Zero or more occurrences
`+`	One or more occurrences

Table 2-2 illustrates the key metacharacters, which obtain meaning in constructing regular expressions.

Table 2-2. Regular expression metacharacters

`{}`	Indicates the number of times to match the preceding pattern, e.g., `\d{3}` matches any three digits in a row.
`[]`	Matches any pattern inside the brackets once and only once, e.g., `[AB]` matches either a single A or B character (case-sensitive) and nothing else.
`-`	When used inside `[]`, defines a range separator, e.g, `[1-5]` matches any single value 1 through 5. More than one range can be used inside a list, e.g., `[1-5A-E]` matches any single value 1 through 5 OR a single case-sensitive character A,B,C,D, or E.
`^`	When used inside `[]`, negates the expression, e.g., `[^0]` matches anything but 0.

Spaces inside brackets are meaningful. Parentheses are used for grouping, and must be escaped if intended literally. Here are some more brief examples:

- `capitali[zs]e` matches the American "capitalize" or the British "capitalise".
- `honou?r` matches the American "honor" or the British "honour".
- `\(?\d{3}\)?[ \-\.]?\d{3}[ \-\.]?\d{4}` matches 888.999.1111 or (888)999-1111 or (888) 999.1111 or (888)-999.1111. Let's dissect part of this phone construct. Take just this part: `\(?\d{3}\)?`. The first slash means escape the opening parenthesis to indicate that you mean to match the parentheses character, not a group. The first ? means that the opening parenthesis character preceding it is optional: there can be 0 or 1. The `\d{3}` matches three digits. You then match the mirror of the opening construct `\)?` to indicate an optional closing parenthesis. Now let's look at the next section: `[ \-\.]?`. The square brackets indicate a range. The space character is meaningful. This snippet indicates that following the area code can be a single space, a hyphen, a dot (`.`), or none of these. The remainder of the phone number regex repeats variations on these patterns.

If you know the structure of a data type, it is probably a good idea to constrain the values with regular expressions. But to ensure the best chance of interoperability, it is probably best to keep your regex constructs fairly simple, and not to use optional extensions that are not available on every platform. These include positioning constructs, such as `\<` to match the beginning of a word, and so on.

See Also

Recipe 2.11.

2.10 Using Schema Enumerations

Problem

You want your schema to define a limited set of known values usable for an element.

Solution

Use an XML Schema enumeration type.

Here is an example using U.S.:

```
<xs:simpleType name="USState">
    <xs:restriction base="xs:string">
        <xs:length value="2" />
        <xs:enumeration value="AL" />
        <xs:enumeration value="AK" />
        <xs:enumeration value="AR" />
        <xs:enumeration value="AZ" />
        ...
    </xsd:restriction>
</xsd:simpleType>
```

Only the characters indicated by the enumeration instances will pass validation in a document instance.

2.11 Generating Java Classes from Schema

Problem

You have taken care to create solid XML schemas representing your data types and now you want to generate Java sources from them.

Solution

Use the XML/Java Compiler XJC tool that comes with Java to compile your schemas into Java classes. If you're using Ant, use Sun's `<xjc>` wrapper task.

Sun does not ship Ant tasks with Java SE, and the task for XJC is no exception. You can find it in the *glassfish/lib* directory *webservices-tools.jar*. You may also need *webservices-rt.jar* on the classpath as well.

Working with JAXB

The purpose of JAXB is to provide a convenient and easy way to bind an XML schema to its corresponding representation in a set of Java classes. It has two primary functions:

Marshaling
: Creating XML document instances from Java objects

Unmarshaling
: Creating Java objects from XML document instances

JAXB used to be a bit more difficult to use than it is now. The 1.0 version came with the Web Services Developer pack as a separate download, and because Java 5 annotations were not yet used, JAXB generated far more code during marshaling and unmarshaling. That code was tricky to read and more rigid to work with. For one thing, JAXB 1.0 generated Java interfaces for everything during unmarshaling, which bloated and complicated the code base, sometimes representing classes with counterintuitive names.

Java SE 1.6.0_05 comes with version 2.1.3 of JAXB. This includes the XJC tool in its *bin* directory, so as long as Java is on your path, which it should be, you'll have no problem invoking it.

The first difference you'll notice is that JAXB 2.1 generates simple and clean annotated POJOs (Plain Old Java Objects) during unmarshaling. The annotations on these concrete classes indicate hints to JAXB for use during marshaling and unmarshaling. We'll examine the use and meaning of the annotations in the next section; for now, let's look at an example.

Say you have the schema in Example 2-8.

Example 2-8. XML schema to bind to a Java class

```
<xs:schema xmlns:xs="http://www.w3.org/2001/XMLSchema"
           targetNamespace="http://ns.soacookbook.com/suits"
           xmlns:tns="http://ns.soacookbook.com/suits"
           elementFormDefault="qualified">

<xs:simpleType name="Suit">
    <xs:restriction base="xs:string">
        <xs:enumeration value="SPADES" />
        <xs:enumeration value="HEARTS" />
        <xs:enumeration value="DIAMONDS" />
        <xs:enumeration value="CLUBS" />
    </xs:restriction>
</xs:simpleType>

</xs:schema>
```

This schema defines the suits available for playing cards. Example 2-9 shows an XML document instance that would validate against that schema.

Example 2-9. XML document matching the suit schema

```
<?xml version="1.0" encoding="UTF-8"?>
<s:suit  xmlns:xsi='http://www.w3.org/2001/XMLSchema-instance'
   xmlns:s='http://ns.soacookbook.com/suits'
   xsi:schemaLocation='http://ns.soacookbook.com/suits Suits.xsd'>HEARTS</s:suit>
```

This could be added to your SOAP message as the payload document. But if you define a web service that accepts an instance of a Java Suit enum, you won't be able to compile your service class unless you have the Suit enum on your classpath.

So you need to create a Java source that matches the schema. To do this, run XJC from the command line to generate the Java sources. Here you will change directories in the console to your project root. You have a directory called *work/gen* that you want to put your files into. Using the -d switch specifies the directory into which you want files generated. You can specify either a single schema filename to perform compilation across only that single schema, or you can specify a directory and XJC will compile all schemas it finds in that directory:

```
> >xjc -verbose -d work/gen src/xml/ch02/Suits.xsd
```

The final argument specifies the directory where XJC should find your files. With this usage, XJC will run against all schemas found in the specified directory. You should see output like this:

```
parsing a schema...
compiling a schema...
[INFO] generating code

com\soacookbook\ns\suits\ObjectFactory.java
com\soacookbook\ns\suits\Suit.java

>
```

The ObjectFactory is present for backward compatibility with JAXB 1.0. For the current example, it will be empty because you are generating an enum type. The resulting class looks like Example 2-10.

Example 2-10. JAXB 2.1 generated Suit.java enum

```
package com.soacookbook.ns.suits;

import javax.xml.bind.annotation.XmlEnum;
import javax.xml.bind.annotation.XmlType;

/**
 * <p>Java class for Suit.
 *
 * <p>The following schema fragment specifies the expected content contained within
     this class.
 * <p>
 * <pre>
 * &lt;simpleType name="Suit">
 *   &lt;restriction base="{http://www.w3.org/2001/XMLSchema}string">
 *     &lt;enumeration value="SPADES"/>
 *     &lt;enumeration value="HEARTS"/>
 *     &lt;enumeration value="DIAMONDS"/>
 *     &lt;enumeration value="CLUBS"/>
 *   &lt;/restriction>
 * &lt;/simpleType>
 * </pre>
 *
 */
@XmlType(name = "Suit", namespace = "http://ns.soacookbook.com/suits")
@XmlEnum
public enum Suit {
```

```
    SPADES,
    HEARTS,
    DIAMONDS,
    CLUBS;

    public String value() {
        return name();
    }

    public static Suit fromValue(String v) {
        return valueOf(v);
    }
}
```

This source file matches your Suits schema, and has been generated in the package corresponding to an inversion of the suits namespace. The namespace `http://ns.soacookbook.com/suits` is translated into the package name `com.soacookbook.ns.suits`.

Now that you have the basic idea, let's look at a more complex real-world example. The *Catalog.xsd* from earlier was declared as shown in Example 2-11.

Example 2-11. Catalog schema declaration

```
<?xml version="1.0" encoding="UTF-8"?>
<xsd:schema xmlns:xsd="http://www.w3.org/2001/XMLSchema"
        xmlns="http://ns.soacookbook.com/catalog"
        targetNamespace="http://ns.soacookbook.com/catalog">
//...
```

I won't repeat the entire listing here. We'll focus only on its `Book` type, as shown in Example 2-12.

Example 2-12. Book type as declared in Catalog.xsd

```
<xsd:complexType name="Book">
    <xsd:sequence>
        <xsd:element name="isbn" type="ISBN"/>
        <xsd:element name="author" type="Author"/>
        <xsd:element name="title" type="xsd:string"/>
        <xsd:element name="category" type="Category"/>
    </xsd:sequence>
</xsd:complexType>
```

Based on this type definition, JAXB will generate a *Book.java* file. The `complexType` is matched with a Java class, and the children of the type sequence are each matched with properties in the order in which they were declared in the sequence. Because none of your elements indicated `nillable="true"`, each field is annotated with `@XmlElement(required = true)`. This acts as a hint to the marshaler that a Java object instance that does not define values for each field should fail validation. See Example 2-13.

Example 2-13. Book.java class generated by JAXB

```
package com.soacookbook.ns.catalog;

import javax.xml.bind.annotation.*;

@XmlAccessorType(XmlAccessType.FIELD)
@XmlType(name = "Book", propOrder = {
    "isbn",
    "author",
    "title",
    "category"
})
public class Book {
    @XmlElement(required = true)
    protected String isbn;
    @XmlElement(required = true)
    protected Author author;
    @XmlElement(required = true)
    protected String title;
    @XmlElement(required = true)
    protected Category category;

//... getters and setters ommitted
```

There are a few more things to look at here. Note that the generated package is named after the namespace from your *Book.xsd*, and the fields are themselves represented by classes matching their `complexType` definitions. For example, the `Book` type is composed in part by a `Category` object:

```
<xsd:simpleType name="Category">
    <xsd:restriction base="xsd:string">
        <xsd:enumeration value="COOKING" />
        <xsd:enumeration value="LITERATURE" />
        <xsd:enumeration value="PHILOSOPHY" />
        <xsd:enumeration value="PROGRAMMING" />
    </xsd:restriction>
</xsd:simpleType>
```

So JAXB generates the *Category.java* file to match. Category happens to be a schema enumeration, and the mapping from a schema enum to a Java enum is very straightforward:

```
@XmlType(name = "Category")
@XmlEnum
public enum Category {
    COOKING,
    LITERATURE,
    PHILOSOPHY,
    PROGRAMMING;

    public String value() {
        return name();
    }
```

```
        public static Category fromValue(String v) {
            return valueOf(v);
        }
    }
```

You can then compile and use these classes as you would any other regular Java class. The `ObjectFactory` class that is generated here is only for backward compatibility with earlier versions of JAXB. So you could use this code in conjunction with code written in JAXB 1.0, and it would still work together.

You can see that `simpleType` string constraints are lost in generation. This is perhaps not what you would expect, but if you are using JAXB for web service model generation, you will still be able to validate your user input into these types using the schema itself at runtime.

For SOA, you might consider starting from XML schemas for entity types, generating sources from them, and then packaging your schemas with your WSDL on the client, which can then validate against any pattern constraints you might have defined.

To see additional options for use with XJC, you can simply invoke `xjc` from the command line with no arguments, and it will print usage information.

Be careful treating generated files as first-class citizens in your project. While the schemas used to generate them may be of primary importance, you should not build on generated Java sources. In general, do not commit generated code to your CVS or SVN repository.

JAXB Annotations

While a complete discussion of JAXB is beyond the scope of this book, it's worthwhile to take a moment to examine the most important annotations that JAXB defines, all of which are in the `javax.xml.bind.annotation` package.

JAXB annotations can be added to packages, classes, fields, or methods. Here we will examine the annotations that XJC might typically add to a Java object that it unmarshals from an XML schema.

XMLRootElement

This annotation at the class level indicates that the Java type is usable as a root element in a schema on marshaling from Java to XML. The Book example defines only a `complexType`, and not an element, and therefore did not receive this annotation during unmarshaling.

Example 2-14 is a schema with a global element that uses `XMLRootElement`.

Example 2-14. XML schema containing a root element

```
<xsd:schema xmlns:xsd="http://www.w3.org/2001/XMLSchema"
        targetNamespace="http://ns.soacookbook.com/book"
```

```
            xmlns:tns="http://ns.soacookbook.com/book"
            elementFormDefault="qualified">

  <xsd:element name="author">

    <xsd:complexType>
        <xsd:sequence>
            <xsd:element name="firstName" type="xsd:string"/>
            <xsd:element name="lastName" type="xsd:string"/>
        </xsd:sequence>
    </xsd:complexType>

  </xsd:element>

</xsd:schema>
```

If you issue this command:

```
> xjc -d . AuthorRootType.xsd
```

JAXB will generate the Java type shown in Example 2-15 (with the appropriate package) in the current directory.

Example 2-15. Author type annotated with XMLRootElement

```
@XmlAccessorType(XmlAccessType.FIELD)
@XmlType(name = "", propOrder = {
    "firstName",
    "lastName"
})
@XmlRootElement(name = "author")
public class Author {

    @XmlElement(required = true)
    protected String firstName;
    @XmlElement(required = true)
    protected String lastName;

//... getters and setter methods ommitted.
```

The getter and setter methods were left out of this output listing because they do not get any annotations attached to them. Notice that the Russian Doll design pattern is employed here, which causes the class to get the `@XMLRootElement` annotation. Had you defined the `complexType` outside of the element and left everything else the same, JAXB would have multiple possible roots to choose from, and leave off the annotation. Put another way, JAXB could not statically guarantee that your `complexType` would not be used in other schemas that might be compiled separately, at another time, which would cause such a collision.

It is illegal to attempt to marshal multiple nested objects annotated with `@XMLRootElement`.

Let's take a quick look at some of the annotations used here.

XMLAccessorType. This annotation indicates which of four possible values will be used to marshal child elements:

`PUBLIC_MEMBER`
: Indicates that the marshaler should marshal every Java bean property (public getter and setter pair).

`FIELD`
: Tells the marshaler to marshal every nonstatic, nontransient field in the class. To prevent a field from being marshaled, annotate it with `XMLTransient`.

`PROPERTY`
: Tells the marshaler to marshal every getter/setter pair, regardless of their access visibility.

`NONE`
: Tells the marshaler not to marshal any properties by default. You must explicitly indicate fields that you want marshaled with their own overriding annotations.

XMLElement. This annotation indicates that the field it annotates should be an element in the XML schema. It has three possible values: `required`, `nillable`, and `defaultValue`. These correspond to the schema values you would expect.

Conclusion

Again, JAXB is a very large topic. The aim here is not to provide a complete tutorial on every aspect of JAXB, but rather to illustrate just the things you need to know in order to use JAXB within an SOA environment. There are a number of tutorials and other resources online. The complete specification is very long (almost 400 pages), but it is certainly the authoritative source for JAXB's capabilities.

2.12 Generating a Schema from Java

Problem

You have a Java class and you want to generate an XML schema that matches it.

Solution

Run the command-line tool `schemagen`, which comes with Java SE 6. Alternatively, generate a schema at runtime with `SchemaOutputResolver`.

XML schemas can be generated from Java classes. You can use the annotations in the `javax.xml.bind.annotations` package to give the marshaler hints during the generation process. The `schemagen` utility comes with the reference implementation of JAXB, and so you can also find it among the Java SE 6 tools. Typing `schemagen` at the command line should give you usage information.

Using schemagen

In its simplest form, you can use schemagen by passing the name of the class you want to create a schema for. To invoke schemagen on Windows, you can use the batch file, and on Linux use the shell script. Here is the quickest example:

```
> schemagen Product.java
```

You may run into problems using schemagen on Windows XP Service Pack 2 with JDK 1.6.0. This was filed as bug 6510966. Thanks to Brian Lee for discovering this.

This will first compile the specified Java class, and then write out a new XSD file called *schema1.xsd* in the current directory by default. To override the directory in which schemagen places its output, use the -d option. Finally, the Product class does not have any external dependencies, but if it did, you would need to specify those with the -cp option. Example 2-16 is what your Java source file looks like.

Example 2-16. Plain Product.java class with no annotations

```
package com.soacookbook.ch02.schemagen;

import java.util.Date;

public class Product {

    private static final long serialVersionUID = 12345L;

    private String name;
    private Date mfrDate;

    public Product() {

    }

    public Date getMfrDate() {
        return mfrDate;
    }

    public void setMfrDate(Date mfrDate) {
        this.mfrDate = mfrDate;
    }

    public String getName() {
        return name;
    }

    public void setName(String name) {
        this.name = name;
    }
}
```

Note that schemagen will ignore private fields in classes that do not also specify getter and setter methods for them. The output after invoking schemagen looks like that shown in Example 2-17.

Example 2-17. Schema generated by schemagen for Product.java

```
<xs:schema version="1.0" xmlns:xs="http://www.w3.org/2001/XMLSchema">

  <xs:complexType name="product">
    <xs:sequence>
      <xs:element name="mfrDate" type="xs:dateTime" minOccurs="0"/>
      <xs:element name="name" type="xs:string" minOccurs="0"/>
    </xs:sequence>
  </xs:complexType>
</xs:schema>
```

There are a few interesting things to discuss here. First, a single complexType, not an element, was created for your class. Also, there is no target namespace for the schema.

Next, the serialVersionUID was ignored, which is intuitive given the fact that it is private, but also given that static fields are not serialized as part of regular Java serialization. So even if the field had not been private, its static status is enough to keep it from being generated into the schema.

The standard schema type xs:dateTime was used to represent the java.util.Date object, and schemagen kept the fields in the same order.

You can decorate your Java class with standard JAXB annotations in order to rearrange your results a little. Here are the changes you'll make:

- Specify a different name for the generated file
- Specify a different name for the class
- Specify a namespace
- Make a global root element
- Keep your static field and maintain its value

Example 2-18 is the same file, but now with JAXB annotations to meet your new goals.

Example 2-18. Product Java class annotated for schema generation

```
package com.soacookbook.ch02.schemagen;

import java.util.Date;
import javax.xml.bind.annotation.XmlElement;
import javax.xml.bind.annotation.XmlRootElement;
import javax.xml.bind.annotation.XmlType;

@XmlRootElement(namespace="com.soacookbook.ch02.schemagen",
    name="Product2")
@XmlType(namespace="com.soacookbook.ch02.schemagen")
public class ProductAnnotated {
```

```
    private static final long serialVersionUID = 12345L;

    @XmlElement(defaultValue="1.0")
    static String VERSION = "1.0";

    private String name;
    private Date mfrDate;

    public ProductAnnotated() { }

    //... getters and setters omitted
}
```

The output of running schemagen this time is a single file shown in Example 2-19.

Example 2-19. Schema file generated using JAXB annotations

```
<?xml version="1.0" encoding="UTF-8" standalone="yes"?>
<xs:schema version="1.0"
    targetNamespace="com.soacookbook.ch02.schemagen"
    xmlns:tns="com.soacookbook.ch02.schemagen"
    xmlns:xs="http://www.w3.org/2001/XMLSchema">

  <xs:element name="Product2" type="tns:productAnnotated"/>

  <xs:complexType name="productAnnotated">
    <xs:sequence>
      <xs:element name="VERSION"
        type="xs:string" default="1.0" minOccurs="0"/>
      <xs:element name="mfrDate"
        type="xs:dateTime" minOccurs="0"/>
      <xs:element name="name"
        type="xs:string" minOccurs="0"/>
    </xs:sequence>
  </xs:complexType>
</xs:schema>
```

Let's take a moment to see how each of the annotations contributed to the creation of this schema. First, the XMLRootElement annotation defined the namespace for the root element. But that's not actually enough to get the namespace declared across the complex type, as that annotation applies only to the root element. So you must repeat that namespace in the XMLType annotation in order to tell schemagen that both the element and the complex type are in the same namespace. This results in the single file that you see here. Had you left off the XMLType annotation, schemagen would have made a conservative guess and left the complex type with no namespace. It then would have been forced to put it in a separate schema file and import the type into the schema defining the element.

Notice that using the XMLElement field-level modifier you get to retain your static field in the schema definition. But you're just overriding the fact that it would have been ignored; there is no concept of "static" in schema you can retain.

Using SchemaOutputResolver

The second way to create a schema based on a Java class is not to use the command-line tool, but rather to write Java code that does it for you. This has the advantage of being usable at runtime within a larger program. Example 2-20 is the listing that writes out a schema for your *ProductAnnotated.java* file.

Example 2-20. Java program to generate a schema at runtime

```
package com.soacookbook.ch02.schemagen;

import static java.lang.System.out;

import java.io.File;
import java.io.IOException;
import javax.xml.bind.JAXBContext;
import javax.xml.bind.JAXBException;
import javax.xml.bind.SchemaOutputResolver;
import javax.xml.transform.Result;
import javax.xml.transform.stream.StreamResult;

/**
 * Generates a schema from a Java class.
 */
public class SchemaMaker {

    SchemaOutputResolver resolver;

    //run the show
    public static void main(String...arg){
        try {
            Class[] classes = {ProductAnnotated.class};

            new SchemaMaker().execute(classes);
        } catch (JAXBException ex) {
           ex.printStackTrace();
        } catch (IOException ex) {
            ex.printStackTrace();
        }
    }

    /**
     * Creates an instance of SchemaMaker with defaults.
     */
    public SchemaMaker() {
        resolver = new MySchemaOutputResolver(".", "MySchema.xsd");
    }

    public void execute(Class...classes)
            throws JAXBException, IOException {

        JAXBContext context = JAXBContext.newInstance(classes);
        context.generateSchema(resolver);

        out.println("All done.");
```

```
    }
}

/**
 * Extends the resolver.
 */
class MySchemaOutputResolver extends SchemaOutputResolver {

    private File output;

    public MySchemaOutputResolver(String dir, String fileName){
        output = new File(dir, fileName);
    }

    public Result createOutput(String namespaceUri,
            String suggestedFileName) throws IOException {

        return new StreamResult(output);
    }
}
```

Running this file produces an identical result to the one achieved by generating the schema with **schemagen** and JAXB annotations earlier, but with the benefit of being able to use it more flexibly at runtime.

2.13 Generating Java Source Files from XML Schema in Ant

Problem

You want to invoke XJC from an Ant script.

Solution

Use the Ant task for XJC, available in *sun-appserv-ant.jar*.

Discussion

In Recipe 2.11, you saw how to use XJC from the command line to generate Java source files based on XML schemas. But that's not a very real-world way to do things. Ideally, you could change your schemas at will and have the Java sources regenerate when you build your service. If you're using Ant to do your building, this is a breeze.

In your build script, you'll be defining the Sun XJC wrapper task, but you need a few JARs from Glassfish on your classpath first. Add these entries to your build script's properties file:

```
sun.app.ant.jar=${glassfish.jars.dir}/sun-appserv-ant.jar
sun.ws.tools.jar=${glassfish.jars.dir}/webservices-tools.jar
sun.ws.rt.jar=${glassfish.jars.dir}/jaxws-rt.jar
xjc.task.path=${sun.app.ant.jar}${path.separator}${sun.ws.tools.jar}${path.separator}
${sun.ws.rt.jar}
```

This will allow Ant to find XJC and the Ant wrapper task. Now in your *build.xml*, define the following:

```
<taskdef name="xjc"
    classname="com.sun.tools.xjc.XJCTask">
    <classpath path="${xjc.task.path}"/>
</taskdef>
```

Then invoke the task before compiling your service code:

```
<target name="schema-to-java">
    <echo message="-----Generating Java sources from Schema-----" />
    <xjc destdir="./src/gen">
    <schema dir="./src/xml/META-INF/wsdl" includes="**/*.schemalet, **/*.xsd"/>
    </xjc>
</target>
```

The `destdir` attribute specifies the directory where XJC should write the generated source files. The schema element points to the location of your schemas and indicates which files to include for generation.

Here a `schemalet` source file was included to customize the bindings. For more on how that works, see Recipe 7.14.

2.14 Generating an XML Document Instance from a Schema

Problem

You want a programmatic way to get from an XML schema to an XML document instance.

Solution

There are, of course, tools that do this. You could use NetBeans 6 or XML Spy, for example, to generate an XML document for you. But if you have a programmatic need to do the same thing, or aren't using one of those tools, try the free Java tool XIG.

First, download XIG from Sourceforge at *http://xml-xig.sourceforge.net*. The current version is xml-xig-0.1.1.

You need to pass XIG the name of the schema and the root element you want to create an instance for. Here you are going to point to your Catalog schema and generate an XML document based on the `searchResults` element. On a command prompt, run the JAR:

```
> java -jar xml-xig-0.1.1.jar "src/xml/META-INF/wsdl/Catalog.xsd" search Catalog.xig
XIG: Generating Template src/xml/META-INF/wsdl/Catalog.xsd.xig...
XIG: Instantiating src/xml/META-INF/wsdl/Catalog.xsd.xml...
```

Two files are created: *Catalog.xsd.xig* and *Catalog.xsd.xml*. We'll look at the XIG file in a moment.

Here is the generated *Catalog.xsd.xml* file:

```
<search>
  <firstName>?{string}</firstName>
  <lastName>?{string}</lastName>
</search>
```

You can then replace the `?{string}` placeholders with your values.

Let's modify this source a little bit in order to run it through a validator to make sure that XIG did its job properly. Let's put the namespace on it with a prefix. Here the *Catalog.xsd* is in the same directory as my instance document:

```
<s:search xmlns:s="http://ns.soacookbook.com/catalog"
xmlns:xsi="http://www.w3.org/2001/XMLSchema-instance"
xsi:schemaLocation="http://ns.soacookbook.com/catalog Catalog.xsd">
  <firstName>James</firstName>
  <lastName>Joyce</lastName>
</s:search>
```

For such a small schema, this doesn't seem to give you much. But the benefit increases with the size and complexity of your schema, and you can use XIG to generate sets of instances.

The XIG file is a template that can be used to generate not just one, but a volume of XML instances based on this type. Moreover, you can pass runtime data to the template to provide distinct values if necessary. Check out the Sourceforge XIG site for details, but here is what the default generated *.xig* file looks like:

```
<xig:template document='search' schema='src/xml/META-INF/wsdl/Catalog.xsd'
xmlns:xds='http://xml-xsd.sourceforge.net/schema/XmlXsd-0.1'>
  <search>
    <firstName>${xs:string}</firstName>
    <lastName>${xs:string}</lastName>
  </search>
  <xig:generate>
    <!-- Generate instance documents from template document above -->
    <loop count='10'>
    </loop>
  </xig:generate>
</xig:template>
```

If you want to invoke it multiple times with differently indexed data, it's ready to go. This is similar to the parameterized test functionality available in JUnit 4.4.

Relaxer

Another popular tool for doing the same work is Relaxer, which works for XML Schema, RELAX NG, Relax Core, and DTD. It's also a free download. Check out the tutorial and documentation at *http://www.asahi-net.or.jp/~dp8t-asm/java/tools/Relaxer*.

2.15 Customizing How a Java Class Is Generated from Schema

Problem

You don't want to accept the default manner in which JAXB generates your Java source and need to customize the behavior.

Solution

Define a Schemalet file, and add it to the `"includes"` attribute of the `"schema"` element in your XJC Ant task. Alternatively, add JAXB-specific annotations inline to your XML schema.

JAXB does a very good job at the difficult task of mapping schema to Java sources. Schema element names map to type names, namespaces map to packages, and enumerations map directly to Java enumerations. But there are times when you want to override the default behavior and specify your own mapping. Perhaps you want to use a different date type than `XMLGregorianCalendar`, which is what JAXB generates for an `xs:dateTime` schema type. This recipe shows you how to do this.

Table 2-3 shows the default mappings from types built-in to XML Schema to Java types.

Table 2-3. Default XML schema mapping to Java data types

XML schema type	Java data type
xs:string	java.lang.String
xs:integer	java.math.BigInteger
xs:int	int
xs:long	long
xs:short	short
xs:decimal	java.math.BigDecimal
xs:float	float
xs:double	double
xs:boolean	boolean
xs:byte	byte
xs:QName and xs:NOTATION	javax.xml.namespace.QName
xs:base64Binary	byte[]
xs:hexBinary	byte[]
xs:unsignedInt	long
xs:unsignedShort	int
xs:unsignedByte	short

XML schema type	Java data type
xs:time, xs:date, xs:dateTime,xs:gDay, xs:gMonth, xs:gMonthDay, xs:gYear, xs:gYear-Month	javax.xml.datatype.XMLGregor-ianCalendar
xs:anySimpleType	java.lang.String
xs:duration	javax.xml.datatype.Duration

If you want to have the binding compiler generate a different Java type than the default, you can do this one of two ways: write the desired types in an external file you pass to the binding compiler, or annotate your XML schema.

In general, you may not have to do this. Remember that you are building an SOA, not just a Java application. You need to keep in mind that clients of your web service will need to be able to do everything that your contract specifies. Working with polymorphic types or getting far into the outer reaches of what schema can do may not serve you well in an SOA.

There are four scopes for binding customizations, each of which specifies the range of schema components to which it applies. They are listed in Table 2-4.

Table 2-4. Binding scopes

Scope	Description
Global (uses `<globalBindings>`)	Applies to all schema elements in the current schema, as well as all schemas imported or included by the current schema, recursively.
Schema (uses `<schemaBindings>`)	Applies to all schema elements in the target namespace of the current schema.
Definition	Applies to the element in which the binding is specified, as well as all other schema elements that reference this type definition.
Component	Applies only to the element in which the binding is specified.

These scopes can override one another, with the most specific scope always overriding any more general scopes that would have covered it.

Now let's look at the two ways to use these bindings.

Using Inline Annotations

The first of two ways to customize your generated code is to use inline annotations. XML Schema makes available the `<appinfo>` child element of `<annotation>` specifically for the purpose of allowing applications to perform customization for their environment. See Example 2-21.

Example 2-21. Customizing JAXB with a Schemalet file

```
<xs:schema elementFormDefault="qualified" version="1.0"
  xmlns:xs="http://www.w3.org/2001/XMLSchema"
  xmlns:jaxb="http://java.sun.com/xml/ns/jaxb"
  jaxb:version="2.0"
```

```
  targetNamespace="urn:schemalet:calendar">

  <xs:annotation>
    <xs:appinfo>

    <jaxb:globalBindings mapSimpleTypeDef="false"
          choiceContentProperty="true">
      <jaxb:javaType name="java.util.Date" xmlType="xs:date"
        parseMethod="javax.xml.bind.DatatypeConverter.parseDate"
        printMethod="javax.xml.bind.DatatypeConverter.printDate"/>

      <jaxb:javaType name="java.util.Date" xmlType="xs:dateTime"
        parseMethod="javax.xml.bind.DatatypeConverter.parseDate"
        printMethod="javax.xml.bind.DatatypeConverter.printDate"/>

    </jaxb:globalBindings>
  </xs:appinfo>
  </xs:annotation>

  //...rest of schema here
</xs:schema>
```

Here you specify the `jaxb` prefix for the namespace `http://java.sun.com/xml/ns/jaxb`, which is required. Then in the `appinfo` section, add your global customizations so that any `dateTime` or `date` type you encounter in the current schema or any schema it reuses will assume your custom type. You can add other annotations here in different scopes, and add your regular comments in the annotation.

The Java type you want to use as the target is indicated by the name attribute, and the type in the schema you will convert to that target is specified by the `xmlType` attribute. You also indicate a `parseMethod` and a `printMethod` as the names of methods in the specified JAXB class that will be intercepted to substitute with your value during parsing and printing.

The values you specify in `parseMethod` and `printMethod` must correspond to the data types you're targeting. For example, if you were customizing the short binding, you'd use something like this:

```
printMethod="javax.xml.bind.DatatypeConverter.printShort"
parseMethod="javax.xml.bind.DatatypeConverter.parseShort"
```

In the next section, we'll look at how to achieve the same thing in an external file.

Using an External File (schemalet)

It might be preferable to put your binding customization annotations in an external file, and not in the schema itself. Like so many things, this has advantages and disadvantages. The advantage is that your schema is not mucked up with Java-specific and JAXB-specific code. You don't leak your implementation out into an otherwise implementation-agnostic schema document. Depending on your environment, this could pose a greater or lesser problem. I recommend preferring the external file method if you don't have constraints preventing it. It leaves your schema easier to read and less cluttered, and won't give pause to implementors in your enterprise using other languages. But the downside to using the external method is that the customization is bound to the schema only at runtime during parsing, and readers of your source schema may be entirely unaware of the potentially significant changes you might be making to code generated from it. This could also be more or less of an issue depending on the extent and scope of your customizations.

Example 2-22 shows a file, sometimes felicitously called a "schemalet," that contains only JAXB customizations. The default schema mapping of an `xs:dateTime` object is an `XMLGregorianCalendar`. It is possible that for some reason you'd like your code to use a `java.util.Calendar` or `java.util.Date` instead. Perhaps the API is a little trickier to use than what you're used to, or you don't want to leak the XML origins of the class to callers if it isn't necessary. You can specify this in a schemalet, an XML file that looks something like the one shown in Example 2-22.

Example 2-22. External file for XML schema binding customization

```
<!-- Changes dates and dateTimes to java.util.Date -->
<jaxb:bindings version="2.0"
  xmlns:jaxb="http://java.sun.com/xml/ns/jaxb"
  xmlns:xs="http://www.w3.org/2001/XMLSchema"
  jaxb:extensionBindingPrefixes="xjc">

  <jaxb:globalBindings mapSimpleTypeDef="false"
      choiceContentProperty="true">
  <jaxb:javaType name="java.util.Date" xmlType="xs:date"
    parseMethod="javax.xml.bind.DatatypeConverter.parseDate"
    printMethod="javax.xml.bind.DatatypeConverter.printDate"/>

  <jaxb:javaType name="java.util.Date" xmlType="xs:dateTime"
    parseMethod="javax.xml.bind.DatatypeConverter.parseDate"
    printMethod="javax.xml.bind.DatatypeConverter.printDate"/>

 </jaxb:globalBindings>
</jaxb:bindings>
```

This file maps both `xs:date` and `xs:dateTime` to `java.util.Date` objects instead of `XMLGregorianCalendar`, leaving `xs:time` (and everything else) to its default. Save it with an *.xjb* extension to have the binding compiler find it automatically.

The code to specify the binding customization in an external file is very similar to that specified inline. In fact, the code within the `<jaxb:globalBindings>` element is identical. But the root is different because in the file its a `<jaxb:bindings>` and with a schema it's, well, `<xsd:schema>`.

Say you have a Library schema that defines a book with a title and a due date. You point to the schemalet using the `-b` switch that allows you to specify either a directory in which to find files with a *.xjb* extension, or, if you're using a different extension, the name of the file. Here I've called the schemalet *dateTime.xjb* and put it in the same directory as my *LibraryBook.xsd*.

Now let's run it, indicating `-d` for the directory to which you want your generated classes to be written, the name of the schema to read, and `-b` for the binding switch, which here tells XJC to look for all *.xjb* files in the current directory:

```
> xjc -d . LibraryBook.xsd -b .
```

Here is the result of the compilation:

```
@XmlAccessorType(XmlAccessType.FIELD)
@XmlType(name = "", propOrder = {
    "title",
    "dueDate"
})
@XmlRootElement(name = "book")
public class Book {

    @XmlElement(required = true)
    protected String title;
    @XmlElement(required = true, type = String.class)
    @XmlJavaTypeAdapter(Adapter2 .class)
    @XmlSchemaType(name = "date")
    protected Date dueDate;

    public Date getDueDate() {
        return dueDate;
    }

    public void setDueDate(Date value) {
        this.dueDate = value;
    }

/...etc
}
```

I removed the comments in the generated code. You might have noticed the `XmlTypeAdapter` annotation indicating that the type is modified using the *Adapter2.class* file. What JAXB does here is create a set of Adapter classes that match your customizations. These customizations extend the XML adapter class, parameterized on two values: a type that JAXB knows how to work with already and the bound type. It defines two methods: marshal and unmarshal, each of which performs the actual translation at runtime.

As a final note, there may be cases where you would want to customize your JAXB source generation. It makes sense to want to encapsulate certain types if it ensures better encapsulation of your web services layers. But excessive customization can make it more difficult to maintain your code, and can potentially introduce interoperability problems. So while customization is powerful and easy to use, and frequently is necessary to get the result you need, use caution and consider not going too far down this road. Make sure that you're working to keep your stuff flexible and maximize your chances for interoperability; this is, after all, the point of web services.

2.16 Validating Against a Schema During Marshaling and Unmarshaling

Problem

You have a Java object object to marshal to XML or an XML document to unmarshal to a Java object. You want to validate that the resulting XML conforms to the specified schema before making the request.

Solution

Use JAXP validation by setting an instance of `javax.xml.validation.Schema` into the JAXB Marshaler. See Example 2-23.

Example 2-23. Validating an XML instance against a schema during unmarshaling

```
package com.soacookbook.ch02.jaxb;

import java.io.File;
import java.io.StringReader;
import javax.xml.XMLConstants;
import javax.xml.bind.JAXBContext;
import javax.xml.bind.JAXBElement;
import javax.xml.bind.JAXBException;
import javax.xml.bind.Unmarshaller;
import javax.xml.transform.stream.StreamSource;
import javax.xml.validation.*;

/**
 * Sets a schema onto the unmarshaller to validate.
 */
public class ValidateUnmarshal {
    private static final String SCHEMA =
            "/home/ehewitt/soacookbook/repository/code/catalog/ws/" +
            "src/xml/ch02/BookVenetianBlind.xsd";

  public static void main(String...arg) {
    try {

        //Create context
        JAXBContext ctx = JAXBContext.newInstance(Book.class);

        //Create marshaller
        Unmarshaller um = ctx.createUnmarshaller();
```

```java
        //Create instance of schema
        SchemaFactory factory =
                SchemaFactory.newInstance(
                  XMLConstants.W3C_XML_SCHEMA_NS_URI);

        //Create factory, add options if necessary
        Schema schema = factory.newSchema(
                new StreamSource(new File(SCHEMA)));

        //This sets us up for validation
        um.setSchema(schema);

        //Read in the XML from anywhere
        //In this case it is a complete XML book as string.
        StringReader sr = new StringReader(getBookXml());

        //Get XML from object.
        //Now that we have a schema set, this throws
        //MarshalException if XML doesn't match XSD
        JAXBElement<Book> b = um.unmarshal(
                new StreamSource(sr), Book.class);

        //We never get this far with invalid XML
        //Start working with object
        Book book = b.getValue();

        System.console().printf("Title: %s", book.getTitle());

    } catch (JAXBException ex) {
        ex.printStackTrace();
    } catch (Exception ex) {
        ex.printStackTrace();
    }
  }

  //NOTE: THIS XML FAILS VALIDATION!
  private static String getBookXml(){
      return "<com.soacookbook.ch02.xstream.Book>" +
              "<title>On Friendship</title>" +
              "<price>39.95</price>" +
              "<author><firstName>Jacques</firstName>" +
              "<lastName>Derrida</lastName>" +
              "</author><category>PHILOSOPHY</category>" +
              "</com.soacookbook.ch02.xstream.Book>";
  }
}
```

Here the validation fails. Because your XML was originally generated from XStream, which caused the package name to prepend the root element name in the generated XML, your root element is `com.soacookbook.ch02.xstream.Book`. This is not valid. So a `javax.xml.bind.UNMarshalException` is thrown, and processing stops immediately. Here is the output:

```
javax.xml.bind.UnmarshalException
 - with linked exception:
```

```
[org.xml.sax.SAXParseException: cvc-elt.1: Cannot find the declaration of element
'com.soacookbook.ch02.xstream.Book'.]
```

So let's go ahead and fix the XML content so that it will validate. Note that it is not enough to simply remove the package name and lowercase the "book" element. The XML needs to specify the namespace it uses for these elements and types just as specified in the schema to actually be valid. But there are more things still wrong with it. You also need to put the elements in the correct order. The `<sequence>` element used in the schema means that content is expected in the specified order. That's the reason that the JAXB `XmlType` mapping annotation provides the order attribute. So you'll have to rearrange the XML to make the proper sequence. Finally, the author tag is invalid because this particular schema has specified it as a `simpleType`, so it must contain only a string and not child elements.

So to fix the XML, substitute the following `getBookXml` method that gives you a book XML instance that validates against the Venetian Blind schema example that you defined earlier:

```
//This is valid according to the schema
private static String getBookXml(){
      return "<b:book xmlns:b='http://ns.soacookbook.com/venetianblind'>" +
            "<title>On Friendship</title>" +
            "<author>Jacques Derrida</author>" +
            "<category>PHILOSOPHY</category>" +
            "<price>39.95</price>" +
            "</b:book>";
}
```

As you might hope, the process is identical whether you're marshaling or unmarshaling. So that's all there is to using simple schema validation. There are a few more advanced options that you can use during validation, such as collecting events emitted by the parser so you can capture more information than just whether you passed or not, and then make that data available to the caller. We'll take a look at some of these advanced options in the next recipe, but this is all you need for general-purpose use.

If you want to explore more options in creating the schema factory, check out these methods:

- `factory.setErrorHandler(errorHandler)`
- `factory.setFeature(string, value)`
- `factory.setResourceResolver(resourceResolver)`
- `factory.setProperty(prop, obj)`

See Also

Recipe 7.12 explains in detail a web service you can deploy and use to generate JAXB types from its schema. You can then use the techniques in this recipe to validate the Java object used to invoke the service.

2.17 Collecting Schema Validation Events During Marshaling and Unmarshaling

Problem

You want to learn more about schema validation errors during unmarshaling so you can report more robust messages back to your user, receive validation failure events as they occur, and generally gain more control over the validation process.

Solution

Implement the `javax.xml.bind.ValidationEventHandler` interface to perform custom operations and set it into your marshaler or unmarshaler object. Also try the `ValidationEventCollector` utility.

This interface defines one method: `handleEvent`, which gives you the opportunity to perform custom event handling. To use it, you implement the interface and then register your implementation with the marshaler or unmarshaler, which will use your handler to collect validation events.

A validation handler is not the appropriate place for modifying the XML content tree, though it might be tempting to do so. Treat your handler as a read-only operator that must return false if any fatal error or runtime exception is thrown.

For your convenience, there are two implementations of `ValidationEventHandler` available in the `javax.xml.bind` package: `DefaultValidationEventHandler` and `ValidationEventCollector`. The default handler is used if you do not set one on the un/marshaler yourself by calling the `setEventHandler` method. This implementation will continue processing if it receives validation warnings, but stop executing immediately upon notice of the first error.

During validation, the `handleEvent` method notifies you of validation warnings or errors using a `ValidationEvent` object. This object indicates the severity of the event (WARNING, ERROR, or FATAL_ERROR), messages from the processor, and any exceptions thrown. But it also gives you access to a `ValidationEventLocator` object via its `getLocator` method. This object gives you access to a rich array of data regarding the file, URL, or DOM node that caused the event to be emitted. You also get line and column number as well, allowing for very precise details to help the user find what went wrong. Let's put some code together that illustrates this usage.

Write a handler implementation and then modify your class used in Recipe 2.16 to accept your handler. Finally, derange your XML document slightly in order to make it emit a warning or error. Here, declare the "b" prefix twice:

```
<b:book xmlns:b='http://ns.soacookbook.com/venetianblind'
            'xmlns:b='http://ns.soacookbook.com/x'> ...
```

Example 2-24 is the implementation of your handler, which simply collects some data and formats a string with some information. You could collect this information in a database or perform some other operation here instead.

Example 2-24. Custom validation handler

```
class MyHandler implements ValidationEventHandler {
    public boolean handleEvent(ValidationEvent event) {
        int severity = event.getSeverity();

        if (severity == ValidationEvent.WARNING) {
            String msg = event.getMessage();

            ValidationEventLocator vel = event.getLocator();
            int line = vel.getLineNumber();

            String warn = "**** WARNING! Msg is %s." +
                    "See source line %d.";
            System.console().printf(warn, msg, line);

            //print warning, but proceed.
            return true;
        } else {
            String err = "**** Got an Error of type %s.";
            System.console().printf(err,
                event.getLinkedException().getClass().getName());
            //ERROR--quit parsing
            return false;
        }
    }

}
```

The main method that performs the actual unmarshaling is basically the same, except that you have to set the handler:

```
            //Create marshaller
            Unmarshaller um = ctx.createUnmarshaller();

            //Create instance of schema...

            //Create instance of our custom handler
            MyHandler myHandler = new MyHandler();

            //Add it to unmarshaller
            um.setEventHandler(myHandler);
    //...
```

Using this handler gives you the following output, indicating that you can't specify the same prefix twice:

```
**** Got an Error of type org.xml.sax.SAXParseException.javax.xml.bind.UnmarshalException
 - with linked exception:
```

```
[org.xml.sax.SAXParseException:
Attribute "xmlns:b" was already specified for element "b:book".]
```

Not all of the data is available for every invocation of the ValidationEventLocator. Depending on the kind of validation, you may or may not be able to access certain fields. Validation during unmarshaling will produce data regarding the XML source data, while ad hoc validation or validation during marshaling will give you locator data referring to Java objects. For example, don't expect much from the getLineNumber method in such a case.

ValidationEventCollector

As previously mentioned, the way that this validation handler works is to immediately halt processing if an error or fatal error is encountered. This might be what you want in order to optimize performance and avoid unnecessary work. You could reject a document out of hand at the first error and instruct the user to fix the content before you'll add it to the body of a SOAP message for transmission.

On the other hand, perhaps you are keeping track of how users invoke your service, and you want to be able to collect more information behind the scenes. Perhaps you want to evaluate the full array of warnings and errors before determining the appropriate action to take. You might have self-correcting code that massages data upon receipt of a payload. That means that you need to continue processing even though you have received warnings and errors. That's where ValidationEventCollector comes in.

Here's how it works: perform your processing, but expect that your warnings and errors will continue being collected as the document is parsed, and processing will complete to the end. Once the call to validate, marshal, or unmarshal returns, invoke the getEvents method to gather the collected events. They will be available as an array of ValidationEvent objects.

Summary

In this chapter, we addressed XML Schema as the foundation of SOA message design. Schemas are vitally important with an SOA that makes use of WSDLs for web service interfaces. Because WSDL uses XML Schema, schemas constitute an important aspect of your service interface. We saw how to design and use schemas in a variety of ways. We also looked at various tools, such as XJC and XIG, and how to use them to simplify your web services development cycle.

Beginning with the next chapter, we'll examine new tools for XML document processing. This will get you on solid footing for dealing with message payloads as you build out your SOA.

CHAPTER 3

Working with XML and Java

3.0 Introduction

This chapter provides some useful techniques for handling XML data in a variety of ways that are important specifically in the context of building out your SOA. We'll also examine some relatively new ways of working with XML as provided by the latest Java APIs. As Java programmers, we've been processing XML in a variety of ways for several years, so I'm going to forego the basics there. I assume that you've worked with SAX and DOM before, so we can get right to the new stuff. Finally, this chapter aims to illustrate how to effectively use XML and data binding specifically within an SOA.

It is not a given, however, that every architect will design an SOA around XML. If you have decided that all your services will be implemented in straight Java using EJBs or RMI, that's fine too. But using XML as your mode of message exchange *is* a very popular approach, and for good reason. SOA is about flexible integration. And while legacy data may live in a variety of formats, if you can get it into XML, you can move it anywhere else, transform it, and give it new life. In this way, XML supports what is, in my view, the core message of SOA: embrace difference. Midrange iSeries computers from IBM whose day job is running 20-year-old COBOL programs now come with SAX parsers out of the box. Native XML databases such as Xindice and Berkeley XML DB are gaining modest popularity. In support of SQL 2003, Microsoft SQL Server, Oracle, and JDBC 4.0 treat XML as a first-class citizen, no longer forcing you to relegate your XML data to CLOBs. Using XML as a translation layer allows you to always select the right tool for the job, rather than resigning yourself to choosing between a world of application silos that don't communicate, or one vendor's idea of what your IT stack should look like. So, using XML for messages is the general approach I take in this book.

Finally, there are a lot of choices out there for XML-to-Java round-trip generation. We'll look at a couple of them, including JAXB and XStream. There are other popular frameworks too, including Castor and the XMLBeans project at Apache. But in working with a Java stack, it is convenient to go with JAXB, as you automatically inherit performance improvements and functionality due to its having been rolled up with Java SE and the JAX-WS reference implementation. It can be comforting to know that the technologies will grow together and remain compatible with minimum fuss. In general, it seems like a good idea to minimize dependencies, but that doesn't mean you shouldn't use the best tool for the job you have to get done. Everyone has exceptions, and I (and everyone I know) still use Log4J even though Java's had its own logging API since 1.4. The corollary of embracing difference is using the right tool for the job.

3.1 Reading an XML Data Stream

Problem

You want to access an XML document in a fast stream. Your dataset is too large for DOM, and you want a more selective API than SAX offers.

Solution

Use the StAX API in Java SE 6 to "pull" parse your document.

Discussion

Java has given us a number of ways to work with XML documents, including the popular DOM and SAX. The most recent addition is StAX, or Streaming API for XML, which is largely the brainchild of Oracle/BEA. While all three of these methods of parsing XML have advantages, they have shortcomings too.

StAX is currently the most efficient method of dealing with XML, and is therefore particularly well suited to working with complex processes such as data binding and SOAP messages. Oracle/BEA's WebLogic 9 and 10 use this parser internally within the application server, as does Glassfish v2.

DOM offers an easy-to-use API, and has an advantage over SAX and StAX in that it is XPath-capable. But it also forces you to read the entire document into memory. This is fine for small documents, but can damage performance for sizeable documents, and can be ultimately prohibitive for very large documents. One European bank network regularly transfers multi-gigabyte XML files within their SOA; they're not using DOM to deal with it.

SAX, on the other hand, handles this problem by working as a "push" parser; that is, events are generated for each structure the parser encounters within the document, and the programmer can choose to deal with those he's interested in. The disadvantage here is that SAX will typically generate a lot of events that the programmer doesn't care about. Moreover, the SAX API does not offer iterative processing of your document, and blasts through the whole thing from beginning to end. In this model, the parser controls the processing of the document.

The StAX API gives you control akin to the Java I/O `RandomAccessFile`—you can skip sections of the document, work with a subsection of the document, pause and resume processing, or stop processing at any time. Using the "pull" model for processing, the application is in charge of how the document is processed, and exerts this control by indicating which items it's interested in working with; the parser then pulls them out of the event stream.

Streaming parsers can work with documents whose format is only loosely known, but you do need to know what you want to work with beforehand: you have to tell the parser what you want to pull.

But the infosets that StAX creates are very small, and are immediate candidates for garbage collection. This gives your XML processing work a small footprint, making it ideal for use not just with small heap devices such as mobile phones, but with long-running server-side applications too.

Unlike SAX, StAX is able to write XML documents. This reduces the number of APIs you have to deal with. That having been said, in addition to reading and writing XML data, there are two different models for parsing data with StAX: the cursor model and the iterator model.

Using the StAX cursor model: XMLStreamReader

The `XMLStreamReader` interface does the heavy lifting here. Using this interface, you can read everything about both the structure of a document and its content in a stream of events. To receive these events, use the `hasNext` method to determine if there are any more events to read, and the `next` method to get an integer token for the next event. Using that token, you switch on the different kinds of parse events, and do some work if the current event represents something in which you're interested.

You can capture events for the following `XMLEvent` subinterfaces, each representing a different aspect of a document's structure:

- `CDATA`
- `CHARACTER`
- `COMMENT`
- `DTD`
- `START_DOCUMENT`
- `END_DOCUMENT`
- `START_ELEMENT`
- `END_ELEMENT`
- `ENTITY_DECLARATION`
- `NAMESPACE`
- `NOTATION_DECLARATION`
- `PROCESSING_INSTRUCTION`
- `SPACE`

The cursor moves forward through the document from start to finish, pointing to each item along the way. If you're used to using SAX, this should be familiar.

Let's start with a very simple and rather poorly defined XML file as an example. Use this XML file as the basis for your parsing:

```
<catalog>
    <book sku="123_xaa">
        <title>King Lear</title>
        <author>William Shakespeare</author>
        <price>6.95</price>
        <category>classics</category>
    </book>
    <book sku="988_yty">
        <title>Hamlet</title>
        <author>William Shakespeare</author>
        <price>5.95</price>
        <category>classics</category>
    </book>
    <book sku="434_asd">
        <title>1984</title>
        <author>George Orwell</author>
        <price>12.95</price>
        <category>classics</category>
    </book>
    <book sku="876_pep">
        <title>Java Generics and Collections</title>
        <authors>
            <author>Maurice Naftalin</author>
            <author>Phillip Wadler</author>
        </authors>
        <price>34.99</price>
        <category>programming</category>
    </book>
</catalog>
```

So here you have a catalog that holds a bunch of books, presumably for sale. Each book has an identifier, a title, one or more authors, and so on. The trickiest part of the *catalog.xml* file is that the authors element is optional, used only if the book has more than one author.

The program in Example 3-1 illustrates how to use the cursor parsing method in StAX. Here the author objects are stored in a `TreeSet` as they are discovered; the `Tree` part provides natural sorting, and the `Set` part ensures uniqueness.

Example 3-1. Using the cursor parsing method in StAX

```
package com.sc.ch02.stax;

import static java.lang.System.out;

import java.io.InputStream;
import java.util.Set;
import java.util.TreeSet;
```

```
import javax.xml.stream.XMLInputFactory;
import javax.xml.stream.XMLStreamException;
import javax.xml.stream.XMLStreamReader;
import javax.xml.stream.events.XMLEvent;

public class StaxCursor {
    private static final String db = "/ch02/Catalog.xml";

    //we'll hold values here as we find them
    private Set<String> uniqueAuthors;

    public static void main(String... args) {
        StaxCursor p = new StaxCursor();
        p.find();
    }

    //constructor
    public StaxCursor() {
        uniqueAuthors = new TreeSet<String>();
    }

    //parse the document and offload work to helpers
    public void find() {
        XMLInputFactory xif = XMLInputFactory.newInstance();
        //forward-only, most efficient way to read
        XMLStreamReader reader = null;

        //get ahold of the file
        final InputStream is =
            StaxCursor.class.getResourceAsStream(db);

        //whether current event represents elem, attrib, etc
        int eventType;
        String current = "";

        try {
            //create the reader from the stream
            reader = xif.createXMLStreamReader(is);

            //work with stream and get the type of event
            //we're inspecting
            while (reader.hasNext()) {
                //because this is Cursor, we get an integer token to next event
                eventType = reader.next();

                //do different work depending on current event
                switch (eventType) {
                case XMLEvent.START_ELEMENT:
                    //save element name for later
                    current = reader.getName().toString();

                    printSkus(current, reader);
                    break;
```

```
                case XMLEvent.CHARACTERS:
                    findAuthors(current, reader);
                    break;
                    }
            } //end loop
            out.println("Unique Authors=" + uniqueAuthors);

            } catch (XMLStreamException e) {
                out.println("Cannot parse: " + e);
            }
    }

    //get the name and value of the book's sku attribute
    private void printSkus(String current, XMLStreamReader r) {
        current = r.getName().toString();

        if ("book".equals(current)) {
            String k = r.getAttributeName(0).toString();
            String v = r.getAttributeValue(0);
            out.println("AttribName " + k + "=" + v);
        }
    }

    //inspect author elements and read their values.
    private void findAuthors(String current, XMLStreamReader r)
        throws XMLStreamException {

        if ("author".equals(current)) {
            String v = r.getText().trim();

            //can get whitespace value, so ignore
            if (v.length() > 0) {
                uniqueAuthors.add(v);
            }
        }
    }
}
```

The reader's `getText` method gives the event value, and the `getAttributeValue` method is used with an integer indicating the index of the attribute you want a value for.

Running the program produces the following results:

```
AttribName sku=123_xaa
AttribName sku=988_yty
AttribName sku=434_asd
AttribName sku=876_pep
Unique Authors=[George Orwell, Maurice Naftalin, Phillip Wadler, William Shakespeare]
```

In this example, you are interested in authors (which are their own element) and SKU values (which are attributes of the `book` element). You save the name of the current node for each iteration of the loop so that you can match it in your two processing methods.

Normally, you'll just want to use the StAX implementation that comes with Java SE 6. But it's worth noting that Sun has an implementation of StAX available as a separate download from *https://sjsxp.dev.java.net/*. This implementation is built on Xerces 2, and is very lazy (a good thing for parsers!). There are other StAX implementations available as well, such as those from Oracle.

Using the StAX iterator model

The iterator API is the more flexible and easily extensible of the two models.

Let's parse the same *Catalog.xml* document just defined with the other StAX model, the iterator. This is shown in Example 3-2.

Example 3-2. Reading XML with StAX iterator

```
public class StaxIterator {
    public void find() {
    XMLInputFactory xif = XMLInputFactory.newInstance();
    //forward-only, most efficient way to read
    XMLEventReader reader = null;

    //get ahold of the file
    final InputStream is =
        StaxIterator.class.getResourceAsStream(db);

    try {
        //create the reader from the stream
        reader = xif.createXMLEventReader(is);

        //work with stream and get the type of event
        //we're inspecting
        while (reader.hasNext()) {
            XMLEvent e = reader.nextEvent();

            if (e.isStartElement()){
                e = e.asStartElement().getAttributeByName(
                new QName("sku"));
                if (e != null){
                    out.println(e);
                }
            }
        } //end loop

    } catch (XMLStreamException e) {
        out.println("Cannot parse: " + e);
    }
  }
}
```

Executing the program gives the following output:

```
sku='123_xaa'
sku='988_yty'
sku='434_asd'
sku='876_pep'
```

As you can see, the two parsing models are very similar, with slightly different ways of handling events.

3.2 Writing XML Data Streams

Problem

You want to write an XML document using a fast new API.

Solution

Use the StAX API in Java SE 6.

This section demonstrates how to use the `XMLStreamWriter` and `XMLOutputFactory` to quickly put together a bit of XML and write it out to a file using the StAX cursor API. See Example 3-3.

Example 3-3. Writing an XML file with XMLStreamWriter

```
package com.sc.ch02.stax;

import static java.lang.System.out;

import java.io.FileNotFoundException;
import java.io.FileOutputStream;
import java.io.IOException;

import javax.xml.stream.XMLOutputFactory;
import javax.xml.stream.XMLStreamException;
import javax.xml.stream.XMLStreamWriter;

public class WriteStax {
    private static final String REPAIR_NS = "javax.xml.stream.isRepairingNamespaces";

    private static final String NS = "http://ns.example.com/books";

    public static void main(String... args) {
        XMLOutputFactory factory = XMLOutputFactory.newInstance();
        // autobox
        factory.setProperty(REPAIR_NS, true);

        try {
            //setup a destination file
            FileOutputStream fos =
            new FileOutputStream("result.xml");
```

```
            //create the writer
            final XMLStreamWriter xsw = factory.createXMLStreamWriter(fos);
            xsw.setDefaultNamespace(NS);

            //open the document. Can also add encoding, etc
            xsw.writeStartDocument("1.0");
            xsw.writeEndDocument();

            xsw.writeComment("Powered by StAX");

            //make enclosing book
            xsw.writeStartElement("book");
            xsw.writeNamespace("b", NS);
            xsw.writeAttribute("sku", "345_iui");

            //make title child element
            xsw.writeStartElement(NS, "title");
            xsw.writeCharacters("White Noise");
            xsw.writeEndElement(); //close title

            xsw.writeEndElement(); //close book

            //clean up
            xsw.flush();
            fos.close();
            xsw.close();

            out.print("All done.");
        } catch (FileNotFoundException fnfe) {
            fnfe.printStackTrace();
        } catch (IOException ioe) {
            ioe.printStackTrace();
        } catch (XMLStreamException xse) {
            xse.printStackTrace();
        }
    }
}
```

The API is very flexible, and allows you to write XML with varying degrees of well-formedness and validity. You can quickly and cleanly produce XML snippets suitable for transfer into the payload of a SOAP body or anywhere else you'd like to stick some markup.

Executing this program gives you the following result:

```
<?xml version="1.0"?>
<!--Powered by StAX-->
<book xmlns="http://ns.example.com/books" xmlns:b="http://ns.example.com/books"
    sku="345_iui">
    <b:title>White Noise</b:title>
</book>
```

You can also use the `setPrefix` method to indicate the prefix to use on elements. Set the `javax.xml.stream.isRepairingNamespaces` on the factory to true to add the default namespace to the root element:

```
<book xmlns="http://ns.example.com/books" xmlns:b="http://ns.example.com/books"
    sku="345_iui">
```

If you do not set the `javax.xml.stream.isRepairingNamespaces` on the factory, or set it to false, the default namespace is left out, resulting in a book element that looks like this:

```
<?xml version="1.0"?>
<!--Powered by StAX-->
<book  xmlns:b="http://ns.example.com/books" sku="345_iui">
//...
```

In general, when deciding between the two modes, if you want to be able to modify the event stream and want the most flexible API, choose Iterator. If you want the fastest possible performance and the smallest footprint, use the Cursor API.

3.3 Filtering Data in an XML Stream

Problem

You want to maximize efficiency while reading an XML file by filtering the StAX event stream to leave out events you're not interested in.

Solution

For data streams, just implement the `javax.xml.stream.StreamFilter` interface and pass it to the `XMLStreamReader` constructor along with your file input stream. Wrap your `XMLStreamReader` with a `FilteredReader`. For event streams, wrap your `XMLEventReader` with an `EventFilter` implementation. You might recognize the Decorator design pattern at work here, as is typical of the standard Java I/O libraries.

The previous StAX cursor example was fine, but could be more efficient. It captured a considerable number of events you weren't interested in receiving. You can use a filter to improve the performance and clarity of your applications by instructing the parser to make available only those events you're interested in hearing about.

When working with cursors, all you have to do is implement the `StreamFilter` interface's `accept` method. Then construct your `XMLStreamReader` with it. When working with an `EventReader`, all you have to do is implement the `EventFilter` interface's `accept` method. Example 3-4 shows how it's done.

Example 3-4. StaxFiltered.java

```
package com.sc.ch02.stax;

import static java.lang.System.out;

import java.io.FileNotFoundException;
import java.io.FileReader;
import java.util.HashMap;
import java.util.Map;
```

```java
import javax.xml.stream.*;
import javax.xml.stream.events.XMLEvent;

public class StaxFiltered {
    private static final String fdb = "path/ch02/Catalog.xml";

    private Map<String, Double> expensiveBooks;

    private String lastTitle;

    //constructor
    public StaxFiltered() {
        expensiveBooks = new HashMap<String, Double>();
    }

    public static void main(String[] args) {
        StaxFiltered p = new StaxFiltered();

        p.findByEvent();
    }

    /*
     * Here our aim is to find book prices over $10. So we use a
     * filter to give us only start elements so we have already
     * filtered out items we know don't help us.
     */
    public void findByEvent() {
        try {
            XMLInputFactory xif = XMLInputFactory.newInstance();

            FileReader fr = new FileReader(fdb);

            // wrap the XMLStreamReader with FilteredReader
            XMLEventReader reader =
                    xif.createFilteredReader(
                            xif.createXMLEventReader(fr),
                            new StartElementEventFilter());

            // work with stream and get the type of event
            // we're inspecting
            while (reader.hasNext()) {

                XMLEvent event = (XMLEvent) reader.next();
                int eventType = event.getEventType();

                switch (eventType) {
                case XMLEvent.START_ELEMENT:

                    findHighPrices(reader, event);
                }

            } // end loop

            out.println("Expensive books=" + expensiveBooks);
```

```
        } catch (FileNotFoundException fnfe) {
            out.println("Cannot find source: " + fnfe);
        } catch (XMLStreamException e) {
            out.println("Cannot parse: " + e);
        }
    }

    private void findHighPrices(XMLEventReader reader,
            XMLEvent event) throws XMLStreamException {

        String currentElem = event.asStartElement().toString();

        // save off the title so we can match the price with it
        if ("<title>".equals(currentElem)) {
            lastTitle = reader.getElementText();
        }

        // get the current price and add to collection if high
        if ("<price>".equals(currentElem)) {
            double price;
            try {
                price = Double.parseDouble(reader
                                .getElementText());

                if (price > 10.0D) {
                    expensiveBooks.put(lastTitle, price);
                }

            } catch (NumberFormatException nfe) {
                nfe.printStackTrace();
            } catch (XMLStreamException xse) {
                xse.printStackTrace();
            }
        }
    }
}

/**
 * Get only start elements for efficiency. If we returned only
 * attributes, for example, we wouldn't be able to read the data
 * we're interested in here (title and price values).
 */
class StartElementEventFilter implements EventFilter {
    // only req'd method to implement
    public boolean accept(XMLEvent event) {
        return event.isStartElement();
    }
}
```

This results in the following output:

```
Expensive books={Java Generics and Collections=34.99, 1984=12.95}
```

3.4 Selecting Values from an XML Document

Problem

After parsing, you need to select only certain values from an XML document to work with.

Solution

Use Java's built-in XPath API to search for elements and attributes that match your criteria.

While the language in previous versions provided for the execution of XPath operations, the updated XPath API was added in Java 5. The libraries are now much easier to work with and are more stable.

XPath is important for SOA work because it is useful in two key areas: searching the payload of SOAP messages for certain values when you're working with the SAAJ API in a server-side provider and working with BPEL assignments in service orchestrations. We'll discuss more in later chapters; for now it is just important to have a good handle on the kinds of things you can do with XPath.

The program listing in Example 3-5 shows how you can parse an XML document and compile a variety of XPath expressions to find different values. Here you will use the *Catalog.xml* file introduced earlier in this chapter.

Example 3-5. BasicXPath.java

```
package com.sc.ch02.xpath;

import static java.lang.System.out;

import java.io.IOException;

import javax.xml.parsers.DocumentBuilder;
import javax.xml.parsers.DocumentBuilderFactory;
import javax.xml.parsers.ParserConfigurationException;
import javax.xml.xpath.*;

import org.w3c.dom.*;
import org.xml.sax.SAXException;

/**
 * Accepts an XPath expression to perform searching against
 * the Catalog.xml document.
 */
public class BasicXPath {

    public static void main(String...args) throws Exception {
        String xmlSource = "src/xml/ch02/Catalog.xml";

        //Get all titles with price between $5 and $9.99
```

```
        xpath = "//book[price > 5.00 and price < 9.99]/title";
        /* Prints:
         * Value=King Lear
           Value=Hamlet
         */

        search(xmlSource, xpath);
    }

    public static void search(String fileIn, String xpathExp)
        throws IOException {

        // Set up the DOM parser
        DocumentBuilderFactory docFactory =
                DocumentBuilderFactory.newInstance();

        try {
            //Parse XML document
            DocumentBuilder docBuilder =
                    docFactory.newDocumentBuilder();
            Document doc = docBuilder.parse(fileIn);

            //Create XPath instance
            XPath xpath = XPathFactory.newInstance().newXPath();

            //Evaluate XPath expression against parsed document
            NodeList nodes = (NodeList) xpath.evaluate(xpathExp,
                doc, XPathConstants.NODESET);

            //We could return these instead to let caller deal
            for (int i = 0, len = nodes.getLength(); i < len; i++) {
                Node node = nodes.item(i);

                String value = node.getTextContent();

                out.println("Value=" + value);
            }

        } catch (XPathExpressionException xpee) {
            out.println(xpee);
            throw new IOException("Cannot parse XPath.", xpee);
        } catch (DOMException dome) {
            out.println(dome);
            throw new IOException("Cannot create DOM tree", dome);
        } catch (ParserConfigurationException pce) {
            out.println(pce);
            throw new IOException("Cannot create parser.", pce);
        } catch (SAXException saxe) {
            out.println(saxe);
            throw new IOException("Error parsing XML document.", saxe);
        }
    }
}
```

Most of the time, this is the sort of thing you'll need to do in SOA. But this is very powerful stuff because you can build the expression string from user-supplied values or another runtime environment supplier, such as a system property.

> **Injection Attack in XPath Expressions**
>
> Use extreme caution in allowing users to directly populate your XPath expressions. XPath expressions, like SQL statements, are very vulnerable to injection attacks. An injection attack can upset your database (whether a SQL-based database or an XML document database) by doing direct damage to the structure, or by revealing far more nodes than you originally intended to return.
>
> The most basic form of injection attack inserts an expression that will always be true into the main expression. For example, say your XPath expression string allowed users to supply a value, as you may have done before with a JDBC statement:
>
> ```
> "//book[price <" + uservalue + "]/title"
> ```
>
> This appears harmless enough. The user could supply "6" to get the titles of all books less than $6. However, this is a bad idea, as it leaves you vulnerable to injection. Imagine that your user-supplied value is `or 1 = 1`.
>
> All of the books are returned. Now, in your book title example that probably isn't a big deal. When dealing with financial data, user credentials, or other sensitive information, however, this can be devastating.
>
> The fix is to simply validate incoming values carefully. For instance, in the previous example, a `NumberFormatException` would have been thrown if you had invoked `Double.parseDouble` on the user-supplied value.

XPath is not only useful for SOAP message data extraction and BPEL assignments, but it is also the foundation of working with a variety of other XML specifications, including XPointer, XQuery, and XSLT.

Discussion

This discussion offers some further characterization of XPath for readers who may be unfamiliar with it, and it gives more detail on how to create advanced XPath expressions.

In the solution example, you were primarily interested in elements and attribute values. In addition to these, XPath is capable of addressing the following document nodes:

- Root
- Text
- Comment
- Processing instruction
- Namespace

The name XPath is appropriate for what XPath does: it defines an expression language that allows you to create a path toward any set of nodes within the tree structure of an XML document. Using an XPath expression, you can yield the following types of results:

- Node set (an unordered set of distinct nodes that match the expression)
- String
- Boolean
- Floating-point number

XPath defines some basic navigational building blocks that you can combine to create address expressions. Table 3-1 illuminates the most basic selectors.

Table 3-1. XPath selectors

/	When this is the first character in an expression, it selects the root node, which is the parent of the document element. In subsequent placements, it acts as an element separator.
.	Selects the current node.
..	Selects the parent of the current node.
@	Selects one or more attributes.
//	Selects all following elements, regardless of their location in the document hierarchy. When used within a path, indicates elements that are direct or indirect descendants of the previously specified element.

XPath also provides a collection of operators that act just as you might hope they would (Table 3-2).

Table 3-2. XPath operators

and, or	Selects according to Boolean meaning.
=, !=	Equal, not equal
<, >, <=, >=	Less than, greater than, LTE, GTE
|	Either/or

Using these elements and some basic operators, you can create a variety of searches. Let's look at some examples:

```
//Find the book titled 'Hamlet' and select its price.
String xpath = "/catalog/book[title='Hamlet']/price";
//Prints: Value=5.95

//Find titles of books with multiple authors
xpath = "/catalog/book[authors]/title";
//Prints:
Value=Java Generics and Collections

//Find all title AND price elements
xpath = "//title | //price";
```

```
//Prints:
Value=King Lear
Value=6.95
Value=Hamlet
Value=5.95
Value=1984
Value=12.95
Value=Java Generics and Collections
Value=34.99

//Get the author of the second book on the list
xpath = "//book[2]/author";
//Prints:
Value=William Shakespeare

//Get the SKU attrib value of the last book on the list
xpath = "//book[last()]/@sku";
//Prints:
Value=876_pep

//Get the entire book node for Hamlet
xpath = "//book[title='Hamlet']";
//Prints the entire Hamlet node

//Get the penultimate (one before the last) book that is a 'classic'
//whose price is between $5 and $10.
xpath = "//book[category='classics' and (price > 5 and price < 10)][last()-1]";
//Prints the entire King Lear node

//Get the title node with the value of Hamlet
xpath = "//title[.='Hamlet']";

//Get the title of the first book whose author starts with 'William'
xpath = "//book[1][author[starts-with(., 'William')]]/title";
//Prints: Value=King Lear

//Gets the categories of the books after the 2nd one in the tree
xpath = "//book[position() > 2]/category";

//Gets any authors that are co-authors,
//that is, all <author> nodes under an <authors> node
xpath = "//authors//author";
//Prints:
Value=Maurice Naftalin
Value=Phillip Wadler
```

As you can see, operator precedence is specified with parentheses. While a complete discussion of XPath is beyond the scope of this book (and beyond what you'll need 90% of the time), you can read the complete specification at *http://www.w3.org/TR/xpath*, or just look there for more string functions.

3.5 Updating a Value in an XML Document

Problem

You want to change a value in an XML document element or attribute. The XML document is on your filesystem and you need to persist the change.

Solution

Parse the document, use XPath to find the value you want to change, change the text content of the node, and then use `StreamResult` with `Transformer` to write out the file again.

The solution is shown in Example 3-6.

Example 3-6. UpdateXMLValue.java

```
package com.sc.ch02.xpath;

import static java.lang.System.out;

import java.io.FileWriter;
import java.io.IOException;

import javax.xml.parsers.DocumentBuilder;
import javax.xml.parsers.DocumentBuilderFactory;
import javax.xml.parsers.ParserConfigurationException;
import javax.xml.transform.*;
import javax.xml.transform.dom.DOMSource;
import javax.xml.transform.stream.StreamResult;
import javax.xml.xpath.*;

import org.w3c.dom.*;
import org.xml.sax.SAXException;

public class UpdateXMLValue {

    public static void main(String[] args) throws Exception {
        String xmlSource = "src/xml/ch02/Catalog.xml";

        //find the book titled 'Hamlet' and select its price.
        String xpath = "/catalog/book[title='Hamlet']/price";

        //this is the new price
        String value = "8.95";

        //we're throwing any exception out
        updateValueInXmlFile(xmlSource, xmlSource, xpath, value);

        out.println("All done.");
    }

    public static void updateValueInXmlFile(String fileIn,
```

```
        String fileOut, String xpathExpression,
        String newValue) throws IOException {

    // Set up the DOM evaluator
    final DocumentBuilderFactory docFactory =
            DocumentBuilderFactory.newInstance();

    try {
        final DocumentBuilder docBuilder =
                docFactory.newDocumentBuilder();
        final Document doc = docBuilder.parse(fileIn);

        final XPath xpath =
                XPathFactory.newInstance().newXPath();
        NodeList nodes =
                (NodeList) xpath.evaluate(xpathExpression,
                        doc, XPathConstants.NODESET);

        // Update the nodes we found
        for (int i = 0, len = nodes.getLength(); i < len; i++) {
            Node node = nodes.item(i);
            node.setTextContent(newValue);
        }

        // Get file ready to write
        final Transformer transformer =
                TransformerFactory.newInstance()
                        .newTransformer();
        transformer.setOutputProperty(OutputKeys.INDENT,
                "yes");
        transformer.setOutputProperty(OutputKeys.ENCODING,
                "UTF-8");

        StreamResult result =
                new StreamResult(new FileWriter(fileOut));
        transformer.transform(new DOMSource(doc), result);

        // Write file out
        result.getWriter().flush();
        result.getWriter().close();

    } catch (XPathExpressionException xpee) {
        out.println(xpee);
        throw new IOException("Cannot parse XPath.", xpee);
    } catch (DOMException dome) {
        out.println(dome);
        throw new IOException("Cannot create DOM tree", dome);
    } catch (TransformerConfigurationException tce) {
        out.println(tce);
        throw new IOException("Cannot create transformer.",
                tce);
    } catch (IllegalArgumentException iae) {
        out.println(iae);
        throw new IOException("Illegal Argument.", iae);
    } catch (ParserConfigurationException pce) {
```

```
            out.println(pce);
            throw new IOException("Cannot create parser.", pce);
        } catch (SAXException saxe) {
            out.println(saxe);
            throw new IOException("Error reading XML document.",
                    saxe);
        } catch (TransformerFactoryConfigurationError tfce) {
            out.println(tfce);
            throw new IOException("Cannot create trx factory.",
                    tfce);
        } catch (TransformerException te) {
            out.println(te);
            throw new IOException("Cannot write values.", te);
        }
    }
}
```

This might not be suitable for very large documents, but will quickly and easily plug into a program that requires you to update values on the fly for a physical file.

3.6 Converting a Java Object into an XML Document Instance

Problem

You have a Java object that you want to convert into an XML document.

Solution

Use the JAXB Marshaler class and invoke its static `marshal` method.

Whether you have written your Java class from scratch or generated it from a schema, you can use JAXB to write out a populated Java object to an XML representation. This representation can take one of the following forms:

- `javax.io.Writer`
- `javax.xml.stream.XMLStreamWriter`
- `javax.xml.stream.XMLEventWriter`
- `javax.xml.transform.Result`
- `org.xml.sax.ContentHandler`
- `org.w3.dom.Node`

The variety of methods for handling the marshaling result gives you a lot of flexibility. You can write the XML result out to a file, to a stream with StAX, as a transformation result, or as a DOM node. Using the Node target is interesting, as it allows you to create the marshaled object as a child on the specified node, using it as a fragment of that object. This can be particularly useful when assembling a SOAP body for a web service request.

You can't just start from a regular POJO (Plain Old Java Object) without annotations and start marshaling. You need to have the appropriate JAXB XML annotations decorating your Java class before you can do this. Recall that these are added automatically when you start from a schema and then generate a Java class. If you have a POJO and you don't want to go through building up from a schema, simply annotate your main composing object with the `XmlRootElement` annotation, and you'll be on your way.

There are two ways to initialize the `JAXBContext`: using a list of package names or using a class array. The first constructor accepts a string, which is a colon-separated list of package names. Each name in the list must contain classes that are annotated with JAXB annotations, or be derived from a schema by JAXB. It might also contain package-level annotations intended for processing. The second constructor accepts an array of classes that you want JAXB to marshal or unmarshal. Note that you don't have to specify all classes in a composition; it's enough to specify the composing class, and JAXB will do the work of marshaling all the rest of them.

Example 3-7 is a basic example of how to perform a marshal and print to the console to see the result. In order to illustrate that JAXB can work with object compositions out of the box, you'll make an example `Book` class to marshal that is composed of an Author type, a Category type, a title string, and a double price.

Example 3-7. Book class to marshal into XML

```
package com.soacookbook.ch02.jaxb;

import javax.xml.bind.annotation.XmlRootElement;

@XmlRootElement
public class Book {

    private String title;
    private double price;
    private Author author;
    private Category category;
//... getters and setters omitted.
}

class Author {
    private String firstName;
    private String lastName;

//... getters and setters omitted.

}

enum Category {
    LITERATURE,
    PHILOSOPHY,
    PROGRAMMING
    ;
}
```

Example 3-8 illustrates how to marshal an instance of your Book class to XML. The result is sent to an output stream, which is, in this case, just the standard out.

Example 3-8. Using JAXB to marshal a Book object into XML and print it to the console

```
package com.soacookbook.ch02.jaxb;

import static java.lang.System.out;

import javax.xml.bind.JAXBContext;
import javax.xml.bind.JAXBException;
import javax.xml.bind.Marshaller;

public class MarshalToConsole {

    public static void main(String...arg) {
        try {

            Book book = new Book();
            Author a = new Author();
            a.setFirstName("Jacques");
            a.setLastName("Derrida");
            book.setAuthor(a);
            book.setPrice(34.95);
            book.setTitle("Of Grammatology");
            book.setCategory(Category.PHILOSOPHY);

            Class[] c = {Book.class};
            JAXBContext ctx = JAXBContext.newInstance(c);
            Marshaller m = ctx.createMarshaller();

            //could also use System.out here
            m.marshal(book, out);

            out.println("\nAll done.");
        } catch (JAXBException ex) {
            ex.printStackTrace();
        }
    }
}
```

Here is the result printed to the console (I added spacing and line breaks for readability):

```
<?xml version="1.0" encoding="UTF-8" standalone="yes"?>
<book>
    <author>
        <firstName>Jacques</firstName>
        <lastName>Derrida</lastName>
    </author>
    <category>PHILOSOPHY</category>
    <price>34.95</price>
    <title>Of Grammatology</title>
</book>
All done.
```

Note that here you get a handle on the Book class instance and pass that to the JAXBContext to create your context for marshaling. There is an alternative way to create the context, which requires you to pass a string to the constructor indicating the name of the package containing the types you're working with.

For simplicity in Example 3-9, you print to the console. Let's look at some drop-in replacements for the output destination of the marshaling line of code. The marshaling, or what is produced, is identical in every case; it is only *where* it gets produced that you're changing.

Example 3-9. Marshal to a DOM node

```
//Create Document
DocumentBuilderFactory dbf =
    DocumentBuilderFactory.newInstance();
dbf.setNamespaceAware(true);
DocumentBuilder db = dbf.newDocumentBuilder();
Document doc = db.newDocument();

//Send marshal result to Document
m.marshal(book, doc);

//Find a value
String title = doc.getDocumentElement().
          getElementsByTagName("title").item(0).getTextContent();

System.console().printf("Read %s now!", title);

/*
Prints: Read Of Grammatology now!
All done.
*/
```

Sometimes you want to marshal an object to XML and directly write out the result to a file. This is shown in Example 3-10. It's just like Example 3-9, with a slight modification.

Example 3-10. Marshal to a new file

```
m.marshal(book, new FileOutputStream(new File("aBook.xml")));
```

This creates a new file on the filesystem in the current directory.

Set the following property on your marshaler instance to pretty-print the XML result with indentation:

```
m.setProperty("jaxb.formatted.output", true);
```

This is false by default.

Finally, Example 3-11 writes your XML content to a string using the StringWriter class.

Example 3-11. Store marshal result in a string using StringWriter

```
StringWriter sw = new StringWriter();
m.marshal(book, sw);

System.out.println(sw);
```

`JAXBContext` is an abstract class, so vendors can implement it as they see fit. JAXB offers a good combination of flexibility and ease of use. There are other options for doing this sort of thing, however, including XStream, XMLBeans, and Castor. Of these, XStream is very fast and does not force you to use annotations on your classes, so in a way it is more flexible than JAXB. Castor is a more general-purpose framework that provides persistence mapping, but it is somewhat more limited in terms of strict binding.

XMLBeans was originally written by BEA and eventually donated to the Apache project. Its most recent release of 2.3 was in June of 2007 and includes XQuery support.

For more alternatives, you could also check out Betwitx and regular Java serialization with XML.

3.7 Converting an XML Document Instance into a Java Object

Problem

You have an XML document instance that you want to convert into a Java object.

Solution

Use JAXB's `Unmarshaller` class with a `JAXBElement<T>`.

With `JAXBElement<T>`, you can specify the class into which you want to unmarshal your XML content without having to first write any mapping. That is, you don't have to use annotations on your XML files during unmarshaling when you use `JAXBElement` and indicate the class of the object you want your result in as its type parameter.

You may get XML from a variety of sources, not just objects that were first marshaled from JAXB, or that you had an opportunity to annotate. You might want to allow a fairly loose interpretation of your object structure that, for example, allows your root element name to be specified differently than it is in the actual class.

XStream produces a root element in the XML serialization process that prepends the package name. So instead of serializing your Book object into a `<book>` element, you end up with a root element of `<com.soacookbook.ch02.xstream.Book>`. So while you and I know that XML document would "fit" into a Book object, it's hard for the tools that actually do the work to know that. Luckily, the tools are pretty smart.

There is a distinction between serialization and marshaling. The term "serialization" is used to express the simple transformation of an object into an output stream, which here happens to be an XML format. Marshaling, which also produces an XML format, does its work specifically through binding, which is achieved in JAXB in the form of annotation mappings.

Example 3-12 uses `JAXBElement<T>` to unmarshal an XML document that was generated entirely outside of JAXB. No XML annotations are used here; this `Book` is just a POJO. Plus, you didn't even use JAXB to do the marshaling in the first place; you used XStream.

Example 3-12. Using JAXBElement<T> to unmarshal an XML string

```
package com.soacookbook.ch02.jaxb;

import java.io.StringReader;
import javax.xml.bind.JAXBContext;
import javax.xml.bind.JAXBElement;
import javax.xml.bind.JAXBException;
import javax.xml.bind.Unmarshaller;
import javax.xml.parsers.DocumentBuilderFactory;
import javax.xml.parsers.DocumentBuilder;
import javax.xml.transform.stream.StreamSource;
import org.w3c.dom.Document;

public class UnmarshalWithElement {

  public static void main(String...arg) {
    try {

        //Create context
        JAXBContext ctx = JAXBContext.newInstance(Book.class);

        //Create marshaller
        Unmarshaller um = ctx.createUnmarshaller();

        //Read in the XML from anywhere
        //In this case it is a complete XML book as string.
        StringReader sr = new StringReader(getBookXml());

        //Get XML from object
        JAXBElement<Book> b = um.unmarshal(
                new StreamSource(sr), Book.class);

        //Start working with object
        Book book = b.getValue();

        System.console().printf("Title: %s", book.getTitle());

    } catch (JAXBException ex) {
        ex.printStackTrace();
    } catch (Exception ex) {
        ex.printStackTrace();
```

```
        }
    }

    private static String getBookXml(){
        return "<com.soacookbook.ch02.xstream.Book>" +
                "<title>On Friendship</title>" +
                "<price>39.95</price>" + //etc...
    }
}
```

The output is what you're hoping for:

```
Title: On Friendship
```

As you can see, JAXBElement allows you to be very flexible in working with XML and Java objects.

3.8 Generating a Schema from an XML Document

Problem

You have an XML document instance and you want to quickly generate a valid schema for it.

Solution

Use Trang, which is available as a free download from *http://www.thaiopensource.com*.

After you unpack the download, you can invoke Trang like this:

```
>java -jar C:/programs/trang/trang.jar C:/repository/src/xml/ch02/Catalog.xml
Catalog.xsd
```

This runs the Trang program and passes it two inputs: the name of the XML file you want to generate a schema for and the name of the output schema file you want Trang to create.

Given your *Catalog.xml* file from Recipe 3.2 as input, Trang generates the following schema:

```
<?xml version="1.0" encoding="UTF-8"?>
<xs:schema xmlns:xs="http://www.w3.org/2001/XMLSchema" elementFormDefault="qualified">
  <xs:element name="catalog">
    <xs:complexType>
      <xs:sequence>
        <xs:element maxOccurs="unbounded" ref="book"/>
      </xs:sequence>
    </xs:complexType>
  </xs:element>
  <xs:element name="book">
    <xs:complexType>
      <xs:sequence>
        <xs:element ref="title"/>
```

```
        <xs:choice>
          <xs:element ref="author"/>
          <xs:element ref="authors"/>
        </xs:choice>
        <xs:element ref="price"/>
        <xs:element ref="category"/>
      </xs:sequence>
      <xs:attribute name="sku" use="required" type="xs:NMTOKEN"/>
    </xs:complexType>
  </xs:element>
  <xs:element name="title" type="xs:string"/>
  <xs:element name="authors">
    <xs:complexType>
      <xs:sequence>
        <xs:element maxOccurs="unbounded" ref="author"/>
      </xs:sequence>
    </xs:complexType>
  </xs:element>
  <xs:element name="price" type="xs:decimal"/>
  <xs:element name="category" type="xs:NCName"/>
  <xs:element name="author" type="xs:string"/>
</xs:schema>
```

Discussion

As you can see, Trang does a good job of inferring appropriate values from your XML source. A book can have one author or a set of authors, and Trang figures out how to make a choice element and add references.

One thing worth noting is that the schema design pattern used in Trang may not be exactly what you want, depending on your use case. The elements in the preceding example are all global and in the default namespace.

When working with SOA, you definitely are going to need to do your best to ensure interoperability. You therefore will probably want to employ the option to disable abstract types, like this:

```
-o disable-abstract-elements
```

In general, you'll want to start with a schema if you can. Sometimes you won't have that luxury, and sometimes it will be much quicker and easier to write the XML instance you know you'll need for your SOAP payload or whatever you're working with, and then generate a schema that you can tweak somewhat (or a lot) to make it conform with a design pattern that you want.

You can use Trang to generate DTD and Relax NG for you as well—that is actually its original purpose. But here we limit our focus to XML schema, as it is the most widely used way of representing a valid XML structure.

Generating a set of schemas from a single XML document

Maybe you have an XML document that defines a variety of namespaces, and you'd like Trang to generate corresponding schemas for each of them. You can do that too.

What you can't do is just prefix your elements and expect Trang to provide some boilerplate defaults. This, for example, won't cut it:

```
<a:address>
  <a:street>1212 Some Street</a:street>
  <a:city>Washington,DC</a:city>
  <a:state>VA</a:state>
</a:address>
```

The answer is clear and simple. You just need to provide a namespace definition for the prefix, and then use Trang normally, as you did in the previous example:

```
<a:address xmlns:a="urn:ns:soacookbook:address">
  <a:street>1212 Some Street</a:street>
  <a:city>Washington,DC</a:city>
  <a:state>VA</a:state>
</a:address>
```

Doing this will give you a new XSD document named for each prefix you define.

See Also

Recipe 2.8.

3.9 Converting XML to Java Without JAXB

Problem

The examples in the previous recipe force you to specify the type that you are working with, and that type has to include mappings in the form of XML annotations. That works fine if in your SOA you are starting from schema, generating to Java with JAXB, letting it provide the mappings, and so on. But maybe you're not doing that, or you want a more general-purpose solution for Java to XML round-trips.

Solution

Try XStream, an open source project available from *http://xstream.codehaus.org*. It is very easy to use, it's customizable, and it performs serialization of full object graphs.

You can use the code in Example 3-13 for general-purpose Java to XML round-trips. It has two methods. The first accepts an object of any type, as long as it implements `java.io.Serializable`, and converts it into an XML string using XStream. The second method accepts a string that has previously been serialized to XML and creates a Java object out of it.

Example 3-13. From Java to XML and back with XStream

```
package com.soacookbook.ch02.xstream;

import com.soacookbook.ch02.jaxb.*;
import com.thoughtworks.xstream.XStream;
import com.thoughtworks.xstream.io.xml.DomDriver;
import java.io.Serializable;
import static java.lang.System.out;

/**
 * Shows Java to XML back to Java with no mapping
 * using XStream.
 */
public class XMLStreamRoundTrip<T extends Serializable>  {

    public static void main(String...arg){

        //Create a complex object to work with
        Book book = new Book();
        Author a = new Author();
        a.setFirstName("Jacques");
        a.setLastName("Derrida");
        book.setAuthor(a);
        book.setPrice(39.95);
        book.setTitle("Glas");
        book.setCategory(Category.PHILOSOPHY);

        //Put the book into XML
        XMLStreamRoundTrip<Book> x = new XMLStreamRoundTrip<Book>();
        String bookXml = x.toXml(book);

        //Print entire XML
        System.console().printf("XML:\n%s\n", bookXml);

        //Create a new object by rehydrating the XML
        Book newBook = x.fromXml(bookXml);

        //Show values
        System.console().printf("Object:\n%s costs $%s\n",
                newBook.getTitle(), newBook.getPrice());

    }

    public String toXml(T model) {
        return new XStream().toXML(model);
    }

    @SuppressWarnings("unchecked")
    public T fromXml(String modelAsString) {
        XStream xstream = new XStream(new DomDriver());
        T model = (T)xstream.fromXML(modelAsString);
        return model;
    }
}
```

This couldn't be easier. Most of the code is setting up the book object itself. The two methods at the bottom of the class do all of the XStream work. The output is just as you would expect:

```
XML:
<com.soacookbook.ch02.xstream.Book>
  <title>Glas</title>
  <price>39.95</price>
  <author>
    <firstName>Jacques</firstName>
    <lastName>Derrida</lastName>
  </author>
  <category>PHILOSOPHY</category>
</com.soacookbook.ch02.xstream.Book>

Object:
Glas costs $39.95
```

Note that in your XStream constructor, you pass a `DomDriver` object. You can also leave that out, and put XPP on the classpath. XPP is the ThoughtWorks XML Pull Parser (also a free download from *http://xstream.codehaus.org*) that is optimized for efficiency.

3.10 Customizing Code Generation in JAXB

Problem

You want to gain advanced capabilities for how JAXB generates your Java code during unmarshaling. For example, you'd like JAXB to add a `hashcode` and an `equals` method to your generated class, or maybe a `toString` method.

Solution

Check out the JAXB plug-ins available at *https://jaxb2-commons.dev.java.net*, or write your own.

At the time of this writing, the JAXB 2 commons project features 16 plug-ins and utilities that extend the capabilities of JAXB. Those hosted at the *jaxb2-commons* site allow you to do some of the useful things that you might normally do if you were writing your own objects instead of generating them. For example, there is a plug-in to generate identifiers using camel case and one to create property listeners around fields.

The plug-ins are easy to use. Simply download the JAR from the website and add it to XJC's classpath along with the necessary plug-in option. Here is an example invocation for using the property listener injector plug-in:

```
> xjc -cp property-listener-injector.jar -Xinject-listener-code Book.xsd
```

If you don't see a plug-in listed that has the functionality you want, you can try writing your own. To do this, first check out the JAXB reference implementation source code to build against. Then extend `com.sun.tools.xjc.Plug-in` to write your plug-in class, which defines a series of methods that your plug-in needs to implement in order to interact with XJC.

Next, you need to package your class into a JAR and indicate its existence to the runtime using Service Provider Interface (SPI), which was introduced internally in Java 1.4 but made publicly available in Java 6. Create a text file in the *META-INF/services* directory of your JAR called *com.sun.tools.xjc.Plugin*. In this file, type the name of your class that implements the plug-in interface. It will be picked up at runtime as an implementor.

Then you need to add an annotation or external binding to indicate that your schema should use this customization. For information on how to do this, see Recipe 2.15.

Finally, invoke XJC as just shown. Or, if you are using Ant, invoke it as usual but make two modifications. First, you need to define your XJC task as using the plug-in. Second, pass the plug-in's argument to the XJC tasks on invocation:

```
<taskdef name="xjc" classname="com.sun.tools.xjc.XJCTask">
  <classpath>
    <pathelement path="/path/jaxb-xjc.jar"/>
    <pathelement path="/path/plugin.jar" />
  </classpath>
</taskdef>

...

<xjc ...>
  <arg value="-Xinject-listener-code" />
</xjc>
```

3.11 Finding the JAR That Contains a Given Class on Linux

Problem

You are developing on the Linux platform and know the name of a class you need to put on your classpath, but you don't know what JAR it is in. There are literally dozens of JARs that ship with a typical Java EE 5 app server, making this a difficult situation.

Solution

Execute the command in Example 3-14, which will examine all of the JAR files in the current directory and print their contents to a file called *tmp*.

Example 3-14. Finding a Java Class within a JAR

```
> find . -name "*.jar" -print -exec jar -tvf {} \; > tmp
```

The resulting file looks like this:

```
./appserv-deployment-client.jar
     0 Tue Apr 24 07:21:00 MST 2007 META-INF/
   449 Tue Apr 24 07:20:58 MST 2007 META-INF/MANIFEST.MF
     0 Tue Apr 24 06:45:36 MST 2007 com/
     0 Tue Apr 24 06:45:34 MST 2007 com/sun/
     0 Tue Apr 24 06:45:34 MST 2007 com/sun/enterprise/
     0 Tue Apr 24 06:45:42 MST 2007 com/sun/enterprise/admin/
     0 Tue Apr 24 06:45:42 MST 2007 com/sun/enterprise/admin/util/
  1821 Tue Apr 24 06:45:28 MST 2007 com/sun/enterprise/admin/util/HostAndPort.class
```

and so on. Each JAR will be named, followed by all of the packages and classes in it. You can then use the `less` tool to quickly jump to the name of your class.

Discussion

This is useful as you're getting started with web services for the sheer volume of JARs you may need to deal with.

You want only the JARs that you actually need on your classpath, not hundreds of modified bundled versions of things that may or may not be in use. Such a project is messy and difficult to maintain. If, for example, your build invokes the `xjc` task, but it complains that it can't find a class like "com/sun/enterprise/cli/framework/InputsAndOutputs.class", you cannot continue your work. You need to find that class. You can tell from the name that it's provided by Sun, so you might start browsing the Glassfish lib directory and just use the brute-force method of opening JARs one by one and eyeballing it.

But if you open the lib directory of Glassfish (or WebLogic 10 or WebSphere), there are dozens of JARs in there! It can be tedious and time-consuming to determine which JAR has the class you want. You don't know what this class does. You don't even care about this class at all. You just need your XJC Ant task to work and apparently some class in there needs some other class that needs this one. But it's not a good practice to throw all of the JARs in there on your classpath—it's slow and misleading and doesn't help you learn about what's happening under the hood. And in my view, it's not good to be dependent on the IDE whatsoever. You should be able to execute Ant from the command line and your build should still work.

As mentioned, each JAR will be named, followed by all of the packages and classes in it. So, you can then use the `less` tool to find your guy. Within the `less` tool, type:

```
> /InputsAndOutputs
```

This will search down the contents for the `InputsAndOutputs` class, and will find and highlight that text (assuming that the JAR that contains your class actually was in the directory you ran this command from).

Or you can Ctrl+G to get to the bottom of the file and then search up the file for the first instance of ".jar". That will be the name of the JAR file containing your class. Run:

```
> ?.jar
```

This highlights *./admin-cli.jar*, which is indeed the Glassfish JAR file containing `InputsAndOutputs.class`. So now you can drop that on your classpath and get on with your build.

If you don't know what JAR file contains the class you're looking for, this is an easy way to find it on Linux. Don't forget to delete the "tmp" file if you don't want to leave it around for another time. The "tmp" files can be very large, depending on the directory in which you run the command.

3.12 Transparently Substituting XML Files

Problem

Your code refers to XML documents such as WSDL or XML Schema using remote addresses, but you want your code to automatically and transparently substitute a saved local copy of the remote resource. Or, you have defined a placeholder location for a WSDL, and you want to substitute a real value at runtime.

Solution

Use an XML catalog.

Discussion

An XML Catalog consists of one or more files that define a logical structure that maps a set of XML entities. XML catalogs cover two basic scenarios: mapping an external entity's public or system identifier to a URI, and mapping one URI reference to another one.

XML catalogs are useful for a few reasons:

Disconnected access
: XML catalogs allow your application to continue working even if you are disconnected from the network that defines the remote resource. If you're using your laptop in a disconnected location and you are developing a web service that uses schemas that are back in the office, you can use an XML catalog to substitute those remote schemas for local copies. You can then continue to develop without having to change code throughout your application that points to those remote resources.

Performance
: XML catalogs are also important for performance reasons. Your application can use catalogs to avoid making expensive remote calls to WSDL documents.

Software development life cycle
: When moving code through development, QA, staging, and production, you may find it useful to employ XML catalogs in resolving new QA entities that map to

existing production resources, for example. Depending on how your environment is configured, XML catalogs could also be useful on large teams.

It is an SOA best practice in some situations to keep your XML schemas located in a central repository. Using XML Catalogs gives you the flexibility to use such an approach practically, as they add a layer of indirection that helps you transparently move, maintain, and scale your application components.

JAX-WS implementations are required to support XML catalogs 1.1, which is a specification published by OASIS. JAX-WS support comes in the form of a processing engine that reads the catalog and resolves the location mappings. When the JAX-WS deployment encounters a reference to an XML file for which there is an entity mapping in the catalog, the runtime substitutes the reference name for the mapped name. Put another way, the engine receives as input, such as a remote URL for a WSDL document that your application code refers to; the engine checks the catalog for a mapped entry for that URL, and if it finds one, it silently substitutes the physical document that is the mapping target. This is generally how they are used within web services, though they can be used to map replacement text for an external entity.

Using an XML catalog within a JAX-WS deployment requires a few steps:

1. Download a local copy of the remote files you want to substitute.
2. Create the XML catalog file that maps the names of the remote resources to their local substitutes.
3. Save the file with the name *jax-ws-catalog.xml*.
4. Package it with your deployment artifact. If this is a WAR, place the catalog file directly in *WEB-INF*. If this is an EAR, place it directly in *META-INF*.

You can read the XML Catalog specification at *http://www.oasis-open.org/committees/download.php/14809/xml-catalogs.html*. It is not very long.

XML catalog entities

XML catalogs are application independent and vendor independent. They are not Java-specific, but they are defined for use in any platform.

Don't map the same entry to different resources. The first one the engine finds will always be the one it uses.

Here is an example. Say that you have a WSDL at `http://localhost:8080/soaCookbookWS/CatalogServiceSN?wsdl`. You have a separate project that implements a client based on this WSDL, and you do not want your application to invoke the remote resource every time the WSDL is encountered in your client code. Define an XML catalog to map this WSDL location to a local copy of the WSDL you store with your client deployment artifact. You can first save a local copy of the WSDL (and any external schemas that it imports) to a directory named *src/xml*. You'll then have your build script include the WSDL and schemas in the *WEB-INF* directory at deploy time.

Here I am using an example of mapping remote to local documents, but this is not the only way to use catalogs; you can also just map one XML document to another that redefines it.

The generated web service client will define annotations like this:

```
@WebServiceClient(name="CatalogServiceSN",
targetNamespace = "http://ns.soacookbook.com",
wsdlLocation = "http://localhost:8080/soaCookbookWS/CatalogServiceSN?wsdl")
public class CatalogServiceSN extends Service { ... }
```

So the catalog file that you'll use will replace the WSDL file and the single schema (defining the `getTitle` and `getTitleResponse` elements) that it imports. This is shown in Example 3-15.

Example 3-15. XML Catalog using system

```
<?xml version="1.0" encoding="UTF-8" standalone="no"?>
<catalog xmlns="urn:oasis:names:tc:entity:xmlns:xml:catalog" prefer="system">
    <system systemId="http://localhost:8080/soaCookbookWS/CatalogServiceSN?wsdl"
        uri="src/xml/CatalogServiceSN.wsdl"/>
    <system systemId="http://localhost:8080/soaCookbookWS/Library.xsd"
        uri="src/xml/Library.xsd"/>
</catalog>
```

This catalog document has a few important elements, which we'll examine now.

The `<system>` element does the heavy lifting. It maps the document that is referenced by the value of its `systemId` attribute to the value of its `uri` attribute. So, in the this example, any application reference to "http://localhost:8080/soaCookbookWS/CatalogServiceSN?wsdl" will be replaced with "src/xml/CatalogServiceSN.wsdl".

Relative URIs defined in your catalog file are always relative to the location of the catalog file itself.

The `<public>` element is constructed very much like `<system>`. It maps a given public identifier specified by its `publicId` attribute with the value of its `uri` attribute:

```
<public publicId="somePublicId" uri="someUri"/>
```

The <uri> element maps one URI to an alternate, and does so regardless of system or public identifier resolution. It has this form:

```
<uri name="http://www.oasis-open.org/committees/docbook/"
        uri="file:///projects/oasis/docbook/website/"/>
```

The root element, catalog, declares its namespace and features a prefer attribute. Valid values are either public or system. This attribute indicates which type of identifier should be preferred if both are available. Let's look at a couple of possible scenarios. If your target document contains both a public and a system identifier, and your catalog contains only a mapping for public, and prefer=public, then the mapping for public will be used. However, if your target document contains only a system identifier, and your catalog contains only a mapping for public, and prefer=public, there is no effect.

Using XML Catalogs in wsimport

The wsimport tool defines a -catalog <filename> option that allows you to specify the path to an XML catalog file during import. This will cause the generated classes to use the catalog to resolve external entity references.

The Ant task wrapper has a corresponding attribute, shown here:

```
<wsimport
  wsdl="${wsdl.url}"
  catalog="jax-ws-catalog.xml"
  destdir="${gen.classes.dir}"
  sourcedestdir="${src.gen.dir}"
  keep="true"
  extension="false"
  verbose="true" >
  <binding dir="${binding.dir}" includes="${binding.file}" />
</wsimport>
```

See Also

Norman Walsh's paper at *https://jax-ws.dev.java.net/nonav/2.1.1/docs/catalog.html*.

Summary

In this chapter, we addressed XML documents, which constitute the basic unit of exchange in an XML-based SOA. In the previous chapter, we saw how to design and use schemas, and here we've extended our reach to query XML documents with XPath, read and write XML documents with StAX, and transform XML instances to and from Java objects using JAXB. We also looked at various industry and open source tools that help us process XML in many useful ways.

Beginning with the next chapter, we'll jump into web services, and see how to write programs that act as web service clients.

PART II
Web Services

CHAPTER 4
Getting Started

4.0 Introduction

JAX-WS, or Java API for XML Web Services, offers a set of three basic choices for connecting to web services: Dynamic Invocation, Proxy, and SAAJ. The first two hide the complexity of dealing with the XML plumbing under the hood. The third gives you full access to the SOAP envelope in an XML view, as well as a few different ways to control the invocation of your SOAP requests.

Given this flexibility, it is easy to use JAX-WS clients to invoke web services. But there is an initial hump to get over in sorting out the differences in the three APIs and determining when to use each. There are a number of standard variations on the basic request and response that can get pretty tricky. Once you need to decorate a request (see Recipe 6.11), or want to add MIME attachments or custom headers to your SOAP message, or invoke your client asynchronously, there's some work to be done.

One initially confusing thing about web services is the way things are named. For example, you might think that the Service class is used to create a web service implementation. But it isn't; instead, it represents a Service Endpoint Interface on the client side, acting as a proxy for the service endpoint you actually want to invoke. Another potentially confusing area is the great number of classes and annotations that you typically won't be using directly, depending on your approach. If you're just browsing the JavaDocs in the Java EE 5 API, you might not know if you're supposed to write a `@WebService` annotation on the same class as a Provider annotation (you're not), or whether Provider implementations go on the client if Services do (they don't). But that's what this chapter is all about.

This chapter is a "convenience chapter" of sorts. It is about getting set up with some tools and getting a sense of the publicly available web service landscape. In the first chapter, we looked at general SOA concepts and terms; this chapter zeroes in on web service-specific concepts, such as SOAP and WSDL. We get together some tools we need to deploy and consume services and make your first Hello World web service, and we close with a brief look at monitoring tools to aid in debugging.

If you are interested in reading the specifications that support modern Java web services development, they include:

JSR 181
: Web Services Metadata for the Java Platform. Provides many of the annotations used to sew together and deploy web services.

JSR 224
: The Java API for XML-Based Web Services (JAX-WS 2.1). Replaces JAX-RPC as the modern way to create web services, and operates at a higher-level object view than SAAJ does.

JSR 109
: Web Services for Java EE. Defines the programming model for web services.

JSR 67
: The SOAP with Attachments API for Java (SAAJ 1.3). Describes how to create and consume web services at a lower-level, XML view, as opposed to the object view provided by JAX-WS.

This book addresses a variety of other specifications, such as those for SOAP, OASIS XML Catalogs, JAXB, and JBI. But those are the code web services specifications from Sun. This chapter assumes you have a basic familiarity with the idea of SOAP. The illustration in Figure 4-1 shows how the basic APIs fit together.

The world of Java web services is a big, complicated, and fascinating place. Let's jump in!

4.1 Using Publicly Available Web Services to Test Against

Problem

You want to eliminate a few variables in the complex world of web services development by using an existing, established WSDL for a real web service to test against. This will allow you to just on the client part for now.

Solution

Use some of the publicly available free web services from places like StrikeIron.com or XMethods.com.

Here are a few places you can look to find WSDLs to run your test clients against:

Web Service X
: This is a pretty good place to start. Their web services are free, have some documentation, require no signup, and are very simple and straightforward to invoke. Moreover, they are written in .NET, so you will be experiencing the real benefit of

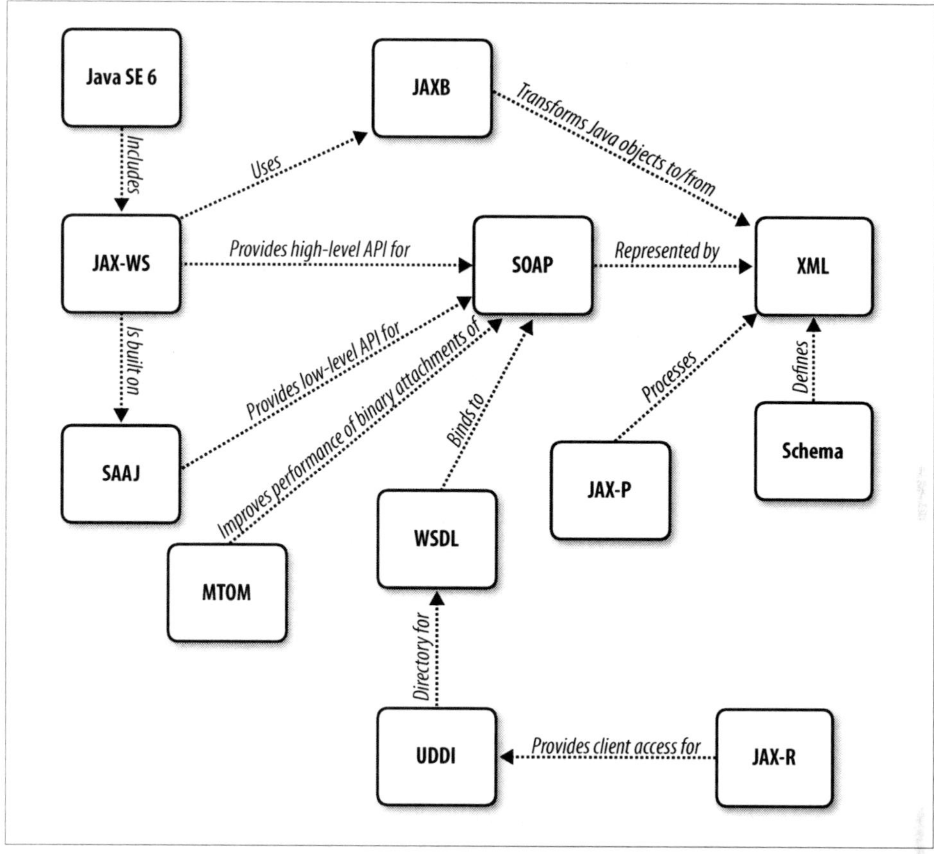

Figure 4-1. The world of JAX-WS

web services (and encountering some of the rough edges) right off the bat. Try them out at *http://www.webservicex.net*.

StrikeIron.com

If you supply your email address, you can invoke a service five times. If you do a full registration, you get 25 times; after that, they'll want you to purchase the service. Note that StrikeIron is not a test bed, and that they make money by having developers and organizations purchase their services for production use. They have real implementations behind them and do real work, such as figuring out the geocode (latitude and longitude) of a certain address. But the services here are real-world with non-trivial interfaces that require passing license info in headers, and the schemas define many composite objects. All of this can make StrikeIron rather tough to start out with. A sample StrikeIron.com service documentation page is shown in Figure 4-2.

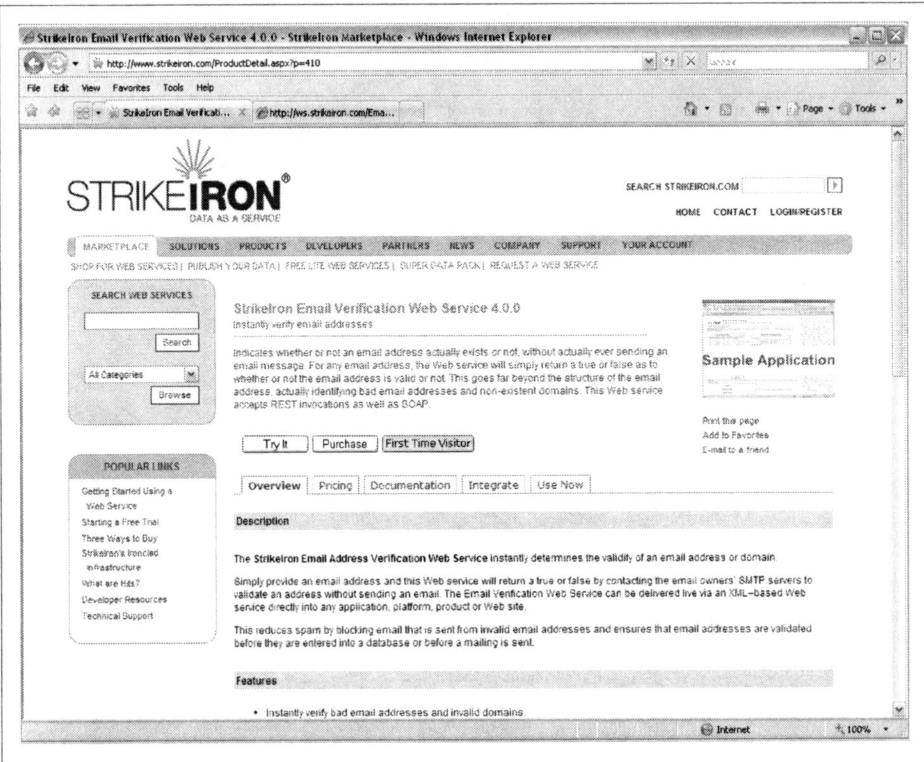

Figure 4-2. StrikeIron web service documentation page

XMethods.com
: There's no signup and no fuss to using many of the services here. The services are not written by XMethods themselves, however; they just host them. So each service will have its own terms of use, and they vary widely in how well they are implemented and documented. Services here are provided by individual developers as well as for-profit companies such as CDyne and StrikeIron. The way that XMethods lists their available services is shown in Figure 4-3.

CDyne.com
: Another web service provider similar to StrikeIron. They also provide a free set of services for developers to use. If you supply a 0 as the credentials key, you can get started with limited usage as with StrikeIron. Their free developer section is available at *http://www.cdyne.com/free/default.aspx*.

FedEx.com
: Offers a Ship Manager web service that you can try out with registration.

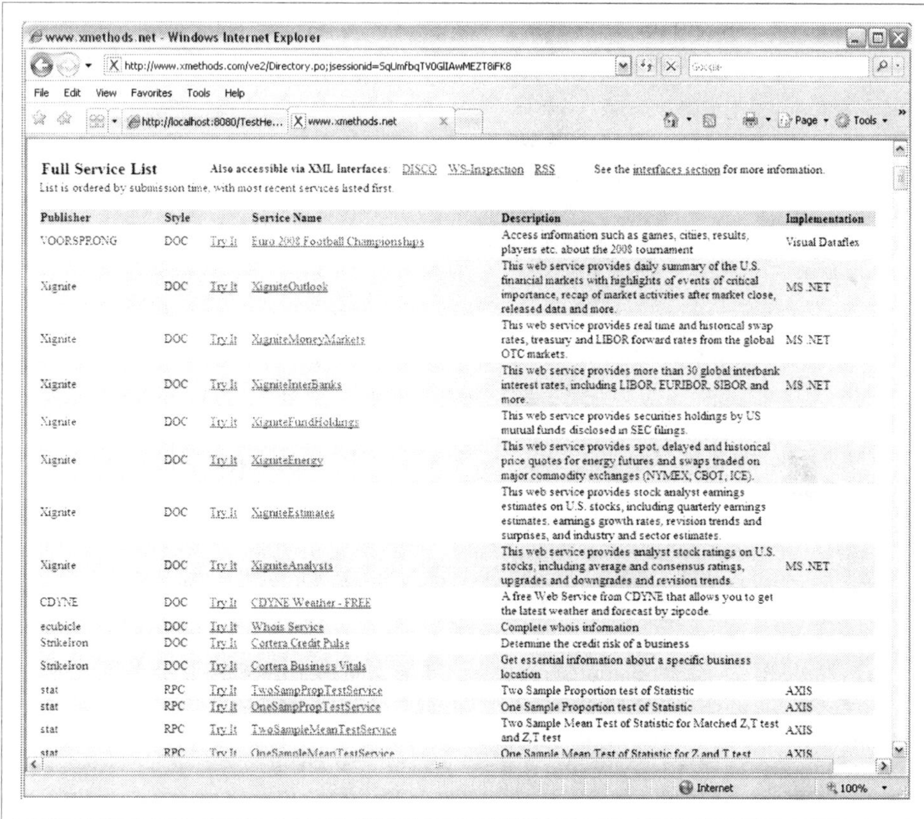

Figure 4-3. XMethods list of available web services

Amazon.com

Amazon provides web services at *http://aws.amazon.com*. At this page you can sign up as a developer, browse their solutions catalog, read whitepapers, and more. Their services include storage (S3), virtual servers (EC2), and database usage (SimpleDB).

Google

Makes a variety of APIs available at *http://code.google.com/*. They are no longer giving out keys to their SOAP-based web service, and the services they offer are primarily focused around JSON and similar technologies.

Discussion

Web services are very complex. Despite the fact that they are wonderful tools for integration across platforms, and that companies like Sun and Microsoft have made great strides in working toward true interoperability with them, services remain just plain hard. They include fussy details that require painstaking attention. The reality of web services today is that there are many slight variations across platforms, versions of the platforms, and different implementations of engines and IDEs. How does one get started in such an environment?

One way to make the enormous web-services pill a little easier to swallow is to eliminate one half of the equation. Instead of writing the service and consuming it too, you can use some web services that are publicly available for free, and just concentrate on getting your client going. That gives you an opportunity to understand the intricacies from one side and see how your client works with an already tested service, so that you can be confident in at least one piece initially.

What Happened to the Public Service Registries?

There used to be public registries at SAP, Microsoft, and IBM. Early in the first decade of this millennium, these companies and others had a vision for something called UBR, or Universal Business Registry. The idea was not dissimilar to the original intent of EJBs. Remember how the vision for EJBs was that developers would make components, then make them publicly available "off the shelf" for others to purchase and consume. We were meant to make a Cart EJB and sell it, allowing frontend developers to easily use our component that "just works" in their Java application. The vision for the UBR was much like this. SAP, Microsoft, and IBM all offered public registries where developers could create a service, upload it with the WSDL and some documentation, and then frontend developers or integrators would be able to browse and shop these registries for the services they wanted. You could pick up a Cart web service from one developer, a Tax Calculator web service from someone else, and a Shipping Calculator service from another party. Then you'd just generate the client-side code to invoke the services, and, presto, you're in the e-commerce business.

Somehow it didn't quite work out that way. Microsoft and IBM have removed their public UDDI (Universal Description, Discovery, and Integration) registries altogether. SAP's registry, shown in Figure 4-4, remains, limping along on an apparently neglected server, a vestigial reminder of the glorious business vision of a honey-bee-like dedication to global commerce that never was to be.

What happened to these registries? In short, there was no one watching the hen house. Well-intentioned developers uploaded their newly minted web services to these public registries, mostly in order to test their use of JAX-R, (the Java API for XML Registries). This API lets you publish a web service, or browse web services available in a UDDI or ebXML registry. The registries became cluttered with hundreds of services called "test2" by `somedude@yahoo.com`. Not surprisingly, interest waned. It also became apparent that certain proclivities within the UDDI spec made it difficult for businesses to justify much automation of the "service discovery" process. While services are still selected at runtime, this is typically based on a set from private registries that have already been vetted. So these public registries ended up suffering a fate similar to the one-time dream of an off-the-shelf EJB-mart.

Eventually, businesses got more sophisticated about setting up their own registries for internal use, and publishing their own services within the firewall for their own teams or selected business partners to browse and consume. This is largely how registries are used today within an SOA.

However, companies like Amazon, Google, and eBay are providing a robust set of services as part of their platform, including functionality that is not only core to their business, but that represents an exposure of their business platforms. Perhaps this model is something we'll see more of in the future.

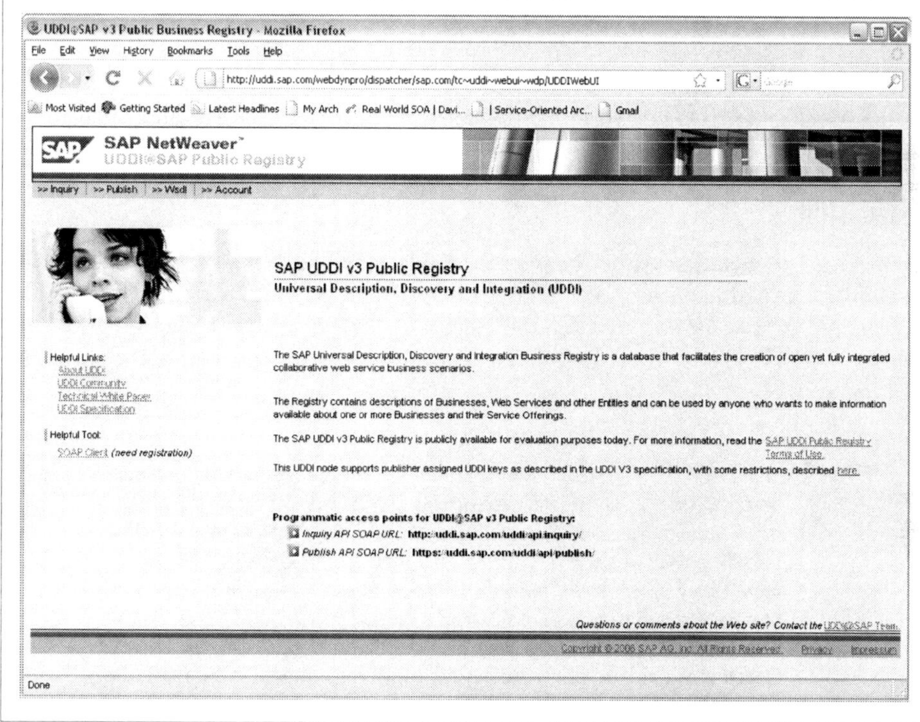

Figure 4-4. SAP Public UDDI 3 Registry

As discussed earlier, publicly available web services that are free to use can be really good for developers who are just getting started with web services. Also, keep in mind that in some cases you actually can purchase the services for real business use, such as with the services from StrikeIron, Amazon, Google, and eBay. Not only that but, these companies are pioneers in the web services space. These two factors can add up to some fairly complex and lengthy WSDLs. If you're still at the Hello World stage, using these services with their wide variety of options and authentication schemes can be overwhelming. Starting with something from XMethods may be a little easier, but many of those services have been developed by well-intentioned people who may be using older versions of their services platform, and you may run into services that don't truly meet your spec or that are just not interoperable. So, if you find yourself banging your head against the wall for a really long time, it may not be you.

4.2 Installing Metro

Problem

You want to use the latest Java APIs available to make it easier to develop interoperable web services.

Solution

Install Metro. Metro is hosted at *https://metro.dev.java.net* as a free and open source project.

Discussion

Metro 1.0.1 is included with Glassfish 9.1 update 1. The JAX-WS Reference Implementation, available within Java SE 6 and Glassfish, provides a rich set of APIs for producing and consuming web services, including WS-Addressing and MTOM capabilities. Metro extends the capabilities of this basic platform but without vendor lock-in.

WSIT, or Web Services Interoperability Technology, is what ensures that JAX-WS applications interoperate with web services and clients from other platforms that conform to the Basic Profile 1.1. WSIT is bundled with JAX-WS 2.1, as included in Glassfish. The WSIT technology is not based on any JSR, and as such is not available as a plug-in for other application servers. Other vendors, such as Oracle WebLogic 10.3, offer roughly equivalent technology, however. In fact, Oracle's WebLogic implementation uses considerable code from the Glassfish and Metro open source projects.

Think of Metro as two basic layers. The core layer gives you the JAX-WS RI, and implementations of key web services specifications to promote interoperability: WS-I Basic Profile, WS-I Attachments Profile, and WS-Addressing. WS-IT, or Web Services Interoperability Technology, provides interoperability with the .NET 3.0 and 3.5 web services platform on Windows. If you download only Glassfish and not the separate Metro 1.1, you get these features.

WSIT and WS-I

WSIT stands for Web Services Interoperabiltiy Technology, and represents a joint effort by Microsoft and Sun, started in 2005, that aims to ensure that web services written in Java can be consumed by .NET clients, and vice versa. This is not to be confused with the WS-I, which is an organization in Boston that promotes interoperability standards. They serve as a central organizing body for the interoperability work for approximately 130 member companies, and most importantly, they are the publishers of the WS-Basic Profile. You can find out more about them at *http://www.ws-i.org*.

The second layer of Metro offers advanced features in four categories: Transports, Reliability, Security, and Transactions, as highlighted in Table 4-1.

Table 4-1. Metro capabilities

Metro capability	Key features implemented
Transports	SOAP over TCP with FastInfoset, JMS and SMTP transports, MTOM and XOP for optimized binary encoding
Reliability	WS-ReliableMessaging implementation
Security	WS-Security and WS-Trust
Transactions	Offers transactional support for web services and implements WS-Coordination and WS-Atomic Transactions

JAX-WS relies on JAXB (Java API for XML Binding) to provide a translation or mapping layer between XML and Java.

WS-Addressing abstracts the physical location of a web service resource for looser coupling. MTOM (Message Transmission Optimization Mechanism) optimizes the transmission of binary data within SOAP messages.

While Metro is available as a separate download that can work in conjunction with other containers such as WebLogic 10.3, it is generally considered as the Sun web services stack, as shown in Figure 4-5.

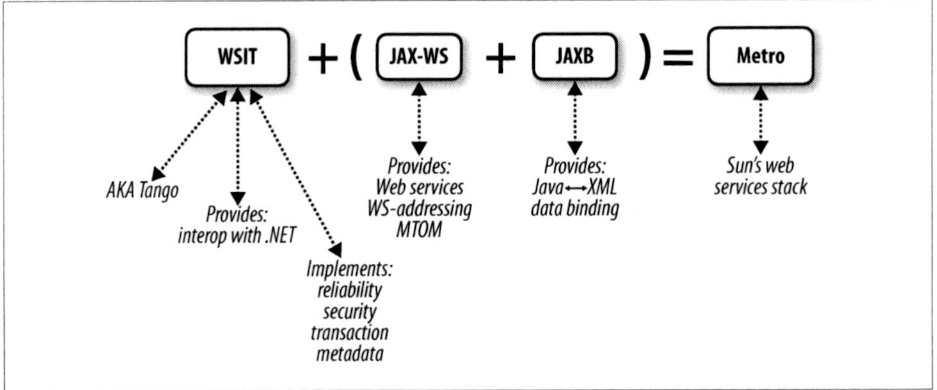

Figure 4-5. Metro: the Java web services stack

In addition to implementing these important specifications, Metro also provides certain conveniences. For example, it offers a single annotation that allows you to perform schema validation against incoming and outgoing message payloads. Metro gives you support for REST via the Jersey project, as well as Spring and JSON (JavaScript Object Notation) integration.

Here's how to get Metro:

1. Download the most recent stable build from *https://metro.dev.java.net*.
2. In a console, navigate to the directory you downloaded it to.
3. Execute > `java -jar metro-installer.jar`. Agree to the license. The installer will expand a directory containing a variety of samples and documentation, as well as a few JARs in the *lib* directory.
4. Navigate to the directory the installer created and run the appropriate Ant script for your platform. First, get the location of your Glassfish home and set that variable on the command. Run *wsit-on-glassfish.xml* as follows:

```
> ant -Denv.AS_HOME=C:\\programs/glassfishv2ur1 -f wsit-on-glassfish.xml
```

You should see that some files were copied and the installation was successful. After restart, the latest version of Metro should now be available for your Glassfish domains.

Metro comes with some tools that are newer versions of the ones that come with the JDK, and some of these are also in Glassfish. For example, the `wsimport` tool that comes with Java SE 1.6.0_05 is version 2.1.1. However, invoking > `wsimport -version` from within the *<glassfish-home>/bin* directory shows "JAX-WS RI 2.1.3-hudson-390-" after installing Metro. It's important to keep your paths straight while using these tools!

This solution assumes that you already have a recent version of Glassfish running locally. It is available at *https://glassfish.dev.java.net*. Glassfish 9.1 update 1, Metro 1.3, and JDK 1.6.0_05 were used to test the examples I've written for this book. If you do not want to use Glassfish, Metro also works with Tomcat, JBoss, and WebLogic.

Using Metro 1.3 in Maven

Here are the dependencies to add to your *pom.xml* if you are using Maven 2 to build your web service and you want to use extra features in Metro:

```
<dependency>
    <groupId>com.sun.xml.ws</groupId>
    <artifactId>webservices-rt</artifactId>
    <version>1.3</version>
    <scope>compile</scope>
</dependency>
<dependency>
  <groupId>javax.xml</groupId>
  <artifactId>webservices-api</artifactId>
  <version>1.3</version>
  <scope>compile</scope>
</dependency>
```

4.3 Installing Oracle WebLogic

Problem

You want to use the latest JAX-WS tools and WS-* implementations, and you also want the support and extensions of a vendor product.

Solution

Get Oracle WebLogic 10gR3 (also known as 10.3). The installation includes WebLogic Server as well as Workshop for WebLogic, which is an Eclipse-based IDE that integrates well with WebLogic server.

Follow these steps on Linux:

1. Download the WebLogic 10.3 file for your platform from *http://www.oracle.com/technology/software/products/ias/bea_main.html*. You can choose the Net installer (smaller download, but requires an Internet connection) or the Package installer (large download of nearly 800MB, but no Internet required). On Linux, the file is *inet_server103_linux32.bin*.
2. Change permissions on the file to allow it to be executed. If you have a GUI in your Linux distribution, just double-click the filename to start the installer. If not, just navigate to the directory you downloaded the binary file to and type *./net_server103_linux32.bin*.

3. Follow the instructions in the wizard. The first step is to create a BEA home (BEA used to make WebLogic until Oracle purchased them in mid-2008). Mine will be */opt/oracle*. Next, you'll specify a temp directory for installer files.
4. Next, specify a custom installation so that you can select everything it will install (there's a lot). If you want detailed information on each item to be installed, click it once, or view the documentation at *http://edocs.bea.com/wls/docs103/getstart/overview.html#wp1062352*.
5. Finally, choose the JDKs to install. By default, these will be Java 1.6.0_05 for the Sun and JRockit JVMs. JRockit is the Oracle implementation of the Java virtual machine, and integrates well with its WebLogic product. This step will get all the remaining files you need to complete the installation.
6. Now set the install directories for WebLogic 10gR3 Server and Workshop. I'll put the server in */opt/oracle/wlserver_10.3*. The installation size is roughly 1.13GB.

Now that the installation is complete, you can run the QuickStart application, which allows you to start the Server and Workshop components.

Starting the server console

Once you have started WebLogic Server, you can start the console by accessing *http://localhost:7001/console*. The console login screen is shown in Figure 4-6.

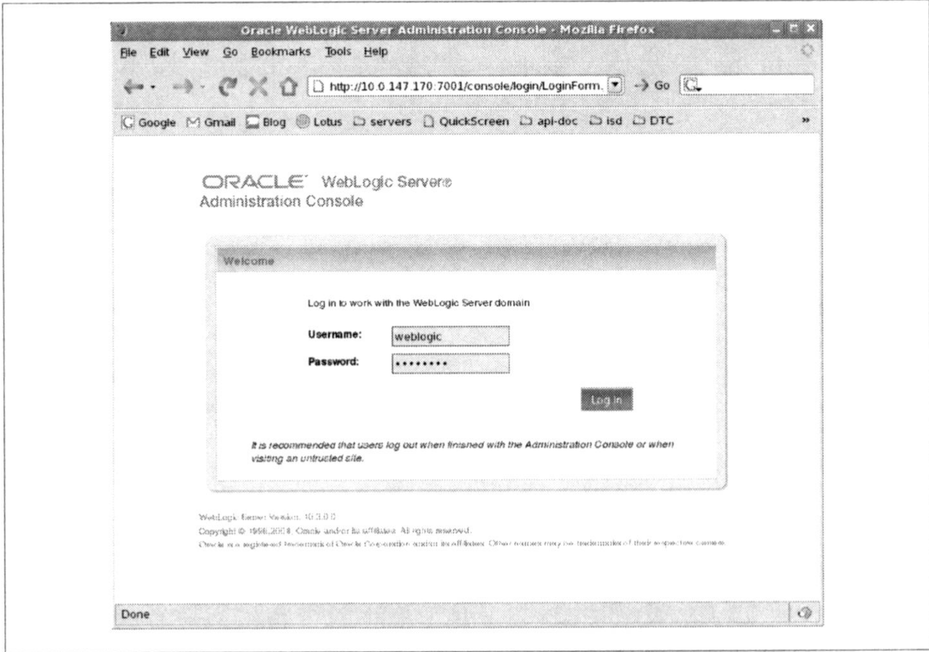

Figure 4-6. WebLogic 10g Release 3 console

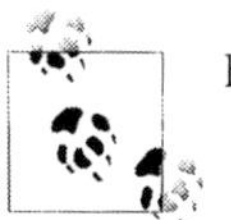

Enter "weblogic" for the username and password.

Now that you are logged in, you are ready to create a web service, package, and deploy it to the console.

See Also

Recipes 4.4 and 4.5.

4.4 Creating and Deploying the Simplest Web Service

Problem

You are new to web services and want to create and deploy the simplest possible functioning web service.

Solution

Write a POJO (Plain Old Java Object) annotated with **`@WebService`** and use `javax.xml.ws.Endpoint` to wrap and publish it within the JVM using the HTTP server built into Java SE 6.

Example 4-1 shows the simplest web service you can write.

Example 4-1. Simple service interface, Hello.java

```
package com.soacookbook.ch03;

import javax.jws.WebService;
import javax.jws.soap.SOAPBinding;

@WebService
@SOAPBinding(style=SOAPBinding.Style.RPC)
public interface Hello {

    String sayHello(String name);
}
```

Here, you created a public interface that clients can use to invoke the service. You used the `@WebService` annotation to indicate that this interface should be made available as a service by the publisher. You then indicated a SOAP binding style of RPC (Remote Procedure Call). Now you need a class to implement the complex business logic (see Example 4-2).

Example 4-2. Simple web service implementation, HelloWS.java

```
package com.soacookbook.ch03;

import javax.jws.WebService;

@WebService(endpointInterface="com.soacookbook.ch03.Hello")
public class HelloWS implements Hello {

    public String sayHello(String name) {
        return "Hello, " + name + "!";
    }
}
```

This service will accept a single parameter and return a string containing the parameter value. Notice that both the interface and the implementation must have the `@WebService` annotation for publishing and invoking using an `Endpoint`. The implementation points to its client-facing interface using the `endpointInterface` attribute of the `@WebService` annotation. This is a fully qualified string.

If you specify a value for the `endpointInterface` attribute in the `@WebService` annotation, the interface will act as the service of record, and its further annotations will be honored while any subsequent annotations in the implementing class will be ignored. This is why you specify the SOAP binding in the interface.

That is all you need to do to create a web service in its most basic form. But it's not quite a real web service until you publish it so that clients can invoke it. You do not need to use a web container for this example. You will use the `javax.xml.ws.Endpoint` class to publish it to the HTTP server internal to the Java SE 6 VM, as shown in Example 4-3.

Example 4-3. Publishing the web service endpoint

```
package com.soacookbook.ch03;

import javax.xml.ws.Endpoint;

public class HelloPublisher {
    public static final String URI = "http://localhost:9999/hello";

    public static void main(String[] args) {

        //Create instance of service implementation
        HelloWS impl = new HelloWS();

        //Make available
        Endpoint endpoint = Endpoint.publish(URI, impl);

        //Test that it is available
        boolean status = endpoint.isPublished();
```

```
        System.out.println("Web service status = " + status);
    }
}
```

The `Endpoint` class has a static `publish` method that binds the annotated service implementation class to a location and makes the service available there. You can then check the status of your service using the `isPublished` method. At this point, your service has been deployed and is available at the specified location.

The endpoint interface allows you to access the complete web service. For instance, you can get the meta data associated with the endpoint by invoking the `getMetadata` method on the endpoint instance. This returns a `List<Source>` of XML documents. You can also get access to the executor that is used to dispatch requests to the service by invoking the `getExecutor` method on the endpoint instance.

See Also

Recipe 4.7 to learn more about what was just generated and how it works.

4.5 Creating and Deploying a Service to WebLogic

Problem

You want to deploy a simple web service to your new Oracle WebLogic 10gR3 installation.

Solution

Follow the steps below.

First, it's probably a good idea to create a new domain for yourself, though you can use the default domain for testing. For this example, I've created one and set it to listen on port 7777.

To set up a domain through WebLogic Workshop, right-click in the Servers tab and choose New Server. At the screen to specify a domain directory, click the Click Here to Launch Configuration Wizard to Create a New Domain and follow the steps. Once your domain is created and your server added, right-click on it and choose Start to start the server. Now you're ready to create and deploy a web service project.

Create a web service project

Follow these steps to create a web service project for WebLogic that uses portable JAX-WS annotations:

1. In WebLogic Workshop, choose File→New→Project.

2. Under the Web Services project type, choose Web Service Project. Click Next.
3. Give your project a name. Choose your new server as the Project Runtime.
4. In the Configurations area, choose Annotated Web Service Facets JAX-WS 10.3. Click Next.
5. Uncheck the box next to WebLogic Web Service Extensions in order to keep your code more readily portable and rely only on the JAX-WS standard.
6. Accept the defaults for the remainder of the wizard and click Finish to create the project.

Now that the project exists, let's add the web service.

Create the web service

1. Under Java Resources, choose the *src* directory, right click, and create a New Package. I've named mine `com.soacookbook`.
2. Right-click on your package, and choose New WebLogic Web Service.
3. In the Filename field, enter HelloWS and finish the wizard.

Now you have a new web service class. Modify the contents of the class to look like this:

```
@WebMethod
public String sayHello(String name) {
  return "Hello, " + name;
}
```

Now you need to create the WSDL for the web service.

Deploy the web service

Now that you have a complete web service, you're ready to deploy it to your WebLogic server. Here are the simple steps to do that:

1. Right-click on the web service implementation class itself (here, `HelloWS.java`) and choose Run As→Run On Server.
2. Choose the local WebLogic server that you installed earlier and click Finish.

Test the service using the built-in test client

Like Glassfish, WebLogic Workshop comes with an easy way to test a web service. When you deploy and run the service through Workshop, it will automatically create a simple graphical client that allows you to test your service.

So after the deploy step, Workshop should launch a screen similar to that shown in Figure 4-7. It shows your web service operation and allows you to enter a value and get a response. In both cases, the SOAP message is shown.

The test client is useful as you are getting started, to see what your messages look like on the wire (without HTTP headers). Also, if you want to view the WSDL for this

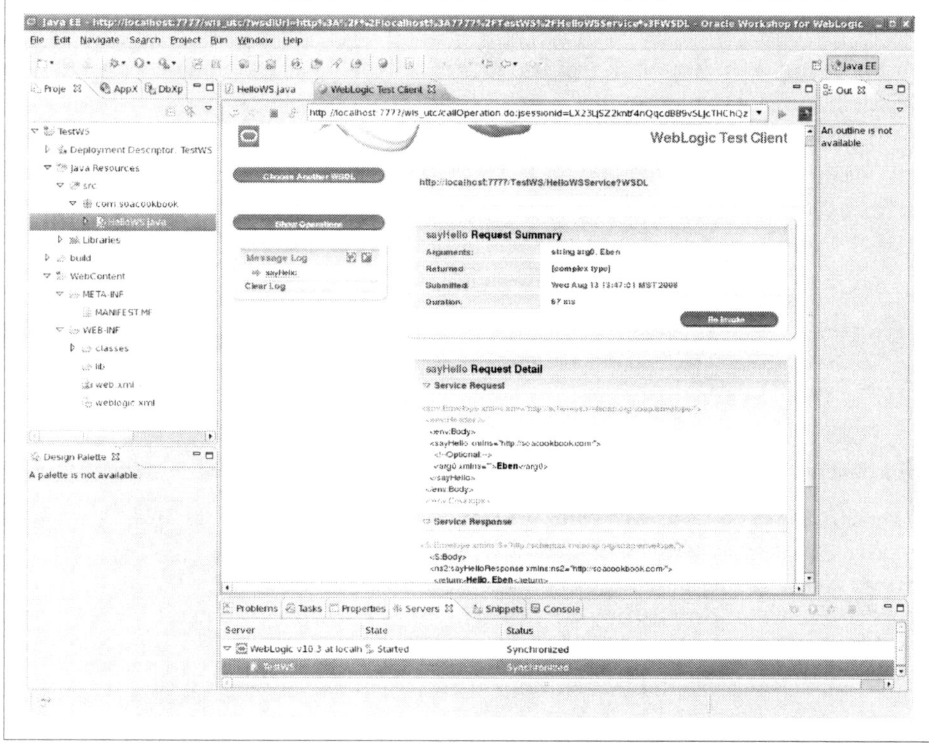

Figure 4-7. WebLogic Workshop test client

service, you can click the link at the top of the test client. In this case, it's *http://localhost:7777/TestWS/HelloWSService?WSDL*.

4.6 Setting Up a Maven 2 Service and Client Project

Problem

You want to create a project to house a web service and its client in Maven 2. You already understand Maven, but you aren't sure what plug-ins you need, what goals to associate them with, or how to structure it.

Solution

Create three projects: one for the service, one for the client, and a parent. Run unit tests in the service and client projects. Also, there are some general dependencies you'll want to set up to work with Java EE 5, and you'll need to update the default Java SDK to 1.6.

Discussion

For the examples in this book that use Java SE 6, you'll need to update your POM to include the compiler plug-in that uses SE 6, as shown below:

```
<build>
  <plugins>
     <plugin>
        <groupId>org.apache.maven.plugins</groupId>
        <artifactId>maven-compiler-plugin</artifactId>
        <version>2.0.2</version>
        <configuration>
          <source>1.6</source>
          <target>1.6</target>
        </configuration>
     </plugin>
...
```

This ensures that the JAX-WS and XML libraries you'll need will be available.

In general, the easiest way to create web services is to use Maven 2, set up a web project (specify `<packaging>war</packaging>`), and then create a POJO that has the `@WebService` annotation on the class. If you stop there, however, your WAR will deploy properly but won't contain any web services. That's because by default Maven 2 uses an older DTD for Servlet 2.3 in the *web.xml* file. To solve this, add the following dependency to your *pom.xml*:

```
<dependency>
  <groupId>javaee</groupId>
  <artifactId>javaee-api</artifactId>
  <version>5</version>
  <scope>provided</scope>
</dependency>
```

Then you have to replace the `web-app` declaration. Look in your project's *src/main/webapp/WEB-INF* folder for the *web.xml* file, and replace the following code:

```
<!DOCTYPE web-app PUBLIC
 "-//Sun Microsystems, Inc.//DTD Web Application 2.3//EN"
 "http://java.sun.com/dtd/web-app_2_3.dtd" >
<web-app>
  <display-name>My Service</display-name>
</web-app>
```

with the Servlet 2.5 version specified here:

```
<?xml version="1.0" encoding="UTF-8"?>
<web-app version="2.5"
  xmlns="http://java.sun.com/xml/ns/javaee"
  xmlns:xsi="http://www.w3.org/2001/XMLSchema-instance"
  xsi:schemaLocation="http://java.sun.com/xml/ns/javaee
  http://java.sun.com/xml/ns/javaee/web-app_2_5.xsd">

   <display-name>My Service</display-name>
</web-app>
```

You also need to set up dependencies for Metro only if you are doing any Metro-specific code (like WS-Addressing on the client, or a stateful web service that relies on Metro's export mechanism):

```
<dependency>
  <groupId>com.sun.xml.ws</groupId>
  <artifactId>webservices-rt</artifactId>
  <version>1.3</version>
  <scope>provided</scope>
</dependency>
<dependency>
  <groupId>javax.xml</groupId>
  <artifactId>webservices-api</artifactId>
  <version>1.3</version>
  <scope>provided</scope>
</dependency>
```

Clean Service Clients

If you're creating a client, the Metro JARs need to be included on its classpath or unjared into your client JAR. In Maven 2, you can do this using the `compile` or default scope for the dependency.

But if you're creating a service application, it's a little different. You need to specify a dependency scope of `provided` if you are deploying to Glassfish because Glassfish already includes these JARs and the classloader will choke on the shell game because it won't be able to find other dependencies. In other containers, use their vendor-specific extensions.

Now when you deploy your projects, they'll know to interpret the annotations and create a service for you.

Overall, the idea is this: you create a parent so that you have a place to build that creates the entire world for you with a single click. It builds the service first, then deploys it, and then builds the client, using the freshly deployed WSDL.

With your JUnit tests, make sure that you test in both the service and client projects. Hopefully, this will seem obvious. But the confusion here can stem from our tendency to think that the web service project must be tested as a web service because that is what's being built. But that would require testing after deployment, which goes against the grain of how Maven works. It's easy enough to get the results you want by following Maven conventions.

Basically, because the deploy phase happens after the test phase, your service project build should test the code directly, as regular Java code, not the code deployed as a web service with a WSDL. To do so, you can make use of mock objects. The Jakarta Commons project is helpful here. It allows you to mock JNDI calls and make connections to a database defined as a `DataSource` in your container. That will make sure that the Java code is thoroughly tested (you can use Cobertura from *http://cobertura.sourceforge*

.net/ to see just how much). The client project will then execute its tests against the live, freshly deployed service.

Creating the service project

The service project is just a regular EAR or WAR project, depending on whether you're using an EJB or a servlet for your service implementation. The only thing to note is that you want to make the service artifact deploy automatically at build time, so that when the client builds too, it can read the new WSDL and get the new implementation of the service. You do that as you would with any regular WAR or EAR. If you're using Glassfish, here's a good plug-in to use:

```
<plugin>
  <groupId>org.nOpe.mojo</groupId>
  <artifactId>asadmin-maven-plugin</artifactId>
  <version>0.1</version>
  <configuration>
    <glassfishHome>${my.glassfish.home}</glassfishHome>
  </configuration>
  <executions>
    <execution>
      <phase>install</phase>
      <goals>
        <goal>redeploy</goal>
      </goals>
    </execution>
   </executions>
</plugin>
```

This plug-in executes during the install phase to deploy your WAR or EAR automatically during your build. This is a nice convenience. The only item of note here is that it's important to use a property for things like paths that might be specific to a given developer's box. Here, I'm referencing a property whose value is specified in my own *settings.xml* file.

Creating the client project

If you are creating a service for public consumption, you may just stop at creating the service itself, and let clients figure out on their own how to use it. But you might want to also create a client JAR that you can make available to users on a Java platform, as a convenience. This is something that Amazon, eBay, Google, and others did in the early days of web services, to make their services easier to work with. They'd distribute a client ZIP file that contained both Java and C# code, allowing developers to get up and running with their services more quickly.

Even if you are developing web services for internal use only, it still may be a good idea to create a client JAR that already contains the generated artifacts off the WSDL so that integrating usage of your service into business applications is not only easier, but also more controlled. For example, if you're creating the client JAR, you can add features such as WS-Addressing, schema validation, and so on without requiring every developer in your shop to understand all those things, or even to be aware that they're happening under the hood. This allows you more flexibility. Of course, if you have business applications written in COBOL or C# that need to invoke your service, they can't use your Java client. You can then either create one for them, or let them do it themselves.

If you're creating both the service implementation and a convenience client, be certain that you are designing your service in a fully encapsulated manner, and not allowing the client to do any real work. That might sound obvious enough, but it's an easy trap to fall into when you are getting started and doing services internally—especially because in order to make the learning curve shorter, the designers of the Java web service APIs made everything build on familiar web technologies.

Here's an easy rule of thumb to make this distinction. If you're making both a client and the service simultaneously, that's fine. It's a common thing to do. But be sure not to have any code in your client JAR that is necessary for the functioning of your solution. It's only a convenience, nothing more. If there's code in your client that would make the overall solution fail were it removed, the service is designed wrong, and you need to find a way to move that functionality back into the service.

Your client and service projects need to be versionable independently of one another. For example, you might add multithreading to your client, but that doesn't mean that anything in your service has changed. You need to be able to redistribute the client to a Maven repository separately, with its own version.

For the client project, use the `wsimport` plug-in like this:

```
<plugin>
 <groupId>org.codehaus.mojo</groupId>
 <artifactId>jaxws-maven-plugin</artifactId>
 <version>1.9</version>
 <executions>
   <execution>
     <goals>
       <goal>wsimport</goal>
     </goals>
   </execution>
 </executions>
 <configuration>
   <packageName>com.myProject</packageName>
     <wsdlUrls>
       <wsdlUrl>${com.myProject.wsdl.url}</wsdlUrl>
     </wsdlUrls>
     <verbose>true</verbose>
  </configuration>
</plugin>
```

The JAX-WS plug-in is available at *https://jax-ws-commons.dev.java.net/jaxws-maven-plugin/*. It allows you to add `wsimport` and `wsgen` functionality to your Maven 2 build. The `<packageName>` is the name of your generated source package.

Creating the parent project

You don't truly need the parent project, but it does allow you to specify shared dependencies, such as Java SE 6, Log4J, JUnit, or other items that both the client and the service require. The parent can declare these dependencies, and also declare its children as the service and client projects, like this:

```
<modules>
   <module>ws</module>
   <module>client</module>
</modules>
```

The purpose of the parent is so that you can build and deploy the service, then immediately build the client against it to make sure that any changes in your WSDL are compatible with your client, and vice versa.

Another reason is so that you have a single umbrella project that makes a convenient target for integration builds. For example, if you're using something like Cruise Control (*http://cruisecontrol.sourceforge.net/*) or Hudson (*https://hudson.dev.java.net/*) to perform continuous integration, it's easier to set up that tool to point to a single POM it needs to build.

However, if you're using a tool like Hudson on its own build server, you will probably need to set up a profile for the build server to use when it specifies WSDL locations, a path to the application server it should deploy to, and so on. Here's a quick example:

```
<profiles>
<!-- For shared Continuous Integration Hudson Build.
     Developers should have their own profile set in profiles.xml,
     which should be ignored by source repository. -->
  <profile>
     <id>myProject-integration-profile</id>
     <activation>
     <!-- This property is passed to Maven from within
          the Hudson build configuration on the build server. -->
     <property>
        <name>integrationBuild</name>
        <value>true</value>
     </property>
     </activation>
     <properties>
       <glassfish.home>/domains/devtools/glassfish/...</glassfish.home>
       <my.wsdl.url>http://example.com:7575/my/MyService?wsdl</my.wsdl.url>
     </properties>
   </profile>
</profiles>
```

Then in the project for this service that you've made in your continuous integration (CI) tool, you can specify a system property that controls what machine this project is being built from. Here I've used the `integrationBuild` property that the Hudson project has configured to pass as an argument to the build, so that the properties for it to use (such as the location of the app server to deploy to and the WSDL URL that the client should read) are triggered.

Thanks to Brian Mericle for his work with me on this solution.

4.7 Understanding WSDL

Problem

You have just deployed a simple web service and want to view its WSDL to understand the relation of your code to the deployed web service.

Solution

Inspect the WSDL by appending `?WSDL` to the end of the service name. This is only a convention and is not required by any specification, but all of the major vendors (IBM, Microsoft, BEA/Oracle, Sun, JBoss) adhere to it.

Check out the following discussion on the key sections of a WSDL in order to better understand this important part of your web service contract.

Discussion

It's hard to have a general discussion of WSDL sections because they change depending on choices you made in a specific service. So in this discussion, we examine the WSDL that is generated for the web service you created in Recipe 4.4, Example 4-3.

Inspect the WSDL published to the Java 6 internal HTTP server by opening your web browser to *http://localhost:9999/hello?wsdl*. You should see something like Example 4-4.

Example 4-4. The Hello WSDL

```
<?xml version="1.0" encoding="UTF-8"?>
<definitions xmlns="http://schemas.xmlsoap.org/wsdl/"
    xmlns:tns="http://ch03.soacookbook.com/"
    xmlns:xsd="http://www.w3.org/2001/XMLSchema"
    xmlns:soap="http://schemas.xmlsoap.org/wsdl/soap/"
    targetNamespace="http://ch03.soacookbook.com/"
    name="HelloWSService">
  <types></types>
  <message name="sayHello">
    <part name="arg0" type="xsd:string"></part>
  </message>
  <message name="sayHelloResponse">
```

```
    <part name="return" type="xsd:string"></part>
  </message>
  <portType name="Hello">
    <operation name="sayHello" parameterOrder="arg0">
      <input message="tns:sayHello"></input>
      <output message="tns:sayHelloResponse"></output>
    </operation>
  </portType>
  <binding name="HelloWSPortBinding" type="tns:Hello">
    <soap:binding style="rpc" transport="http://schemas.xmlsoap.org/soap/http">
    </soap:binding>
    <operation name="sayHello">
      <soap:operation soapAction=""></soap:operation>
      <input>
        <soap:body use="literal" namespace="http://ch03.soacookbook.com/"></soap:body>
      </input>
      <output>
        <soap:body use="literal" namespace="http://ch03.soacookbook.com/"></soap:body>
      </output>
    </operation>
  </binding>
  <service name="HelloWSService">
    <port name="HelloWSPort" binding="tns:HelloWSPortBinding">
      <soap:address location="http://localhost:9999/hello"></soap:address>
    </port>
  </service>
</definitions>
```

There are a few things to notice about the WSDL published by the endpoint. Let's look at them to gain a better understanding of how this all works.

Types

This Types section of the WSDL is empty. Types is where a WSDL either imports or locally defines the XML schema types that the messages your web service exchanges will use. The reason this section is empty is that the messages defined by this web service use only strings, which are defined as a simple type in XML Schema—all web services will be able to use them out of the box. So it's not necessary to put anything there.

Frequently, WSDLs will define a Types section that points to an external schema. In your WebLogic service created in Recipe 4.5, the WSDL indicates the location of a schema, generated by the server at deploy time, that defines the types the messages will use:

```
<types>
<xsd:schema>
  <xsd:import namespace="http://soacookbook.com/"
    schemaLocation="http://localhost:7777/TestWS/HelloWSService?xsd=1"/>
</xsd:schema>
</types>
```

That URI references a complete XML Schema document that indicates the values of the complex types used in the request and response messages.

If you are writing your own WSDL, you can define your types this way in an external schema, or define them entirely inline, like this:

```
<types>
<xsd:schema>
  <xsd:simpleType name="ID">
    <xsd:restriction base="xsd:string">
      <xsd:pattern value="[0-9]{5}"/>
    </xsd:restriction>
  </xsd:simpleType>
</xsd:schema>
</types>
```

In general, it's considered a best practice not to define your types inline in order to keep the interface separate from the implementation as much as possible. Instead, refer to an external schema.

Messages

The Messages section of the WSDL contains definitions for the request and responses to be used in communicating with the service. You'll notice that there is one message each for the request and response. The request message has the same name as the method invocation because you are doing RPC style here. The response is given the name of the operation appended with "Response", which is the default according to the JAX-WS specification. Each of these messages has a `part` child. A message part is similar to a parameter to a method in that it has a name and a type. The name for the first part is "arg0", which is the default. Subsequent arguments would be named "arg1", and so forth. These names can be customized to make them easier to read and follow, which becomes increasingly important for more complicated WSDLs.

For the response, there is an element `<part name="return" type="xsd:string">`. Because the default parameter style value is "wrapped," the value that gets returned by the web service will be wrapped within a single element with a name of "return" from which you can extract the rest of the payload. This is discussed in more detail in Recipe 7.3.

Binding

The Bindings section of the WSDL indicates the transport used to send messages to and from a web service. The default is SOAP, and other advanced options include HTTP, JMS, SMTP, and TCP. Because you specified that you wanted to bind your service to SOAP using the `@SOAPBinding(style=SOAPBinding.Style.RPC)` annotation on your Hello service interface implementation class, you get SOAP bindings as the message transport.

The `<soap:binding>` element features a `transport` attribute with a value of *http://schemas.xmlsoap.org/soap/http*. That means that the service will use SOAP 1.1 for the send and receive protocol for your messages. You can also specify SOAP 1.2, but 1.1 is the default, and using SOAP 1.2 is not widely recommended just yet, as the overwhelming majority of implementations currently are for 1.1.

You can also see that the `<soap:binding>` element features a `style` attribute with a value of "rpc", which was written in this WSDL because of the `@SOAPBinding(style=SOAPBinding.Style.RPC)` annotation on the Hello service interface. The other option you could have provided there is "document." This is discussed in detail in Recipe 7.3.

The service is given a namespace of *http://ch03.soacookbook.com*, which matches an exact reversal of the package name of the Java class defining the endpoint. Likewise, the operation name matches the method name in that class because you have not customized it.

Service

The Service section of the WSDL indicates that the name of the service will be `HelloWSService`. This is the name of the class that defined your service, with "Service" appended to it, which is how services with no customizations are named according to the JAX-WS specification. It also indicates that the "HelloWSPort" port will be bound using SOAP. The elements in that section are prefixed with soap, indicating that they are from the *http://schemas.xmlsoap.org/wsdl/soap/* namespace.

The important `location` attribute here indicates where you can invoke the service, and this is what clients will use to invoke it. The next recipe shows you how to invoke this service.

4.8 Using References in NetBeans to Generate Web Service Clients

Problem

You have grown tired of manually generating client-side code based on a WSDL from the command line, and want that to become part of your regular development workflow. You just want a quick and easy way to generate the portable JAX-WS objects based on a WSDL so that you can start using the service as you would any other dependency.

Solution

Use NetBeans 6 Web Service References from within a regular Java project.

Discussion

Many modern IDEs come with the ability to create web service references for client projects. This saves you from some of the error-prone drudgery of performing many manual steps on the command line. First, set up your client project as a regular Java project and add a service reference by pointing to the WSDL location. Then, once you run the clean and build Ant targets through the IDE, it generally will insert a `wsimport` step and compile the generated service client code along with yours, making it available on the classpath. This makes it very easy to create clients of existing web services and incorporate that code into your project.

Here is how to use a web service reference in NetBeans 6, which is representative of how various IDEs typically do it:

1. Create a new client project. This could be a web page, but for this example, you'll just create a regular Java console-based project, and create a class with a main method to run.
2. Right-click on the project name and choose New→Web Service Client.
3. When the wizard comes up, as shown in Figure 4-8, enter the local or remote WSDL address, and a name for the package that you want generated code to be put into.

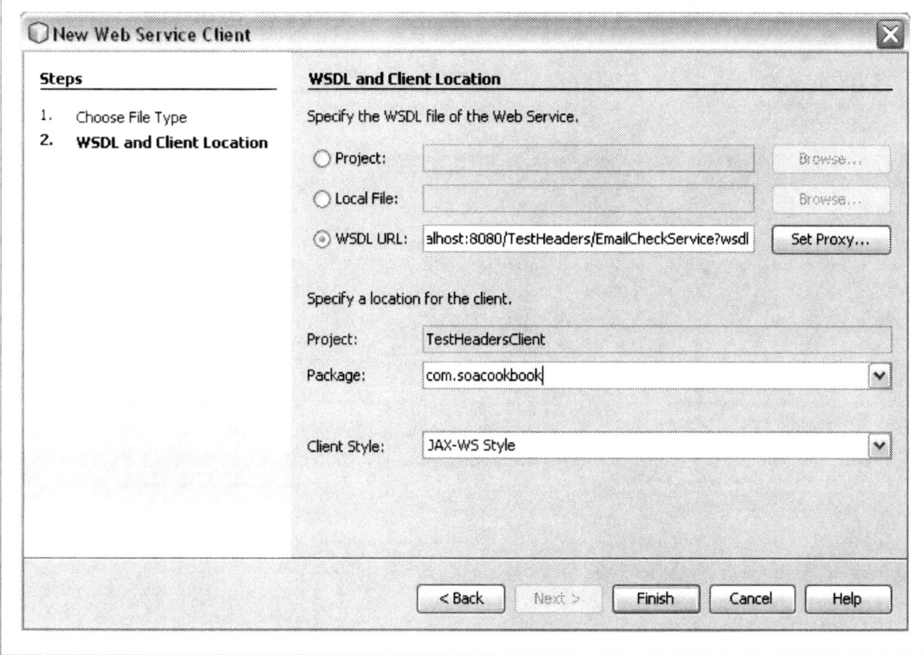

Figure 4-8. NetBeans 6 Web Service Client Wizard

4. Once you click Next, NetBeans will create a local catalog for the WSDL and generate portable JAX-WS objects based on it. It puts them in a folder under your *build* directory called *generated/wsimport/client*. You will see a new folder available under your project called *Web Service References*. This stores a list of the web services that your project is using (that NetBeans knows about).

5. Now that your service is available, you can drag and drop from the name of the service operation you want to invoke directly onto your main method. This will generate inline the necessary code skeleton, as shown in Figure 4-9.

   At this point you can add the necessary values to the skeleton code and right-click to clean, build, and run the client project.

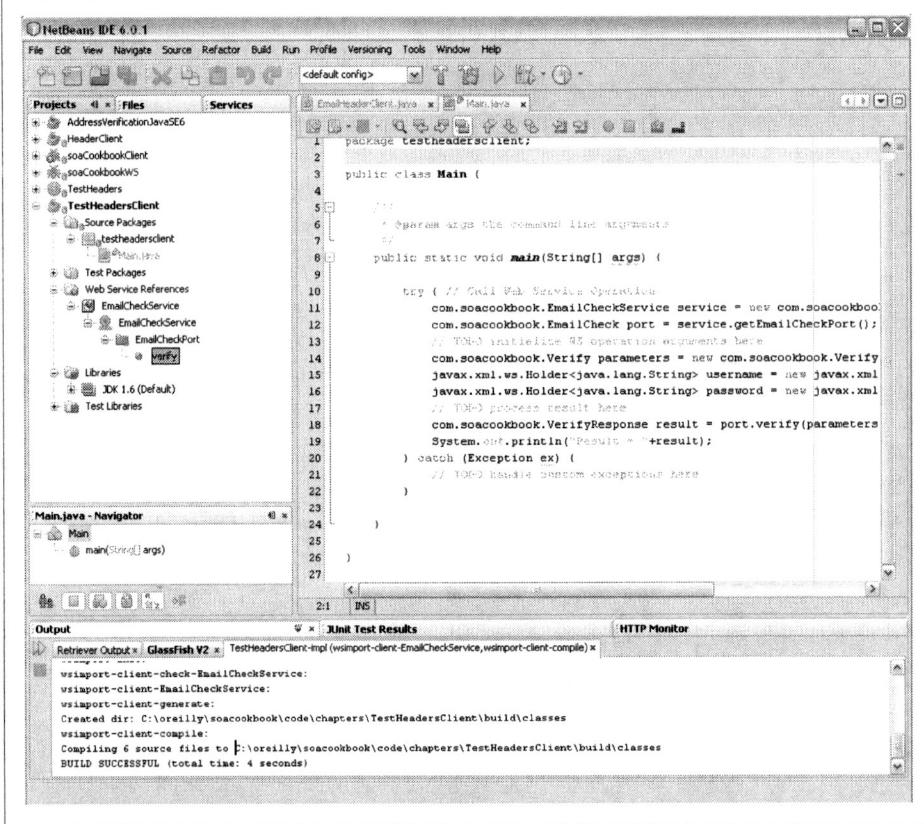

Figure 4-9. Generated skeleton code for invoking a service reference

If your WSDL is not stable, you'll need to refresh the web service reference to make sure that your client still compiles. The WSDL gets downloaded locally and referenced with an XML catalog by the IDE. If the parameters on your web service operation change, you'll need to refresh it. In such a case, you'll often have to delete the web service reference altogether and regenerate it. If you have client code that used to work against a given WSDL and now it won't compile, try deleting the reference and adding it back. This will freshly import the WSDL and run the generator against it again.

4.9 Monitoring SOAP Traffic with Metro

Problem

You're using Glassfish/Metro and you want to dump the transport-level traffic that your web service client sends and receives to the console.

Solution

Pass the flag `-Dcom.sun.xml.ws.transport.http.client.HttpTransportPipe.dump=true` to your JVM.

This dump technique shows you the bytes representing the message as it is sent and received on the wire. That means that you also get transport-specific information, such as all HTTP headers, which can be useful.

You can also do this in Ant with `jvmarg`:

```
<target name="run">
    <java classname="com.soacookbook.ch03.MyClient" fork="true">
        <arg value="someArg"/>
        <classpath>
          <path refid="jaxws.classpath"/>
          <pathelement location="..."/>
        </classpath>
        <jvmarg value="-Dcom.sun.xml.ws.transport.http.client.HttpTransportPipe.dump=
         true"/>
    </java>
</target>
```

Note that the JUnit Ant task will accept the `jvmarg` element too, so you can easily add it to invocations that you test on your client as well. See Example 4-5.

Example 4-5. JUnit Ant task with SOAP message dumping enabled

```
<target name="run-test" depends="compile-test">
<echo message="-----Running Tests-----" />
<junit fork="true" printsummary="true"
       errorProperty="test.failed"
       failureProperty="test.failed">
    <classpath refid="cp.test" />

    <jvmarg
    value="-Dcom.sun.xml.ws.transport.http.client.HttpTransportPipe.dump=true"/>

    <formatter type="brief" usefile="false"/>
    <formatter type="xml"/>
    <batchtest todir="${test.report.dir}">
        <fileset dir="${test.classes.dir}"
          includes="**/*Test.class" />
    </batchtest>
</junit>
```

```
<echo message="-----Creating JUnit Report-----" />
<junitreport todir="${test.report.dir}">
    <fileset dir="${test.report.dir}" includes="TEST-*.xml"/>
    <report format="frames" todir="${test.report.dir}"/>
</junitreport>

<fail if="test.failed"
   message="Tests failed. Check log and/or reports."/>
</target>
```

This is an easy way to get lots of information about what's going on behind the scenes in your SOAP message invocation. If you have improperly constructed a message, for example, this can be a terrific aid in finding the issue.

Example 4-6 shows the output that the `HttpTransportPipe` dump operation gives you during a JUnit test invocation of a web service client talking to a credit authorizer web service (I added line breaks only for readability).

Example 4-6. Output of HttpTransportPipe during JUnit test

```
4/27/08-14:40 DEBUG  com.soacookbook.ch03.test.SchemaValidateTest.testCreditAuth -
Invoking Credit Authorizer Service.
---[HTTP request]---
SOAPAction: ""
Accept: text/xml, multipart/related, text/html, image/gif, image/jpeg, *; q=.2, */*; q=.2
Content-Type: text/xml;charset="utf-8"
<?xml version="1.0" ?>
<S:Envelope xmlns:S="http://schemas.xmlsoap.org/soap/envelope/">
<S:Body><creditCard xmlns="http://ns.soacookbook.com/credit">
<cardNumber>4011111111111111</cardNumber>
<name>
<firstName>Phineas</firstName>
<middleInitial>J</middleInitial>
<lastName>Fogg</lastName>
</name>
<expirationDate>2015-04-27-07:00</expirationDate>
</creditCard>
</S:Body></S:Envelope>--------------------

---[HTTP response 200]---
Transfer-encoding: chunked
null: HTTP/1.1 200 OK
Content-type: text/xml;charset="utf-8"
Server: Sun Java System Application Server 9.1_01
X-powered-by: Servlet/2.5
Date: Sun, 27 Apr 2008 21:40:44 GMT
<?xml version="1.0" ?>
<S:Envelope xmlns:S="http://schemas.xmlsoap.org/soap/envelope/">
<S:Body>
<authorization xmlns="http://ns.soacookbook.com/credit">
<amount>2500.0</amount>
</authorization>
</S:Body></S:Envelope>--------------------
```

There is a corresponding class available on the server side that lets you dump messages for incoming traffic to the console.

If you are invoking your web services through a web page, it is also convenient to use the Firefox plug-in called Live HTTP Headers, which shows the HTTP headers for every request and response in a window. You can get it at *https://addons.mozilla.org/en-US/firefox/addon/3829*.

Discussion

The disadvantage to using monitoring GUI tools, other than the fact that you need a GUI environment to run them, is that they use a man-in-the-middle strategy that requires rerouting the destination of your messages. Here's how they work: the monitor receives your request, dumps the payload, and then forwards your request to its intended destination. So, you are forced to change your service client to point to the port on which the monitor listens. Setting `HttpTransportPipe.dump=true` allows you to see the content of your messages with less error-prone twiddling. It can be easier, quicker, and cleaner to set up a console dumper like this as you are getting started.

Using the console dumper is not appropriate for production situations, but it can save you lots of time during development.

Dumping during a Maven unit test run

It is useful to see the SOAP messages being passed during an execution of unit tests. This is easy to do if you are running your build directly from the command line or from within an IDE, both of which offer a clear way to send arguments to the VM during execution.

But if you're building from Maven 2, it may not be immediately apparent how to get this to work. All you have to do is add a system property to the Surefire plug-in, like this:

```
<plugin>
  <groupId>org.apache.maven.plugins</groupId>
  <artifactId>maven-surefire-plugin</artifactId>
  <version>2.4.3</version>
  <configuration>
    <systemProperties>
      <property>
        <name>wsdlLocation</name>
        <value>${my.wsdl.url}</value>
      </property>
      <property>
        <name>com.sun.xml.ws.transport.http.client.HttpTransportPipe.dump</name>
        <value>true</value>
      </property>
```

```
        </systemProperties>
      </configuration>
    </plugin>
```

This will create the same effect as passing the argument directly to the VM as you would with -D.

Transport-independent logging

The preceding examples work if you are using HTTP as the transport layer. If you are using a different protocol, you need a transport-agnostic class. Using basically the same mechanism just described, you can substitute this invocation instead:

```
com.sun.xml.ws.util.pipe.StandaloneTubeAssembler.dump=true
```

See Also

Other tools are available as well. Check out the WS Monitor tool at *https://wsmonitor.dev.java.net*, and for Axis, TCPMon at *http://ws.apache.org/axis/java/user-guide.html*.

4.10 Monitoring SOAP Traffic with TCPMon

Problem

You want to monitor SOAP traffic without putting anything on your classpath.

Solution

Use TCPMon, an open source monitor for TCP traffic, available from *https://tcpmon.dev.java.net*. You'll need to change the values in your local WSDL to use it.

Discussion

You can run the tool a few ways—directly from the Web using Java Web Start, or by downloading the JAR. It will listen on an available port, and you must route requests through it for it to be able to dump the traffic data. TCPMon will then forward the requests on to the actual destination.

Running TCPMon

The easiest way to get started with TCPMon is to visit the website and find the link that says "Click here to run directly from the web." If you don't want to do that, you can download it and execute it on Windows by double-clicking it or on Linux by typing this command:

```
$ java -jar tcpmon.jar
```

This will start up the Java Web Start program. Here are the steps to get it up and running. You'll use a NetBeans sample project because it gets in the way the least. If you have another web service and client you want to use, the general instructions are still relevant:

1. Start the application. In the GUI, change the default values to the following:
   - Local Port: 8090
   - Server Port: 8080
2. Click "Add Monitor," which will run the listener.
3. You want to send a SOAP request to port 8080 because that's the port your service is listening on. So you need to change your WSDL to point to 8090 so that TCPMon can dump the message. Then the value you supplied in the Server Port field is the target to which TCPMon will forward each request. Because all you care about here is illustrating the traffic dump, and not the service itself, you'll just create a new web service sample project in NetBeans. To do so, click File→New Project→Samples→Web Service→Calculator. Of course, you can use any project you like. Doing so will also create a Calculator Client project, containing a web service reference.

   When the client project was created, it imported a copy of the WSDL from the service. This is the copy you need to change to point to TCPMon. To access the WSDL, navigate to Configuration Files→xml-resources→web-service-references, and find the WSDL under it. If you're using a different web service client project, just locate the local copy of the WSDL that is being invoked. Find this section at the end of the WSDL file:

   ```
   <soap:address location="http://localhost:8080/CalculatorApp/CalculatorWSService">
   ```

   Change the location to *http://localhost:8090/CalculatorApp/CalculatorWSService*.
4. Now you need to change your application to use the modified WSDL. If you're using the NetBeans sample, find the *ClientServlet* Java source file in the `org.me.calculator.client` package. Find this line:

   ```
   @WebServiceRef(wsdlLocation =
   "http://localhost:8080/CalculatorApp/CalculatorWSService?wsdl")
   ```

   Modify it to use the TCPMon port number of 8090. Because you're in a servlet, the container will inject the service instance at runtime, and use the modified WSDL location.

   If you weren't using a servlet, but had generated portable artifacts from `wsimport`, you could use code similar to this:

   ```
   URL wsdlLocation = new URL("file:///C:/projects/etc/CalculatorWSService.wsdl");
   QName serviceName = new QName("http://calculator.me.org/",
   "CalculatorWSService");
   CalculatorWSService service =
     new CalculatorWSService(wsdlLocation, serviceName);
   CalculatorWS port = service.getCalculatorWSPort();
   int result = port.add(2, 3);
   ```

The thing that you're doing here is overriding the WSDL that the client will use when invoking the service; you're pointing to the file that you've modified manually.

5. Now you'll make a request, routed through the monitor. If necessary, clean and build the web service Calculator project, and make sure it is deployed using the Undeploy and Deploy target.

   Now right-click on the web service Calculator Client project and choose Run.

   Then go to the monitor application and click Submit to Server. The monitor will display a timestamp of your request and show the request and response contents, including HTTP headers, in the windows.

TCPMon is shown in action in Figure 4-10.

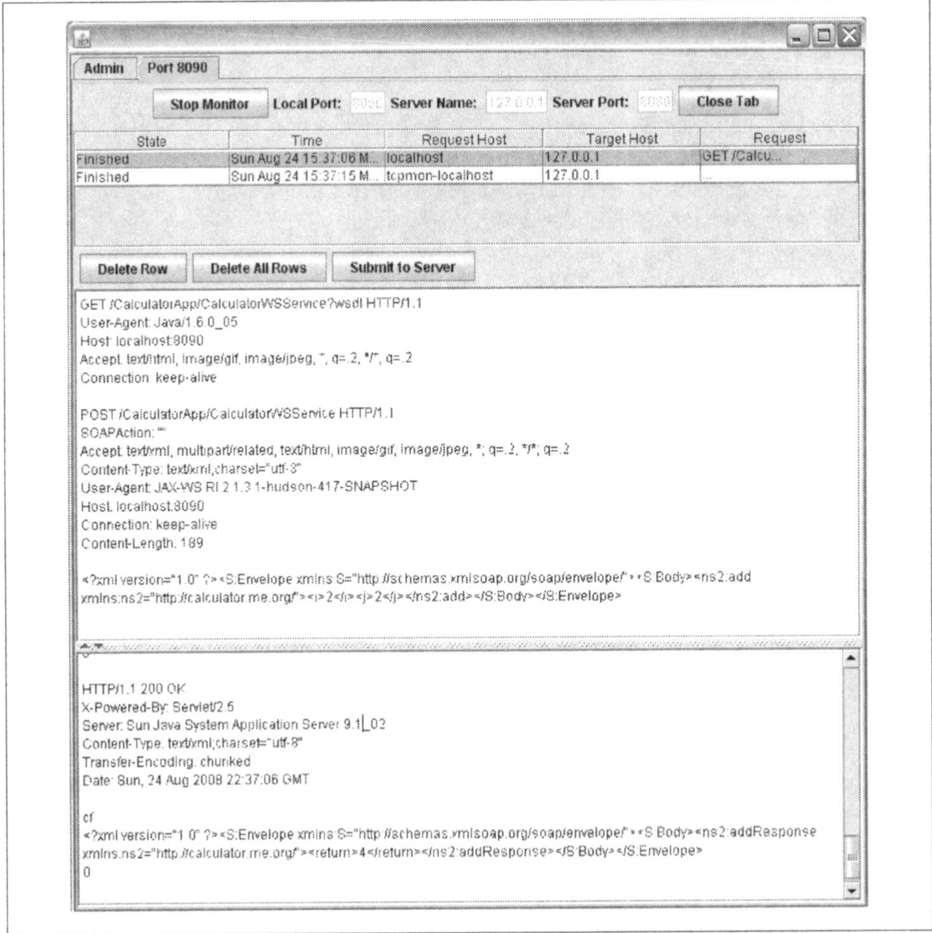

Figure 4-10. TCPMon showing a SOAP request and response

Using TCPMon is pretty easy to use given all it's doing for you, and it's a terrific aid when you're debugging. Just remember to change your WSDLs back.

CHAPTER 5
Web Services with SAAJ

5.0 Introduction

This chapter examines how to build Java clients that can talk to SOAP-based web services using the SOAP with Attachments API for Java (SAAJ) API.

SOAP, standardized by the W3C in 2000, is a platform-agnostic way of creating and sending messages in a distributed system.

You may be familiar with SOAP as an acronym for Simple Object Access Protocol, but version 1.2 of the spec, published in 2003, throws out the explanation of the acronym with the direct, clear, and yet mysterious statement that "This is no longer the case." Perhaps they decided it wasn't so simple after all....

Because SOAP is based on XML, it is relatively easy for humans to read and understand, and the structure of a SOAP message itself is simple. SOAP messages are always wrapped in a container called the *envelope*; the envelope always contains a *body*, which carries the payload of the message in one or more XML documents. Optionally, your envelope can include headers, very similar to HTTP headers. If something goes wrong during processing, a SOAP fault will be added as the body content. The structure of a SOAP 1.1 envelope is depicted in Figure 5-1. The * in the figure denotes that there can be multiple instances of that type.

Developers on either end of the web service can extract the content of the SOAP envelope using XML tools for processing.

SOAP-ENV:Envelope
SOAP-ENV:Header
Header Entry*
SOAP-ENV:encodingStyle
SOAP-ENV:mustUnderstand
SOAP-ENV:actor
SOAP-ENV:Body
Body Entry*
SOAP-ENV:Fault*
SOAP-ENV:faultCode
SOAP-ENV:faultString
SOAP-ENV:faultActor
SOAP-ENV:Detail
DetailEntry*

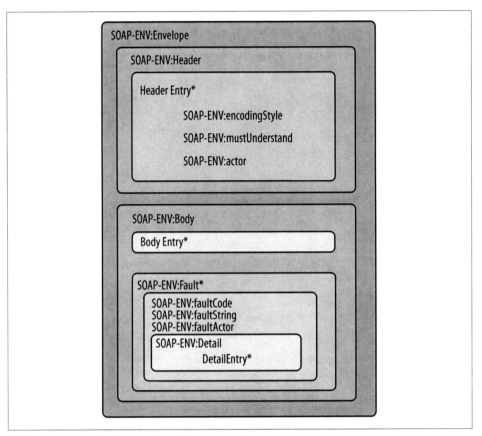

Figure 5-1. Structure of a SOAP envelope

SAAJ 1.3 creates messages that adhere to both the SOAP 1.1 and SOAP 1.2 specifications. Which version of SOAP you use will depend on your vendor. I have tried to make distinctions between these versions where they matter. The namespace for SOAP 1.1 (the default for most tools still as of this writing) is *http://schemas.xmlsoap.org/soap/envelope/*. The namespace for SOAP 1.2 is *http://www.w3.org/2003/05/soap-envelope*.

SOAP messages typically travel over HTTP (though sometimes JMS and other mechanisms can be used). Corporate firewalls generally allow exchange of HTTP traffic already, and have sophisticated mechanisms, including firewall rules, subnets, and so forth, in place to deal with that traffic. Because SOAP reuses the HTTP transport layer, adopting SOAP as a standard for web services was convenient, contributing to SOAP's early popularity. Moreover, developers found it easy to use SOAP because XML was already familiar to them, and many platforms have native XML tools. Quickly, SOAP became a popular way of doing web services.

The SOAP with Attachments API for Java (SAAJ) was created to specifically address the needs of burgeoning SOAP-based web services developers. It allows you to programmatically manipulate SOAP envelopes. Using its classes and methods, you can create an envelope, add a header to the envelope, put data in the header, create a SOAP body, add an XML document to the SOAP body, and add the body to the envelope. Once your message is complete, you can ship the complete SOAP message off over HTTP to invoke a web service using a dispatcher. SAAJ 1.3, which we examine in this chapter, is the foundational API for working with web services in Java. Every Java EE vendor provides a SAAJ implementation.

There is a charter at the W3 for SOAP-JMS. This work is in the early stages as of this writing, but the idea is to ensure standardize the binding mechanism to interoperability between implementations created by web services vendors for SOAP over JMS. You can read more about it at *http://www.w3.org/2007/08/soap-jms-charter.html*.

It should be noted, however, that in recent years SAAJ has been superseded by JAX-WS (Java API for XML Web Services). SAAJ operates at the plumbing level, requiring you to build every aspect of your SOAP envelopes by hand. The code can get long and somewhat tedious, and requires in-depth knowledge of the internal structure of the requests and responses you must work with when invoking web services. JAX-WS reuses SAAJ and acts as a layer of abstraction above it. Think of SAAJ as the XML view and JAX-WS as the object view of a message exchange.

Here's an example of a SOAP envelope in XML with HTTP header data:

```
POST /StockQuote HTTP/1.1
Host: www.soacookbook.com:8080
Content-Type: text/xml; charset="utf-8"
Content-Length: n
SOAPAction: ""
<SOAP-ENV:Envelope
  xmlns:SOAP-ENV="http://schemas.xmlsoap.org/soap/envelope/"
  SOAP-ENV:encodingStyle="http://schemas.xmlsoap.org/soap/encoding/">

  <SOAP-ENV:Body>
    <m:GetStockQuote xmlns:m="urn:com:soacookbook">
      <ticker>JAVA</ticker>
    </m:GetStockQuote>
  </SOAP-ENV:Body>

</SOAP-ENV:Envelope>
```

Once you have used SAAJ to create a SOAP message structure, you can send requests and receive responses using a `SOAPConnection` object. SAAJ connections are based on the `java.net.URL` class, which is extendable to support any network protocol.

Like email messages, SOAP envelopes may also contain attachments of any type of document (XML, binary image, or any valid MIME type). The SAAJ API allows you to work with such attachments as well.

You can read more about SAAJ at *https://saaj.dev.java.net*.

Relation to JAX-M

You may have heard of the JAX-M API. The Java API for XML Messaging was released in December 2001 as JSR-67. By June of 2002, the SAAJ API was born as a spin-off project from that original JAX-M 1.0 specification. The classes in JAX-M are all in the `javax.xml.messaging` package. JAX-M is no longer maintained.

SAAJ and JAX-WS

This chapter shows you how to perform common and useful tasks with the SAAJ API. Because it is a foundational layer, I thought it would be helpful to illustrate how to work with it, and it should help you get familiar with SOAP exchanges, so you'll know what's happening under the hood once you start working with JAX-WS later in this book. That having been said, nowadays it's frequently not necessary to work with SOAP at this lower level, and most of the things you'd want to do in SAAJ are all wrapped as domain objects for you in JAX-WS.

From a practical standpoint, using SAAJ means that you don't use tools such as `wsimport` or `wsdl2java`. Those are for use with JAX-WS, and are the means by which a client can generate domain objects and operate almost as if they weren't using web services at all. With SAAJ, you have no domain view of a service. You're really working with the plumbing. Development with JAX-WS can be much quicker and easier, and generally doesn't cause you any loss in control. But JAX-WS is a convenience layer, and it can be comforting to know that if you wield some command of SAAJ, you'll be ready to do anything that a WSDL interface requires of you.

SAAJ Packages and Classes

Let's first take a quick overview of the structure of the API itself. The SAAJ API is part of Java SE after version 5, so you don't need to get the old web services developer pack or anything like that to work with it. The classes you need are all in the package `javax.xml.soap` and its subpackages, and they work with both SOAP 1.1 and the current version, SOAP 1.2.

In general, the SAAJ class names clearly match the structure of a SOAP message. The `SOAPMessage` class is the root of all SOAP classes. The API makes heavy use of factories, so you can use `MessageFactory.newInstance.createMessage` to get a new instance of a `SOAPMessage`.

Once you've got a message, you're ready to create its envelope. But messages directly contain "SOAP parts," which are wrappers for the SOAP-specific portions of the message; this is in distinction to any message attachments, which don't count as SOAP parts (they count, happily, as `AttachmentParts`). So because the `SOAPPart` object contains the envelope, which is in turn the wrapper for the header and the body, to create them you need to first get the SOAP part object from the message. You do this using the `soapMessage.getSOAPPart` method.

Once you have the `SOAPEnvelope` object, you're ready to create instances of the `SOAPBody` and `SOAPHeader` classes. To sum it all up, here is a typical series of invocations as you work with SAAJ:

```
MessageFactory mf = MessageFactory.newInstance();
SOAPMessage message = mf.getMessage();
SOAPPart soapPart = message.getSOAPPart();
SOAPEnvelope env = soapPart.getEnvelope();
SOAPBody body = env.getBody();
SOAPHeader header = env.getHeader();
```

It's worth noting that in SAAJ, the objects described in the SOAP specification (envelope, body, header, fault, etc.) all implement the `SOAPElement` interface. This interface gives you basic methods to work with their content. For example, you can use methods on this interface to get meta-information such as the namespace or the encoding style. You can also use its methods to manipulate the XML tree data: for example, you can add an attribute, add a child element, or get the text value of the content.

At this point, I think we're ready to jump in and get to work.

5.1 Creating a SOAP Element with a Qualified Name

Problem

You need to add an element to a SOAP message that you're building, and it needs to have a namespace URI, a prefix, and a local part.

Solution

Use a `javax.xml.namespace.QName`, which represents a qualified name, and allows you to define a namespace URI, a prefix, and a local part.

Discussion

`QNames` are new with Java SE 5, replacing the older `Name` class. They are immutable, and therefore must be wholly created using the constructor.

Let's recall the basic components of an XML qualified name, using the following element as a model:

```
QName bodyName = new QName("http://example.com", "getQuote", "e");
```

This name defines a namespace URI, a local part, and a prefix:

- The namespace URI is "http://example.com", which acts somewhat like a Java package in that it demarcates a logical division of a set of elements as distinct from some other set. They allow multiple elements with the same name but different properties to contain the same local part but not collide during processing.
- The local part is "getQuote", which defines the element name.
- The prefix is "e". It is not meaningful in the document, but used only as a shortcut pointer to the namespace.

That will result in an XML element that looks like this:

```
<e:getQuote xmlns:e="http://example.com">
```

You can also create a `QName` that uses only the namespace URI and the local part, as is sometimes required by public web services. For example, the WebServicesX services, written in .NET, use this format:

```
QName portQName = new QName("http://www.webserviceX.NET/", "StockQuoteSoap");
```

This Java code creates a `QName` that looks like this in XML:

```
<StockQuoteSoap xmlns="http://www.webserviceX.NET/">
```

An interesting thing about `QNames`, should you ever need to compare two instances, is that the prefix is not used by the `equals` or `hashcode` methods. It seems obvious why this would be the case: the prefix is user-defined and incidental to the current document; it doesn't really distinguish two names.

The third and final constructor allows you to create a `QName` with a local part only.

URIs, URLs, and URNs in namespaces

`QName` documentation refers to "URI references" as the value allowed for the `namespaceURI` field. The Uniform Resource Identifier is the superset of the other two. URLs are, obviously, *locators*: they identify a place, or imply a physical resource. These are by far the most commonly used as namespaces for a variety of reasons, not the least of which is their popularity due to the ubiquity of the Web. In addition, they are hierarchical in structure, they are commonly understood, and companies that create things that need namespaces generally have a domain name that can be used to readily differentiate their namespaces from anyone else's (like Java packages).

But for the more, um, academically inclined among us, there are certain disadvantages to using URLs. First, they specify a protocol, which is out of place in a namespace; also, they imply that there is a physical resource associated with the element that the namespace marks (which is, of course, their purpose).

So some people have turned to using URNs, or Uniform Resource Names. While these carry a syntax similar to URLs and are still usually hierarchical in structure (depending on the author), they also have the advantages of appearing purely as a namespace and implying no other purpose or object. URNs also allow you to maintain the hierarchical structure we love about URLs.

URNs have this basic format: "urn:". For example:

```
<Namespace Identifier> ":" <Namespace Specific String>
```

These are often seen specified as a colon-separated list, preceded by "urn", sometimes with version information at the end, as follows:

```
<e:getQuote xmlns:e="urn:example:quotes:2:0">
```

Here is a valid, formal URN definition that identifies this book: `urn:isbn:9780596520724`. This URN is *formal* because it uses the officially registered namespace `isbn`, where officially registered means "defined and recognized by IANA (Internet Assigned Numbers Authority)." You may see other variations around as well, such as `urn:example.com/quotes`, but these lack a degree of formality.

This book uses URLs and informal URNs on different occasions, to highlight that both are allowed. My URNs are informal in order to be short, and invalid because IANA doesn't recognize them. Your SOAP messages will work the same, regardless of which one you use. It is important in an SOA context, however, to establish a clear and concrete convention for namespaces early and stick to it.

See Also

To find out more about URIs, URLs, and URNs, read the original paper by Tim Berners-Lee and others at *http://www.ietf.org/rfc/rfc2396.txt*.

Go to *http://www.iana.org/assignments/urn-namespaces/* for a complete list of official namespace assignments.

5.2 Creating a Complete SOAP Message

Problem

You want to create a complete SOAP request programmatically, and you don't have a complete SOAP envelope in a physical file you can use to send your SAAJ request.

Solution

Use the `javax.xml.ws.soap.SOAPMessage` class to construct an envelope, any headers, the body, and any attachments you need.

`SOAPMessage` is part of the SAAJ 1.3 API built-in to Java SE 6, so you only need to build a SOAP message manually like this if you have not generated objects based on the WSDL.

SAAJ is defined by the contents of the `javax.xml.ws.soap` package, which gives you complete, low-level programmatic control over the contents of your SOAP messages. Instead of working with an object view of a service, SAAJ gives you an XML view.

Using SAAJ, you can do the following:

- Create a SOAP message
- Extract the content from the body of a SOAP message
- Create attachments for a SOAP message
- Create and extract content from SOAP headers
- Work with SOAP faults (exceptions)
- Send a SOAP message

The following code listing shows how to build a simple message whose body wraps a basic string. You'll use this as the ISBN number to pass to the `getBook` method of your web service.

As you know, a SOAP message consists of an envelope, which is the single outer wrapper type. SOAP 1.1 is represented by the *http://schemas.xmlsoap.org/soap/envelope/* namespace and defines an optional set of headers similar to HTTP headers, an optional fault child, an optional set of attachments, and one mandatory element: `body`.

The SOAP 1.1 message you will build with Java will represent the following text under the hood:

```
<SOAP-ENV:Envelope xmlns:SOAP-ENV="http://schemas.xmlsoap.org/soap/envelope/">
<SOAP-ENV:Header/>
<SOAP-ENV:Body>
<isbn xmlns="http://ns.soacookbook.com/catalog">12345</isbn>
</SOAP-ENV:Body>
</SOAP-ENV:Envelope>
```

So, let's get to work building the envelope. For clarity, I included the entire method that builds the SOAP envelope, uses an appropriate `Dispatch<SOAPMessage>`, dumps the contents of the message to the console, and then invokes the server. This listing is shown in Example 5-1.

Example 5-1. Building a complete SOAP message manually

```
public void buildSoapEnv() {
try {
    URL wsdl = new URL("http://localhost:8080/CatalogService/Catalog?wsdl");

    String ns = "http://ns.soacookbook.com/ws/catalog";

    //Create the Service name
```

```
        String svcName = "CatalogService";
        QName svcQName = new QName(ns, svcName);

        //Get a delegate wrapper
        Service service = Service.create(wsdl, svcQName);

        //Create the Port name
        String portName = "CatalogPort";
        QName portQName = new QName(ns, portName);

        Dispatch<SOAPMessage> dispatch =
                service.createDispatch(portQName,
                SOAPMessage.class, Service.Mode.MESSAGE);

        //Create the message
        SOAPMessage soapMsg =
                MessageFactory.newInstance().createMessage();

        //Get the body from the envelope
        SOAPPart soapPart = soapMsg.getSOAPPart();
        SOAPEnvelope env = soapPart.getEnvelope();
        SOAPBody body = env.getBody();

        //Create a qualified name for the namespace of the
        //objects used by the service.
        String iNs = "http://ns.soacookbook.com/catalog";
        String elementName = "isbn";
        QName isbnQName = new QName(iNs, elementName);

        //Add the <isbn> element to the SOAP body
        //as its only child
        body.addBodyElement(isbnQName).setValue("12345");

        //debug print what we're sending
        soapMsg.writeTo(out);

        out.println("\nInvoking...");

        //send the message as request to service and get response
        SOAPMessage response = dispatch.invoke(soapMsg);

        //just show in the console for now
        response.writeTo(System.out);

    } catch (Exception ex) {
        ex.printStackTrace();
    }
    }
```

The main focus of this example is the creation of the `SOAPMessage` itself. I included the surrounding `Dispatch` creation and invocation because there are so many different possible options to use, and it's frustrating to have short fragments without enough context for you to recreate the example. But the main point here is that if you have a string you want to use to pass into a web service, you can do it pretty quickly by following these basic steps:

1. Create `Dispatch<SOAPMessage>`.
2. Create a `SOAPMessage` instance from the factory.
3. Get the `SOAPPart` from the message and use it to get the envelope and body.
4. Create a `QName` for your element matching the expected namespace for that element given its schema type.
5. Invoke the `addBodyElement` method, pass it the `QName`, and set the element value.
6. Invoke your dispatch with the SOAP message to send the request.

This example uses the previously defined catalog web service that lets you pass an ISBN number and returns the matching book object. In that example, there are two namespaces: the one used by the web service itself, and the one that matches the schema that defines the parameters and return types. The parameter namespace must then be used when creating the qualified name object for the `<isbn>` element.

5.3 Writing a SOAP Response to an Output Stream

Problem

You want to print the contents of your SOAP envelope to an output stream, such as to the console or to a file.

Solution

Use the `SOAPMessage.writeTo` method, and pass it an output stream such as `System.out`.

Discussion

This is an easy way to do a little debugging. As you build your SOAP envelopes with SAAJ, it is easy to get tripped up and forget a header or a namespace declaration, or try to add a child in the wrong place. It is very convenient that the `SOAPMessage` class includes this method to dump the contents to the given output stream. See Example 5-2.

Example 5-2. Writing the contents of a SOAP message to the console

```
package writesoapmessage;

import java.io.IOException;
import javax.xml.namespace.QName;
import javax.xml.soap.MessageFactory;
import javax.xml.soap.SOAPBody;
import javax.xml.soap.SOAPEnvelope;
import javax.xml.soap.SOAPException;
import javax.xml.soap.SOAPMessage;
import javax.xml.soap.SOAPPart;
```

```java
/**
 * Creates a SOAP Message and writes it to the console.
 */
public class Main {
    public static void main(String[] args) {
        try {
            SOAPMessage soapMsg =
                    MessageFactory.newInstance().createMessage();

            //Get the body from the envelope
            SOAPPart soapPart = soapMsg.getSOAPPart();
            SOAPEnvelope env = soapPart.getEnvelope();
            SOAPBody body = env.getBody();

            //Create a qualified name for the namespace of the
            //objects used by the service.
            String iNs = "http://ns.soacookbook.com/catalog";
            String elementName = "isbn";
            QName isbnQName = new QName(iNs, elementName);

            //Add the <isbn> element to the SOAP body
            //as its only child
            body.addBodyElement(isbnQName).setValue("12345");

            //debug print what we're sending
            soapMsg.writeTo(System.out);
        } catch (SOAPException ex) {
            ex.printStackTrace();
        } catch (IOException ex) {
            ex.printStackTrace();
        }
    }
}
```

The code doesn't invoke any web service, it just creates a message that is suitable for sending to some WSDL that requires a message in this format. Here is the result of running the program:

```xml
<SOAP-ENV:Envelope
  xmlns:SOAP-ENV="http://schemas.xmlsoap.org/soap/envelope/">
  <SOAP-ENV:Header/>
  <SOAP-ENV:Body>
    <isbn xmlns="http://ns.soacookbook.com/catalog">12345</isbn>
  </SOAP-ENV:Body>
</SOAP-ENV:Envelope>
```

If there are no attachments on the message, it is just written out as XML. If there are attachments on the message, a MIME-encoded byte stream is written. Also, the method throws an `IOException` if it can't write to the given stream.

5.4 Creating a Web Service Client Based on an Existing SOAP Envelope

Problem

You want to manually create a client to invoke a web service. You have a SOAP envelope in a plain-text file, perhaps as the result of some XSL transformation.

Solution

Use the SAAJ 1.3 API to build your message by hand. Then use a `Dispatch<T>` to call the service with your message. There are several steps involved:

1. Create a URL based on the WSDL location.
2. Create a `QName` object representing the service.
3. Create a `QName` object representing the port to invoke.
4. Create a `Dispatch` object using the port `QName`. Parameterize `Dispatch` on `javax.xml.soap.SOAPMessage` to indicate that you will build the entire SOAP envelope yourself and provide it to the `Dispatch`.
5. When creating the `Dispatch`, indicate Message for the mode and use `SOAPMessage.class` as the data type.
6. Read in the text file containing a complete SOAP envelope for Message mode and use it to create an instance of `SOAPMessage`.
7. Call the invoke method of your dispatch. Because your `Dispatch` is parameterized on `SOAPMessage`, that is what you'll get back in response.

Discussion

Let's turn to the business at hand. It can be very tricky getting started, so I'll spell things out along the way.

On the server side, you have an EJB web service with the definition as shown in Example 5-3. This is the service your client will invoke.

Example 5-3. Catalog EJB web service

```
@WebService(serviceName="CatalogService", name="Catalog",
    targetNamespace="http://ns.soacookbook.com/ws/catalog")
@Stateless
@Local
public class CatalogEJB {

    @WebMethod
    @SOAPBinding(style=SOAPBinding.Style.DOCUMENT,
        use=SOAPBinding.Use.LITERAL,
        parameterStyle=SOAPBinding.ParameterStyle.BARE)
    public @WebResult(name="book",
```

```
            targetNamespace="http://ns.soacookbook.com/catalog") Book
            getBook(
            @WebParam(name="isbn",
            targetNamespace="http://ns.soacookbook.com/catalog") String isbn) {

        LOG.info("Executing. ISBN=" + isbn);
        Book book = new Book();

        //you would go to a database here.
        if ("12345".equals(isbn)) {
            LOG.info("Search by ISBN: " + isbn);
            book.setTitle("King Lear");
            Author shakespeare = new Author();
            shakespeare.setFirstName("William");
            shakespeare.setLastName("Shakespeare");
            book.setAuthor(shakespeare);
            book.setCategory(Category.LITERATURE);
            book.setIsbn("12345");

        } else {
            LOG.info("Search by ISBN: " + isbn + ". NO RESULTS.");
        }

        LOG.info("Returning book: " + book.getTitle());
        return book;
    }
    //...
}
```

The web service operates using the `http://ns.soacookbook.com/ws/catalog` namespace, and the schema-based artifacts are defined in the `http://ns.soacookbook.com/catalog` namespace. Your build process uses XJC to generate Java objects based on the schemas before compiling the service. The robust business logic in this example just indicates that you'll get a book result back if you pass in "12345" as the ISBN, and an empty book otherwise.

The `getBook` method accepts a string ISBN code and returns the book object that matches it. In this example, you want to invoke the service without creating portable wrapper objects on the client with a tool like `wsimport`. So, you'll write a file that contains a complete SOAP envelope, and then read that into a SAAJ `Dispatch` to invoke the service. Here is the SOAP message in your client, *isbnMsg.txt*:

```
<?xml version="1.0" encoding="utf-8"?>
<soap:Envelope xmlns:soap="http://schemas.xmlsoap.org/soap/envelope/">
<soap:Body>
<i:isbn xmlns:i="http://ns.soacookbook.com/catalog">12345</i:isbn>
</soap:Body>
</soap:Envelope>
```

Note that the line breaks are optional; you will be able to invoke your service successfully whether you include them or not. I included them here for readability.

So, now create a dispatch client. There are a few steps involved. The listing in Example 5-4 represents a complete example.

Example 5-4. Manually invoking a web service with Dispatch using SOAPMessage in message mode

```
import static java.lang.System.out;

import java.io.FileInputStream;
import java.net.MalformedURLException;
import java.net.URL;
import javax.xml.namespace.QName;
import javax.xml.soap.MessageFactory;
import javax.xml.soap.SOAPMessage;
import javax.xml.ws.Dispatch;
import javax.xml.ws.Service;
import javax.xml.ws.WebServiceException;

public class CatalogTest {

public void dispatchMsgIsbnTest() {
try {
    URL wsdl =
            new URL("http://localhost:8080/CatalogService/Catalog?wsdl");

    String ns = "http://ns.soacookbook.com/ws/catalog";

    //Create the Service qualified name
    String svcName = "CatalogService";
    QName svcQName = new QName(ns, svcName);

    //Get a delegate wrapper
    Service service = Service.create(wsdl, svcQName);

    //Create the Port name
    String portName = "CatalogPort";
    QName portQName = new QName(ns, portName);

    //Create the delegate to send the request:
    Dispatch<SOAPMessage> dispatch =
            service.createDispatch(portQName,
            SOAPMessage.class, Service.Mode.MESSAGE);

    String dataFile = "/path/src/xml/ch03/isbnMsg.txt";

    //read in the data to use in building the soap message from a file
    FileInputStream fis = new FileInputStream(dataFile);

    //create the message, using contents of file as envelope
    SOAPMessage request =
            MessageFactory.newInstance().createMessage(null, fis);

    //debug print what we're sending
    request.writeTo(out);

    out.println("\nInvoking...");
```

```
    //send the message as request to service and get response
    SOAPMessage response = dispatch.invoke(request);

    //just show in the console for now
    response.writeTo(System.out);

} catch (MalformedURLException mue) {
    mue.printStackTrace();
} catch (WebServiceException wsex) {
    wsex.printStackTrace();
} catch (Exception ex) {
    ex.printStackTrace();
}
}
}
```

In this example, you have specified a few options that go together. In Recipe 5.6, we'll examine how to use different options, such as `PAYLOAD` instead of `MESSAGE`, and `Dispatch<Source>` instead of `Dispatch<SOAPMessage>`.

Here is the program's output (I added line breaks for clarity):

```
<?xml version='1.0' encoding='utf-8'?>
<soap:Envelope xmlns:soap="http://schemas.xmlsoap.org/soap/envelope/">
<soap:Body>
<i:isbn xmlns:i="http://ns.soacookbook.com/catalog">12345</i:isbn>
</soap:Body>
</soap:Envelope>

Invoking...

<S:Envelope xmlns:S="http://schemas.xmlsoap.org/soap/envelope/">
<S:Header/>
<S:Body>
<ns2:book xmlns:ns2="http://ns.soacookbook.com/catalog">
<isbn>12345</isbn>
<author>
<firstName>William</firstName><lastName>Shakespeare</lastName>
</author>
<title>King Lear</title>
<category>LITERATURE</category>
</ns2:book>
</S:Body>
</S:Envelope>
```

The SOAP envelope must specify the namespace for messages that the service annotations indicate.

It is unusual to get a SOAP envelope fully constructed from a physical file. There are a lot of options for creating your SOAP message, but I chose to illustrate the file version because it keeps the focus on the invocation mechanism, and it is the most explicit. This is a good starting point for the round-trip that other recipes can refer to.

5.5 Extracting Content from a SOAP Message

Problem

You have invoked a web service with `Dispatch<SOAPMessage>` and now you want to work with an XML view of the message response.

Solution

Use the `SOAPMessage` response to get the SOAP body, and then invoke its `extractContentAsDocument` method. That gives you an `org.w3.dom.Document` object to work with. You can then execute XPath queries against it, or just use the DOM 3 API as you otherwise would.

This code is identical to that in the previous example, except that instead of just using the convenience method `writeTo` to send the response to the console, you will get a DOM view of the response and then pull out the author's last name. Example 5-5 shows how this works.

Example 5-5. Getting a DOM view of a SOAP response

```
public void extractDOMFromSOAPResult() {
try {
    URL wsdl =
            new URL("http://localhost:8080/CatalogService/Catalog?wsdl");

    String ns = "http://ns.soacookbook.com/ws/catalog";

    //Create the Service name
    String svcName = "CatalogService";
    QName svcQName = new QName(ns, svcName);

    //Get a delegate wrapper
    Service service = Service.create(wsdl, svcQName);

    //Create the Port name
    String portName = "CatalogPort";
    QName portQName = new QName(ns, portName);

    Dispatch<SOAPMessage> dispatch =
            service.createDispatch(portQName,
            SOAPMessage.class, Service.Mode.MESSAGE);

    //create the message
    SOAPMessage soapMsg =
            MessageFactory.newInstance().createMessage();

    SOAPPart soapPart = soapMsg.getSOAPPart();
    SOAPEnvelope env = soapPart.getEnvelope();
    SOAPBody body = env.getBody();

    //Create a qualified name for the namespace of the
```

```
        //objects used by the service.
        String iNs = "http://ns.soacookbook.com/catalog";
        String elementName = "isbn";
        QName isbnQName = new QName(iNs, elementName);

        //Add the <isbn> element to the SOAP body
        //as its only child
        body.addBodyElement(isbnQName).setValue("12345");

        //debug print what we're sending
        soapMsg.writeTo(out);

        out.println("\nInvoking...");

        //send the message as request to service and get response
        SOAPMessage response = dispatch.invoke(soapMsg);

        //Extract response content as DOM view
        Document doc =
                response.getSOAPBody().extractContentAsDocument();

        NodeList isbnNodes = (NodeList)
                doc.getElementsByTagName("lastName");

        //just get by index; we know there's only one
        String value = isbnNodes.item(0).getTextContent();
        out.println("\nAuthor LastName=" + value);

        //just show in the console for now
        //response.writeTo(System.out);

    } catch (Exception ex) {
        ex.printStackTrace();
    }
    }
```

Here is the result of running the program:

```
Author LastName=Shakespeare
```

If you have worked with DOM before, this should be very straightforward. You are basically indicating to JAX-WS that you want a view of the message as `SOAPMessage` type, but then when you invoke the `extractContentAsDocument` method, JAX-WS will create a new DOM node, remove the `SOAPElement` part, and add the SOAP body as the document element to the new DOM node.

You can then run XPath queries, use an iterator on the `NodeList`, or whatever you like.

5.6 Creating a Web Service Client Using Raw XML Source and DOM

Problem

You want to invoke a web service without generating any artifacts first, and you have some simple data in a string that you want to use as the payload of your SOAP message.

Solution

Use the `Service.create` factory to create an instance of `Service`, make a `Dispatch` object parameterized on `javax.xml.transform.Source`, and use a `StringReader` to construct your message. Make sure to specify `Service.Mode.PAYLOAD`.

If you forget to change your `Dispatch` to be parameterized on `Source`, you will get a message like this:

```
Can not create Dispatch<SOAPMessage> of PAYLOAD. Must be MESSAGE.
```

The type parameter to `Dispatch` is telling it how much of the work you want to do in specifying the content of the request. In the previous example, you wrote the entire SOAP envelope in a file. Here, you want to minimize that work and let the `Dispatch` wrap your payload (the `soap:body` child) with the appropriate envelope.

The idea of this solution is the same as in the previous recipe where you used a `Dispatch<SOAPMessage>`. But there are key differences. You won't get your SOAP message from a file, but rather from a string. And it won't be a complete envelope, but just the payload. That means you also can't write the request and response so easily to `System.out`. Here are the steps:

1. Create a URL based on the WSDL location.
2. Create a `QName` object representing the service.
3. Create a `QName` object representing the port to invoke.
4. Create a `Dispatch` object using the port `QName`. Parameterize `Dispatch` on `javax.xml.transform.Source` to indicate that you will not provide a complete SOAP envelope yourself and provide it to the `Dispatch`, but will instead just give the kernel of the message the value of the SOAP body.
5. When creating the `Dispatch`, indicate Payload mode and use `Source.class` as the data type.
6. Read in the data you want to specify in the request as the child of the `soap:body`.
7. Call the invoke method of your `Dispatch`. Because your `Dispatch` is parameterized on `Source`, that is what you'll get back in response.
8. There isn't much you can do with a `Source` directly, so transform the result into a DOM tree you can work with.

9. Use the XPath API to extract the data you're interested in.

You're using the same method on the server side. Example 5-6 shows the complete client listing.

Example 5-6. Web service client using Dispatch<Source> with an XML string in payload mode

```
public void dispatchPayloadIsbnTest() {
try {
    URL wsdl =
            new URL("http://localhost:8080/CatalogService/Catalog?wsdl");

    String ns = "http://ns.soacookbook.com/ws/catalog";
    String objNs = "http://ns.soacookbook.com/catalog";

    //Create the Service name
    String svcName = "CatalogService";
    QName svcQName = new QName(ns, svcName);

    //Get a delegate wrapper
    Service service = Service.create(wsdl, svcQName);

    //Create the Port name
    String portName = "CatalogPort";
    QName portQName = new QName(ns, portName);

    //Create the dispatcher on Source with Payload
    Dispatch<Source> dispatch =
            service.createDispatch(portQName,
            Source.class, Service.Mode.PAYLOAD);

    //Change to tick marks or escape double quotes
    String payload =
         "<i:isbn xmlns:i='http://ns.soacookbook.com/catalog'>12345</i:isbn>";

    //Create a SOAP request based on our XML string
    StreamSource request = new StreamSource(new StringReader(payload));

    out.println("\nInvoking...");

    //Send the request and get the response
    Source bookResponse = dispatch.invoke(request);

    //Now we have to transform our result source object
    //into a DOM tree to work with it
    DOMResult dom = new DOMResult();
    Transformer trans = TransformerFactory.newInstance().newTransformer();
    trans.transform(bookResponse, dom);

    //Extract values with XPath
    XPathFactory xpf = XPathFactory.newInstance();
    XPath xp = xpf.newXPath();
    NodeList resultNodes = (NodeList) xp.evaluate("//title",
            dom.getNode(), XPathConstants.NODESET);
```

```
        //Show the result
        String title = resultNodes.item(0).getTextContent();
        out.println("TITLE=" + title);

    } catch (MalformedURLException mue) {
        mue.printStackTrace();
    } catch (WebServiceException wsex) {
        wsex.printStackTrace();
    } catch (Exception ex) {
        ex.printStackTrace();
    }
    }
```

The value of the response SOAP envelope contained in the `Source` looks like this:

```
<S:Envelope xmlns:S="http://schemas.xmlsoap.org/soap/envelope/">
<S:Header/>
<S:Body>
<ns2:book xmlns:ns2="http://ns.soacookbook.com/catalog">
     <isbn>12345</isbn>
     <author><firstName>William</firstName><lastName>Shakespeare</lastName>
     </author>
     <title>King Lear</title>
     <category>LITERATURE</category>
</ns2:book>
</S:Body>
</S:Envelope>
```

The results of running the program are:

```
Invoking...
TITLE=King Lear
```

After specifying `Source` as your parameter to `Dispatch<T>`, you have to transform the results into something usable within the application. You parse the result into a DOM tree and then use XPath to extract the title of the book you got back in response.

In general, you probably won't need to use such a low-level API and can instead rely on generated artifacts from a tool such as `wsimport` to do this work for you. Either way you'll get good flexibility. Notice that using SAAJ requires a lot of knowledge about the structure of the XML you are sending and receiving. You do not have to go through a stub generation step when using SAAJ. But you still need to know the WSDL location and the service name and ports, and you need to understand how to use the returned XML. It is fair to argue, however, that if you were working with JAXB to give you a Java view, you'll have the same entity structure regardless of the implementation semantics, and if you don't know that a book has a title, you're out of luck either way.

You may already have your data in an XML format, however, in which case using SAAJ is a terrific fit.

5.7 Adding a MIME Header

Problem

You want to add an outgoing MIME header on the HTTP transport wrapper of your message (not a SOAP header).

Solution

Use the `SOAPMessage.getMimeHeaders.addHeader` method.

Discussion

Try something like this:

```
MessageFactory factory = MessageFactory.newInstance();
SOAPMessage message = factory.createMessage();
message.getMimeHeaders().addHeader("X-Powered-By", "Duff");
```

5.8 Adding Namespace Declarations

Problem

You want to add a namespace declaration to your SOAP message.

Solution

Use the `SOAPEnvelope.addNamespaceDeclaration` method to add a namespace to the envelope, then create a `QName` and use the **`SOAPBody.addBodyElement`** method using the namespace.

Discussion

The following code will create a namespace and associate it with the SOAP envelope and then create an empty body element that uses that namespace:

```
//Declare the namespace
SOAPEnvelope env = msg.getSOAPPart().getEnvelope();
env.addNamespaceDeclaration("e", "http://example.com/myNs");

//Use the new namespace in the body
SOAPBody body = msg.getSOAPPart().getEnvelope().getBody();
QName bodyName = env.createQName("Quote", "e");
SOAPBodyElement q = body.addBodyElement(bodyName);
```

To use the namespace within the SOAP body, you create a qualified name and add it to the body as an element. Here you see the resulting SOAP message that uses this namespace in the body:

```
<SOAP-ENV:Envelope
  xmlns:SOAP-ENV="http://schemas.xmlsoap.org/soap/envelope/"
  xmlns:e="http://example.com/myNs">
  <SOAP-ENV:Header/>
  <SOAP-ENV:Body>
    <e:Quote/>...
```

Note that you must declare the namespace before trying to use it, or you'll get a `javax.xml.soap.SOAPException` indicating that it can't find the namespace.

5.9 Specifying SOAPAction

Problem

You need to specify the `SOAPAction` MIME header to invoke a web service that requires one.

Solution

You need to enable the ability to send a `SOAPAction` on your `Dispatch` or `Call` object. Then set its value to the URI that is required by the service, as specified by the operation's `soapAction` attribute.

Discussion

`SOAPAction` is an HTTP header that is specified on SOAP requests. It was originally used to provide routing information in headers. Because headers don't require inspecting the SOAP payload, they are quick to access, and were found to improve performance. Firewalls, filters, or routing agents can simply check the value of `SOAPAction` to determine the endpoint and operation the message is destined for.

The decision whether to employ `SOAPAction` is left to the implementer of the web service. If you choose to, it is specified on the concrete aspect of the WSDL in the SOAP binding:

```
<wsdl:operation name="GetQuote">
  <soap:operation style="document"
    soapAction="http://www.webserviceX.NET/GetQuote" />
...
```

In a SOAP request, the `SOAPAction` value must be a string, in quotes, that matches the value specified by the `soapAction` attribute in the WSDL. The following HTTP header would need to be set to match the `soapAction` specified in the WSDL just shown:

```
SOAPAction: "http://www.webserviceX.NET/GetQuote"
```

While performance can certainly still be an issue with SOAP-based web services, this approach has disadvantages. For the more academically inclined, relying on the transport protocol (HTTP) to include SOAP-specific information is problematic. While taking advantage of headers for certain incidental data or metadata may be acceptable, allowing the internal details of the contained message to ooze out into the transport layer is not encapsulated. It's like passing a JPanel into a DAO. It is suggested that rather than specifying routing information externally, it should be located instead in the SOAP message itself. This argument makes a good deal of sense. In fact, that's some of the basis for the justification for creating the WS-Addressing specification. WS-Addressing still provides routing information in a manner similar to `SOAPAction`, but it does so in structured SOAP headers, not HTTP headers.

The Basic Profile (the specification from the Web Services Interoperability consortium that provides guidelines for ensuring that web services are interoperable across multiple platforms) requires that `SOAPAction` be present and its value must be a quoted string. But the string can be empty. Java implementations, including the SAAJ and JAX-WS reference implementations, will automatically add `SOAPAction` as a header, and give it a value of "" (empty string). This complies with the Basic Profile and doesn't break encapsulation.

Another thing to consider is that the WSDL 1.2 and 2.0 specifications make `soapAction` optional, so they may be deprecated before too long in favor of elements provided by the WS-Addressing specification.

Some web services, particularly those implemented in .NET, require you to specify a real value for a `SOAPAction` header. In Java, this will be created, but its value will be an empty string.

The `SOAPAction` will typically look something like this:

```
POST /stockquote.asmx HTTP/1.1
Host: www.webservicex.net
Content-Type: text/xml; charset=utf-8
Content-Length: length
SOAPAction: "http://www.webserviceX.NET/GetQuote"
```

If you don't specify it, the service will complain. Adding a `SOAPAction` is turned off by default on both the `Dispatch` and `Call` objects that are used to send messages. In order to use services that require a `SOAPAction`, you have to do two things: enable the message to provide a value for `SOAPAction` and then provide the value.

Because you have to enable it this way, `SOAPAction` is *not* just another MIME header like any other you might want to add. So let's look at a web service from the good folks at *http://webservicesx.net*, which has been around for a few years.

This example uses a publicly available free web service available at *http://webservicex.net*. The web services on the site are implemented using Microsoft.NET. There are a few things that are done slightly differently on their side of the WSDL that have a subtle effect on how you must create your requests. For example, in Java, you may be used to specifying namespaces with a prefix such as "tns:". But if you read the WebserviceX schema, its `GetQuoteResponse` is specified without a prefix, like this:

```
<GetQuoteResponse xmlns="http://www.webserviceX.NET/">
```

You have to keep that in mind when creating your `QName`, and do so like this:

```
QName q = new QName("http://www.webserviceX.NET/","GetQuote");
```

If you do specify a prefix, you'll get an error back in the response.

The web service you're going to invoke is available at *http://www.webservicex.net/WCF/ServiceDetails.aspx?SID=19* if you'd like to read the WSDL and schema. It asks for a ticker symbol and returns some data about the stock in response. The code in Example 5-7 shows how to build the complete client. Here you just build a SAAJ client, specify the `SOAPAction` as required, and send your request for information about the JAVA symbol.

Example 5-7. Adding a SOAPAction header as required by this .NET web service

```
package addSoapAction;

import java.net.MalformedURLException;
import java.net.URL;
import javax.xml.namespace.QName;
import javax.xml.soap.MessageFactory;
import javax.xml.soap.SOAPMessage;
import javax.xml.soap.SOAPEnvelope;
import javax.xml.soap.SOAPBody;
import javax.xml.soap.SOAPBodyElement;
import javax.xml.soap.SOAPElement;
import javax.xml.soap.SOAPException;
import javax.xml.ws.Dispatch;
import javax.xml.ws.Service;

/**
 * Shows how to add a MIME header, of which SOAPAction is one.
 */
public class AddSoapAction {
    private static final String WSDL =
       "http://www.webservicex.net/stockquote.asmx?wsdl";

    private static final String NS =
        "http://www.webserviceX.NET/";

    public static void main(String...arg) {
        new AddSoapAction().invoke();
```

```java
    System.out.println("\nAll done.");
}

public AddSoapAction() {  }

private void invoke(){
    try {
        //Prepare service to call
        Service service = createService();
        QName portQName = new QName(NS, "StockQuoteSoap");
        Dispatch<SOAPMessage> dispatch =
            service.createDispatch(portQName,
            SOAPMessage.class, Service.Mode.MESSAGE);

        //Add SOAPAction
        dispatch.getRequestContext().put(
                Dispatch.SOAPACTION_USE_PROPERTY, "1");
        dispatch.getRequestContext().put(
                Dispatch.SOAPACTION_URI_PROPERTY,
                "http://www.webserviceX.NET/GetQuote");

        //Prepare request
        SOAPMessage request = createMessage();

        //send request and get response
        SOAPMessage response = dispatch.invoke(request);

        //Write response to console
        System.out.println("\nGot Response:\n");
        response.writeTo(System.out);
        System.out.println("\n");

    } catch (Exception ex) {
        ex.printStackTrace();
    }
}

private SOAPMessage createMessage() throws SOAPException {
    //Create a SOAPMessage
    MessageFactory messageFactory =
            MessageFactory.newInstance();
    SOAPMessage message = messageFactory.createMessage();

    try {
        SOAPEnvelope env = message.getSOAPPart().getEnvelope();
        SOAPBody body = env.getBody();

        //Create a SOAPBodyElement
        QName bodyName = new QName("http://www.webserviceX.NET/",
            "GetQuote");

        SOAPBodyElement bodyEl = body.addBodyElement(bodyName);

        //Add our data
```

```
            QName name = new QName("symbol");
            SOAPElement symbol = bodyEl.addChildElement(name);
            symbol.addTextNode("JAVA");

            System.out.println("\nCreated Request:\n");
            message.writeTo(System.out);
            System.out.println("\n");

        } catch (Exception e) {
            System.out.println(e.getMessage());
        }

        return message;
    }

    private Service createService() throws MalformedURLException {
        URL wsdl = new URL(WSDL);

        //Create the Service name
        String svcName = "StockQuote";
        QName svcQName = new QName(NS, svcName);

        //Get a delegate wrapper
        Service service = Service.create(wsdl, svcQName);
        System.out.println("Created Service: " + service.getServiceName());

        return service;
    }
}
```

The important part of this code is getting the `RequestContext` from the `Dispatch` object, and using constants in the `Dispatch` class to specify that you want to use the `SOAPAction` header, allowing that to specify the action that the service dictates:

```
//Say we want to use SOAPAction
dispatch.getRequestContext().put(
  Dispatch.SOAPACTION_USE_PROPERTY, "1");

//Specify our value
dispatch.getRequestContext().put(
  Dispatch.SOAPACTION_URI_PROPERTY,
    "http://www.webserviceX.NET/GetQuote");
```

The preceding code indicates that you want to specify the `SOAPAction` property ourselves, overriding the default. Next, you indicate the actual value to use. It will produce a header in the HTTP request that looks like this:

```
SOAPAction: "http://www.webserviceX.NET/GetQuote"
```

Here you use "1" to indicate a Boolean true. But you could spell out the word true as well; the SOAP specification is happy with either. This works for false and 0 too, and not just with `SOAPAction`—you can also use these values on items like `mustUnderstand` and others.

The result includes data about the market and share activity:

```
Created Service: {http://www.webserviceX.NET/}StockQuote

Created Request:
<SOAP-ENV:Envelope xmlns:SOAP-ENV="...">
<SOAP-ENV:Header/>
<SOAP-ENV:Body>
<GetQuote xmlns="http://www.webserviceX.NET/">
<symbol>JAVA</symbol>
</GetQuote>
</SOAP-ENV:Body>
</SOAP-ENV:Envelope>

Got Response:

<soap:Envelope
  xmlns:soap="http://schemas.xmlsoap.org/soap/envelope/"
  xmlns:xsd="http://www.w3.org/2001/XMLSchema"
  xmlns:xsi="http://www.w3.org/2001/XMLSchema-instance">
<soap:Header/>
<soap:Body>
  <GetQuoteResponse xmlns="http://www.webserviceX.NET/">
  <GetQuoteResult>
  <StockQuotes>
  <Stock>
  <Symbol>JAVA</Symbol>
  <Last>10.10</Last>
  <Date>7/24/2008</Date>
  <Time>4:00pm</Time>
  <Change>-0.42</Change>
  <Open>10.47</Open><High>10.48</High>
  <Low>10.06</Low><Volume>18796276</Volume>
  <MktCap>7.896B</MktCap>
  <PreviousClose>10.52</PreviousClose>
  <PercentageChange>-3.99%</PercentageChange>
  <Name>SUN MICROSYSTEMS </Name>
  </Stock>
  </StockQuotes>
  </GetQuoteResult>
  </GetQuoteResponse>
</soap:Body>
</soap:Envelope>
```

5.10 Adding an Attribute to an Element

Problem

You want to add an attribute to an element in the body of your SOAP message.

Solution

Create a `QName` for your attribute and add it to the desired element using the `SOAPElement.addAttribute` method.

Discussion

When you create the `QName` for the attribute, you don't need to give it the namespace because it will inherit from its enclosing parent. Just create it using the local part, specifying the name of your attribute as the `QName`. Then give it a value as the second argument to the `addAttribute` method. That's really all there is to it.

Example 5-8 shows the complete listing that adds an attribute to a message element.

Example 5-8. Adding an attribute to an element

```
package addAttribute;

import javax.xml.namespace.QName;
import javax.xml.soap.MessageFactory;
import javax.xml.soap.SOAPMessage;
import javax.xml.soap.SOAPEnvelope;
import javax.xml.soap.SOAPBody;
import javax.xml.soap.SOAPBodyElement;
import javax.xml.soap.SOAPElement;

public class SAAJCreateAttribute {
    public static void main(String args[]) {
    try {
        //Create a SOAPMessage
        MessageFactory messageFactory =
                MessageFactory.newInstance();
        SOAPMessage message = messageFactory.createMessage();
        SOAPEnvelope env = message.getSOAPPart().getEnvelope();
        SOAPBody body = env.getBody();

        //Create a SOAPBodyElement
        QName bodyName = new QName("http://example.com",
                "getQuote", "e");

        SOAPBodyElement bodyEl = body.addBodyElement(bodyName);

        //Add our data
        QName name = new QName("ticker");
        SOAPElement ticker = bodyEl.addChildElement(name);
        ticker.addTextNode("JAVA");

        //to ticker element, add our countryCode attribute
        //with a value of US
        QName attributeName = new QName("countryCode");
        ticker.addAttribute(attributeName, "US");

        message.writeTo(System.out);
```

```
        } catch (Exception e) {
            System.out.println(e.getMessage());
        }
        }
}
```

As you can see, you've just created a QName for the attribute, passing it the name you want the attribute to have. Then you specify its value when you add it to the ticker element.

Here is the resulting output:

```
<SOAP-ENV:Envelope
  xmlns:SOAP-ENV="http://schemas.xmlsoap.org/soap/envelope/">
  <SOAP-ENV:Header/>
  <SOAP-ENV:Body>
    <e:getQuote xmlns:e="http://example.com">
        <ticker countryCode="US">JAVA</ticker>
    </e:getQuote>
  </SOAP-ENV:Body>
</SOAP-ENV:Envelope>
```

The attribute has been added to your ticker element as shown in the highlighted code.

5.11 Removing a Header from a SOAP Message

Problem

You want to remove a header from a SOAP message. Perhaps you have processed it already and want to relay the message to the next processor, or you just don't want it taking up unnecessary space in the byte stream because you're not using it.

Solution

Use the SOAPHeader.detachNode method.

Discussion

If you know that you won't be using the header section of the envelope, you can remove it to lighten the load you're sending across the wire. Here is the code to make it happen:

```
SOAPHeader header = env.getHeader();
header.detachNode();
```

The resulting SOAP envelope looks like this, just the envelope and the body:

```
<SOAP-ENV:Envelope xmlns:SOAP-ENV="...">
<SOAP-ENV:Body>...
```

That's all there is to it.

5.12 Adding Headers to a SOAP Request

Problem

You want to add custom header information to a SOAP request.

Solution

Use the `SOAPEnvelop.addHeader` method.

Discussion

The SOAP 1.2 specification covers headers at length, and they are a popular choice for storing all manners of data concerning message exchanges within a SOA. There are also a number of SOAP headers that can be defined to comply with the specification when you need to use certain kinds of behavior. Some of the headers defined by the specification include `mustUnderstand`, `role`, and `relay`. So, it's important to understand how to use them.

Any user-defined header can also be defined by service clients and providers. Headers can be used to indicate vendor extensions (typically beginning with "X-"), or processing instructions such as what parts of an infoset can be cached, security codes, or other bits of meta-data.

There are a few basic ways to do work with SOAP headers. You can use the SAAJ API, which ensures portability, and add the headers to your code on invocation. That's what we'll examine here.

In this example, you'll create a web service, examine the schema and WSDL that define it, and then write the client program to contact it. We'll walk through every step to make sure that it's clear how all of the parts get wired together.

Creating the web service

The first thing you'll do is create a web service. It will specify some header value that it wants clients to provide as a SOAP header, which it can then read on the server side and perform some processing on it. You'll be creating a `passwordHeader` header. (You won't actually do any security stuff with it because that's not the point here, but you could.) The service itself is kept as simple as possible in order to stay focused on the task at hand. It just adds two integers together.

In Example 5-9, you see the web service you've defined that requires the headers. You'll create this quickly using JAX-WS. This will give you something to test against.

Example 5-9. A web service operation that defines headers

```
import javax.jws.WebMethod;
import javax.jws.WebParam;
import javax.jws.WebService;
```

```
@WebService(targetNamespace="urn:soacookbook.saaj")
public class CalculatorWS {

    @WebMethod(operationName="add", action="add")
    public int add(@WebParam(name = "i") int i,
            @WebParam(name="j") int j,
            @WebParam(header=true, name="passwordHeader",
            mode=WebParam.Mode.IN) String passwordHeader) {

        System.out.print("Header value was: " + passwordHeader);
        System.out.print("i=" + i + ". j=" + j);

        return i + j;
    }
}
```

The highlighted code shows how you are adding the header to your web service definition. Using the `@WebParam` annotation, you specify `header=true`, and then give the parameter a name and a Java type. The Java type will get translated to an XML schema type when the WSDL is generated. This method of creating a header is quick and easy, but can have certain implications for services and clients. We'll examine this more later, when we look at how to deal with headers in JAX-WS.

For now, you'll just package this service in a WAR's *WEB-INF/classes* directory, deploy, and the WSDL will be generated for you. You can then examine the WSDL to determine how you need to structure a SOAP message that will comply with the interface.

Examining the WSDL

Now that you've deployed your service, here is the WSDL that `wsgen` generates for you in the JAX-WS reference implementation (in Glassfish) at deploy time:

```
<?xml version="1.0" encoding="UTF-8"?>
<definitions xmlns:wsu="http://docs.oasis-open.org/wss/
  2004/01/oasis-200401-wss-wssecurity-utility-1.0.xsd"
  xmlns:soap="http://schemas.xmlsoap.org/wsdl/soap/"
  xmlns:tns="urn:soacookbook.saaj"
  xmlns:xsd="http://www.w3.org/2001/XMLSchema"
  xmlns="http://schemas.xmlsoap.org/wsdl/"
  targetNamespace="urn:soacookbook.saaj"
  name="CalculatorWSService">

<types>
  <xsd:schema>
  <xsd:import namespace="urn:soacookbook.saaj"
  schemaLocation="http://localhost:8080/SecureCalculatorApp/
    CalculatorWSService?xsd=1">
  </xsd:import>
</xsd:schema>
</types>

<message name="add">
```

```
    <part name="parameters" element="tns:add"></part>
    <part name="passwordHeader" element="tns:passwordHeader"></part>
  </message>
  <message name="addResponse">
    <part name="result" element="tns:addResponse"></part>
  </message>

  <portType name="CalculatorWS">
    <operation name="add" parameterOrder="parameters passwordHeader">
      <input message="tns:add"></input>
      <output message="tns:addResponse"></output>
    </operation>
  </portType>

  <binding name="CalculatorWSPortBinding" type="tns:CalculatorWS">
    <soap:binding transport="http://schemas.xmlsoap.org/soap/http"
      style="document"></soap:binding>
    <operation name="add">
    <soap:operation soapAction="add"></soap:operation>
    <input>
    <soap:body use="literal" parts="parameters"></soap:body>
    <soap:header message="tns:add" part="passwordHeader"
      use="literal"></soap:header>
    </input>
    <output>
    <soap:body use="literal"></soap:body>
    </output>
    </operation>
  </binding>

  <service name="CalculatorWSService">
    <port name="CalculatorWSPort" binding="tns:CalculatorWSPortBinding">
    <soap:address location="http://localhost:8080/SecureCalculatorApp/
      CalculatorWSService"></soap:address>
    </port>
  </service>

  </definitions>
```

As you can see, there are two primary aspects of the WSDL that have been modified by the presence of a header. The first is that an element was created for `passwordHeader` as part of the `add` message in the abstract WSDL. In the concrete definition, where you specify the protocol the message will use as transport, you see an entry for `<soap:header part="passwordHeader"/>`. That's because you must wire up the abstract idea of a header (something that accompanies the message, but which lies outside the body content that contains the payload that you're really interested in) to a concrete implementation of how that header will accompany the message. The answer, in this case, is via a standard SOAP header.

There are a couple of parts of the WSDL that merit special attention. First, take a look at the `add` operation. It specifies that the data used as input to the `add` operation (incoming SOAP message) will be represented by the `add` message, which actually combines the header and regular method parameters. The operation indicates an order in which its two parameters should arrive, separated by a space.

Next, take a look at the `<soap:header...>` element in the WSDL. You're indicating that you're going to use SOAP as the concrete transport mechanism, and declaring that inbound messages must include a header, which is defined in the `passwordHeader` part of the `add` message definition in the namespace that matches the `tns` prefix, or the target namespace. Note that the header is defined separately, as its own element in the schema that matches this WSDL. It is not part of the `add` complex type.

Examining the schema

The web service imports a schema that defines the types that the messages must exchange. Following is the entire schema that was generated based on your annotations in the service. So these are the XML info sets that you need to create with SAAJ over on the client side:

```
<xs:schema xmlns:tns="urn:soacookbook.saaj"
  xmlns:xs="http://www.w3.org/2001/XMLSchema" version="1.0"
  targetNamespace="urn:soacookbook.saaj">

<xs:element name="add" type="tns:add"></xs:element>

<xs:element name="passwordHeader" nillable="true"
  type="xs:string"></xs:element>

<xs:element name="addResponse"
  type="tns:addResponse"></xs:element>

<xs:complexType name="add">
<xs:sequence>
<xs:element name="i" type="xs:int"></xs:element>
<xs:element name="j" type="xs:int"></xs:element>
</xs:sequence>
</xs:complexType>
//... response omitted
</xs:schema>
```

According to the schema, you'll need to create an element called `add` that has two child elements in the given namespace, which will in turn hold integer values. Here's what it should look like:

```
<tns:add xmlns:tns="urn:soacookbook.saaj">
  <i>5</i><j>4</j>
</tns:add>
```

Of course, you need to have the XML structure for the header itself.

Headers in SOAP 1.2 are not simply key/value pairs, as you may be used to seeing in SMTP or HTTP headers. They must be full-blown XML info sets, including a namespace.

Here is a snippet of XML that conforms to the definition of the schema element `passwordHeader`:

```
<SOAP-ENV:Header>
  <passwordHeader xmlns="urn:soacookbook.saaj">
    s3cr3t
  </passwordHeader>
</SOAP-ENV:Header>
```

Now that you have an idea of what XML structure you need to create, let's go for it. Of course, you could have a SOAP message template and replace values in it at runtime, or read it in from a file, as we've seen in earlier recipes. But creating the entire thing programmatically is more common and straightforward, so that's what we'll do here.

Building the client program

Now, you finally get to the point of this recipe, which is to write a program that creates a SOAP client message, including an XML info set header, and invokes a remote web service. In this case, you're pretending that there's some security on the web service and you need to supply a password in the header, so you need to account for those in your message creation. The SAAJ client that fulfills your requirements is shown in Example 5-10.

Example 5-10. SAAJ client that passes headers

```
package createHeader;

import java.io.IOException;
import java.net.MalformedURLException;
import java.net.URL;
import javax.xml.namespace.QName;
import javax.xml.soap.MessageFactory;
import javax.xml.soap.SOAPBody;
import javax.xml.soap.SOAPBodyElement;
import javax.xml.soap.SOAPEnvelope;
import javax.xml.soap.SOAPException;
import javax.xml.soap.SOAPHeader;
import javax.xml.soap.SOAPHeaderElement;
import javax.xml.soap.SOAPMessage;
import javax.xml.ws.Dispatch;
import javax.xml.ws.Service;

/**
 * Invokes the SAAJ header service.
 */
public class SAAJCreateHeader {

    private static final String NS = "urn:soacookbook.saaj";

    public static void main(String...arg) {
        new SAAJCreateHeader().invoke();
        System.out.println("\nAll done.");
    }
```

```
public SAAJCreateHeader() {  }

private void invoke(){
    try {
        //Prepare service to call
        Service service = createService();
        QName portQName = new QName(NS, "CalculatorWSPort");
        Dispatch<SOAPMessage> dispatch =
            service.createDispatch(portQName,
            SOAPMessage.class, Service.Mode.MESSAGE);

        //Prepare Request
        SOAPMessage request = createMessage();

        //Send request and get response
        SOAPMessage response = dispatch.invoke(request);

        //Write response to console
        response.writeTo(System.out);

    } catch (Exception ex) {
        ex.printStackTrace();
    }
}

private SOAPMessage createMessage() throws SOAPException {
   SOAPMessage msg = MessageFactory.newInstance().createMessage();

   try {

        SOAPEnvelope env = msg.getSOAPPart().getEnvelope();
        SOAPHeader header = env.getHeader();

        //Create header
        QName passwordQName =
                new QName(NS, "passwordHeader");
        SOAPHeaderElement headerElement =
                header.addHeaderElement(passwordQName);
        headerElement.addTextNode("s3cr3t");

        //Create body
        SOAPBody body = msg.getSOAPPart().getEnvelope().getBody();
        QName addQName =
               new QName("urn:soacookbook.saaj", "add", "tns");

        SOAPBodyElement bodyEl = body.addBodyElement(addQName);

        bodyEl.addChildElement("i").addTextNode("5");
        bodyEl.addChildElement("j").setValue("4");

        System.out.println("\nCreated Message:\n");
        msg.writeTo(System.out);
        System.out.println("\n");
```

```
        } catch (SOAPException ex) {
            ex.printStackTrace();
        }catch (IOException ex) {
            ex.printStackTrace();
        }
       return msg;
    }

    private Service createService() throws MalformedURLException {
        URL wsdl =
            new URL("http://localhost:8080/SecureCalculatorApp/" +
            "CalculatorWSService?WSDL");

    //Create the Service name
    String svcName = "CalculatorWSService";
    QName svcQName = new QName(NS, svcName);

    //Get a delegate wrapper
    Service service = Service.create(wsdl, svcQName);
    System.out.println("Created Service: " + service.getServiceName());

    return service;
    }

}
```

Let's examine this code to see what's going on. First, this is just a simple console-based Java program with a main method. You don't have any libraries on your classpath, only what you get with Java SE 6. When the program runs, the main method creates a new instance of the class and calls its `invoke` method. This method, in turn, does the three things that make the round-trip. First, it creates a reference to the service using the `createService` method; next, it creates a conforming SOAP message using the SAAJ API that can be effectively sent to the service; and finally, it wires these together and uses the message to call the service, printing out the request and response from the server.

The primary element that we're concerned with in this program is the header. Get a header object directly from the envelope, just as you do the body. That returns an object of type `SOAPHeader`. Here you will add a single header element to the header, though you could add more if necessary. You create a `QName` for the header element you want to add, which in this case is `passwordHeader`. Then you'll call the `addHeaderElement` method on the header in order to place this new element as its child. That will create and return the element as a type of `SOAPHeaderElement`. Then you can add your XML data to it. In this case, it's just a text node containing your password.

Assessing the results

Here is the result of executing the program, with a little formatting added for readability:

```
Created Service: {urn:soacookbook.saaj}CalculatorWSService
Created Message:

<SOAP-ENV:Envelope
  xmlns:SOAP-ENV="http://schemas.xmlsoap.org/soap/envelope/">
  <SOAP-ENV:Header>
    <passwordHeader xmlns="urn:soacookbook.saaj">s3cr3t</passwordHeader>
  </SOAP-ENV:Header>
  <SOAP-ENV:Body>
    <tns:add xmlns:tns="urn:soacookbook.saaj">
      <i>5</i>
      <j>4</j>
    </tns:add>
  </SOAP-ENV:Body>
</SOAP-ENV:Envelope>

<S:Envelope xmlns:S="http://schemas.xmlsoap.org/soap/envelope/">
  <S:Header/>
  <S:Body>
  <ns2:addResponse xmlns:ns2="urn:soacookbook.saaj">
    <return>9</return>
  </ns2:addResponse>
</S:Body>
</S:Envelope>

All done.
```

This shows the SOAP envelopes for both the outgoing request and the response that the service returns. You can see that your header value is in the right place, and your body's `add` child conforms to the schema. Obviously, if you don't structure your SOAP message in conformance with the schema and other expectations surrounding the service, the service will not be able to read the incoming data properly. Depending on how you messed it up, the behavior at that point is undefined.

Here is what's printed on the server side:

```
Header value was: s3cr3t
i=5. j=4
```

This snippet from the server logs shows that you're getting the right parameters to the operation and that the service is able to read (and thereby process) the value of the header.

See Also

Recipe 6.10 for a more in-depth discussion and alternate methods. (There are a variety of other ways to add headers to an outgoing SOAP message.)

5.13 Accessing All SOAP Header Elements

Problem

You want to process all of the SOAP elements on an inbound message.

Solution

Use the `SOAPHeader.examineAllHeaderElements` method to get an iterator. Use the iterator to inspect the `SOAPHeaderElement` objects one at a time.

Discussion

Example 5-11 shows how this works.

Example 5-11. Shows all headers in a message

```
package allHeaders;

import java.io.IOException;
import java.util.Iterator;
import javax.xml.namespace.QName;
import javax.xml.soap.MessageFactory;
import javax.xml.soap.SOAPBody;
import javax.xml.soap.SOAPBodyElement;
import javax.xml.soap.SOAPException;
import javax.xml.soap.SOAPHeader;
import javax.xml.soap.SOAPEnvelope;
import javax.xml.soap.SOAPHeaderElement;
import javax.xml.soap.SOAPMessage;

/**
 * Loops over headers in a message.
 */
public class AllHeaders {
    private static final String NS = "urn:soacookbook.saaj";

    public static void main(String args...) {
        try {
            AllHeaders me = new AllHeaders();
            me.showHeaders(me.createMessage());
        } catch (SOAPException ex) {
            ex.printStackTrace();
        }
    }

    @SuppressWarnings("unchecked")
    private static void showHeaders(SOAPMessage message)
            throws SOAPException {
        SOAPHeader header = message.getSOAPHeader();

        Iterator<SOAPHeaderElement> allHeaders =
             header.examineAllHeaderElements();
```

```
        while (allHeaders.hasNext()) {
            SOAPHeaderElement headerElement =
                    allHeaders.next();
            QName headerName = headerElement.getElementQName();
            System.out.println("\nHeader name=" +
                    headerName.getLocalPart());
            System.out.println("Actor=" +
                    headerElement.getActor());
        }
    }

    private SOAPMessage createMessage() throws SOAPException {
        SOAPMessage msg = MessageFactory.newInstance().createMessage();
        try {
            SOAPEnvelope env = msg.getSOAPPart().getEnvelope();
            SOAPHeader header = env.getHeader();

            //Create header
            QName passwordQName =
                    new QName(NS, "passwordHeader");
            SOAPHeaderElement headerElement =
                    header.addHeaderElement(passwordQName);
            headerElement.addTextNode("s3cr3t");

            //Create body
            SOAPBody body = msg.getSOAPPart().getEnvelope().getBody();
            QName addQName = new QName("urn:soacookbook.saaj", "add", "tns");

            SOAPBodyElement bodyEl = body.addBodyElement(addQName);

            bodyEl.addChildElement("i").addTextNode("5");
            bodyEl.addChildElement("j").setValue("4");

            System.out.println("\nCreated Message:\n");
            msg.writeTo(System.out);
            System.out.println("\n");

        } catch (SOAPException ex) {
            ex.printStackTrace();
        } catch (IOException ex) {
            ex.printStackTrace();
        }
        return msg;
    }
}
```

All you have to keep in mind here is that you are dealing with SOAPHeaderElement objects in the iterator.

Here is the output of running the code:

```
Header name=passwordHeader
Actor is null
```

5.14 Adding an Attachment to an Outbound SOAP Message

Problem

You want to add an attachment to an outbound SOAP message.

Solution

Use the `SOAPMessage.createAttachmentPart` method and add the data to your `AttachmentPart` using its `setContent` method.

Discussion

There are four possible content types that you can use in setting attachment values:

- `String`
- `Stream`
- `javax.xml.transform.Source`
- `javax.activation.DataHandler`

Here is the basic idea:

```
AttachmentPart attachment = message.createAttachmentPart();
String data = "Some attachment data";
attachment.setContent(data, "text/plain");
attachment.setContentID("my-data");
message.addAttachmentPart(attachment);
```

This is the simplest way to do it if your attachment uses data that fits into a string. If you have binary data, such as an image or PDF, or an XML `Source`, you can use the `javax.activation.DataHandler` class and add the contents to the attachment using the `DataHandler`:

```
URL url = new URL("http://java.sun.com/im/logo_sun_small_sdn.gif");
DataHandler dataHandler = new DataHandler(url);
AttachmentPart att = msg.createAttachmentPart(dataHandler);
msg.addAttachmentPart(att);
```

The `javax.activation.DataHandler` class has been around for some time in the JavaBeans Activation Framework, but it is a new addition to Java SE 6. This class provides a unified interface for working with data in a variety of formats and from a variety of sources. `DataHandler` can automatically detect the MIME type of the object passed to it, so it is able to add the MIME content type to the attachment transparently. Because you constructed it with a URL, it privately creates a `URLDataSource` object, which is also new in Java SE 6. This class implements the `DataSource` interface, giving you access to the data as input and output streams. There are two main things that you need to know about `DataHandler` in this context: it is the most convenient way to get non-string data into a SAAJ attachment, and when you need to deal with the data once you've retrieved it from the attachment, you can use a standard `InputStream` to read it and an `OutputStream` to write it.

You saw how to use a source with SAAJ messages earlier, so I won't belabor that here.

See Also

Recipe 5.16.

5.15 Accessing Inbound Attachment Data

Problem

You need to access an attachment to a SOAP message you are receiving.

Solution

Use the `AttachmentPart.getContent` method to retrieve all of the attachments from the message, iterate over each one, and check their content type before processing.

Discussion

This is very straightforward. You just need to iterate over the result returned from invoking `SOAPMessage.getAttachments`. The following servlet code receives a request from a client that has passed it an attachment. You read the attachment from the SOAP message, and create an attachment of your own. You then put the attachment onto the SOAP message to return with the response to the client.

The following method is defined within a SAAJ provider servlet. This private method accepts a `SOAPMessage` and calls its `getAttachments` method, which returns an attachment part. Then you can call any of the available methods to check the content ID, check the content type, and so on. In this case, you print out the contents of the attachment ID, the content type, and the attachment data:

```
@SuppressWarnings("unchecked")
private void printReceivedAttachmentData(SOAPMessage msg)
            throws SOAPException {

  System.out.print("Getting attachment...");

  Iterator<AttachmentPart> it = msg.getAttachments();
  while (it.hasNext()) {
    AttachmentPart attachment = it.next();

    String id = attachment.getContentId();

    //Check the ID, just to pretend some business logic
    if ("clientVersion".equals(id)){
      String type = attachment.getContentType();
      System.out.print("Attachment ID=" + id +
```

```
                        ". Content Type=" + type);

        if ("text/plain".equals(type)) {
          Object content = attachment.getContent();
          System.out.println("Attachment data: " + content);
        }
      }
    }
  }
```

You can find the complete code listing for this method in the file *SAAJProviderAttachServlet.java*. It accepts a request that has attachment data, prints the incoming attachment data, and then creates an attachment for the response. The result of printing the incoming attachment data is as follows:

```
Getting attachment...
Attachment ID=clientVersion. Content Type=text/plain
Attachment data: Client-Version=1.1
```

Note that because the Servlet API has not yet been fitted with Java SE 5 language features such as generics and annotations (that will have to wait until Java EE 6), you indicate that you're suppressing the compiler warnings regarding your Iterator's type parameter. If you prefer, you can forget the `@SuppressWarnings` annotation, use Iterator's raw type, and just cast `Object` to `AttachmentPart` when you call `it.next`.

See Also

Recipe 5.20.

5.16 Connecting to a SAAJ Endpoint Without a WSDL

Problem

You want to create a connection to a SAAJ endpoint. You know the data structure required for messages, but it doesn't present a WSDL, and `Service.create` requires a WSDL.

Solution

Create a `SOAPConnectionFactory` and use it to get a `SOAPConnection` object.

Discussion

The SOAP connection allows you to send a SOAP message to a resource at the end of a URL. This is convenient to use in any situation, but necessary if that service does not have a defined WSDL. That's because calling `Service.create` requires passing in the location of the WSDL. It may be rare that you don't have a WSDL with a SOAP-based service, but it does happen, and you'll be prepared.

```
//Prepare Request
SOAPMessage request =
     MessageFactory.newInstance().createMessage();

//add data to request SOAP Message here...

//Create connection object
SOAPConnectionFactory scf = SOAPConnectionFactory.newInstance();
SOAPConnection connection = scf.createConnection();

//Create an endpoint to invoke
URL endpoint = new URL("http://localhost:8080/" +
                    "SAAJProvider/SAAJProviderServlet");

// Send request to endpoint, get response
SOAPMessage response = connection.call(request, endpoint);
```

To create a connection to a web service that does not expose a WSDL, you can use the `SOAPConnection` class to communicate directly with the remote resource. First, create a SOAP message for your request as you normally would, and populate its body with data as necessary. Then get an instance of the `SOAPConnection` object using the `SOAPConnectionFactory` class. You then create a URL object representing the remote resource (servlet) you want to call. Pass the SOAP request message and the endpoint you want to invoke to the `call` method on your connection object, and then wait for it to return a SOAP response.

Overall, this is very simple and straightforward to use. Here are a couple of minor usage notes:

- The endpoint URL passed to the `connection.call` method can be either a string or a `java.net.URL`.
- Don't forget to close the connection when you're done with it, as you would a JDBC connection. You can close the connection right after you call it and still use the response it returns later.

Implementing the `SOAPConnection` class is optional; if your implementation does not support it, calling `SOAPConnectionFactory.newInstance` will throw an `UnsupportedOperationException`. Sun's SE 6 VM supports it.

5.17 Working with SOAP Actors

Problem

You want to specify the SOAP actor that should handle a certain aspect of your message.

Solution

Just create a regular SOAP header, add a header element to it, and call the `setActor` method on the header element.

Discussion

Attributes that appear as `SOAPHeaderElements` provide instructions on how a node should process a message. They allow you to indicate whether a message must be processed by a given node, how transactions should be managed, what kinds of policies apply to the message, and so forth.

In SOAP 1.2, the term *actor* has been replaced with *role*. The role, defined in section 5.2.2 of the specification, indicates a particular node to which a particular header block is assigned. The named node should process a message once it is received by that node.

Most SOAP messages are processed by a single node, called the Ultimate Receiver. This is the default actor if none is specified. A client sends a message to a service endpoint, which processes the contents of the message, and perhaps returns a response. It is possible, however, to create a series of nodes that process different parts of a received SOAP message, using a pipe and filter design. In this scenario, every node along a chain of SOAP handlers examines every header element to determine if any of the headers must be processed by a role that this node supports. If there is only one processor, that is by definition acting in the Ultimate Receiver role, and it does all of the processing.

The actor attribute is optional, and if it is not specified, the message will route directly to the Ultimate Receiver. SOAP actors and roles are identified by URIs. Each node in a processing path can support multiple roles.

As an example, suppose that an incoming message represents an invoice. Its `SOAPHeader` might define a variety of `SOAPHeaderElements` that each specify a different actor attribute that routes the message to different applications, such as customer management, inventory, accounts, or cross-cutting aspects such as logging and security. Once an intermediary processor receives a message, it processes the appropriate header blocks, removing the headers it has processed, and optionally adding new headers, and sends the message on. Ultimate Receivers simply process all headers and all body information and return a response.

Here is the basic construction for specifying an actor on a header:

```
//Create header
QName passwordQName = new QName(NS, "passwordHeader");
SOAPHeaderElement passwordHeader =
                  header.addHeaderElement(passwordQName);
passwordHeader.addTextNode("s3cr3t");
passwordHeader.setActor("http://example.com/authenticator");
```

```
//Set the Actor on it
passwordHeader.setActor("http://example.com/authenticator");
```

This code uses the `setActor` method on the header element, creating a SOAP envelope that looks like this:

```
<SOAP-ENV:Envelope
  xmlns:SOAP-ENV="http://schemas.xmlsoap.org/soap/envelope/">
<SOAP-ENV:Header>
  <passwordHeader xmlns="http://soacookbook.com/saaj"
    SOAP-ENV:actor="http://example.com/authenticator">
      s3cr3t
  </passwordHeader>
</SOAP-ENV:Header><SOAP-ENV:Body
```

Only the nodes in the message path that identify themselves with an actor value of *http://example.com/authenticator* will process the `passwordHeader` header element.

There is a special actor called `next`, whose URI value is *http://schemas.xmlsoap.org/soap/actor/next*. This indicates that the next recipient in the chain should process the message. Using next means that no matter what roles the next node in the processing path supports, it must process the message.

After a node processes a header, it must remove it from the SOAP message. Some developers don't like the idea of removing data from a message, as this can make it difficult to trace the history of a message and can disturb its integrity. So instead, they may choose to modify the existing header, which in effect removes the actual header that they did process, and adds one that no one else will process.

5.18 Asynchronous Invocation with Dispatch

Problem

You are using the SAAJ API's `Dispatch` class to invoke a web service, and you want to perform the invocation asynchronously.

Solution

Create your `Dispatch` object as you normally would, and instead of calling the `invoke` method, call `invokeAsync` using one of the two supplied methods:

```
Response<T> invokeAsync(T msg)
Future<?> invokeAsync(T msg, AsyncHandler<T> handler)
```

Here is an example:

```
Dispatch<SOAPMessage> dispatch =
    service.createDispatch(portQName, SOAPMessage.class,
                          Service.Mode.MESSAGE);

//Send the request and get the response
Response<Source> bookResponse = dispatch.invokeAsync(request);
```

Discussion

Other than the fact that you are getting the methods from the `Dispatch` object, the behavior of the responses for both polling and callbacks is the same as with an SEI. With this method, you haven't generated an SEI, but the work being done under the hood is the same, as JAX-WS reuses SAAJ.

> Remember that before you attempt to call `invokeAsync`, you need to enable asynchronous mappings on the WSDL using the `JAX-WS:bindings` element. Otherwise, your invocations may appear to succeed, but they won't actually be asynchronous. That is, they'll block, just like a normal call to `invoke`.

See Also

Recipe 6.18 to learn how to use the asynchronous methods and their return types in JAX-WS.

Recipe 7.14 to enable asynchronous invocations on the server side. The JAX-WS specification covers asynchronous bindings and other customizations in Chapter 8; you can read it at *http://jcp.org/aboutJava/communityprocess/pfd/jsr224/index.html*.

5.19 Validating Your Payload Against a Schema on the Client

Problem

You want to consume a web service whose schema defines constraints (such as min and max length of strings, or pattern restrictions using regular expressions), and you want your generated Java objects on the client to conform to that schema; however, when you use `wsimport`, the generated objects have "forgotten" the constraints. You want to do this in a portable way, without using vendor extensions.

Solution

Populate the Java objects in your client application as usual, and then create a JAXB `Marshaller` and set the schema reference on it. Then, when it's time to invoke the service, pass a populated Java object representing the generated parameter type to a `Dispatch` that uses the marshaler to populate the payload. JAXB will do the validation for you.

Discussion

The basic problem that this recipe addresses is this: you want to invoke a service whose schema defines constraints that your payloads must conform to, but those constraints are no longer present in Java objects that have been generated by JAXB from that schema. When it's time to invoke your service, there's nothing to ensure that the data populating your object actually matches the schema-defined constraints. You don't want to duplicate those constraints elsewhere, but you do want to make sure that your service is passed only valid objects that actually conform to the schema. So, you need a way to validate those objects. While you could hope that the service does validation (and it should), you don't want to incur unnecessary network overhead if someone just fat-fingered a phone number.

This recipe shows you how to do this by hand if you are not using the latest version of JAX-WS. If you are, however, it's easier to do it by using the `com.sun.xml.ws.developer.SchemaValidation` feature, specifying a handler for it, and passing that to your proxy. This is specific to Metro 1.1, however, and is not portable.

There are a few steps to doing this, so we'll take it step by step. This solution will use the schema and WSDL for the Credit Authorization service defined in Chapter 7.

This recipe is the client side of the Credit Authorization example using custom schema with JAXB-generated types from Recipe 7.12. You can also reference Recipe 2.16 for a discussion on schema validation in JAXB.

Here's an overview of what you'll do:

1. Import a copy of the schema into your local project. This is easy to do within NetBeans 6, which will snag all schemas referenced from a single WSDL. Alternatively, you can get them from a browser and copy them based on the schema location in the WSDL.
2. Generate and compile the Java types that are defined in the schema associated with the WSDL. Use these Java objects in your application.
3. Validate the Java objects during marshaling into XML, as shown in Recipe 2.16. Basically you do this by reading in the schema and attaching it to the JAXB Marshal object.
4. Attach the raw XML in a DOM object as the child of the body of a SOAP message that you create with SAAJ. Use `Dispatch<T>` to invoke your web service directly with the XML representation.
5. The SAX parser will throw any validation exceptions as `SAXParseExceptions` during marshaling, before the service is invoked. You can then handle those exceptions, probably by reporting them back to the client.

Let's first look at the JUnit 4.4 test, which you'll use as your service consumer. The list of imports required is retained for clarity. The test defines a physical path to the locally saved schema file that will be used for validation. That schema defines the `CreditCard`,

Name, and Authorization types that are used in request and response messages. These classes are generated from the WSDL into the com.soacookbook.ns.credit package using the wsimport tool.

The test will start off creating credit card and name objects and populating them just as you would with a client GUI. But instead of using the Service derivative that was also generated during import, you'll call your own validateAndInvoke method. It will use other methods to do the translation into XML manually using JAXB and then pass the payload into a method, so you can construct the SOAPMessage ourselves. The process at that point becomes a blackbox to the caller, and the SOAP invocation returns an Authorization object, just as it would had you used the JAX-WS proxy.

It is unusual to include such helpers within a test case; ideally these should be encapsulated within a client class. It is presented this way for simplicity.

```
package com.soacookbook.ch03.test;

import javax.xml.validation.Schema;
import javax.xml.validation.SchemaFactory;
import static org.junit.Assert.*;

import com.soacookbook.ns.credit.*;
import java.io.File;
import java.io.IOException;
import java.util.Calendar;
import java.util.GregorianCalendar;
import javax.xml.XMLConstants;
import javax.xml.bind.JAXBContext;
import javax.xml.bind.JAXBElement;
import javax.xml.bind.JAXBException;
import javax.xml.bind.Marshaller;
import javax.xml.bind.Unmarshaller;
import javax.xml.datatype.DatatypeFactory;
import javax.xml.datatype.XMLGregorianCalendar;
import javax.xml.datatype.DatatypeConfigurationException;
import javax.xml.namespace.QName;
import javax.xml.parsers.DocumentBuilder;
import javax.xml.parsers.DocumentBuilderFactory;
import javax.xml.parsers.ParserConfigurationException;
import javax.xml.soap.MessageFactory;
import javax.xml.soap.SOAPBody;
import javax.xml.soap.SOAPEnvelope;
import javax.xml.soap.SOAPException;
import javax.xml.soap.SOAPMessage;
import javax.xml.transform.stream.StreamSource;
import javax.xml.ws.Dispatch;
import javax.xml.ws.Service;
import javax.xml.ws.soap.SOAPBinding;
import org.apache.log4j.Logger;
```

```
import org.junit.*;
import org.w3c.dom.Document;
import org.xml.sax.SAXException;

/**
 * Tests that JAXB-generated objects validate against a schema
 * at runtime.
 */
public class SchemaValidateTest {
    private static final Logger LOGGER =
            Logger.getLogger(SchemaValidateTest.class);

    private static final String schemaFile =
            "C:/oreilly/soacookbook/code/" +
            "chapters/client/config/ch03/Credit.xsd";

//Tests that our schema constraints are not violated.
@Test
public void testCreditValidating() throws Exception {
    LOGGER.debug("Executing.");

    //JAXB-generated types from schema
    CreditCard card = new CreditCard();
    Name cardholder = new Name();
    cardholder.setFirstName("Eliza");
    cardholder.setLastName("Doolittle");
    card.setName(cardholder);
    //4222222222222222
    card.setCardNumber("4");

    //see setup method which creates this
    card.setExpirationDate(expiryDate);

    LOGGER.debug("Invoking Credit Authorizer Service.");
    //invoke service using SAAJ here:
    Authorization auth = validateAndInvoke(card);

    assertTrue(2500.0D == auth.getAmount());
}

//This is called by the test
private Authorization validateAndInvoke(CreditCard card){

    Authorization auth = new Authorization();

    try {
    //Create DOM from CreditCard obj and validate against schema
    Document domCC = marshalCC(card);

    LOGGER.debug("Got card. " + domCC);

    //Create SOAP Message from DOM
    SOAPMessage soapCC = createSoapMessage(domCC);

        //Dispatch SOAP Message: invoke svc
```

```
        SOAPMessage soapAuth = invoke(soapCC);

        //unmarshall back into Authorization object
        auth = unmarshal(soapAuth);

    } catch (JAXBException iae){
        LOGGER.warn("JAXB: Invalid data! ", iae);
    } catch (SAXException se){
        LOGGER.warn("SAX: Invalid data! " + se);
    }

    return auth;
}

/**
 * Creates a SOAP Envelope with a SOAP Body containing this
 * document as its child. */
public SOAPMessage createSoapMessage(Document document) {
    LOGGER.debug("Executing.");

    SOAPMessage message = null;
    try {
        message = MessageFactory.newInstance().createMessage();
        final SOAPEnvelope env = message.getSOAPPart().getEnvelope();
        final SOAPBody body = env.getBody();

        body.addDocument(document);
        message.saveChanges();

        LOGGER.debug("Created SOAP Message.");

    } catch(SOAPException se){
        LOGGER.error("Could not create SOAP message. ", se);
    }

    return message;
}

/**
 * Uses the previously created request message to call the
 * web service and return a response.
 */
public SOAPMessage invoke(SOAPMessage request) {
    LOGGER.debug("Executing.");

    String ns = "http://ns.soacookbook.com/credit";

    QName svcQName = new QName(ns, "CreditService");
    QName portQName = new QName(ns, "CreditAuthorizer");
    String wsdlUrl = "http://localhost:8080/soaCookbookWS/CreditService?wsdl";

    final Service service = Service.create(svcQName);
    service.addPort(portQName,
            SOAPBinding.SOAP11HTTP_BINDING, wsdlUrl);
    LOGGER.debug("Invoking Service: " + service.getServiceName() +
```

```
            ". Port: " + portQName + ". WSDL Location: " + wsdlUrl);

    final Dispatch<SOAPMessage> dispatch =
            service.createDispatch(portQName,
              SOAPMessage.class, Service.Mode.MESSAGE);

    //Call the Service with our message
    return dispatch.invoke(request);
}

@SuppressWarnings(value = "unchecked")
public static Authorization unmarshal(SOAPMessage soapMsg){
    LOGGER.debug("Executing.");

    String pkg = "com.soacookbook.ns.credit";
    Authorization auth = null;
    try {
        JAXBContext ctx = JAXBContext.newInstance(pkg);
        Unmarshaller unmarshaller = ctx.createUnmarshaller();

        //Show returned SOAP Message
        soapMsg.writeTo(System.out);

        //Get the payload of the response
        Document doc =
                soapMsg.getSOAPBody().extractContentAsDocument();

        //turn DOM document paydload into JAXBElement
        JAXBElement<Authorization> el =
                (JAXBElement<Authorization>) unmarshaller.unmarshal(doc);

        //extract the payload as object
        auth = el.getValue();

        LOGGER.debug("DOM AUTH: " + auth);

    } catch (IOException ioe) {
        ioe.printStackTrace();
    } catch (SOAPException se) {
        se.printStackTrace();
    } catch (JAXBException je) {
        je.printStackTrace();
    }
    return auth;
}

private static Document marshalCC(final CreditCard card)
        throws JAXBException, SAXException {

    Document doc = null;
    try {
        Class[] clazz = {CreditCard.class};
        JAXBContext ctx = JAXBContext.newInstance(clazz);

        String ns = "http://ns.soacookbook.com/credit";
```

```
        QName qName = new QName(ns, "creditCard", "");
        JAXBElement<CreditCard> root =
           new JAXBElement<CreditCard>(
                qName, CreditCard.class, card);

        Marshaller m = ctx.createMarshaller();

        SchemaFactory sf = SchemaFactory.newInstance(
            XMLConstants.W3C_XML_SCHEMA_NS_URI);

        Schema schema = sf.newSchema(
            new StreamSource(new File(schemaFile)));
        m.setSchema(schema);

        DocumentBuilderFactory dbf =
                DocumentBuilderFactory.newInstance();
        DocumentBuilder db = dbf.newDocumentBuilder();
        doc = db.newDocument();

        m.marshal(root, doc);

        LOGGER.debug("DOM object has elements: " +
                doc.getChildNodes().getLength());

    } catch (ParserConfigurationException pce) {
        pce.printStackTrace();
    }

    return doc;
}
```

The `createSoapMessage` method serves to accept the content of the `CreditCard` object as a DOM document and add it as the only child payload of the SOAP message you construct. Once you have a complete SOAP message, you pass that to the invoke method, which will set up the mechanism to actually call the service.

You build `QNames` that match the port and the service as defined in the specified WSDL, and then create a service, adding the known port to it. You specify SOAP 1.1 as the protocol the service will be bound to. Finally, the dispatch is created with a type parameter of SOAP message; you will pass it your constructed SOAP message as the request, and it will return a value of type `SOAPMessage` as the response that will contain the authorization XML.

The marshal and unmarshal methods are mirror images of one another, with the marshal handling Java to XML and the unmarshal handling XML to Java. So, in addition to validating outgoing requests, you can use the same technique to validate response payloads in the unmarshal method. However, you have to be careful doing so because if your response is actually a SOAP fault instead of a poorly formed authorization, you will get JAXB errors because it will find a child it was not expecting in the SOAP body.

If you invoke the service with data that is not valid given the schema constraints, you get a `SAXParseException` that has the following message:

```
org.xml.sax.SAXParseException: cvc-pattern-valid:
Value '4' is not facet-valid with respect to pattern '\d{16}' for type 'CardNumber'.
```

You've tried to invoke the service with a credit card number of 4 digits, but the constraint dictates that you must pass 16 digits for it to be valid.

This is a portable and flexible way to work with your objects for validation against a schema.

It is relatively straightforward to modify this solution to make it a more general case to handle any kind of request and response. That is, here you have hardcoded the schema location, package name, class names, and `QNames` for port and service into the methods. These could easily be passed into the method to create a schema validation handler that would work for any schema, object, and service.

5.20 Providing a Web Service with SAAJ

Problem

You want to use SAAJ on the server side to return a response to a SOAP request.

Solution

Create a regular servlet and use the SAAJ API to create a SOAP message response, much as you do on the client. This is rarely done in practice because annotations make it so much easier and less brittle to do. But there are always times when you want to do things by hand, or perhaps experiment to see what JAX-WS is doing under the hood.

Discussion

Here are the basic steps to follow to create a SAAJ-based service:

1. Create a regular web application structure as you would to create any WAR.
2. Create a servlet class that extends `javax.servlet.http.HttpServlet`.
3. In a static constructor, instantiate a static `javax.xml.soap.MessageFactory` field.
4. Override the `doPost` method, and create the SOAP message for the response using SAAJ.
5. Return the response in the servlet's output stream using the `SOAPMessage.writeTo` method.

In this example, we'll walk through creating a Hello World type application. To keep it as simple as possible, you are just going to invoke the servlet with a regular HTTP request, but return a SOAP response.

The code listing in Example 5-12 shows the servlet that implements the SAAJ SOAP provider. There really is no magic here at all. You're just using standard SAAJ stuff that you've seen throughout this chapter, and building a regular servlet that returns the SOAP message as a response.

Example 5-12. Servlet SOAP provider

```
package saaj.provider;

import java.io.IOException;
import java.io.InputStream;
import java.io.OutputStream;
import java.util.Enumeration;
import javax.servlet.ServletException;
import javax.servlet.http.HttpServlet;
import javax.servlet.http.HttpServletRequest;
import javax.servlet.http.HttpServletResponse;
import javax.xml.namespace.QName;
import javax.xml.soap.MessageFactory;
import javax.xml.soap.MimeHeaders;
import javax.xml.soap.Name;
import javax.xml.soap.SOAPBody;
import javax.xml.soap.SOAPBodyElement;
import javax.xml.soap.SOAPEnvelope;
import javax.xml.soap.SOAPException;
import javax.xml.soap.SOAPMessage;
import javax.xml.soap.SOAPPart;

/**
 * SAAJ servlet to act as web service provider.
 */
public class SAAJProviderServlet extends HttpServlet {

    static MessageFactory mf;
    static {
        try {
            mf = MessageFactory.newInstance();
        } catch (Exception ex) {
            ex.printStackTrace();
        }
    }

    @Override
    protected void doPost(HttpServletRequest request,
            HttpServletResponse response)
            throws ServletException, IOException {

        System.out.println("\nGot Http Request: " +
                request.getMethod());

        try {

            SOAPMessage reply = createReply(request);

            if (reply != null) {
                response.setStatus(HttpServletResponse.SC_OK);
                response.setHeader("X-Powered-By", "SOA Cookbook");
```

```java
                response.setContentType("text/xml");
                //Log for debug:
                System.out.println("\nSending Response:\n");
                reply.writeTo(System.out);

                //Return response
                OutputStream os = response.getOutputStream();
                reply.writeTo(os);
                os.flush();
                os.close();
            } else {
                response.setStatus(HttpServletResponse.SC_BAD_REQUEST);
            }
        } catch (Exception ex){
            throw new ServletException("SAAJ could not " +
                    "understand request. " + ex.getMessage());
        }
    }

    private SOAPMessage createReply(HttpServletRequest request)
            throws SOAPException, IOException {

        String ns = "urn:soacookbook:saaj";

        //Get all HTTP Headers
        MimeHeaders headers = getHeaders(request);

        //Get incoming request as stream
        InputStream is = request.getInputStream();

        //use headers and request stream to create SOAP Msg
        SOAPMessage reqMsg = mf.createMessage(headers, is);

        //Create new message for response
        SOAPMessage msg = mf.createMessage();
        SOAPPart part = msg.getSOAPPart();
        SOAPEnvelope env = part.getEnvelope();
        SOAPBody body = env.getBody();

        //Add Namespace
        env.createName("message", "soa", ns);

        //Put data in response
        Name bn = env.createName("message", "soa", ns);
        SOAPBodyElement be = body.addBodyElement(bn);

        //Inspect request and get data from it as necessary...
        String name = request.getParameter("name");
        be.addTextNode("Hello, " + name + "!");

        msg.saveChanges();

        return msg;
    }
```

```
    //Here we inspect HTTP Request headers
    @SuppressWarnings("unchecked")
    private MimeHeaders getHeaders(HttpServletRequest request)
                        throws SOAPException {
        MimeHeaders headers = new MimeHeaders();
        Enumeration<String> names = request.getHeaderNames();
        while (names.hasMoreElements()){
            String key = names.nextElement();
            String value = request.getHeader(key);
            headers.addHeader(key, value);
            System.out.println("Added MIME Header: " +
                    key + "=" + value);
        }
        return headers;
    }

    @Override
    public void init() throws ServletException {
        super.init();
    }

    @Override
    protected void doGet(HttpServletRequest request,
            HttpServletResponse response)
            throws ServletException, IOException {

        doPost(request, response);
    }

    public SAAJProviderServlet() { }
}
```

Because you're just clicking a link, the HTTP method will come in as a GET, and you'll just forward that to the doPost override. You do some basic housekeeping here, such as setting the content MIME type and setting the HTTP status code to 200. And then you do some real-world things, like adding a custom header that can be useful in a chain.

Here's the real meat and potatoes of this example: you can use the request to get an input stream that can be used in constructing the SOAP message for the response. You'll have access to the headers and data in the request, and can use them to base your response on as necessary.

For the response, you set the content type to "text/xml" for a SOAP message. If you kept the default of "text/html", the browser would attempt to interpret the response as HTML. For this example, that would mean that it would show only your greeting in the browser because it would suppress the tags it doesn't understand (which in the case of SOAP is all of them). By changing the content type to "text/xml", the entire message will show in the browser. Of course, in the real world, you probably wouldn't have a use case for doing that, and you might instead be calling this servlet in another manner and be prepared to handle a SOAP response.

Finally, the `SOAPMessage.writeTo` method is used to send the constructed response to the output stream retrieved from the `HttpServletResponse`. That sends the response containing the SOAP message and all of your regular HTTP header information back to the client.

To invoke your web service, you'll cheat a little bit. That is, you won't send it a SOAP request, but rather create a quick JSP that invokes the servlet with a link. The link will pass the servlet a person's name as a request parameter, which you'll use to return a SOAP response containing a classic greeting.

So your JSP looks like this:

```
<html>
  <body>
    <a href="SAAJProviderServlet?name=Eben">CLICK ME</a>
  </body>
</html>
```

There's no real SOAP client and no handling of a SOAP response here, just a link that calls the servlet. This chapter provides many examples of getting a SOAP response, so we'll just stick to the server here.

The servlet is deployed with a mapping in the *web.xml* that is easily invoked relative to the JSP (they're in the same WAR in this example):

```
<web-app version="2.5" xmlns="http://java.sun.com/xml/ns/javaee"
  xmlns:xsi="http://www.w3.org/2001/XMLSchema-instance"
  xsi:schemaLocation="http://java.sun.com/xml/ns/javaee
      http://java.sun.com/xml/ns/javaee/web-app_2_5.xsd">
  <servlet>
    <servlet-name>SAAJProviderServlet</servlet-name>
    <servlet-class>saaj.provider.SAAJProviderServlet</servlet-class>
    <load-on-startup>1</load-on-startup>
  </servlet>
  <servlet-mapping>
    <servlet-name>SAAJProviderServlet</servlet-name>
    <url-pattern>/SAAJProviderServlet</url-pattern>
  </servlet-mapping>
...
```

Clicking the link gives you this response in the browser:

```
HTTP/1.x 200 OK
X-powered-by: SOA Cookbook
Server: Sun Java System Application Server 9.1_02
Content-Type: text/xml
Transfer-Encoding: chunked
Date: Fri, 25 Jul 2008 18:21:21 GMT

<SOAP-ENV:Envelope
xmlns:SOAP-ENV="http://schemas.xmlsoap.org/soap/envelope/">
<SOAP-ENV:Header/>
<SOAP-ENV:Body>
<soa:message xmlns:soa="urn:soacookbook:saaj">
  Hello, Eben!
```

```
</soa:message>
</SOAP-ENV:Body>
</SOAP-ENV:Envelope>
```

The SOAP message contains your happy greeting, and if you dump the entire contents of the message, you see your user-defined HTTP header.

5.21 Sending and Receiving SOAP Faults

Problem

You want to deal with a web service that has returned a SOAP fault to your SAAJ client.

Solution

Use the SAAJ fault classes to work with the data.

Discussion

When a web service provider throws an exception or error, a SOAP fault is generated. This bears obvious similarity to exceptions in Java, such as details regarding the exception, human-readable explanations, and codes.

But there are a number of differences to be aware of. To begin with, there is no linguistic structural mechanism surrounding the use of faults as there is with Java exceptions. That is, there is no try-catch mechanism. A fault *replaces* the body content of the SOAP response; therefore, the body element must contain the fault as its only child. Clients must then be prepared to read a fault from the body in much the same way they are prepared to read the data expected on a successful invocation. What this means is that the fault is simply data in SOAP. It cannot reroute or stop processing the way a Java exception can. It is just a message, the same as anything else.

If the message exchange is request-reply, the fault message is returned to the caller as a type of `soap:Fault`. If the invocation is one-way, the fault is not returned to the caller.

The only possible child elements of `soap:Fault` in SOAP 1.1 are the following:

`faultstring`
: A required element. It provides a human-readable explanation of the fault.

`faultactor`
: A required element in the event that an actor is specified. If no actors are specified, the node is considered the Ultimate Receiver, in which case this element is optional. It is specified by a URI that identifies the actor causing the fault.

`detail`
: A required element if the error is related to the processing of the SOAP body, in which case it provides details concerning what went wrong.

`faultcode`
: A required element in a Fault. It must be a fully qualified name (that is, it must contain a prefix and local part).

The SOAP 1.1 specification defines four fault codes, and they are listed in Table 5-1.

Table 5-1. SOAP 1.1 fault codes

Local name	Purpose
Client (called Sender in SOAP 1.2)	The node processing the SOAP message found that the message was improperly formed, or did not contain sufficient data to complete processing.
Server (called Receiver in SOAP 1.2)	There is nothing wrong with the message itself, but the node throwing the fault was unable to process the message due to some problematic condition with the receiver. This generally means that the same message can be sent again later, and that the receiver may be able to process it at that point.
`MustUnderstand`	The node throwing the fault doesn't understand part of the message that a header in the message asserts that it should.
`VersionMismatch`	The node throwing the fault expected a valid envelope containing the proper namespace and local name, but found something else.

The only possible child elements of `soap:Fault` in SOAP 1.2 are the following:

`Reason`
: Provides a human-readable explanation of the fault

`Node`
: Indicates the node that was processing the message when the fault occurred

`Role`
: Indicates the role in which the processor was acting when the fault occurred

`Detail`
: Carries application-specific error information, and may be used for additional explanation of fault codes used

`Code`
: Classifies faults according to one of several local names and provides a context for the detail items that may follow

Of these, only `Code` and `Reason` are mandatory. SOAP 1.2 defines one additional fault code than SOAP 1.1, as you can see in Table 5-2. You'll note that some of the codes have survived to SOAP 1.2, and others have been renamed.

Table 5-2. SOAP 1.2 fault codes

Local name	Purpose
`DataEncodingUnknown`	SOAP 1.2 only. The node throwing the fault can't read the data encoding used by the message.
`Sender`	Called `Client` in SOAP 1.1.
`Receiver`	Called `Server` in SOAP 1.1.
`MustUnderstand`	Same as SOAP 1.1.
`VersionMismatch`	Same as SOAP 1.1.

Sending a fault

Now that you're familiar with the basic structure of a fault, let's look at how to put one together on the server side.

The basic idea is to get the body from the message, and call the `addFault` method. You can use additional methods defined on the `SOAPFault` object to add a name, code, actor, and fault string, as shown here:

```
//SOAP 1.1
Name codeName = soapFactory.createName("Server", "",
                    SOAPConstants.URI_NS_SOAP_ENVELOPE);
fault.setFaultCode(codeName);
fault.setFaultActor("http://soacookbook.com/books");
fault.setFaultString("The remote susbsytem host is unavailable.");
```

Getting fault information

Because of the lack of structured exception handling, and the fact that fault content replaces body content, you need a way to check if a fault occurred. To do so, use the convenience method, `SOAPBody.hasFault`:

```
SOAPBody body = responseMessage.getSOAPBody();
if (body.hasFault()) {
  SOAPFault fault = body.getFault();

  Name code = fault.getFaultCodeAsName();
  String string = fault.getFaultString();
  String actor = fault.getFaultActor();
}
```

If this check determines that you have received a fault, you can retrieve the contents of the fault object using the `body.getFault` method. Then use the various accessor methods to get the code, string, and actor values from the fault.

There are a few different methods regarding the fault code.

Getting fault details

Recall that the SOAP fault will contain details in the form of a `javax.xml.soap.Detail` object and one or more `DetailEntry` objects *only* in the event that the node was not able to process the contents of the body. `Detail` objects are containers for `DetailEntry` objects. There are only three real methods available on `Detail`; the first gets all of the `DetailEntry` objects it contains, while the others let you create and add a `DetailEntry` object to a detail, using either a `Name` or a `QName`:

```
Detail d = body.getFault().getDetail();

Iterator<DetailEntry> it = d.getDetailEntries();
while (it.hasNext()) {
    DetailEntry e = it.next();
    System.out.println("Detail Entry = " + e.getValue());
}
```

Here you get the detail object from the fault so that you can iterate the list of entries. Back on the server side, entries get created as shown here:

```
QName name = new QName("http://example.com/quotes",
                       "getQuote", "e");

//Create the DetailEntry and add it
d.addDetailEntry(name);
```

In this listing, we've created a fully qualified name to represent the detail entry. This method both creates and adds the entry.

See Also

Recipe 5.20 to check out the code listing if you want to test this from a server point of view, and modify it to return your fault under certain circumstances.

Summary

In this chapter, we looked at several different ways to put together SOAP messages using the SAAJ API and create and invoke web services with them. Now you have an XML-level view of working with SOAP-based services. Next, we'll see how to use the JAX-WS API to take away some of the boilerplate code and respond more quickly to service description changes.

CHAPTER 6

Creating Web Service Applications with JAX-WS

6.0 Introduction

The SAAJ API, introduced in Chapter 5, offers a powerful, flexible way to work with web services at a low level. The Java API for XML Web Services (JAX-WS) is a high-level API for consuming and providing web services. This chapter introduces JAX-WS and shows you how to use it for a wide variety of practical tasks.

JAX-WS in Relation to Other APIs

JAX-WS replaces the older JAX-RPC API. Unlike SAAJ, JAX-WS doesn't require you to know very much about XML or WSDL. The entire XML layer is hidden from developers, who can instead just work with objects generated by web services tools that come with Java SE 6 and EE 5. These objects encapsulate all of the work of creating SOAP messages, invoking the service, and parsing responses, hiding significant complexity from developers. This can be convenient, and can make client maintenance much easier.

JAX-WS actually is built on top of SAAJ, using it under the hood to do its parsing and communication work. As you know, a web service as represented in a WSDL will define XML types for each of the message parts used in service requests and responses. In order to create object representations of these types, you need a binding language to convert (marshal) from Java to XML and back again. In the older API, this was done directly within JAX-RPC, which defined its own conversion mechanism. However, this was later deemed to complicate the specification, and Java to XML conversion came to be viewed as something that deserved a standalone specification. So instead of defining its own such mechanism as JAX-RPC did, JAX-WS uses the external JAXB 2.0 (Java API for XML Binding) spec. JAX-WS supports message-oriented and RPC-oriented web services.

Different Java EE vendors have implemented JAX-WS. The reference implementation, called Metro, was introduced in Recipe 4.2, and provides a number of other features, including implementations of key WS-* specifications that support, in particular, interoperability, security, and reliable messaging. JAX-WS also supports WS-Basic Profile 1.1, which is a standard that service implementations can conform to in order to ensure interoperability across platforms.

Three Approaches

There are three different ways to approach developing applications with JAX-WS:

The WSDL to Java approach
: Point to a WSDL and use tools such as `wsimport` to generate portable web service artifacts.

The Java to WSDL approach
: Create a Service Endpoint Interface as Java source files. Use them as inputs to generate the WSDL and other required portable artifacts.

The Start from Java and WSDL approach
: This can be a smart way of working. Write Java classes and let `wsgen` create WSDL and schema for you. Then save the generated artifacts locally, modify them as necessary, and point your service implementation to them via the `wsdlLocation` attribute of the `@WebService` annotation. This means you have to keep your classes in synch with your schema and WSDL, but it puts you in the sweet spot that maximizes convenience and control.

With any approach, JAX-WS will generate significant amount of code for you, and reduce the challenges of dealing with what was designed to be machine-readable code. Moreover, these generated artifacts are portable across vendors. As with EJBs or any other "portable" Java artifact, there can be slight variations in generated code that either do not conform entirely to the specification, or do conform to the specification but touch on an area of the spec that was slightly ambiguous or left the implementation decision up to vendors. In these cases, you can have portability issues. So if that's a concern for you, then you may consider taking an extra look at the generated artifacts for potential areas of conflict.

Annotations

JAX-WS makes heavy use of Java 5 annotations. Therefore, the source code that you write will be fairly slim, and then tools will process your annotations to create the infrastructure artifacts necessary to run or consume the service. The generated artifacts themselves, including clients, services, and JAXB 2.0 value classes, all are heavily annotated as well.

That has certain ramifications for developers. For example, because annotations don't allow runtime arguments, you have to work around the annotation attributes if you need to specify something different than what was generated. There are recipes in this chapter that show you how to do that with certain items, such as changing the WSDL location on a client proxy. But there are also ways to deal with this limitation that are provided by the general framework. For example, you can use handlers to modify outbound messages if necessary.

Service Endpoints

A web service endpoint is a server-side component that receives SOAP messages, does some processing, and returns a SOAP message result. Because they execute on an application server, there are two types of service endpoint components you can create:

A servlet
: Note that while documentation refers to this type of web service implementation as a "servlet" implementation, this is actually an annotated POJO (Plain Old Java Object) class, and *not* a class that extends the `javax.servlet.http.HttpServlet` class. This kind of service implementation is packaged in a WAR and deployed just as you would a servlet, but the actual servlet implementation will be provided by JAX-WS, which handles the HTTP requests and responses, translates the SOAP messages, and is multithreaded. In some web containers, you need to provide a regular servlet mapping in *web.xml* as you would for a regular servlet. In Glassfish, you can just package the class in a WAR and deploy it; it will provide the mapping for you at deploy time.

A stateless session bean
: This is the only kind of EJB that can be implemented as a web service. As with the servlet version, you consume your EJB web service endpoint via a WSDL interface, HTTP, and SOAP messages, all of which is handled by JAX-WS.

So you do not need an EJB container to provide a web service if you go the regular "servlet" route.

Packages and Classes

The core JAX-WS APIs are in the `javax.xml.ws` package and its subpackages, which include several packages related to HTTP, SOAP, and using handlers.

JAX-WS can be found in two packages, the primary package being `javax.jws`. This package is small, but mighty, consisting of no classes, no interfaces, six annotations, and a single enum. The annotations here are the primary means of creating portable web services:

```
package com.soacookbook;

import javax.jws.WebService;
import javax.jws.WebMethod;

@WebService public class Hello {
  public String sayHello(String name) {
    return "Hello, " + name";
```

```
    }
}
```

We'll get into details throughout this chapter, but for now, this should give you an idea of the basic programming model.

The second JAX-WS package is `javax.jws.soap`, which contains no classes, no interfaces, one annotation, and four enums (there are actually four annotations in that package, but three are deprecated and should not be used). This package is used by developers to override defaults with alternate values for binding to SOAP (the concrete aspect of the WSDL) when creating a web service.

Here's an example. The Hello web service will use a SOAP style, use, and parameter style of "Document/Literal Wrapped" by default if you don't specify these three attributes otherwise. If you want to override this, you would use the annotations in the `javax.jws.soap` package. Here's an example:

```
package com.soacookbook;

import javax.jws.WebService;
import javax.jws.WebMethod;

@WebService public class Hello {

  @SOAPBinding(parameterStyle=SOAPBinding.ParameterStyle.BARE)
  public String sayHello(String name) {
    return "Hello, " + name";
  }
}
```

Here you specified a non-default parameter style (the manner in which parameters will be packaged in SOAP messages). So you indicate the only choice other than the default of "document", which is "bare", and the enum will modify the generated WSDL to conform to your wishes. Again, the details of what's happening here or why you would want to choose a "bare" parameter style aren't important for now; this should just give you a taste of how to use this package.

This chapter takes a close look at JAX-WS and how to use it to create web services. Enjoy!

6.1 Calling a Web Service from the Command Line

Problem

You want a quick and simple way to call a web service that is already deployed.

Solution

Follow these basic steps:

1. Make sure that you are running Java SE 6.
2. Use the `wsimport` tool by passing it the location of your service's WSDL. This will generate classes that conform to the WSDL messages, and convenience classes to invoke it.
3. Create a class with a main method that will invoke the service use the generated classes.
4. Compile and run the program.

Discussion

These steps represent an easy way to call an existing web service using JAX-WS. You can then transfer this basic idea onto more sophisticated Java projects. By doing everything from scratch, outside any IDE, you can better understand how the pieces all work. Let's follow the steps to create the client and call a service.

Here you'll use a service that is available publicly for free at *http://WebServiceX.net*. If you are testing against another service, such as one within your own organization, just replace the WSDL location string. The `wsimport` tool will then of course generate a different set of classes that match your WSDL, and you'll have to put the objects together in a way that creates a meaningful message for that service. But the basic idea is always the same.

The web service you'll invoke is described at *http://www.webservicex.net/WCF/ServiceDetails.aspx?SID=44*. It's called USA Weather Forecast: you pass it a zip code, and it returns a forecast. I chose this service because while it accepts only a simple string, it returns a composite object consisting of a variety of classes, which gives `wsimport` more to do.

Now let's walk through the steps and put it all together.

Verifying wsimport

To verify that you're running Java SE 6, which makes the `wsimport` tool available, open a command terminal and run the following command, which should print a version number of JAX-WS:

```
$ wsimport -version
JAX-WS RI 2.1.1 in JDK 6
```

As long as your version number is 2.0 or higher, you should be in business. If you don't have `wsimport` on your path, you won't get a version number, but rather an error indicating that the OS couldn't find the program. In that case, you'll need to either add it to an environment variable or invoke the program using the complete path.

Generating client code

Now you'll point to the WSDL and generate the portable client-side artifacts you can use to construct a SOAP message that the service is expecting. By using JAX-WS to do this instead of SAAJ, you avoid having to deal with XML directly.

Create a new directory on your filesystem to contain your program. Mine will be *~/weatherTest*.

Now navigate to this directory in your terminal. Create a directory called *gen* under it. This is where you'll tell `wsimport` to put the generated classes based on the WSDL.

This web service is written in .NET, which presents a good opportunity to test the promise of web services. But its WSDL is written in a non-standard manner, using HTTP POST and GET operations, without specifying SOAP bindings. So you will likely see some warnings when you run `wsimport`.

For this web service, the WSDL is located at *http://www.webservicex.net/WeatherForecast.asmx?wsdl*. Here is the command to generate the client objects:

```
wsimport -verbose -d gen -extension
-keep http://www.webservicex.net/WeatherForecast.asmx?wsdl
```

Using the `-keep` option retains the Java source files so that you can examine how the objects are put together to make a request. The `-d` option allows you to specify the directory where JAX-WS should put the generated files. Running this command should create about a dozen Java files that correspond to the types defined in the schema.

Creating the client class

With a text editor, create a Java source file that puts together the objects required to make a message that conforms to the WSDL. This is shown in Example 6-1.

Example 6-1. Client class that invokes the weather forecast service at WebServiceX.net

```
import net.webservicex.*;
import java.math.*;

/*
 Calls the forecast service at WebServiceX.net.
*/
public class WeatherClient {
 public static void main(String...arg) {
    System.out.println("Invoking...");
    WeatherForecast service = new WeatherForecast();
    WeatherForecastSoap port = service.getWeatherForecastSoap();

    //Invoke Service and Get Result
    WeatherForecasts forecasts = port.getWeatherByZipCode("85255");
```

```
        //Use the generated objects in the result
        String placeName = forecasts.getPlaceName();

        ArrayOfWeatherData arr = forecasts.getDetails();
        WeatherData data = arr.getWeatherData().get(0);

        System.out.println("Place=" + placeName);
        System.out.println("Day=" + data.getDay());
        System.out.println("High Temp (F)=" + data.getMaxTemperatureF());

        System.out.println("All done.");
    }
}
```

The client class creates an instance of the service proxy, and gets the port that has the business method we're interested in. When you call `getWeatherByZipCode`, the service is invoked, and that returns the result if everything goes well. Now all you have to do is compile and run the client.

The best way to start putting a JAX-WS client together is to begin with the service and work your way backwards to the individual data points. First, find the class that extends `javax.xml.ws.Service`, and use it to get the appropriate port. That will tell you what type is returned by the port. That type will be a domain object that will expose accessor (getter) methods that you can inspect to get the information you want. In your case, this service returns much more data than we're showing for this example.

Compiling the client

To compile the client, use the following command:

```
$ javac -cp gen WeatherClient.java
```

Running the client

On Linux, run the client using the following command:

```
$ java -cp gen:. WeatherClient
```

On Windows systems, you need to use the ; character to separate paths, so replace the preceding with:

```
gen;
```

This will produce a result such as the following:

```
Invoking...
Place=SCOTTSDALE
Day=Tuesday, July 29, 2008
High Temp (F)=94
All done.
```

You can follow these same basic steps to invoke any web service using JAX-WS.

6.2 Using JAX-WS Annotation Name Properties

Problem

You want to know what the impact of changing certain annotation properties that refer to names of some kind will be on your overall design.

Solution

Read the following Discussion section.

Discussion

In general, naming can be tricky with JAX-WS. There are many properties of web service name variations that do not directly indicate how setting their values will impact your service and clients, and even the specification does not clearly and state the practical ramifications of populating certain JAX-WS annotation properties. The listings below should clarify some of the most common cases.

WebService.targetNamespace

```
@WebService(targetNamespace="http://ns.soacookbook.com",
  name="CatalogService")
```

The `@WebService` annotation indicates that a Java class implements a web service. If used on an interface, it serves as a web service interface definition. A service endpoint interface maps to a `wsdl:portType` element. In a `@WebService` annotation, the `targetNamespace` property changes the namespace your service will be defined in. The WSDL for a class with the annotation just shown reads like this:

```
<definitions targetNamespace="http://ns.soacookbook.com"
  name="CatalogService">
```

If you do not specify a `WebService.targetNamespace` property, the default used in its place will be the reverse of the package name. For example:

```
<definitions targetNamespace="http://ch03.soacookbook.com/"
```

WebService.name

```
@WebService(targetNamespace="http://ns.soacookbook.com",
  name="CatalogService")
```

In a `@WebService` annotation, the `name` property changes the *port* name on your generated `@WebServiceClient` classes. As a consequence, the following method will become available on your service client:

```
service.getCatalogServicePort
```

The element `@javax.jws.WebService.name` cannot be used with the element `@javax.jws.WebService.endpointInterface`.

If you do not specify a @WebService.name property, it will default to the class name. For example:

```
@WebService(serviceName="CatalogService", targetNamespace="http://ns.soacookbook.com")
public class CatalogWS implements Catalog { ... }
```

requires client code like this:

```
private CatalogService service;
CatalogWS port = service.getCatalogWSPort();
```

It is important to differentiate between the generated stub, which is an interface annotated with @WebService (and which gets its name from the value of the name property in the @WebService annotation on the class that actually does implement the business logic of the web service), and the actual class implementation, if you are operating with a web service client and provider in the same JVM, as you might with a servlet.

WebService.serviceName

This property defines the URL of your deployed service. For example, the following @WebService annotation above a class:

```
package com.soacookbook.ch03;
//...
@WebService(serviceName="CatalogServiceSN",
    targetNamespace="http://ns.soacookbook.com")
```

will generate the following deployed URL:

```
http://localhost:8080/soaCookbookWS/CatalogServiceSN?wsdl
```

This also modifies the name of the generated service class. That same @WebService annotation also generates the following when you execute wsimport:

```
@WebServiceClient(name = "CatalogServiceSN",
targetNamespace = "http://ns.soacookbook.com",
wsdlLocation = "http://localhost:8080/soaCookbookWS/CatalogServiceSN?wsdl")
public class CatalogServiceSN
    extends Service { ... }
```

Also, notice that it is used to populate the value of the @WebServiceClient.name annotation property. And though it doesn't make much difference to the client coder, it also is used to define the name of the constant used in the generated service class:

```
private final static URL CATALOGSERVICESN_WSDL_LOCATION;
```

The annotation property @WebService.serviceName is not allowed on an interface.

WebService.portName

This property changes the name of the method that returns the service implementation stub from the generated service class. It has no effect within an interface. The following:

```
@WebService(serviceName="CatalogServiceSN",
  portName="CatalogPort",
  targetNamespace="http://ns.soacookbook.com")
```

will create this:

```
public class CatalogServiceSN extends Service {

  @WebEndpoint(name = "CatalogPort")
  public CatalogWS getCatalogPort() { ...}
```

Its `QName` (qualified name) in the WSDL is no longer `CatalogWSPort`, which is the default name assigned by concatenating the service implementation class name with "Port". The WSDL now looks like this:

```
<service name="CatalogServiceSN">
<port name="CatalogPort" binding="tns:CatalogPortBinding">
```

`WebService.portName` has no effect when indicated on an interface.

Service Ref with dependency injection

Using the `@WebServiceRef` annotation, you can easily refer to a web service from within a container-managed component, such as a servlet. Just use dependency injection as you normally would:

```
@WebServiceRef
private CatalogServiceSN catalogServiceIT;
```

If this annotated field is included in a servlet called "InjectionServlet," at deploy time, something like the following is automatically generated into *web.xml* for you:

```
<service-ref>
<display-name>com.soacookbook.ch03.InjectionServlet/catalogServiceIT
</display-name>
<service-ref-name>com.soacookbook.ch03.InjectionServlet/catalogServiceIT
</service-ref-name>
<service-interface>com.soacookbook.ch03.CatalogServiceSN
</service-interface>
<wsdl-file>http://localhost:8080/soaCookbookWS/CatalogServiceSN?wsdl
</wsdl-file>
<service-qname xmlns:service-qname_ns__="http://ns.soacookbook.com">
service-qname_ns__:CatalogServiceSN</service-qname>
<injection-target>
  <injection-target-class>com.soacookbook.ch03.InjectionServlet
  </injection-target-class>
  <injection-target-name>catalogServiceIT</injection-target-name>
```

```
    </injection-target>
    </service-ref>
```

The `injection-target-name` element here is based on the variable name you give your service. In your invoking code, we've defined a variable named `catalogServiceIT` in a class called `com.soacookbook.ch03.InjectionServlet`. So the injection target gets populated appropriately in the generated *web.xml*. Beyond the `<service-ref>` element, this is not particular to web services, but is simply how Java EE 5 injection works with servlets. While you can do web services for a very long time and not need to know that this is being generated in this manner for you, such knowledge may be helpful in a debugging effort.

6.3 Invoking the Simplest Web Service

Problem

You deployed the Hello web service using `Endpoint` in Recipe 4.4, and now you want to call it.

Solution

This solution assumes that you have already deployed the web service according to Recipe 4.4. Recall that this service is deployed within the HTTP server that ships with JDK 6, and not to a container.

To call the web service, create a URL that points to the WSDL location, and then create a `QName` object to represent the name of the service as specified in the name attribute of the WSDL's `<service>` element. Then create a service instance based on those two locators. The service instance gives you a representation of the port, which corresponds to the interface. You can think of this process as being somewhat analogous to getting the business interface from an EJB Home. This is the same process you would do if you had used the `wsimport` tool.

Once you have the port type, which will be your interface type, you can start invoking business methods. Example 6-2 shows a complete listing.

Example 6-2. Hello web service client, HelloClient.java

```
package com.soacookbook.ch03;

import java.net.URL;
import java.util.Iterator;
import javax.xml.namespace.QName;
import javax.xml.ws.Service;

public class HelloClient {
  public static void main(String[] args) throws Exception {

    //Specify the WSDL
```

```
        URL wsdlLocation = new URL("http://localhost:9999/hello?wsdl");

        //Create a Qualified Name that represents the
        //namespace and local part of the service
        QName serviceName = new QName("http://ch03.soacookbook.com/",
                "HelloWSService");

        //Create a proxy to get a port stub from
        Service service = Service.create(wsdlLocation, serviceName);

        // Return a list of QNames of ports
        System.out.println("QNames of service endpoints:");
        Iterator<QName> it = service.getPorts();
        QName lastEndpoint = null;
        while (it.hasNext()) {
        lastEndpoint = it.next();
            System.out.println("Name: " + lastEndpoint);
            //prints: Name: {http://ch03.soacookbook.com/}HelloWSPort
        }

        // Get the Hello stub
        Hello hello = service.getPort(lastEndpoint, Hello.class);

        //Invoke the business method
        String result = hello.sayHello("Duke");
        System.out.println("\nResponse: " + result);
    }
}
```

The comments within the file should indicate what's happening. I want to show the simplest possible invocation of a service. The only part of the client that is not strictly necessary is the iterator over the available endpoints. You could just have invoked the business method after getting the port from the service.

Here is the output from invoking this program:

```
QNames of service endpoints:
Name: {http://ch03.soacookbook.com/}HelloWSPort

Response: Hello, Duke!
```

The client program lists the `QNames` available by reading the `<port>` child elements of the `<service>` element on the WSDL, and there is a `QName`: `{http://ch03.soacookbook.com/}HelloWSPort`. A `QName` is a combination of namespace and local part. The namespace in `QName`'s `toString` method is enclosed in curly braces, and the local part is appended.

During invocation, the `binding` attribute of this `QName` is read, and the invoker is referred to the `<binding>` element of the WSDL, which lists the operations that can be performed, and the types necessary to use in messages during invocation of those operations. A stub is generated based on the interface specified, which the client program uses to call methods as if they were local to the same JVM.

See Also

Recipe 6.4.

6.4 Creating a Client Proxy

Problem

You are tired of doing all of this work by hand to create your SOAP invocation with SAAJ. You want to have Java generate everything necessary for you to invoke a service based only on its WSDL.

Solution

Use the `wsimport` tool to generate the necessary client-side stubs and invoke them as you would a regular Java object.

Discussion

When you are new to web services the whole enterprise can be very daunting. This discussion will walk you through the use of the `wsimport` tool from a client developer's perspective. It will touch on schema, JAXB, and how the parts hook up together under the hood so that you will have enough of a foundation going forward to know which items you need to concern yourself with and what gets taken care of for you.

The `wsimport` tool will read the WSDL of a deployed web service and generate the Java objects necessary to invoke it, including a class that extends `javax.xml.ws.Service`, which provides the client view of a web service. This can be a confusing concept because we tend to think of the service as being located on the server. But a service instance acts as a factory to create proxies that allow you to invoke a web service as if it was local. These proxies are sometimes referred to as SEI (Service Endpoint Interface) objects.

The tool generates portable artifacts that use only standard Java means. It will automatically call on JAXB to create value types that map Java to XML tand the result can be used to perform web services operations.

> **Dynamic Proxy**
>
> The creation of a dynamic proxy within JAX-WS is sometimes referred to as the "static" client programming model. The client uses the generated SEI that specifies the types for you; you build the object tree using factory methods required for the service invocation, and the actual request processing is performed by a delegate under the hood.
>
> This delegate is implemented on the fly by a dynamic proxy object. Dynamic proxies were introduced in Java SE 1.3. They are supported by `java.lang.reflect.Proxy`, and exist to implement a list of interfaces specified at runtime. Because of this, the artifacts that JAX-WS creates are fully portable. You can move your client code to another

platform and not have to use that platform's tools to regenerate it. This is similar to how stubs worked with the older JAX-RPC model that JAX-WS replaces, inasmuch as JAX-RPC also used the SEI. Beyond ease of use, the major difference is that with JAX-RPC, the tools generated platform-specific stubs, forcing you to recreate the client for the new platform.

Dynamic proxies stand in distinction to the SAAJ model, in which no SEI is generated for you beforehand and you piece together the SOAP message yourself, as we saw in Chapter 5. This is a lot of work if you are just performing a straightforward invocation as an SEI might, without any tinkering. But if you want your client program to sew up a SOAP request on the fly based on runtime properties, SAAJ is fantastic.

You can use `wsimport` from the command line, or within Ant or Maven. Let's use a simple calculator web service as an example. The WSDL of your service is located at *http://localhost:4933/CalculatorApp/CalculatorWSService?wsdl*. It defines a single port type, as in the following code:

```
<portType name="CalculatorWS">
<operation name="add">
<input message="tns:add"></input>
<output message="tns:addResponse"></output>
</operation>
</portType>
//The service name element is:
<service name="CalculatorWSService">
```

In order to use this recipe, you need a real WSDL deployed somewhere. If you are using NetBeans, you can set up and deploy this web service in just a few moments. You could also try deploying the Endpoint from Recipe 4.4, or using a publicly available service from somewhere like StrikeIron.com. Each of these options will give you a different level of complexity in the generated artifacts, as based on the message types.

Now run the `wsimport` tool to create a proxy so you can invoke the service. Here is the command and the output:

```
>wsimport  -d /home/ehewitt/soacookbook/code/imported -target 2.1 \
    -verbose http://localhost:4933/CalculatorApp/CalculatorWSService?wsdl
parsing WSDL...
generating code...

org\me\calculator\Add.java
org\me\calculator\AddResponse.java
org\me\calculator\CalculatorWS.java
org\me\calculator\CalculatorWSService.java
org\me\calculator\ObjectFactory.java
org\me\calculator\package-info.java

compiling code...
```

```
javac -d /home/ehewitt/soacookbook/code/imported -classpath //...
>
```

The `wsimport` tool has a variety of options, many of which have to do with customization. But in the basic invocation, you pass the tool the options you want and the final argument is the location of the WSDL. The first option, `-d`, indicates the directory where you want the imported source code to be written. The `-target` option is used to specify the version of JAX-WS you want to be compatible with (2.0 is the default), and the `-verbose` option tells the tool to indicate the work it is doing as it does it. Let's look at what the tool generated for you.

First it generated a set of packages that correspond to the namespace of the service, which in this example is `org.me.calculator`. Inside the package is a set of Java classes. We will discuss the key Java classes the tool generated below.

If you want to have `wsimport` retain the Java source files it generates in addition to the class files, use the `-keep` option.

The generated Service class

In this example, the `Service` class is called `CalculatorWSService.java`, which corresponds to the value of the `name` attribute of the WSDL `<service>` element. The generated `Service` class allows you to:

- Get available ports (service endpoint interfaces)
- Get the location of the WSDL document associated with the service
- Get the Executor instance associated with the service, which provides threading capability to service invocations
- Create a `Dispatch`
- Create a `Service` instance
- Call the `getPort` method on the `Service` instance to invoke web service operations

This class extends `javax.xml.ws.Service`, and is annotated with a `@WebServiceClient` annotation that specifies the location of the WSDL representing the service to be invoked. It contains factory methods that return the Java object that represents the WSDL port you can invoke operations on. The generated `Service` class looks like this:

```
@WebServiceClient(name = "CalculatorWSService",
  targetNamespace = "http://calculator.me.org/",
  wsdlLocation = "http://localhost:4933/CalculatorApp/CalculatorWSService?wsdl")
public class CalculatorWSService extends Service { //...
  @WebEndpoint(name = "CalculatorWSPort")
    public CalculatorWS getCalculatorWSPort() {
        return super.getPort(new QName("http://calculator.me.org/",
          "CalculatorWSPort"), CalculatorWS.class);
    }
```

The `wsdlLocation` attribute must allow for the use of the XML Catalog facility specified by OASIS, if one is available. This is discussed in Recipe 3.12.

Here the `getCalculatorWSPort` method returns an object that implements the `CalculatorWS` interface, which is discussed next. The no-arg `getPort` method can be used in general; the second `getPort` method accepts a variable-length array of `javax.xml.ws.WebServiceFeature` objects that can be used by clients to configure certain aspects of the invocation, such as whether to enable MTOM or WS-Addressing.

The generated Port class

Because the WSDL port as shown in the earlier listing has a value of `CalculatorWS` for the name attribute, that is the name of the generated Java interface representing the port. This interface is (somewhat confusingly) annotated with `@WebService`, to indicate that it is a service endpoint interface that will be used as a proxy. There is not an implementation for this class generated by JAX-WS. The runtime will do the work behind the scenes by delegating the invocation to an implementation of `javax.xml.ws.spi.ServiceDelegate`, which the `Service` class decorates.

The Service Provider Interface (SPI) was introduced publicly in Java SE 6, though it was used internally within the Java APIs since version 1.4. It allows a pluggable architecture by indicating the name of a class that implements a given interface within the META-INF directory of a JAR. Though the developer does not need to worry about it, this is how the `ServiceDelegate` implementation is supplied at runtime.

In the calculator example, the port has one method, to match the single `add` operation defined in the WSDL. Let's take a step back and unpack this for a moment, as there's a lot going on here:

```
@WebMethod
@WebResult(targetNamespace = "")
@RequestWrapper(localName = "add",
  targetNamespace = "http://calculator.me.org/",
  className = "org.me.calculator.Add")
@ResponseWrapper(localName = "addResponse",
  targetNamespace = "http://calculator.me.org/",
  className = "org.me.calculator.AddResponse")
public int add(
    @WebParam(name = "i", targetNamespace = "")
    int i,
    @WebParam(name = "j", targetNamespace = "")
    int j);
```

As you can see, your seemingly simple, innocuous `add` method suddenly has a variety of annotations adorning it. We'll account for these one by one.

First, your WSDL specifies the following in the messages section:

```
<message name="add"> <part name="parameters" element="tns:add"></part> </message>
```

So the SEI needs to account for this message, and creates an annotation indicating that the runtime will create a message with a `QName` that contains a local part of `add`, in the specified namespace. That message is derived from the Java class that is also generated, `org.me.calculator.Add`, which looks like this:

```
@XmlAccessorType(XmlAccessType.FIELD)
@XmlType(name = "add", propOrder = {
    "i",
    "j"
})
public class Add {
    protected int i;
    protected int j;
    //getters and setters omitted
```

That class acts as the wrapper for each of the integers that will be sent in the request. The `@Xml` annotations on this class come from JAXB. They indicate how JAXB should marshal and unmarshal instances of this class to and from XML. The `@XmlType` annotation is used to specify that this `Add` class matches a top-level complex type (or an enum) within an XML schema, and the "name" property is specified as "add" in it, to match the item's name within the schema. If you look at the schema that your WSDL refers to, you see the following complex type, which matches your `Add` class:

```
<xs:complexType name="add">
<xs:sequence>
<xs:element name="i" type="xs:int"></xs:element>
<xs:element name="j" type="xs:int"></xs:element>
</xs:sequence>
</xs:complexType>
```

But why does this type get created for you? Integers are defined as basic types provided with XML Schema; they are not custom types that you have written that require something special. The complex type that wraps these two integers is created in order to match your WSDL, which uses the document/literal style. Here is the portion of the WSDL that tells you this:

```
<soap:binding transport="http://schemas.xmlsoap.org/soap/http"
  style="document"></soap:binding>
<operation name="add">
<soap:operation soapAction=""></soap:operation>
<input>
<soap:body use="literal"></soap:body>
</input>
```

Had you been using RPC and not document, the values would have been passed separately to the operation invocation just like method parameters.

For more information on document versus RPC and literal versus Encoding, see Recipe 7.3.

The `@RequestWrapper` and `@ResponseWrapper` annotations capture information that JAXB needs to perform the marshaling and unmarshaling operations. If your service is defined as using document/literal mode, as ours is, this annotation also serves to resolve overloading conflicts.

Now, let's write a quick program to invoke the generated client code and get a result from your service. Here are the steps in their simplest form, stripped of any unnecessary items so you can get the clearest picture.

First, write the invoker called `CalculatorInvoker.java` (Example 6-3). Navigate to the top-level directory that you passed to the `wsimport` tool earlier. For me this was "/home/ehewitt/soacookbook/code/imported". You'll write your client there.

Example 6-3. CalculatorInvoker.java will invoke the generated service endpoint code

```
import org.me.calculator.*;

public class CalculatorInvoker {
  public static void main(String... arg) {

    CalculatorWSService service = new CalculatorWSService();
    CalculatorWS port = service.getCalculatorWSPort();

    int result = port.add(2, 3);

    System.out.println("Result: " + result);
  }
}
```

The class in Example 6-3 simply creates a service instance, uses it to get the port, and uses the port to call the business method, `add`. Let's compile it, making sure the generated classes in the current directory are on your classpath:

```
>javac -cp . CalculatorInvoker.java
```

Then you can run it:

```
>java -cp . CalculatorInvoker
Result: 5
```

That's all there is to a basic client. Web services have come a long way with JAX-WS.

For more information on using `wsimport` specifically, you can invoke it with no arguments to print the help.

Finally, there are a few considerations to keep in mind with using generated clients:

- As you might imagine, the client cannot create or destroy web service implementations and has no view into its life cycle, which is handled entirely on the server.
- A port object has no identity. It cannot meaningfully be compared to other port objects. You cannot ask for a specific instance of a port.
- Treat service invocations as stateless. There is no mechanism within `Service` to handle state across requests.
- All data binding is performed by JAXB, so no JAX-RPC mapping file is required.

6.5 Consuming a Web Service from a Servlet or EJB

Problem

You have an EJB, servlet, or other container-managed resource that you want to act as the client for your web service.

Solution

Use the `@WebServiceRef` annotation to inject a reference to the service you want to invoke. Note that this does not have to be only a servlet or EJB. You might also want to invoke a web service from other container-managed resources, such as a `Filter`, a `SessionContextListener`, a `ServletContextListener`, or a `TagHandler` depending on your use case.

Using `@WebServiceRef`, you can get a reference to a web service and an injection target for it. Items annotated with `@WebServiceRef` follow the standard rules for resource injection within Java EE 5. It defines five attributes or properties, as are described in Table 6-1.

Table 6-1. @WebServiceRef properties

Property	Description
`name`	A name that identifies the reference to the component using the resource, as a JNDI name. If annotating a field, the default is the name of the field. If annotating a method, the default is the name of the Java Bean property the method defines. If annotating a class, there is no default.
`wsdlLocation`	The URL pointing to the WSDL for the referenced web service. This is necessary if you define your own WSDL in a physical file and include it with your WAR or EAR.
`type`	The resource class type. If annotating a field, the default value is the type of the field. If annotating a method, the default is the same as the Java Bean property. If annotating a class, there is no default, and a value must be specified.
`value`	The service class type, which must extend `javax.xml.ws.Service`. If the reference type is an SEI, this value must be specified.
`mappedName`	A name, such as a JNDI name, that maps from the value of the "name" property to a resource known to the server. Any `mappedName` value is specific to the application server platform, and is non-portable. It is not required that application servers support them.

Here you will write a servlet that invokes the web service by injection using the `@WebServiceRef` annotation. There are a few steps, which are exactly the same for using the reference from an EJB client:

1. Create the interface that the web service will implement, and to which clients, such as your servlet, will refer.
2. Implement the web service.
3. Add the reference annotation to the servlet; an instance of the generated SEI will automatically be injected.

Let's get to work.

`Catalog.java` in Example 6-4 is the interface that clients will refer to. It defines a simple operation that returns a book title for a given identifier.

Example 6-4. Catalog.java defines the service interface

```
package com.soacookbook.ch03;

import javax.jws.WebMethod;
import javax.jws.WebParam;
import javax.jws.WebResult;
import javax.jws.WebService;

/**
 * Public interface for CatalogWS impl.
 */
@WebService(targetNamespace="http://ns.soacookbook.com")
public interface Catalog {

    @WebMethod
    @WebResult(name="title")
    String getTitle(
        @WebParam(name="id") String id);

}
```

Note that you need to include the `@WebService` annotation on the interface, or the client will complain. Also, the `@WebService` annotation must include the `targetNamespace` because you want to customize it in your service implementation as well.

`CatalogWS.java`, shown in Example 6-5, implements the service interface.

Example 6-5. CatalogWS.java implements the service interface

```
package com.soacookbook.ch03;

import javax.jws.WebMethod;
import javax.jws.WebParam;
import javax.jws.WebResult;
import javax.jws.WebService;
import org.apache.log4j.Logger;
```

```
/**
 * This annotation will produce a WSDL URL of:
 * http://localhost:8080/soaCookbookWS/CatalogService?wsdl
 * That's because it is in the web context of "soaCookbookWS",
 * which is the WAR name, appended with the value of the
 * serviceName property.
 *
 * Use that value in the properties file to generate client
 * artifacts.
 */
@WebService(serviceName="CatalogService", name="Catalog",
    targetNamespace="http://ns.soacookbook.com")
public class CatalogWS implements Catalog {
    private static final Logger LOGGER =
            Logger.getLogger(CatalogWS.class);

    @WebMethod
    public @WebResult(name="title") String
            getTitle(
            @WebParam(name="id") String id)  {

        if ("12345".equals(id)) return "Hamlet";
        if ("98765".equals(id)) return "King Lear";
        if ("55555".equals(id)) return "Macbeth";

        return "--Item not in catalog--";
    }

    public CatalogWS() { }
}
```

The code in Example 6-6 is the servlet that will get the `@WebServiceRef` annotation and receive the service injection from the container at runtime.

Example 6-6. InjectionServlet.java uses @WebServiceRef to refer to a web service

```
public class InjectionServlet extends HttpServlet {

    @WebServiceRef(type=Catalog.class)
    private CatalogService service;

    protected void processRequest(HttpServletRequest request,
        HttpServletResponse response)
        throws ServletException, IOException {

        response.setContentType("text/html;charset=UTF-8");
        PrintWriter out = response.getWriter();

        //service instance injected...
        Catalog port = service.getCatalogPort();
        String title = port.getTitle("12345");

        try {
            out.println("<html>");
            out.println("<head>");
```

```
            out.println("<title>WebServiceRef Test</title>");
            out.println("</head>");
            out.println("<body>");
            out.println("<h1>Title= " + title  + "</h1>");
            out.println("</body>");
            out.println("</html>");

        } finally {
            out.close();
        }
    }
}
```

The servlet itself contains the reference to the generated SEI proxy instance, and the container does the injection as it would with any other injectable resource.

The following is the client that can invoke this web service using an SEI generated from a call to `wsimport`:

```
CatalogService svc = new CatalogService();
Catalog port = svc.getCatalogPort();

return port.getTitle("12345");
```

Figure 6-1 shows the output in a browser window.

Figure 6-1. Output of WebServiceRef InjectionServlet.java

That's all there is to it.

Discussion

There are two ways to use the `@WebServiceRef` annotation:

- Make your annotation refer to a generated service class. If the default value cannot be inferred from the field or method your annotation modifies, then you must at a minimum supply a value for the `type` property, which refers to the generated service class type.
- Make your annotation refer to an SEI. With this option, you must supply a service type class object for the `value` property. This object must be a generated service class type (a subtype of `javax.xml.ws.Service`).

The value of the `wsdlLocation` property will override the URL established in the generated service class (the class annotated with `@WebService`).

WebServiceRefs

Annotations in Java prevent you from defining the same annotation more than once on the same type. So if your client class needs to refer to more than one web service, you can use the `@WebServiceRefs` annotation to wrap multiple instances of `@WebServiceRef`. That curtails the ability of JAX-WS to infer appropriate values for the name and type properties because more than one `@WebServiceRef` is defined, and they are defined at the class level. To address this, each `@WebServiceRef` annotation wrapped within a `@WebServiceRefs` annotation must define `name` and `type` values.

`@WebServiceRefs` contains only a single implicit value property, which is an array of `@WebServiceRef` annotations.

6.6 Consuming a Web Service from a JSP

Problem

You have a JSP that you want to act as a client of a web service.

Solution

Generate a client based on the WSDL and include those resources within your WAR deployment. Use a scriptlet in the JSP to instantiate the client.

Discussion

In your JSP application, make sure the web service is deployed by testing the WSDL URL in a browser. Use the WSDL location to generate a client with `wsimport` either during your build or at the command line. Write a scriptlet that invokes the client, just as you would within a servlet. Include the client classes with your WAR when you deploy.

As with any other Java class-based resource that your web application uses, it does not matter if you package your classes together as a library and include them in *WEB-INF/lib* or whether you just place the classes directly in the *WEB-INF/classes* directory. Of course, regular classloader concerns apply as usual.

Example 6-7 is the JSP code that executes after following these steps.

Example 6-7. Invoking a web service from a JSP

```
<%@page import="com.soacookbook.client.CatalogServiceSN,
  com.soacookbook.client.CatalogService"
  contentType="text/html" pageEncoding="UTF-8"%>

<!DOCTYPE HTML PUBLIC "-//W3C//DTD HTML 4.01 Transitional//EN"
   "http://www.w3.org/TR/html4/loose.dtd">

<html>
    <head><title>JSP Client</title></head>
    <body>
        <h2>Catalog Service Client</h2>
 <%
    try {
      CatalogServiceSN service = new CatalogServiceSN();
      CatalogService port = service.getCatalogPort();

      String id = "98765";
      String result = port.getTitle(id);
      out.println("Result for ID 98765= "+result);
    } catch (Exception ex) {
        //...
    }
  %>

    </body>
</html>
```

Notice that you import the service stub and the port you'll use to invoke the operation using the page directive. The result in the browser is shown in Figure 6-2.

There is no need to use a JNDI lookup or add anything to the deployment descriptor.

6.7 Using a JAXB-Annotated Instance in a SOAP Message

Problem

You want to work with an object view of the contents of your SOAP request, rather than working with low-level XML plumbing to build messages. You have a Java object that was created from a JAXB-annotated class. You want to want to automatically marshal this into XML and use it as the child element of the body of a SOAP request.

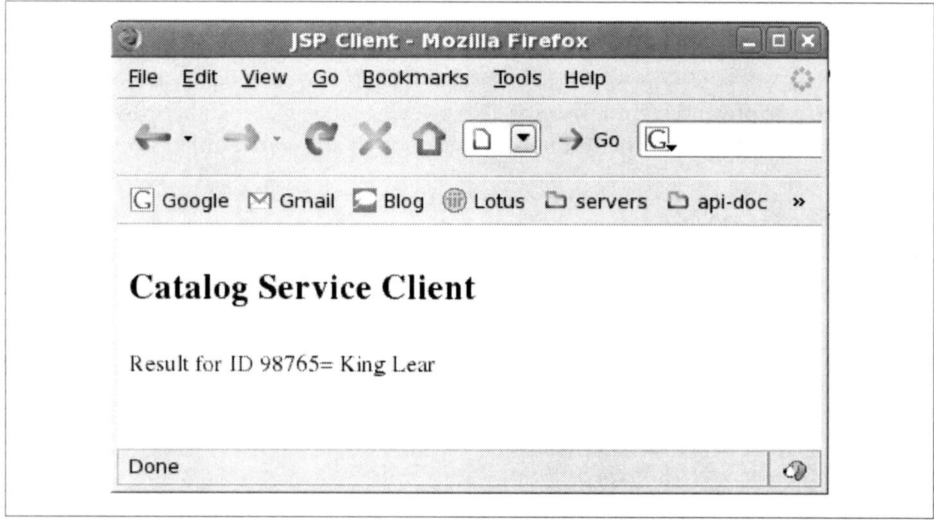

Figure 6-2. Catalog web service invoked from JSP

Solution

Generate the client-side objects with a tool such as wsimport (or, if using Apache Axis, the WSDL2Java tool). Then use the generated object model normally. All of the necessary XML is hidden from you.

Discussion

The important aspect of this recipe is that it shows you that with JAX-WS, it's almost as easy to use complex types as it is to use primary types for service operation parameters.

In this example, you'll use a catalog service that represents a database of books, as shown in the following code:

```
@WebService(serviceName="CatalogService", name="Catalog",
    targetNamespace="http://ns.soacookbook.com/ws/catalog")
@Stateless
@Local
public class CatalogEJB {

    @WebMethod
    @SOAPBinding(style=SOAPBinding.Style.DOCUMENT,
        use=SOAPBinding.Use.LITERAL,
        parameterStyle=SOAPBinding.ParameterStyle.BARE)
    public @WebResult(name="searchResults",
            targetNamespace="http://ns.soacookbook.com/catalog") SearchResults
            authorSearch(
            @WebParam(name="author",
            targetNamespace="http://ns.soacookbook.com/catalog") Author author)
```

```
    //...

}
```

For comparison purposes, the following JUnit test creates a Book instance that you know the service should return. The test makes use of JAXB annotated objects generated off of the WSDL:

```
public class CatalogTest {
    private Book hamlet;

    @org.junit.Before
    public void init(){
        hamlet = new Book();
        Author shakespeare = new Author();
        shakespeare.setFirstName("William");
        shakespeare.setLastName("Shakespeare");
        hamlet.setAuthor(shakespeare);
        hamlet.setIsbn("1234");
        hamlet.setCategory(Category.LITERATURE);
        hamlet.setTitle("Hamlet");
    }

    public CatalogTest() { }


    @Test
    public void searchByAuthorTest() {
        Author shakespeare = new Author();
        shakespeare.setFirstName("William");
        shakespeare.setLastName("Shakespeare");

        CatalogService svc = new CatalogService();
        Catalog catalog = svc.getCatalogPort();

        SearchResults results = catalog.authorSearch(shakespeare);

        Book book = results.getBookList().get(0);

        assertTrue(book.getTitle().equals(hamlet.getTitle()));

    }
```

The unit test illustrates how working with domain objects generated from JAXB allow for a familiar, object-oriented style when programming against a web service. There are no XML or low-level plumbing details here.

The SearchResults object returned from the authorSearch method holds a List<Book>, so you can just use regular methods in the List interface, such as get, to navigate the results. In this way, JAX-WS affords a very natural programming model.

6.8 Using wsimport in a Maven Project

Problem

You want to create a web client project using Maven 2, and you need to run `wsimport` as part of the build.

Solution

Use the `jaxws-maven-plugin` from Java.net.

Discussion

If you're comfortable with Maven, just download the plug-in and get started at *https://jax-ws-commons.dev.java.net/jaxws-maven-plugin/*.

This plug-in started as a project at Codehaus, but in 2007 all work on it was transferred to the Java.net website that is also home to Glassfish, Metro, OpenESB, and related projects.

The plug-in is easy to use, and works well out of the box. All you need to do is specify the plug-in in your *pom.xml*, as shown in Example 6-8.

Example 6-8. Maven 2 POM using the JAX-WS plug-in

```
<build>
    <plugins>
       <plugin>
           <groupId>org.codehaus.mojo</groupId>
           <artifactId>jaxws-maven-plugin</artifactId>
           <version>1.9</version>
           <executions>
                <execution>
                    <goals>
                        <goal>wsimport</goal>
                    </goals>
                </execution>
           </executions>
           <configuration>
               <packageName>com.example</packageName>
               <wsdlUrls>
                   <wsdlUrl>${my.wsdl.url}</wsdlUrl>
               </wsdlUrls>
               <verbose>true</verbose>
           </configuration>
       </plugin>
//...
```

Of course, to use the plug-in, you need to be able to reach the Maven 2 repository that stores it. This is located at *http://download.java.net/maven/2/*. Adding this to your organization's internal Maven repository (for example, Archiva) will allow the repository to act as a proxy and will simplify the process of managing plug-ins across developers or teams.

To use an internal repository, you must specify it in your *settings.xml* file, typically located in your user home. If your organization doesn't have an internal repository, that's fine—you can just skip this part:

```
<mirrors>
    <mirror>
        <id>my-internal</id>
        <mirrorOf>*</mirrorOf>
        <url>http://repo.example.com/archiva/repository/internal</url>
        <name>My - Archiva</name>
    </mirror>
</mirrors>
```

Using a variable for the WSDL location

In this example, you run the `wsimport` goal of the plug-in using a variable as the WSDL URL. The variable exists in order to account for a variety of WSDL locations that your environment may require. For example, if you're using a development workstation and running a local server, your WSDL may be located at localhost. Once it's time to promote your work to an integration build server, your WSDL may need to use a different address. This problem is solved by using variables in your Maven profile.

To follow this example, you might have a developer profile and an integration server profile, each of which is activated depending on different variables in the environment.

To set this up, create a *profiles.xml* file within the root folder of your project. Here you define a variable matching the name of the variable used within the POM for the value of the `wsdlUrl`. The text within the variable name element is used as the value at build time, so your *http://localhost:8080/myProject/SomeService?wsdl* value will be inserted as the URL for the `wsimport` plug-in to use:

```
<profilesXml xmlns="http://maven.apache.org/POM/4.0.0"
    xmlns:xsi="http://www.w3.org/2001/XMLSchema-instance"
    xsi:schemaLocation="http://maven.apache.org/POM/4.0.0
      http://maven.apache.org/xsd/profiles-1.0.0.xsd">
<profiles>
  <profile>
    <id>development</id>
    <properties>
      <my.wsdl.url>
        http://localhost:8080/myProject/SomeService?wsdl
      </my.wsdl.url>
    </properties>
  </profile>
  //...other profiles
</profiles>
```

6.9 Dealing with Version Errors in wsgen and wsimport

Problem

There are two different versions of the main web services tools (`wsimport` and `wsgen`). One version is included in Java SE 6, and the other is included with Glassfish/Metro. You want to use the newer libraries, but Java SE includes the older one. In other words, you're getting this error:

```
You are running on JDK6 which comes with JAX-WS 2.0 API, but this tool
requires JAX-WS 2.1 API. Use the endorsed standards override mechanism
(http://java.sun.com/javase/6/docs/technotes/guides/standards/),
or use -Xendorsed option.
```

Solution

Get Java SE 1.6.0_4 or higher, as it ships with JAX-WS 2.1. Or override the older version using the endorsed directory mechanism.

Discussion

If you're using Java 5, you must include the *jaxws-api.jar* and *jaxb-api.jar* on your classpath, as there is no native support for JAX-WS before Java SE 6, which includes JAX-WS 2.0.

Java SE 6 update 4 is the first release to include JAX-WS 2.1 API within the *rt.jar*. The easiest way to deal with this problem is to install that version or newer of Java. If you can't do that for some reason, then you'll need to pull the proverbial wool over your classloader's eyes.

Let's unpack this a bit. If you open a command prompt and issue the command `wsimport -version`, you should see something like the following output, assuming that your Java SE 1.6.0_04+ bin directory is on the path:

```
JAX-WS RI 2.1.1 in JDK 6
```

If you're using an older version, it will print JAX-WS 2.0 in JDK 6. So you can upgrade to a newer version of the JDK that ships with JAX-WS 2.1.

If you have Glassfish/Metro, you can navigate to the *bin* directory under your Glassfish installation and run the same command, `wsimport -version`. Doing that from within the Glassfish *bin* directory gives me the following output:

```
JAX-WS RI 2.1.3-hudson-390-
```

This difference of minor version matters if you need the JAX-WS runtime JAR (*jaxws-rt.jar*) to perform certain tasks that represent extensions to the basic functionality. For example, the `WSBindingProvider` class, which gives you easy access to setting outbound headers, is in the `com.sun.xml.ws.developer` package.

Do not be misled by the fact that these classes are in the `com.sun` package. Sun itself advocates not using any such packages because they are not part of the public interface, are frequently undocumented, and are subject to change at any given time. They are not guaranteed to work in future versions of the platform, and are considered risky and experimental. However, that is *not* what's happening with these JAX-WS classes. Sun's admonition against using `com.sun` classes refers only to classes that ship within Java SE itself. The JAX-WS classes are defined within the JAX-WS standalone library, which should be included as part of your application. The package name starts the same, but the rule doesn't apply. That said, carefully consider how far down the road of proprietary extensions you want to go when writing your apps.

So if a very new version of JAX-WS, such as 2.1.3, includes some feature you want to use, you may still have some work to do. You can't just get a newer version of Java in this case (as of yet). You need to override those JARs, unless you can do everything from the console.

If you have downloaded Metro 1.1, then you can point your `JAVA_HOME` environment variable to your Java SE 6 update 4 installation, and run the web service tools from Metro. Metro 1.1 includes a directory called *jax-ws-latest-wsit/bin* that contains the updated `wsgen` and `wsimport` tools. But if you want to make sure that your environment always has the same features available and you don't want to point to Metro, you can use the endorsed directories mechanism.

Using endorsed directories

If you are using Java SE 6 with an update release version of less than 4 (i.e., 1.6.0._03 or less) and you are using Metro or WSIT (Web Services Interoperability Technology), you may be familiar with the following error message:

```
You are running on JDK6 which comes with JAX-WS 2.0 API, but this tool requires
JAX-WS 2.1 API. Use the endorsed standards override mechanism
(http://java.sun.com/javase/6/docs/technotes/guides/standards/),
or use -Xendorsed option.
```

The basic problem is classloader confusion because Java SE ships with a slightly older version of JAX-WS than is required by the operation you're performing. You need to get newer versions of two API JARs on your classpath: JAX-WS 2.1.x and JAXB 2.1.x. These are found in *jaxws-api.jar* and *jaxb-api.jar*. But because Java already includes these classes, it's not just a simple matter of placing them on your classpath as you would with a third-party JAR. You need to get Java to read your new JAR before it reads its own. You do that using the endorsed directory.

There is no support for the endorsed directories mechanism using Web Start (JNLP) technology. This may be addressed in Java SE 7.

Because the classes that Java uses at runtime are in the *rt.jar*, you need to get your classes into the bootstrap classpath, which loads before *rt.jar*. You do this by creating a new directory called "endorsed" under `<java-home>/lib`, and place your new JARs in there.

Alternatively, you can point to a different directory using the `java.endorsed.dirs` property; the Java runtime will search the directories listed there for classes to load. If you use multiple directories, they must be separated with your OS directory separator character, which is equivalent to the value of `File.pathSeparatorChar`.

Using with Ant

You really only want *jaxws-api.jar* and *jaxb-api.jar* in your endorsed directories. Do not copy every JAX-WS-related JAR into this directory, as doing so can cause an Ant task to fail, and it is more likely that you are using Ant rather than the command line to do your `wsimport` work. You may see an error such as the following:

```
taskdef A class needed by class com.sun.tools.ws.ant.WsImport cannot
be found: org/apache/tools/ant/taskdefs/MatchingTask
```

Use the classpath task in Ant to specify the two JARs if necessary.

6.10 Adding Headers to a SOAP Request

Problem

You want to add custom header information to a SOAP request using JAX-WS.

Solution

There are a few basic ways to do this. You can use the SAAJ API, which ensures portability, and add the headers to your code on invocation. Alternatively, depending on the structure of the WSDL you have to invoke, you can create a `Holder<T>` that will add the headers as message parameters.

You can also use vendor-specific convenience code for this. With Metro, for example, you can use `Headers.create`.

Discussion

We'll look at these alternatives here.

A new option, -XadditionalHeaders, was added to the wsimport task in JAX-WS RI 2.1.3. This option automatically maps headers as method parameters. You may have a slightly earlier version of Java, such as 2.1.1, that does not support this.

If you are using CXF, you can specify -exsh true instead.

Let's say that you have the following simple WSDL defined:

```
<message name="usernameHeader">
    <part name="usernameHeader" element="types:usernameHeader"/>
</message>

<wsdl:portType name="SecureCatalogPortType">
    <wsdl:operation name="execute">
        <wsdl:input message="tns:aRequest"/>
        <wsdl:output message="tns:aResponse"/>
    </wsdl:operation>
</wsdl:portType>

<wsdl:binding name="SecureCatalogBinding" type="tns:SecureCatalogPortType">
     <soap:binding style="document"
       transport="http://schemas.xmlsoap.org/soap/http"/>
     <wsdl:operation name="execute">
        <soap:operation/>
        <wsdl:input>
            <soap:body message="tns:aRequest"/>
            <soap:header message="tns:usernameHeader" part="usernameHeader"/>
        </wsdl:input>
        <wsdl:output>
            <soap:body message="tns:aResponse"/>
        </wsdl:output>
    </wsdl:operation>
</wsdl:binding>
```

In this WSDL, you have one operation, called execute, which accepts a single parameter, aRequest, and returns aResponse. The binding also specifies that there is a single header, usernameHeader, that will be passed along with the SOAP message. This header is not specified within the portType, but is present in the operation definition, which means that it is not part of the abstract contract for the service. Because of this, when you use wsimport to create an SEI, nothing will be generated to account for the header. Only wsdl:part information, representing the abstract contract, is mapped to method parameters in the SEI. The method would map to the following signature:

```
public String execute(String arg0)
```

There's no accounting for the header. So you need another mechanism to allow clients to pass a value for it. That mechanism, if you're using the RI, is to pass -Xadditional Headers to the wsimport tool.

While it is convenient to generate SEIs with a tool such as `wsimport`, be aware that you are limiting your portability by using the `-XadditionalHeaders` option.

By using this option, the `wsimport` tool will generate a signature such as this:

```
public String execute(String arg0, String additionalHeader);
```

Using Holder<T>

If the concrete WSDL defines header parameters, then you can use `wsimport` as you normally would, and then use a `Holder` to represent the outgoing headers. The type parameter on the `Holder` is whatever type your header is. For example, consider the following WSDL snippet:

```
<message name="verify">
<part name="parameters" element="tns:verify"></part>
<part name="username" element="tns:username"></part>
<part name="password" element="tns:password"></part>
</message>

<portType name="EmailCheck">
<operation name="verify" parameterOrder="parameters username password">
<input message="tns:verify"></input>
<output message="tns:verifyResponse"></output>
</operation>
</portType>

<binding name="EmailCheckPortBinding" type="tns:EmailCheck">
<soap:binding transport="http://schemas.xmlsoap.org/soap/http"
  style="document"></soap:binding>
<operation name="verify">
<soap:operation soapAction=""></soap:operation>
<input>
<soap:body use="literal" parts="parameters"></soap:body>
<soap:header message="tns:verify" part="username"
  use="literal"></soap:header>
<soap:header message="tns:verify" part="password"
  use="literal"></soap:header>
</input>
<output>
<soap:body use="literal" parts="result"></soap:body>
<soap:header message="tns:verifyResponse" part="username"
  use="literal"></soap:header>
<soap:header message="tns:verifyResponse" part="password"
  use="literal"></soap:header>
</output>
</operation>
</binding>

<service name="EmailCheckService">
<port name="EmailCheckPort" binding="tns:EmailCheckPortBinding">
<soap:address location="http://localhost:8080/TestHeaders/EmailCheckService">
</soap:address>
```

```
</port>
</service>
</definitions>
```

This WSDL allows headers to be passed as method parameters, using the SOAP headers element. Just as you might add HTTP headers in a regular HTTP request when using a servlet, this WSDL specifies that the username and password headers are to be added as child elements of the SOAP `<header>` element in the envelope.

Note the `verify` operation on the `EmailCheck` `portType`. It specifies an attribute called `parameterOrder`. This attribute indicates what order the `Holder` will assign to the parameters within its array, following any regular parameters to the method. In this example, the `parameters` message will come first, followed by the username header and then the password header.

This WSDL was generated using the following web service implementation class:

```
public String verify(
    @WebParam(mode=WebParam.Mode.IN,
        name="email")String email,
    @WebParam(mode=WebParam.Mode.INOUT, header=true,
        name="username") Holder<String> username,
    @WebParam(mode=WebParam.Mode.INOUT, header=true,
        name="password") Holder<String> password){
```

This is perhaps the easiest way to define a web service that requires headers. You need to do a few things to make this work. First, define the parameters as regular parameters on the method using `@WebParam`, set `header=true`, and then indicate the headers as method parameters of type `Holder<T>`, where `T` is the type that you want clients to define. Finally, indicate that the headers are inbound using the `Mode` enum. This is easy for clients to work with because a standard `wsimport` will do all of the right things, making it very straightforward to include the appropriate header values.

This can work because in JAX-WS 2.1, the `wsdl:parts` from the abstract part of the WSDL (that is, those defined within the `portType`) are mapped to Java method parameters. But not all WSDLs are defined this way, so you may need to do a little extra work to deal with different kinds of WSDLs. We'll examine these different methods now.

Remember that you can see the outgoing SOAP message traffic by using the `HttpTransportPipe` class that comes with the *webservices-rt.jar* in Glassfish. Even if you're developing on another platform, this is very easy and helpful. Just add the following line to your command-line invocation:

```
-Dcom.sun.xml.ws.transport.http.client.HttpTransportPipe.dump=true
```

Of course, if you're running from within an IDE, you can include this VM argument in your run configuration. In NetBeans 6, just right-click on the project name, click Run, and add it to the VM options field. In Eclipse, click Run→Open Run Dialog, then choose the Arguments tab. Enter the value in the VM Arguments field and click Apply.

Making the client invocation sends the following SOAP message to the server:

```
---[HTTP request]---
SOAPAction: ""
Accept: text/xml, multipart/related, text/html, image/gif, image/jpeg, *;
q=.2, */*; q=.2
Content-Type: text/xml;charset="utf-8"
<?xml version="1.0" ?>
<S:Envelope xmlns:S="http://schemas.xmlsoap.org/soap/envelope/">
<S:Header>
<ns2:username xmlns:ns2="http://soacookbook.com/">eben</ns2:username>
<ns2:password xmlns:ns2="http://soacookbook.com/">secret</ns2:password>
</S:Header>
<S:Body>
<ns2:verify xmlns:ns2="http://soacookbook.com/">
<email>me@example.com</email></ns2:verify>
</S:Body>
</S:Envelope>
```

So despite the Java client view, which has you send headers wrapped in a holder for the regular method invocation, the username and password values do actually get sent to the service as SOAP headers as expected.

Using Headers.create and JAXB

There is an option to use `Headers.create` as a convenience. However, this works only with the reference implementation, although similar functionality may be available in other platforms such as WebLogic (after all, WebLogic 10gR3 is a modified Glassfish under the hood). Also, you cannot use this method with a WSDL such as the one in the previous example if you create proxies for it. That is, the operations accept the headers as if they were regular method parameters, so the proxy method will be expecting the holders.

In this example, you'll use a WSDL that is defined by a third party, representing a real-world web service. It is somewhat long and complicated (at least more so than some of our simpler examples), and is written in ASP.NET and not Java. It defines complex objects for use in SOAP headers. So it's a little more challenging to use, and doesn't let you get away with any contrived toy code.

Beyond the fact that the header objects are composite objects and not merely strings, the WSDL also defines its use of headers differently. In the previous username and password example, the WSDL was generated by JAX-WS, which also conveniently can be used for the consumer side. Let's take a look at how this works with a WSDL from StrikeIron.com that defines headers as composite Java objects:

```
<wsdl:definitions xmlns:s1="http://ws.strikeiron.com"
  xmlns:http="http://schemas.xmlsoap.org/wsdl/http/"
  xmlns:soap="http://schemas.xmlsoap.org/wsdl/soap/"
  xmlns:s="http://www.w3.org/2001/XMLSchema"
  xmlns:si="http://www.strikeiron.com"
  xmlns:soapenc="http://schemas.xmlsoap.org/soap/encoding/"
  xmlns:tm="http://microsoft.com/wsdl/mime/textMatching/"
```

```
xmlns:mime="http://schemas.xmlsoap.org/wsdl/mime/"
targetNamespace="http://www.strikeiron.com"
xmlns:wsdl="http://schemas.xmlsoap.org/wsdl/">
<wsdl:types>
      //...all types omitted for brevity
</wsdl:types>

<wsdl:message name="AddressToAddressDistanceSoapIn">
  <wsdl:part name="parameters" element="si:AddressToAddressDistance" />
</wsdl:message>
<wsdl:message name="AddressToAddressDistanceSoapOut">
  <wsdl:part name="parameters" element="si:AddressToAddressDistanceResponse" />
</wsdl:message>
<wsdl:message name="AddressToAddressDistanceResponseInfo">
  <wsdl:part name="ResponseInfo" element="si:ResponseInfo" />
</wsdl:message>
<wsdl:message name="GetRemainingHitsSoapIn">
  <wsdl:part name="parameters" element="s1:GetRemainingHits" />
</wsdl:message>
<wsdl:message name="GetRemainingHitsSoapOut">
  <wsdl:part name="parameters" element="s1:GetRemainingHitsResponse" />
</wsdl:message>
<wsdl:message name="LicenseInfoMessage">
  <wsdl:part name="LicenseInfo" element="s1:LicenseInfo" />
</wsdl:message>
<wsdl:message name="SubscriptionInfoMessage">
  <wsdl:part name="SubscriptionInfo" element="s1:SubscriptionInfo" />
</wsdl:message>

<wsdl:portType name="AddressDistanceCalculatorSoap">
  <wsdl:operation name="AddressToAddressDistance">
    <wsdl:input message="si:AddressToAddressDistanceSoapIn" />
    <wsdl:output message="si:AddressToAddressDistanceSoapOut" />
  </wsdl:operation>
  <wsdl:operation name="GetRemainingHits">
    <wsdl:input message="si:GetRemainingHitsSoapIn" />
    <wsdl:output message="si:GetRemainingHitsSoapOut" />
  </wsdl:operation>
</wsdl:portType>

<wsdl:binding name="AddressDistanceCalculatorSoap"
      type="si:AddressDistanceCalculatorSoap">
  <soap:binding transport="http://schemas.xmlsoap.org/soap/http" style="document" />

  <wsdl:operation name="AddressToAddressDistance">
    <soap:operation soapAction="http://www.strikeiron.com/AddressToAddressDistance"
      style="document" />
    <wsdl:input>
      <soap:body use="literal" />
      <soap:header message="si:LicenseInfoMessage" part="LicenseInfo"
              use="literal" />
    </wsdl:input>
    <wsdl:output>
      <soap:body use="literal" />
      <soap:header message="si:AddressToAddressDistanceResponseInfo"
```

```
                part="ResponseInfo" use="literal" />
          <soap:header message="si:SubscriptionInfoMessage"
                part="SubscriptionInfo" use="literal" />
      </wsdl:output>
    </wsdl:operation>
    <wsdl:operation name="GetRemainingHits">
      <soap:operation soapAction="http://ws.strikeiron.com/StrikeIron/
        AddressDistanceCalculator/GetRemainingHits" />
      <wsdl:input>
        <soap:body use="literal" />
        <soap:header message="si:LicenseInfoMessage"
          part="LicenseInfo" use="literal" />
      </wsdl:input>
      <wsdl:output>
        <soap:body use="literal" />
        <soap:header message="si:SubscriptionInfoMessage"
                part="SubscriptionInfo" use="literal" />
      </wsdl:output>
    </wsdl:operation>
  </wsdl:binding>

  <wsdl:service name="AddressDistanceCalculator">
    <wsdl:port name="AddressDistanceCalculatorSoap"
        binding="si:AddressDistanceCalculatorSoap">
      <soap:address
        location="http://ws.strikeiron.com/StrikeIron/AddressDistanceCalculator" />
    </wsdl:port>
  </wsdl:service>
</wsdl:definitions>
```

Here, the WSDL does not indicate its headers as method parameters, and you cannot therefore use generated `Holder` objects to pass the headers along with your request. Put more precisely, it doesn't declare that it uses headers in the abstract part of the WSDL, the port type. But the concrete aspect, the binding element whose `AddressToAddressDistance` operation you're going to invoke, does declare headers. Because they're missing from the abstract part, JAX-WS won't generate them. You'll have to add them to the message another way.

The object that needs to get added is a `LicenseInfo`, which also contains a `RegisteredUser`, which has a string user ID and password. I've omitted the types to save space, but they are all fairly straightforward, and make clear and direct translations to the JAXB objects generated by JAX-WS that you use in your Java client to invoke the operation.

If you want to see the complete WSDL this service uses in order to view the types, go to*http://ws.strikeiron.com/AddressDistanceCalculator?WSDL*. You might first check out a web-based client that allows you to test it before trying to tie all of the objects together; this is located at *http://www.strikeiron.com/sample/AddressDistanceCalculator_v2_0/AddressDistanceCalculator.aspx*.

You don't have to entirely forego the convenience of JAX-WS and return to lengthy stanzas of SAAJ code, however. You just have to make a few minor adjustments that are perfectly simple and elegant once you understand what's involved.

The class in Example 6-9 shows how you construct a client that uses JAX-WS generated objects from that WSDL as well as the `Headers.create` reference implementation convenience method to set a complex object into a header.

Example 6-9. Setting a complex object into a SOAP header with JAXB and Headers.create

```
package headersclientsiaddress;

import com.sun.xml.ws.api.message.Headers;
import com.sun.xml.ws.developer.WSBindingProvider;
import javax.xml.namespace.QName;

import com.strikeiron.*;
import javax.xml.bind.JAXBContext;
import javax.xml.bind.JAXBElement;
import javax.xml.bind.Marshaller;
import javax.xml.parsers.DocumentBuilderFactory;

/**
 * Creates a compound object (License) generated by JAX-WS as
 * a JAXB object so we can marshall it into XML to attach as
 * a SOAP header before invoking service.
 */
public class Main {
  public static void main(String... args) {
    try {
        //instantiate JAX-WS service object and its port
        AddressDistanceCalculator service =
                new AddressDistanceCalculator();
        AddressDistanceCalculatorSoap port =
                service.getAddressDistanceCalculatorSoap();

        //After registering, use your values here.
        RegisteredUser registeredUser = new RegisteredUser();
        registeredUser.setUserID("eben@example.com");
        registeredUser.setPassword("secret");

        LicenseInfo licenseInfo = new LicenseInfo();
        licenseInfo.setRegisteredUser(registeredUser);

        //setup a context to marshall our license header info
        JAXBContext jaxbContext = JAXBContext.newInstance(
                LicenseInfo.class);

        Marshaller marshaller = jaxbContext.createMarshaller();
        marshaller.setProperty(Marshaller.JAXB_ENCODING, "UTF-8");
        marshaller.setProperty(Marshaller.JAXB_FRAGMENT, Boolean.TRUE);

        //must do this because LicenseInfo is not a root element
        QName q = new QName("http://ws.strikeiron.com",
```

```
            "LicenseInfo");
    //set up the license as XML so we can attach as header
    JAXBElement<LicenseInfo> jaxbLicense =
            new JAXBElement<LicenseInfo>(
            q, LicenseInfo.class,licenseInfo);

    //set up a parser to hold the XML result of marshalling
    javax.xml.parsers.DocumentBuilderFactory dbf =
            DocumentBuilderFactory.newInstance();

    //this will store the XML result after marshalling
    org.w3c.dom.Document doc =
            dbf.newDocumentBuilder().newDocument();

    //turn our JAX-WS object into XML
    marshaller.marshal(jaxbLicense, doc);

    //JAX-WS RI Only--downcast
    WSBindingProvider bp = (WSBindingProvider)port;

    //use RI convenience method to create header
    //using the Document object
    bp.setOutboundHeaders(
        Headers.create(doc.getDocumentElement()));

    //Starting address bean
    AddressInput location1 = new AddressInput();
    location1.setAddress1("10 Columbus Circle");
    location1.setCityStateZip("New York,NY,10019");
    location1.setCountry(CountryCode.US);

    //End address bean
    AddressInput location2 = new AddressInput();
    location2.setAddress1("301 Park Avenue");
    location2.setCityStateZip("New York,NY,10022");
    location2.setCountry(CountryCode.US);

    UnitOfMeasure unitOfMeasure = UnitOfMeasure.MILES;

    //make the call--no explicit headers
    double result = port.addressToAddressDistance(
            location1, location2, unitOfMeasure);

    //show result
    System.out.println("Distance: " + result);
  } catch (Exception ex) {
    ex.printStackTrace();
  }
}
}
```

This code is doing a lot, so let's break it up a bit. Here you're getting a JAXB context on the `LicenseInfo` class. That means that the JAXB runtime will "recognize" an instance of `LicenseInfo` and any classes it references. You then create a `JAXBElement`, parameterized on the `LicenseInfo` class, which will allow you to marshal an instance of that class into XML, even though it may not be annotated with `@XmlRoot`. You then create a DOM document instance that will hold the XML tree of the license info object; the XML content is populated in the DOM tree at the invocation of the `marshal` method.

Now that your headers are prepared, you downcast the port you get off of the proxy to an instance of `WSBindingProvider`. This allows you to call the convenience method `setOutboundHeaders`. Because so far you only have the license info XML content that is bound in your DOM document's root element, you need to wrap them as SOAP headers before setting them on the port. You do that using the `Headers.create` method, which will wrap your XML license info content into SOAP headers.

You can read the JavaDoc for JAXB at *https://jaxb.dev.java.net/nonav/jaxb20-pfd/api/index.html*.

So at this point, you are home free. All you have to do is continue to populate your generated objects as you normally would, and invoke the `addressToAddressDistance` method on your port, as you normally would. The `WSBindingProvider` has already taken care of setting the headers for any outbound invocations off of that port, so you don't need to do anything further. This is in contrast to the prior method of sending headers with a request; no holder is required, and the operation invocation isn't as confusing. The downside, however, is that this client invocation requires classes in the reference implementation, making your client less portable.

You may need to add the *webservices-rt.jar* to your project's classpath in order to use the tools in the `com.sun.xml.ws` packages.

This is the SOAP message you're sending as the request:

```
---[HTTP request]---
SOAPAction: "http://www.strikeiron.com/AddressToAddressDistance"
Accept: text/xml, multipart/related, text/html, image/gif, image/jpeg,
*; q=.2, */*; q=.2
Content-Type: text/xml;charset="utf-8"
<?xml version="1.0" ?>
<S:Envelope xmlns:S="http://schemas.xmlsoap.org/soap/envelope/">
<S:Header>
  <LicenseInfo xmlns="http://ws.strikeiron.com">
    <RegisteredUser>
    <UserID>eben@example.com</UserID>
    <Password>secret</Password>
    </RegisteredUser>
  </LicenseInfo>
</S:Header>
```

```
<S:Body>
    <ns2:AddressToAddressDistance xmlns="http://ws.strikeiron.com"
     xmlns:ns2="http://www.strikeiron.com">
        <ns2:Location1>
          <ns2:address1>10 Columbus Circle</ns2:address1>
          <ns2:city_state_zip>New York,NY,10019</ns2:city_state_zip>
          <ns2:country>US</ns2:country></ns2:Location1>
          <ns2:Location2><ns2:address1>301 Park Avenue</ns2:address1>
          <ns2:city_state_zip>New York,NY,10022</ns2:city_state_zip>
          <ns2:country>US</ns2:country>
        </ns2:Location2>
        <ns2:UnitOfMeasure>Miles</ns2:UnitOfMeasure>
    </ns2:AddressToAddressDistance>
</S:Body>
</S:Envelope>
```

The headers appear in the envelope as you would hope, using a composite service-defined object, rather than merely a built-in schema type.

This is the output resulting from successfully invoking the service to calculate the distance between the Waldorf Hotel on Park Avenue and Thomas Keller's Per Se restaurant on Columbus Circle, both in New York City:

```
---[HTTP response 200]---
null: HTTP/1.1 200 OK
Cache-control: private
Content-type: text/xml; charset=utf-8
Content-length: 1009
X-powered-by: ASP.NET
Server: Microsoft-IIS/6.0
Date: Mon, 07 Jul 2008 00:33:18 GMT
X-aspnet-version: 1.1.4322

<?xml version="1.0" encoding="utf-8"?>
<soap:Envelope xmlns:soap="http://schemas.xmlsoap.org/soap/envelope/"
xmlns:xsi="http://www.w3.org/2001/XMLSchema-instance"
xmlns:xsd="http://www.w3.org/2001/XMLSchema">

  <soap:Header>
    <ResponseInfo xmlns="http://www.strikeiron.com">
      <ResponseCode>0</ResponseCode>
      <Response>Success</Response>
    </ResponseInfo>
    <SubscriptionInfo xmlns="http://ws.strikeiron.com">
      <LicenseStatusCode>0</LicenseStatusCode>
      <LicenseStatus>Valid license key</LicenseStatus>
      <LicenseActionCode>0</LicenseActionCode>
      <LicenseAction>Decremented hit count</LicenseAction>
      <RemainingHits>24</RemainingHits>
      <Amount>0</Amount>
    </SubscriptionInfo>
  </soap:Header>

  <soap:Body>
```

```
    <AddressToAddressDistanceResponse xmlns="http://www.strikeiron.com">
      <AddressToAddressDistanceResult>
            1.0286261980640472
      </AddressToAddressDistanceResult>
    </AddressToAddressDistanceResponse>
  </soap:Body>
</soap:Envelope>--------------------

Distance: 1.0286261980640472
```

This response message illustrates a few things. First, it indicates that the service is implemented in ASP.NET in the HTTP header, and you also see its version in an extension header. You see that there is considerable subscription information in the SOAP headers, and finally you see that the SOAP body contains the elements you were expecting: in particular, you got the actual distance in miles between the restaurant and the hotel you supplied.

If you don't want to do this work directly in the client code you're writing, you can also put it in a registered handler so that the headers are added just before the message is sent over the wire.

Additional workarounds

In the event that your provider insists on defining implicit headers that don't make it into your generated code, and you can't or don't want to use one of the methods just specified, perhaps you can use one of the following workarounds:

- Modify the generated SEIs by adding the parameters to their methods. In general, however, you want to avoid modifying generated code because then you will need to maintain it under version control. And this solution is not feasible if you regenerate this code during builds. Therefore, this is probably not something you would ever really want to do.
- Kick it old school and use the SAAJ API.
- Use your vendor's IDE to add headers.
- Add the headers to their own message, that is, send them prior to sending your actual content message. This is possible with multiple vendor implementations, including Apache CXF, but it is optional in the JAX-WS specification, and is therefore not recommended.

See Also

Recipe 5.12.

6.11 Intercepting the Request to Perform Protocol-Specific Work

Problem

You want to decorate your service request by intercepting it immediately prior to invocation so that you can modify certain protocol-specific parts of your request, such as SOAP headers. You don't want to bake this code into your message construction, or you aren't using SAAJ.

Solution

Implement the `javax.xml.ws.handler.soap.SOAPHandler<T extends SOAPMessageContext>` interface to use a `ProtocolHandler`. Write a class that implements the `HandlerResolver` interface and puts your handler in a list. Add an instance of your resolver to your service proxy before you get its port. The handler will be invoked at each request sent and each response received by the runtime.

Discussion

There are two types of message handlers defined in JAX-WS: `SOAPHandlers` and `LogicalHandlers`. If you want to operate on the payload of your message itself or its message context properties, use a logical handler (discussed in Recipe 6.12). If you want to operate on some part of the message that is specific to the binding protocol in use, such as SOAP, then you can use a protocol handler. One such handler, defined out of the box by JAX-WS, is the `SOAPHandler`, which allows you to operate on the SOAP envelope, such as its headers, attachment, or fault. This recipe examines that class.

Handlers are similar to EJB 3 interceptors or servlet filters. On the client side, handlers are used to modify or simply access SOAP messages immediately before they are sent across the wire to the service.

Message handlers can also be used on the server side, but that's covered in the next chapter.

With JAX-RPC, considerable configuration in *webservices.xml* was required to provide support for your handler within the runtime. Java EE 5 removes much of this burden by employing annotations.

Handlers are very useful within SOA, as they provide an easy and standard means of employing many of the decorations that some of the SOAP specifications make available. For example, you could use a handler to add a security block to an outbound message, or take advantage of WS-ReliableMessaging. You might wish to log outbound messages or even save them to disk so that you could resend them in the event of a network failure. It could be useful to add a unique ID to your message header.

> In fact, adding a unique ID to your message headers is probably a good idea. This does two things: it ensures that you have a useful reference key for extending the work of operating on a message across a grid or other distributed workflow; and it can also help prevent message replay attacks. A message replay attack happens when a malicious user records a message in transit and resends it. The only way to avoid replay is to ensure message uniqueness using an ID or timestamp. You can then register that the message with a given ID has been handled, and it shouldn't be processed any further.

Another use for handlers, as indicated in the JAX-WS specification, is to ensure that messages conform with one or more WS-I profiles.

The `javax.xml.ws.handler.Handler<C extends MessageContext>` interface defines three methods, each of which makes use of a context. The context used as the handler type parameter allows developers to pass properties between the multiple handlers processing the same message:

`boolean handleMessage(C context)`
: The primary method handler developers are interested in, as it gets invoked for normal processing of messages, inbound or outbound. Return true if you want to continue processing, or false to stop further processing.

`boolean handleFault(C context)`
: The method that determines what to do when a SOAP fault is thrown during message processing. Return true if you want to continue processing, or false to stop further processing.

`boolean close(MessageContext context)`
: The method used to perform any clean-up work necessary at the end of processing. It is invoked by the runtime immediately prior to dispatch.

In order to specify programmatically that your handler should be attached to a proxy instance, use a `javax.xml.ws.handler.HandlerResolver`. This interface allows the developer to control the handler chain that is set on a service proxy or dispatch object.

The `handleMessage` method is invoked at two different times in a typical SOAP request/response message exchange pattern: when sending the message and when receiving the request. More specifically, outbound messages are processed by handlers immediately following binding provider processing, and inbound messages are processed by handlers immediately before binding provider processing.

Implementing a simple handler

Let's implement a simple handler to see how they work. This protocol handler class will simply write all SOAP messages to a file output stream.

Do a quick check of the message context to find out if the current message is a request (outbound) or a response (inbound), and write a new file based on that. Note that in a production system, you wouldn't want to use a static name for all inbound and outbound messages, as each message would get overwritten with the new set. The thing to do is to set a unique message ID in the header on an outbound message (you could do this using a handler too, using SAAJ), and then use that as the filename to help you look it up later. Or, more simply, you could append to the file instead of creating a new one with each invocation. But that's not the point here. (See Example 6-10.)

Example 6-10. SaveMessageHandler.java

```
package com.soacookbook.ch03.handler;

import java.io.File;
import java.io.FileOutputStream;
import static java.lang.System.out;

import java.io.IOException;
import java.util.Set;
import javax.xml.namespace.QName;
import javax.xml.soap.SOAPException;
import javax.xml.ws.handler.MessageContext;
import javax.xml.ws.handler.soap.SOAPHandler;
import javax.xml.ws.handler.soap.SOAPMessageContext;
import org.apache.log4j.Logger;

public class SaveMessageHandler implements
            SOAPHandler<SOAPMessageContext> {

    private static final Logger LOGGER =
            Logger.getLogger(SaveMessageHandler.class);

    public boolean handleMessage(SOAPMessageContext ctx) {
        LOGGER.debug("Handling SOAP MESSAGE.");

        //determine if the message is coming or going
        Boolean outbound = (Boolean)
            ctx.get(MessageContext.MESSAGE_OUTBOUND_PROPERTY);

        //different file name for request and response
        String msgFileName = "";
        //auto-unbox
        if (outbound) {
            LOGGER.debug("Message is OUTBOUND");
            msgFileName = "outMsg.xml";
        } else {
            LOGGER.debug("Message is INBOUND");
            msgFileName = "inMsg.xml";
        }
```

```
        try {
            //do business logic here. We'll just log msg to file
            LOGGER.debug("Logging....\n");
            String dirName = "/tmp";
            File logFile = new File(dirName, msgFileName);
            logFile.createNewFile();
            FileOutputStream fos = new FileOutputStream(logFile);
            ctx.getMessage().writeTo(fos);
            fos.close();

            LOGGER.debug("Log complete.");
        } catch (SOAPException ex) {
            LOGGER.error("SOAP Exception--", ex);
        } catch (IOException ex) {
            LOGGER.error("IO Exception--", ex);
        }

        LOGGER.debug("Exiting handler normally.");
        //indicate that we want to continue processing
        return true;
    }

    public boolean handleFault(SOAPMessageContext ctx) {
        LOGGER.error("SOAP FAULT! Quitting.");
        return false;
    }

    public void close(MessageContext ctx) {
        LOGGER.debug("Closing handler.");
    }

    public Set<QName> getHeaders() {
        return null;
    }
}
```

Implementing the `SOAPHandler` interface gives you access to SOAP-specific properties, such as SOAP headers, in the messages to be handled. There are a few methods you need to implement, but the main one is `handleMessage`.

Now that you have a handler, you need to make it accessible to the service proxy. The way to do this is to associate it with a resolver. The handler resolver specifies the handlers in the chain for the service instance you set it on. The implementation for the resolver is shown in Example 6-11.

Example 6-11. HelloHandlerResolver.java

```
package com.soacookbook.ch03.handler;

import java.util.ArrayList;
import java.util.List;
import javax.xml.ws.handler.Handler;
```

```
import javax.xml.ws.handler.HandlerResolver;
import javax.xml.ws.handler.PortInfo;
import org.apache.log4j.Logger;

public class HelloHandlerResolver implements HandlerResolver {
    private static final Logger LOGGER =
            Logger.getLogger(HelloHandlerResolver.class);

    private final List<Handler> chain;

    //constructor. we'll set up chain here.
    public HelloHandlerResolver() {
        chain = new ArrayList<Handler>();
        chain.add(new SaveMessageHandler());
    }

    public List<Handler> getHandlerChain(PortInfo portInfo) {
        LOGGER.debug("Returning handler chain...");
        return chain;
    }
}
```

Each handler implementation acts within the context of a `HandlerChain`. A `HandlerChain` is similar in concept to a filter chain, which allows the programmer to specify multiple handlers for a given request and the order in which those handlers will be invoked. Your resolver class must implement the `HandlerResolver` interface, which defines the single method `getHandlerChain`, and the chain itself is simply represented as a `List<Handler>`. Note that you don't have to call that method yourself from your client or test class; JAX-WS will do it for you. All you need to do is implement that method to indicate what handlers are in this chain and then set the chain into the service.

Outbound messages (requests) are processed in the order specified in the handler chain list. Inbound messages (responses), however, are processed in the opposite order.

Now that everything is set up, you'll use the JUnit test case in Example 6-12 to invoke the service. All you have to do is attach an instance of the handler to the service proxy using its `setHandlerResolver` method. As long as the instance you specify implements the `Handler` interface or one of its subinterfaces (such as `SOAPHandler`), you should be in business.

Example 6-12. TestHandler.java

```
package com.soacookbook.ch03.test;

import static org.junit.Assert.*;

import com.soacookbook.ch03.*;
```

```
import com.soacookbook.ch03.handler.HelloHandlerResolver;
import com.soacookbook.ns.bin.*;
import org.apache.log4j.Logger;
import org.junit.Test;

import java.io.*;

/**
 * Tests that the handler is called on an invocation to
 * a service operation.
 */
public class HandlerTest {
    private static final Logger LOGGER =
            Logger.getLogger(HandlerTest.class);

    private String name;

    public HandlerTest() {
        name = "Eben";
    }

    @Test
    public void testHandler(){
        HelloWSService service = new HelloWSService();

        //Set handler resolver into service.
        service.setHandlerResolver(new HelloHandlerResolver());

        // Get the Hello stub
        Hello hello = service.getHelloWSPort();

        //Invoke the business method
        String result = hello.sayHello(name);

        assertEquals("Hello, " + name + "!", result);

        //Now go check your log file to see if handler worked.
      }
}
```

The client here is just a standard invocation of a proxy following a call to `wsimport` in your Ant script. That generates the service and port classes for you based on the WSDL. Before you invoke the `getXXXPort` method, make sure to set the handler resolver instance on the service.

This test performs the usual assertion check to make sure that what you got back in the response matches what you expected to get. But the real test lies in checking to make sure that the filesystem has the files the handler writes. If you open the contents of the file written by the handler on the response, it contains the entire SOAP envelope, as follows:

```
<S:Envelope xmlns:S="http://schemas.xmlsoap.org/soap/envelope/">
<S:Body>
<ns2:sayHello xmlns:ns2="http://ch03.soacookbook.com/">
```

```
<arg0>Eben</arg0>
</ns2:sayHello>
</S:Body></S:Envelope>
```

This is the entire request SOAP envelope written to *outMsg.xml* in the */tmp* directory. The response message will get written to the file *inMsg.xml* and has the following contents:

```
<S:Envelope xmlns:S="http://schemas.xmlsoap.org/soap/envelope/">
<S:Header/><S:Body>
<ns2:sayHelloResponse xmlns:ns2="http://ch03.soacookbook.com/">
<return>Hello, Eben!</return>
</ns2:sayHelloResponse>
</S:Body></S:Envelope>
```

The handler illustrated here just performs a simple pass through in order to focus on the skeleton of the handler interface. But handlers, like filters and EJB interceptors, offer an important opportunity for client developers to access or modify the contents of their messages, especially when they need to supply security credentials, add headers, change the message contents on the fly (for example, by encrypting them), or ensure that their outbound message conforms with a policy of some kind.

More About Handlers

There's a lot to working with handlers, so it's worth taking a moment to illustrate some of their darker corners. Here are several things to consider when working with handlers in general:

- JAX-WS handlers have a life cycle that is managed by the container. The life cycle defines two methods, similar to EJB 3 life cycle methods. The first is a method annotated with `@PostConstruct`, which acts as an initializer. The container will always call this method before calling any other method. The second is a method annotated with `@PreDestroy`, which can perform clean up before the handler instance is removed. You can define these life cycle methods in your handler if you wish to receive callbacks from the container notifying you of these events. These methods must have a `void` return type and take no arguments.
- If a `RuntimeException` is thrown during handler processing, the method annotated with `@PreDestroy` will be invoked so you have an opportunity to do cleanup before the handler instance is removed.
- Containers can pool handler instances if they like, but they aren't required to. If handler instances are pooled, they will be associated with only a single port type.
- Handlers are stateless. The container does not have to use the same handler instance when invoking the `handleMessage` or `handleFault` methods because of the potential to pool instances. Handlers do not maintain any client-specific state across requests.
- The transactional context in which handlers run is dictated to them by their associated component. Handlers are not allowed to specify their own transactions using `javax.transaction.UserTransaction`.

- The security context in which handlers run is dictated to them by the container. A handler may not perform security checks using role-based authorization, and cannot access the principal associated with the request.
- Different threads can be used to invoke each handler, and containers are not required to use the same thread to invoke a handler as it uses to invoke its service implementation.
- You can declare that your handler will process certain headers in the WSDL using the `getHeaders` method. This returns a `Set<QName>`. It's OK to return null if your handler doesn't process any headers or your WSDL doesn't define any.
- Logical handlers are always executed before all protocol handlers. Even if you define them as interspersed within your handler chain, they will be sorted with logicals first.
- Handlers are allowed to specify the `@Resource` annotation to define injectable resources for their use if they are running inside a managed environment (i.e., a container).

See Also

Recipe 6.12 to see how to write a handler that deals only with the payload, not the protocol wrapper (the SOAP envelope in this example).

6.12 Intercepting the Request to Perform Work on Your Payload

Problem

You want to access or modify only the payload of your request or response by intercepting it, and you don't want to bake this code into your message construction. You're not interested in the protocol wrapper, such as the SOAP envelope.

Solution

Use a `LogicalHandler` by implementing the `javax.xml.ws.handler.LogicalHandler` interface.

Discussion

Logical handlers are useful if you need to operate only on the payload of a message, whether you are using SOAP or REST. They are also the appropriate choice if you want to use JAXB for processing the message payload.

The framework for logical handlers is similar to that for protocol handlers, so for more background you may want to also read Recipe 6.11, in particular the sidebar "More About Handlers" on page 279.

The `printMetaData` method illustrates that even in a logical handler you can get access to certain aspects of the transport, and understand a lot about the message you're working with. The result of running the code for the meta data print method looks like this on a response for the client (inbound message):

```
********** HEADERS:
List of headers for Transfer-encoding: [chunked]
List of headers for null: [HTTP/1.1 200 OK]
List of headers for Content-type: [text/xml;charset="utf-8"]
List of headers for Server: [Sun Java System Application Server 9.1_01]
List of headers for X-powered-by: [Servlet/2.5]
List of headers for Date: [Thu, 15 May 2008 17:02:12 GMT]
********** RESPONSE CODE: 200
********** ATTACH: {}
```

6.13 Sharing Data Between Handler Invocations

Problem

You want to share data between invocations of your handlers within a chain during processing, but handler instances cannot rely on thread-local state.

Solution

Obtain the message context from the parameter to your handler, and add data to it. There are predefined properties you can set and access later, or you can add your own. These properties are exposed as a map.

The following code illustrates using a custom property and a built-in property with the message context to share data between two handlers defined on the same service.

Your test client adds the handler resolver to the service before getting the port:

```
@Test
public void testMessageContext(){
    HelloWSService service = new HelloWSService();

    //Set handler resolver into service.
    service.setHandlerResolver(new MultipleHandlerResolver());

    // Get the Hello stub
    Hello hello = service.getHelloWSPort();

    //Invoke the business method
    String result = hello.sayHello(name);

    assertEquals("Hello, " + name + "!", result);
}
```

This is a new handler resolver that defines more than one handler:

```
public class MultipleHandlerResolver implements HandlerResolver {
    private static final Logger LOGGER =
            Logger.getLogger(MultipleHandlerResolver.class);

    private final List<Handler> chain;

    //constructor. we'll set up chain here.
    public MultipleHandlerResolver() {
        chain = new ArrayList<Handler>();
        chain.add(new SetVersionHandler());
        chain.add(new VersionInstructionsHandler());
    }
//...
```

This resolver defines one handler that will set the version that the client is using into the message context. Another handler is defined to add additional instructions to the outgoing SOAP message given a certain client version. The handler that modifies the message context is shown in Example 6-13.

Example 6-13. SetVersionHandler.java

```
package com.soacookbook.ch03.handler;

import static java.lang.System.out;

import java.util.Set;
import javax.xml.namespace.QName;
import javax.xml.ws.handler.MessageContext;
import javax.xml.ws.handler.soap.SOAPHandler;
import javax.xml.ws.handler.soap.SOAPMessageContext;
import org.apache.log4j.Logger;

public class SetVersionHandler implements
            SOAPHandler<SOAPMessageContext> {

    private static final Logger LOGGER =
            Logger.getLogger(SetVersionHandler.class);

    public boolean handleMessage(SOAPMessageContext ctx) {
        LOGGER.debug("Handling SOAP MESSAGE.");

        //determine if the message is coming or going
        final Boolean outbound = (Boolean)
            ctx.get(MessageContext.MESSAGE_OUTBOUND_PROPERTY);

        if (outbound){
            ctx.put("SVC-VERSION", "1.0");
        }
        return true;
    }

    public boolean handleFault(SOAPMessageContext ctx) {
        LOGGER.error("SOAP FAULT! Handle here...");
        return false;
    }
```

```
    public void close(MessageContext ctx) {
        LOGGER.debug("Closing handler.");
    }

    public Set<QName> getHeaders() {
        return null;
    }
}
```

The handler here simply adds a string key/value pair to the message context. That key can be used by other handlers in the chain to retrieve the value. Note that you only set the version metadata if the message is outbound.

> Recall that handlers are invoked in the order specified in the resolver when outgoing, and in the reverse order when inbound. Logical handlers are always called before protocol handlers.

Now the next handler in the chain is invoked before the message is dispatched. It specifies instructions for the service if a certain version is in use, and adds them to an attachment to the outbound message, as shown in Example 6-14.

Example 6-14. Returning binary data from a web service

```
public class VersionInstructionsHandler implements
                SOAPHandler<SOAPMessageContext> {

public boolean handleMessage(SOAPMessageContext ctx) {
        LOGGER.debug("Handling SOAP MESSAGE.");

        //determine if the message is coming or going
        final Boolean outbound = (Boolean)
            ctx.get(MessageContext.MESSAGE_OUTBOUND_PROPERTY);

        //is message incoming?
        if (outbound) {

            //get the version from context
            final String version = (String)ctx.get("SVC-VERSION");

            LOGGER.debug("Service Version: " + version);


            //if the version is 1.0, give user instructions
            //for upgrading to coming version.
            if ("1.0".equals(version)) {
                try {
                SOAPMessage msg = ctx.getMessage();
                SOAPBody body = msg.getSOAPBody();
                SOAPElement content =
                        (SOAPElement)body.getFirstChild();
```

```
                String value = content.getTextContent();

                LOGGER.debug("Print value: " + value);

                //because version is old, attach instructions
                //for migrating to new version

                //Create SOAP attachment
                AttachmentPart ap = msg.createAttachmentPart();
                String s = "Client will support JMS in " +
                        "version 1.5.";
                ap.setContent(s, "text/plain");
                ap.setContentId("Version-1.5-Notice");
                msg.addAttachmentPart(ap);

                LOGGER.debug("Attachment added.");

                } catch (Exception ex) {
                    LOGGER.error("Problem.", ex);
                }
            }
        }
        return true;
    }
//...
```

The attachment mechanism itself is not important at this point. What you want to focus on here is the idea that you can pass data between handlers using the context, and then take some action based on it. It is perhaps unusual to have a client sending the service some sort of notice in this way, but the demonstration is useful for our purposes here.

The handler chain is complete, and the message is dispatched. But because you modified it on the way out, it results in a multipart SOAP request. Along with the data in the SOAP body, it sends the attachment as well. The final SOAP message looks like Example 6-15.

Example 6-15. Passing binary data to a web service

```
---[HTTP request]---
SOAPAction: ""
Accept: text/xml, multipart/related, text/html,
image/gif, image/jpeg, *; q=.2, */*; q=.2
Content-Type: multipart/related; type="text/xml";
boundary="uuid:002fa642-b700-47c4-a298-ed1e1fb03795"
--uuid:002fa642-b700-47c4-a298-ed1e1fb03795
Content-Type: text/xml

<?xml version="1.0" ?>
<S:Envelope xmlns:S="http://schemas.xmlsoap.org/soap/envelope/">
<S:Body>
<ns2:sayHello xmlns:ns2="http://ch03.soacookbook.com/">
<arg0 xmlns="">Eben</arg0>
</ns2:sayHello></S:Body>
</S:Envelope>
```

```
--uuid:002fa642-b700-47c4-a298-ed1e1fb03795
Content-Id:<Version-1.5-Notice>
Content-Type: text/plain
Content-Transfer-Encoding: binary

Client will support JMS in version 1.5.
--uuid:002fa642-b700-47c4-a298-ed1e1fb03795
```

The attachment was added to the message associated with the given UUID, and this will be dispatched to the service.

Discussion

Message contexts are used to share state related to message processing. The `javax.xml.ws.handler.MessageContext` is the super-interface for message contexts in JAX-WS. You may recall from Recipe 6.11 that the `handleMessage` and `handleFault` methods of `Handler` accept a generic type parameter of `<C extends MessageContext>`. `LogicalMessageContext` and `SOAPMessageContext` both extend `MessageContext` to provide properties useful for their respective handler types, therefore fulfilling the generic type parameter contract. We'll look at the capabilities of these subinterfaces in a moment. But `MessageContext` provides a number of keys out of the box that can give you useful information about the current message being processed by the handler.

MessageContext properties

Many properties are available in the `MessageContext` interface, including:

- HTTP-related properties that allow you to inspect the headers, the request method, the response code, and the response headers.
- Serlvet and path-related properties that give you the path info object, the query string, and the servlet request and response objects.
- Handler-specific properties. For example, `MESSAGE_OUTBOUND_PROPERTY` is used to determine whether you are processing an inbound or outbound message (it's true if your message is outbound, false if inbound). Checking this property allows a simplification of the interface over the old JAX-RPC way that required defining two methods in the handler interface. You can also get access to MIME attachments using these properties.
- WSDL-specific properties. Using these properties gives you access to information about the service, port, and operation that this handler is associated with.

See the JavaDoc available at *http://java.sun.com/javaee/5/docs/api/javax/xml/ws/handler/MessageContext.html* for a complete list.

SOAPMessageContext

The `SOAPMessageContext` interface defines methods to get the SOAP message itself from the context, set the message back into the context, get the headers according to their

QName from the message in the context, and get the SOAP actor roles associated with the processing across a chain.

LogicalMessageContext

The LogicalMessageContext interface extends MessageContext to provide access to the message. The message is represented in a protocol-independent format. To this end, this interface adds only a single method to the MessageContext interface: getMessage, which returns a LogicalMessage.

6.14 Passing Binary Data in a Request

Problem

You need to send binary data, such as an image file or PDF, within the body of a SOAP message.

Solution

Use a byte array to represent your binary data. The WSDL will represent this as xs:base64 or xs:hexBinary.

Example 6-16 demonstrates this. The use case idea here is a web service operation called getImage, which accepts a string as input. The string is an identifier for an image in a database that has been previously stored as a BLOB (Binary Large Object). You could use the ID to perform a SQL query and get the BLOB out, returning it as a byte array. To keep it simple and focused, though, just create a regular byte array and return it.

Example 6-16. Binary data method

```
@WebMethod
public @WebResult(name="imageResponse",
    targetNamespace="http://ns.soacookbook.com/ch03")
    byte[]
    getImage(
    @WebParam(name="imageRequest",
    targetNamespace="http://ns.soacookbook.com/ch03")
    String imageId) {

    //Use the passed ID to find this instance in the database
    //This is our fake image data...
    byte[] imageBytes = {1,0};

    //If you want to save your image data to a database,
    //create a PreparedStatement and use:
    ...
    ps.setBinaryStream(1,
        new ByteArrayInputStream(sigImageData), imageBytes.length);
```

```
    return imageBytes;
}
```

Note that this example shows how you would convert a BLOB to a returnable byte array for the service operation, as that's the more real-world use case.

The WSDL generated by these JAX-WS annotations will generate the basic XML schema `xs:base64` type for the byte array returned. The important consideration here is that handling binary data will probably require a conversation with clients out of band so that they know what to expect. If, as in this example, you request image data based on an identifier, how does the client know what image codec to expect? Is this a GIF, a JPG, or a PNG? If it is a bitmap or a TIFF, as many credit card readers produce, that file format is not natively supported within Java SE, and the client must have the Advanced Imaging API on its classpath.

Use care when packaging binary data in SOAP messages, or clients may not know what to expect. You can advertise in comments the type or codec of your binary data, or you could advertise it in making specific method names. A method to retrieve mugshots could be more appropriately named `getMugshotTiff()` or `getMugshotJpg()`, for instance.

See Also

Recipe 7.22.

6.15 Using Binary Data in a SOAP Message

Problem

You have binary data, such as an image or a PDF, that you need to pass to a web service.

Solution

Use a byte array as the parameter type.

Discussion

Using a byte array as the parameter type will allow you to read a stream of bytes on the client and pass it straight into the method. The SOAP mechanism will encode it as `xs:base64Binary` content and pass it to the service. Here is such a method as defined on the web service:

```
@WebMethod
@SOAPBinding(parameterStyle=SOAPBinding.ParameterStyle.WRAPPED)
public @WebResult(name="putResponse",
        targetNamespace="http://ns.soacookbook.com/bin")
        String
```

```
        put(
        @WebParam(name="putData",
        targetNamespace="http://ns.soacookbook.com/bin")
        byte[] binaryData) {
```

The matching generated schema looks like this:

```
<xs:element name="put" type="tns:put"></xs:element>
<xs:complexType name="put">
  <xs:sequence>
    <xs:element name="putData" type="xs:base64Binary"
      form="qualified" nillable="true" minOccurs="0" />
  </xs:sequence>
</xs:complexType>
```

Let's make a client in the form of a unit test that will read in some image data and post it to the service. Here you will pass in a JPG image as the value of the parameter to the put request on the service. The service will return an ID, which for the purposes of the unit test will be "007". See Example 6-17.

Example 6-17. BinaryDataTest.java

```
package com.soacookbook.ch03.test;

import static org.junit.Assert.*;

import com.soacookbook.ns.bin.*;
import org.apache.log4j.Logger;
import org.junit.Test;

import java.io.*;
/**
 * Tests the BinaryData service.
 */
public class BinaryDataTest {
    private static final Logger LOGGER =
            Logger.getLogger(BinaryDataTest.class);

    private static final String FILE_PATH =
            "/home/ehewitt/soacookbook/repository/code/" +
            "chapters/client/winchesterHouse.jpg";

    public BinaryDataTest() { }

    /**
     * Client has a binary file such as image or PDF it would
     * like to send to service for storage or processing.
     * This client reads it in and passes to service, which
     * generates an ID for it and returns the ID so client
     * can get back data later if necessary.
     */
    @Test
    public void testPutBinaryData(){
        LOGGER.debug("");
        try {
            BinaryDataService svc = new BinaryDataService();
```

```
            BinaryData port = svc.getBinaryDataPort();

            File f = new File(FILE_PATH);
            byte[] imageData = getFileAsBytes(f);

            LOGGER.debug("*** Read in file of bytes: " +
                    imageData.length);

            String id = port.put(imageData);

            LOGGER.debug("Got id returned from service: " + id);

            assertEquals("007", id);
        } catch (IOException ex) {
           fail();
           ex.printStackTrace();
        }
    }

    // Returns file contents in a byte array.
    private static byte[] getFileAsBytes(File file) throws IOException {
        InputStream is = new FileInputStream(file);

        // Get file size
        long length = file.length();
        if (length > Integer.MAX_VALUE) {
            throw new IOException("File is too big to read: " +
                    file.getName());
        }

        // Create the byte array to hold the data
        byte[] bytes = new byte[(int)length];

        // Read the bytes in
        int offset = 0;
        int numRead = 0;
        while (offset < bytes.length
               && (numRead=is.read(bytes, offset,
                    bytes.length-offset)) >= 0) {
            offset += numRead;
        }

        // Make sure we read all bytes
        if (offset < bytes.length) {
            throw new IOException("Could not read file " +
                    file.getName());
        }

        is.close();
        return bytes;
    }
}
```

As you can see, the hard part is handled by the JAX-WS runtime. All you have to do is read the image file in from the local filesystem so you can use it as the argument to the operation.

Here is what the SOAP message looks like on the wire:


```
<?xml version="1.0" ?>
<S:Envelope xmlns:S="http://schemas.xmlsoap.org/soap/envelope/">
<S:Body>
<put xmlns="http://ns.soacookbook.com/bin">
<putData>/9j/4AAQSkZJRgABAgEBLAEsAAD/4RFdRXhpZgAATU0AKgAAAAgABwE
SAAMAAAABAAEAAAEaAAUAAAABAAAAYgEbAAUAAAABAAAAagEoAAMAAAABAAIAAAE
xAAIAAAAUAAAAcgEyAAIAAAAUAAAAhodpAAQAAAABAAAAnAAAAMgAAAEsAAAAAQA
AASwAAAABQWRvYmUgUGhvdG9zaG9wIDcuD2qDO1Kt9Vv+Cr7f0fyvp11DwJ//9k=
//....

</putData>
</put>
</S:Body>
</S:Envelope
```


See Also

Recipe 6.16 to see how to optimize the transmission of binary data on the client side.

6.16 Enabling Binary Optimization on the Client

Problem

Your client must send binary data to a SOAP-based web service, and you want to optimize it for performance.

Solution

Encode your binary data as `xs:base64Binary` content. Then enable MTOM on the client side by passing `javax.xml.ws.MTOMFeature` to the proxy constructor.

MTOM stands for Message Transmission Optimization Mechanism. It is a specification created by the W3C to support the selective encoding of portions of a message. The XML infoset is still available within the SOAP message, so it is not obfuscated by this process.

JAX-WS-compliant vendors are required to support MTOM, so this code is portable.

So how do you set it up? If you review the `WebServiceClient` classes generated by JAX-WS, you will notice that each includes two `get<X>Port` methods: one that takes no arguments, and another that takes a variable length argument of `WebServiceFeature` objects. The catalog `WebServiceClient` as generated by JAX-WS during wsimport is shown in Example 6-18.

Example 6-18. Generated web service client

```
@WebEndpoint(name = "CatalogPort")
public Catalog getCatalogPort() {
    return super.getPort(new QName("http://ns.soacookbook.com",
            "CatalogPort"), Catalog.class);
}

@WebEndpoint(name = "CatalogPort")
public Catalog getCatalogPort(WebServiceFeature... features) {
    return super.getPort(new QName("http://ns.soacookbook.com",
            "CatalogPort"), Catalog.class, features);
}
```

A `WebServiceFeature` is a standard manner of enabling and disabling support for a variety of useful mechanisms at runtime. Some features come built in with JAX-WS, and vendors can provide additional features. You can also write your own.

The class `javax.xml.ws.soap.MTOMFeature` extends `WebServiceFeature`. The generated client interfaces make it easy to invoke your service operations using a built-in or custom feature. To use MTOM on the client, simply retrieve the port using the factory that accepts a variable-length argument of `WebServiceFeature` objects, passing in an instance of the `MTOMFeature`. Here's how you can enable MTOM using the `getCatalogPort` method:

```
Catalog catalogPort = service.getCatalogPort(new MTOMFeature());
```

The implementation is handled for you by the runtime.

The `MTOMFeature` constructor also accepts an optional integer argument indicating the threshold, or the number of bytes that the binary data should be before being sent as an attachment. The default value for the threshold is 0.

See Also

Recipe 7.22.

6.17 Validating a SOAP Payload Against a Schema with Metro

Problem

You want an easier way to validate your messages against an XML schema than the one you saw using SAAJ in Recipe 5.19.

Solution

Use the annotation `com.sun.xml.ws.developer.SchemaValidation` from Metro on your service class. You can also use the `handler` attribute on this annotation to point to a particular class that implements the `Handler` interface that can respond to the validation events.

On the client side, create a new `SchemaValidationFeature` and pass it to your port.

Discussion

If you want to validate payloads against a schema on the client, you can use the schema validation feature, like this:

```
SignatureCapture port = null;

try {
  final SigCapService service =
          new SigCapService(wsdlLocation, QNAME);

  port = service.getSignatureCapturePort(
          new AddressingFeature(),
          new SchemaValidationFeature(
            SigCapClientValidationHandler.class));

//invoke service...
```

Here you have used `wsimport` to generate artifacts to use in invoking the service. The variable-length argument list that the generated port proxy accepts allows you to pass zero or more features that you'd like the JAX-WS runtime to manage for you. Here I'm using two: WS-Addressing, and schema validation. This will examine the payload of the outbound SOAP message during marshaling of the Java object to XML, and create an instance of the `SigCapClientValidationHandler` class. Inside this handler class, you implement the required interface and respond to SAX parsing events as they occur. Example 6-19 shows a simple handler implementation.

Example 6-19. Validation handler implementation

```
import com.sun.xml.ws.developer.ValidationErrorHandler;
import org.xml.sax.SAXParseException;
import org.xml.sax.SAXException;
import org.apache.log4j.Logger;

/**
 * The error handler that catches validation problems against
 * the schema.
 *
 * @author ehewitt
 * @author bmericle
 */
public final class SigCapClientValidationHandler
        extends ValidationErrorHandler {
```

```
    private static final Logger LOGGER =
      Logger.getLogger(SigCapClientValidationHandler.class);

    public SigCapClientValidationHandler() {
        LOGGER.debug("Schema Validation Handler created.");
    }

    @Override
    public void warning(final SAXParseException e) throws SAXException {
        LOGGER.warn("Schema Validation Warning: " +
          e.getLocalizedMessage());
        // Store warnings in the packet so that they can be retrieved
        //from the endpoint
        packet.invocationProperties.put("Schema Validation Warning.", e);
        throw e;
    }

    @Override
    public void error(final SAXParseException e) throws SAXException {
        LOGGER.error("Schema Validation Error: " + e.getLocalizedMessage());
        throw e;
    }

    @Override
    public void fatalError(final SAXParseException e) throws SAXException {
        LOGGER.warn("Schema Validation Fatal Error: " +
          e.getLocalizedMessage());
        throw e;
    }
}
```

What's happening here is fairly straightforward. The parser emits events when it stumbles onto something in the XML instance that doesn't match the schema. Here I'm just logging the problems and rethrowing the exceptions, but you could do something more interesting as your needs suggest.

Adding Metro to the client in Maven

The obvious drawback to this solution is that you need to include the Metro JAR on the client. If you're building your Java client application in Maven, here's what you need to add to your POM's <dependencies>:

```
<dependency>
  <groupId>com.sun.xml.ws</groupId>
  <artifactId>webservices-rt</artifactId>
  <version>1.3</version>
  <scope>compile</scope>
</dependency>

<dependency>
  <groupId>javax.xml</groupId>
  <artifactId>webservices-api</artifactId>
  <version>1.3</version>
```

```
    <scope>compile</scope>
  </dependency>
```

6.18 Making Asynchronous Calls with a JAX-WS Client

Problem

You want to invoke an operation on your service endpoint interface asynchronously.

Solution

Add the `<enableAsyncMapping>` custom binding on the server side in the WSDL, then use one of the `invokeAsync` methods available on your SEI.

Asynchronous web service clients can be constructed in one of two ways: with a callback, or with polling. Both methods become available when using a single `<enableAsyncMapping>` customization.

Before you attempt to call `invokeAsync`, you need to enable asynchronous mappings on the WSDL using the `jaxws:bindings` element. Otherwise, your invocations may appear to succeed, but they won't actually be asynchronous. That is, they'll block, just like a normal call to `invoke`.

With the polling method, the client blocks, checking repeatedly for the response. This is not suitable for a GUI application where the main thread must be free to keep the application responsive to user interaction. With the callback method, clients must pass a `Handler<T>` to the web service operation at invocation, and the handler object will be populated when the response is ready. This allows the application thread to continue with other business in the meantime.

In order to allow a client to invoke an operation asynchronously, you must first specify the binding customization in a file that you point to during client generation with `wsimport`.

It does not matter what name you give the binding customization file or what extension you use, but .xml is the convention for JAX-WS custom binding files. This is opposed to .xjb, which is the convention for JAXB custom binding files.

An example of a custom binding file that enables asynchronous mappings is shown in Example 6-20.

Example 6-20. Custom JAX-WS binding to enable asynchronous operations

```
<bindings
    xmlns:xsd="http://www.w3.org/2001/XMLSchema"
    xmlns:wsdl="http://schemas.xmlsoap.org/wsdl/"
    wsdlLocaption="http://localhost:8080/soaCookbookWS/SoaCookbookService?wsdl"
    xmlns="http://java.sun.com/xml/ns/jaxws">
    <bindings node="wsdl:definitions">
        <package name="com.soacookbook.ch03"/>
        <enableAsyncMapping>true</enableAsyncMapping>
    </bindings>
</bindings>
```

In this file, you're using the binding customizations available in the `http://java.sun.com/xml/ns/jaxws` namespace to indicate what nodes you want to adapt.

When you include binding customizations in `wsimport`, you must create a child element of the `wsimport` task that points to your binding file, like this:

```
<binding dir="..." includes="..." />
```

So you will need to update your *build.xml* file to include this code. The new `wsimport` task looks like Example 6-21.

Example 6-21. The wsimport Ant task including binding customizations

```
<wsimport
    wsdl="${wsdl.url}"
    destdir="${gen.classes.dir}"
    sourcedestdir="${src.gen.dir}"
    keep="true"
    extension="false"
    verbose="true" >
    <binding dir="${binding.dir}" includes="${binding.file}" />
</wsimport>
```

You can use a wildcard to specify all files with a given extension if you have multiple binding customization files in the given directory. If you want to point to multiple directories, you can use more than one `<binding>` element.

If you are executing from the command line, use the `-b` option to specify the location of the binding file. You don't have to put all of your customizations in a single file; if you want to separate them for greater flexibility, just use a new `-b` option for each file. Likewise, you can specify multiple binding elements in the Ant task.

Running your build script now modifies your generated code. It generates two separate methods within the SEI (here, `SoaCookbook.java`) in addition to the regular synchronous method that was generated. Each asynchronous method has a different manner of handling the asynchronous behavior: polling and callbacks. We'll examine these in the following sections.

Using Asynchronous Polling

This section assumes that you have performed the steps earlier in this recipe to generate the asynchronous SEI. This looks like the code in Example 6-22.

Example 6-22. Generated polling method

```
@WebMethod(operationName = "doLongJob")
@RequestWrapper(localName = "doLongJob",
    targetNamespace = "http://ns.soacookbook.com",
    className = "com.soacookbook.ns.DoLongJob")
@ResponseWrapper(localName = "doLongJobResponse",
    targetNamespace = "http://ns.soacookbook.com",
    className = "com.soacookbook.ns.DoLongJobResponse")
public Response<DoLongJobResponse> doLongJobAsync(
    @WebParam(name = "jobName", targetNamespace = "http://ns.soacookbook.com")
    String jobName);
```

The polling operation signature does not return a `DoLongJobResponse`, as the regular blocking method does. Instead it returns a `Response<DoLongJobResponse>`. The `javax.xml.ws.Response<T>` is a standard JAX-WS class that wraps the regular return type. It extends `Future<T>`, and gives you access to the context map for operation responses. For asynchronous operations it offers an `isDone` method to check if the operation has finished, and a `cancel` operation to allow clients to interrupt the call.

A client using polling will need to manually perform this check. Let's add a method to your client class that will handle all of the interaction with the SEI. This class, shown in Example 6-23, will act as a business delegate within a larger application in order to encapsulate the fact that the work is being performed by a web service.

Example 6-23. Using polling to invoke operation asynchronously

```
package com.soacookbook.ch03;

import java.util.*;

import javax.xml.bind.*;
import javax.xml.soap.*;

import org.apache.log4j.Logger;
import com.soacookbook.ns.*;
import javax.xml.ws.Response;

public class AsynchClient {
  private static final Logger LOGGER = Logger.getLogger(AsynchClient.class);

    public String doLongJobPolling(String jobName) throws Exception {
        LOGGER.debug("Executing.");

        SoaCookbookService svc = new SoaCookbookService();
        SoaCookbook port = svc.getSoaCookbookPort();
        Response<DoLongJobResponse> response =
                port.doLongJobAsync(jobName);
```

```
        LOGGER.debug("Invoked service.");
        while(!response.isDone()){
          LOGGER.debug("Waiting...");
          Thread.sleep(1000); //do something
        }

        DoLongJobResponse res = response.get();
        String status = res.getJobDone();

        LOGGER.debug("Status: " + status);

        return status;
    }
}
```

Once the isDone method returns true, the response object is available.

Running this client from a unit test using a fabricated job name of "My Batch" has this output:

```
Executing.
Invoked service.
Waiting...
Waiting...
Waiting...
Waiting...
Status: Job is done running: My Batch
```

Using Asynchronous Callbacks

This section assumes that you have performed the steps earlier in this recipe to generate the asynchronous SEI.

The second generated method uses a callback defined by the client that will receive the response from the service operation when it is complete. The method signature is as follows:

```
@WebMethod(operationName = "doLongJob")
@RequestWrapper(localName = "doLongJob",
    targetNamespace = "http://ns.soacookbook.com",
    className = "com.soacookbook.ns.DoLongJob")
@ResponseWrapper(localName = "doLongJobResponse",
    targetNamespace = "http://ns.soacookbook.com",
    className = "com.soacookbook.ns.DoLongJobResponse")
public Future<?> doLongJobAsync(
    @WebParam(name="jobName", targetNamespace="http://ns.soacookbook.com")
    String jobName,
    @WebParam(name = "asyncHandler", targetNamespace = "")
    AsyncHandler<DoLongJobResponse> asyncHandler);
```

Notice that there are two changes to the regular method signature. The method does not return a DoLongJobResponse, which the WSDL defines, nor does it return a Response<DoLongJobResponse> as with the asynchronous polling method. Rather, it returns a `Future<?>`. The second change is that, unlike the polling method, which does not modify the argument list from the original method, this adds a parameter, which is an `AsyncHandler`, parameterized on `DoLongJobResponse`. But where does this `AsyncHandler` implementation come from? You have to write it, and pass an instance of it to the service invocation. The interface contains only one method, called `handleResponse`, which accepts a `Response<T>`.

About Future<?>

While GUI programmers might be used to it by now, `Future<?>` is perhaps not something commonly encountered by web programmers. `Future`s were first introduced in Java 5 as part of the concurrency library. A `Future` represents an abstract task that bears some result, and provides methods for managing the life cycle of such a task. These methods allow you to check if a task has been cancelled, to check if it is complete, and to collect the result of the task. You can also cancel the task if desired, and specify an amount of time you want to wait for the task to complete before throwing a `TimeoutException`. The tasks themselves are usually described by an implementation of the `Runnable` or `Callable` interfaces, and `Future` generally wraps them.

The method used to collect the result of the task the `Future` represents is `get`, which waits if necessary.

Behind the scenes, the `Future` will put the result into the handler, which you can use to perform additional work once the result is ready.

Given the way that `Future<?>` works, you do not want to retrieve the result directly from the `Future` object itself. The "?" represents a wildcard with no upper bound and has no standard type, which means the effective type is `Object`. So while it is possible to do this:

```
DoLongJobResponse r = (DoLongJobResponse)task.get();
```

clients are discouraged from casting the result in this manner, as it could lead to non-portable behavior. Instead, use the handler implementation to retrieve the result if necessary.

Make sure that you invoke `isDone` before attempting to use the result. If it is not yet ready, the future's `get` returns null.

Writing the callback handler

A callback handlers can be implemented for dispatch clients or SEI clients. It is just a class that implements the `AsyncHandler` interface, which defines the single method `handleResponse`.

Within a callback handler, the developer has access to the following:

- The JNDI context at `java:comp/env`
- The resource managers
- Enterprise Java Beans

Dependency injection is not available within a callback handler. Vendors may allow this, but the spec does not require it, so such behavior, if available, is not portable. You can use JNDI to look up your resource if it is bound.

There are just a few rules regarding writing the handler. First, it cannot itself be an EJB or a servlet. Also, there is no transaction context specified for callback handlers. That means that while you can create a `UserTransaction` within your `handleResponse` method, you cannot propagate it to another resource; it must be either committed or rolled back before your method exits. Otherwise, the callback handler implementation is fairly straightforward. This is shown in Example 6-24.

Example 6-24. AsyncHandler<T> implementation

```
class MyHandler implements AsyncHandler<DoLongJobResponse> {
  private static final Logger LOGGER =
        Logger.getLogger(MyHandler.class);

  private DoLongJobResponse response;

  public void handleResponse(Response<DoLongJobResponse> in) {
    LOGGER.debug("Executing callback handler.");

    try {
      response = in.get();
      LOGGER.debug("Got response! " +
                   response.getJobDone());

    } catch (ExecutionException e) {
        e.printStackTrace();
    } catch (InterruptedException e) {
        e.printStackTrace();
    }
  }

  public DoLongJobResponse get() {
    return response;
  }
}
```

The implementation requires only the single `handleResponse` method. Because you save the response to an instance field, there's an additional method to retrieve the result of the operation. In general, you should not need to return the result, but rather work with it directly in the handler.

Example 6-25 shows the client code that uses this handler to produce the callback.

Example 6-25. Asynchronous Callback Client

```
public void doLongJobCallback(String jobName) throws Exception {
    LOGGER.debug("Executing.");

    SoaCookbookService svc = new SoaCookbookService();
    SoaCookbook port = svc.getSoaCookbookPort();

    MyHandler handler = new MyHandler();
    Future<?> task = port.doLongJobAsync(jobName, handler);

    LOGGER.debug("Invoked service.");

    while(!task.isDone()){
        LOGGER.debug("Waiting...");
        Thread.sleep(1000); //do something
    }
}
```

This code gets the SEI, and then invokes its overloaded `doLongJobAsync` method. You create an instance of your custom handler and remember that no such method is actually defined in the WSDL, but is generated due to your binding customizations on the client side. This method returns a `Future`, which will eventually receive and wrap the result of the operation, making it available to operate on within your handler.

The output of running this code is as follows:

```
AsynchClient.doLongJobCallback - Executing.
AsynchClient.doLongJobCallback - Invoked service.
AsynchClient.doLongJobCallback - Waiting...
AsynchClient.doLongJobCallback - Waiting...
AsynchClient.doLongJobCallback - Waiting...
AsynchClient.doLongJobCallback - Waiting...
MyHandler.handleResponse - Executing callback handler.
MyHandler.handleResponse - Got response! Job is done running: Some Batch
```

In the event that a web operation call fails when using one of the asynchronous invocation methods, the spec requires that a `java.util.concurrent.ExecutionException` is thrown from the `Response.get` method. The cause is the original exception that was thrown, which is always a `WebServiceException` or a subclass.

6.19 Overriding the Endpoint Address in an SEI

Problem

You want to create a JAX-WS client and pass it a different endpoint address at runtime.

Solution

Get the request context from the port and use its map to set the `BindingProvider.ENDPOINT_ADDRESS_PROPERTY` constant as a key with the new endpoint location as its value.

Discussion

When you generate a service proxy from a WSDL, the endpoint address is hardcoded into the class. But it is possible to override the endpoint location your client will contact using constants in the `javax.xml.ws.BindingProvider` interface. This interface defines constants for endpoint location as well as those for indicating a SOAP action, maintaining session state across requests, and others.

It's very simple to use, as shown in Example 6-26.

Example 6-26. Setting the endpoint address property

```
public class ClientServlet extends HttpServlet {
    @WebServiceRef(wsdlLocation=
       "http://localhost:8080/CalculatorApp/CalculatorWSService?wsdl")
    public CalculatorWSService service;

protected void processRequest(HttpServletRequest request, HttpServletResponse response)
    throws ServletException, IOException {

  org.me.calculator.client.CalculatorWS port = service.getCalculatorWSPort();

  ((BindingProvider)port).getRequestContext().put(
    BindingProvider.ENDPOINT_ADDRESS_PROPERTY,
    "http://localhost:4933/CalculatorApp/CalculatorWSService?wsdl");


  int i = Integer.parseInt(request.getParameter("value1"));
  int j = Integer.parseInt(request.getParameter("value2"));

  int result = port.add(i, j);
```

At the point in the code where you get the proxy from the service instance, the address is set to call whatever is specified within the SEI. The request context is not a wrapper, but a simple map that is used to specify key/value pairs. In this example, the client is a servlet whose `@WebServiceRef.wsdlLocation` property indicates a WSDL on port 8080; use the `BindingProvider.ENDPOINT_ADDRESS_PROPERTY` to specify a WSDL on a different port. At runtime, the SEI will use the WSDL at 4933.

There are many uses for such code. Because the WSDL location value is specified by a string, you can dynamically override the location that is set in the `@WebServiceRef` annotation. This might be useful, for example, if you want to point certain clients to a different version of the WSDL that specifies different policies.

This only works, of course, if the service and ports represented at the target endpoint location match those on the WSDL from which the client was originally created. Otherwise, you'll get an error.

Summary

In this chapter, we looked at how to do a variety of things with the new web services API, which makes heavy use of Java 5 annotations. In some cases, these examples replaced the more complex and lower-level work we would have had to do with SAAJ. In general, the code in this chapter is portable between different vendor implementations of JAX-WS, including Glassfish, Oracle WebLogic, and Apache products such as CXF and Axis.

CHAPTER 7

Providing SOAP-Based Web Services

7.0 Introduction

Web services have been available in Java for years, but working with them as a developer has been a complicated process, involving a great number of brittle steps. With the advent of Java EE 5, much of this complexity has been reduced. Deployment descriptors have given way to annotations, and much of the boilerplate work is generated for you.

Despite this good news, doing web services in the real world remains very tricky. The actual complexity of web services is still very real; the fact that we are shielded from some of the grunt work does not change how the plumbing works. Writing maintainable, flexible code that prevents vendor lock-in as much as possible is a challenge on any project. The added flexibility in Java EE 5 gives us more options; which is terrific, but it also presents us with a new array of configuration and implementation choices that can be daunting to the novice. So we have a lot of work ahead of us to figure out how all of the pieces go together.

If you have worked with web services in previous versions of Java, you can build on your background knowledge, but the new APIs represent a fundamental change in how we as web services developers approach our work. Here are some of the ways in which the world has changed with Java EE 5:

- No need to write *webservices.xml* deployment descriptor. This file used to be mandatory. Now, instead of a single web services-related descriptor file, annotations handle all of that work. Of course, you now have to learn to write all those annotations.
- No JAX-RPC file for mapping Java to WSDL needs to be packaged with your deployment.
- No need for an interface. JAX-RPC required developers to have their service implementation implement an interface that extends Remote. Now, a single class annotated with `@WebService` is all that is required.
- No JNDI lookups. Clients such as servlets or EJBs no longer need to use `<service-ref>` elements in their deployment descriptors (*web.xml* or *ejb-jar.xml*) to look up

services in order to invoke them. Using the new JAX-WS generated clients with a `@WebServiceRef` or `@WebServiceClient` annotation will do this work for you.

- Using `Endpoint` in a regular Java SE 6 JVM is a very simple way to get started with web services for testing purposes. This lowers the barrier to entry. And now it's simplified even further—you used to have to run the APT tool separately over such an `Endpoint`, but this is no longer necessary.

This chapter examines web services from the provider side, illustrating how to create and publish web services with different options and using different APIs.

7.1 Assembling a Service for Deployment

Problem

You are new to web services and want to assemble the pieces you need to create a deployment.

Solution

There are three options here. You can:

- Publish a `javax.xml.ws.Endpoint`. This is the simplest option because you do not need to create a deployable artifact such as a WAR or an EAR. The Endpoint API takes care of that for you, and makes the service available in the HTTP server built-in to Java SE 6. It is suitable for testing, or if you want to allow the creation and publication of a service at runtime.
- Write a servlet decorated with the JAX-WS annotation `@WebService` and publish it in a WAR. Include a WSDL and schemas, or allow Glassfish to generate them for you at deployment time according to the values in your annotations. Structure your WAR just as you would to deploy a regular web application. You must include all of the regular WAR descriptors such as *web.xml*.
- Write a stateless session EJB decorated with the JAX-WS annotation `@WebService` and publish it in an EAR. Structure your EAR just as you would to deploy a regular enterprise application.

Discussion

There are some options within each of these three basic choices as well, discussed in the following sections.

Web service or provider

You can use the SAAJ `@Provider` annotation on your service instead of the `@WebService` annotation. This gives you the ability to examine incoming and outgoing messages at the raw XML level, and in this way `Provider` is the counterpart to `Dispatch` on the client.

Interfaces

It is good form to write an interface for your stateless session EJB, and it makes your EJB accessible as a resource from other enterprise resources. For example, your EJB must implement an interface if you want to invoke it with a context listener in the web tier. Strictly speaking, though, it is not necessary to have one in order for your web service to deploy and execute properly if you are only going to invoke it as a service, and not use it as an EJB component.

Likewise, if you use a WAR to package your service, it is not strictly necessary that the class containing your `@WebService` annotation actually implement the `javax.servlet.http.HttpServlet` interface. It can just be a POJO (Plain Old Java Object) class packaged under WEB-INF.

Ignoring these interfaces may or may not be what you want. It seems to be bad form not to define them as intended, and may be confusing to other developers. On the other hand, it does restrict their use purely as web service objects, disallowing any invocation as a straight servlet or straight EJB. Still, I recommend defining your servlets and components as they were intended to be defined, and using the interfaces.

Packaging WSDL

You must also decide if you want to package your WSDL with your deployment or not. When you are getting started, it is probably easier to allow the container to generate your WSDL for you at deploy time based on your annotations. If you choose to write the WSDL yourself, you will need to maintain it separately, but you will also have total control.

You might try deploying your archive without a WSDL at first and let the container generate one that is certain to be correct. You can strip out items that you don't need, make it more abstract, and so forth. Just remember to modify your `@WebService` annotation so that it includes the `wsdlLocation` attribute. That value should be something like `wsdlLocation="META-INF/wsdl/My.wsdl"`.

If you are deploying in a WAR and want to include your own WSDL file instead of letting the container generate it for you at deploy time, set the WSDL location to something like `wsdlLocation="WEB-INF/wsdl/Some.wsdl"`. This should work across containers, including Glassfish and Oracle WebLogic.

If you choose to include the WSDL yourself, modify the `@WebService` to indicate its location using the `wsdlLocation` property. That should point to the *META-INF/wsdl* directory, or one of its subdirectories. If you are deploying in a WAR, you must place it in *WEB-INF/wsdl*. If you have written schemas, you should include them here as well and make sure the WSDL points to them locally. The container may massage the schema location value to make them publicly accessible, as the contents of the META-INF directory in an EAR are not open to the public.

Generally, when you start your development from Java, you do not want to specify the WSDL—just allow JAX-WS to create it for you. Glassfish has had uneven support surrounding this issue, and the specification indicates that starting from Java and WSDL is optional. If you want to specify your own schemas, however (because there are restrictions you want to add, for example), it's the only way.

Deployment descriptors

You might see references to deployment descriptors such as *sun-JAX-WS.xml*. This is the deployment descriptor for Metro, and is used to describe service endpoints. Each endpoint represents a different port in the WSDL and contains information on binding, implementing class, and the URL pattern that can be used to invoke it. In general, you can forget about this file. The elements it defines are all replicated as annotations. Instead of having to create and maintain and package a separate file to include a description of your service deployment, in many cases, you can just use the corresponding annotations. For example, to indicate that you want to enable MTOM (Message Transmission Optimization Mechanism), just use the `@MTOM(enable=true)` annotation on your service endpoint interface. The same is true for handler chains. Here is an example of a basic file:

```
<?xml version="1.0" encoding="UTF-8"?>
<endpoints xmlns="http://java.sun.com/xml/ns/jax-ws/ri/runtime" version="2.0">
  <endpoint name="HelloService"
      implementation="com.soacookbook.ch04.HelloServer" url-pattern="/hello" />
</endpoints>
```

This descriptor would configure your servlet to be published as *http://localhost:8080/HelloService/hello* if you are using the default port.

There are recipes throughout this chapter that illustrate how to use some of these options.

7.2 Determining a Service Development Model

Problem

You need to start developing the web services for your SOA solution, but there are so many different pieces to put in place that you are not sure where to begin. You need to determine what has to be written by hand and what doesn't.

Solution

Use one of the three basic development models accounted for in the specifications: "Start from Java," "Start from WSDL," or "Start from WSDL and Java." There is also a corollary development model, which I'll refer to as "Start from Schema." You need to write different items depending on what starting point you choose.

Discussion

In this section, we'll discuss the four development models just listed.

Start from Code (Java)

Using this development model, the Java developer writes a single Java class that represents the web service implementation. Using special web services annotations on the implementation, you can have Java generate for you the many other web services-related artifacts, such as schemas, the WSDL, and deployment descriptors.

Here are the basic steps to using a code-first approach:

1. Write a plain old Java class, servlet, or EJB, and annotate it with the `@WebService` annotation.
2. Deploy it to a JAX-WS-compliant container.
3. The JAX-WS runtime will generate a WSDL for you, and handle the translations between Java and SOAP/XML.

This is probably the easiest way for Java developers to start, as most of the manual work is performed using the tools and APIs we already know.

But the more you work with all of your web service artifacts, especially when it's time to advertise your service to others, you may find that you are not entirely happy with the default values that have been generated for you. For instance, by default the names of method parameters get generated into a WSDL as `arg0`, `arg1`, and so on according to their index in the parameter list. This is not particularly clear in communicating your intent, and may end up being confusing to clients.

So the second step is to customize the values that will be generated by your Java class when the preprocessor creates the WSDL and other artifacts. For example, you might use the `@WebService.serviceName` property to indicate the value of the `wsdl:service` element in your WSDL.

The names and implementations of the code generation tools for creating portable client-side artifacts are not standard. For example, if you are running Glassfish, you can create a client using the `wsimport` tool. If you're using Axis, this tool is called `WSDL2Java` (or, going the other way, `Java2WSDL`).

You can use these tools manually from the command line, or you can automate code generation as part of your build by writing customizations to affect how those generated artifacts are created.

Once you have used standard means to customize the values in your generated artifacts, you may choose to branch out to external customizations. These include modifying how JAXB code generates Java classes that will be used by your client.

At this point, you might be concerned that your web service has a larger scope than a regular Java class, even more than an EJB component; you want to start really thinking of your service as a service, and not a glorified Java class. Or you might realize that you don't want to leak implementation details out into your WSDL, which some tools can do. You might want to include schemas that you write by hand. This last point is particularly important if you're going to create a canonical data model to represent common types throughout your organization.

Not all data types in a given programming language map to interoperable types in XML. Watch your tools carefully, to ensure that they do not introduce implementation-specific mappings or dependencies. For example, consider the `Java2WSDL` tool, which comes with Apache Axis 1.2. It creates a WSDL from a Java service implementation, but it introduces custom types in the Apache SOAP namespace that represent image data, an octet stream, and a few others. Your generated WSDL could look like this:

```
<wsdl:definitions targetNamespace="http://example.org/ns";
  xmlns:apachesoap="http://xml.apache.org/xml-soap";
//...
<element name="anImage">
  <complexType>
    <sequence>
      <element name="image" type="apachesoap:Image">
    <sequence>
  <complexType>
</element>
```

You don't want such implementation details in your WSDL, especially when it isn't necessary.

Another issue with starting from code is that you may end up with either much stronger or much weaker typing in your WSDL than you want. While strong typing is considered a feature of languages like Java, you must consider your purpose in SOA. There are many popular dynamically typed languages (Ruby, Python, etc.), and you can't blindly assume that the strongest possible typing is always best. Your service is not a "Java Program++"—it is a service, and the Java platform just offers a way to create it. But on the other hand, you do not want to forsake control for convenience. If your service really demands an array of length 12, make sure that constraint is expressed in the WSDL. Generated WSDLs often gloss over such details, and you wind up with a WSDL that accepts any kind of array.

Finally, you might decide that the whole point of web services is to interoperate with external clients based on a strong, clear, implementation-independent contract. In web services, that contract is a WSDL. Perhaps instead of generating it as an afterthought, it should be your focus as a developer/architect. In addition, there are a number of detractors from this approach. It has been considered problematic from the early days of Java web services.

Community Thoughts on the "Start from Java" Approach

There have been a number of detractors over the years of the "Start from Java" model, for a few different reasons.

Early web services were largely implemented using RPC/encoded because the SOAP encoding scheme would generate XML models directly from service provider data structures and duplicate them for use within client applications. This was expedient, making RPC/encoded a popular approach. But it also meant that the clients were tightly coupled with the SOAP encoding itself, forcing clients to regenerate their code if data structures changed. Moreover, SOAP encoding is a serialization mechanism; because it is driven by SOAP itself, there is little or no use for it outside such a protocol. Validation is not possible using that scheme, and the resulting data structures are not transferable.

Modern web services applications employ data binding, which serves as a layer of indirection between the programmatic representation of a data structure (e.g., a JavaBean) and its XML representation. The data binding layer, as performed by Castor, BEA's XMLBeans or JAXB (all of which are Java-XML binding technologies), isolates each of these representations, allowing developers to maintain independent control over them, using each to its best advantage.

All in all, the new Java web services specs, including JAXB (JSR 222) and JAX-WS 2.1 (JSR 224), have answered those charges handily. So maybe the reasons for being leery of this approach in the past years have faded.

Such objections might lead one instead to start from the opposite end of the spectrum: writing the WSDL by hand and generating the service, which we'll explore in the next section.

Start from contract (WSDL)

For SOAP-based services, the WSDL represents the contract. This model has a single overarching paradigm: the WSDL defines the primary features of the contract for the service, and implementation-independent contracts are one of the cornerstone necessities of SOA. The contract is not an afterthought, but rather a central concern. With this model, you write the WSDL yourself by hand, generate a Java code shell for the service implementation, and then fill in the business logic for the service implementation. This method is also sometimes referred to as "Contract First."

You start by taking a preexisting abstract WSDL and pointing it to a tool such as `wsimport` that produces a service endpoint interface in addition to Java classes that represent the schema definitions and message parts specified in the WSDL. Once the endpoint interface has been generated, write a Java class that implements that interface. The basic steps are as follows:

1. Write a WSDL representing the service you want to deploy.
2. Generate client-side code using `wsimport`. Among other things, this will generate a service interface for each `portType`.
3. Implement each interface by writing your web service implementation class. That means doing something like this:

```
@WebService
(endpointInterface="com.soacookbook.MyGeneratedInterface",
wsdlLocation="/META-INF/wsdl/MyWsdl.wsdl")
public class MyService implements MyGeneratedInterface { ... }
```

4. Deploy the service endpoint implementation to a JAX-WS-compatible container.

In this example, the endpoint interface is specified as a fully qualified name of the interface that `wsimport` generated, written as a string. The WSDL location property allows you to specify either a relative or an absolute URI. If relative, it must be in *META-INF/wsdl*.

One benefit to this approach is that the vendor implementation is obligated to inform you if the service implementation you created does not actually conform to the WSDL.

In order to round out the implementation, you can use JSR-181 (Web Services Metadata) annotations to specify the concrete aspect of the WSDL, such as protocol binding.

Because the purpose of web services is to develop a strong contract that is free of implementation dependencies, this may seem like a good approach. And while its theoretical purity may be attractive, for many Java developers, it can be a difficult way to start. If you have little experience with WSDL, the thought of writing one by hand is daunting. They are not simple documents to create, in particular because considerable knowledge about how web services work under the hood is required to understand the implications of your choices. In part this is due to the fact that Java IDEs are very powerful, and readily perform sophisticated code refactorings at the click of a button. On the other hand, tools that can perform even basic refactoring of XML schemas or WSDLs are hard to come by at any price.

So despite the fact that the "Start from Contract" method can be very powerful, Java developers often shy away from it because their core competency is in Java, not WSDL. However, although WSDL is complex, perhaps overly complex, it can certainly be learned. A given WSDL instance document itself is complicated by the fact that choices such as parameter style and use change the structural features of the document. But conceptually WSDL will reflect only a few basic constructs, making it relatively straightforward to read and write.

XML Schema, on the other hand, is nearly as rich and expressive as many programming languages. There are a wide variety of advanced features that will not comfortably find their way into an interface definition that can easily interoperate as a web service. Fluency in schema can be an important prerequisite for this approach.

You must rely on considerable generation of code when working with modern web services, whether you decide to generate schema and WSDL or Java. But the bottom line with generation of any kind is that you should never generate what you don't understand. Generation is wonderful, and saves lots of time and trouble, but it can cause a lot of trouble if you get in over your head.

It is common to hear the term "contract" used to refer solely to the WSDL. I and others consider the "contract" to include not only all of the elements within the WSDL, such as data types, operations, bindings, and policies, but also items external to the WSDL. For services, and SOA in particular, a service contract is not only the WSDL, but it can also include items such as policies, service-level agreements, user authorizations, and other items that might be presented from an enterprise registry/repository.

On a practical level, your organization might benefit from having a published WSDL released early in the project, so that client- and server-side development teams can work independently.

Another key benefit to starting from WSDL is that XML schema affords a far richer set of data types than many programming languages. Starting from WSDL, you can offer a set of type options, maximizing interoperability.

Start from Java and WSDL

This approach takes a realistic middle road. If you have a mature organization with a large catalog of diverse systems that your SOA intends to interconnect, you might find yourself needing to implement your web services atop legacy systems that provide their own APIs and schema sets. Your service implementation Java class might use annotations such as `@WebMethod.operationName` to associate an operation defined in the WSDL to a particular method of the class.

The "Start from WSDL and Java" model, outlined in JSR 181, is optional. Because vendors are not required to support it, using this development model could limit your portability.

This approach can prove very difficult to maintain because once you've generated classes using the tools, you still need to manually tweak a variety of resources. The "Start from Java" approach, by distinction, gives you considerable flexibility during the development process because you can all but forget about the WSDL and the schemas it uses, and focus on your business logic. Starting from WSDL, you can focus on only the contract. But starting from both requires that you keep your eye on more than one moving part.

Start from Schema

This is a somewhat rarer solution, but one that I have used successfully in the past. With this model, you do not start from WSDL or from Java, but begin by defining your business documents in XML Schema. Starting from either WSDL or Java gives you a more process-oriented view: you write operations or methods first and you're starting from verbs. When starting from schema, there are no verbs, only nouns, so your focus is more on the business documents that your service must exchange. Here are the steps involved:

1. Write a set of XML schemas that represent the data types your business model requires.
2. Use JAXB to generate Java classes based on the schemas.
3. Create an annotated service endpoint implementation in Java. This implementation refers to the JAXB-generated types in the method signatures. If you use a document/literal bare style, each type will be used only once within the service. If you use a wrapped style, you will need to create wrapper elements.
4. Package and deploy the application, allowing the tool to generate the WSDL.
5. Perform runtime validation during marshaling against the schemas.

With the "Start from Schema" view, your SOA becomes more about a document exchange and less about performing remote procedure calls, which can be an advantage in the long run when building orchestrations around your services. This method encourages you to primarily focus on your business documents, such as Invoice, Purchase Order, Customer, and Credit Application. Your service then becomes more of an intake for such documents, serving as a facade for possibly complex enterprise workflows.

The "Start from Schema" approach works well with a document/literal style and use. RPC, like start from Java, can in subtle ways lead you toward considering your service from the view of parameter lists. This is generally not desirable with an enterprise SOA context because it is not business document-oriented, and you can end up with a service that is less likely a candidate for reuse.

Of course, there are disadvantages to this approach. One is added complexity. You cannot rely on certain constructs you've become not only accustomed to, but adamant about using within your Java code, such as `toString`, `equals`, and `hashcode` implementations (without customization using third-party tools). In fact, if you are using this approach, it will become important to use data binding customization in order to ensure that you are not at the mercy of tool defaults.

Another danger to this approach is a susceptibility to tight coupling . By putting schemas at the forefront, you risk tightly coupling services together within composite applications if they share root schemas. Such tight coupling is partly what services are intended to combat in the first place. Canonical data models are very important in SOA, but they must be handled properly. For more discussion on the canonical data model, see Recipe 2.2.

If you don't make sure to refer to your source schemas in your WSDL and package them with your service deployment, your service might still deploy and work, depending on the container. But you will likely suffer from a slight of hand, and end up actually referring to schemas generated at deploy time based on the Java beans generated by JAXB from your schemas. That means that you would lose any schema-based validation restrictions that may have been written into your original schemas. If you want to keep your XSD restrictions, you must package them with your service deployment. Another useful trick here is the use of XML Catalogs (see Recipe 3.12), which would allow you to put placeholder schema locations in your WSDL and then substitute them in your deployment.

One advantage to starting from schema is that you maintain a clear focus on XML. You can validate data within its native XML format and not lose sight of your goals for interoperability. Keeping your code as general as possible can be very beneficial in the long run within a SOA. "Starting with Java" can work out just fine, as long as you're not doing it just because it's more comfortable. You also need to be careful with the "Start from Java" method because it can lead to inadvertent dependency on programming language features, and allow you to slip into using advanced Java constructs such as generics.

You can also get help from tools here, such as WebLogic Workshop, so that you don't have to go through the entire regeneration process every time you build. However, you do not need to rely on any IDE tools; once you have written the schemas, you can do all of the other steps right through unit testing in a single build.

If you are using WebLogic 9.2 or 10gR3, you can substitute XMLBeans for JAXB here.

Note that using any of these "Start from" methods ultimately allows you to create much the same service. The differences here are largely in nuance and style, and are influenced by the development environment in which you work, your SOA maturity level, and your ultimate goals for SOA within your organization.

7.3 Choosing Encoding, Use, and Parameter Styles

Problem

You need to determine the best encoding style, parameter style, and use values for your web service.

Solution

Check out the discussion below for advantages and disadvantages of the different combinations.

Discussion

A web service definition is mapped to a WSDL binding in order to indicate the transport mechanism used to communicate with the service. Consider the following WSDL binding:

```
<binding name="CartEJBPortBinding" type="tns:CartEJB">
<soap:binding transport="http://schemas.xmlsoap.org/soap/http" style="document">
</soap:binding>
<operation name="getVersion">
<soap:operation soapAction=""></soap:operation>
<input>
<soap:body use="literal"></soap:body>
</input>
<output>
<soap:body use="literal"></soap:body>
</output>
</operation>
</binding>
```

There are three items at work here, two of which are explicit and one that is implicit:

- The SOAP binding style ("document")
- The SOAP binding use ("literal")
- The SOAP binding parameter Style ("wrapped")

The two explicit items are style and use. They are specified in the `soap:binding` style attribute and the `soap:body` use attribute, respectively. We'll talk about parameter style in a moment.

Style

The `soap:binding` element's style attribute can have the value of "rpc" or "document". A value of "rpc" indicates that you want to use SOAP messages containing parameters and return values. In this way, your web service will mimic an RMI call. A value of "document" indicates you want your SOAP messages to use XML document instances. "Document" is the default.

JAX-WS is the replacement technology for JAX-RPC. The name for the older technology is telling. Much of Oracle's WebLogic web services implementations and documentation simply assumes that you are using RPC style. This is in part due to the fact that RPC was simpler for vendors to implement and more familiar and straightforward for developers to use. According to one manager on the Oracle web services team I spoke with, this is also due to the fact that customers have a lot of JAX-RPC web services already out in the field and asked for lots of support for it. However, in recent years, the implementations have become more sophisticated and developers more comfortable, and the industry has largely moved beyond RPC for new work, choosing document instead. Document is more interoperable than RPC, and more message-centric.

RPC style. In an RPC-based service, clients interact with the service as if it is a single, monolithic application that exposes methods to that you pass parameters to. The messages map directly to inputs and outputs.

An RPC-style SOAP request will wrap message parameters in an element named after the current operation. By default, RPC responses are wrapped in an element named after the operation with "Response" appended.

Document style. In a document-based service, clients interact with the service using XML document instances based on schemas that represent a complete business entity, such as Author, Order, Invoice, or Product. The XML document instances are self-describing, and offer you the best chance for interoperability.

Document style essentially means that each message part will reference a concrete schema type using its element attribute. The schema completely describes SOAP requests and responses, and requires no intrusion of external encoding rules.

Document-style services have been more difficult to create than RPC style. That's because you typically need to create schemas, which requires a corresponding shift in thinking as you consider your service as a service and not simply as a wrapper for an existing set of methods that happens to use SOAP.

Because document messages represent complete and self-describing entities rather than method parameters, which are available to you as the SOAP message payload, document style allows greater processing flexibility. You can create the incoming payload as a complete XML document and run XSL transformations against it, validate it according to a schema, or manually massage it however you like.

Maintaining state is easier with document style because you have only a single entity rather than a set of entities to manage.

Use

The `soap:body` element's use attribute specifies the manner in which the body content of your SOAP message will be serialized into XML. Possible values are "literal" or "encoded". Literal indicates that your message will be serialized as an XML document, whereas "encoded" indicates that a default SOAP encoding will be applied to it.

Style and use combinations

In the following sections, let's look at the implications of combining the style and uses in various ways.

RPC/encoded

There is a single strength to RPC/encoded: WSDLs written with this formatting are the most simple and straightforward to read.

Everything else is bad news. The WS-I recommends that the `soap:body` have only one child element. RPC/encoded violates this recommendation by allowing multiple children of the SOAP body element. Using this style means that complex types will be SOAP encoded and referenced by "href" elements that point to `multiref` elements outside the operation wrapper element. This makes the message harder to read and understand.

RPC/encoded bindings must maintain type encoding information for every parameter, adding unnecessary overhead to every invocation. This formatting style has the worst performance of all the possible styles.

RPC/encoded is not compliant with WS-I Basic Profile 1.1, so it's not a good candidate for creating web services you expect to interoperate with clients or services implemented with a different platform.

With RPC/encoded, SOAP encoding is typically used to serialize complex types, causing you to lose the more specific and sophisticated functionality you get with XML schemas.

RPC/literal

This is a weird choice. Specifying RPC/literal prevents you from being able to perform schema-based validation. It is complicated by the fact that RPC/literal must handle both RPC element naming conventions and WSDL namespaces.

RPC/literal strips you of the benefits of working with document/literal, but it does offer an advantage over RPC/encoded in that it is WS-I compliant. Despite this fact, Microsoft offers only limited support for this style, so it is rarely used.

Document/literal

This is the best choice to ensure interoperability with services and clients written on other platforms. You can use any XML validator to validate the contents of the message. With document/literal, your operation type gets written as a complex type declared in your schema.

It's interesting to note that .NET initially supported only document/literal. Document/literal does away with the operation name inside the SOAP message. RPC focuses on the method call, whereas document focuses on the document instance you are sending.

Document/encoded

The combination of document and encoded is dead. Nobody uses it. Even in the earliest days of JAX-RPC this mode was not supported. Just pretend it doesn't exist.

Using parameter styles

In JAX-WS, there are two choices for specifying the parameter style: wrapped or bare. The parameter style indicates how parameters will be encapsulated. WSDL itself does not make this distinction. The choice is only relevant for a document/literal style service. The following sections discuss the differences.

Wrapped. Using the wrapped parameter style indicates that the child of the `<soap:body>` will be a wrapper element that is named for the operation. As a wrapper, it is not part of the payload. The advantage here is that a SOAP engine will have a clear and simple naming convention during unmarshaling.

With document/literal wrapped services that define their schemas externally, you have the best chance for ensuring interoperability, and for leveraging the built-in advantages of schema restrictions. The chief disadvantage to the document/literal wrapped style is that it generally results in the most complex WSDL.

There is another wrinkle, however: if you plan to use document/literal wrapped, the content type of the wrapper element must be specified as `sequence` in the XML schema. This indicates that its constituent elements will be ordered, which is key to modeling method signatures in Java, where parameter order matters.

If you want an element to be optional, it must be declared `nillable` in your schema.

With document/literal wrapped, your WSDL looks like this:

```
<message name="authorSearch">
<part name="parameters" element="tns:authorSearch"></part>
</message>
<message name="authorSearchResponse">
<part name="parameters" element="tns:authorSearchResponse"></part>
</message>
<portType name="Catalog">...</portType>
```

Bare. Using the bare (non-wrapper) parameter style indicates that the service operation will receive the complete XML document instance. The glaring drawback to using a bare style is that because you are passing your entire XML document instance and are foregoing using the name of any operation, you have only one shot. That is, you can only define one method per service that accepts that particular document type. Your operation is also limited to defining only a single parameter.

Say that you want to define a service operation called "authorSearch" using document/literal bare. Your operation will accept an Author matching an Author type in a schema, and search for books written by that author.

But what if you want to define an operation in the same service to allow you to add an author to your database? You're painted into a corner because you didn't specify the operation name. The runtime must select which operation to perform based on trying to match the parameter it was passed with the operation signatures. If you had an `add(Author a)` operation and a `search(Author a)` operation, the runtime wouldn't know which one you meant. During invocation of `wsimport`, you would receive an error such as this:

```
[ERROR] Non unique body parts! In a port, as per BP 1.1 R2710 operations must have
unique operation signaure on the wire for successful dispatch. In port CatalogPort,
Operations "authorSearch" and "add" have the same request body block
{http://ns.soacookbook.com/catalog}author. Try running wsimport with
-extension switch, runtime will try to dispatch using SOAPAction
  line 70 of http://localhost:8080/CatalogService/Catalog?wsdl
```

Follow the advice in the error message and see if that helps. Set your `wsimport` task attribute extension to true, and rebuild. This allows you to perform the import, so you get farther along:

```
Testcase: searchByAuthorTest(com.soacookbook.catalog.test.CatalogTest):
Caused an ERROR
Cannot find dispatch method for Request=[SOAPAction="",
Payload={http://ns.soacookbook.com/catalog}author]
javax.xml.ws.soap.SOAPFaultException: Cannot find dispatch method
for Request=[SOAPAction="",Payload={http://ns.soacookbook.com/catalog}author]
```

So making this work requires setting the `SOAPAction` header. This header is optional in JAX-WS implementations, and it can only be used if HTTP is your transport layer, which defeats the purpose of specifying bare in the first place. While it gives you a sense of very loose coupling, which is certainly a goal, if you plan to perform CRUD operations or make your intentions explicit, bare becomes a tricky choice.

Of course, there is a clever workaround for this. If the only requirement keeping you from having both of your operations accept a single `Author` parameter is that each element must be represented by a different element in the schema, you could simply define a second element with a different name that happens to be of the exact same type:

```
<xs:schema xmlns:tns="http://ns.soacookbook.com/catalog" ...>
<xs:element name="searchAuthor" nillable="true" type="tns:Author"></xs:element>
<xs:element name="addAuthor" nillable="true" type="tns:Author"></xs:element>
```

```
<xs:complexType name="Author">
<xs:sequence>
<xs:element name="firstName" type="xs:string"></xs:element>
...
</xs:sequence>
</xs:complexType>
```

In my view, this is a hack, and I don't recommend doing it. But there it is nonetheless.

I sort of like the theoretical purity that the bare style affords, and I wouldn't necessarily rule it out entirely. But wrapped is probably going to get you better mileage in the long run.

A document/literal bare WSDL looks like this:

```
<message name="authorSearch">
<part xmlns:ns4="http://ns.soacookbook.com/catalog" name="author"
element="ns4:author"></part> </message>
<message name="authorSearchResponse">
<part xmlns:ns5="http://ns.soacookbook.com/catalog" name="searchResults"
element="ns5:searchResults"></part> </message>
<portType name="Catalog">...</portType>
```

The contents of the `wsdl:portType` are the same for both styles.

Summary

It's worth noting that selecting and specifying the style and use combination is a configuration matter. It will change the semantics of your service implementation, and you will be able to identify differences in your WSDL, but overall the usability should be transparent to developers; it doesn't change how your service appears to behave.

The main lesson is this: interoperability can either be enhanced or thwarted depending on the combination you specify here, primarily because it affects your schema. When possible, for the sake of interoperability and validation, I encourage you not to rely on tools to generate your schemas for you. Rather, design your service from the schema up. This will help you to focus the idea of your SOA as an infrastructure for enterprise integration via document exchange. This will in turn encourage you to keep individual service implementations focused on their core business logic and allow you to move decorating business logic into orchestrations.

7.4 Generating a WSDL and Portable Artifacts Based on a Java Service Endpoint Implementation

Problem

You want to generate a WSDL and portable web service artifacts (classes based on the WSDL) starting from a service implementation class.

Solution

Use the wsgen command-line tool, included with JAX-WS.

Discussion

Create a Java class annotated with @WebService, and then execute the wsgen tool that comes with Java. It will generate the following portable artifacts for you:

- A WSDL file, if you indicate so using the -wsdl option. The wsgen tool will only generate a WSDL if you explicitly specify this option.
- JAXB classes required to marshal and unmarshal the messages exchanged in the service definition.

There is only one argument required by wsgen: the name of the Java class that implements your web service. You can also specify a variety of options. The form of using the tool is:

```
$ wsgen [options] service-implementation-class
```

Table 7-1 illustrates the set of options available for wsgen.

Table 7-1. Options for the wsgen tool

Option	Purpose
-classpath <path> or -cp <path>	Specifies where to find input class files.
-d <directory>	Specifies where to place generated output files. This directory must exist before running wsgen.
-extension	Specifies whether to allow vendor extensions.
-help	Shows the usage.
-keep	Specifies whether to retain generated files.
-r <directory>	Specifies Destination directory for resource files such as WSDLs. Can only be used when the -wsdl option is also used.
-s <directory>	Specify where to place generated Java source files.
-verbose	Provides output messages about what the compiler is doing.
-version	Prints version information, e.g., JAX-WS RI 2.1.3-hudson-390-.
-wsdl[:protocol]	Indicates that you want wsgen to generate a WSDL file. The protocol is optional. Valid protocols are soap1.1 (the default) and Xsoap1.2 (which is not standard). Can only be used when the -extension option is also used.
-servicename <name>	Specifies the Service name to use in the generated WSDL. Can only be used when the -wsdl option is also used.
-portname <name>	Specifies the Port name to use in the generated WSDL. Can only be used when the -wsdl option is also used.

Using extensions (functionality not specifically outlined by the specifications) may result in applications that are not portable or may not interoperate with other implementations.

Here is an example. In the following class, you have a web service definition, for which you'll create a WSDL:

```
package com.soacookbook;

import javax.jws.WebMethod;
import javax.jws.WebParam;
import javax.jws.WebResult;
import javax.jws.WebService;

/**
 * Used to manually run the wsgen tool against.
 */
@WebService(targetNamespace="http://ns.soacookbook.com",
  name="GenCatalog", serviceName="GenCatalog")
public class CatalogToGen {

    @WebMethod
    @WebResult(name="title")
    public String getTitle(
        @WebParam(name="id") String id) {

      return "King Lear";
    }
}
```

Given this source file, you'll compile it like this from the directory that stores the top-level package:

```
javac com/soacookbook/CatalogToGen.java
```

Now you can run the `wsgen` tool across this class to generate a WSDL, schema, and appropriate JAX-WS artifacts:

```
$ wsgen -verbose -cp . -wsdl -servicename {http://ns.com/}Catalog \
-keep -r gen -s gen com.soacookbook.CatalogToGen

Note:   ap round: 1
[ProcessedMethods Class: com.soacookbook.CatalogToGen]
[should process method: getTitle hasWebMethods: true ]
[endpointReferencesInterface: false]
[declaring class has WebSevice: true]
[returning: true]
[WrapperGen - method: getTitle(java.lang.String)]
[method.getDeclaringType(): com.soacookbook.CatalogToGen]
[requestWrapper: com.soacookbook.jaxws.GetTitle]
[ProcessedMethods Class: java.lang.Object]
com\soacookbook\jaxws\GetTitle.java
com\soacookbook\jaxws\GetTitleResponse.java
Note:   ap round: 2
```

You see the output as a result of running the command with the `-verbose` option. Because you used the `-keep` option, your generated Java source files are not deleted after compilation. The tool makes two classes, `GetTitle` for request messages and `GetTitleResponse` for response messages, and places them in the package name you used, appended with `jaxws`. The classes are put in the directory named *gen*, as specified with the `-s` option.

The tool also creates two WSDLs. The first is the abstract WSDL, containing only the `<messages>`, the `<types>` element (which imports all types from the generated schema), and the `<portType>` element. The WSDLs are placed in the *gen* directory, in accordance with the value in the `-r` option in the command. The abstract WSDL, called *GenCatalog.wsdl* here, looks like this:

```
<definitions targetNamespace="http://ns.soacookbook.com"
  xmlns="http://schemas.xmlsoap.org/wsdl/"
  xmlns:tns="http://ns.soacookbook.com"
  xmlns:xsd="http://www.w3.org/2001/XMLSchema">
  <types>
    <xsd:schema>
      <xsd:import namespace="http://ns.soacookbook.com"
        schemaLocation="GenCatalog_schema1.xsd"/>
    </xsd:schema>
  </types>
  <message name="getTitle">
    <part name="parameters" element="tns:getTitle"/>
  </message>
  <message name="getTitleResponse">
    <part name="parameters" element="tns:getTitleResponse"/>
  </message>
  <portType name="GenCatalog">
    <operation name="getTitle">
      <input message="tns:getTitle"/>
      <output message="tns:getTitleResponse"/>
    </operation>
  </portType>
</definitions>
```

On its own, of course, the abstract WSDL is not enough to run your service. That requires a concrete WSDL, which the tool also generates, as follows:

```
<definitions targetNamespace="http://ns.com/" name="Catalog"
  xmlns="http://schemas.xmlsoap.org/wsdl/"
  xmlns:tns="http://ns.com/"
  xmlns:xsd="http://www.w3.org/2001/XMLSchema"
  xmlns:soap="http://schemas.xmlsoap.org/wsdl/soap/">
  <import namespace="http://ns.soacookbook.com" location="GenCatalog.wsdl"/>
  <binding name="GenCatalogPortBinding"
    type="ns1:GenCatalog" xmlns:ns1="http://ns.soacookbook.com">
    <soap:binding transport="http://schemas.xmlsoap.org/soap/http"
      style="document"/>
    <operation name="getTitle">
      <soap:operation soapAction=""/>
      <input>
        <soap:body use="literal"/>
```

```
      </input>
      <output>
        <soap:body use="literal"/>
      </output>
    </operation>
  </binding>
  <service name="Catalog">
    <port name="GenCatalogPort" binding="tns:GenCatalogPortBinding">
      <soap:address location="REPLACE_WITH_ACTUAL_URL"/>
    </port>
  </service>
</definitions>
```

There are a few items of interest in this WSDL. First, it accepts the target namespace that you specified between the curly braces with the **`-servicename`** option, and it preserves the name for the **`<definitions>`** element. Next, it imports the abstract WSDL, a technique similar to separating a Java interface from its implementation. Finally, the SOAP address location is not specified and must be replaced with a URI value.

Note that you must run `wsgen` against a Java class that has already been compiled (not against the source program), and if you specify a directory in which the tool should place generated files such as the WSDL, that directory must exist before you run the program. Also, you must run the tool against an implementation class, and not an interface.

Using the wsgen Ant task

If you want to run `wsgen` as part of an Ant build, an Ant task wrapper is available for the tool in the usual location. It has the following structure:

```
<wsgen
  sei="..."
  destdir="directory for generated class files"
  classpath="classpath" | cp="classpath"
  resourcedestdir="directory for generated resource files such as WSDLs"
  sourcedestdir="directory for generated source files"
  keep="true|false"
  verbose="true|false"
  genwsdl="true|false"
  protocol="soap1.1|Xsoap1.2"
  servicename="..."
  portname="...">
  extension="true|false"
  <classpath refid="..."/>
</wsgen>
```

This task mirrors the command-line tool, so I won't explain it further except to mention that the nested `classpath` element is a regular Ant path like any other. In order to use the `<wsgen>` task, you need to point to the implementing class in your Ant build script:

```
<taskdef name="wsgen" classname="com.sun.tools.ws.ant.WsGen">
  <classpath path="jaxws.classpath"/>
</taskdef>
```

Using wsgen in Maven 2

If you want to use `wsgen` as part of a Maven 2 build, you can get the plug-in at *http://mojo.codehaus.org/jaxws-maven-plugin/wsgen-mojo.html*. It will automatically execute during the `generate-sources` phase.

7.5 Creating a Basic Web Service

Problem

You want to create a basic but real-world web service in Java EE 5.

Solution

Create an EJB or servlet and annotate it with `@WebService`. Then package it as you normally would and deploy it; JAX-WS will take care of creating the WSDL and the necessary mappings at deploy time.

Here is the simplest possible way to do it with an EJB:

```
package com.soacookbook.catalog.ejb;

import com.soacookbook.ns.catalog.*;
import javax.ejb.*;
import javax.jws.*;

/**
 * Basic Web Service does shopping cart operations.
 */
@WebService
@Stateless
@Local
public class CartEJB {
    public Double getVersion() {
        return 5.0;
    }
}
```

This is enough to create a web service that accepts the default mappings. It is important to examine for a moment what those mappings are. In later recipes, you'll customize the mappings for the generated WSDL so that the names of your elements are more user friendly.

Note that the bean does not implement a business interface. This may be something that you'd want to do in the real world, as it makes your bean available to other enterprise processes such as web-based context listeners, but as of EJB 3, it is no longer strictly necessary.

See Recipe 4.4 for how to create and invoke the simplest possible web service in Java.

Discussion

Let's take a look at each of the important sections of the WSDL to see how it maps. This might not seem important at this stage because you can just use the `wsdimport` tool to generate the artifacts necessary to invoke the service. But this will be very important to be able to do later when you're working with orchestrations, and it's good to know a little about what's happening under the hood in case something breaks.

In this discussion, I will use the qualified name `wsdl:<elementName>` in referring to WSDL elements in the namespace `xmlns="http://schemas.xmlsoap.org/wsdl/"`. By default, JAX-WS generates a WSDL that does not qualify these elements, making WSDL the default namespace. I use the prefix for clarity, though your WSDL document won't be qualified in this way. For example, a reference to `wsdl:service` here will appear in your generated WSDL as service.

Package and types

Notice that your EJB that defines the service is with the `com.soacookbook.catalog.ejb` package. Without customizations, JAX-WS will generate a namespace for your imported types that matches the package name:

```
<types>
<xsd:schema>
  <xsd:import namespace="http://ejb.catalog.soacookbook.com/"
    schemaLocation="http://localhost:8080/CartEJBService/CartEJB?xsd=1">
  </xsd:import>
</xsd:schema>
</types>
```

It also generated a schema document and placed it in the location specified by the `schemaLocation` attribute. Unlike IBM's implementation in WebSphere, which generates inline types in WSDLs, Glassfish follows the best practice of writing the schemas to an external file and importing it into the WSDL to keep the WSDL abstract. The generated schema looks like this:

```
<xs:schema xmlns:tns="http://ejb.catalog.soacookbook.com/"
  xmlns:xs="http://www.w3.org/2001/XMLSchema" version="1.0"
  targetNamespace="http://ejb.catalog.soacookbook.com/">

<xs:element name="getVersion" type="tns:getVersion">
</xs:element>

<xs:element name="getVersionResponse" type="tns:getVersionResponse">
</xs:element>

<xs:complexType name="getVersion">
<xs:sequence></xs:sequence>
</xs:complexType>

<xs:complexType name="getVersionResponse">
```

```
<xs:sequence>
<xs:element name="return" type="xs:double" minOccurs="0"></xs:element>
</xs:sequence>
</xs:complexType>
</xs:schema>
```

This schema defines a target namespace that matches the package name that defined the service. It features two elements: `getVersion` and `getVersionResponse`. The `getVersion` element is empty because the operation takes no arguments. The response is named after the Java method, suffixed with "Response".

Class and service

The Java class that implements your service endpoint interface (SEI), which in this case is the `CartEJB`, gets mapped to the `wsdl:service` element. (If you look back at the WSDL, the `wsdl:service` element is at the bottom.)

```
<service name="CartEJBService">
<port name="CartEJBPort" binding="tns:CartEJBPortBinding">
<soap:address location="http://localhost:8080/CartEJBService/CartEJB"></soap:address>
</port>
</service>
```

By default, the name of the service is the name of the SEI ("CartEJB") appended with "Service".

In this case, you're exposing the underlying implementation as an EJB given your naming convention. It is a best practice to hide such matters. Keep them from being exposed to clients by using the `serviceName` element of the `@WebService` annotation.

In WSDL 1.1, a service is a collection of port elements. A port element defines the URI you can use to connect to a web service.

Class and PortType

Think of a `wsdl:portType` as a class, and its `wsdl:operation` child elements as methods:

```
<portType name="CartEJB">
    <operation name="getVersion">
       <input message="tns:getVersion"/>
       <output message="tns:getVersionResponse"/>
    </operation>
</portType>
```

Each method in your Java service is defined within the `portType` as a `wsdl:operation` to indicate the abstract operations that your service can perform. But each is also repeated as a child element of a `wsdl:binding` (which we will look at next). You can see that your `getVersion` method name was used as the WSDL operation name by default. See Recipe 7.21 for more details on the `soapAction` attribute.

The input of the operation is used to specify method arguments, and the output element specifies the return type.

Method and binding

Methods in the Java service are defined as operations in the WSDL. The WSDL must describe the physical manner of invoking the service on the wire, and it does so in the `wsdl:binding` element. The operation as defined in `wsdl:portType` tells you what you can do, and the operation child of the `wsdl:binding` element tells you how it must be done.

Because no binding customization was added when you generated this WSDL, JAX-WS selects the default binding of SOAP over HTTP. Other bindings, such as REST over HTTP or SOAP over JMS, are possible.

That section of the generated WSDL looks like this:

```
<binding name="CartEJBPortBinding" type="tns:CartEJB">
<soap:binding transport="http://schemas.xmlsoap.org/soap/http" style="document">
</soap:binding>
<operation name="getVersion">
<soap:operation soapAction=""></soap:operation>
<input>
<soap:body use="literal"></soap:body>
</input>
<output>
<soap:body use="literal"></soap:body>
</output>
</operation>
</binding>
```

The binding element also identifies what SOAP encoding style and use the service employs. See Recipe 7.3 for more discussion on choosing an appropriate encoding style, parameter style, and use.

With no customization, the WSDL will be available at: *http://localhost:8080/CartEJBService/CartEJB?wsdl*.

The use of `?wsdl` (or `?WSDL`—it's case-insensitive) appended to a service URL is only a convention; most application servers—including Glassfish, WebLogic 10, and WebSphere 6.1—will make a WSDL available this way, but they aren't required to. If you let JAX-WS generate your WSDL as we've done here, the clients created with `wsimport` will point to this remote WSDL.

7.6 Specifying Namespaces

Problem

You are starting from Java, and want to indicate the namespace(s) your service should define in the generated WSDL because you don't care for the default.

Solution

Use the `targetNamespace` property of the `@WebService` annotation to indicate the namespace for the web service itself.

Discussion

The `targetNamespace` property is optional. If you do not use it, your service will get assigned a namespace that is an inversion of the package name your implementation class is in. For example, if your class is in the package `com.soacookbook.ch04`, the default namespace for your service will be `http://ch04.soacookbook.com/`. This property allows you to override the default with whatever you like.

You can also use the `targetNamespace` property on other items beside the service. Both the `@WebResult` and `@WebParam` annotations take a `targetNamespace`. Each of them either comes from schema originally or match have schema representations generated, so their namespaces do not have to match, nor do they have to match the service namespace.

If you do not specify a namespace for web params or web results, they will inherit the target namespace for the service.

If you want to specify the empty namespace, use `@WebParam(targetNamespace="")`.

It is a best practice to use separate namespaces for your WSDL and your schemas.

7.7 Creating a Web Service Operation

Problem

You want to define an operation on a web service.

Solution

Simply add a public method to the service implementation class that defines the `@WebService`, and it will automatically be added to the generated WSDL.

Any public methods you add to an annotated service class will automatically be added to the WSDL operations; if you want to accept the default mappings, you don't need to do anything else.

Discussion

You can explicitly specify a Java method as a service operation by annotating it with the `@WebMethod` annotation. But the annotation also allows you to specify certain properties of how the operation will be represented in the WSDL and how it will behave. These properties are listed in Table 7-2.

Table 7-2. @WebMethod properties

Property	Purpose
operationName	Customizes the value of the `wsdl:operation` if starting from Java, or mapping to an existing WSDL.
action	In SOAP, sets the value of the action.
exclude	Indicates that you explicitly do not want this method exposed as an operation in the WSDL. It is illegal to specify this on endpoint interfaces. It is illegal to specify any other properties of `@WebMethod` if you specify this one.

If you use the `@WebMethod` annotation on a single method in your Java class, you must explicitly set it on all remaining methods you want to be included in the service definition. Otherwise, JAX-WS will think you intend to exclude them, and they won't be added to the WSDL.

The `@WebMethod` annotation is used in a Start from Java approach to indicate what should be generated on the WSDL as the operation name; if the annotation is not used, the operation name will match the method name.

If you are using a Start from WSDL approach, the annotation's `operationName` property gives you the opportunity to call your Java method whatever you like but map it to the WSDL operation.

7.8 Specifying a Web Service Message Part

Problem

You want to specify the mapping from your method's parameter name to a `wsdl:part` name instead of using the defaults.

Solution

Use the `@WebParam` annotation. It features ways to specify the target namespace in which this part is defined, whether this parameter should be pulled from the header, what its name will be in the WSDL, and the direction of the parameter flow (in, out, or in/out).

Discussion

The simplest and most visible change to make is to the `WebParam.name` property. Setting this parameter is *required* if all three of the following are true of your service:

- The operation style is document.
- The parameter style is bare.
- The mode is either OUT or INOUT.

You can also specify a value for the `WebParam.partName` property, as shown here:

```
@WebMethod(operationName = "add")
    public int add(@WebParam(name = "i", partName="iPart")
```

Setting `@WebParam.partName` only has an effect if the operation style is RPC or if the operation style is document and the parameter style is bare.

7.9 Specifying an Operation Return Value

Problem

You want to define a return value for a Java method so that it maps to a WSDL output.

Solution

Use the `@WebResult` annotation to map to an existing `wsdl:output` or to customize how it's generated.

Discussion

You can explicitly specify a Java method as a service operation by annotating it with the `@WebResult` annotation. But the annotation also allows you to specify certain properties of how the operation will be represented in the WSDL. These are shown in Table 7-3.

Table 7-3. @WebResult properties

Property	Purpose
name	The name of the return value. This will match the element name in the schema that is mapped from the WSDL's message for the response. If the style is RPC and no `@WebResult.partName` has been specified, this value will be used as the `wsdl:part` that represents the return value. If the operation is document style or the return type maps to a header, this will be the name of the schema element that represents the return value.
partName	The name of the `wsdl:part` that represents this return value. This is only used if the operation is RPC style or if the operation is document style and the parameter style is bare.

Property	Purpose
targetNamespace	The XML target namespace for the element representing the return value if the style is RPC or if the style is document and the parameter style is bare.
header	If set to true, the result will be pulled from a value set as a message header instead of one set into the message body.

Here is an example of how specifying the name property affects the WSDL. Assume the following Java method in a service implementation annnotated with an empty `@WebService` (which gives you the default style of document/literal):

```
@WebMethod
public @WebResult(name="doItOne") int
        doIt(int x) {
    return 1;
}
```

From this method, JAX-WS will generate the following WSDL fragment:

```
<message name="doItResponse">
  <part name="parameters" element="tns:doItResponse"></part>
</message>

<portType name="Worker">
  <operation name="doIt">
    <input message="tns:doIt"></input>
    <output message="tns:doItResponse"></output>
  </operation>
</portType>
```

This fragment indicates an operation whose response type is defined in the associated schema's `doItResponse` element type. Because of your customization, that will look like this:

```
<xs:complexType name="doItResponse">
<xs:sequence>
<xs:element name="doItOne" type="xs:int"></xs:element>
</xs:sequence>
</xs:complexType>
```

The schema element name gets the value of the `@WebResult.name`.

7.10 Defining Zero-Argument Operations

Problem

You are using a Start from Schema approach to develop your service, and you need to know how to represent a Java method that does not take any arguments.

Solution

Say you have the following Java method that takes no arguments:

```
@WebMethod
public boolean startBatch(){
    return true;
}
```

If you want to have JAX-WS generate the WSDL for you, you're done. But if you are starting from schema, what do you type to represent nothing? Use the following schema definition:

```
<xs:schema xmlns:tns="urn:myNs"
  xmlns:xs="http://www.w3.org/2001/XMLSchema"
  version="1.0" targetNamespace="urn:myNs">

  <xs:element name="startBatch" type="tns:startBatch" />

  <xs:element name="startBatchResponse" type="tns:startBatchResponse" />

  <xs:complexType name="startBatch">
    <xs:sequence />
  </xs:complexType>

  <xs:complexType name="startBatchResponse">
    <xs:sequence>
      <xs:element name="return" type="xs:boolean"/>
    </xs:sequence>
  </xs:complexType>
</xs:schema>
```

The key is to define a schema element and have it refer to a complex type, but to have the complex type define an empty sequence.

7.11 Defining Operations with Void Return Type

Problem

You want to create a web service operation that does not return any value.

Solution

Define a Java method with a void return type and then add to it the `@OneWay` annotation.

Discussion

This is perhaps not common, but there are times when you want to update a service with a new value, and do not need a response. You cannot simply define a Java method with a void return type. Say that we want to create the following web service operation:

```
@WebMethod(operationName="update")
public void update(int status) {
  System.out.println("The new status is: " + status);
}
```

The WSDL operation generated from this method will not have the desired effect. It will look like this:

```
<operation name="update">
  <input message="tns:update" />
  <output message="tns:updateResponse" />
</operation>
```

Of course, we could just go ahead and call it at this point, like this:

```
//Remember WebServiceRef only works in managed environment
@WebServiceRef(wsdlLocation=
"http://localhost:8080/CalculatorApp/CalculatorWSService?wsdl")
public CalculatorWSService service;

service.getCalculatorWSPort();
port.update(200);
```

and this invocation would go through using JAX-WS. However, it's not really what we want because we're getting a result and we're just ignoring it. Moreover, there are SAAJ clients that would have a hard time with this, as the runtime complains because it's not getting a response when one is expected (at least according to the WSDL).

In fact, what's written in the XML schema associated with this operation's response type is an empty sequence:

```
<xs:element name="updateResponse" type="tns:updateResponse" />
<xs:complexType name="updateResponse">
  <xs:sequence />
</xs:complexType>
```

A cleaner and more interoperable way to do this is just to add the `javax.jws.Oneway` annotation to any service method that has a void return type. Let's modify the method and see what the new WSDL says:

```
@Oneway
@WebMethod(operationName="update")
public void update(int status) {
  System.out.println("The new status is: " + status);
}
```

Now there is nothing in the XML schema to represent the void response (which is as it should be). The WSDL no longer contains a message for the void response:

```
<message name="update">
  <part name="parameters" element="tns:update" />
</message>
```

and the SOAP operation is fixed to just include an input:

```
<operation name="update">
  <soap:operation soapAction="" />
    <input>
      <soap:body use="literal" />
    </input>
  </operation>
```

7.12 Creating a Web Service That Uses Complex Types Based on Custom WSDL and a Custom Schema

Problem

You have to program in the real world, not Hello World, so you want to write a web service that sends and receives complex types based on a schema that you have written. That schema is referred to by a WSDL that you have written, and you want to be sure to maintain the constraints specified in your schema. You are not using a Provider, but a class annotated with `@WebService`, so you need to generate portable types from the schema before your web service will compile.

Solution

Basically, you will use the `@WebService.wsdlLocation` annotation and generate your classes at the right point in your build with the XJC Ant task.

Discussion

You will create a `Credit` web service that defines a single operation: `authorize`. It will accept a `CreditCard` complex type and execute some business logic to determine what amount the card should be authorized for. It will then return a custom `Authorization` Java type.

You'll write each artifact in the order you would in the real world: the schema, the WSDL, the Java web service, and the build script that puts it all together and deploys it.

Schema

The schema in Example 7-1 contains elements that specify parts of a credit card and an authorization amount. The idea in this solution is to create a complex schema, such as you might use in the real world, that is still not overly long.

This schema is suitable for use with a parameter style of bare because the two elements defined (`creditCard` and `authorization`) represent the actual documents we want to exchange in the invocation. If you want to use a wrapped parameter style, specify elements that act as the wrappers for your real elements.

Example 7-1. Credit.xsd credit card schema

```
<?xml version="1.0" encoding="UTF-8"?>
<xs:schema
    version="1.0"
    targetNamespace="http://ns.soacookbook.com/credit"
    xmlns:xs="http://www.w3.org/2001/XMLSchema"
    xmlns:tns="http://ns.soacookbook.com/credit"
    elementFormDefault="qualified">
```

```
<xs:element name="creditCard" type="tns:CreditCard" />

<xs:element name="authorization" type="tns:Authorization" />

<xs:annotation>
    <xs:documentation xml:lang="en">
        A Credit Card contains a number, a cardholder name,
        and an expiry date. The date is just an XSD date,
        and the others are custom types with constraints.
    </xs:documentation>
</xs:annotation>
<xs:complexType name="CreditCard">
    <xs:sequence>
        <xs:element id="cardNumber" name="cardNumber"
                type="tns:CardNumber"
                minOccurs="1" maxOccurs="1"/>

        <xs:element id="name" name="name" type="tns:Name" />

        <xs:element id="expirationDate" name="expirationDate"
                type="xs:date" nillable="true" />
    </xs:sequence>
</xs:complexType>

<xs:complexType name="Name">
    <xs:sequence>
        <xs:element name="firstName" type="tns:NameString"/>
        <xs:element name="middleInitial" type="tns:InitialString"
            nillable="true"/>
        <xs:element name="lastName" type="tns:NameString"/>
    </xs:sequence>
</xs:complexType>

<!-- Names must be at least 2 characters, no more than 35
  characters, and consist of alphabetic characters, hyphens,
  single quotes, periods and spaces -->
<xs:simpleType name="NameString">
    <xs:restriction base="xs:string">
        <xs:minLength value="2" />
        <xs:maxLength value="35" />
        <xs:pattern value="[A-Za-z\-. ]{2,35}" />
    </xs:restriction>
 </xs:simpleType>

 <xs:simpleType name="InitialString">
    <xs:restriction base="xs:string">
        <xs:minLength value="0" />
        <xs:maxLength value="1" />
        <xs:pattern value="[A-Za-z]?" />
    </xs:restriction>
 </xs:simpleType>

 <!--Just simple constraint to keep it this short.
 Not good enough for real world.-->
<xs:simpleType name="CardNumber">
```

```
    <xs:restriction base="xs:string">
        <xs:pattern value="\^(\d{4}[- ]){3}\d{4}|\d{16}$" />
        <xs:minLength value="10" />
        <xs:maxLength value="16" />
    </xs:restriction>
</xs:simpleType>

<xs:complexType name="Authorization">
    <xs:sequence>
        <xs:element name="amount" type="xs:double"/>
    </xs:sequence>
</xs:complexType>

</xs:schema>
```

This schema defines two global elements: `creditCard` and `authorization`. The credit card is a composite type consisting of three elements: `cardNumber`, `name`, and `expirationDate`. Each of these types is in turn specified by other types.

The `cardNumber` is defined as a `simpleType` with a restriction on the allowable structure of the number and a minimum and maximum length. The cardholder name actually points to another complex type, `Name`, which defines a first, last, and middle initial. These are then assigned their own constraints for acceptable data length and acceptable characters.

The second element, `authorization`, defines an amount of money for which a given card can be authorized. It's simpler because I wanted to show a custom type for the return as well, but I didn't want to be redundant.

While it may be tempting to place clues about the relation between schema elements and WSDL parts in your schema, do not. Schemas have more jobs in life than being tied to our WSDLs. If you are certain they will never do anything else, it may be simpler to inline them within the WSDL and save maintainers the puzzle. This does undermine the modularity of your WSDL, however.

Your web service implementation itself does not specify anything about your schema, but the WSDL must point to it.

Once you deploy your service, the schema's annotations may be the only thing visible if you open it in Internet Explorer for viewing. You can use the view source option to see the entire schema contents. This is not necessary in Firefox, which just shows the entire schema regardless.

WSDL

This WSDL in Example 7-2 is very simple. It defines a target namespace that is shared by the schema and the service implementation. In the `wsdl:types` section, import the

Credit.xsd schema defined in the previous listing. In this example, it is located in the same directory as the WSDL, though it could be specified as a URL or within another directory relative to the WSDL.

You might notice that Glassfish rewrites the WSDL to have the `schemaLocation` attribute of `xsd:import` point to an absolute URL (in the form of *http://localhost:8080/soaCookbookWS/CreditService?xsd=1*) if you've passed it a relative path.

The WSDL defines a single `wsdl:portType`, `CreditAuthorizer`, which is similar to a Java interface that defines one operation, `authorize`. The `soap:address` element indicates the URL at which the service is available. The `soap` prefix is used because you are binding the service using the SOAP protocol.

Recall that if you want to view the WSDL associated with a service you can bring up the service location as specified by `soap:address` in a browser, and just append `?wsdl` to the end. This is not defined in the specification, but all vendors (including Sun, IBM, JBoss, and Oracle) honor it.

Example 7-2. Credit.wsdl

```
<?xml version="1.0" encoding="UTF-8"?>
<definitions
xmlns:soap="http://schemas.xmlsoap.org/wsdl/soap/"
xmlns:tns="http://ns.soacookbook.com/credit"
xmlns:xsd="http://www.w3.org/2001/XMLSchema"
xmlns="http://schemas.xmlsoap.org/wsdl/"
targetNamespace="http://ns.soacookbook.com/credit"
name="CreditService">

<types>
<xsd:schema>
<xsd:import namespace="http://ns.soacookbook.com/credit"
  schemaLocation="Credit.xsd"/>
</xsd:schema>
</types>

<message name="authorizeRequest">
<part name="creditCard" element="tns:creditCard" />
</message>
<message name="authorizeResponse">
<part name="authorization" element="tns:authorization" />
</message>

<portType name="CreditAuthorizer">
<operation name="authorize">
<input message="tns:authorizeRequest" />
<output message="tns:authorizeResponse" />
```

```
</operation>
</portType>

<binding name="CreditAuthorizerPortBinding"
  type="tns:CreditAuthorizer">
<soap:binding transport="http://schemas.xmlsoap.org/soap/http"
  style="document" />
<operation name="authorize">
<soap:operation soapAction="" />
<input>
<soap:body use="literal" />
</input>
<output>
<soap:body use="literal" />
</output>
</operation>
</binding>

<service name="CreditService">
<port name="CreditAuthorizerPort"
  binding="tns:CreditAuthorizerPortBinding">
<soap:address
  location="http://localhost:8080/soaCookbookWS/CreditService" />
</port>
</service>
</definitions>
```

The service implementation class will refer directly to this WSDL file, which will be packaged alongside the service implementation in the *WEB-INF/wsdl* folder at build time. Also notice that your schema is defined as *Credit.xsd* because it is deployed to the same directory as the WSDL in the WAR.

This WSDL specifies document/literal style and use and the parameter style is bare, just so you understand how your service will be invoked. Your web service will make this relationship explicit.

Remember that if you use the mechanism within Glassfish that automatically generates a WSDL for you, it will redefine your schema and lose the constraints. That's why you package the schemas with the application instead of letting Glassfish write them for you, which would be more expedient.

Service implementation

The implementation of the web service is a simple class. Despite the fact that it will be available as a servlet within the container, you don't have to actually implement the `HttpServlet` interface. You can just define a regular class and package it in a WAR. You don't need to write anything into *web.xml* either.

This file is a standard service implementation for deployment in a WAR. It could be an EJB without many changes, but then you'd have to do more packaging work in the build script and put it in an EAR.

Let's examine the file in some detail.

Notice that you're importing the `com.soacookbook.ns.credit` package in order to use the parameter and the return type. That's the package you know JAXB will generate the types to, but they don't exist until we run the build.

When you first create the class, the web service operation accepts types that are based on schema, and which don't exist until you generate them with JAXB. You then have to make sure they're on the classpath at service compile time, and then include them with the WAR. Your build will handle that for you, as we'll see later.

The service implementation uses the `@WebService` annotation and specifies a few properties:

- The `@WebService.name` value matches the value of the `wsdl:portType` name. Here this is `CreditAuthorizer`.
- The `@WebService.serviceName` value matches the value specified in the WSDL's service name as `<service name="CreditService">`.
- The `@WebService.targetNamespace` property is used to indicate the namespace. While the namespace is the same here for the schema types, that is for convenience, and there is no restriction there. In general, it is a best practice to separate your type namespaces and your WSDL namespace.
- Finally, specify the `wsdlLocation`, which must be physically present in the WAR with the service implementation. Because you're specifying the WSDL by hand and including it along with a schema you have written, the Glassfish deployment tool will honor the schema so that it still contains your type constraints.

Take a look at the code listing in Example 7-3 and we'll unpack the business method annotations.

Example 7-3. CreditService.java

```
package com.soacookbook.ch03.validate;

import com.soacookbook.ns.credit.*;

import javax.jws.WebMethod;
import javax.jws.WebParam;
import javax.jws.WebResult;
import javax.jws.WebService;
import javax.jws.soap.SOAPBinding;
import org.apache.log4j.Logger;

/**
```

```
 * Demonstrates a service that uses JAXB-generated types as
 * parameters for a start-from-schema-and-java method.
 * Uses Credit.wsdl and Credit.xsd.
 */
@WebService(
  name="CreditAuthorizer",
  serviceName="CreditService",
  targetNamespace="http://ns.soacookbook.com/credit",
  wsdlLocation="WEB-INF/wsdl/ch03/Credit.wsdl")
public class CreditService {
  private static final Logger LOGGER =
          Logger.getLogger(CreditService.class);

    /** Creates an instance of CreditService.
     */
    public CreditService() {
        LOGGER.debug("Created provider instance.");
    }

    //business method
    @WebMethod(operationName="authorize")
    @SOAPBinding(style=SOAPBinding.Style.DOCUMENT,
     use=SOAPBinding.Use.LITERAL,
     parameterStyle=SOAPBinding.ParameterStyle.BARE)
    public @WebResult(name="authorization",
            targetNamespace="http://ns.soacookbook.com/credit")
            Authorization

            authorize(

            @WebParam(name="creditCard",
            mode=WebParam.Mode.IN,
            targetNamespace="http://ns.soacookbook.com/credit")
            CreditCard creditCard)  {

        LOGGER.debug("Authorizing.");

        LOGGER.debug("Card Number: " + creditCard.getCardNumber());

        //get data from compound type
        String cardNumber = creditCard.getCardNumber();

        //create custom type for return
        Authorization auth = new Authorization();
        //business logic here
        if (cardNumber.startsWith("4")) {
            auth.setAmount(2500.0);
        } else {
            auth.setAmount(0.0);
        }

        LOGGER.debug("Returning auth for amt: " + auth.getAmount());

        return auth;
```

```
    }
}
```

Let's first examine the authorize business method. It accepts a CreditCard type and returns an Authorization type. Neither of these exists anywhere as Java classes; they are generated by XJC within your build before compiling the service. You need to do some tweaking in the annotations to make your service match up with the WSDL we've defined.

You annotate your method with the @WebMethod annotation. Normally all of the public methods in a class that is annotated with @WebService will be exposed in a generated WSDL as operations. But you hand-coded ouyr WSDL, so you want to match up the method name with the name of the operation specified in the WSDL as <operation name="authorize">. We use the @WebMethod.operationName property to do so.

Next include binding information, indicating that you want to use a style of document, a use of literal, and a parameterStyle of bare. (You can read more about these in Recipe 7.13.) The main thing here is that you don't have any wrapper types, so you need to use a bare parameter style. Notice that you specify this on the class, and not a particular method because you cannot mix these styles within the same service.

Both the return type and the method parameter specify their namespace, and their name properties match the part names in the WSDL.

As for the body of the method, your business logic simply returns an authorization in the amount of $2,500 if your card number starts with a 4, and it returns 0 otherwise. It sets this return value into the generated Authorization type, which is returned to the client.

Example 7-4 shows what the messages for each of these types looks like on the wire.

Example 7-4. SOAP message credit card request

```
<?xml version="1.0" ?>
<S:Envelope xmlns:S="http://schemas.xmlsoap.org/soap/envelope/">
<S:Body>
<creditCard xmlns="http://ns.soacookbook.com/credit">
<cardNumber>4011111111111111</cardNumber>
<name>
<firstName>Phineas</firstName>
<middleInitial>J</middleInitial>
<lastName>Fogg</lastName>
</name>
<expirationDate>2015-04-27-07:00</expirationDate>
</creditCard></S:Body></S:Envelope>
```

If you were going to construct a credit card SOAP message by hand on the client to invoke this service, this is what you would need to build using SAAJ. If you used wsimport and let JAX-WS generate a CreditCard Java type for you on the client, you could just populate the object as you would any other and pass it to the proxy to let it do the marshaling into this same XML.

Example 7-5 shows what the SOAP message for the `Authorization` return type looks like on the wire.

Example 7-5. SOAP message XML for authorization return

```
<?xml version="1.0" ?>
<S:Envelope xmlns:S="http://schemas.xmlsoap.org/soap/envelope/">
<S:Body>
<authorization xmlns="http://ns.soacookbook.com/credit">
<amount>2500.0</amount>
</authorization>
</S:Body>
</S:Envelope>
```

These XML documents are what's actually exchanged during service invocation, and in each case the only child element of the SOAP body is a type that matches the corresponding schema element exactly.

JAXB generated types

As mentioned, your parameter and return type are based on schema elements that XJC generates into Java types. Example 7-6 shows the `CreditCard.java` type. This is what you can compile and use on the client side if you import the WSDL.

Example 7-6. CreditCard.java

```
package com.soacookbook.ns.credit;

import javax.xml.bind.annotation.XmlAccessType;
import javax.xml.bind.annotation.XmlAccessorType;
import javax.xml.bind.annotation.XmlElement;
import javax.xml.bind.annotation.XmlSchemaType;
import javax.xml.bind.annotation.XmlType;
import javax.xml.datatype.XMLGregorianCalendar;

/**
 * Java class for CreditCard complex type. Comments ommitted.
 */
@XmlAccessorType(XmlAccessType.FIELD)
@XmlType(name = "CreditCard", propOrder = {
    "cardNumber",
    "name",
    "expirationDate"
})
public class CreditCard {

    @XmlElement(required = true)
    protected String cardNumber;
    @XmlElement(required = true)
    protected Name name;
    @XmlElement(required = true, nillable = true)
    @XmlSchemaType(name = "date")
    protected XMLGregorianCalendar expirationDate;
```

```
//getters and setters for each field ommitted.
```

The generated type for the Authorization looks similar. The XML annotations allow you to marshal an instance of this type back into XML using JAXB on the client side if you want to work with a SAAJ XML view. But you can treat it like a regular Java class on the server side, and on the client side as well if you use a proxy.

Notice that the type as represented in Java has "forgotten" all of the constraints you placed on the element in the schema. A Java proxy will let you populate these fields regardless of those constraints.

For the sake of completeness, let's now look at the build file to see how all these items are packaged.

Build file

Here is the build file that puts all of these pieces together and deploys it to Glassfish:

```
<project name="soacookbookServer" default="all">
    <property file="soacookbookServer.properties"/>

    <!-- PATHS -->
    <path id="cp">
        <pathelement location="${classes.dir}"/>
        <pathelement location="${gen.classes.dir}"/>
        <pathelement location="${javaee.jar}"/>
        <pathelement location="${common.jar}"/>
        <pathelement location="${config.dir}"/>
        <pathelement location="${commons.lang.jar}"/>
        <pathelement location="${service.schemas.classes.dir}"/>
        <pathelement location="${sun.ws.rt.jar}"/>
        <pathelement location="${log4j.jar}"/>
        <pathelement location="${client.jar}"/>
    </path>

    <path id="cp.test">
        <!-- Added src.test.dir to allow a specific log4j.xml
            file just for the tests -->
        <pathelement location="${src.test.dir}"/>
        <pathelement location="${test.classes.dir}"/>
        <pathelement location="${junit.jar}"/>
        <path refid="cp" />
    </path>

    <path id="srcs.path">
        <pathelement path="${src.dir}" />
        <pathelement path="${src.gen.dir}" />
    </path>

    <!-- BUILD TARGETS -->
    <target name="all" depends="init,clean,prepare,
        schema-class-gen,compile,build-war,deploy" />
```

```
<!-- INIT & TASK DEFS -->
<target name="init">
    <echo message="Testing for glassfish root directory"/>
    <fail>
        <condition>
            <not>
                <available file="${javaee.jar}"/>
            </not>
        </condition>
        Please open the user.properties file and set the
        gf.root property to point
        to your glassfish install directory.
        (default /opt/glassfish on Linux and
        c:/glassfish-v2 on windows)
    </fail>

    <echo message="Testing for gf.password.file setting in user.properties"/>

    <fail>
        <condition>
            <not>
                <available file="${gf.password.file}"/>
            </not>
        </condition>

        Please open the user.properties file and set the gf.password.file property
        to point to the absolute path on your machine of this file.  This is
        required for the glassfish deploy task (which does not work on
        relative paths).
    </fail>

    <echo message="Using Path Separator: ${path.separator}"/>

    <taskdef name="junit" classname=
     "org.apache.tools.ant.taskdefs.optional.junit.JUnitTask">
        <classpath path="${junit.task.path}" />
        <classpath path="${junit.jar}" />
    </taskdef>

    <taskdef name="xjc" classname="com.sun.tools.xjc.XJCTask">
        <classpath path="${xjc.task.path}"/>
    </taskdef>

    <taskdef name="gf-deploy"
             classname=
             "org.apache.tools.ant.taskdefs.optional.sun.appserv.DeployTask"
             classpath="${deploy.cp}" />
</target>
<!-- END INIT -->

<!-- CLEAN -->
<target name="clean">
    <echo message="-----Cleaning-----" />
    <delete dir="${dist.dir}"/>
    <delete dir="${build.dir}"/>
```

```
    <delete dir="${test.dir}"/>
    <delete dir="${src.gen.dir}" />
</target>

<!-- PREPARE -->
<target name="prepare">
    <mkdir dir="${dist.dir}"/>
    <mkdir dir="${build.dir}"/>
    <mkdir dir="${ear.lib.dir}"/>
    <mkdir dir="${src.gen.dir}"/>
    <mkdir dir="${classes.dir}"/>
    <mkdir dir="${gen.classes.dir}"/>
    <mkdir dir="${ejb.dependencies.classes.dir}"/>
    <mkdir dir="${test.dir}"/>
    <mkdir dir="${test.classes.dir}"/>
    <mkdir dir="${test.report.dir}"/>
</target>

<!-- RUN JAXB TO GENERATE JAVA FROM SCHEMA-->
<target name="schema-class-gen">
    <echo message="---Generating Java src from Schema---" />
    <xjc destdir="${src.gen.dir}"
         extension="false">
        <schema dir="${schemas.dir}"
                includes="**/*.schemalet,
                ${schemas.includes.pattern}"/>
    </xjc>
</target>

<!-- COMPILE CLASSES-->
<target name="compile">
    <echo message="-----Compiling-----" />
    <javac compiler="modern" debug="${debug}" fork="true"
        source="${source.java.version}"
        target="${target.java.version}"
        excludes="**/client/**"
        destdir="${classes.dir}">

        <src path="${src.gen.dir}"/>
        <src path="${src.dir}"/>
        <classpath refid="cp"/>
    </javac>
</target>

<!-- BUILD WAR -->
<target name="build-war">
    <echo message="-----Building WAR-----" />
    <war destfile="${build.dir}/${war.name}"
        webxml="${webinf.dir}/web.xml">
        <manifest>
            <attribute name="Manifest-Version" value="1.0"/>
            <attribute name="Built-By" value="${user.name}"/>
        </manifest>
        <webinf  dir="${config.meta.inf.dir}"
            includes="**/*.wsdl,**/*.xsd"/>
```

```
            <lib file="${client.jar}" />
            <classes dir="${build.dir}/classes"
                excludes="**/ejb/**"/>

            <fileset dir="${root.dir}/jsp" includes="*.jsp" />
        </war>
    </target>

    <!-- DEPLOY TO GLASSFISH-->
    <!-- Undeploy happens automatically on a new deploy so it
      does not need to be called explicitly -->
    <target name="deploy">
        <echo message="Deploying ${war.name}"/>
        <gf-deploy user="${gf.username}"
                   passwordfile="${gf.password.file}"
                   host="${gf.server.address}"
                   port="${gf.adminport}"
                   file="${build.dir}/${war.name}"
                   asinstalldir="${gf.root}"/>
        <property name="artifact.deployed" value="true" />
    </target>

</project>
```

This is a fairly standard build file, but it is useful to clarify the class names of the tasks that are involved, and to illustrate a reasonable way to set up an Ant build. It is also worth noting that this is about as simple as you can get in Ant. It cleans out temporary directories, generates Java sources from schema, compiles the Java classes, and packages everything up in a WAR with the WSDL and the schema. It then deploys the resulting WAR to Glassfish.

If you are using Maven 2, you probably want to break up the build process illustrated here into separate modules. One idea, for example, is to create a module for the service, a module for supporting required classes, a module for the generation of client-side artifacts, and a module for a client JAR if you are doing those too. The client JAR can then depend on the JAR of the generated artifacts.

I have included the properties file (Example 7-7) for the sake of completeness. You can see what classes and JARs are involved, and easily do some mapping to your environment for source directories and other items.

Example 7-7. soacookbookServer.properties

```
project.name=soaCookbookWS

#USER PROPERTIES: LINUX
#gf.password.file=/home/ehewitt/soacookbook/repository/code/chapters/ws/
soacookbookServer.properties
#gf.root=/opt/glassfish91u1
```

```
#USER PROPERTIES: WINDOWS
gf.password.file=C:\\oreilly/soacookbook/code/chapters/ws/soacookbookServer.properties
gf.root=C:\\programs/glassfishv2ur1

#GENERAL JAVA
source.java.version=1.6
target.java.version=1.6
debug=on

#DIRS
root.dir=.
build.dir=./build
classes.dir=${build.dir}/classes
gen.classes.dir=${build.dir}/gen-classes
dist.dir=dist
docs.dir=./docs
src.dir=./src/java
src.gen.dir=./src/gen
src.xml.dir=./src/xml
src.test.dir=./src/test
test.dir=./test
test.classes.dir=${test.dir}/classes
test.report.dir=${test.dir}/report
tmp.dir=${build.dir}/tmp

config.dir=./config
webinf.dir=${config.dir}/WEB-INF
config.meta.inf.dir=${config.dir}/META-INF

ear.lib.dir=${build.dir}/lib
schemas.dir=${config.meta.inf.dir}/wsdl/ch03

ejb.dependencies.classes.dir=${build.dir}/ejb-dependency-classes
#location of the .class files for classes generated from schemas used by the service
and the client service.schemas.classes.dir=${root.dir}/../ws/build/classes
#generated classes from wsimport go here
gen.client.package.name=com.dte.soa.soacookbook.wsclient

#PATTERNS
ejb.dir.pattern=**/ejb/**
spi.includes.pattern=**/*.spi.*
schemas.dir=config/META-INF/wsdl/ch03
schemas.includes.pattern=**/*.xsd

#DEPENDENCIES: LIB DIR
lib.dir=../../lib
commons.lang.jar=${lib.dir}/commons-lang-2.3.jar
javaee.jar=${lib.dir}/javaee.jar
junit.jar=${lib.dir}/junit-4.4.jar
log4j.jar=${lib.dir}/log4j-1.2.9.jar
webservices-rt.jar=${lib.dir}/webservices-rt.jar

#From the Client project, to be included in WAR
client.jar=../client/dist/soaCookbookClient.jar
```

```
#ARTIFACT NAMES
client.classes.jar=${project.name}-client.jar
ejb-jar.name=${project.name}-ejb.jar
ear.name=${project.name}.ear
log4j.xml=${config.dir}/log4j.xml
log4j.props.jar=log4jProps.jar
war.name=${project.name}.war
war.name=${project.name}.war
svc.common.jar.name=svc-common.jar

#GLASSFISH DEPLOYMENT
deploy.target=glassfish
gf.server.address=localhost
gf.domain.name=soacookbookdomain

#You may need to modify these for your system
# Glassfish requires the AS_ADMIN_PASSWORD to be in a file.
# The task requires an absolute path.  We are pointing directly
# to this file.
gf.username=admin
gf.adminport=5050
gf.port=8080
gf.esb.port=18181

AS_ADMIN_PASSWORD=adminadmin
deploy.cp=${sun.app.ant.jar}${path.separator}${gf.root}/lib/
admin-cli.jar${path.separator}${gf.root}/lib/
appserv-rt.jar${path.separator}${gf.root}/lib/appserv-admin.jar
server.location=http://${gf.server.address}:${gf.port}

#2.1
sun.app.ant.jar=${lib.dir}/sun-appserv-ant.jar
sun.ws.tools.jar=${lib.dir}/webservices-tools.jar
sun.ws.rt.jar=${lib.dir}/webservices-rt.jar

#TASKS
junit.task.path=${lib.dir}/ant-junit.jar
xjc.task.path=${sun.app.ant.jar}${path.separator}${sun.ws.tools.jar}
${path.separator}${sun.ws.rt.jar}
```

Run the "all" target on the Ant build and you should be up and running.

Don't forget that you may want clients to use your original schema; the JAXB types generated from them will lose all type restriction information. There are ways of validating Java objects against a service schema, which we examine in other recipes. If you have only Java clients, you can bundle the generated classes and the original schema in a client JAR for them to invoke.

See Also

Recipe 2.16 for further discussion on schema validation options and Recipe 5.19 to see how to validate client data using this schema, WSDL, and service as an example.

7.13 Specifying the SOAP Binding Style, Use, and Parameter Style

Problem

You want to customize the SOAP binding style, SOAP body use, and parameter style for your web service operation.

Solution

Use the @SOAPBinding annotation on your web method and specify its attributes using enums within the javax.jws.soap.SOAPBinding class, like this:

```
@WebMethod
@SOAPBinding(style=SOAPBinding.Style.DOCUMENT,
    use=SOAPBinding.Use.LITERAL,
    parameterStyle=SOAPBinding.ParameterStyle.WRAPPED)
public @WebResult(name="searchResults",
        targetNamespace="http://ns.soacookbook.com/catalog") SearchResults
        authorSearch(
        @WebParam(name="author", mode=WebParam.Mode.IN,
        targetNamespace="http://ns.soacookbook.com/catalog") Author author) {
//...
```

DOCUMENT and RPC are possible values for SOAPBinding.Style, LITERAL and ENCODED are possible values for SOAPBinding.Use, and WRAPPED and BARE are possible values for SOAPBinding.ParameterStyle. If no values are specified, that is, if no @SOAPBinding annotation is used on your web method, the defaults will be document/literal wrapped.

See Recipe 7.3 for a discussion on how to choose among these combinations.

7.14 Configuring Standard Custom Bindings

Problem

You want to customize the binding between Java and WSDL in order to enable asynchronous operations, dictate client Java package names, specify MIME content, or enable wrapper style.

Solution

Write your custom bindings either inline within the WSDL or in an external binding file. Your generated SEI will provide asynchronous methods based on the methods defined. If you are using SAAJ, asynchronous methods are defined already for you on Dispatch<T>. These are:

```
Response<T> invokeAsync(T msg)

Future<?> invokeAsync(T msg, AsyncHandler<T> handler)
```

Discussion

There are four standard customizations that the JAX-WS specification defines out of the box:

`package`
: Used to dictate to clients the name of the Java package for the target namespace indicated in the `wsdl:definitions` element, and to insert package-level JavaDoc text for a client *package-info.java* file

`enableWrapperStyle`
: Turns on wrapper style processing for all qualifying operations

`enableAsyncMapping`
: Allows clients to invoke specified operations asynchronously

`enableMIMEContent`
: Enables use of MIME content by default for all specified operations

Because a client's only view of your service is the WSDL, that's where you have to indicate whether your service supports any of these capabilities. JAX-WS defines a separate binding element for each of these items, and you tie them to your WSDL using one of two methods: an external binding file that your WSDL imports, or inline elements, directly within your WSDL.

Either way, you enable these options by specifying simple values for these elements, which are defined within the `http://java.sun.com/xml/ns/jaxws` namespace, and use a prefix of `JAX-WS` by convention. Regardless of method (inline or file), the element `JAX-WS:bindings` is used to contain all other binding declarations. You can specify the declarations in any order.

But each of the standard custom bindings is allowed only in certain places. If you are using an external file, you must specify the proper node using XPath on the bindings `@node` attribute. If you specify bindings inline within the WSDL, you must take care to place the bindings only on the elements to which you want them to apply (and on which they are allowed to apply) or you will get a deployment error, rendering your service unavailable.

If you are using bindings within a WSDL document, you cannot use either the `@node` or the `@wsdlLocation` element.

The following sections discuss the use of these two methods.

Using the external binding file

With this approach, you group all binding declarations for your WSDL into a single document, which is a standalone file. You write the `jaxws:bindings` element, and specify a value for the `wsdlLocation` property to indicate what WSDL this binding applies to. You also supply an XPath expression to the `node` property to signal what aspect of the WSDL this binding applies to. A standalone binding file that enables asynchronous operations is shown in Example 7-8.

Example 7-8. Standalone file with JAX-WS binding customizations

```
<jaxws:bindings wsdlLocation="http://ns.soacookbook.com/Calculator.wsdl">
    <jaxws:packageName="com.soacookbook.calc">
      <jaxws:javadoc>The 'add' operations in this package will be
      available asynchronously.
      </jaxws:javadoc>
    </jaxws:packageName>
    <jaxws:bindings node="wsdl:operation[@name='add']">
      <jaxws:enableAsyncMapping>true</jaxws:enableAsyncMapping>
    </jaxws:bindings>
<jaxws:bindings>
```

This file applies to the single WSDL at the given location, and it specifies two binding customizations. The first is that the package name specified will contain the JavaDoc of the given string. The second is that the SEI will contain additional methods to make an invocation of the `add` operation asynchronously.

There are two other attributes allowed on the bindings element. The first is `version`, which by default is 2.0 and refers to the JAX-WS version. The other is `node`, which allows you to limit the application of this binding customization to an element within the target WSDL that you specify in an XPath expression.

Using inline elements

With this approach, you must not specify a WSDL location in the `jaxws:bindings` element, as any customization can apply only to the current WSDL, nor are you allowed to use an XPath expression indicating the node this declaration applies to.

Example 7-9 shows how to use the inline declaration to `enableAsyncMapping`.

Example 7-9. An inline jaxws:bindings element

```
<wsdl:definitions targetNamespace="..."
  xmlns:jaxws="http:java.sun.com/xml/ns/jaxws">
  <wsdl:portType name="CalculatorWS">
    <wsdl:operation name="add">
        <wsdl:input message="tns:add"></input>
        <wsdl:output message="tns:addResponse"></output>
    </wsdl:operation>
    <jaxws:bindings>
        <jaxws:enableAsyncMapping>true</jaxws:enableAsyncMapping>
    <jaxws:bindings>
```

```
  </wsdl:portType>
</wsdl:definitions>
```

In terms of how your customizations are applied by the runtime, there is no semantic difference between specifying your bindings externally or inline. There is a difference for your maintenance program, however. You may find that it is more flexible to put unrelated customizations in separate files, and have them all applied to the same WSDL as necessary. This gives you a separation of concerns but also makes it harder to determine what exactly is being applied to your WSDL because the binding files refer to the WSDL, and not the other way around.

Also, you might decide that you do not want to advertise certain capabilities directly in the WSDL in order to keep it free of platform-specific code.

If you annotate a port with `jaxws:provider`, no SEI will be generated for it. In its place, the application code will use a `javax.xml.ws.Provider` interface. This means that there will be no `getXXXPort` method created in the generated service type (otherwise, a clients could call a method to get a port that doesn't exist).

Be careful what implementation details you allow to creep into your public interface.

See Also

Chapter 8 in the JAX-WS specification to see what custom bindings are allowed on which elements.

7.15 Excluding a Public Method from a Service

Problem

You have a service implementation that uses the `@WebService` annotation, but this automatically makes all public methods available on a generated WSDL.

Solution

There are three ways to deal with this:

- Write the WSDL yourself. If you don't generate the WSDL, the method you want to leave out won't be there.
- If you are generating the WSDL, you can annotate every method that you explicitly want to appear in the WSDL with `@WebMethod`. Do not add the annotation to the method you want to leave out.
- Explicitly indicate `@WebMethod(exclude=true)` on the method you want to leave out.

Discussion

There are a few reasons that you might encounter this situation. You might have a web service that relies on a third-party application to run, such as credit processor software. You want to make sure that the life cycle of the dependency matches that of the EJB that defines your service. This EJB is a stateless session bean that also implements `TimedObject`. The EJB is set up as a timer so that you can have a web-based context listener that gets a callback when your application starts and invokes a method on the EJB to start the dependency. That setup may be fine, but you definitely don't want to expose that life cycle method web service. Still, it needs to be public so the context listener can find it.

There are many ways to deal with the life cycle of a dependency. One obvious design choice here is to have the context listener invoke a public method in another class in the same package as the EJB, and have it invoke a package-private method in the EJB. This is simply a hypothetical. It could very well be the case, however, as this alternate solution proposes, that you may want to reconsider a design that appears to require using `@WebMethod(exclude=true)`.

7.16 Creating a Service Provider with an XML View

Problem

You want to create a service implementation that works directly with the SOAP XML in the requests and responses, rather than the object view.

Solution

Have your service implement the `javax.xml.ws.Provider<T>` interface.

Discussion

JAX-WS-based web services are typically implemented using annotations, which allow the developer to get up and running quickly. Such endpoint implementations are very easy to work with and save developers the trouble of having to deal with a lot of plumbing. They offer an object-level view of messages and port types as described in the WSDL, allowing developers to work comfortably with abstractions over the XML contents of the messages passed back and forth in service invocations.

But there are times when you want to have a raw XML view of the requests and responses coming through your service. That's where `Provider<T>` comes in.

`Provider<T>` is part of JAX-WS, but it lets you work with the SAAJ API, and it offers an alternative to working with annotated SEIs. It is the server-side analog to

Dispatch<T>, providing an XML message-level view of requests. The interface defines a single method for you to implement:

```
T invoke(T request)
```

Every time a new message is received, the invoke method is called.

Vendor implementations of JAX-WS are required to support at least three values for the type parameter on the provider:

- javax.xml.transform.Source
- javax.activation.DataSource
- javax.xml.soap.SOAPMessage

A Source acts as a container for XML source, and it can include implementations such as DOMSource and SAXSource. SOAPMessage represents a SOAP message containing the header, the body, any attachments, and so on. A DataSource works with HTTP bindings to provide an abstraction of an arbitrary collection of data, providing access to the data in the form of InputStream and OutputStream.

Working with a Provider requires detailed knowledge of the structure of the payload or message.

Creating a Provider<T>

To create a provider, you must do three things:

1. Supply a public no-arg constructor.
2. Implement the Provider<T> interface, supplying one of the three acceptable values for the type parameter.
3. Annotate the class with the @WebServiceProvider annotation.

Along with the @WebServiceProvider interface, the developer can supply a @javax.xml.ws.Service.Mode annotation with one of two values: Mode.PAYLOAD or Mode.MESSAGE. This value indicates the view of the data the provider instance will have access to.

Using Mode.PAYLOAD will give the provider access to only the children of the SOAP body element. Using Mode.MESSAGE gives the provider the entire SOAP envelope, including headers. Note that here my example uses SOAP, but the MESSAGE mode is actually intended in a more general way, meaning that it applies to the protocol message itself, whatever that protocol is. The default value is PAYLOAD.

With a provider, you are also allowed to use handlers. Handlers are discussed further in Recipe 7.17.

Example 7-10 shows the basic WSDL that you'll write by hand. Your `Provider` will indicate that it conforms to that WSDL using the `wsdlLocation` property. Because the provider is not an EJB, you'll just package this in a WAR, and have your Ant script place the WSDL in the *WEB-INF/wsdl* directory. Your service interface indicates that a request should contain a username, and if the service authorizes the user, it will return an SSO token placed in the header as well as a child of the SOAP body indicating the role that user is in.

Example 7-10. The WSDL for an authorizer service

```
<?xml version="1.0" encoding="UTF-8"?>
<definitions name="GatewayService"
    xmlns="http://schemas.xmlsoap.org/wsdl/"
    xmlns:soap="http://schemas.xmlsoap.org/wsdl/soap/"
    targetNamespace="http://ns.soacookbook.com/gateway"
    xmlns:tns="http://ns.soacookbook.com/gateway">

    <types>
        <xs:schema xmlns:xs="http://www.w3.org/2001/XMLSchema"
            targetNamespace="http://ns.soacookbook.com/gateway">
          <xs:element name="gatewayRequest" type="xs:string" />
          <xs:element name="gatewayResponse" type="xs:string" />
        </xs:schema>
    </types>

    <message name="gatewayRequest">
        <part name="parameters" element="tns:gatewayRequest"></part>
    </message>

    <message name="gatewayResponse">
        <part name="parameters" element="tns:gatewayResponse"></part>
    </message>

    <portType name="Gateway">
        <operation name="authorize">
            <input message="tns:gatewayRequest"></input>
            <output message="tns:gatewayResponse"></output>
        </operation>
    </portType>

    <binding name="GatewayPortBinding" type="tns:Gateway">
        <soap:binding transport="http://schemas.xmlsoap.org/soap/http"
            style="document"></soap:binding>

        <operation name="authorize">
            <soap:operation soapAction=""></soap:operation>
            <input>
                <soap:body use="literal"></soap:body>
            </input>
            <output>
                <soap:body use="literal"></soap:body>
            </output>
        </operation>
    </binding>
```

```
    <service name="GatewayService">
        <port name="GatewayPort" binding="tns:GatewayPortBinding">
            <soap:address
              location="http://localhost:8080/GatewayService/Gateway">
            </soap:address>
        </port>
    </service>
</definitions>
```

For the sake of simplicity, this example puts the types directly into the schema itself. That's acceptable for an example this straightforward, but is probably not something you'd want to do in practice. You define one operation named `authorize`, which takes and returns a string.

Now you'll define your provider. Because you want to add headers, you'll use `SOAPMessage` as the type parameter, which means you also have to specify `@ServiceMode(Mode.MESSAGE)`.

There are certain combinations of service mode that don't make sense with your provider's type parameter. For example, it is an error to attempt to parameterize your provider on `javax.xml.soap.SOAPMessage`, and then specify `Mode.PAYLOAD` (which is also the default). To rectify this, if you really only want the payload, use a `Source` type; if you really want access to the whole SOAP message, including its headers and attachments, employ `@ServiceMode(Mode.MESSAGE)`.

Example 7-11 shows a simple `Provider` implementation.

Example 7-11. Provider<SOAPMessage> implementation

```
package com.soacookbook.ch04;

import java.io.IOException;
import java.util.UUID;
import javax.xml.namespace.QName;
import javax.xml.soap.MessageFactory;
import javax.xml.soap.SOAPBody;
import javax.xml.soap.SOAPElement;
import javax.xml.soap.SOAPException;
import javax.xml.soap.SOAPFactory;
import javax.xml.soap.SOAPHeader;
import javax.xml.soap.SOAPHeaderElement;
import javax.xml.soap.SOAPMessage;
import javax.xml.ws.Provider;
import javax.xml.ws.Service.Mode;
import javax.xml.ws.ServiceMode;
import javax.xml.ws.WebServiceProvider;
import org.apache.log4j.Logger;

/**
 * Demonstrates simple Provider.
```

```
 */
@WebServiceProvider(
  serviceName="GatewayService",
  portName="GatewayPort",
  targetNamespace="http://ns.soacookbook.com/gateway",
  wsdlLocation="WEB-INF/wsdl/Gateway.wsdl")
@ServiceMode(Mode.MESSAGE)
public class MyProvider implements Provider<SOAPMessage> {
  private static final Logger LOGGER =
           Logger.getLogger(MyProvider.class);

    public MyProvider() {
        LOGGER.debug("Created provider instance.");
    }

    public SOAPMessage invoke(SOAPMessage request) {
        SOAPMessage response = null;

        try {
            LOGGER.debug("Received request:\n");

            //Dump request to console
            request.writeTo(System.out);

            LOGGER.debug("Building SOAP Response.");
            String user = request.getSOAPBody().getTextContent();
            response = createResponse(user);

        } catch (SOAPException ex) {
            ex.printStackTrace();
        } catch (IOException ex) {
            ex.printStackTrace();
        }

        return response;
    }

    public SOAPMessage createResponse(String user)
                throws SOAPException, IOException {

        LOGGER.debug("Creating SOAP Response for user: " + user);

        //Create a response message
        MessageFactory mf = MessageFactory.newInstance();
        SOAPFactory sf = SOAPFactory.newInstance();
        SOAPMessage response = mf.createMessage();

        //Could go to database here to check creds
        if ("jgosling".equals(user)) {
            //Create Header
            QName q = new QName("urn:myNS", "sso");
            SOAPHeader h  = response.getSOAPHeader();
            SOAPHeaderElement headerEl = h.addHeaderElement(q);
            headerEl.addAttribute(new QName("gateway"),
                    "192.168.1.102");
```

```
            headerEl.addAttribute(new QName("authToken"),
                    UUID.randomUUID().toString());

            //Create Body
            SOAPBody body = response.getSOAPBody();
            SOAPElement respContent =
                    body.addChildElement("gatewayResponse");
            respContent.setValue("ADMIN");

        } else {

            //Create body for unauthorized user, and no header
            SOAPBody body = response.getSOAPBody();
            SOAPElement respContent =
                    body.addChildElement("gatewayResponse");
            respContent.setValue("N/A");
        }

        response.saveChanges();

        LOGGER.debug("Returning response.");

        response.writeTo(System.out);

        return response;
    }
}
```

The provider implements the required `invoke` method; it reads the request and returns a response, delegating the work of sending authentication tokens to valid users, and denying invalid users. The example demonstrates a few things:

- How to implement a `Provider`
- How the `Provider` relates to the given WSDL
- How to create a complete SOAP message for a response
- How to add a complete element to a SOAP header

Here you've used a message mode to ensure that you can access the entire SOAP envelope. The WSDL is packaged with the WAR, and the other properties of the annotation indicate the service and port that this provider will respond to requests for.

So you can build and deploy this now, and start listening for requests. Your deployment message will indicate that your provider class is available at the specified address if all goes well:

```
DPL5306:Servlet Web Service Endpoint [com.soacookbook.ch04.MyProvider]
listening at address [http://localhost:8080/soaCookbookWS/GatewayService]
```

Glassfish provides a web page representing your service that allows you to view the service name, port name, and implementing class, as shown in Figure 7-1.

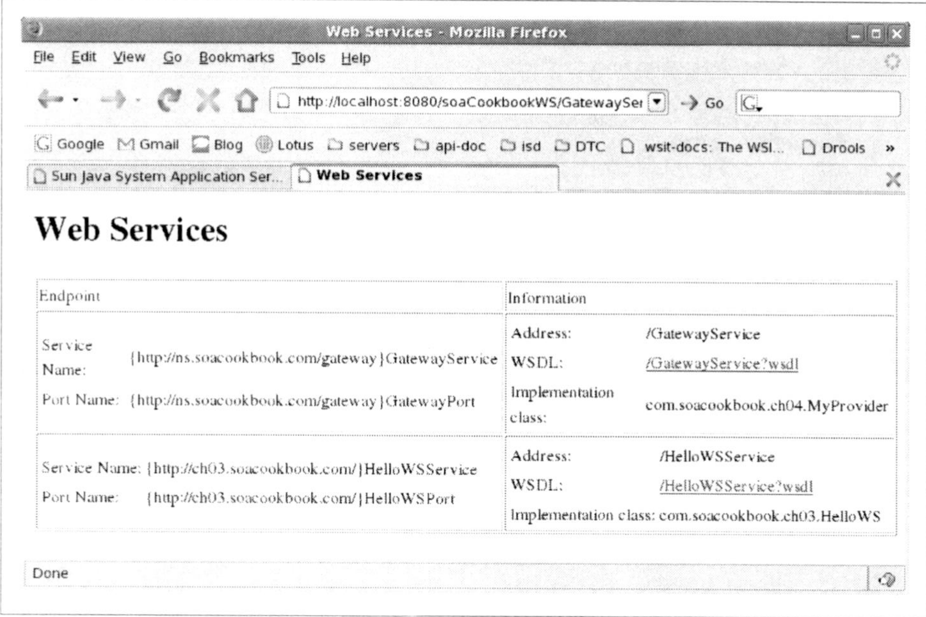

Figure 7-1. Glassfish service list page

At this point, a provider instance will have been created, and you can send it a SOAP request to test it.

Testing the provider

In this section, you'll create a JUnit test to send requests to your provider. You can create the JUnit 4.4 class shown in Example 7-12 to execute two tests. This class will test the single method `authorize` that accepts a username string and returns a string indicating the role that user is in.

Using the username `jgosling`, you expect to get authorized to the Admin role and to get an `<sso>` header element sent that could be used for routing. Invoking the service with a username that's not in the database gives a value of "N/A."

Example 7-12. Provider unit test

```
package com.soacookbook.ch04.test;

import static org.junit.Assert.*;
import com.soacookbook.ns.gateway.*;
import java.util.*;
import org.apache.log4j.Logger;
import org.junit.*;

/**
 * JUnit test for the authorization provider.
 */
```

```
public class ProviderTest {
    private static final Logger LOGGER =
            Logger.getLogger(ProviderTest.class);

    private GatewayService authService;
    private Gateway gateway;

    @Before
    public void setup() {
        authService = new GatewayService();
        gateway = authService.getGatewayPort();
    }

    //This user should get authorized in Admin role
    @Test
    public void testProviderAuth() throws Exception {
        LOGGER.debug("Executing.");

        String response = gateway.authorize("jgosling");

        LOGGER.debug("Response: " + response);
        assertEquals("ADMIN", response);
    }

    //This user should fail authorization
    @Test
    public void testProviderNotAuth() throws Exception {
        LOGGER.debug("Executing.");

        String response = gateway.authorize("bgates");
        assertEquals("N/A", response);
    }
}
```

Using JUnit 4.4, you can set up your proxies only once, and JUnit's `@Before` annotation will set up a fresh instance of the service and the port for each test method to use.

The following shows the output of running the JUnit test:

```
Received request:
<S:Envelope xmlns:S="http://schemas.xmlsoap.org/soap/envelope/">
<S:Header/>
<S:Body>
<gatewayRequest
  xmlns="http://ns.soacookbook.com/gateway">jgosling</gatewayRequest>
</S:Body>
</S:Envelope>

Building SOAP Response.

Creating SOAP Response for user: jgosling

4/15/08-15:05 DEBUG  com.soacookbook.ch04.MyProvider.createResponse - Response ready:
<SOAP-ENV:Envelope xmlns:SOAP-ENV="http://schemas.xmlsoap.org/soap/envelope/">
<SOAP-ENV:Header>
  <sso xmlns="urn:myNS" authToken="2878f38f-5515..."
```

```
        gateway="192.168.1.102"/>
    </SOAP-ENV:Header>
    <SOAP-ENV:Body>
      <gatewayResponse>ADMIN</gatewayResponse>
    </SOAP-ENV:Body>
    </SOAP-ENV:Envelope>
```

The unit test sends two messages. One containing a username that should be authorized and get a temporary authorization Single Sign On token. The other contains a username that should not be authorized, and gets no header element set with no token, and the response indicates "N/A" for "Not Authorized."

7.17 Implementing Server-Side Handler Chains

Problem

You need to specify the handlers you want your service to invoke against incoming and outgoing messages, and you want your chain to be defined externally in a configuration file rather than have it embedded in the code.

Solution

Write an XML file that defines the chain in accordance with the Java EE rules, and then add a `javax.jws.HandlerChain` annotation to your web service to specify the name of the handler chain file. This file will be an XML file that you put in the *WEB-INF/classes* directory or elsewhere on the application's classpath.

Let's look at how to do this.

If you are starting from Java, create a WAR project in whatever way you like and add a web service POJO to it. Then add the `@HandlerChain` annotation to the class, and use the `file` attribute to indicate the name of the XML file that lists your handlers. This is shown in Example 7-13.

Example 7-13. HandlerService.java

```
package com.soacookbook;

import javax.jws.HandlerChain;
import javax.jws.WebMethod;
import javax.jws.WebParam;
import javax.jws.WebService;

/**
 * Uses a handler chain on the server.
 */
@WebService
@HandlerChain(file="myHandlers.xml")
public class HandlerWebService {

    @WebMethod(operationName = "doWork")
```

```
    public String doWork(
        @WebParam(name = "msg") String msg) {

        System.out.println("doing work");
        return "Processed work for: " + msg;
    }
}
```

Other than the new annotation, there's nothing noteworthy about this web service. You then need to write the actual handler implementation classes. You can have as few as one if you like, and I'll do that here. This will be a simple class that spits out the messages to the system output stream. I've kept it simple on purpose so that it doesn't get in the way. You would implement anything you would normally want to do in a servlet filter, for example.

The last step is to create your *myHandlers.xml* file (as shown in Example 7-14). Put it in the *WEB-INF/classes* directory of your WAR.

Example 7-14. myHandlers.xml

```
<?xml version="1.0" encoding="UTF-8"?>
<handler-chains xmlns="http://java.sun.com/xml/ns/javaee">
<handler-chain>
    <handler>
        <handler-class>com.soacookbook.LogHandler</handler-class>
        <handler-class>com.soacookbook.LateNotifyHandler</handler-class>
    </handler>
</handler-chain>
</handler-chains>
```

The handlers are dynamically loaded based on the implementations specified, and they are executed for both inbound and outbound messages. Handlers are executed in the order listed.

Testing the service produces the following output, which illustrates the order in which the runtime invokes the handler interface methods:

```
LH: handleMessage
LH: logToOut
Inbound message:
<S:Envelope xmlns:S="http://schemas.xmlsoap.org/soap/envelope/">
<S:Header/>
<S:Body><ns2:doWork xmlns:ns2="http://soacookbook.com/">
<msg>SOME IMPORTANT JOB</msg></ns2:doWork></S:Body>
</S:Envelope>

doing work
LH: handleMessage
LH: logToOut
Outbound message:
LH: close
```

Just like a servlet filter, the handler receives the request before the service does, allowing you time to do some additional processing or massaging of the data.

Example 7-15 shows the implementation of the handler class.

Example 7-15. LogHandler.java

```
package com.soacookbook;

import java.io.IOException;
import javax.xml.namespace.QName;
import javax.xml.soap.SOAPException;
import javax.xml.ws.handler.MessageContext;
import javax.xml.ws.handler.soap.SOAPHandler;
import javax.xml.ws.handler.soap.SOAPMessageContext;
import java.util.Set;

/**
 * Logs inbound SOAP messages to the console.
 */
public class LogHandler
    implements SOAPHandler<SOAPMessageContext> {

    public Set<QName> getHeaders() {
        System.out.println("LH: getHeaders");
        return null;
    }

    public boolean handleMessage(SOAPMessageContext ctx) {
        System.out.println("LH: handleMessage");
        logToSystemOut(ctx);
        return true;
    }

    public boolean handleFault(SOAPMessageContext ctx) {
        System.out.println("LH: handleFault");
        logToSystemOut(ctx);
        return true;
    }

    // nothing to clean up
    public void close(MessageContext messageContext) {
        System.out.println("LH: close");
    }

    private void logToSystemOut(SOAPMessageContext ctx) {
        System.out.println("LH: logToOut");
        Boolean outboundProperty = (Boolean)
            ctx.get (MessageContext.MESSAGE_OUTBOUND_PROPERTY);

        if (outboundProperty.booleanValue()) {
            System.out.println("\nOutbound message:");
        } else {
            try {
                System.out.println("\nInbound message:");
```

```
                ctx.getMessage().writeTo(System.out);
            } catch (SOAPException ex) {
                ex.printStackTrace();
            } catch (IOException ex) {
                ex.printStackTrace();
            }
        }
    }
}
```

Recall that there are two kinds of handlers: protocol handlers and logical handlers. Because you've used a protocol handler, you have access to the SOAP envelope via the SAAJ API. Protocol handlers are concerned with processing related to the binding information in the WSDL, so the message appears to the handler as a SOAP message. Logical handlers, on the other hand, see the message payload as either a `javax.xml.transform.Source` or a JAXB annotated instance.

You can mix and match handler types within the same chain.

7.18 Providing Stateful Services

Problem

You want your web service to keep track of client sessions, much as you could do with a servlet.

Solution

This is a tricky one—at least as of this writing. There are a few different solutions, none of them is optimal. Here are your options:

- If you are using HTTP as the transport layer, declare a `WebServiceContext` object as a `Resource`, and use it to get the `HttpSession` object. Use the `HttpSession` as you normally would in a servlet. The only downside is that it does not work for transports other than HTTP. But it's straightforward and portable.
- If you are using the JAX-WS reference implementation, you can use a simple annotation, `@HttpSessionScope`. This is a nice solution that wraps the first solution just mentioned, so there is a little less coding. There is no need to do anything but store your desired state in regular instance variables, and the runtime will hand out one service instance per HTTP session. However, it is specific to the RI and it does not work just yet. (See *https://jax-ws.dev.java.net/issues/show_bug.cgi?id=545*.)
- Finally, you can use WS-Addressing, which works outside of HTTP, but this is very complex. WS-Addressing is outlined in Chapter 12.

Discussion

HTTP is a stateless protocol, meaning that each new connection bears no relation to any previous connection; state is not held between requests. While this is a fundamental feature of HTTP, there are many times when keeping state (particular knowledge of each request as it relates to other requests from the same client) is necessary. It's this mechanism that allows you to store items in a shopping cart, for example.

Using WebServiceContext

Let's examine keeping state using the `WebServiceContext` object, which is similar to the `ServletContext` object in a web container. You can declare the context as a `Resource` to be injected by the container, and then use it to store data that you want to associate with all requests coming from the same client. Let's look at an example. First you need to create the service, as shown in Example 7-16.

Example 7-16. Stateful web service using WebServiceContext

```
package com.soacookbook;

import javax.annotation.Resource;
import javax.jws.WebService;
import javax.servlet.http.HttpSession;
import javax.xml.ws.WebServiceContext;
import javax.xml.ws.handler.MessageContext;

@WebService
public class CounterContextWS {
    @Resource
    private WebServiceContext wsContext;

    public int getCounter(){
        MessageContext mc = wsContext.getMessageContext();
        HttpSession session = ((javax.servlet.http.HttpServletRequest)mc.get(
            MessageContext.SERVLET_REQUEST)).getSession();

        Integer count = (Integer)session.getAttribute("count");
        if (count == null) {
            count = 0;
            System.out.println("New Session ID=" + session.getId());
        }
        count++;
        session.setAttribute("count", count);
        return count;
    }
}
```

Here you take advantage of auto-boxing and auto-unboxing of the counter primitive. The service class simply stores the session in the `WebServiceContext`. The counter associated with the given session is stored as an attribute, like you would a shopping cart item or anything else in a servlet session. But you're not done yet. Notice that in the service the count variable is method local. You can't just store it as an instance variable, for the same reason you couldn't with a regular servlet. While it would appear to work in a simple test, multiple clients would get the shared variable.

At this point, if a client invokes the service in the regular fashion, the counter would not appear to increment. That's because the session ID is not being sent along with each request, so you need to configure the client to maintain the session across requests. Example 7-17 shows the client that will invoke the service and get a counter incremented.

Example 7-17. Stateful web service client JSP

```
<%@page contentType="text/html" pageEncoding="UTF-8"
  import="com.soacookbook.*, javax.xml.ws.*"%>
<html>
    <head><title>Counter Service</title></head>
    <body>
        <h1>Counter Context Service</h1>
        <hr/>
    <%
    try {
        CounterContextWS port = null;
        if (session.isNew()){
            CounterContextWSService service = new CounterContextWSService();
            port = service.getCounterContextWSPort();

            session.setAttribute("port", port);

            ((BindingProvider)port).getRequestContext().put(
            BindingProvider.SESSION_MAINTAIN_PROPERTY, true);
        }
        port = (CounterContextWS)session.getAttribute("port");

        int result = port.getCounter();
        out.print(result);
        result = port.getCounter();
        out.print("<br/>");
        out.print(result);

    } catch (Exception ex) {
        ex.printStackTrace();
    }
    %>
    </body>
</html>
```

Let's unpack this client code a bit. The `BindingProvider` class is in the `javax.xml.ws` package, so you import that at the top, along with the generated JAX-WS artifacts for your service. Then check if the session is new, and if so, create a new stub and associate it with this session by setting it as an attribute. You now get the request context, and use the `BindingProvider` class to indicate that you want to maintain session state across requests for this service. Whether the session is new or not, you are going to use the port that you previously associated with this session in order to call its business method (getCounter).

To test this, open a browser and point to the location where you deployed the WAR and visit the JSP. You can refresh this page, and it will increment the counter. To prove that you're not getting your counters mixed up, open a different browser and you'll see that a new session is started, and that page refreshes for each browser are maintained separately. The output in the console of opening a second browser instance shows this:

```
New Session ID=2aece0c189a202a05699f7e44893
New Session ID=2af2bfb1860fdd0f7debc1286ea9
```

But the JSP will show the incremented and independent counter values with each page refresh, as they are associated with the two different sessions. Once the service proxy is created with the session state maintenance property, save the port in the servlet application context. Otherwise, you'll get a new port every time, and the instance won't appear to increment.

7.19 Adding a Header with a Method Parameter

Problem

You want to indicate that your service operation accepts a SOAP header.

Solution

Use the @WebParam annotation properties header=true and mode=WebParam.Mode.IN. Here is an example:

```
@WebMethod
public @WebResult(name="title") String
  secureGetTitle(
  @WebParam(name="id") String id,
  @WebParam(name="usernameToken",
  header=true, mode=WebParam.Mode.IN)
  String usernameToken) {...}
```

Discussion

Using the header=true property of the @WebParam annotation as in the example just shown will cause a WSDL to be generated that accounts for the header in the abstract WSDL. The parameter will be pulled from the header of the message instead of from the body. The @WebParam.Mode.IN enum constant indicates that the parameter is only available on incoming requests, and not on the response. That's true for the example here, but it is possible to map header parameters to OUT modes.

Example 7-18 is a partial listing of what the resulting WSDL looks like when specifying a header value as just shown.

Example 7-18. Partial WSDL with headers specified

```
<message name="secureGetTitle">
<part name="parameters" element="tns:secureGetTitle"></part>
<part name="usernameToken" element="tns:usernameToken"></part>
</message>

<portType name="CatalogService">
  <operation name="secureGetTitle"
    parameterOrder="parameters usernameToken">
  <input message="tns:secureGetTitle"></input>
  <output message="tns:secureGetTitleResponse"></output>
  </operation>
</portType>

<binding name="CatalogPortBinding" type="tns:CatalogService">
  <soap:binding transport="http://schemas.xmlsoap.org/soap/http"
    style="document"></soap:binding>
  <operation name="secureGetTitle">
  <soap:operation soapAction=""></soap:operation>
  <input>
    <soap:body use="literal" parts="parameters"></soap:body>
    <soap:header message="tns:secureGetTitle" part="usernameToken"
      use="literal">
    </soap:header>
  </input>
  <output>
    <soap:body use="literal"></soap:body>
  </output>
  </operation>
</binding>
```

Because the part element, which is part of the abstract contract, specifies the header information, clients should be able to address the headers easily.

However, not all WSDLs will specify headers like this one does—it depends on whether it is written by hand, is working but non-compliant, uses a different tool, or what have you. The JAX-WS specification indicates that tools are not required to consider the binding section when generating SEIs—they need only inspect the `portType`, as it is part of the abstract WSDL.

There is a bit of a gray area with respect to proper header usage. Many public services, such as some posted by the United States Post Office, use what are sometimes called "implicit headers." These headers are not defined as part of the `wsdl:portType` as you have done here. At first glance, not including information necessary to the contract within the operation may seem like bad practice. The argument is that if the header information is really metadata regarding the request, it should not be part of the signature proper, as it isn't part of the business operation. The net effect for you is that, whichever route you choose, you need to consider how clients will interact with your code, and communicate to them what they are required to pass when invoking service operations.

7.20 Accessing Incoming Header Parameters in a Service

Problem

You want to access all parameters set in the header of an incoming request.

Solution

You can use `JAXWSProperties.INBOUND_HEADER_LIST_PROPERTY` in the message context if you are using the reference implementation. You can also do it with SAAJ.

Discussion

The following code works only with the reference implementation. It pulls WS-Addressing headers:

```
@WebService
public class MyService {
  private static final QName MY_HEADER =
    new QName("http://ns.soacookbook.com","headerName");

@Resource
WebServiceContext context;

@WebMethod
public void sayHello(String name) {
  //RI only
  HeaderList headers = context.getMessageContext().get(
    JAXWSProperties.INBOUND_HEADER_LIST_PROPERTY);
  Header header = headers.get(MY_HEADER);
  //do something with header
}
}
```

Here you're in a web service, which is a managed code situation. This means that you can just declare the `WebServiceContext` as a `Resource`, and let the container inject it for you. From this context, you can get the message context and use the specified property to get the name of the header you're interested in, using its `QName`.

Recipe 5.13 shows how to use the SAAJ API to read the values of SOAP headers. But if you're in a JAX-WS provider class, you want to use code for that API.

7.21 Providing a Value for SOAP Action or WS-Addressing Action

Problem

You want to specify a value for the `soapAction` in your WSDL. Or, you want to specify an action value if you're using WS-Addressing.

Solution

Use the @WebMethod annotation, and specify a value for the action attribute.

Discussion

There is an HTTP header called SOAPAction that accompanies SOAP requests. The value of this header is dictated by the soapAction attribute value on the soap:operation. Its value must be a URI that indicates the intended processing resource for the operation. In compliance with the Basic Profile 1.1, the JAX-WS runtime will specify a set of empty double quotes ("") as the value of the soap:operation element's soapAction attribute if not present.

The following code shows an example of indicating the value for SOAPAction in a Java service endpoint implementation:

```
@WebMethod(operationName="greet",
    action="http://soacookbook.com/Hello/sayHello")
public String greet(
    @WebParam(name="name") String name) {
    return "Hi " + name;
}
```

By including this attribute in the annotation of your service operation, you'll get two things. The first is a value in the generated WSDL for the soapAction attribute on the operation, as shown here:

```
<operation name="greet">
   <soap:operation soapAction="http://soacookbook.com/Hello/sayHello"/>
```

You will also get an HTTP header accompanying every request you make with this operation that contains the specified value.

The WSDL 1.1 specification (section 3.4) expressly forbids the use of the SOAPAction attribute when using a transport layer other than HTTP. Also, it's worth noting that SOAPAction has been made optional in WSDL 1.2 and 2.0.

The purpose of SOAPAction is to allow firewalls and other processing nodes on a message's path to filter or help route messages. However, the WS-Addressing standard subsumes the functionality offered by this header. WS-Addressing deals with routing information in a far more robust fashion that SOAPAction does, and it does so native to the SOAP message itself (rather than out of band by relying on the underlying transport layer).

It is a good idea to specify a value for the `soapAction` if you are planning on having any .NET WCF (Windows Communication Foundation) with your service using WS-Addressing. The WCF client will generate the proper values based on your WSDL if it has a value other than the default empty string.

Using BindingProvider

There are other ways of specifying the SOAP action as well. You can use the `javax.xml.ws.BindingProvider` too, as follows:

```
//indicate to use soap action
((javax.xml.ws.BindingProvider)port).getRequestContext().put(
  javax.xml.ws.BindingProvider.SOAPACTION_USE_PROPERTY, Boolean.TRUE);

//Specify the soap action uri
((javax.xml.ws.BindingProvider)port).getRequestContext().put(
  javax.xml.ws.BindingProvider.SOAPACTION_URI_PROPERTY,
"http://soacookbook/myService/myOp");
```

7.22 Optimizing Transmission of Binary Content on the Server

Problem

You have a web service that must send and receive binary data, such as an image or a PDF, and you want to optimize performance.

Solution

Use the `javax.xml.ws.soap.MTOM` annotation on your web service endpoint implementation.

Discussion

When you define a web service that includes operations for sending and receiving binary data, the encoding to `xs:base64Binary` can get very verbose, as all binary content must be encoded and set with the message as text. A character encoding of `base64Binary` will increase the size of the message by 1.33 times the original size when UTF-8 is used. It's necessary to compress this content, much as you might use HTTP compression in a web server. Luckily, it's very easy to do.

By default, JAX-WS disables MTOM-encoding. To enable it on your web service, just use the `MTOM` annotation:

```
@WebService
@MTOM
public class MyService { ... }
```

MTOM is intended to replace MIME attachments (Microsoft's DIME attachments are all but obsolete) as a method for binary optimization, relying on XOP (XML Binary Optimized Packaging). Though the optimized form compacts the character sequence of the binary content in the message, the content can still be reconstructed at the receiver.

Visit *http://www.w3.org/TR/soap12-mtom/* to read the MTOM specification.

MTOM is widely supported, portable, and interoperable. In addition to Glassfish and WebLogic10gR3, MTOM is implemented in Axis 2. You can read about how to use MTOM in Axis 2 at *http://ws.apache.org/axis2/1_0/mtom-guide.html*.

The WS-I Basic Profile 1.2 incorporates the SOAP 1.1 binding for MTOM, ensuring even greater support and interoperability going forward.

See Also

Recipe 6.16 to see how to call an MTOM-enabled service from a client.

7.23 Getting and Sharing Data About Users and the Request

Problem

You want to get data regarding your service invocations, such as the user invoking the service, information about HTTP statuses, and web service-specific information such as attachments and the WSDL. You want something similar to `ServletContext`, but for a web service. Or, you want a way to share processing-related state between handlers within a handler chain.

Solution

Refer to the `javax.xml.ws.WebServiceContext` inside your web service implementation. Use it to get the `MessageContext`, the user principal, or to find out if the user is in a given role.

Discussion

The `WebServiceContext` interface is implemented behind the scenes by the SOAP container. It has three methods:

- MessageContext getMessageContext
- Principal getUserPrincipal
- boolean isUserInRole(String role)

An endpoint implementation class will get a WebServiceContext instance injected when a field of that type is declared as a Resource, as shown here:

```
@WebService
public class Hello {
    @Resource
    private WebServiceContext wsContext;

    public void doWork(){
        MessageContext mContext = wsContext.getMessageContext();
    ...}
}
```

As with any injected resource in Java EE 5, the context will be populated by the container at runtime. Once you have a message context object from the web service context, you can share data between handlers within a handler chain using the standard Map methods to put and get data (MessageContext extends Map).

If you want to get data about some specific aspect of the request, you can do so using one of the many field constants that are provided with the WebServiceContext class as the parameter to a get call.

7.24 Using Header References with Holder<T>

Problem

You want to define an operation that requires SOAP headers and invoke it from a client.

Solution

In the service, use the @WebParam annotation with your operation parameter. Specify header=true, and wrap your parameter in a Holder<T>, where T is the actual type of the parameter you want. On the client, use a Holder<T> to set the values of the parameter elements and get the return values with a reference.

Discussion

The following examples illustrate how to use a Holder to handle the SOAP headers required for using a web service. This is a command-line client for the web service, and it is totally portable; it doesn't rely on proprietary extensions within Glassfish or another container. The web service and WSDL are shown as well to help aid your understanding the process.

First, you'll create a web service using the "Start from Java" approach. This is easy to do, and lets you generate a WSDL with `wsgen` that indicates the required header values. Most containers will automatically generate a WSDL for you on deployment, so all you should need to do is create the Java class as part of a WAR project within your favorite IDE, and package the class in *WEB-INF/classes* as you would any other regular Java class. The web service is shown in Example 7-19.

Example 7-19. Email verifier web service requiring credentials in SOAP headers

```
package com.soacookbook;

import javax.jws.WebParam;
import javax.jws.WebService;
import javax.xml.ws.Holder;

/*
 * Very simple web service that shows how to define a service
 * that accepts SOAP headers. This is frequently useful for user
 * credentials, an authorization token, or some other
 * identifier.
 *
 * Making param mode INOUT means your type must be a Holder.
 */
@WebService
public class EmailCheck  {

    private static String NO_CREDENITALS_MSG =
            "You must be registered and supply a " +
            "valid username and password to use this service.";

    /**
     * The single op we'll expose on the service. Checks the
     * value of the email address passed in.
     * @param email The address clients want to verify.
     * @param username The username of a hypoethetically
     * pre-registered user so that only authorized users
     * can access the service.
     * @param password the passsword for this 'registered' user.
     * @return a string indicating if the email address is
     * valid or not.
     */
    public String verify(
        @WebParam(mode=WebParam.Mode.IN,
            name="email")String email,
        @WebParam(mode=WebParam.Mode.INOUT, header=true,
            name="username") Holder<String> username,
        @WebParam(mode=WebParam.Mode.INOUT, header=true,
            name="password") Holder<String> password){

        if (!isValidUser(username, password))
            return NO_CREDENITALS_MSG;

        //Silly check. Robust business logic here...
        if (email != null && email.endsWith(".com")) {
```

```
            return "VALID";
        } else {
            return "INVALID";
        }
    }

    /*Checks that the supplied username/password combination
     is valid. Replace this with a run to a database or LDAP.
     */
    private boolean isValidUser(Holder<String> username,
            Holder<String> password) {

        boolean suppliedUsername = username != null &&
                !username.value.isEmpty();

        boolean suppliedPassword = password != null &&
                !password.value.isEmpty();

        if (suppliedUsername && suppliedPassword) {
            //log
            System.out.println("Username: " + username.value);
            System.out.println("Password: " + password.value);

            //check registered user credentials in LDAP
            //or database or something
            boolean validUser = username.value.equals("eben") &&
                    password.value.equals("secret");
            if (validUser) {
                return true;
            }
        }
        return false;
    }
}
```

The highlighted code indicates the part of the service devoted to handling the SOAP headers and their values.

In order to use this web service, you first need to use the `wsimport` tool to import the WSDL and generate client classes that match it, as you've done before. See Example 7-20.

Example 7-20. Email verifier web service client that passes SOAP headers

```
package headerclient;

import com.soacookbook.headerClient.EmailCheckService;
import com.soacookbook.headerClient.EmailCheck;
import com.soacookbook.headerClient.Verify;
import com.soacookbook.headerClient.VerifyResponse;

import javax.xml.ws.Holder;

/**
 * Invokes a web service that checks the validity of an
```

```
 * email address. The web service requires a registered
 * user's credentials as SOAP headers, so we use a
 * {@code javax.xml.ws.Holder<T>}  to pass the username
 * and password.
 */
public class EmailHeaderClient {

    /**
     * Command-line client invokes the web service,
     * passing header data along with the operation parameter.
     */
    public static void main(String... args) {

        String emailToCheck = "me@example.com";
        try {

            EmailCheckService service = new EmailCheckService();
            EmailCheck port = service.getEmailCheckPort();

            //This is the email address we want to check
            Verify params = new Verify();
            params.setEmail(emailToCheck);

            //Used for header data, because username is a String
            Holder<String> username = new Holder<String>();

            //Holder's value is of type T
            username.value = "eben";

            //Same deal for password header
            Holder<String> password = new Holder<String>();
            password.value = "secret1";

            //Note that we pass the SOAP header into the op
            VerifyResponse result =
                    port.verify(params, username, password);

            System.out.println("Email check result:  " +
                    result.getReturn());

        } catch (Exception ex) {
            ex.printStackTrace();
        }
    }
}
```

Here is the result if you pass an invalid username and password combination:

```
C:\oreilly\soacookbook\code\chapters\HeaderClient>java -jar dist/HeaderClient.jar
Email check result:  You must be registered and supply a valid username and password
to use this service.
```

If you use a valid username and password combination, you should be treated to a happier message:

```
C:\oreilly\soacookbook\code\chapters\HeaderClient>java -jar dist/HeaderClient.jar
Email check result:  VALID
```

Summary

In this chapter, we examined a number of different ways to deal with the sorts of challenges you're confronted with specifically when providing web services, as opposed to when you're consuming them. We looked at using holders and headers, MTOM for receiving binary data, and using constructs like `SOAPAction`, and discussed the fundamentals of providing a service.

CHAPTER 8

RESTful Web Services

8.0 Introduction

SOAP is a specification. WSDL is a specification. XML Schema is a specification. Although developers and architects may hotly debate exactly how implementations of SOAP-based web services should be written or how they should be used, there is no question about *what* these things are. They are concrete, and exist. Like a cup.

SOA, and even ESB, on the other hand, are more conceptual in nature. Their principles are clear, but they really represent architectural styles and strategies. They are therefore more open to interpretation than the likes of SOAP and WSDL; their very definitions are open to considerable debate. So while people can generally agree on the key principles of SOA (loose coupling, etc.) and on key features of an ESB (routing, mediation, transformation, etc.), the devil is always in the details.

SOA, ESB, and REST have no specifications. As a result, vendors may take whatever 15-year-old EAI software they have lying around and re-brand it as their "SOA Stack" now that SOA has become the chief topic of conversation at every dinner table in the country. (Or at least in every software-company lunchroom.) And as with SOA and ESB, there are many contributing factors to the sense that REST is in the middle of a lot of contention out there. Java developers who may be used to having clearly defined APIs have to make a slight shift when it comes to thinking about SOA, ESB, and REST. Sun can't simply tell us exactly what they are—we have to really understand the concepts. Anyone with an IDE who knows that JSPs exist can write and deploy a JSP in under a minute without necessarily having to understand what's happening under the hood. But anyone with an IDE *can't* sit down to write and deploy a RESTful application in under a minute: it's a matter of knowing the principles.

REST is the brainchild of Roy T. Fielding, cofounder of the Apache HTTP server project and coauthor of the HTTP and URI standards. In 2000, he wrote a doctoral dissertation for the University of California at Irvine called *Architectural Styles and the Design of Network-based Software Architectures*, wherein he defined REST.

You can read Dr. Fielding's dissertation at *http://www.ics.uci.edu/~fielding/pubs/dissertation/top.htm*. REST developers frequently cite this work directly (even as they misinterpret it), as does JSR 311. It's a terrific read.

Fielding's assertion is that since 1994, "the REST architectural style has been used to guide the design and development of the architecture of the modern Web" (page 107). This is important to understand: REST is not, as the popular imagination might have it, a different way of doing web services that appeals more to the kind of people who prefer PHP and Rails to .NET and Java. REST doesn't build on the principles of the Web—the Web was built based on RESTful principles. They just weren't so named until a few years later. The idea of REST is essentially a reverse-engineering of how the Web works. HTTP itself, and URIs themselves, are written with REST principles.

REST is very important in the modern services landscape, its popularity is growing, and it is often radically misunderstood. It seems that the popular imagination has taken hold of the idea of REST as POX over HTTP, or any web services that are not SOAP with WS-*. Such designs are popular and abundant, and may have many laudable qualities, but they are *not* an embodiment of REST just because they aren't SOAP.

This chapter is not here to tell you how theoretically pure your REST implementations must be. But it is important to outline what REST really is, so that you can implement your services with clarity. There are some interesting convenience frameworks available, such as JSR 311, and we'll work with that framework a lot in this chapter. I've tried to keep examples short and to the point, but they still can get rather long given all of the moving parts. Remember that you have to balance the little local code solution with the general overarching principles that make a sound RESTful architecture.

Industry analysts have recently coined the term WOA, or Web Oriented Architecture. This is typically used to refer to something like a SOA-lite, or a service architecture that uses XML, JSON (JavaScript Object Notation), and HTTP. The term is generally intended to imply two things: an architecture that 1) does not use WS-* specifications and 2) is an application of RESTful principles that is much looser than Fielding's dissertation actually allows (you can use cookies, etc.).

So let's try to examine, beyond the considerable noise, what REST really is.

The Principles of REST

REST is an acronym for REpresentational State Transfer. Because it is an architectural style, there's room for variety in how certain constraints are understood. What follows are the basic points that distinguish REST, as Fielding stated in Chapter 5 of his dissertation.

REST services are stateless

REST services should not require state stored on the server. Fielding states it best himself: "each request from client to server must contain all of the information necessary to understand the request, and cannot take advantage of any stored context on the server" (pages 78–79). Having all of the state reside in the client improves stability and scalability. Cache-ability is important too, especially for GETs.

Server sessions should *not* be used, and everything that you need to process a request should be contained in that request. There are certain constraints that make cookies a popular way to store state on the client. Some sites that advertise a RESTful architecture use cookies to store recently viewed items, currency preference, and shopping cart identifiers, for example. That's OK, but it's not strictly RESTful.

The reason cookies violate REST is stated in Fielding's dissertation, section 6.3.4.2. To summarize his comments, cookies typically store information that encompasses a user's interaction with an entire site and not just the current request, which violates encapsulation. Furthermore, cookies pass data without defining the semantics that define that data, thereby raising concerns regarding both security and privacy.

REST services have a uniform interface

There is no WSDL in REST. This constraint on the architectural style of REST is generally understood as the interface provided by the standard HTTP methods (PUT, GET, POST, DELETE, etc.), but Fielding doesn't say that. He actually stresses protocol independence, despite the popular reliance on HTTP.

Resources are manipulated through representations

The components in the system exchange data (usually XML documents) that represents the resource. For example, if you wanted to update customer information, you would post the XML document representing that resource to its URI. A representation is simply a sequence of bytes and metadata in the form of name/value pairs that describe the resource.

Resources have multiple representations. The resource is not the HTML page that might be returned to a browser when you request it—that is simply one out of many possible representations of the resource. You could return a variety of formats representing a given resource, as stated in section 5.2.1 of Fielding's dissertation:

- XML
- JSON
- XHTML
- JPEG image

Messages are self-describing

No out-of-band negotiation can be required to determine how to communicate with the service.

RESTful architectures are built with resources

RESTful architectures are built through *resources*, each of which has its own unique URI. A resource is an item that "might be the target of an author's hypertext reference" (section 5.2.1.1). The URI serves as the ID of the resource. Any information item that can be named can be a resource. This could be a stock price at a given point in time, a purchase order, the current weather in Scottsdale, and so on. Here are some examples:

- `http://soacookbook.com/customers`
- `http://soacookbook.com/customers/1234`
- `http://soacookbook.com/orders/456/customer`

And here is a real-life example from Overstock.com, which was created with a RESTful architecture:

- `http://www.overstock.com/Home-Garden/Tiffany-style-Table-Lamp/2260849/product.html`

This URI drills down through the category representing home and garden to the Tiffany-style lamp subcategory to a particular product ID. From this page, you can get to help pages, customer care pages, and more. The "View a Particular Product" state allows for transitions to each of these other states.

RESTful identifiers may be long-lived and stable. Because of the use of URIs, everything that matters to users in REST can be bookmarked, cut and pasted, or cataloged with RDF (Resource Description Framework) in a metadata model. Every unit of information carries its address, and is wholly independent of the underlying framework or implementation producing the API. That is, there is no domain-specific object or resources in view; clients simply act on the representations they receive.

Hypermedia as the engine of application state

Hypertext is generally considered to be text that is interactive and nonlinear, that branches and gives the reader a set of choices. Fielding's definition of hypertext does not simply mean HTML in a browser, though that is perhaps the most popular form. Fielding's site defines hypertext as "the simultaneous presentation of information and controls such that the information becomes the affordance through which the user (or automaton) obtains choices and selects actions."

The idea of "hypermedia as the engine of application state" is mentioned, but not elaborated upon, in section 5.1.5 of Fielding's dissertation. As a result, it is probably the least understood aspect of REST, though it is also one of its most important tenets. Despite Fielding's brevity, it is clear what this means: every document returned by the server will include all the URIs to any next step. That is, all possible application states that the user can transition to from the current state are represented as resource URIs (hypermedia links). Application state is driven (transitioned to a next state) by selecting and following a URI.

On his website, Fielding recently restated the case that hypertext is a constraint: "if the engine of application state (and hence the API) is not being driven by hypertext, then it cannot be RESTful and cannot be a REST API. Period. Is there some broken manual somewhere that needs to be fixed?" (*http://roy.gbiv.com/untangled/2008/rest-apis-must-be-hypertext-driven*)

In many web applications, developers use cookies to retain state on the client. But cookies, which are a function of HTTP, are considered unreliable and insecure, and they side-step the semantic constraints of REST. Therefore, using cookies to keep state on the client (login status, preferences, etc.) is explicitly disallowed by the Fielding dissertation (section 6.3.4.2).

This constraint is frequently ignored, however, in "RESTful" framework implementations in the real world, not the least of which is JSR 311, which includes the `@CookieParam` annotation to allow a provider to extract information from cookies, as well as access to the `Cookie` class. So there are competing degrees of "purity" among REST practitioners.

REST really takes issue with cookies because they carry state and are intended to be sent to the server in future requests. Because some state is set in the cookie, the application avoids representing all possible next-state transition possibilities directly in the hypertext.

It's fine to use cookies if you need to. We've been using them for many years. There are loads of popular websites that use cookies. Just don't call that application RESTful.

So in REST, how do you keep state for something like a shopping cart? Fielding's suggestion, instead of using cookies to identify a set of cart products within a server-side database, is to define the semantics of the products within hypermedia data formats, so that the user can store selected items client-side and use a URI to check out. To restate the point, the URI serves as the ID of the resource. Any information item that can be named can be a resource. "Bob's shopping cart on Tuesday at 9 a.m." is a valid resource. Hypermedia as the engine of application state (sometimes abbreviated HATEOS) is one of the key tenets of REST, and we will revisit this idea throughout the chapter.

Other Tenets of REST

There are a number of related tenets that Fielding has identified on his website in recent years to help clarify some of the complexity or abstraction of his doctoral dissertation. These include the following:

- A REST API should not be dependent on any single communication protocol.

- A REST API "should spend almost all of its descriptive effort in defining the media types used for representing resources and driving application state." Do this to ensure that hypertext is actually the driver that transitions application state, and not out-of-band information.
- A REST API must not define fixed resource names that are written in stone, as doing so will lead to coupling of the client and server. Instead, you want to define the instructions for constructing valid URIs through the media types and link relations. If you don't find a way to do this, you'll ultimately end up with an API that looks and acts very much like RPC, except that you're maybe using HTTP methods and doing lots of out-of-band homegrown IDL work.
- A REST API should have an initial entry point URI that is stable (bookmarkable). From that point, all state transitions must take place with the client choosing from among a set of server-provided choices. Those choices must be present in the representations received by the client. The set of transition possibilities can be narrowed down by something like an `Accept` header, for example.

Advantages of REST

This architecture provides several benefits on the server side. These include the additional ability to scale horizontally and an easy and clear mechanism for caching, as well as a simple failover strategy. These benefits are directly inherited from building on the architecture of the Web in its static form.

There are advantages to working with REST on the client side as well. These include the ability to cache and bookmark representations, and the flexibility to choose data formats that are most appropriate for your use case.

REST Versus SOAP

As you may be aware, there is considerable debate among developers and architects on the topic of REST versus SOAP. The following points seem most pertinent to me regarding the importance of REST:

- The Web is the most successful software application on the planet (with the possible exception of email). It is therefore general enough, with sufficient clarity and definition, to create robust and scalable applications according to a particular style (a style whose interface generally includes the methods provided by HTTP).
- Developers love complexity. They approach complex problems with complex solutions, though it is a fallacy to think one is required to do so. In other words, posit a thing that is the simplest possible thing that works; this is the best thing. REST is simpler than SOAP and represents a small, incremental set of constraints over the Web, which are widely understood. SOAP, on the other hand, is new and different, making it harder to adopt.
- SOAP-based web services are hard, which often translates to "needlessly complex."

In general, people who write books about SOAP take an attitude of refusing to weigh in on the matter. They point to the debate, but then don't make a statement regarding their personal view.

On the other hand, proponents of REST tend to be very vocal regarding their preference. The popular O'Reilly book *RESTful Web Services* by Leonard Richardson and Sam Ruby (*http://oreilly.com/catalog/9780596529260*) describes SOAP-based systems as "Big Web Services." Ruby on Rails founder David Heinemeier Hansson has termed the WS-* specifications "WS-Death Star," and recently pulled the SOAP libraries from within Rails and replaced them with REST libraries.

For their part, SOAP developers refer to the other side as "RESTafarians," in an apparent effort to reduce their simple web interface predilections to the status of hippy-dippy tomfoolery.

It's an exciting time to be in the software business!

RESTful web services are a perfectly acceptable way to build your SOA (though some REST proponents might not even like to hear the word SOA). However, SOAP-based services are more common at this point, probably because the big software stack vendors have a lot of skin in that game. SOAP and all of the attendant WS-* specs take a long time to understand and to implement, and many of the top software vendors were the brains behind these specifications. But then the specifications had to be implemented of course. And guess who is happy to provide you with implementations....

I speculate that REST will grow considerably in popularity in the coming years. That's because the simplest thing that works usually does well, even if it takes a while for us to see it given all the noise.

It's a reasonable argument, in my view, to suggest that SOAP-based web services, and in particular the WS-* stack, do little more than move the interoperability problem. Once you're using tools like BPEL to orchestrate web services within a SOA, you become dependent in some way on vendor implementations, or you can succumb to proprietary extensions if you aren't very careful. If that jeopardizes your interoperability efforts, you've defeated the whole purpose.

So when you go to implement your SOAP/WS-* SOA, you face a couple of choices, neither of which seems particularly appealing:

- Go with a stack vendor. Buy an ESB, SOAP engine, application server, BPEL, Registry/Repository, BAM (Business Activity Monitoring), and BPMN (Business Process Management Notation) tools all from one company. This may reassure you that your own complex service processes will work seamlessly together. But even within a single platform these tools don't always integrate perfectly. That's because the big stack vendors often OEM a popular product, or buy an entire company or product because that company has a piece of the stack they need, or they wrap an open source product and put a logo on it. Now instead of trying to make Java interoperate with .NET, you're trying to make all of these particular stripes across your SOA interoperate with your business partner, who may have the same problem. The bottom line is that in order to decrease coupling from one system (the one you're wrapping with a service), you may have increased coupling with another one (the vendor implementation).

- Seeing the difficulties presented by the first choice, you may decide to go with best of breed vendors. That is, instead of going with a single vendor, you get the best ESB, the best orchestration and process engine, and so on, regardless of vendor. This is difficult to manage, can be far more expensive, and can make it tough to get an answer when something goes south. You soon realize you still have many of the problems presented by the first choice. At least you still have throats to choke.

Of course, if you don't like these choices, you can always build your own. This raises an interesting question. If you were going to start from a green field, and wanted to have machines intercommunicate by exchanging platform-independent XML documents, how would you do it? Would you define your business entities (Customer, Product, and so on) and then represent them in a canonical way and exchange these documents over a well-understood, simple, clear, and popular protocol? Or would you create a new idea, like SOAP, to wrap some functionality on an existing system, and have that idea require an XML document of its own to represent it, and require some software to hook that interface to your application, and then define the entities, and then exchange them not directly on HTTP, but rather on another new idea for a protocol, which also requires new software to run?

There's an answer there if you want to make your systems work together as simply and inexpensively as possible, and there's another answer if you are in the business of selling software.

That said, I'm aware that this book devotes hundreds of pages to the WS-* stuff and only a single chapter to REST. The world is full of SOAP and WS-*, and for many of us it's important to know how to work with them. It does speak, however, to the comparative complexity. And before we dump too much on Big Web Services (as Leonard Richardson and Sam Ruby term them), the WS-* stack does work together to create more functionality than you get with the basic ideas found in REST. That is, Big Web Services are bigger than REST because they're talking about a lot more than REST is. That's not a value judgment; it's just pointing out a fact. REST isn't trying to solve a lot of problems that the specs are tackling. For example, WS-AtomicTransaction and WS-MetaDataExchange offer standard ways for disparate components to participate in distributed transactions or for independent clients to negotiate policies at runtime. And security in the form of SAML (which specifies SOAP as its binding) makes complex federated security policies across business partnerships realizable and straightforward to implement with minimum manual and error-prone negotiation.

Moreover, many REST proponents argue that Remote Procedure Calls (RPC) are what opponents object to most in SOAP-based services. But you can achieve a level of document exchange with SOAP. Using the document/literal bare style, which specifies no operation but only presents an XML document as the child of the SOAP body, offers some of the features of a RESTful architectural style. The operation invoked on the WSDL is matched by the schema type presented. Notice, too, that the early Flickr REST API was in some ways RPC masquerading as REST. Just because you don't have SOAP doesn't mean you're doing REST.

To settle this question, you must ask yourself what problem you're trying to solve with your SOA. Assess your current architecture and the WS-* specs to determine the right target architecture for your organization. Do not forget that while many resources, including many recipes in this book, show a code-first approach to building web services, you are free (and in this book very much encouraged) to build your services contract-first, and present the ideal interface to the world. Just because tools such as binding customization let you bleed implementation-specific business out into what's supposed to be a platform-independent interface doesn't mean you should use them all over the place.

The WS-* specs are really about enterprise integration. REST is an architectural style. Ultimately, I reject the REST versus SOAP battle as a false dichotomy. These two technologies can be complementary to one another and can work in tandem. After all, the very point of SOA is to not force you into a single stack, but to support heterogeneous environments. A good SOA and integration practitioner or software architect has both REST and SOAP available to him, and can apply them as necessary.

Many enterprise information systems, including PeopleSoft, SAP, and JDA, expose their systems with WSDL. At the point where you need to integrate with two decades of existing programs comprising two million lines of custom code, it becomes irrelevant very quickly if we think REST is neater. If the legacy interface is already exposed as a WSDL, that helps decide the matter for you.

Finally, remember that you can write bad code in any language. You can create big, sloppy, monster designs that paint you into a really expensive corner using any tool. Some might say, "a fool with a tool is still a fool." Use the right tool for the job. The best hammer in the world doesn't help you if your problem isn't a nail.

Strides have been made to take the best ideas from both SOAP and REST and incorporate them into the other. For example, WS-Addressing can be said to provide a unique URI for SOAP operations in a manner similar to how REST URIs provide unique IDs to resources. If you have both REST and SOAP in your toolbox, you can do what's best for your customer.

So let's get out of the middle of this touchy subject already and start looking at how to put together REST applications in Java.

Restlet

In 2005, Jérôme Louvel founded the Restlet project, hosted at *http://www.restlet.org*. Louvel needed to build a website and wanted to do so using the REST architectural style as much as possible. But he noticed a lack of Java support for REST using the Servlet API, which led him to develop his own.

The Restlet project is divided into two parts: the API, which provides utilities and a way to register API implementations, and a reference implementation of that API. The reference implementation is called Noelios, which includes connectors for clients of different protocols, including HTTP, SMTP, and JDBC. The project allows you to work with multiple protocols within a single API and forego the context switching required by JavaMail, Servlet, JDBC, and so on as you work.

The primary aim of Restlet is to provide Java developers with a way to "think RESTfully": its core classes are named directly for the key concepts within REST, including resource, representation, connector, and so on. The API is intended to bridge the impedance mismatch between an object-oriented and a RESTful mode of development. However, if you want to use the Restlet API within the context of a servlet container, there is a lightweight adapter that allows you to do that.

JAX-RS

JSR 311 represents the Java API for RESTful Web Services. Like JAX-WS, JAX-RS uses annotations on POJOs (Plain Old Java Objects) to map to the RESTful style of presenting web applications. For example, methods on classes that represent a resource use the `@Path` annotation to indicate their URI, and a set of annotations are provided that map to each of the HTTP methods (`@GET`, `@PUT`, etc.).

Jersey

The Jersey project is Sun's reference implementation of JAX-RS 1.0. The project aims primarily to make it easy for REST developers to build web services using Java. Jersey is also scheduled to ship within Glassfish and will be formally incorporated as a standard part of the Java EE platform in Java EE 6.

Jersey also provides support for Spring and Google Guice.

While Jersey provides a client API, this is *not* part of the JAX-RS specification.

RESTEasy

This is a JBoss project that implements JAX-RS. RESTEasy is portable (it runs in any servlet container) and provides a client API that allows you to map outbound HTTP requests to remote servers with JAX-RS annotations.

The project also provides a RESTful facade to JMS, which is very interesting.

You can get RESTEasy from *http://wiki.jboss.org/wiki/RESTeasyJAXRS*.

RESTpack

The open source Mule ESB (*http://www.mulesource.org*) also distributes Jersey within its RESTpack download. It provides connectors for Jersey, Restlet, and Apache Abdera (which is an implementation of the Atom Publishing Protocol) to help you get REST applications going.

REST in Java

In the last section, we noted a few examples of REST framework implementations. These frameworks are useful in jump-starting your applications, and we'll look at JAX-RS rather closely in this chapter. Because REST is an architectural style, you don't need a framework to use it, and just because you're using a framework doesn't mean you're adhering to the principles.

Non-Java REST Resources

Because SOA is about interoperability, you likely have more than one language at work in your organization. Here are a few resources to check out if you want to work with REST in platforms other than Java.

If you are interested in writing RESTful applications for the .NET 3.5 WCF (Windows Communication Foundation) platform, check out the O'Reilly book *RESTful .NET* by Jon Flanders (*http://oreilly.com/catalog/9780596519209*).

For information on implementing RESTful services in Ruby, check out O'Reilly's *RESTful Web Services* by Leonard Richardson and Sam Ruby, and of course the Ruby on Rails framework at *http://www.rubyonrails.org*. `ActiveResource` is the main class used for mapping resources within Rails.

For the Python lovers out there, check out Django at *http://www.djangoproject.com*.

Coming Up

Now that you have an overview of what REST is and how it fits into SOA, and have seen a few of the open source tools that help you build RESTful applications, you're ready to start getting down to business. In this chapter, we'll examine how to create RESTful web services, with an emphasis on their use within SOA. RESTful applications are commonly written in PHP, Ruby on Rails, and other popular platforms, but we'll focus on Java implementations. Because it's slated for inclusion in Java EE 6, we'll mostly focus on JAX-RS.

8.1 Creating a POX over HTTP Service with Servlets

Problem

You want to get started writing RESTful web services without getting bogged down by an external framework. All you want is a class available at a URI that returns some XML.

Solution

Create a class that extends `javax.servlet.http.HttpServlet`; make sure that you set the response content type to `text/xml`. Use a transformer to write the XML out to your response.

Discussion

This is the simplest way to create an XML service without using any frameworks. For large-scale solutions, you probably want to at least consider using one of the available frameworks mentioned previously, but this approach represents the simplest thing that works.

In this example, you will define a servlet that returns XML to the requester. There is no schema associated with the XML, and no interface definition such as a WSDL. In a real-world service, this servlet would act as a frontend to some sort of enterprise information system. Here I just mock that out with a `ProductCatalog` class that contains a list of `Product` instances. The service itself consists of a servlet that invokes this "backend system" and transforms the result to XML for the output stream of the response.

First let's look at the `Product` class because it uses no other class (Example 8-1).

Example 8-1. Product.java

```
package com.soacookbook;

import javax.xml.bind.annotation.XmlType;

@XmlType
public class Product {

    private String id;
    private String name;
    private double price;

    public Product() { }

//Getters and Setters omitted...
```

The `Product` class represents a basic item in the catalog that users want to view. The `ProductCatalog` class consists of a few items of this type. There are only two things required here. You need this class to conform to the JavaBean conventions so that JAXB can marshal instances of it into XML for the servlet response. Then you need to add the @XmlType annotation above the type declaration as a hint to JAXB. In the real world, you would likely have some other mechanism for getting your products represented as XML; that's not the point of this example. What you care about here is the servlet and how it returns the response, so let's take only a precursory look at the ProductCatalog class (Example 8-2).

Example 8-2. ProductCatalog.java

```
package com.soacookbook;

import java.util.ArrayList;
import java.util.List;
import javax.xml.bind.annotation.XmlRootElement;

@XmlRootElement
public class ProductCatalog {

  private List<Product> products;

  public ProductCatalog() {
    products = new ArrayList<Product>();
    Product p = new Product();
    p.setId("123");
    p.setName("Shirt");
    p.setPrice(159.95D);

    Product p2 = new Product();
    p2.setId("456");
    p2.setName("Monkey");
    p2.setPrice(2500D);

    products.add(p);
    products.add(p2);
  }

  public List<Product> getProducts() {
    return products;
  }

  public void setProducts(List<Product> products) {
        this.products = products;
  }

  @Override
  public String toString() {
      return products.toString();
  }
}
```

This class represents the complete catalog of products in your store. You want to return the whole catalog as a response to a GET request from your RESTful servlet. So you identify to JAXB that this class is the root XML element that can be marshaled to XML from Java. The constructor sets up a couple of Product instances. Again, in the real world, this class might be set up rather differently, depending on your Enterprise Information Systems (EIS). You just need something for the servlet to return.

So now we get to the interesting part of this example. The servlet will return the product catalog as XML to the output stream provided by the `HttpServletResponse` object (Example 8-3).

Example 8-3. SimpleRestfulServlet.java

```
package com.soacookbook;

import java.io.IOException;

import javax.servlet.ServletException;
import javax.servlet.ServletOutputStream;
import javax.servlet.http.HttpServletRequest;
import javax.servlet.http.HttpServletResponse;
import javax.xml.bind.JAXBContext;
import javax.xml.bind.JAXBException;
import javax.xml.bind.Marshaller;
import javax.xml.parsers.DocumentBuilder;
import javax.xml.parsers.DocumentBuilderFactory;
import javax.xml.parsers.ParserConfigurationException;
import javax.xml.transform.Source;
import javax.xml.transform.Transformer;
import javax.xml.transform.TransformerFactory;
import javax.xml.transform.dom.DOMSource;
import javax.xml.transform.stream.StreamResult;

import org.w3c.dom.Document;

/**
 * Implements a simple RESTful service.
 */
 public class SimpleRestServlet extends javax.servlet.http.HttpServlet
     implements javax.servlet.Servlet {

    public SimpleRestServlet() {
        super();
    }

    protected void doGet(HttpServletRequest request, HttpServletResponse response)
        throws ServletException, IOException {

        System.out.println("DoGet invoked on RESTful service.");
        ProductCatalog catalog = new ProductCatalog();

        Source xmlSource = asXml(catalog);

        ServletOutputStream out = response.getOutputStream();
        response.setContentType("text/xml");

        StreamResult st = new StreamResult(out);

        try {
```

```
        Transformer t =
             TransformerFactory.newInstance().newTransformer();
        t.transform(xmlSource, st);
    } catch (Exception e) {
        throw new ServletException(e);
    }

    System.out.println("All done.");
  }

  private static Source asXml(ProductCatalog pc) throws ServletException {
        System.out.println("Marshalling...");

        Source source = null;
        Document doc = null;

        try {
            JAXBContext ctx = JAXBContext.newInstance(ProductCatalog.class);
            Marshaller m = ctx.createMarshaller();

            DocumentBuilder parser =
            DocumentBuilderFactory.newInstance().newDocumentBuilder();
            doc = parser.newDocument();

            System.out.println("Products=" + pc);
            m.marshal(pc, doc);

            System.out.println("Marshalled catalog to XML.");

        } catch (JAXBException je) {
            throw new ServletException(je);
        } catch (ParserConfigurationException pce) {
            throw new ServletException(pce);
        }

        source = new DOMSource(doc);

        System.out.println("Returning XML source.");
        return source;
        }

   protected void doPost(HttpServletRequest request, HttpServletResponse response)
        throws ServletException, IOException {

        doGet(request, response);
   }
}
```

The `asXml` method here hides the JAXB business of marshaling the catalog populated with products into XML. Here's how you do it. First, create a `JAXBContext` on the `ProductCatalog` class because that's your root element. Then create a new DOM document node and pass in both the populated catalog object and the empty DOM node to the marshaler. JAXB will then create the product catalog instance as XML for you, and put its result into the DOM document. You can create the DOM document as a

DOMSource using that constructor. The DOMSource acts as a holder for a transformation source in the form of a tree. Because it implements the Source interface, you can use it to pass to the transformer. There is no XML transformation actually happening at this point because it's already done; you're just using the transformer to write to the output stream.

So once you have your product catalog as XML, the only work left to do is to put it together as a response within the body of the doGet method. You get the output stream from the HttpServletResponse object so that you can write your response out to it. Then set the response MIME type as text/xml. Next wrap the response object in a StreamResult and then use a Transformer instance to send your source object to the response stream.

Then you need to set up your servlet in *web.xml* as usual. Here you map the servlet to the /Products path:

```
<web-app version="2.5" xmlns="http://java.sun.com/xml/ns/javaee"
  xmlns:xsi="http://www.w3.org/2001/XMLSchema-instance"
  xsi:schemaLocation="http://java.sun.com/xml/ns/javaee
    http://java.sun.com/xml/ns/javaee/web-app_2_5.xsd">

    <servlet>
        <servlet-name>SimpleRestServlet</servlet-name>
        <servlet-class>com.soacookbook.SimpleRestServlet</servlet-class>
    </servlet>
    <servlet-mapping>
        <servlet-name>SimpleRestServlet</servlet-name>
        <url-pattern>/Products</url-pattern>
    </servlet-mapping>
/...
```

You can invoke the servlet using a simple JSP that includes a link like this:

```
<a href="Products">Get Products</a>
```

When you run the application, you're presented with the *index.jsp* page at *http://local host:8080/SimpleRestServlet/*. Click the link, and the servlet returns the following response:

```
<?xml version="1.0" encoding="UTF-8" standalone="no"?>
<productCatalog>
  <products>
    <id>123</id>
    <name>Shirt</name>
    <price>159.95</price>
  </products>
  <products>
    <id>456</id>
    <name>Monkey</name>
    <price>2500.0</price>
  </products>
</productCatalog>
```

This simple example is a good introduction to REST because it builds on powers that you already have. But if you've worked on Java web applications of any size, you probably used some kind of framework, such as Struts. Making services using a simple servlet as shown here can become inefficient, which is why a framework can be handy. The reason it becomes inefficient specifically for REST is that you need to map multiple URIs to the same servlet as base paths, and then dispatch specific requests from that servlet to individual services in order to manage your representations. This makes your *web.xml* complicated, and also means that you are doing a lot of that work out of the purview of the application itself, through the descriptor. We'll look at alternatives to this in other recipes.

See Also

Recipe 8.2 to build on this example using ideas from JAX-WS we've already learned about.

8.2 A RESTful Service with JAX-WS

Problem

You want to build a RESTful web service using a lightweight framework such as JAX-WS, giving your service a little more order than a plain servlet does.

Solution

Implement the `Provider<Source>` interface on your POJO with the annotation `@WebServiceProvider` and a binding type of `HTTPBinding`.

Discussion

As you may recall, the `@WebServiceProvider` annotation is defined in the JAX-WS specification. This annotation allows you to work at the XML message level. If you're doing straight JAX-WS, the alternatives to parameterizing on `Source` are either `DataSource` or `SOAPMessage`, but you can't use those here. Because the `Provider` gives you access to the XML in the message, you don't have to use JAXB anywhere in this example.

Recall that `Provider` defines only one method, which has the following signature:

```
public T invoke(T request)
```

Parameterize on `Source` here and use the required annotation. The final thing you need to do is specify the `BindingType` as HTTP. So this is the basic shell of a RESTful service done in this fashion:

```
import javax.xml.transform.Source;
import javax.xml.ws.Provider;
import javax.xml.ws.WebServiceProvider;
import javax.xml.ws.http.HTTPBinding;
```

```
@WebServiceProvider
@BindingType(HTTPBinding.HTTP_BINDING)
public class JaxWsRestfulService implements Provider<Source> {
    public Source invoke(Source request) {
        //do work...
    }
}
```

The binding type specification is crucial here, as it tells the container to talk straight XML over HTTP, and not to use SOAP messages (which is what you would get by default).

Next you need to specify in *web.xml* that you are going to use the class `com.sun.xml.ws.transport.http.servlet.WSServlet` available in the *webservices-rt.jar* to route the requests through. Map the URL path for your service through this servlet.

8.3 Creating a Client for a RESTful Service Using Sockets

Problem

You want to invoke a publicly available RESTful service to work with a real API.

Solution

Use the URL class to get a socket connection. Post the data in the URL and create the HTTP headers from scratch. Then use the input stream on the socket to read the XML response.

Discussion

The Digital Library for Earth System Education is a free library of articles available online for learners from grade school through graduate school. It exposes its catalog as a RESTful API. You can read about its services at *http://www.dlese.org/dds/services/ddsws1-1/service_specification.jsp*. I'm using it here because it's simple and requires no registration, so you can focus on the example.

Example 8-4 is a Java class that kicks it old school. It simply performs a basic search and gets an XML response, which you print to the console.

Example 8-4. DigitalLibraryRestSearch.java

```
package simplerestclient;

import java.io.BufferedReader;
import java.io.BufferedWriter;
import java.io.InputStream;
import java.io.InputStreamReader;
import java.io.OutputStreamWriter;
import java.net.InetAddress;
```

```
import java.net.Socket;
import java.net.URLEncoder;

/**
 * Invokes a RESTful service.
 */
public class DigitalLibraryRestSearch {
    public static void main(String... args) throws Exception {
        doDigLib();
    }

    public static void doDigLib() throws Exception {
        System.out.println("Invoking Digital Library.");

        //Create socket
        String hostname = "www.dlese.org";
        int port = 80;
        InetAddress addr = InetAddress.getByName(hostname);
        Socket socket = new Socket(addr, port);

        String path = "/dds/services/ddsws1-1?";

        //Create query string
        String query = "verb" + "=" + URLEncoder.encode("Search", "UTF-8");
        query += "&" + "q" + "=" + URLEncoder.encode("web services", "UTF-8");
        query += "&" + "s" + "=" + URLEncoder.encode("0", "UTF-8");
        query += "&" + "n" + "=" + URLEncoder.encode("10", "UTF-8");
        query += "&" + "client" + "=" + URLEncoder.encode("ddsws-explorer", "UTF-8");

        //write content to create HTTP request
        BufferedWriter bw = new BufferedWriter(
            new OutputStreamWriter(socket.getOutputStream(), "UTF8"));
        bw.write("POST " + path + " HTTP/1.0\r\n");
        bw.write("Content-Length: " + query.length() + "\r\n");
        bw.write("Content-Type: application/x-www-form-urlencoded\r\n");
        bw.write("\r\n");

        //Submit request
        bw.write(query);
        bw.flush();

        //Read response off socket input
        InputStream is = socket.getInputStream();
        BufferedReader br = new BufferedReader(new InputStreamReader(is));
        String line = "";
        while ((line = br.readLine()) != null) {
          System.out.println(line);
        }

        socket.close();
        System.out.println("\nAll done.");
    }
}
```

This service is available from the URL *http://www.dlese.org/dds/services/ddsws1-1?verb=Search&q=web+services&s=0&n=10&client=ddsws-explorer*. Here you create the Socket instance on the base URL of the server and then append the path to create the URL for the POST. Then create a BufferedWriter to write the data of the bare HTTP request to the server. The server generates its response, which you get off the socket's input stream and wrap in a BufferedReader instance, allowing you to read the response line by line. Then just print it to the console.

The response is lengthy, so I'll abbreviate it significantly here just to give you an idea of what it returns:

```
HTTP/1.1 200 OK
Set-Cookie: UCARcwebsession=7e985be83e45b9e8baeebb58; path=/;
expires=Sun, 14-Sep-2008 21:51:42 GMT
Date: Sun, 14 Sep 2008 20:21:46 GMT
Server: Apache-Coyote/1.1
Cache-Control: max-age=0
Expires: Sun, 14 Sep 2008 20:21:46 GMT
Set-Cookie: JSESSIONID=09E46564A820483FBF30D95190B5F48C; Path=/dds
Content-Type: text/xml;charset=UTF-8
X-Cache: MISS from www.dlese.org
Connection: close

<?xml version="1.0" encoding="UTF-8" ?>
<DDSWebService xmlns="http://www.dlese.org/Metadata/ddsws"
 xmlns:xsi="http://www.w3.org/2001/XMLSchema-instance"
 xsi:schemaLocation="http://www.dlese.org/Metadata/ddsws
  http://www.dlese.org/Metadata/ddsws/1-1/ddsws.xsd">
 <Search>
    <resultInfo>
       <totalNumResults>34</totalNumResults>
      <totalNumRecordsInLibrary>14494</totalNumRecordsInLibrary>
       <numReturned>10</numReturned>
       <offset>0</offset>
   </resultInfo>
   <results>
     <record>...</record>
   </results>
 </Search>
```

This is perhaps a somewhat rudimentary way to create a client. But it works, it's fast enough, and it requires no external libraries. There are alternative ways to do this sort of thing, most notably the Jakarta Commons HTTP Client class.

8.4 Application: Using SSL, Atom Publishing, and the Google Finance REST API

This is not a recipe but rather a complete application, as it addresses all at once a variety of issues found in the real world of dealing with RESTful web services.

Years ago, Google used to publish SOAP-based APIs to let developers work with different aspects of its platform. It has since deprecated those web services in favor of RESTful APIs. You can interact with Google in lots of ways with REST, including interacting with Blogger, Feedburner, AdSense, Calendar, CheckOut, Maps, OpenSocial, YouTube, Earth, Search, and lots more. To see a complete list, visit *http://code.google.com* and click "APIs & Tools."

In this application, you'll address several things at once:

- Interacting with a real-world RESTful web service that goes well beyond "Hello World." In this example, you'll use the Google Finance API to authenticate and get a user token, create a new portfolio, and read the list of portfolios associated with an account.
- Working with the Atom Publishing Protocol, which has grown into a popular way to implement REST.
- Using a secure socket to communicate over SSL with a RESTful service.
- Interacting with a RESTful service across multiple invocations in a "session."
- Authenticating using raw HTTP.
- Working at a low level to establish connections at the socket layer in the absence of a framework.
- Reading and writing data using GET and POST in REST.
- Dealing with some of the issues of working with services in the absence of WSDL.

It's a lot to cover, but this single example will encapsulate it all. One problem you confront in dealing with RESTful services is that they do not present a WSDL. That means that you have to negotiate the contract through some external means. In this example, you'll need to read the documentation on the Google website to determine what the valid parameters are.

Before You Start

Running this example requires that you have a Google account set up. If you use Gmail or another Google application that requires authentication, you're all set. Just use the username and password associated with that account in these examples.

If you need to get an account, visit *https://www.google.com/accounts/NewAccount* to sign up.

Otherwise, this example requires nothing but Java 5. You don't need anything on your classpath, and there is no setup. That's refreshingly lightweight compared to some of the SOAP examples we've seen, and part of why REST is gaining popularity.

Documentation and clients

You might want to check out *http://code.google.com/apis/finance/developers_guide_protocol.html*. This document describes the operations available with the API, and gives an overview of the terminology. If you want to use an API other than Finance or a different operation, or if you are having a little trouble, check out the documentation at *http://code.google.com/apis/gdata/basics.html*.

See the document at *http://code.google.com/apis/gdata/reference.html* for more information on the Google Data API.

You'll notice that you can download clients written in Java, Python, .NET, and Objective-C. These are pre-compiled clients that make it much easier to get started working with the language of your choice. You probably would want to download and use the Google Java client if you were going to add this functionality to your application. But because the point here is to learn what's going on under the hood and acquire the tools to invoke any kind of RESTful service, you won't use these clients in this example.

About Atom

The Google APIs use the Atom Publishing Protocol (APP). Let's take a moment to find out what Atom is because not only is it useful in this exercise, but it's a popular choice for RESTful web services.

APP is a standard for content publishing and management, created by the Internet Engineering Task Force. It builds a wrapper around standard HTTP operations such as POST, GET, DELETE, and PUT, allowing you to create, read, and edit web-based resources. It's popularly used to represent calendars, wikis, blogs, and other social web entities. Collections of editable documents are represented by Atom feeds and entries.

There is also the Atom format, which was invented as an alternative to RSS. The Atom format describes the usable entity definitions for documents exchanged with APP.

If you're interested in working with Atom, check out the Apache Abdera project, which implements both the Atom Publishing Protocol and the Atom Syndication Format. As of this writing, it is still in Incubator status. You might also check out *https://rome.dev.java.net/*, which is a Sun open source project that implements both Atom and various versions of RSS.

Here are a few simple examples of working with Atom. To retrieve a document, you might provide an HTTP request like this:

```
GET http://finance.google.com/finance/feeds/default/portfolios HTTP/1.1
```

No content is required in the body of the request. The service at that URI should then respond with a list of available entries in the collection, indicating the choices for your next path. Here is how the Google Finance API responds to a request for retrieving the list of a given user's portfolios:

```
<feed xmlns='http://www.w3.org/2005/Atom'
    xmlns:gf='http://schemas.google.com/finance/2007'
    xmlns:gd='http://schemas.google.com/g/2005'>
  <id>http://finance.google.com/finance/feeds/someUser@gmail.com/portfolios</id>
  <updated>2008-09-14T01:29:50.000Z</updated>
  <category scheme='http://schemas.google.com/g/2005#kind'
    term='http://schemas.google.com/finance/2007#portfolio'/>
  <title type='text'>Portfolio Feed</title>
  <link rel='alternate' type='text/html'
    href='http://finance.google.com/finance/portfolio?action=view'/>

//...
```

This is a standard Atom response, indicating a set of available links that represent the actions you could take next. Notice that certain key RESTful properties are at work here: the documents (representations) are given unique URIs, allowing the client to remain in charge of transferring state. This is also lightweight, requiring no external platform-specific libraries. If the platform can talk HTTP, it can work with the service. This is not always the case in the world of WS-*, where different platforms may or may not implement different specifications, making out-of-band negotiation and client alternatives more important and complex.

One minor adjustment that you'll have to make only when posting is to set the HTTP `Content-Type` header to `application/atom+xml`.

You also see the standard use of RESTful URIs at work in this example. The typical way to create URIs uses a "container" pattern to drill down from general to specific resources. For example, in the following URI, you drill down through the finance container to the feeds, then to "default" (which represents the current user in this case), then to that user's portfolios, and then to the specific portfolio with the ID of 1:

```
http://finance.google.com/finance/feeds/default/portfolios/1
```

Without further ado, let's get into the example.

Creating the Client

A Google Finance Portfolio is a collection of stocks or mutual funds that you want to watch. This client will interact with the RESTful API to create a new portfolio. You could then use additional aspects of the API to add or remove stocks to update the portfolio.

Example 8-5 shows the complete Java program that runs the show. This will authorize you with your Google account, create a new Finance Portfolio in your account called "My Restful Portfolio," and then retrieve a list of all the portfolios associated with your account (including your new one).

Example 8-5. GoogleFinanceRestClient.java

```
package simplerestclient;

import java.io.BufferedReader;
import java.io.InputStream;
import java.io.InputStreamReader;
import java.io.OutputStreamWriter;
import java.io.Writer;
import java.net.InetAddress;
import java.net.Socket;
import java.net.URLEncoder;
import java.security.Security;
import javax.net.ssl.SSLSocketFactory;
import javax.net.ssl.SSLSocket;

/**
 * Google finance API client authenticates over SSL, then
 * uses the Auth token to create a new portfolio, then
 * reads the list of portfolios for this user.
 * See:
 * http://code.google.com/apis/gdata/reference.html
 * http://code.google.com/apis/accounts/docs/AuthForInstalledApps.html#Request
 * https://www.google.com/accounts/ClientLogin
 */
public class GoogleFinanceRestClient {

    //replace with your account username and password
    private static String ACCOUNT = "me@gmail.com";
    private static String PASSWORD = "xxx";

    //use this to connect to API for auth token
    private static String AUTH_URL = "www.google.com";

    //use this to interact with API once authorized
    private static String FINANCE_URL = "finance.google.com";

    //This is a formattable string. You must replace
    //the %s to add your title
    private static String ATOM_PORTFOLIO_ADD_XML =
           "<entry xmlns='http://www.w3.org/2005/Atom' " +
           "xmlns:gf='http://schemas.google.com/finance/2007' " +
           "xmlns:gd='http://schemas.google.com/g/2005'>" +
           "<title type='text'>%s</title>" +
           "<gf:portfolioData currencyCode='USD'/></entry>";

    public static void main(String... arg) throws Exception {

        //Create an instance of this class
        GoogleFinanceRestClient client = new GoogleFinanceRestClient();
```

```
        //authenticate over SSL to get a session token
        String token = client.getAuthToken();

        //Create a new portfolio
        client.addPortfolio(token, "My Restful Portfolio");

        //Retrieve list of current portfolios
        client.getPortfolios(token);
    }

    /**
     * Retrieve the list of available portfolios for
     * the authorized user.
     */
    public void getPortfolios(String token) throws Exception {
        //Now that we have auth token, lose the SSL
        InetAddress addr = InetAddress.getByName(FINANCE_URL);
        Socket socket = new Socket(addr, 80);

        //Create HTTP request using headers
        Writer out = new OutputStreamWriter(socket.getOutputStream());
        out.write("GET /finance/feeds/default/portfolios HTTP/1.0\r\n");
        out.write("Content-Length: " + 0 + "\r\n");
        out.write("Content-Type: " +
                "application/x-www-form-urlencoded\r\n");
        out.write("Authorization: GoogleLogin auth=" +
                token + "\r\n");
        out.write("\r\n");

        //there is no body to this request
        out.flush();

        //Read response off socket input
        System.out.println("\nReading GET PORTFOLIOS Response...");
        InputStream is = socket.getInputStream();
        BufferedReader br = new BufferedReader(
                new InputStreamReader(is));
        String line = "";
        while ((line = br.readLine()) != null) {
          System.out.println(line);
        }

        socket.close();
        System.out.println("\nAll done.");
    }

    /**
     * Creates a new portfolio of the given name using the
     * current auth token.
     */
    public void addPortfolio(String token, String portfolioName)
            throws Exception {

        //Now that we have auth token, lose the SSL
```

```
    InetAddress addr =
            InetAddress.getByName(FINANCE_URL);
    Socket socket = new Socket(addr, 80);

    //you can get a Bad Request response if length is wrong
    String request = String.format(ATOM_PORTFOLIO_ADD_XML, portfolioName);

    Writer out = new OutputStreamWriter(socket.getOutputStream());
    out.write("POST /finance/feeds/default/portfolios HTTP/1.0\r\n");
    out.write("Content-Length: " + request.length() + "\r\n");
    out.write("Content-Type: application/atom+xml\r\n");
    out.write("Authorization: GoogleLogin auth=" + token + "\r\n");
    out.write("\r\n");

    out.write(request);

    System.out.println("\nADD REQUEST BODY:\n" + request);

    out.flush();

    //Read response off socket input
    System.out.println("\nReading ADD PORTFOLIO POST Response...");
    InputStream is = socket.getInputStream();
    BufferedReader br = new BufferedReader(new InputStreamReader(is));
    String line = "";

    //Just print response to console.
    while ((line = br.readLine()) != null) {
      System.out.println(line);
    }

    socket.close();
    System.out.println("\nAll done.");
}

/**
 * Use your existing account to get an auth token for
 * this session. You will use the string returned by
 * this method in subsequent requests interacting with
 * the service.
 */
public String getAuthToken() throws Exception {
    System.out.println("Invoking Google to get Auth Token.");

    //get an SSL connection
    SSLSocket socket = getSecureSocket();

    //build request
    String query = q("Email", ACCOUNT);
    query += "&" + q("Passwd", PASSWORD);
    query += "&" + q("accountType", "GOOGLE");
    query += "&" + q("service", "finance");
    query += "&" + q("source", "myco-test-1");

    //Create a request
```

```
        Writer out = new OutputStreamWriter(socket.getOutputStream());
        out.write("POST /accounts/ClientLogin HTTP/1.0\r\n");
        out.write("Content-Length: " + query.length() + "\r\n");
        out.write("Content-Type: application/x-www-form-urlencoded\r\n");
        out.write("\r\n");
        out.write(query);

        //send request
        out.flush();

        //Get Response
        InputStream is = socket.getInputStream();
        BufferedReader br = new BufferedReader(new InputStreamReader(is));
        String line = "";
        String authToken = "";

        //this call returns a few items. We need to get
        //the AuthToken only out of it.
        while ((line = br.readLine()) != null) {
          System.out.println(line);
          if (line.startsWith("Auth=")){
              authToken = line.substring(
                      line.indexOf("Auth=")+5, line.length());
          }
        }
        if (!"".equals(authToken)){
            System.out.println("Got AUTH TOKEN=" + authToken);
        }

        //clean up and return token for future calls
        socket.close();
        return authToken;
    }

    //Convenience to create Secure Socket connection
    private SSLSocket getSecureSocket() throws Exception {
        int HTTPS_PORT = 443;
        Security.addProvider(
                new com.sun.net.ssl.internal.ssl.Provider());

        SSLSocketFactory sf = (SSLSocketFactory)SSLSocketFactory.getDefault();
        SSLSocket socket = (SSLSocket)sf.createSocket(
                AUTH_URL, HTTPS_PORT);
        String[] suites = socket.getSupportedCipherSuites();
        socket.setEnabledCipherSuites(suites);

        //allows encrypted connection
        return socket;
    }

    //Convenience to build and encode key/values used in headers
    private static String q(String key, String value) throws Exception {
        return key + "=" + URLEncoder.encode(value, "UTF-8");
    }
}
```

This code listing is long, but the entire client is contained in this single class, and each part of it is fairly straightforward. First, create a few constants for your Google account username and password, as well as the base URL to interact with the API. The main method creates an instance of the class, and then invokes the `getAuthToken` method, which creates a secure connection to Google using the `getSecureSocket` method. There is nothing specific to REST at this point, and you can use this method any time you want to obtain an HTTPS connection. The `getAuthToken` method is specific to the Google API, requiring you to indicate your username and password, and then use the HTTP POST method to write the data to Google, which will respond with a security token that you can use for the rest of your session to interact with the API. In this way, you don't have to re-authenticate on every invocation. The token looks something like this:

```
SID=DQAAAHOAAAA3FKWU...-AtltIlsfPdU62RPOB31cqnRzErHL9ppsg
LSID=DQAAAH8AAAAffNC...-E_kPEN76bcZewVajOu3s6zjVlmPaOqUzyuzRUaw
Auth=DQAAAH8AAAAffNC...-AYIySHu9BMnDrJ4UDZA3Jrb1n4mCaoBg
```

You are only interested in the `Auth` token here, so substring this response to extract only that part, and then save it in an instance variable.

Once you have the token, invoke the `addPortfolio` method, which is where the real interaction with the API begins. Create a new connection using your finance URL constant, and then use a string formatter (added in Java 5) on `ATOM_PORTFOLIO_ADD_XML` to insert the name of the portfolio you want to create into the Atom XML boilerplate. This text represents an Atom `<entry>`, which you post to the URL. Then immediately read the HTTP response off the socket, which consists of an Atom `<entry>` element indicating that you have successfully added the portfolio: the response contains a RESTful URI representing your new portfolio on the Web.

Finally, you'll illustrate another aspect of the API, and prove that your portfolio creation method worked, by getting the list of all of the portfolios associated with this account. All you have to do in the `getPortfolios` method is create a new socket connection and invoke the RESTful URI at */finance/feeds/default/portfolios*, which returns the list of portfolios for this account, using the security token you saved earlier.

Here is the output from running the program, with a touch of formatting for readability and the replacement of account data:

```
Invoking Google to get Auth Token.
HTTP/1.0 200 OK
Content-Type: text/plain
Cache-control: no-cache, no-store
Pragma: no-cache
Expires: Mon, 01-Jan-1990 00:00:00 GMT
Date: Mon, 15 Sep 2008 03:28:23 GMT
Content-Length: 563
Server: GFE/1.3
Connection: Close

SID=DQAAAHOAAAA3FKWU...-AtltIlsfPdU62RPOB31cqnRzErHL9ppsg
```

```
LSID=DQAAAH8AAAAffNC...-E_kPEN76bcZewVajOu3s6zjVlmPaOqUzyuzRUaw
Auth=DQAAAH8AAAAffNC...-AYIySHu9BMnDrJ4UDZA3Jrb1n4mCaoBg
Got AUTH TOKEN=DQAAAH8A...-AYIySHu9BMnDrJ4UDZA3Jrb1n4mCaoBg

ADD REQUEST BODY:
<entry xmlns='http://www.w3.org/2005/Atom'
  xmlns:gf='http://schemas.google.com/finance/2007'
  xmlns:gd='http://schemas.google.com/g/2005'>
  <title type='text'>My Restful Portfolio</title>
  <gf:portfolioData currencyCode='USD'/>
</entry>

Reading ADD PORTFOLIO POST Response...
HTTP/1.0 201 Created
Content-Type: application/atom+xml; charset=UTF-8
Cache-Control: max-age=0, must-revalidate, private
GData-Version: 1.0
Location: http://finance.google.com/finance/feeds/default/portfolios/3
Content-Location: http://finance.google.com/finance/feeds/default/portfolios/3
Date: Mon, 15 Sep 2008 03:28:24 GMT
Server: GFE/1.3
Connection: Close

<?xml version='1.0' encoding='UTF-8'?>
<entry xmlns='http://www.w3.org/2005/Atom'
xmlns:gf='http://schemas.google.com/finance/2007'
xmlns:gd='http://schemas.google.com/g/2005'>
<id>http://finance.google.com/finance/feeds/me@gmail.com/portfolios/3</id>
<updated>2008-09-15T03:28:24.000Z</updated>
<category scheme='http://schemas.google.com/g/2005#kind'
term='http://schemas.google.com/finance/2007#portfolio'/>
<title type='text'>My Restful Portfolio</title>
<link rel='self' type='application/atom+xml'
href='http://finance.google.com/finance/feeds/default/portfolios/3'/>
<link rel='edit' type='application/atom+xml'
href='http://finance.google.com/finance/feeds/default/portfolios/3'/>
<gd:feedLink
href='http://finance.google.com/finance/feeds/me@gmail.com/portfolios/3/positions'/>
<gf:portfolioData currencyCode='USD'
gainPercentage='0.0' return1w='0.0' return1y='0.0'
return3m='0.0' return3y='0.0' return4w='0.0' return5y='0.0'
returnOverall='0.0' returnYTD='0.0'/>
</entry>

All done.

Reading GET PORTFOLIOS Response...
HTTP/1.0 200 OK
Content-Type: application/atom+xml; charset=UTF-8
Cache-Control: max-age=0, must-revalidate, private
GData-Version: 1.0
Last-Modified: Mon, 15 Sep 2008 03:28:24 GMT
Date: Mon, 15 Sep 2008 03:28:24 GMT
Server: GFE/1.3
Connection: Close
```

```
<?xml version='1.0' encoding='UTF-8'?><feed xmlns='http://www.w3.org/2005/Atom'
xmlns:openSearch='http://a9.com/-/spec/opensearchrss/1.0/'
xmlns:gf='http://schemas.google.com/finance/2007'
xmlns:gd='http://schemas.google.com/g/2005'>

<id>http://finance.google.com/finance/feeds/me@gmail.com/portfolios</id>
<updated>2008-09-15T03:28:24.000Z</updated>
<category scheme='http://schemas.google.com/g/2005#kind'
term='http://schemas.google.com/finance/2007#portfolio'/>
<title type='text'>Portfolio Feed</title>
<link rel='alternate' type='text/html'
href='http://finance.google.com/finance/portfolio?action=view'/>
<link rel='http://schemas.google.com/g/2005#feed'
type='application/atom+xml'
href='http://finance.google.com/finance/feeds/default/portfolios'/>
<link rel='http://schemas.google.com/g/2005#post'
type='application/atom+xml' href='http://finance.google.com/finance/feeds/
default/portfolios'/>
<link rel='self' type='application/atom+xml'
href='http://finance.google.com/finance/feeds/default/portfolios'/>
<openSearch:totalResults>2</openSearch:totalResults>
<openSearch:startIndex>1</openSearch:startIndex>
<openSearch:itemsPerPage>2</openSearch:itemsPerPage>
<entry><id>http://finance.google.com/finance/feeds/me@gmail.com/portfolios/1</id>
<updated>2008-09-14T22:58:41.000Z</updated>

<category scheme='http://schemas.google.com/g/2005#kind'
term='http://schemas.google.com/finance/2007#portfolio'/>
<title type='text'>Eben Portfolio</title>
<link rel='self' type='application/atom+xml'
href='http://finance.google.com/finance/feeds/default/portfolios/1'/>
<link rel='edit' type='application/atom+xml'
href='http://finance.google.com/finance/feeds/default/portfolios/1'/>
<gd:feedLink href='http://finance.google.com/finance/feeds/me@gmail.com/portfolios/
1/positions'/>
<gf:portfolioData currencyCode='USD' gainPercentage='0.0' return1w='0.0'
return1y='0.0' return3m='0.0' return3y='0.0' return4w='0.0' return5y='0.0'
returnOverall='0.0' returnYTD='0.0'/>
</entry>

<entry>
<id>http://finance.google.com/finance/feeds/me@gmail.com/portfolios/3</id>
<updated>2008-09-15T03:28:24.000Z</updated>
<category scheme='http://schemas.google.com/g/2005#kind'
term='http://schemas.google.com/finance/2007#portfolio'/>
<title type='text'>My Restful Portfolio</title>
<link rel='self' type='application/atom+xml'
href='http://finance.google.com/finance/feeds/default/portfolios/3'/>
<link rel='edit' type='application/atom+xml'
href='http://finance.google.com/finance/feeds/default/portfolios/3'/>
<gd:feedLink
href='http://finance.google.com/finance/feeds/me@gmail.com/portfolios/3/positions'/>
<gf:portfolioData currencyCode='USD' gainPercentage='0.0'
return1w='0.0' return1y='0.0' return3m='0.0'
```

```
returnЗy='0.0' return4w='0.0' return5y='0.0'
returnOverall='0.0' returnYTD='0.0'/></entry></feed>

All done.
```

After executing the application, check the Google website to make sure that your portfolio was added. The update is instant, adding "My Restful Portfolio" to the list, as illustrated in Figure 8-1.

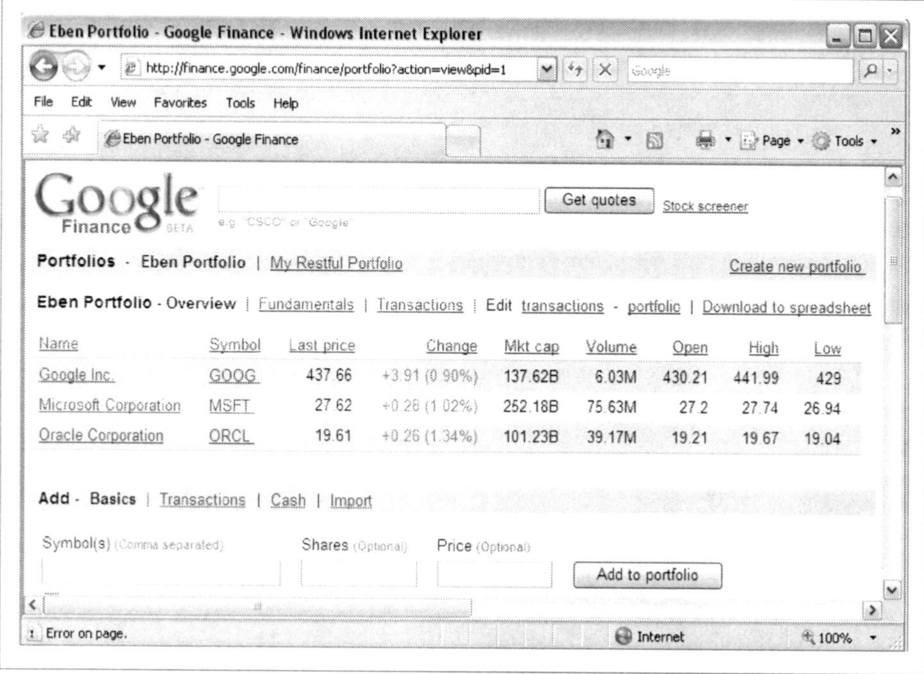

Figure 8-1. Your RESTful Atom application adds the portfolio to Google Finance

Atom is a lightweight, powerful, and standard way to interact with resources on the Web, and the Google applications illustrate how to create invocation flows that follow best practices for resource representation, request/response for following links, and ease of use.

8.5 Setting Up the Jersey JAX-RS Implementation

Problem

You want to work with JAX-RS so that you can build RESTful applications in a standard Java fashion.

Solution

Get Jersey, available from *https://jersey.dev.java.net*.

Discussion

Jersey is a Maven 2 project, so you can get the JARs, sources, and JavaDocs all from the Maven repository at *http://download.java.net/maven/2/com/sun/jersey*.

If you use NetBeans 6 or better, Jersey IDE support is available as a plug-in. Just go to Tools→Plugins and check if it's there. If it is, you should be able to create a Hello World-type project by navigating to New Project→Samples→RESTful Web Services→Hello World.

The JavaDoc for JAX-RS is available at *https://jsr311.dev.java.net/nonav/javadoc/index.html*. The JavaDoc for the Jersey implementation is available at *https://jersey.dev.java.net/source/browse/*checkout*/jersey/tags/jersey-1.0/api/jersey/index.html*.

You can use any servlet container, such as Tomcat 6, to run Jersey (and these examples). As long as you have made the necessary servlet mapping (shown below) and included all of the necessary JARs on the classpath, you won't have any problems.

Dependencies

It will be easier to integrate Jersey into your project if you're using Maven 2. That's because Jersey has a variety of runtime dependencies, including:

- The core server.
- The core client.
- Container, which is a set of container dependencies, such as for Grizzly (the NIO implementation), a lightweight HTTP server, or a servlet container.
- Entity, the set of dependencies required for serializing Java types with JAXB, for working with JSON, Atom, and Mail. If you're already using Java SE 6, you don't need any additional dependencies.
- WADL support requires no additional JARs if you're using Java SE 6.

To successfully run the JAX-RS reference implementation, you need a lot of JARs. It's probably easiest to put them on your server's classpath, but you can certainly add them to your WAR's *WEB-INF/lib* directory if you like. As of the current release, they are:

- *activation.jar*
- *asm-3.1.jar*
- *grizzly-servlet-webserver-1.7.3.2.jar*

- *http.jar*
- *jaxb-api.jar*
- *jaxb-impl.jar*
- *jaxb-xjc.jar*
- *jaxws-api.jar*
- *jdom-1.0.jar*
- *jersey.jar*
- *jettison-1.0-RC1.jar*
- *jsr173_api.jar*
- *jsr250-api.jar*
- *jsr311-api.jar*
- *rome-0.9.jar*
- *wadl2java.jar*

Of course, not every example will require the use of all of these, and they do all come with the Jersey download. If you're using Ant and need a complete list of dependencies based on how you're using Jersey, visit the project page at *https://jersey.dev.java.net* for more information.

Modifying the web.xml file

You need to modify your *web.xml* file to use the Jersey adapter servlet, much as you would when using JavaServer Faces:

```
<web-app version="2.5" xmlns="http://java.sun.com/xml/ns/javaee"
  xmlns:xsi="http://www.w3.org/2001/XMLSchema-instance"
  xsi:schemaLocation="http://java.sun.com/xml/ns/javaee
    http://java.sun.com/xml/ns/javaee/web-app_2_5.xsd">

  <servlet>
    <servlet-name>ServletAdaptor</servlet-name>
    <servlet-class>
     com.sun.jersey.spi.container.servlet.ServletContainer
    </servlet-class>
    <load-on-startup>1</load-on-startup>
  </servlet>
  <servlet-mapping>
    <servlet-name>ServletAdaptor</servlet-name>
    <url-pattern>/resources/*</url-pattern>
  </servlet-mapping>
...
```

8.6 Creating a Jersey Project with Eclipse and Tomcat

Problem

You want to create a Jersey-based project in Eclipse and use Tomcat as the container to deploy your project to.

Solution

Create a web project as you normally would. Add three JARs to the project's configuration: *jersey-bundle-1.0.jar*, *jsr311-api.jar*, and *asm-3.1.jar*. These are all available from *https://jersey.dev.java.net/source/browse/*checkout*/jersey/tags/jersey-1.0/jersey/dependencies.html*; just click on the links provided to download them. Right-click on the project name and choose Configure Build Path... to add them as external JARs, and don't forget to add them to the J2EE module dependencies as well. Once you've created your REST application, right-click on the project, choose Export...→Web→WAR File, and save the WAR to the Tomcat *webapps* directory. Your application will be picked up by Tomcat and deployed. If all goes well during deployment and all of your dependencies are straight, you'll see some output like this in the Tomcat console:

```
Oct 25, 2008 3:38:34 PM org.apache.catalina.startup.HostConfig deployWAR
INFO: Deploying web application archive restexamples.war
Oct 25, 2008 3:38:34 PM com.sun.jersey.api.core.ClasspathResourceConfig init
INFO: Scanning for root resource and provider classes in the paths:
  C:\programs\tomcat\apache-tomcat-6.0.16\webapps\restexamples\WEB-INF\lib
  C:\programs\tomcat\apache-tomcat-6.0.16\webapps\restexamples\WEB-INF\classes
Oct 25, 2008 3:38:34 PM com.sun.jersey.api.core.ClasspathResourceConfig init
INFO: Root resource classes found:
  class com.soacookbook.ProductResource
Oct 25, 2008 3:38:34 PM com.sun.jersey.api.core.ClasspathResourceConfig init
INFO: Provider classes found:
```

The output in bold indicates that the deployment knows it is a Jersey application and found a resource it could instantiate.

If you're using the NetBeans IDE, you may want to structure your project from scratch this way instead of using the wizard to create a Jersey project. That wizard comes with the Jersey plug-in, which uses an older version of Jersey that doesn't support all of its features.

As you're getting started, you may see a message like this in the Tomcat console:

```
Oct 25, 2008 3:58:19 PM com.sun.jersey.impl.application.WebApplicationImpl
processRootResources
SEVERE: The ResourceConfig instance does not contain any root resource classes.
```

This is a Bad Thing. It means that your application, while it may appear to have classes in it that represent root resources by indicating a `@Path` annotation at the class level, is misconfigured. Take a look at your JAX-RS annotations and make sure they are properly constructed.

See Also

Recipe 8.7 to find out how to build a RESTful application with Jersey so that you have something to deploy.

8.7 Creating Hello World with Jersey

Problem

You want to create the simplest REST application with the Jersey implementation of JAX-RS.

Solution

Put the Jersey JARs on your project's classpath, and then create a POJO for your resource annotated with `@Path` to indicate the path at which your resource will be available. Then add a method annotated with one of the HTTP method annotations such as `@GET` to indicate that it should be invoked when the resource receives a request using that HTTP method. Indicate the MIME type that the method will respond with. Make sure that you've updated your *web.xml* file to cause the Jersey adapter servlet to be invoked against your resource path.

Discussion

Getting started with Jersey could hardly be easier. Creating a Hello World class is simple and straightforward, as shown in Example 8-6.

Example 8-6. A RESTful Hello World application using Jersey

```
package com.soacookbook;

import javax.ws.rs.Path;
import javax.ws.rs.GET;
import javax.ws.rs.ProduceMime;

/**
 * Simplest REST web service.
 */
@Path("/helloRest")
public class HelloRest {

    /**
     * Retrieves representation of an instance of
     * com.soacookbook.HelloRest.java
     * @return a string with HTML text.
     */
```

```
    @GET
    @ProduceMime("text/html")
    public String sayHello() {
        return "<html><body><h1>Hello from REST!</body></h1></html>";
    }
}
```

Using REST is easy with Jersey. Here you create a POJO that is annotated with `javax.ws.rs.Path`. Its value attribute indicates the path where this resource will be made available. The resource path follows the adapter servlet path, so you will be able to reach an instance of this class at `<server>:<port>/<context>/<jersey-servlet-mapping>/<path-value>`. The Jersey servlet mapping is defined in the *web.xml* file.

You also need to annotate your method that does the work. By using the JAX-RS `@GET` annotation, you indicate that the `sayHello` method is the one you want to respond to HTTP GET requests. Then use the `@ProduceMime` annotation to indicate the MIME type you want to return on response. Here you use `text/html`, but you can use any MIME type that makes sense for your application, including `text/xml` and `image/gif`.

Example 8-7 is the *web.xml* file that causes Jersey to intercept requests that follow the `resources` path. If you've used JavaServer Faces before, this intercepting servlet idea should be familiar.

Example 8-7. The web.xml file specifying the Jersey Adapter servlet

```
<web-app version="2.5" xmlns="http://java.sun.com/xml/ns/javaee"
 xmlns:xsi="http://www.w3.org/2001/XMLSchema-instance"
 xsi:schemaLocation="http://java.sun.com/xml/ns/javaee
  http://java.sun.com/xml/ns/javaee/web-app_2_5.xsd">
    <servlet>
        <servlet-name>JerseyAdapter</servlet-name>
        <servlet-class>com.sun.jersey.spi.container.servlet.ServletContainer</servlet-class>
        <load-on-startup>1</load-on-startup>
    </servlet>
    <servlet-mapping>
        <servlet-name>JerseyAdapter</servlet-name>
        <url-pattern>/resources/*</url-pattern>
    </servlet-mapping>
    <welcome-file-list>
        <welcome-file>index.jsp</welcome-file>
    </welcome-file-list>
</web-app>
```

Now you can deploy your WAR and open a browser at *http://localhost:8080/Hello World/resources/helloRest* to see your message.

Resource methods

In JAX-RS, annotations that correspond to the HTTP methods are called *resource methods*. These include `@GET`, `@POST`, `@PUT`, `@DELETE`, and `@HEAD`. Like your `sayHello` method, these methods must be declared `public`. You can define your own custom request method designator, if, for example, you'd like to create an alternate for one of the HTTP methods.

The return types for resource methods are limited to `void`, `javax.ws.rs.core.Response`, `javax.ws.rs.core.GenericEntity`, or another Java type.

If your method returns `void`, the response will be an empty method body with a 204 status code, which indicates that the request was successfully processed but the response doesn't have a message body. We'll look at the other response types in later sections.

The annotation value in `@Path` is automatically encoded, so `@Path("product list")` is identical to `@Path("products%20list)`.

8.8 Creating a Single Path for Variable Resources of the Same Type

Problem

You want to create a class that can respond for many instances of the same type. That is, you don't want to have a separate individual class for each individual resource, as this would be a maintenance nightmare. You want, for example, to have representations for `/products/1` and `/products/2` map to the same class.

Solution

Use a template in the `@Path` element on your class, defining the variable part in curly braces. Then use the `@PathParam` annotation on your method parameters.

Discussion

In a RESTful URL, such as that for the Google Finance Portfolio application in Recipe 8.4, you see a drill-down structure that moves from general categories to specific instances. In the case of the Google Finance app, you can access a specific portfolio using a URL that includes the ID for the portfolio you want to get data for, like this: `/finance/feeds/default/portfolios/3`. Here, 3 is the ID of the specific portfolio you want to view. You need to be able to create URIs like this in JAX-RS, without having to create a separate class for every single resource you might want to return a representation of. Doing so would be a maintenance nightmare, and isn't how good applications are designed.

For this reason, the JAX-RS API provides a way to handle just this situation, called *URI templates*. A root resource is assigned a specific URI root path using the `@Path` annotation at the class level. This path follows the context path of the application, and allows you to assign dynamic resources using what's called a *path parameter*. A path parameter is defined in curly braces inside the value of the path itself. You then match that parameter value to a method parameter using the annotation `@PathParam`. This sounds much more complicated than it is. An example will make it clear.

In Example 8-8, you define a method that will respond to GET requests for products, accept a parameter for a product ID, and return the appropriate representation.

Example 8-8. Using a PathParameter to get specific products in a RESTful URI

```
package com.soacookbook;

import javax.ws.rs.Path;
import javax.ws.rs.GET;
import javax.ws.rs.PUT;
import javax.ws.rs.ProduceMime;
import javax.ws.rs.ConsumeMime;
import javax.ws.rs.POST;
import javax.ws.rs.PathParam;
import javax.ws.rs.core.Context;
import javax.ws.rs.core.UriInfo;

/**
 * API for Products.
 */
@Path("/products/{id}")
public class ProductResource {
    @Context
    private UriInfo context;

    /** Creates a new instance of ProductResource */
    public ProductResource() { }

    @GET
    @ProduceMime("text/plain")
    public String getProduct(@PathParam("id") int productId) {
        switch (productId) {
            case 1: return "A Shiny New Bike";
            case 2: return "Big Wheel";
            case 3: return "Taser: Toddler Edition";
            default: return "No such product";
        }
    }
}
```

Building this class into a WAR with the Jersey JARs and the servlet mapping in the *web.xml* is all you need to do to deploy this example. The string value of the template must make a valid URI path. If you open a browser to *http://localhost:8080/JaxrsExamples/resources/products/3*, you should see this response:

```
Taser: Toddler Edition
```

Obviously, in the real world you would go to a database delegate or something here to get the product info. The only trick to this example is that the value you pass to the `@PathParam` annotation must match the text inside the curly braces that define your template in the `@Path` annotation, as that's what provides the necessary mapping.

8.9 Restricting the Structure of Values in a Path Template

Problem

You don't want just a simple template that accepts any string (such as `/products/{id}`) to match your resource; you need to define a template with a more powerful mechanism for handling variation, and ensure that only values matching a certain complex structure are passed to your method.

Solution

Use a regular expression after a colon in your template, like this: `@Path("products/{id}:[a-zA-Z][a-zA-Z_0-9]}"}`. Parameters that don't match the expression will return a 404 HTTP status code.

Discussion

JAX-RS path parameters allow you to define your templates using regular expressions. Just create your path template as you normally would, but add a colon and then your regular expression within the path.

You need to use the latest version of the Jersey implementation for this functionality. Version 0.8, which may be included by default in the plug-in for your IDE (as it was the first general release), does not support this. Version 1.0 supports regular expressions.

Example 8-9 provides an illustration.

Example 8-9. A path template using a regular expression

```
@Path("/products/{id: \\d{3}}")
public class ProductResource {

    public ProductResource() { }

    @GET
    @Produces("text/plain")
    public String getProductPlainText(@PathParam("id") int productId) {

        return "Your Product is: " + productId;
    }
}
```

In this regular expression, you indicate that product IDs must be exactly three digits. If you compile and deploy this resource and open your browser to the URL *http://localhost:8080/restexamples/resources/products/555*, you'll see the following output:

```
Your Product is: 555
```

But if you open it to the URL *http://localhost:8080/restexamples/resources/products/3* (which has only a single-digit number in the ID parameter), you'll get a 404. The application is responding properly, and there is a resource there, but the ID doesn't match the constraints of the expression. So in effect, in the REST world, there is no resource there. This may require a slight adjustment in thought.

8.10 Accessing Query Parameters

Problem

You want to access the query parameters in the URI (the `name=value` pairs following a ?) within your method implementation.

Solution

Use the `@QueryParam` annotation on your method parameter. Optionally, include the `@DefaultValue` in case the query parameter you're expecting is not passed.

Discussion

The use of query parameters is prevalent in the REST world, and JAX-RS makes it easy to access them. All you need to do in your code is create a parameter on your implementation method that you want to hold the specific query parameter value you need access to. If the user does not access your resource with that parameter, you can specify a default value so that things don't go haywire. See Example 8-10.

Example 8-10. Accessing a query parameter value

```
package com.soacookbook;

import javax.ws.rs.DefaultValue;
import javax.ws.rs.GET;
import javax.ws.rs.Path;
import javax.ws.rs.PathParam;
import javax.ws.rs.Produces;
import javax.ws.rs.QueryParam;
import javax.ws.rs.core.Context;
import javax.ws.rs.core.UriInfo;

/**
 * Shows accessing Query Parameters.
 */
@Path("/products")
public class ProductQuery {
```

```
    @Context
    private UriInfo context;

    /** Creates a new instance of ProductResource */
    public ProductQuery() { }

    @GET
    @Produces("text/xml")
    public String getProducts(
        @PathParam("id") int productId,
        @QueryParam("results")
        @DefaultValue("5") int numResults) {

        StringBuilder result = new StringBuilder("<products>");

        //return the number of results requested
        for (int i = 0; i < numResults; i++) {
          result.append("<p>Product " + i + "</p>");
        }
        result.append("</products>");
        return result.toString();
    }
}
```

In this example, you have a loop that runs to create the number of product results the user wants to see in this search. The `numResults` integer is declared in the method signature and annotated with `@QueryParam` to indicate that it should receive the value from the browser address's query parameter called **`results`**. This value will be coerced into an integer; if the runtime can't do that, it will throw a 404 exception. You then fake out a search and loop, appending to the result the number of rows the user asked for.

Accessing this resource with the URL *http://localhost:8080/restexamples/resources/products?results=3* gives the following XML result:

```
<products><p>Product 0</p><p>Product 1</p><p>Product 2</p></products>
```

If you access it without the query parameter, you get 5 product results, as specified by the `@DefaultValue` annotation.

8.11 Marshaling a Custom Type to XML in a Response

Problem

You want your service to provide an XML view of a custom Java type you've defined.

Solution

Use JAXB annotations on your custom type, and let JAX-RS handle the rest. JAX-RS requires that vendors support certain built-in marshalers, and JAXB is one of them. All you have to do is annotate the class you want to return as XML with

@XmlRootElement, and create a JAX-RS service that indicates that it produces XML with the @Produces("application/xml") annotation.

Discussion

Example 8-11 shows a basic Java type that your service can automatically marshal to XML using JAXB.

Example 8-11. Employee.java with JAXB annotations to assist in automatic marshaling

```
package com.soacookbook.rest.xml;

import javax.xml.bind.annotation.XmlElement;
import javax.xml.bind.annotation.XmlRootElement;

@XmlRootElement(name="employee")
public class Employee {
    @XmlElement(name="id")
    int id;

    @XmlElement(name="name")
    String name;
}
```

This class is just a regular POJO that might as well be a product or line item or some other type. The only thing that matters here is that the class itself is annotated with @XmlRootElement to indicate that instances of this class can be marshaled into XML as complete documents. The fields feature the related **@XmlElement** annotation to allow them to customize their names in the resulting XML elements.

Now you'll create a JAX-RS service that makes use of this element. Because you're taking advantage of one of the built-in marshalers, it's very straightforward. The service is shown in Example 8-12.

Example 8-12. EmployeeService.java using automatic JAXB marshaling

```
package com.soacookbook.rest.xml;

import java.util.HashMap;
import java.util.Map;

import javax.ws.rs.GET;
import javax.ws.rs.Path;
import javax.ws.rs.PathParam;
import javax.ws.rs.Produces;

@Path("/emps")
public class EmployeeService {

    private static Map<Integer, Employee> emps = populateDatabase();

    public EmployeeService() { }
```

```
    @GET
    @Path("{id}")
    @Produces("application/xml")
    public Employee getEmployee(@PathParam("id") int empId) {

        return emps.get(empId);
    }

    private static Map<Integer, Employee> populateDatabase(){
        Map<Integer, Employee> emps = new HashMap<Integer, Employee>();

        Employee e1 = new Employee();
        e1.id = 1;
        e1.name = "Bill Gates";

        Employee e2 = new Employee();
        e2.id = 2;
        e2.name = "Larry Ellison";

        Employee e3 = new Employee();
        e3.id = 3;
        e3.name = "Steve Jobs";

        emps.put(1, e1);
        emps.put(2, e2);
        emps.put(3, e3);
        return emps;
    }
}
```

In this class, you use the `/emps` path, which will follow the context, and then map the dynamic `id` parameter to select the employee whose data you're interested in.

Now if you deploy this in a WAR with the servlet mapped to `/resources` as with all of the other examples in this chapter, you'll get an XML representation of a given employee. Let's try `http://localhost:8080/restexamples/resources/emps/2`, which shows the following in a browser:

```
<?xml version="1.0" encoding="UTF-8" standalone="yes"?>
<employee>
<id>2</id>
<name>Larry Ellison</name>
</employee>
```

That's it. Here you're using the JAXB entity provider, but JAX-RS actually requires several of them. They are discussed in section 4.2 of the specification. Here's a complete list:

- `byte[]`
- `java.lang.String`
- `java.io.InputStream`
- `java.io.Reader`

- `java.io.File`
- `javax.activation.DataSource`
- `javax.xml.transform.Source`
- `javax.xml.bind.JAXBElement` and application-supplied JAXB classes (used for XML media types only)
- `MultivaluedMap<String, String>` for form content only (`application/x-www-form-urlencoded`)
- `StreamingOutput`

JAX-RS vendors are required to offer `MessageBodyReader` and `MessageBodyWriter` implementations for each of these means of providing entities. Each must support the `*/*` media type unless otherwise specified.

8.12 Offering Different Representations of the Same Resource

Problem

You want your service to provide alternate views of the same resource.

Solution

Provide separate methods that respond to the HTTP protocol you're interested in (e.g., multiple methods with a `@GET` annotation) and specify a different `@Produces` for each one that indicates the MIME type it returns.

Discussion

A standard browser will pass the MIME types it can handle by passing the HTTP `Accept` header in its request. A typical request header sent from Firefox looks like this:

```
Accept: text/html,application/xhtml+xml,application/xml;q=0.9,*/*;q=0.8
```

The client is telling the server that it would prefer to get HTML or XHTML, and its next preference is to accept XML. The preferences are indicated not only by the order in which they appear, but with the `q` parameter, used to specify a relative "quality factor" or how strong the preference is for the given media type on a scale of 0 to 1.

You can read more about the HTTP `Accept` header at *http://www.w3.org/Protocols/rfc2616/rfc2616-sec14.html*.

So to test the client, you'll need to indicate an alternative HTTP `Accept` header. Building a client programmatically using something like the HTTP Commons Client library will do this for you. To run this example, you'll also need Apache Commons Logging, Logging API, and Codec on your classpath, as the Apache HTTP client requires them.

Apache Commons Codec and Logging are available at *http://commons.apache.org/*. This example uses version 3.1 of the HTTP Commons Client, available at *http://hc.apache.org/*.

The REST service that presents three different representations of the same resource is shown in Example 8-13. This class has three different methods, all annotated with `@GET`. The client will automatically be routed to the appropriate method based on either its declared `Accept` content type or its preferences.

Example 8-13. DifferentRepresentations.java

```
package com.soacookbook.rest.ex;

import java.io.File;

import javax.activation.MimetypesFileTypeMap;
import javax.ws.rs.GET;
import javax.ws.rs.Path;
import javax.ws.rs.Produces;
import javax.ws.rs.WebApplicationException;
import javax.ws.rs.core.Response;

/**
 * If we put a @Produces annotation on the class level,
 * that will be the value matched despite browser preferences
 * in the Accept header.
 */
@Path("/duke")
@Produces("text/plain")
public class DifferentRepresentations {
    private static final String IMG_PATH =
        "C:\\programs/eclipse/workspace/restexamples/WebContent/duke.gif";

    @GET
    @Produces("text/html")
    public String doGetAsHtml() {
        return "<html><h1>Html Duke</h1></html>";
    }

    //notice no override, as this method returns the default
    @GET
    public String doGetAsPlainText() {
        return "Plain Duke";
    }

    @GET
    @Produces("image/*")
    public Response doGetAsImage() {
```

```
        File image = new File(IMG_PATH);

        if (!image.exists()) {
            throw new WebApplicationException(404);
        }

        String type = new MimetypesFileTypeMap().getContentType(image);
        return Response.ok(image, type).build();
    }

    @GET
    @Produces("text/xml")
    public String doGetAsXml() {
        return "<?xml version='1.0' encoding='utf-8'?>" +
               "<mascot>Xml Duke</mascot>";
    }
}
```

This service is fairly straightforward except for a few things. One is that there are multiple methods that claim to respond to HTTP GET requests, but they each respond with a different MIME type, as indicated by their `@Produces` annotations. Note that in the `doGetAsImage` method, the value of the `@Produces` annotation indicates that it produces any image type. You might instead specify `image/gif` as the produces type, but this allows that clients interested in receiving an image type might match this with their `Accept` header more easily.

The class itself also contains an `@Produces` annotation, which means that the default MIME will be `text/plain`. So despite the browser's declared preference for receiving HTML, this class produces plain text unless you specifically indicate a single type you'll accept (you'll do this later in your client). Therefore, if you open a regular browser and point to the class, you'll see plain text, not HTML. All of the remaining GET methods are overrides for this default, and will only be invoked in the event that there is a fairly specific match for the client's accept type. For this reason, the `doGetAsPlainText` method needs no `@Produces` annotation.

The other thing that needs some clarification here is the way that you build the response in the `doGetAsImage` method. It uses the `MimetypesFileTypeMap` class from the Java Activation framework to create a string representation of the actual MIME type of the file as read from the server-side filesystem. In this case, the class examines the file you've passed to the `getContentType` method and determines its MIME, and then returns a string `image/gif`. So the advantage of using that class is that you don't have to hardcode the content type; this class could serve a `.png` instead, and you wouldn't have to change any code.

But there is another new item in the body of this method; the `Response` class and its `ok` method haven't been discussed. The `javax.ws.rs.core.Response` class and its inner `ResponseBuilder` class allow you to create your own custom responses. `ResponseBuilder` allows you to create a response that contains metadata instead of an entity, or contains metadata as well as an entity. The `ok` method is a convenience method that builds a response that returns an HTTP 200 OK response along with the actual body of the response.

As we just discussed, if you point to this service using your regular web browser as a client, it passes along the browser's default `Accept` header, but you'll still only ever see the plain-text representation because that's the default as long as the client will accept that type (which a browser will). So you need to build a client to manipulate the outgoing headers. In the next class, you'll use the Apache HTTP Commons Client library to programmatically create the HTTP request so that you can specify your own `Accept` header and test each of the three different representations in the same program all at once.

This example assumes that you're deploying the service in a WAR using a *web.xml* entry so that the service resolves at *http://localhost:8080/rest examples/resources/duke*.

Example 8-14 shows the code for the client that programmatically creates an HTTP request, allowing you to specify your own HTTP `Accept` headers. This way you can see each of the different representations the service provides.

Example 8-14. DifferentRepClient.java

```
package com.soacookbook.rest.ex;

import java.awt.image.BufferedImage;
import java.io.File;
import java.io.IOException;
import java.io.InputStream;

import javax.imageio.ImageIO;

import org.apache.commons.httpclient.HttpClient;
import org.apache.commons.httpclient.HttpException;
import org.apache.commons.httpclient.HttpStatus;
import org.apache.commons.httpclient.methods.GetMethod;

/**
 * Gets three different representations of the same
 * resource (Duke): HTML, XML, and an image.
 * Note that all three methods point to the exact same URL,
 * and specify only a different "Accept" header; there's no
 * query parameter, etc.
 *
 * This class is used with DifferentRepresentations.java which
 * is the REST service.
 */
public class DifferentRepClient {

    private static String RESOURCE_URL =
        "http://localhost:8080/restexamples/resources/duke";
```

```
//client path to save image in current execution dir
private static String SAVE_TO =
    System.getProperty("user.dir") + "/dukeClient.gif";

/**
 * Use with HTTP client in Apache Commons to
 * get alternative content from DifferentRepresentations
 * REST service.
 */
public static void main(String... args) {

    getXml();
    System.out.println("Got XML. Now getting HTML...");

    getHtml();
    System.out.println("Now getting image...");

    getImage();
    //now that it's saved on client, show image:
    new ImageViewer(SAVE_TO).show();

    System.out.println("All done.");
}

private static void getXml() {
    HttpClient client = new HttpClient();
    GetMethod get = new GetMethod(RESOURCE_URL);
    get.setRequestHeader("Accept", "text/xml");

    try {
        int httpStatus = client.executeMethod(get);

        if (HttpStatus.SC_OK == httpStatus) {
            String xmlResponse = get.getResponseBodyAsString();
            System.out.println("Xml Response: " +
                    xmlResponse);
        }

    } catch (HttpException e) {
        e.printStackTrace();
    } catch (IOException e) {
        e.printStackTrace();
    } finally {
        //clean up
        get.releaseConnection();
    }
}

private static void getHtml() {
    HttpClient client = new HttpClient();
    GetMethod get = new GetMethod(RESOURCE_URL);
    get.setRequestHeader("Accept", "text/html");

    try {
```

```
            int httpStatus = client.executeMethod(get);

            if (HttpStatus.SC_OK == httpStatus) {
                String htmlResponse = get.getResponseBodyAsString();
                System.out.println("Html Response: " +
                        htmlResponse);
            }

        } catch (HttpException e) {
            e.printStackTrace();
        } catch (IOException e) {
            e.printStackTrace();
        } finally {
            //clean up
            get.releaseConnection();
        }
    }

    private static void getImage() {
        HttpClient client = new HttpClient();
        GetMethod get = new GetMethod(RESOURCE_URL);
        get.setRequestHeader("Accept", "image/gif");

        try {
            int httpStatus = client.executeMethod(get);

            if (HttpStatus.SC_OK == httpStatus) {
                InputStream responseBody = get.getResponseBodyAsStream();

                System.out.println("Response Size=" +
                        get.getResponseContentLength());
                System.out.println("Response Type=" +
                        get.getResponseHeader("Content-Type"));


                //save retrieved file on local path
                File outputFile = new File(SAVE_TO);
                BufferedImage img = ImageIO.read(responseBody);
                ImageIO.write(img, "gif", outputFile);
            }

        } catch (HttpException e) {
            e.printStackTrace();
        } catch (IOException e) {
            e.printStackTrace();
        } finally {
            //clean up
            get.releaseConnection();
        }
    }
}
```

The methods in the `DifferentRepClient` class all follow the same basic pattern: they create an `HttpClient` instance, create a class representing the HTTP GET method to send a request, and then specify the HTTP `Accept` header on the outgoing request to match the representation they want to get back. This is fairly straightforward for the HTML and XML types; the main difference within the image getter method is that it gets the body as a stream, and then saves the response out as an image to the current directory using the Java Image IO library.

All of the invocations of the service point to the exact same URL—the single difference between them is the use of the `Accept` header. There is no query parameter or any other mechanism to distinguish what method the service should dispatch to for generating a response.

The third class required in this application is just a little Swing image viewer helper class used by the client to prove that it successfully retrieved the representation presented in GIF image format. There's nothing REST-specific about it, but I show it here for completeness (Example 8-15).

Example 8-15. ImageViewer.java displays the image retrieved by the client

```
package com.soacookbook.rest.ex;

import java.awt.BorderLayout;
import java.awt.EventQueue;
import java.awt.image.BufferedImage;
import java.io.File;
import java.io.IOException;

import javax.imageio.ImageIO;
import javax.swing.Icon;
import javax.swing.ImageIcon;
import javax.swing.JFrame;
import javax.swing.JLabel;

/**
 * Shows an image in a window given a file path.
 * Used by the DifferentRepClient class to prove the client
 * got the image.
 */
public class ImageViewer {
    final private JFrame frame = new JFrame("Image Viewer");

    //constructor reads image and sets up frame
    public ImageViewer(String fileLocation) {
        try {
            //read newly saved image file
            File input = new File(fileLocation);
            BufferedImage image = ImageIO.read(input);

            //set up window
            frame.setDefaultCloseOperation(JFrame.EXIT_ON_CLOSE);

            //put image on it
            Icon icon = new ImageIcon(image);
```

```
            JLabel label = new JLabel(icon);
            frame.getContentPane().add(
                    label, BorderLayout.CENTER);

            //make image fit window
            frame.pack();

            //now it's all set to show

        } catch (IOException ie) {
            System.out.println("Error:" + ie.getMessage());
            System.exit(-1);
        }
    }

    //creates the thread and shows it
    public void show() {
        Runnable runner = new FrameDisplay();
        EventQueue.invokeLater(runner);
    }

    private class FrameDisplay implements Runnable {
        public void run() {
            frame.setVisible(true);
        }
    }
}
```

In short, this helper simply reads the image that the client class saved off at the specified location and adds it to a frame, which it then displays in a runnable.

Running the program prints the following output:

```
Xml Response: <?xml version='1.0' encoding='utf-8'?><mascot>Xml Duke</mascot>
Got XML. Now getting HTML...
Html Response: <html><h1>Html Duke</h1></html>
Now getting image...
Response Size=13715
Response Type=Content-Type: image/gif

All done.
```

Once the text representations are printed, the program creates a `JFrame` and shows the image you received as the GIF representation response in the window to prove that the client got it intact. The screenshot is shown in Figure 8-2.

And that's all there is to it!

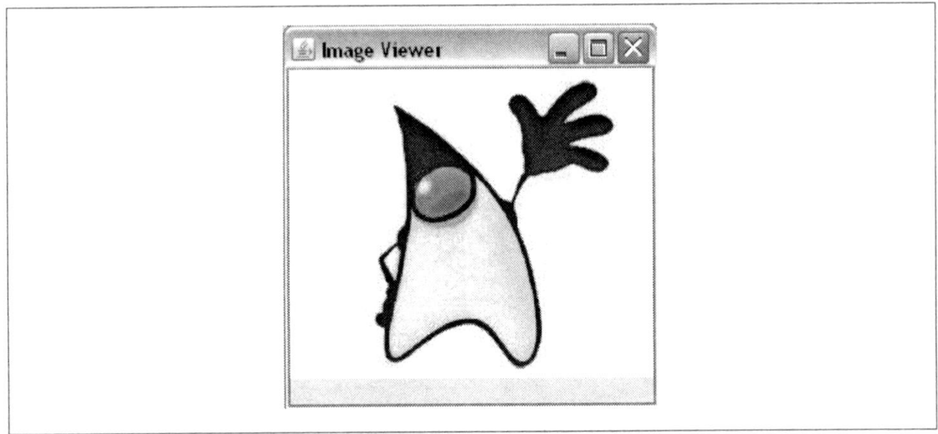

Figure 8-2. The image representation of Duke

8.13 Creating a Resource

Problem

You want to provide a way for users to create a RESTful resource in JAX-RS.

Solution

Use the `@POST` annotation on a resource method to indicate that it accepts HTTP POST data, and add the entity in the method with the incoming data.

If you're not using JAX-RS, post the data from an HTML form. Create the URI for the new resource, and return the proper set of links to allow users to perform any new state transitions they might want. Remember not to store state on the server.

Discussion

In this example, you'll use the `@POST` annotation on a method to add a resource to the server, and then retrieve it. Using POST to create data is common, though PUT may sometimes be used. POST is the more common idiom because HTML works readily with it, even though PUT may make more sense conceptually.

An HTTP POST response in REST will result in a 201 response (typically including a representation indicating what happened and offering another idea of what states you can transition to next). Some designers might choose to have a POST result in a 204 status code that includes a location header containing the URI of the new resource.

Strictly speaking, the HTTP status code 201 means that the request has been fulfilled and a new resource has been created. 204 means the request has been fulfilled and produces a response of No Content, meaning it does not include a message body. So 201 is preferred here.

In this example, you'll use the Apache Commons HTTP Client to do post data programmatically. First you'll create a service using JAX-RS, and then create the client that can add entities and get them later.

Example 8-16 shows the code for the service.

Example 8-16. Post and get user service

```
package com.soacookbook.rest.post;

import java.net.URI;
import java.util.HashMap;
import java.util.Map;

import javax.ws.rs.Consumes;
import javax.ws.rs.GET;
import javax.ws.rs.POST;
import javax.ws.rs.Path;
import javax.ws.rs.PathParam;
import javax.ws.rs.core.Response;
import javax.ws.rs.core.UriBuilder;

import com.sun.jersey.spi.resource.Singleton;

@Path("user/{id}")
@Singleton
public class UserService {

    private Map<Integer, User> userDatabase;

    //create fake user database to keep example simple
    public UserService() {
        userDatabase = new HashMap<Integer, User>();
    }

    @POST
    @Consumes("application/xml")
    public Response postUser(User user) {
        System.out.println("Post User.");

        //save to database here...
        userDatabase.put(user.getId(), user);
        System.out.println("Posted user: " + user);

        URI createdUri = UriBuilder.fromPath("user/" +
             user.getId()).build(user);

        System.out.println("post: createdUri: " + createdUri);

        //return a 201 'created' status
        return Response.created(createdUri).build();
    }

    @GET
    public Response getUser(@PathParam("id") int id) {
```

```
        System.out.println("Get User.");

        //get from database...
        User user = userDatabase.get(id);

        Response.ResponseBuilder responseBuilder =
        Response.ok(user).entity(user);
        Response response = responseBuilder.build();

        System.out.println("get: Found User: " + user);
        return response;
    }
}
```

This class uses the Jersey implementation's extension `@Singleton` to indicate that the service should be instantiated only once and that each request should be processed by the same instance. That's obviously not portable, but it's just a convenience in order to make a complete example that doesn't use a database. The map field stands in for a relational database and isn't an integral part of the solution.

Some interesting things are happening in this service. It responds to GET and POST requests against the `user/{id}` template, which we've seen before. The POST accepts XML that represents a user, and then saves it to the "database" so that invokers of the GET method can retrieve it later. But to use the GET method to view the representation, you respond to the POST with the URI for the newly created user object. You use the `UriBuilder` class to create the URI for the new entity, and then pass the URI to the `Response` instance.

The GET method responds to requests of this service by retrieving the ID parameter from the request path and using it to look up the user in the database. Once you find that user, you return it in the `Response` method to be read on the client.

The next class in the application is the `User` class itself (Example 8-17). It's just a bean with an ID and a string username. The only thing you do to it is add a JAXB annotation for `@XmlRootElement`. You can do this in your own applications to make it easier to marshal and unmarshal entities to and from XML. JAX-RS implementations are guaranteed to support automatic translation using JAXB, so this will be portable. But if you don't want to pollute your entities with binding-specific information, that's fine. You would just need to provide `MessageBodyWriter<User>` and `MessageBodyReader<User>` implementations to be picked up by the JAX-RS runtime.

Example 8-17. User entity class

```
package com.soacookbook.rest.post;

import javax.xml.bind.annotation.XmlRootElement;

@XmlRootElement
public class User {
    private int id;
    private String username;
```

```
    public int getId() {
        return id;
    }
    public void setId(int id) {
        this.id = id;
    }
    public String getUsername() {
        return username;
    }
    public void setUsername(String username) {
        this.username = username;
    }

    @Override
    public String toString() {
        return "[ID=" + id + ". Username=" + username + "]";
    }

}
```

So `User` is your entity in this example and is just a standard bean annotated with `@XmlRootElement` so that you don't have to write a custom reader and writer.

The last class in the application is the client (Example 8-18). This class uses the Apache Commons HTTP library to execute the POST and GET operations programmatically. There are a couple of other dependencies you'll need for this example, including Commons Logging and Commons Codec. You don't use them directly, but the HTTP library requires them.

Example 8-18. Post user client

```
package com.soacookbook.rest.post;

import java.io.IOException;

import org.apache.commons.httpclient.HttpClient;
import org.apache.commons.httpclient.HttpException;
import org.apache.commons.httpclient.HttpStatus;
import org.apache.commons.httpclient.methods.GetMethod;
import org.apache.commons.httpclient.methods.PostMethod;

/**
 * Invokes the User service to add a resource and then
 * retrieve it to prove it worked.
 */
public class UserClient {
    private static String SERVICE_URL =
        "http://localhost:8080/restexamples/resources/user/";

    public static void main(String... args) {
        System.out.println("Creating new user.");

        createUser(777, "eben");
```

```
        getUser(777);

        System.out.println("All done.");
    }


    private static void createUser(int id, String username) {
        HttpClient client = new HttpClient();
        PostMethod post = new PostMethod(SERVICE_URL + id);

        String userXml = "<?xml version='1.0' encoding='UTF-8' ?>" +
                "<user>" +
                "<id>" + id + "</id>" +
                "<username>" + username + "</username>" +
                "</user>";
        post.setRequestBody(userXml);

        try {
            int httpStatus = client.executeMethod(post);

            if (HttpStatus.SC_OK == httpStatus) {
                String xmlResponse = post.getResponseBodyAsString();
            }

        } catch (HttpException e) {
            e.printStackTrace();
        } catch (IOException e) {
            e.printStackTrace();
        } finally {
            //clean up
            post.releaseConnection();
        }
    }

    private static void getUser(int id) {
        HttpClient client = new HttpClient();
        GetMethod get = new GetMethod(SERVICE_URL + id);
        get.setRequestHeader("Accept", "text/xml");

        try {
            int httpStatus = client.executeMethod(get);

            if (HttpStatus.SC_OK == httpStatus) {
                String xmlResponse = get.getResponseBodyAsString();

                System.out.println("Xml User Response: " +
                        xmlResponse);
            }

        } catch (HttpException e) {
            e.printStackTrace();
        } catch (IOException e) {
            e.printStackTrace();
        } finally {
            //clean up
```

```
            get.releaseConnection();
        }
    }
}
```

The client creates a new instance of the POST method for interacting with the service. It then sends that XML to the service, which will select the `postUser` method and invoke the JAXB framework to translate the XML into a `User` object and then save it to the database.

In the next method invocation, you use a GET method to look up the user you just created. Running the client produces the following output on the console:

```
Creating new user.
Xml User Response:
<?xml version="1.0" encoding="UTF-8" standalone="yes"?>
<user><id>777</id><username>eben</username></user>
All done.
```

Here you do not return to the client any additional state transition possibilities. You just return the entity itself, and that's the end of the road. But it does illustrate how to use POST and GET together, and one way of creating objects on the server, as well as some of the supporting plumbing in JAX-RS, such as `UriBuilder` and `ResponseBuilder`.

Because you are using the Jersey-specific `@Singleton` annotation, there is only one instance of the service for the entire container. That is not an intrinsic aspect of this example; I'm only doing it as a convenience to save the added users in the map, instead of having to go to a database. If you didn't use that annotation, the user instance data would not be saved across requests. Note that in general, you want RESTful services to be stateless so that they scale (this service could be stateless if you were actually going to a database), so don't get too used to the idea of this annotation. Plus, it's only part of the reference implementation, and not the JAX-RS API, so your code here wouldn't be portable to something like RESTEasy.

8.14 Working with Forms and URIs

Problem

You want an easy way to get data from an HTML form.

Solution

For each item in the form that you want to capture, use the `@FormParam` annotation within the method parameters.

Discussion

The form parameters annotation works like many other annotations in JAX-RS, such as @QueryParam and @PathParam—the values are injected by the runtime. So if you have either a short form with just a few input controls, or are only interested in a few values, it's very easy to access form data using @FormParam.

Example 8-19 shows the code for the User entity that the form will create and that you'll show in a static representation.

Example 8-19. User.java is the business entity the form creates

```
package com.soacookbook.rest.forms;

import java.util.Date;

/**
 * A business entity created by form input.
 */
public class User {

    private String id;
    private String name;
    private Date createdDate;

    //getters and setters omitted...
}
```

In a real-world application, you would use a database or some other persistent store to save created users. For the purposes of this example, you'll just save them in a static map, as shown in Example 8-20.

Example 8-20. A mock database for saving users

```
package com.soacookbook.rest.forms;

import java.util.HashMap;
import java.util.Map;

/**
 * Mocks a database. When users are created by the form, they
 * are stored here for later retrieval.
 */
public class Database {
    static Map<String, User> users = new HashMap<String, User>();
}
```

The class that runs the show is the FormsService; this is shown in Example 8-21.

Example 8-21. The FormsService class represents the user in a form, in a list, and in detail

```
package com.soacookbook.rest.forms;

import java.net.URI;
```

```
import java.util.Date;
import javax.ws.rs.Consumes;
import javax.ws.rs.FormParam;
import javax.ws.rs.GET;
import javax.ws.rs.POST;
import javax.ws.rs.Path;
import javax.ws.rs.PathParam;
import javax.ws.rs.Produces;
import javax.ws.rs.core.Context;
import javax.ws.rs.core.Response;
import javax.ws.rs.core.UriBuilder;
import javax.ws.rs.core.UriInfo;

/**
 * REST service produces a form for users to provide input,
 * reads the data from the form, creates a user, and returns
 * navigation control. Allows viewing all users.
 *
 * Shows using @FormParam, Response variations, URI building,
 * and putting together a complete application.
 *
 * 'Forms' shouldn't be part of the path probably; I only use
 * it here for the book example to keep demos clear.
 */
@Path("/forms/user")
@Produces("text/html")
public class FormsService {

    //no user selected, so present form to create one
    @GET
    public Response create() {

        return Response.ok(NEW_USER_FORM_HTML).build();
    }

    //get form data and create and save user
    @POST
    @Consumes("application/x-www-form-urlencoded")
    @Produces("text/html")
    public Response doCreate(
            @FormParam("id") String id,
            @FormParam("fname") String fname,
            @Context UriInfo uriInfo) {

        //add user to database
        User user = new User();
        user.setId(id);
        user.setName(fname);
        user.setCreatedDate(new Date());
        Database.users.put(id, user);

        //create URI here with entity response
        URI createdUri =
                UriBuilder.fromUri(
                uriInfo.getRequestUri().toString())
```

```
                .path("{a}").build(user.getId());

        System.out.println("Created URI: " + createdUri);

        //Set the Location header and indicate 201 (Created) response
        //Setting the entity in the response returns
        //the object that was created, by first running it through
        //the writer implementation.
        Response response = Response.created(createdUri)
                .entity(user)
                .location(createdUri)
                .build();

        return response;
    }

    @GET
    @Path("/{id}")
    public Response viewOne(@PathParam("id") String id) {
        User u = Database.users.get(id);

        StringBuilder sb = new StringBuilder("<html><body>");

        sb.append("<h1>View User Details</h1>");

        sb.append("User ID: ").append(u.getId()).append("<br/>");
        sb.append("Name: ").append(u.getName()).append("<br/>");
        sb.append(String.format("Created On: %1$tm.%1$te.%1$tY",
              u.getCreatedDate()) );

        sb.append("</body></html>");

        Response response = Response.ok(sb.toString()).build();

        System.out.println("Built response.");

        return response;
    }

    private static String NEW_USER_FORM_HTML =
         new StringBuilder("<html><body>")
        .append("<h1>Create User</h1>")
        .append("<form name='userForm' method='POST' action=''>")
        .append("ID: <input type='text' name='id' size='3' />")
        .append("<br/>")
        .append("Name: <input type='text' name='fname' />")
        .append("<br/>")
        .append("<input type='submit' name='submit' value='Create'/>")
        .append("</form>")
        .append("</body></html>").toString();
}
```

There is a lot going on in this class, but some of it we've seen before. Let's walk through what it does, focusing on the most interesting aspects. A view of the application is shown in Figure 8-3.

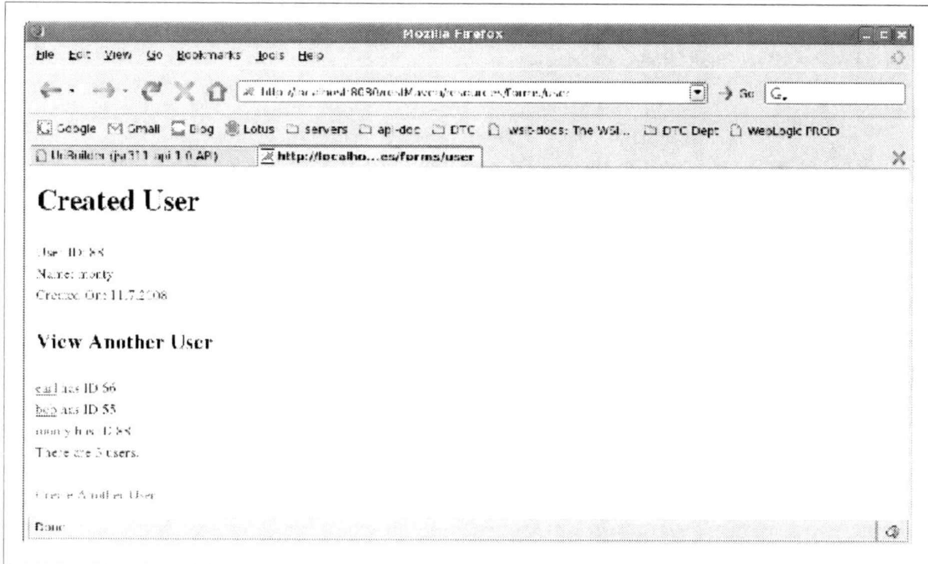

Figure 8-3. The user service representation after creating a user

When the user requests the service at *http://localhost:8080/restMaven/resources/forms/user*, the runtime selects the `create` method. That's because it's annotated with GET, which matches your request type, and because it's the best match for your path. The class is annotated with a root `@Path`, and that is used as the basis for other path calculations later. But in the `create` method, you have to return only a 200 OK response containing the HTML for the user creation form.

Once the user enters some data into the form and clicks the submit button, the runtime matches the only method for this path annotated with `@POST`, which is the `doCreate` method. As an alternative to using `@FormParam`, this method could instead accept a `User` type, if you wanted to write an implementation of `MessageBodyReader<User>`. That would probably be a good idea in the real world, especially if your entity has more than a couple of fields, but here you want to see how the `@FormParam` annotation works. The `MessageBodyReader<T>` interface is examined closely in Recipe 8.23.

So the `doCreate` method accepts two `@FormParam` instances. These are injected automatically by the runtime; you don't have to do anything special to assign them values. Jersey will simply look in the submitted form for a parameter matching the string you gave as the annotation value, and assign it to your local variable.

Using the values injected into the form parameter annotations, create a new `User` object and save it in your mock database. Then use the `UriBuilder` class to create the URI that represents the user you just created. This is important in REST because you want resources to have bookmarkable URIs. So you've decided that your URI scheme will be `...user/{id}`, which is a template where the part between the curly braces represents the user's ID. So if you create a user with ID 007, that bookmarkable URI will be `...resources/forms/user/007`.

To follow the basic REST style, you need to create this URI now so that you can return in the HTTP response the `Location` header populated with the value of the unique URL for the user you created. This provides the client with metadata about the response and also a choice for the client to transition state (among others). Remember, *hypermedia as the engine of application state*.

So in order to build your URI, use the `UriBuilder` class in conjunction with the `UriInfo` object, which was injected into the method via the `@Context` parameter to this method. Again, you don't have to do anything special to get that `UriInfo` object; its values are populated by the runtime.

Using the `UriInfo` instance, you get the value for the path the current request is answering, and then use the path method to indicate to your template that you need to populate (`"{a}"`). The value within the template (in this case, `a`) is not special. It gets substituted for the value passed to the build method (in this case, the ID of the user you created). Note that the `UriBuilder` class follows a standard builder pattern, and works like `StringBuilder` and other builder classes (`ResponseBuilder` in JAX-RS, for instance).

Once your URI is created, pass it into your response-building process. The `Response` class actually has `ResponseBuilder` as an inner class. By using the `created` method initially, you set the HTTP response code to 201 Created. By using the `entity` method and passing it your user object (the entity you created), you're able to return the representation of the entity along with the response. The runtime will look for an available `MessageBodyWriter<User>` implementation in order to create that entity representation. Finally, by using the location method, you can automatically add the new URI as the value of the `Location` header in the HTTP response.

Note that it's enough to simply post the form to itself by specifying `action=''` because you have different HTTP methods answering. While there are two GETs in the service, they respond to different paths, as the `viewOne` method only responds when an ID is supplied.

The last class in this little service is the `MessageBodyWriter` implementation that returns your `User` representation as requested by your invocation of the `entity` method on the `Response` builder. The writer is shown in Example 8-22.

Example 8-22. UserHtmlWriter.java creates an HTML representation of the user entity

```
package com.soacookbook.rest.forms;

import javax.ws.rs.Produces;
import javax.ws.rs.ext.MessageBodyWriter;
```

```
import javax.ws.rs.ext.Provider;
import java.io.IOException;
import java.io.OutputStream;
import java.lang.annotation.Annotation;
import java.lang.reflect.Type;

import javax.ws.rs.core.MediaType;
import javax.ws.rs.core.MultivaluedMap;

/**
 * Creates an HTML representation of a user.
 */
@Produces("text/html")
@Provider
public class UserHtmlWriter
    implements MessageBodyWriter<User> {

    //match type parameter to make sure runtime picks up
    //this class as writer for User
    public boolean isWriteable(Class<?> type, Type genericType,
      Annotation[ ] annotations, MediaType mediaType) {

      return User.class.isAssignableFrom(type);
    }

    public long getSize(User data,
      Class<?> type, Type genericType,
      Annotation annotations[ ], MediaType mediaType) {

      return -1;
    }

    /**
     * Gets executed by putting entity in Response and by
     * matching that same class to the isWriteable method.
     */
    public void writeTo(User user,
            Class<?> type, Type genericType,
            Annotation[ ] annotations, MediaType mediaType,
            MultivaluedMap<String, Object> headers,
            OutputStream out) throws IOException {

        System.out.println("writeTo.");

        StringBuilder sb = new StringBuilder("<html><body>");

        sb.append("<h1>User</h1>");
        sb.append("User ID: ").append(user.getId()).append("<br/>");
        sb.append("Name: ").append(user.getName()).append("<br/>");
        sb.append(String.format("Created On: %1$tm.%1$te.%1$tY",
              user.getCreatedDate()) );

        sb.append("<h2>View Another User</h2>");

        int count = 0;
```

```
        for (User u : Database.users.values()) {
            sb.append("<a href='user/").append(u.getId());
            sb.append("'>");
            sb.append(u.getName()).append("</a> has ID ");
            sb.append(u.getId());
            sb.append("<br />");
            count++;
        }
        sb.append("There are ").append(count).append(" users.");

        //will create another GET request
        sb.append("<br/><br/><a href=''>Create Another User</a>");
        sb.append("</body></html>");

        out.write(sb.toString().getBytes());
    }
}
```

The `UserHtmlWriter` class is pretty standard stuff. Its main job is to produce HTML representing a user on creation, along with a list of existing users to give the client some navigation choices. Clients can view details for specific users by clicking their names, or navigate to create another user. Clicking on the "Create Another User" link has an `href` value of `''` because it simply sends a new GET request to the same page, so you'll run back through the service and end up at the start page of the application.

The important thing about the writer implementation is that you have to use the type parameter correctly. On encountering an invocation of the `entity` method in a root resource class, the runtime will look through the list of all writer implementations it loaded at startup and invoke their `isWriteable` methods in an attempt to find a match. If the entity created is assignable to the type parameter of a given writer, the runtime will invoke that implementation's `writeTo` method. The only thing to note about the HTML is that you ultimately have to call `getBytes` on the string you produce because that's what the `OutputStream` accepts.

Here is the request that gets sent once you click the button on the form:

```
http://localhost:8080/restMaven/resources/forms/user

POST /restMaven/resources/forms/user HTTP/1.1
Host: localhost:8080
User-Agent: Mozilla/5.0 (X11; U; Linux i686; en-US; rv:1.8.0.7)
  Gecko/20061011 Fedora/1.5.0.7-7.fc6 Firefox/1.5.0.7
Accept: text/xml,application/xml,application/xhtml+xml,text/html;
  q=0.9,text/plain;q=0.8,image/png,*/*;q=0.5
Accept-Language: en-us,en;q=0.5
Accept-Encoding: gzip,deflate
Accept-Charset: ISO-8859-1,utf-8;q=0.7,*;q=0.7
Keep-Alive: 300
Connection: keep-alive
Referer: http://localhost:8080/restMaven/resources/forms/user
Content-Type: application/x-www-form-urlencoded
```

```
Content-Length: 31
id=88&fname=monty&submit=Create
```

The important thing to note about the request is that you have specified with the `@Consumes` tag that a particular method will consume data for requests declaring that they send an `application/x-www-form-urlencoded` `Content-Type`.

And here is the accompanying response:

```
HTTP/1.x 201 Created
Server: Apache-Coyote/1.1
Location: http://localhost:8080/restMaven/resources/forms/user/88
Content-Type: text/html
Content-Length: 314
Date: Fri, 07 Nov 2008 23:59:08 GMT
```

The important thing about the response is that it returns not a 200 OK HTTP status, but a 201 Created status. That's because you created an entity once the user posted the form data. But you also return a `Location` header specifying the unique URI of the entity that you created. This header is added by calling the `location(createdUri)` method on the `ResponseBuilder` object.

8.15 Using SAAJ to Access a RESTful Service

Problem

You want to use the SAAJ library to access a RESTful web service, or at least have an easy way to talk POX (Plain Old XML) over HTTP.

Solution

No problem. Get a `RequestContext` object from your `Dispatch`. Then invoke `requestContext.put(MessageContext.HTTP_REQUEST_METHOD, "GET")`.

Discussion

You used these classes throughout the JAX-WS chapters, so I won't belabor the point now. But Example 8-23 shows a complete example of the sort of thing you want to do.

Example 8-23. Using a SAAJ client to invoke a RESTful service that talks over HTTP and returns plain XML

```
package com.soacookbook.rest.saaj;

import java.net.URI;
import java.util.Map;

import javax.xml.namespace.QName;
import javax.xml.transform.Source;
import javax.xml.transform.Transformer;
import javax.xml.transform.TransformerFactory;
```

```
import javax.xml.transform.dom.DOMResult;
import javax.xml.ws.Dispatch;
import javax.xml.ws.Service;
import javax.xml.ws.handler.MessageContext;
import javax.xml.ws.http.HTTPBinding;
import javax.xml.xpath.XPath;
import javax.xml.xpath.XPathConstants;
import javax.xml.xpath.XPathExpressionException;
import javax.xml.xpath.XPathFactory;

import org.w3c.dom.NodeList;

/**
 * Using SAAJ to call a REST service that produces raw XML
 * over HTTP.
 */
public class SaajRestClient {

    public static void main(String[] args) throws Exception {
        new SaajRestClient().call();
    }

    public void call() throws Exception {
        //these can be any value here, as we're not NS qualified
        //I leave them to illustrate usage in other contexts
        URI nsURI = new URI("urn:emps");
        QName serviceName = new QName("empsSvc",nsURI.toString());
        QName portName = new QName("empsPort",nsURI.toString());
        Service s = Service.create(serviceName);

        String address = "http://localhost:8080/restexamples/resources/emps/1";

        s.addPort(portName, HTTPBinding.HTTP_BINDING, address);

        Dispatch<Source> d = s.createDispatch(portName,
                Source.class, Service.Mode.PAYLOAD);

        Map<String, Object> requestContext = d.getRequestContext();
        requestContext.put(MessageContext.HTTP_REQUEST_METHOD, "GET");

        //no body in this example. you would build it here if necessary
        Source result = d.invoke(null);

        if (result != null) {
            //got result, so drill down to find data.
            DOMResult domResult = new DOMResult();
            Transformer trans = TransformerFactory.newInstance().newTransformer();
            trans.transform(result, domResult);

            printResult(domResult);

        } else {
            System.out.println("No result.");
        }
    }
```

```
//use XPath to drill down to data we want
    private void printResult(DOMResult domResult)
        throws XPathExpressionException {

        String name = "";

        XPathFactory xpf = XPathFactory.newInstance();
        XPath xp = xpf.newXPath();
        NodeList resultList = (NodeList)xp.evaluate(
                "/employee/name", domResult.getNode(),
            XPathConstants.NODESET);

        name = resultList.item(0).getTextContent();

        System.out.println("Employee Name: " + name);
    }
}
```

The service, which you built in Recipe 8.11, produces XML that looks like this:

```
<?xml version="1.0" encoding="UTF-8" standalone="yes"?>
<employee>
    <id>1</id>
    <name>Bill Gates</name>
</employee>
```

Once you specify the address of the service, you pass it into the `Service.addPort` method along with the `HTTPBinding` constant instead of the SOAP binding you used earlier. Then use the request context you get from the `Dispatch` to indicate that you're using the HTTP GET method. The runtime will use the properties in this map to help it create the proper request and send it off.

The `Dispatch` returns a `Source`, which can be transformed into a number of `Source`-related objects suitable for different purposes. Here, you'll examine the result as a `DOMResult`, so pass a new, empty `DOMResult` object to a `Transformer` along with your `Source` result. The transformer will create a DOM view of the returned XML that you can traverse using XPath.

The `printResult` method just applies the XPath expression `/employee/name` to the DOM tree. You get the text content of the first matching node in the tree, and finally print the result.

8.16 Setting Metadata on Representations

Problem

You want to follow the RESTful principle of setting metadata on representations you return to clients.

Solution

Use the Response and ResponseBuilder classes to set your metadata using some of their built-in methods.

Discussion

One of the tenets of REST is that representations can include metadata. In JAX-RS, this idea is enabled by the ResponseBuilder class, which is an inner class of Response. The build pattern employed by this class means that a modified instance of Response is returned by each invocation so that you can append any amount of metadata you need to, one item at a time. Here's an example:

```
@POST
 public Response addUser(...) {
   User user = ...
   URI userId = UriBuilder.fromResource(User.class)...
   return Response.created(userId).build();
 }
```

The use of the created method here modified the response by setting the HTTP status code to 201 Created. Table 8-1 highlights the metadata methods available from Response.ResponseBuilder.

Table 8-1. Metadata methods available on Response.ResponseBuilder

Method	Description
cacheControl(CacheControl cacheControl)	Abstracts the value of an HTTP Cache-Control response header.
contentLocation(java.net.URI location)	Sets the content location HTTP header.
cookie(NewCookie... cookies)	Allows you to create a variable-length set of cookies to add to the response.
expires(java.util.Date expires)	Sets the HTTP Expires header.
header(java.lang.String name, java.lang.Object value)	Allows you to create a custom HTTP header in a key/value pair.
language(java.util.Locale language)	Sets the Content-Language HTTP header.
lastModified(java.util.Date lastModified)	Sets the last modified date on the response.
location(java.net.URI location)	Usually used to specify the unique URI of a created entity, this sets the Location header on an HTTP 201 Created response. If a relative URI is supplied, it will be converted into an absolute URI by resolving it relative to the base URI of the application. Setting it to null removes any existing value.
status(Response.Status status)	Sets a value from the Status enumeration representing standard HTTP status codes, such as OK, BAD_REQUEST, FORBIDDEN, INTERNAL_SERVER_ERROR, and so forth.

Method	Description
type(MediaType type)	Sets the media type of the response, with enum instances for standard media types, such as APPLICATION_ATOM_XML, APPLICATION_JSON, APPLICATION_OCTET_STREAM, MULTIPART_FORM_DATA, TEXT_HTML, TEXT_XML, and more.

Example 8-24 is a quick illustration of how some of these methods can be combined to tailor your HTTP response.

Example 8-24. Metadata service uses Response.ResponseBuilder

```
package com.soacookbook.rest.metadata;

import java.util.Calendar;
import java.util.Date;
import java.util.GregorianCalendar;
import java.util.Locale;

import javax.ws.rs.GET;
import javax.ws.rs.Path;
import javax.ws.rs.core.CacheControl;
import javax.ws.rs.core.MediaType;
import javax.ws.rs.core.Response;

@Path("/meta")
public class MetaDataService {

    @GET
    public Response get() {
        CacheControl cacheCtl = new CacheControl();
        cacheCtl.setMaxAge(500);
        cacheCtl.setMustRevalidate(true);
        cacheCtl.setNoStore(true);

        Calendar cal = new GregorianCalendar();
        cal.roll(Calendar.YEAR, 1);
        Date expy = cal.getTime();

        Response response = Response.noContent()
            .header("MY_KEY", "MY_VALUE")
            .cacheControl(cacheCtl)
            .expires(expy)
            .language(Locale.ENGLISH)
            .type(MediaType.TEXT_HTML)
            .build();

        return response;
    }
}
```

You can append these builder methods in arbitrary order, with each method adding its own metadata to the response. In this example, you specify a custom header of your own, set the cache control to expire after 500 seconds, create a date representing one year in the future and set that on your expires header, and so forth.

If you deploy the example and open a browser to *http://localhost:8080/restexamples/resources/meta*, you won't see a response in the window (because you specified 204 No Content), but the headers produced by the response are as expected:

```
(Status-Line) HTTP/1.1 204 No Content
Server: Apache-Coyote/1.1
Cache-Control: no-store, no-transform, must-revalidate, max-age=500
Expires: Sun, 08 Nov 2009 16:41:49 GMT
MY_KEY: MY_VALUE
Content-Language: en
Date: Sat, 08 Nov 2008 16:41:49 GMT
```

You can also use the `Variant` class to set a collection of metadata values at once. This class is intended for setting representation metadata on the `ResponseBuilder`, and encapsulates content type, supported content languages using a variable-length argument, and supported content encodings all separately, using the values you indicate in the variant's properties.

8.17 Deleting a Resource

Problem

You want to provide a way for users to delete a resource in JAX-RS.

Solution

Use the `@DELETE` annotation on a resource method to indicate that it responds to HTTP DELETE requests, and then remove the resource in the method body.

Discussion

This annotation works like some of the other HTTP annotations we've examined from JAX-RS, with one primary difference: browsers only natively support GET and POST, not PUT and DELETE. So if you want to permanently remove a resource, you can mark the method with `@DELETE` and the runtime will invoke that method automatically. Then use whatever code necessary to remove the resource from your persistent store.

8.18 Redirecting to Another Service

Problem

You want to redirect clients from one RESTful service to another and keep attendant details and metadata such as parameters intact.

Solution

Create a URI using `javax.ws.rs.core.UriBuilder` that maps the parameters and other data you want to preserve. Then use `Response.temporaryRedirect` to return a redirect to the client and pass it the URI you've built.

Discussion

The code in Example 8-25 redirects clients from one service to another. It maintains the query string that was passed in the original request. You have one service, `OldService`, that responds on the URI the client actually requests. It redirects to the new service.

Example 8-25. OldService.java redirects clients to the service at NewService

```
package com.soacookbook.rest.response;

import java.net.URI;

import javax.ws.rs.GET;
import javax.ws.rs.Path;
import javax.ws.rs.QueryParam;
import javax.ws.rs.core.Response;
import javax.ws.rs.core.UriBuilder;

/**
 * Redirects the client from the requested URI to another,
 * and maintains the query parameters.
 */
@Path("/oldversion")
public class OldService {

    private static final String REDIR_PATH =
        "http://localhost:8080/restexamples/resources/";

    private static final String REDIR_SERVICE = "newversion";

    @GET
    public Response doGet(@QueryParam("user") String user) {

        System.out.println("In Old doGet.");

        URI uri = UriBuilder.fromUri(REDIR_PATH).
        path("{a}").
        queryParam("user", "{value}").
        build(REDIR_SERVICE, user);

        Response response = Response.temporaryRedirect(uri).build();

        System.out.println("Redirecting to " + uri);

        return response;
    }
```

```
}
```

The simplest new part of this code is that you just have your method return a `Response` instance, and build that response using the factory method based on the HTTP status you want to send. In this case, you want to redirect, so you'll use the `temporaryRedirect` method (there are others for `ok`, `noContent`, `serverError`, and so forth). Once you have the URI instance representing where you want to redirect to, it's easy. You just pass that to the response and call `build`.

This class expects these query parameters, so if you don't pass them, your client will see a 500 server error indicating that the necessary values to build the template don't exist.

The tricky part of this code is the URI. This class is part of the REST core, and follows the Gang of Four Builder pattern. Like with `StringBuilder`, each method invocation on `UriBuilder` returns the newly modified object, allowing you to make further modifications. Here's the basic idea:

1. Create the initial URI object by passing it the base path of the service you want to redirect to. At this point, you have a URI of *http://localhost:8080/restexamples/resources/*.
2. Use the `path` method to create a new instance of the `UriBuilder` that uses the template notation (here, `{a}`) to append the service name once you call build.
3. Use the `queryParam` method to create a new instance of the builder that extracts the query parameter called "user" and stores its value in the `{value}` part of the template. This will handle the equals sign appropriately.
4. When you're done with the builder, call build, and it will put together all of these parts into a URI that can be passed to the response redirector.

See section 3.7 of the JAX-RS specification for the rules on request preprocessing and URI templates. Also, if you need to have anything unusual in the query string or other data with your request, the `UriBuilder` class generally behaves in the way you would hope. For example, `UriBuilder.fromPath("{p}").build("foo#bar")` will result in the encoding of the # sign so that the result is `foo%23bar`.

Redirecting can be useful when you are migrating clients to newer versions of your service. Checking for the data that they may have provided and then mapping default values if anything is missing can be helpful in this area. Example 8-26 shows a service that accepts the redirect returned from the old service in Example 8-25 and returns the result to the client.

Example 8-26. NewService.java

```
package com.soacookbook.rest.response;

import javax.ws.rs.GET;
import javax.ws.rs.Path;
import javax.ws.rs.QueryParam;

@Path("/newversion")
public class NewService {

    @GET
    public String doGet(@QueryParam("user") String user) {
        System.out.println("In New doGet.");
        return "Hello from New Version, " + user;
    }
}
```

Now open a browser and point it to *http://localhost:8080/restexamples/resources/oldversion?user=Indiana Jones*.

Your browser's address bar will change, and you'll see this: *http://localhost:8080/restexamples/resources/newversion?user=Indiana+Jones*. And of course, the message you expect is displayed, with the proper formatting: `Hello from New Version, Indiana Jones`.

Redirecting based on class

In the preceding example, you want to redirect to a new service that replaces your existing service. That may not always be the case, however; that method of build URIs allows you to create some complex values that could redirect to any outside address. But if you simply want to point to a new service that is a Java class in your application, there's an easy way to do that.

Just use the `UriBuilder.fromResource` method, and pass it the name of the class that you want to invoke. Then pass the build method the string that represents your service name:

```
URI uri = UriBuilder.fromResource(NewService.class).build("newversion");
```

8.19 Accessing HTTP Headers

Problem

You want your JAX-RS service to access the HTTP headers sent with a request.

Solution

Access the headers using the `HttpHeaders` class as a parameter to the method in which you want to work with them, annotating the parameter with `@Context`.

Alternatively, use the @HeaderParam annotation.

Discussion

Example 8-27 illustrates how to access HTTP headers using the @Context annotation.

Example 8-27. Accessing HTTP headers using the @Context annotation

```
package com.soacookbook.rest.headers;

import javax.ws.rs.GET;
import javax.ws.rs.Path;
import javax.ws.rs.core.Context;
import javax.ws.rs.core.HttpHeaders;
import javax.ws.rs.core.MultivaluedMap;

@Path("headers")
public class Headers {

    @GET
    public String doGet(@Context HttpHeaders headers) {

        System.out.println("Looking at headers.");

        //list all incoming headers
        MultivaluedMap<String,String> map = headers.getRequestHeaders();
        for (String header : map.keySet()) {
            System.out.println(header + "=" + map.get(header));
        }

        return "All done";
    }
}
```

The @Context annotation gives you access to a variety of other contextual variables too, including UriInfo, SecurityContext, ContextResolver, and ServletContext. The MultivaluedMap interface is part of JAX-RS, and allows you to specify more than one value for the same key. This is unlike a standard Java Map, which would just overwrite any new values added for the same key.

In my case, this code prints the following:

```
Looking at headers.
accept-encoding=[gzip, deflate]
cache-control=[no-cache]
connection=[Keep-Alive]
host=[localhost:8080]
accept-language=[en-us]
user-agent=[Mozilla/4.0 (compatible; MSIE 7.0; Windows NT 5.1; .NET CLR 2.0.50727)]
ua-cpu=[x86]
accept=[*/*]
```

Using @HeaderParam

Another way to set and get the value of a specific field is to use the `@HeaderParam` annotation. The class in Example 8-28 illustrates setting a custom response header and also shows how to examine the value of the `User-Agent` header.

Example 8-28. Using the @HeaderParam annotation

```
package com.soacookbook.rest.header;

import javax.ws.rs.GET;
import javax.ws.rs.HeaderParam;
import javax.ws.rs.Path;
import javax.ws.rs.Produces;
import javax.ws.rs.core.Response;

@Path("/header")
@Produces("text/html")
public class HeaderService {

    //set custom header
    @GET
    @Path("/home")
    public Response home() {

        System.out.println("Header Home page.");

        String html = "<html><body><a href='step2'>Click</a> " +
          "to go to the next step.</body></html>";

        //include header in 200 OK response
        Response response = Response.ok(html).header(
                "X-Powered-By", "JAX-RS/Jersey").build();

        System.out.println("Built response.");

        return response;
    }

    //retrieve standard header
    @GET
    @Path("/step2")
    public String step2(@HeaderParam("User-Agent") String agent) {

        System.out.println("Header Step 2.");

        String html = "";

        if (agent != null) {
            System.out.println("Header Value: " + agent);

            html = "<html><body>Your User-Agent is: " +
                 agent + "</body></html>";
        } else {
            html = "<html><body>Could not find header. :(</body></html>";
```

```
        }

        System.out.println("Sending response for step2.");

        return html;
    }
}
```

This class does two things with headers. First, it sets a custom header that you create. The name of the header is "X-Powered-By" and the value is "JAX-RS/Jersey". This header will get returned to the client for the current request, but it won't persist across subsequent invocations automatically. The key here is that you use the `Response` builder pattern to create a response template representing 200 OK, and then add the header key/value pair to your response object using the `header` method. Once your response is prepared, call the build method to finalize it.

The `@HeaderParam` annotation uses resource injection to make the named header available in a read-only local copy to the `step2` method. Here it is in action. This shows the HTTP response to invoking the service at *http://localhost:8080/restMaven/resources/header/home*:

```
HTTP/1.x 200 OK
Server: Apache-Coyote/1.1
X-Powered-By: JAX-RS/Jersey
Content-Type: text/html
Transfer-Encoding: chunked
Date: Wed, 05 Nov 2008 23:57:59 GMT
```

Your custom HTTP header has been set. Clicking on the link sent back with the HTML that takes you to `step2` shows the following in my browser:

```
Your User-Agent is: Mozilla/5.0 (X11; U; Linux i686; en-US; rv:1.8.0.7)
  Gecko/20061011 Fedora/1.5.0.7-7.fc6 Firefox/1.5.0.7
```

8.20 Working with Cookies

Problem

You want your JAX-RS service to set and accept an HTTP cookie.

Solution

Use the `@CookieParam` annotation on your method parameters.

Discussion

All of the parameter types in JAX-RS work by injection. You can simply add a parameter to your business method that is of the appropriate type (`HeaderParam`, `CookieParam`, `FormParam`, etc.), and the runtime will inject the value so you can work with it locally.

Example 8-29 demonstrates the setting and reading of a cookie.

Example 8-29. CookieService.java

```
package com.soacookbook.rest.cookie;

import javax.ws.rs.CookieParam;
import javax.ws.rs.GET;
import javax.ws.rs.Path;
import javax.ws.rs.Produces;
import javax.ws.rs.core.Cookie;
import javax.ws.rs.core.NewCookie;
import javax.ws.rs.core.Response;

@Path("/cookie")
@Produces("text/html")
public class CookieService {

    //set cookie on home page
    @GET
    @Path("/home")
    public Response home() {

        System.out.println("Home page.");

        //create a cookie object
        NewCookie cookie = new NewCookie("MY_KEY", "MY_VALUE");

        String html = "<html><body><a href='step2'>Click</a> " +
            "to go to the next step.</body></html>";

        //include cookie in 200 OK response
        Response response = Response.ok(html).cookie(cookie).build();

        System.out.println("Built response.");

        return response;
    }

    //retrieve cookie previously set
    @GET
    @Path("/step2")
    public String step2(@CookieParam("MY_KEY") Cookie cookie) {

        System.out.println("Step 2.");

        String html = "";

        if (cookie != null) {
            System.out.println("Cookie Name: " + cookie.getName());
            System.out.println("Cookie Value: " + cookie.getValue());

            html = "<html><body>The value in your cookie was: " +
                 cookie.getValue() + "</body></html>";
        } else {
```

```
            html = "<html><body>Could not find cookie. :(</body></html>";
        }

        System.out.println("Sending response for step2.");

        return html;
    }
}
```

Open your browser to *http://localhost:8080/restMaven/resources/cookie/home*, and you'll send a request to the service that looks like this (it's just a snippet):

```
http://localhost:8080/restMaven/resources/cookie/home
GET /restMaven/resources/cookie/home HTTP/1.1
```

So you're accessing the GET method that corresponds to the `/home` mapping. That makes the `home` method in the `CookieService` class respond to the request. Note that you have a class-level path mapping, and then the additional GET methods respond to the same path appended with their annotation's values.

To create the cookie you use the `NewCookie` class, which will also accept a `Cookie` instance as a constructor argument. Then write some HTML that you'll send as your response, and pass them both into the response builder chain. The `ok` factory method creates a 200 OK response template; set your cookie on it and call build to prepare the final response.

Here are the HTTP headers in the response you get from the service after accessing the home page:

```
HTTP/1.x 200 OK
Server: Apache-Coyote/1.1
Set-Cookie: MY_KEY=MY_VALUE;Version=1
Content-Type: text/html
Transfer-Encoding: chunked
Date: Wed, 05 Nov 2008 21:05:42 GMT
```

As you can see from this response, the cookie has been set. Clicking the link on the returned HTML will then pass the newly set cookie along with the request, allowing you to read the value back on the server. The request containing the cookie looks like this:

```
http://localhost:8080/restMaven/resources/cookie/step2
GET /restMaven/resources/cookie/step2 HTTP/1.1
Host: localhost:8080
User-Agent: Mozilla/5.0 (X11; U; Linux i686; en-US; rv:1.8.0.7)
  Gecko/20061011 Fedora/1.5.0.7-7.fc6 Firefox/1.5.0.7
Accept: text/xml,application/xml,application/xhtml+xml,text/html;
  q=0.9,text/plain;q=0.8,image/png,*/*;q=0.5
Accept-Language: en-us,en;q=0.5
Accept-Encoding: gzip,deflate
Accept-Charset: ISO-8859-1,utf-8;q=0.7,*;q=0.7
Keep-Alive: 300
Connection: keep-alive
```

```
Referer: http://localhost:8080/restMaven/resources/cookie/home
Cookie: MY_KEY=MY_VALUE
```

The standard Cookie header contains the cookie data just as you set it.

Here is the total output in the server log:

```
Home page.
Built response.
Step 2.
Cookie Name: MY_KEY
Cookie Value: MY_VALUE
Sending response for step2.
```

And here is the output to the browser, as you would expect:

```
The value in your cookie was: MY_VALUE
```

You can also use other methods on the NewCookie, as well as additional arguments to its constructor, to do things like set an expire time, set a domain and path name, or set a version number.

If you're using the Firefox browser, a terrific plug-in for debugging HTTP applications is Live HTTP Headers, which shows you the headers being sent with requests and responses.

Using HttpHeaders to access cookies

You can also get a Map<String, Cookie> that contains all cookies in the request by using the getCookies method off of HttpHeaders. The string type parameter on the map is the key to the cookie value. You can then iterate the map using a key set:

```
//retrieve cookie using injected HttpHeaders
@GET
@Path("/step3")
public String step3(@Context HttpHeaders headers) {

    System.out.println("Step 3.");

    String html = "";

    if (headers != null) {
        html = "<html><body>Headers:<br/>";

        final Map<String, Cookie> cookies = headers.getCookies();
        for (String key : cookies.keySet()) {
            html += "Cookie " + key + "=" +
                    cookies.get(key) + "<br>";
        }

        html += "</body></html>";
    } else {
        html = "<html><body>Could not find cookies. :(</body></html>";
    }
```

```
        return html;
    }
```

You just inject the HttpHeaders using the @Context annotation, and then invoke the getCookies method. If you add this method onto the class you used in the cookie example, it returns the following response to the browser:

```
<html><body>Headers:<br/>
Cookie MY_KEY=$Version=0;MY_KEY=MY_VALUE<br>
</body></html>
```

8.21 Working with Exceptions and Response Status Codes

Problem

You want your service to throw exceptions under certain conditions, and deal with them appropriately on the client.

Solution

Create a response with the status code you want to set, and then set it into a WebApplicationException instance and throw it out of the method.

Discussion

Example 8-30 shows the class that handles this.

Example 8-30. Creating an exception and setting your own HTTP status

```
package com.soacookbook.rest.response;

import javax.ws.rs.GET;
import javax.ws.rs.Path;
import javax.ws.rs.WebApplicationException;
import javax.ws.rs.core.Response;

@Path("statuscode")
public class CustomStatusCode {

    @GET
    public Response doGet(){
        Response.ResponseBuilder responseBuilder =
            Response.status(Response.Status.BAD_REQUEST);
        Response response = responseBuilder.build();
        throw new WebApplicationException(response);
    }
}
```

The WebApplicationException is a runtime exception that you can use to issue clients standard HTTP response codes. The primary downside to the class is that it doesn't allow you to set your own message. The default message and description will be sent with the exception to clients. In the case of BAD_REQUEST, there is no message, and the description is merely "The request sent by the client was syntactically incorrect ()." There's no way that I'm aware of to change that message as of the current API, and still specify the response status directly using the WebApplicationException. You would think that something like this would do the trick:

```
RuntimeException re = new RuntimeException("My forbidden message...");
throw new WebApplicationException(re, 403);
```

But it doesn't. Your custom message is ignored, though your status code is retained (you could also have used the Status enum here). So if you really, really want to create a more descriptive response, you'll have to create another exception first, pass it into the WebApplicationException instance, and just return that.

I don't recommend the following code; it doesn't allow you to specify a meaningful status code with the exception (everything is just a 500 Internal Server Error), which is an important part of REST. Still, it does get your message to the client:

```
@GET
public Response doGet(){
   throw new RuntimeException("My forbidden message...");
}
```

The problem with this code is that it's confusing because it's lying. You're saying that the client tried to access a forbidden resource, but you're returning a status code of 500. You may be able to get away with such squirrelly things in the regular world of servlets and JSPs, where any exception just returns a web page anyway, but this is a real problem in REST. Of course, returning an entire stack trace to the client isn't exactly a best practice anyway, especially when it's in conflict with what's ostensibly the issue:

```
java.lang.RuntimeException: My forbidden message...
 com.soacookbook.rest.response.CustomStatusCode.doGet(CustomStatusCode.java:16)
 sun.reflect.NativeMethodAccessorImpl.invoke0(Native Method)
...
```

This is where custom exception mappers come in.

Using exception mappers

The response builder feature allows you to build responses that correspond to particular HTTP response types, including those that represent an error state such as Not Found. But JAX-RS also provides the WebApplicationException class as a general exception mechanism, as Java developers may be more accustomed to using exceptions in this way during development. If necessary, the WebApplicationException class can be extended to provide your own message, as in the following example:

```
public class MyException extends WebApplicationException {

    //creates a custom 404 Not Found exception
    public MyException() {
        super(Responses.notFound().build());
    }

    //msg represents the entity of the 404 response
    public MyException(String msg) {
        super(Response.status(Responses.NOT_FOUND).
                entity(msg).type("text/plain").build());
    }

}
```

Alternatively, you might find use for the web exception mapping feature. If there's an existing exception that you want to throw, you can use the `ExceptionMapper` interface. First, you annotate the mapper implementation with `@Provider` so that the JAX-RS runtime will pick it up. When a resource throws an exception that the runtime has a mapping for, it uses the exception provider (in the case of the next example, `FileNotFoundExceptionMapper`) to get its response, which you can build however you like. The response is processed as if the method in your service that threw the checked or runtime exception had instead returned the response built by the mapping implementation.

Example 8-31 illustrates a service that uses the exception mapping facility. The example simply throws a `FileNotFoundException` in order to demonstrate the execution mapping capability.

Example 8-31. ExceptionService.java

```
package com.soacookbook.rest.except;

import java.io.File;
import java.io.FileNotFoundException;

import javax.ws.rs.GET;
import javax.ws.rs.Path;
import javax.ws.rs.core.Response;

/**
 * Purposefully throws an exception in order to demonstrate
 * the Exception mapping capability.
 */
@Path("exception")
public class ExceptionService {

    @GET
    public Response doGet() throws FileNotFoundException {

        //build entity from file
        File file = new File("/path/doesnt/exist/file.txt");
        if( !file.exists() ) {
            System.out.println("Couln't find file.");
```

```
            throw new FileNotFoundException("My custom message.");
        }
        Response response = Response.ok(file).build();

        System.out.println("Returning exception response.");

        return response;
    }
}
```

In this example, you have a regular method that looks for a file on the server and, if it isn't found, throws a standard `java.io.FileNotFoundException`. This is a checked exception, so you declare it in the `throws` clause on the method. Because the path specified doesn't exist, invoking the service will throw this exception, and the `Response.ok` will never be built. Instead, the JAX-RS runtime will look in its list of provider implementations and attempt to map the exception to a suitable mapping implementation.

If an exception mapping provider can be found that matches the exact exception thrown or one of its superclasses, then JAX-RS will take the exception mapping provider implementation that represents the nearest match to the runtime type of the exception and use that to build the response.

If an exception is thrown during an attempt to put together a response inside an exception mapping implementation, the runtime will return a 500 Internal Server Error to the client.

Example 8-32 shows how `FileNotFoundExceptionMapper` implementation builds a 404 response with a custom message.

Example 8-32. FileNotFoundExceptionMapper.java

```
package com.soacookbook.rest.except;

import java.io.FileNotFoundException;

import javax.ws.rs.core.Response;
import javax.ws.rs.ext.ExceptionMapper;
import javax.ws.rs.ext.Provider;

/**
 * Maps a FileNotFoundException to a 404 and uses its message
 * in the response.
 */
@Provider
public class FileNotFoundExceptionMapper implements
ExceptionMapper<java.io.FileNotFoundException> {

    public Response toResponse(FileNotFoundException ex) {
        System.out.println("Returning mapped exception.");
```

```
        return Response.status(404)
          .entity(ex.getMessage())
          .type("text/plain")
          .build();
    }
}
```

If you deploy and then open the service URL at *http://localhost:8080/restexamples/resources/exception* in Firefox, you'll see the message indicated in the constructor of the `FileNotFoundException`: "My custom message". The response status code is still a 404, so browsers such as IE or Chrome may display their own standard error pages. But the point of this example is that you're getting your own message in there, and, more importantly, you're getting to program with exceptions in the way that Java developers are accustomed to doing. The mapping capability is also nice because the runtime loads your mapping and invokes it automatically as necessary, keeping your implementation loosely coupled.

8.22 Working with WADL

Problem

You've found a web service that exposes a WADL (Web Application Description Language) file and you want to generate portable Java objects based on the WADL. Or, you are publishing a "RESTful" web service and want to provide an interface for it that is simpler than WSDL and allows clients to generate code, and WADL seems perfect.

Solution

You can check out the WADL whitepaper at *http://research.sun.com/techrep/2006/abstract-153.html.*

If you want to use the `wadl2Java` tool to generate client code, it's available for the command line, Ant, and Maven at *https://wadl.dev.java.net/.*

Discussion

The WADL project started in 2006. WADL was created by Marc Hadley at Sun, and was conceived to "provide a machine processable protocol description format for use with...HTTP-based Web applications, especially those using XML." In other words, it's an attempt at an IDL for web apps.

That's just fine, and it may have some laudable uses. But it's not REST. The concern is not really about WADL itself, but rather that WADL subverts one of the central tenets of REST, which is *hypermedia as the engine of application state.*

Appendix A of the WADL specification uses an example similar to this (I've tightened it up):

```
<resources base="http://example.com/widgets">
  <resource>
    <path_variable>
    <method id="ItemSearch" name="GET">
      <request>
        <query_variable name="Operation" fixed="ItemSearch">
      </request>
      <response>
        <representation mediaType="text/xml"
          element="aws:ItemSearchResponse" />
      </response>
    </method>
  </resource>
</resources>
```

Now, to be fair, the WADL whitepaper never mentions the term REST a single time. However, this code example uses the terms *resource* and *representation* as if there is something RESTful going on. This is not RESTful. This is straight RPC.

It is not RESTful to provide a service that does not use hypermedia as the engine of application state, and rather acquiesces to a total reliance on out-of-band negotiation and code generation in order to communicate successfully with the service. The interface is completely described in terms of operations and parameters.

It's good to know about WADL, as it may be useful in situations where, for example, you want to provide some machine-readable description for test automation. That's actually a pretty interesting use for such a description. It's less clear how useful it is for something like documentation generation, as there is no room for commentary in the format, and you may as well generate documentation from a format more specifically suited to that purpose, and closer to the code itself.

Again, I have nothing against WADL in particular, but if you're a purist, it isn't RESTful.

8.23 Interacting with a Resource Using a Custom Reader and Writer

Problem

You want to create a web page that produces a representation of an item with HTML forms and allows the user to interact with it. You have a real-world compound object, such as a list of products, and you want to read and write its representation in an interactive HTML form.

Solution

Create a resource, and then create two classes: one that implements `MessageBodyWriter<T>` and another that implements `MessageBodyReader<T>`. Use the `@Produces` and

`@Consumes` annotations on them respectively. In the writer, produce the HTML form; in the reader, parse the incoming form data and create your objects with them.

This gets complex fairly quickly, so we'll look at a complete example in the discussion below. This example uses only JAX-RS standard code, so it's portable across implementations. I'm using Jersey here, but this would work in JBoss RESTEasy too.

Discussion

This application consists of four classes: a `Product` class that is a POJO containing two strings and an integer; a REST `Resource` class that manages the resource on the server; a `MessageBodyWriter` implementation that writes out the HTML form; and a `MessageBodyReader` implementation that gathers the form data and creates `Product` instances from it.

Figure 8-4 shows a screenshot of the application running in Tomcat, after submitting the form a few times. Open your browser to *http://localhost:8080/restexamples/resources/order* after deploying the application to see it working.

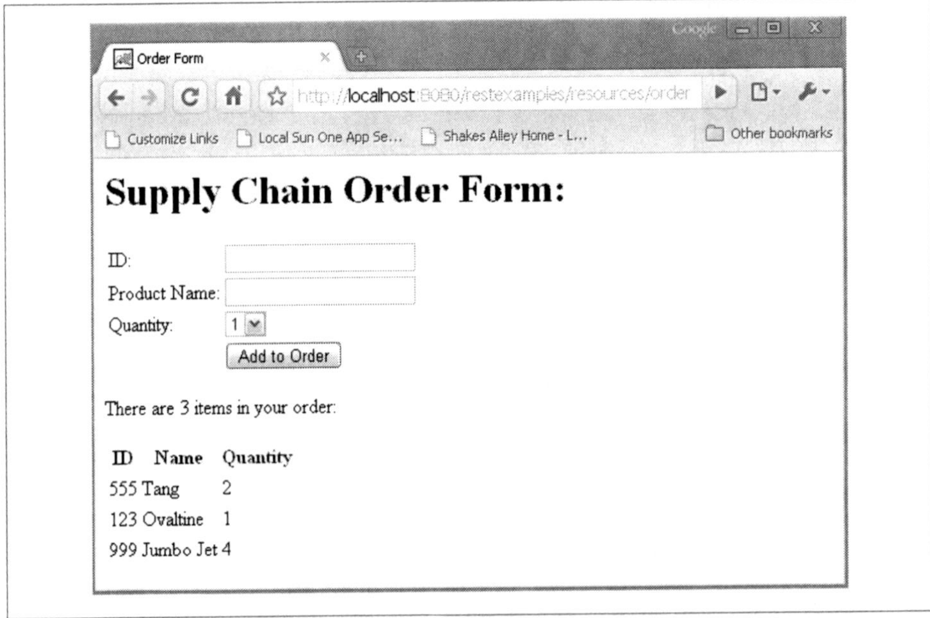

Figure 8-4. HTML form accepting data using a complex object

The primary purpose of this example, which is loosely based on an example that ships with the Jersey implementation, is to illustrate how to create an HTML form that represents your resource, and allow users to interact with that resource via the form representation. The resource in this example is a proxy for a list of products. The product is the basic unit of exchange in this example, and comprises two strings (ID and

Name) and an integer representing the quantity, in order to illustrate how to deal with complex, real-world objects. The Product class (which is a standard POJO) is shown in Example 8-33.

Example 8-33. The Product.java class

```
package com.soacoobook.rest.order;

public class Product {
    private String id;
    private String name;
    private int qty;

    public Product() {
        System.out.println("Creating empty product.");
    }

    public Product(String id) {
        System.out.println("Creating product: " + id);
        this.id = id;
        this.name = "";
        this.qty = 1;
    }

//setters and getters left out...

    @Override
    public String toString() {
        return "ID=" + id;
    }
}
```

The Product class doesn't contain any JAX-RS-specific code. It's just a regular class that might wrap a row in a database, and it follows the JavaBeans conventions.

The REST resource is shown in Example 8-34. It has both GET and POST methods for the list of products.

Example 8-34. The OrderResource.java class

```
package com.soacoobook.rest.order;

import java.util.ArrayList;
import java.util.List;
import javax.ws.rs.GET;
import javax.ws.rs.POST;
import javax.ws.rs.Produces;
import javax.ws.rs.Path;

/**
 * Collects the products that an inventory manager wants
 * to order from a vendor.
 */
@Path("order")
public class OrderResource {
```

```
    //holds products user adds to order
    private List<Product> products = new ArrayList<Product>();

    //constructor
    public OrderResource() {
        System.out.println("Constructing OrderResource");
    }

    @GET
    @Produces("text/html")
    public List<Product> getOrderHtml() {
        System.out.println("getOrderData. Items: " + products);

        return products;
    }

    @POST
    @Produces("text/html")
    public List<Product> addToOrder(List<Product> items) {
        System.out.println("addToOrder. Items: " + items);

        products.addAll(items);
        return products;
    }
}
```

The `OrderResource` class advertises a path using the `@Path` annotation, and returns an empty HTML form on GET requests. The `@GET` annotation on the `getOrderHtml` method indicates that this is the method that handles GET requests for this resource, and the method annotated with `@POST` handles any HTTP POST requests. An HTTP POST request posts the multi-part data that is generated for this request back to the same URI, and adds an instance of the `Product` class to the "database" represented by the `OrderResource` products list. Both methods produce HTML, as indicated by their `@Produces` annotation.

You can see that no HTML code is produced by these methods, despite what the annotations declare. They just deal with the list of `Product` POJOs. The JAX-RS API encourages strong separation of concerns, allowing the representations to be matched to the appropriate `Provider` classes at runtime. The runtime examines the HTTP method used to interact with the resource, finds a `Provider` that matches the `Content-Type`, and uses the matching `Writer` to create a response. Following a form post, the `addToOrder` method will be invoked by the runtime *after* the reader class has executed.

So the real sequence of events on the first visit to the page is as follows:

1. When you deploy the application, the JAX-RS runtime will search for available root resources and providers and store them so that it's ready to do mapping once requests come in.
2. On the first request for the order page, the runtime constructs the `OrderResource`. It will have an empty products list.

3. The resource's `getOrderData` method is invoked because the request is an HTTP GET, and that method features the `@GET` annotation.
4. The runtime checks to make sure that it can use an available provider to create a response. It finds the `@Produces` annotation with a value of `text/html`, and checks its `isWriteable` method to see whether the invoked method parameter (`List<Product>`) matches. It does, so the runtime selects the `ProductHtmlFormWriter` class to create its response.
5. The writer's `writeTo` method gets invoked to write the HTML response containing the empty form to the output stream.

Now that you've written the response to the browser, the user can fill out the form to add a product. Here's the sequence of events:

1. Once the user fills out the form and clicks Submit, the runtime determines that it needs to read the incoming response because its `@Consumes` annotation declares that it is a handler for the `application/x-www-form-urlencoded` MIME type.
2. The runtime further determines that your `ProductHtmlFormReader` class is the appropriate handler because it implements `MessageBodyReader<List<Product>>`. It does this with the `isReadable` method, which finds that the matching type is a `List`.
3. Your helper methods in this `Reader` class then break up the incoming request into a single string and parse that string for the form data. Form data is separated in HTML with ampersands (&) and can be inspected as key/value pairs. So once you parse that, you can create a new `Product` instance using the submitted data.
4. The reader method then adds the new product to the list that it's maintaining of all ordered products.
5. The runtime returns control to the `Resource` class and invokes its `addToOrder` method, which is mostly a pass-through.
6. You still have to write a response, so the runtime invokes your same `ProductHtmlFormWriter` class and returns the form. Because the writer receives the list of products from the resource, it can append to the bottom of the form something new: the previously ordered products. The HTML is written and returned to the output stream.

Now we'll look at the rest of the classes that make up the application. The `MessageBodyWriter` implementation is shown in Example 8-35.

Classes that implement the `MessageBodyReader<T>` and `MessageBodyWriter<T>` interfaces are called *entity providers*. Their job is to map representations to their associated Java types. The runtime uses the reader entity provider to map HTTP requests, and the writer is used to map HTTP responses.

Example 8-35. ProductHtmlFormWriter.java

```
package com.soacoobook.rest.order;

import javax.ws.rs.Produces;
import javax.ws.rs.ext.MessageBodyWriter;
import javax.ws.rs.ext.Provider;
import java.io.IOException;
import java.io.OutputStream;
import java.lang.annotation.Annotation;
import java.lang.reflect.Type;
import java.util.List;

import javax.ws.rs.core.MediaType;
import javax.ws.rs.core.MultivaluedMap;

/**
 * Creates an HTML form representing an order for a
 * supply chain. Users can submit the form back to this resource
 * to add items. The page shows all items from ordering analysts.
 */
@Produces("text/html")
@Provider
public class ProductHtmlFormWriter
    implements MessageBodyWriter<List<Product>> {

    public boolean isWriteable(Class<?> type, Type genericType,
        Annotation[] annotations, MediaType mediaType) {

        System.out.println("isWriteable");
        return List.class.isAssignableFrom(type);
    }

    public long getSize(List<Product> data,
        Class<?> type, Type genericType,
        Annotation annotations[], MediaType mediaType) {

        System.out.println("Writer.getSize");
        return -1;
    }

    /**
     * Here we create the representation of the order as an
     * HTML form. Note that we are dealing with a custom Java
     * type (List<Product>) directly.
     * The headers param shows Content-Type=[text/html].
     */
    public void writeTo(List<Product> products,
            Class<?> type, Type genericType,
            Annotation[] annotations, MediaType mediaType,
            MultivaluedMap<String, Object> headers,
            OutputStream out) throws IOException {

        System.out.println("writeTo");

        out.write(ORDER_HTML_FORM.getBytes());
```

```
        if (products.isEmpty()) {
            out.write(ORDER_EMPTY_HEADER.getBytes());
        } else {
            //there are items in order; show table of them
            out.write(String.format(
                    ITEMS_HEADER, products.size()).getBytes());

            for (Product p : products) {
                out.write("<tr><td>".getBytes());
                out.write(p.getId().getBytes());
                out.write("</td><td>".getBytes());
                out.write(p.getName().getBytes());
                out.write("</td>".getBytes());
                out.write("<td>".getBytes());
                out.write(Integer.toString(p.getQty()).getBytes());
                out.write("</td></tr>".getBytes());
            }
            out.write("</table></form>".getBytes());
        }
        out.write(END_HTML.getBytes());
    }

    private static String ORDER_HTML_FORM =
        "<!DOCTYPE HTML PUBLIC '-//W3C//DTD HTML 4.01 Transitional//EN'>\n" +
        "<html><head><title>Order Form</title></head>" +
        "<body><h1>Supply Chain Order Form:</h1>" +
        "<form name='order' action='order' method='POST'>" +
        "<table><tr>" +
        "<td align='left'>ID:</td>" +
        "<td><input type='text' name='id' value='' size='20' /></td>" +
        "</tr><tr>" +
        "<td align='left'>Product Name:</td>\n" +
        "<td><input type='text' name='name' value='' size='20' /></td>" +
        "</tr><tr>" +
        "<td align='left'>Quantity:</td>" +
        "<td><select name='qty' value='' />" +
        "<option>1</option><option>2</option>" +
        "<option>3</option><option>4</option></select>" +
        "</td></tr>" +
        "<tr><td></td>" +
        "<td><input type='submit' value='Add to Order' name='submit' />" +
        "</td></tr></table>";

    private static String ORDER_EMPTY_HEADER =
        "<p>There are no items in your order.</p>";

    private static String ITEMS_HEADER =
        "<p>There are %d items in your order:</p>" +
        "<table>" +
        "<tr><th>ID</th><th>Name</th><th>Quantity</th></tr>";

    private static String END_HTML = "</body></html>";
}
```

Once the runtime determines that the ProductHtmlFormWriter class is the appropriate handler for the incoming request (by invoking the isWriteable method), the writeTo method is invoked. The @Produces annotation indicates that the class creates HTTP responses. It is responsible for creating the HTTP response body. There are a few static strings that contain boilerplate HTML that make up the form, which you use to keep the main body of the method clear. All the writeTo method does is loop over the list of accumulated products and write them out as a table, and then present the HTML form.

After the user fills out the form and clicks Submit, the reader eventually gets invoked to accept the submitted form data and do something with it. The ProductHtmlForm Reader class is shown in Example 8-36.

Example 8-36. The ProductHtmlFormReader class accepts incoming HTML form data and parses it

```
package com.soacoobook.rest.order;

import java.io.BufferedReader;
import java.io.IOException;
import java.io.InputStream;
import java.io.InputStreamReader;
import java.lang.annotation.Annotation;
import java.lang.reflect.Type;
import java.net.URLDecoder;
import java.util.ArrayList;
import java.util.HashMap;
import java.util.List;
import java.util.Map;
import javax.ws.rs.Consumes;
import javax.ws.rs.core.MediaType;
import javax.ws.rs.core.MultivaluedMap;
import javax.ws.rs.ext.MessageBodyReader;
import javax.ws.rs.ext.Provider;

/**
 * Accepts the values from the HTML form to create our custom
 * Java type, Product.
 */
@Consumes("application/x-www-form-urlencoded")
@Provider
public class ProductHtmlFormReader implements MessageBodyReader<List<Product>> {

    private static String ENC = "UTF-8";

    //remembers all products
    private List<Product> cartProducts = new ArrayList<Product>();

    public boolean isReadable(Class<?> type, Type genericType,
            Annotation[] annotations, MediaType mediaType) {

        System.out.println("isReadable");

        return type.equals(List.class);
    }
```

```
    /*
     * Returns the list of products represented by this
     * application. If this only returned a single product,
     * you'd only see the last one added.
     */
    public List<Product> readFrom(Class<List<Product>> type,
            Type genericType,
            Annotation[] annotations, MediaType mediaType,
            MultivaluedMap<String, String> headers,
            InputStream inputFormData)
            throws IOException {

        System.out.println("readFrom");

        // get form data as a string
        String formData = formToString(inputFormData);

        // access elements from form data
        Map<String, String> form = formToMap(formData);

        // create a new product based on form data
        Product product = new Product();
        product.setId(form.get("id"));
        product.setName(form.get("name"));
        product.setQty(Integer.parseInt(form.get("qty")));

        cartProducts.add(product);

        System.out.println("Returning all products.");
        return cartProducts;
    }

    /*
     * Now that we have form data in a single string, parse it
     * to find the key/value pairs, bust them up, and put them
     * in a map.
     */
    private Map<String, String> formToMap(String formData)
        throws IOException {

        System.out.println("Breaking string of form into map.");

        Map<String, String> form = new HashMap<String, String>();
        String[] keyValuePairs = formData.split("&");
        for (int i = 0; i < keyValuePairs.length; i++) {
            String[] s = keyValuePairs[i].split("=");
            form.put(URLDecoder.decode(s[0], ENC),
                    URLDecoder.decode(s[1], ENC));
        }
        return form;
    }

    /*
     * Helper converts the form data input stream to a string
```

```
     * so we can read its values.
     */
    private String formToString(InputStream is) throws IOException {

        System.out.println("getting request input as string.");

        BufferedReader reader = new BufferedReader(
                new InputStreamReader(is));

        StringBuilder sb = new StringBuilder();
        String line;
        while ((line = reader.readLine()) != null) {
            sb.append(line);
        }

        is.close();
        reader.close();
        return sb.toString();
    }
}
```

The `ProductHtmlFormReader` class implements the `MessageBodyReader<T>` class. Its type parameter is `List<Product>` because that's what your resource deals with. The reader is invoked on an incoming POST request containing multi-part form data, as indicated by its `@Consumes` annotation. Once the runtime determines that this is the appropriate handler (using the `isReadable` method), the `readFrom` method is invoked. That method reads the incoming request to do something with its data payload. In this example, you use two helper methods to prepare the form data for creating the product posted by the user to add to the order. The `formToString` method takes the request input stream and wraps it with a buffered reader so that it's easy to break up into a single string. The resulting string is passed to the `formToMap` method, which parses the string for the key/value pairs that make up the form. Those key/value pairs represent the user's selections in the form, and match one-to-one the properties of your `Product` bean. So you use that data to construct a new `Product`, add it to the accumulating list, and return control to the resource.

Summary

The JAX-RS specification is slated to be included in Java EE 6, so it's not only a fun and easy API to use, but an important one as well. REST has gained significant popularity recently, and it will be interesting to see what impact on the world of web services JAX-RS will have in the future.

That having been said, JAX-RS != REST. The Atom Publishing Protocol != REST. These are useful frameworks for making lightweight web applications. They are covered in this chapter because they are important starting points for Java developers, and can certainly be used to create RESTful applications. Just don't fall into the trap of thinking that because you're using Jersey you're doing REST.

When designing a RESTful application, which you can do (or fail to do) with these frameworks, keep this in mind above all else: *hypermedia as the engine of application state*. Your application is a state machine, with every response containing the means to transition to any next possible state. This does three important things: it allows your applications to scale because state is not kept on the server; it frees the client from relying on out-of-band negotiations (as is the case with WSDL client code generation); and it allows the server to change the shape of URIs (other than the root) as it sees fit, which gives your infrastructure team some real flexibility.

PART III

Business Processes

CHAPTER 9
Service Orchestrations with BPEL

9.0 Introduction

In previous chapters, we've seen how to build well-formed web services. Services represent the basic building blocks of a service-oriented architecture. But by definition, a well-made service must be loosely coupled from other services. It must, in general, leave routing logic up to an external component such as an enterprise service bus. The real promise of SOA is not realized by building services alone, but by defining clear services with high cohesion, that wholly describe their interactions and that are then capable of being reused, through composition, in a variety of process-based services.

The key design principles of SOA include:

- Loose coupling, which means that a change to one component results in minimal or no change to other related components.
- Interoperability, which builds on the idea of loose coupling to suggest that services should be able to exchange messages with other services, even if they are implemented in different languages and their platforms differ dramatically.
- Reusability, which means that more than one application can act as a client of your service without resorting to internal service changes. Services must be autonomous, or capable of running independently, and be designed in logical divisions that fully encapsulate their business logic.
- Discoverability, which means that a service's execution environment and contract allow it to be looked up, bound to, and invoked at runtime.

These goals are interrelated, so fulfilling one or two of them usually gives you a head start on fulfilling the others. At this point, you know how to create a single service that can be invoked by one or more clients, such as a website or point of sale system. But what about more complex systems that require invoking multiple services? If the client is your point of sale system, and you need to create a workflow surrounding an invoice, you are immediately faced with the choice of where to put the flow logic. Your first thought might be to bake it into the client system itself. But that process cannot then be captured very easily as an abstraction; it encourages tighter coupling between the client and each service it invokes in the flow. If you later create another point of sale-like system, say one that works from a handheld device or a website or even a lighter version of the system that can be used out in the field, you have to recreate that work. Moreover, such a strategy begins to undermine the whole point of using web services in the first place. Flow logic is likely to grow or change somewhat as business processes change, and versioning or updates can become difficult. You may find that the application is "chattier" than you want between client and server as well, and it would be nice if you could reduce some of the load on that part of the network and move it to the server where you can balance things better and distribute the load.

In order to address these problems, you might then think to move the flow logic into a wrapper service that can be used on the server side. This service could act as the use case director, expose a WSDL that the client communicates with, and that service could define all of the steps in the flow. This is closer to what you want, but it bakes the logic into a platform-specific language, such as Java, making the process less transparent, and it puts the responsibility for the process firmly in the hands of the developer. If you want more robust features of workflows, such as parallel execution and correlation, you have to home-grow a complex threading mechanism to handle it. You are also dealing with the messages in a platform-specific manner, that is, in Java code, and not in their raw XML format. This can have performance benefits that may be required in some cases, but it also takes you further away from the fundamental goals of SOA, highlighted earlier. You are suddenly spending more time dealing with your platform than we are solving business problems.

What you really want is a way to express the flow in the language of the business, something that is sufficiently abstract and catered more to analysts and architects. Such a language could be expressed visually and easily, but ultimately be exposed as a WSDL and execute on the server so that it's invokable as a service. What you want, in the world of SOA, is called an orchestration. And orchestrations are often executed using BPEL, or Business Process Execution Language.

Let's look at a slightly different example to tie all of this together. Imagine you have defined a small catalog of web services for the following tasks:

- A service that allows HR to modify employee data in your payroll system
- A service that captures signatures on a reader device used in your retail stores
- A service that wraps communication to and from a benefits provider

These services can operate independently in different areas of your business, under different problem domains. Each of them fulfills its function appropriately and is self-contained. But consider how they might be combined as a composite service for handling new hires in your company. You could create a new process that indicates each step required for employee intake: adding someone to the payroll system, having them sign a variety of HR documents by capturing their digital signature, and passing the necessary collected data to the benefits provider service to get the new hire set up with insurance or 401K enrollment. The process would indicate the order in which each service should be invoked, and how to respond to different messages. For example, you might want to invoke the benefits service only if the employee will be working full time. Or perhaps the payroll system takes some length of time to complete an internal operation, so instead of sitting around waiting for it to finish, you'd like to have certain parts of the process execute concurrently.

Such a business process that defines a new service by reusing existing services in a composition would require an environment of its own in which to execute. Of course, you could just write some procedural Java code to perform each step in your process, but you'd like to expose the process itself as a service.

BPEL (commonly pronounced "BEE-pell" or "bipple") provides the orchestration layer within a SOA. Orchestrations define the business process around which services will be invoked. A deployed BPEL application represents a new, complex composite service that is composed of basic services. A BPEL is an XML document, with a *.bpel* extension, that conforms to the WS-BPEL standard and executes in its own environment, a BPEL engine.

Benefits of BPEL

There are several benefits to using BPEL as a central component within a SOA:

- It's an industry standard. BPEL was originally released as a specification in July of 2002 in a joint effort by BEA, Microsoft, and IBM. More recent versions of the spec contain contributions from SAP and Siebel Systems. Since its original release, it has undergone revision and close scrutiny, and was eventually released to OASIS Open for maintenance by a technical committee as an open standard. Therefore, you can implement BPEL processes without fear of vendor lock-in, and without worrying that you are basing your work on an untested fad that only operates in a tiny corner of the IT universe.
- It's designed as part of the web services stack. While you aren't limited to using SOAP messages in your orchestrations, it does use WSDL, and you can leverage SOAP, WS-Addressing, security, and other integral aspects of the WS-* specifications.
- It's purely XML, so it's portable across platforms and vendors. It relies on XML schema for its data model, and BPEL documents are human-readable and can be processed and transformed with any XML tools.
- It abstracts business logic, and acts as a reusable container for service compositions. Because processes are exposed as WSDLs, sophisticated orchestrations may invoke other orchestrations along with other individual service implementations. Because the flow directives are abstracted up to a BPEL, your service implementations are free to remain highly cohesive.

BPEL Engine and Designer Implementations

The BPEL engine is a new component in your SOA, and there are a variety of commercial and open source products available.

Open source and free implementations include Apache ODE and Sun's BPEL Service Engine, available within OpenESB. The Active BPEL engine, provided by Active Endpoints, is available either as a free community edition or as a commercial product with support. Other commercial products include Microsoft's BizTalk server and Oracle BPEL Process Manager. Because BPEL is a standard, you can generally port a BPEL across any of these platforms (assuming that you don't go off the deep end using vendor-specific extensions).

The second aspect of working with BPEL is the process designer. Because BPEL is just XML, you could write BPEL using a plain-text editor. The same is true for Java or C#, of course, although in practice, we often prefer to use tools to aid us, especially important when we're first learning. In the same way, a good BPEL designer can clarify and validate your work and present a visual representation akin to UML modeling tools.

Some of the companies that offer execution engines also offer visual process designers. For example, Active Endpoints' ActiveBPEL Designer has tight integration with their engine. Processes for deployment to Sun's BPEL Service Engine for OpenESB can be created using NetBeans 6.X. There is an Eclipse plug-in project that turns Eclipse into a BPEL editor. (However, the plug-in is in milestone release and doesn't seem to have been updated in a while, so the status of that project isn't clear.) Many of the big-ticket stack vendors (IBM, Sun, etc.) offer designer solutions specific to their runtime engines as well. Overall, you have a lot of options here.

BPMN (Business Process Management Notation)

In your search to achieve SOA greatness, you may have heard discussion of BMPN, or Business Process Management Notation. This notation is similar to UML in that it allows analysts and architects to create diagrams that represent a business flow. There is a defined relationship between BPMN and BPEL that's worth noting.

The OMG (Object Management Group), which maintains the UML specification, has published the BPMN specification. It is available at *http://www.bpmn.org*. The purpose of BPMN is to allow business people to describe a process flow from a high level. BPEL is more suited to technical people, and BPMN is more suited to managers and analysts who wish to monitor a process, and visualize it in a flow chart format using a graphical language. To this end, BPMN describes a variety of standard constructs, such as flow objects, connectors, events, gateways, artifacts, associations, and swim lanes, which are used to logically group the other constructs.

In general, the vision for BPMN is that business analysts can create BPMN flows outside of IT. These documents serve purely as executable representations of how a business actually does its work. Some of the tools offer ways to test the flows. When the business analyst is satisfied with the result, she can then turn it over to IT. IT will use tools to generate a set of more technical BPEL documents from that higher-level notation. Each BPMN pool will map to a different BPEL document, which can then be executed in an engine. The BPMN specification is fairly specific about how its constructs should map to BPEL constructs.

Some platform-agnostic tools, such as MagicDraw UML 10.5, offer a way to create BPMN and then export it to BPEL. Many other vendors also offer BPMN products. Prominent among them is AquaLogic BPM from BEA (now Oracle). These tools handle artifacts in different ways. BEA's designer, for example, will export to portlets. Software AG's BPM suite will export to BPEL, but that isn't necessary, as it rolls up its BPM files into a proprietary format that is itself deployable and executable on its server platform. The same is true for Savvion's BPM Server product (*http://www.savvion.com*). An important advantage of using BPMN is that it can represent workflows that include human tasks.

Overview

In this chapter, we'll look at how to get up and running with a couple of the more popular BPEL engines. Some of them execute as a process, and some are easily installed as a WAR within a servlet container. We'll learn BPEL by walking through the problems it solves, step by step. Overall, you have some choices to make about which engine best suits your environment, so we'll try a variety of them before jumping into the standard constructs. While the design tools ostensibly allow you to do all of your work using visual models, in practice I've usually found it easier to work directly with the XML, or toggle back and forth between the graphical and source code views. The emphasis in this chapter is on getting the source-level constructs straight so that you can always solve your problems in a standard, portable manner.

9.1 Determining a Process Design Method

Problem

You want to start designing a business process, but you're not sure where to start.

Solution

Use the Top-Down approach, the Bottom-Up approach, or a combination of the two, the Meet in the Middle approach.

Discussion

These three approaches are discussed in the following sections.

The Top-Down approach

With the Top-Down approach, you sketch out the process that you want to create. You might conduct interviews with stakeholders in your organization and determine exactly what needs to happen for a given business process. You could record this information on pencil and paper or a white board, and eventually transfer the flow to a visual BPEL process designer.

You can then start designing composite services. Break up tasks into hierarchies, and be sure to keep the service granularity at the appropriate level of abstraction, as described in Chapter 1. In short, you want to view your services and the compositions from the invoker's perspective, and consider what that invoker would like to see as parameters and returns. What would a dream invocation of your service look like? It must be simple and clear, but also complete.

Once all that is done, you can start to add technical details to the process, such as the port type data and the WSDLs of the services involved. Build out the composite service as an orchestration by adding conditional logic, transformations, and error handling.

This approach is best when someone in your organization has come up with a new business idea or when you are charged with streamlining an existing process, such as purchasing. You may not have all of the services that you need to complete the orchestration already available, but once you've identified what you need, you can build or purchase them.

This can also be a good approach when your team is organized into architects or business modelers and analysts who can represent the abstract process itself, and developers who can implement the concrete services and bindings. With the Top-Down approach, both teams can work somewhat concurrently, with little overlap of work.

The Bottom-Up approach

With the Bottom-Up approach, you use a collection of services that you already have available (perhaps, within an enterprise repository in your organization) to build out a service composition. You already have complete and valid WSDLs, and you want to combine existing functionality to make something new.

Of course, this approach only works when you have a large variety of services available that you can combine to create a new process. You may find that if you have designed services at an appropriate level of granularity within your organization, you can find new uses for existing services within compositions. For example, a service that is used to capture customer signatures in a retail store could also be used in designing a service for new hires who have extensive paperwork to fill out.

The Meet in the Middle approach

This approach combines the qualities of the previous two techniques. This is typically most realistic once you have developed several services or have a business partner whose services you subscribe to. In general, you can accept a workflow from a designer and create service interfaces with stub implementations; this allows you to work concurrently. The analyst can fine tune the process while you implement the services.

9.2 Selecting a Business Process Language

Problem

You want to begin implementing your defined business process in an executable process modeling language that supports visualization by analysts and architects.

Solution

In Java environments, choose between BPMN, BPEL, and jPDL. Or use them in tandem.

Discussion

There are many good ways to represent workflows. Let's take a quick look at how the most popular business process languages relate to one another and so that you can determine which is most appropriate for your environment.

BPMN

BPMN is a graphical language that is executable; see the sidebar "BPMN (Business Process Management Notation)" on page 480. Many BPMN tools are fairly high level, and come bundled within product suites that define separate roles for developers and analysts. Typically, these design tools (many of which are based on Eclipse or ship as Eclipse plug-ins) deploy a completed business process into a proprietary format that runs on a given vendor's server software.

jPDL

Like BPEL, jPDL (Java Process Definition Language) was created to express long-running processes. The chief difference between the two is that developers write BPEL processes using an XML grammar, and jPDL uses Java directly. The XML grammar is an advantage if you want to perform some sort of transformation on process code itself or port your process to another environment. It's a disadvantage, however, if you have limited resources because it does force you to learn that grammar pretty well. For this reason, Java developers may find jPDL more native and intuitive.

Because jPDL won't be covered in much depth in this book, let's take a moment to get a feel for it here. Following are a few of its important distinguishing characteristics:

Swimlanes
: jPDL supports the notion of swimlanes much as BPMN does. BPEL does not offer an analogous way to organize partners into roles within a process.

Expression Language
: The robust support for jPDL within the JBoss suite of products means that developers can take advantage of integration with Seam/Web beans. Using the Expression Language, you can integrate your process with any named object in any Seam context.

Human tasks
: jPDL offers support for defining business processes that are composed in part of steps that humans must complete. In BPEL, human tasks are not handled directly, and require an extension.The competing specifications in the BPEL realm are WS-HumanTask and an IBM whitepaper called "BPEL4People." WS-HumanTask was published by a consortium, including Oracle, SAP, Active Endpoints, IBM, and Adobe in June 2007.

Embeddable
: Because it is pure Java, jPDL can be embedded easily in libraries, databases, or other Java-based tools.

Ultimately, I think that the difference between BPEL and jPDL comes down to this: jPDL is about task management in Java, and BPEL is focused on creating composite applications in XML. You might consider using jPDL when you have existing Java POJOs (Plain Old Java Objects) that you want to combine within a task management flow, and BPEL when your process steps need to be executed by external web services. Because of the growing popularity of BPMN, and the fact that it exports (if roughly) to BPEL, we won't cover jPDL much further in this book. However, it's an interesting and useful technology. It is also worth noting that JBoss's jBPM platform supports not only jPDL, but also BPEL, pageflows, and others because its runtime is implemented on top of a "process virtual machine." Which is pretty slick.

BPEL

We're going to be spending a lot of time covering BPEL, so I won't rehash its features here. BPEL is the focus of this chapter because it is written in an XML grammar and does not require you to write Java code, which is a potential advantage over jPDL in flexibility. Also, despite solid support for jPDL from vendors such as JBoss/RedHat, BPEL is more widely supported.

Microsoft products such as BizTalk can execute BPEL, as can a variety of Java engines.

9.3 Getting Apache ODE BPEL Engine

Problem

You want to try a free and open source orchestration engine. BPEL is new to you, and it's a complex world, so you'd like to get up and running quickly with minimum fuss.

Solution

Download Apache ODE (Orchestration Director Engine) from *http://ode.apache.org*. It is distributed as a WAR, which you can install in the servlet container of your choice.

The download will contain a variety of items. Extract the compressed download, and in the root directory will be a file called *ode.war*, which is the deployable BPEL engine. If you're using Tomcat, simply drop that file into the *webapps* directory. In Glassfish or WebLogic, you can use their web consoles to deploy the WAR.

As an alternative, ODE is available as a JBI Service Engine for you to plug into a JBI container such as OpenESB or Apache ServiceMix. If that's your aim, there's a separate ZIP file you can download containing the JBI service assembly. We'll look at JBI more later.

For now, I'll assume you're using Tomcat 6. Start Tomcat by executing the *startup.bat* (Windows) or *startup.sh* (Linux) script, and if you have already copied *ode.war* into the *webapps* directory, ODE will start up after Tomcat does. Otherwise, drop it in now, and the poller will pick up your new application.

To test your installation, open *http://localhost:8080/ode* in a browser. You should see a page like the one shown in Figure 9-1.

Now you should be ready to deploy a process to the engine. We'll see how to do that in Recipe 9.4.

Discussion

Apache ODE is compliant with WS-BPEL 2.0. The current version as of this writing is 1.2.

All build artifacts are also available via the Maven 2 repository available at *http://repo1.maven.org/maven2/org/apache/ode*.

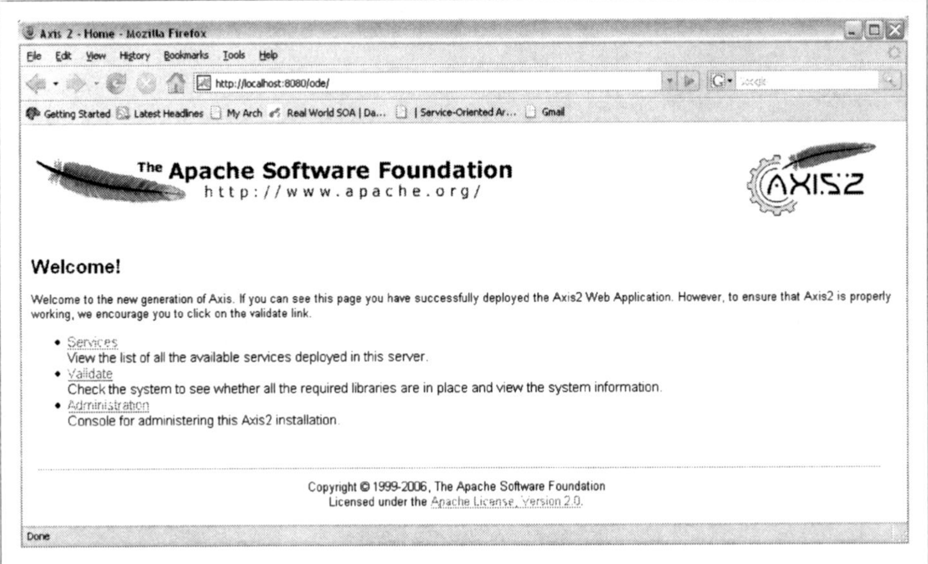

Figure 9-1. Apache ODE/Axis 2 welcome page

9.4 Deploying a Process to Apache ODE

Problem

You have Apache ODE up and running, and you want to deploy a process to it.

Solution

Deploy one of the examples that ships with ODE by copying the examples folder from the ODE distribution into the *$TOMCAT_HOME/webapps/ode/WEB-INF/processes* directory and then invoking the provided sample client, which sends a SOAP message to the process.

If you already have a process developed that ODE can handle, copy the entire directory contents and the enclosing directory itself into the processes folder under *WEB-INF/processes* directory, which is located in your application server's exploded ODE WAR file.

In Glassfish, you can put the process under the exploded ODE WAR at *$GLASSFISH_HOME/domains/domain_name/applications/j2ee-modules/ode/WEB-INF/processes*.

Discussion

The ODE examples are easy to use and are self-contained. By deploying the examples and browsing the code, you can quickly get a feel for how BPEL works, which will give you a larger context when we examine local BPEL constructs later.

The examples use an executable script to send SOAP messages from the filesystem into the BPEL process. We'll start with the HelloWorld2 example.

Running the HelloWorld2 example

Navigate to the directory into which you inflated the ODE ZIP distribution. This will be something like *apache-ode-war-1.1.1*. Navigate to the *bin* directory, and you should see a file called *sendsoap*. This executable will set up your classpath to include libraries in the *ode/lib* directory, and then invoke a class called `HttpSoapSender` in *ode-tools.jar*.

The first thing to do is get the BPEL executables deployed so that you have something to invoke. To do this, copy the *$ODE_HOME/examples/HelloWorld2* directory into the *$TOMCAT_HOME/webapps/ode/WEB-INF/processes* directory. If the process deployed successfully, you should see some Tomcat log entries like this:

```
DEBUG - GeronimoLog.debug(66) | Activated {http://ode/bpel/unit-test}HelloWorld2-1
DEBUG - GeronimoLog.debug(66) | Rehydrating process {http://ode/bpel/unit-test}
HelloWorld2-1
DEBUG - GeronimoLog.debug(66) | Creating process DAO for {http://ode/bpel/unit-test}
HelloWorld2-1
(guid=hqejbhcnphr3cqjo1clone)
INFO - GeronimoLog.info(79) | Registered process {http://ode/bpel/unit-test}
HelloWorld2-1.
INFO - GeronimoLog.info(79) | Deployment of artifact HelloWorld2 successful:
[{http://ode/bpel/unit-test}HelloWorld2-1]
```

If you return to the ODE home page at *http://localhost:8080/ode*, you should now see your Hello World process listed along with the others. The URL to invoke the process will be displayed, along with available operations. If you click the link around the name, you will be taken to the process WSDL.

It looks much like any other WSDL. You'll notice that there is a message defined in the inline schema that indicates what type of message the process expects to receive when it's invoked:

```
<xsd:element name="hello">
<xsd:complexType>
<xsd:sequence>
    <xsd:element form="unqualified" name="TestPart" type="xsd:string"/>
</xsd:sequence>
</xsd:complexType>
</xsd:element>
```

And the following element indicates what type of response it will generate:

```
<xsd:element name="helloResponse">
<xsd:complexType>
```

```
<xsd:sequence>
    <xsd:element form="unqualified" name="TestPart" type="xsd:string"/>
</xsd:sequence>
</xsd:complexType>
</xsd:element>
```

You may also notice that at the bottom of the WSDL, there are multiple bindings provided in the bindings and service sections:

```
<wsdl:service name="helloWorld">
<wsdl:port name="helloWorldSOAP11port_http" binding="tns:helloWorldSOAP11Binding">
    <soap:address location="http://localhost:8080/ode/processes/helloWorld"/>
</wsdl:port>
<wsdl:port name="helloWorldSOAP12port_http" binding="tns:helloWorldSOAP12Binding">
    <soap12:address location="http://localhost:8080/ode/processes/helloWorld"/>
</wsdl:port>
<wsdl:port name="helloWorldHttpport" binding="tns:helloWorldHttpBinding">
     <http:address location="http://localhost:8080/ode/processes/helloWorld"/>
</wsdl:port>
</wsdl:service>
```

This design allows clients to choose either SOAP 1.1 or SOAP 1.2 for communicating with the service.

So to invoke a client that will send a message to the process, run this command from the ODE distribution's *bin* directory:

```
$ sendsoap http://localhost:8080/ode/processes/helloWorld examples/HelloWorld2/
testRequest.soap
```

The initial request may take a second, and then you'll see the log of the SOAP response if it's successful:

```
$ bin/sendsoap http://localhost:8080/ode/processes/helloWorld examples/Hello
World2/testRequest.soap
WARN - 2008-06-14 14:41:04,820 - <org.apache.commons.httpclient.HttpMethodBase>
Going to buffer response body of large or unknown size. Using getResponseBodyAsStream
instead is recommended.
<?xml version='1.0' encoding='UTF-8'?>
<soapenv:Envelope xmlns:soapenv="http://schemas.xmlsoap.org/soap/envelope/">
<soapenv:Body>
<axis2ns1:helloResponse xmlns:axis2ns1="http://ode/bpel/unit-test.wsdl">
  <TestPart xmlns:SOAP-ENV="http://schemas.xmlsoap.org/soap/envelope/"
    xmlns:ns1="http://ode/bpel/unit-test.wsdl">Hello World</TestPart>
</axis2ns1:helloResponse>
</soapenv:Body></soapenv:Envelope>
```

Buried in some considerable text is the venerable message, "Hello World". This SOAP response of course matches the element described in the inline schema.

As you can see, from this perspective there is not really any difference between invoking a BPEL process and invoking any other web service. Its interface is defined with WSDL, and you send and receive messages, usually in SOAP. The only thing that's really new here is the BPEL itself, so in the next recipe, we'll peek over the other side of the wall and see what is happening to your `TestPart` request once the service receives it.

9.5 Understanding BPEL Process Basics

Problem

You want to see a simple BPEL process to get an overview of how to create composite service orchestrations, without getting in too much detail.

Solution

If you deployed the Apache ODE Hello World example in the previous recipe, navigate to the *$TOMCAT_HOME/webapps/ode/WEB-INF/processes/HelloWorld2* folder and open the *HelloWorld2.bpel* file with a text editor.

Discussion

Here's a quick overview of the sorts of things you can do with BPEL to give you an idea of the scope of the language:

- Receive a client request message with `<receive>`.
- Invoke other web services within the composition using `<invoke>`.
- Send a response back to invoking clients using `<reply>`.
- Copy data from part of one message or variable into another using `<assign>`.
- Represent exceptions and handle them using `<throw>`, `<catch>`, and `<catchAll>`.
- Implement conditional logic using `<switch>`, `<if>`, `<else>`, and `<pick>`.
- Loop using `<while>`.
- Perform a step in the process after a duration or on a certain date and time using `<wait>`.

There are a variety of other constructs to help you create robust workflows in BPEL, but these are the basic items that you'll use most frequently.

In the last recipe, you deployed the Hello World example that ships with the Apache ODE BPEL engine. Let's open the file to see that there really isn't any magic to putting these puzzle pieces together.

Other than the standard Apache license, Example 9-1 shows the complete, portable HelloWorld2 process file.

What's not portable across BPEL engines is the way in which you deploy a process to the engine. While the process itself can easily be moved, you generally need to supply some sort of deployment descriptor to give the engine hooks into the process.

Example 9-1. Apache ODE's HelloWorld2.bpel

```
<process name="HelloWorld2"
    targetNamespace="http://ode/bpel/unit-test"
    xmlns="http://docs.oasis-open.org/wsbpel/2.0/process/executable"
    xmlns:tns="http://ode/bpel/unit-test"
    xmlns:xsd="http://www.w3.org/2001/XMLSchema"
    xmlns:test="http://ode/bpel/unit-test.wsdl"
    queryLanguage="urn:oasis:names:tc:wsbpel:2.0:sublang:xpath2.0"
    expressionLanguage="urn:oasis:names:tc:wsbpel:2.0:sublang:xpath2.0">

  <import location="HelloWorld2.wsdl"
    namespace="http://ode/bpel/unit-test.wsdl"
     importType="http://schemas.xmlsoap.org/wsdl/" />

   <partnerLinks>
      <partnerLink name="helloPartnerLink"
         partnerLinkType="test:HelloPartnerLinkType"
         myRole="me" />
   </partnerLinks>

   <variables>
     <variable name="myVar" messageType="test:HelloMessage"/>
     <variable name="tmpVar" type="xsd:string"/>
   </variables>

   <sequence>
       <receive
          name="start"
          partnerLink="helloPartnerLink"
          portType="test:HelloPortType"
          operation="hello"
          variable="myVar"
          createInstance="yes"/>

      <assign name="assign1">
          <copy>
              <from variable="myVar" part="TestPart"/>
              <to variable="tmpVar"/>
          </copy>
          <copy>
              <from>concat($tmpVar,' World')</from>
              <to variable="myVar" part="TestPart"/>
          </copy>
      </assign>
       <reply name="end"
              partnerLink="helloPartnerLink"
              portType="test:HelloPortType"
              operation="hello"
              variable="myVar"/>
   </sequence>
</process>
```

The process life cycle includes a receiving a message, working with the message data in the form of variables, invoking partner web services to complete different steps in the process, and then replying to the invoker. Let's now examine each of the basic building blocks of a BPEL process.

The <process> element

The root element is `<process>`, which opens all BPEL documents. It declares namespaces used within the process, and it indicates a variety of optional directives. The namespace declaration is `http://docs.oasis-open.org/wsbpel/2.0/process/executable`, which is the standard namespace for BPEL 2.0 processes.

The `<process>` element also defines a set of attributes (see Table 9-1) that can be used as directives to the engine for how to handle various aspects of the executing workflow.

Table 9-1. Attributes of the <process> element

Attribute	Purpose
`queryLanguage`	Specifies the language to use when selecting nodes within the XML messages. The default value is "urn:oasis:names:tc:wsbpel:2.0:sublang:xpath1.0", which indicates that the process uses XPath 1.0.
`expressionLanguage`	Indicates what expression language will be used for `assign` activities. The default value is "urn:oasis:names:tc:wsbpel:2.0:sublang:xpath1.0", which indicates that the process uses XPath 1.0.
`suppressJoinFailure`	Indicates whether or not to expose the fault generated when a join has failed. The default value is "no". This can be overridden by child activities or local scopes; if they don't define this attribute themselves, then the value will be inherited from the closest enclosing scope.
`exitOnStandardFault`	If the value is "yes", the process will immediately stop in the event that any fault is thrown during execution. If the value is "no", the process can execute any fault handlers that have been defined. The default value is "no". This can be overridden by child activities or local scopes; if they don't define this attribute themselves, the value will be inherited from the closest enclosing scope.

BPEL Portability

While it's generally true that BPELs are portable, there are often things you have to tweak, just like when porting Java code from one platform to another. The most prominent is clearly proprietary vendor extensions. If you use vendor shortcuts purposefully, or use their tools and don't realize that they are baking in proprietary extensions, you may find your porting effort more difficult.

There are also minor differences in implementations that might not allow you to simply copy-and-paste a *.bpel* file from one engine to another and have it work right out of the box. While one might hope that something as simple as "Hello World" would have the best chance of being instantly portable, there are subtleties that could catch you. An example with the ODE Hello World BPEL is the declaration of `expressionLanguage="urn:oasis:names:tc:wsbpel:2.0:sublang:xpath2.0"`. Their engine implementation supports the use of XPath 2.0 expressions when working with message data; Sun's BPEL Service Engine supports only XPath 1.0 (which is the standard that BPEL 2.0 supports). Also, not all engines support expression language dictation for all elements. Just something to be aware of.

The <import> element

The `<import>` is used to declare a dependency on either an XML schema or a WSDL. In this example, the `<import>` looks like this:

```
<import location="HelloWorld2.wsdl"
    namespace="http://ode/bpel/unit-test.wsdl"
    importType="http://schemas.xmlsoap.org/wsdl/" />
```

Of the three attributes, only the `importType` is required, as the standard namespaces are used to define WSDL or schema.

If you want your import type to be XML schema, use `http://www.w3.org.2001/XMLSchema`.

If you do not specify a namespace, the imported definitions will not be namespace qualified. If you do not specify a location, the BPEL processor will not be required to retrieve the imported document.

According to the specification, "if an external item is used by a WS-BPEL process, then a document (or namespace) that defines that item *must* be directly imported by the process." Elements are not transitively imported—this is explicitly disallowed by the BPEL 2.0 spec.

As an example, say that you have defined a business process P1 that imports a schema S1 that defines a type T1. T1 refers to another type T2, defined in a second schema document S2. If P1 imports S1, it can refer to S1 and use its element T1 successfully in the process execution. However, it cannot directly refer to T2 anywhere in the process, unless it also explicitly imports the S2 schema that defines it.

In the Hello World example here, the process imports a WSDL that is concretely defined and available in the same directory as the BPEL file. The WSDL defines some partner links that the process uses, which is the reason for the import. Specifically, if you look at that WSDL file, it has a section like this:

```
<plnk:partnerLinkType name="HelloPartnerLinkType">
     <plnk:role name="me" portType="tns:HelloPortType"/>
     <plnk:role name="you" portType="tns:HelloPortType"/>
</plnk:partnerLinkType>
```

Partner links can be thought of as business partners; they define the different parties that are consulted during the execution of the business process. Here, both the `<receive>` activity, which receives new messages, and the `<reply>` activity, which sends the response back to the invoker, use the partner link type `test:HelloPartnerLinkType`. This type is not defined directly in the process but rather in the imported WSDL. We'll look into partner links more later; for now, all you need to know is that is how the process communicates with other web services.

The <sequence> activity

The `<sequence>` activity is just a wrapper that defines a collection of activities that should be executed sequentially.

The <receive> activity

The `<receive>` activity is really the port of entry for a process. It represents the first item in a process that will be invoked when a message arrives. Essentially, processes wait for a message to arrive that matches the definition in the `<receive>` activity, which is complete once the message arrives. The `<receive>` activity captures the incoming message in a variable (in this case, "myVar") so that it is available for the remainder of the process, does a few other things, and exits.

Just as it can be helpful to think of a WSDL `portType` as a Java interface, you can think of a BPEL `<receive>` activity like a `main` method in Java; it's the first thing that happens when a process is invoked.

Here is the Hello World `<receive>` activity again:

```
<receive
   name="start"
   partnerLink="helloPartnerLink"
   portType="test:HelloPortType"
   operation="hello"
   variable="myVar"
   createInstance="yes"/>
```

The `createInstance` attribute indicates whether a new instance should be dedicated to the execution of this process. The `<receive>` activity is known as a "start" activity because it is capable of receiving messages and marks the beginning of a process. There is one other start activity, `<pick>`, which waits for a message to arrive that corresponds to one within a set of possible messages, and then executes the activity associated with it.

The <assign> activity

Now that the incoming message has been captured, the next activity is almost always an `<assign>`, as is the case in this example. Assignment consists of copying variable data. It can also be used to create new data based on expressions.

The <reply> activity

The `<reply>` activity is usually the final activity within a BPEL process. Once the message has been received and the main message exchange processing is complete, you may want to return a response of some kind to the invoker. You do this with a `<reply>` activity.

This brief overview of basic building blocks within BPEL should have given you a feel for how BPEL works in general. Upcoming recipes will look more closely at various activities and language constructs.

9.6 Using a Free Graphical Designer to Create BPEL Processes

Problem

You want to create your BPEL processes quickly and easily using a graphical notation, but you don't want to pay for expensive commercial tools.

Solution

Get the BPEL designer plug-in for NetBeans 6.X.

Discussion

BPEL is XML-based, and because it is a structured procedural language (meaning it contains constructs such as if/then, while, sequences, and so on), it is not difficult to write. However, there are times when it is easier to use a graphical tool to generate the XML for you by just dragging and dropping items onto a process page. You can then switch to the XML source view as necessary to tweak various aspects of your process. Using the NetBeans or Active Endpoints graphical designers can give you a jump start as you are learning BPEL.

The NetBeans plug-in offers a rich set of constructs and activities to work with in various palettes. It is fairly intuitive to use, and, with the exception of default namespaces, it does not add proprietary hooks into your process source. Because BPEL is a standard, you can still use the BPEL processes you design with the NetBeans BPEL plug-in with BPEL engines other than the one that comes with OpenESB.

Figure 9-2 shows the NetBeans 6.1 BPEL editor, loaded with one of the sample processes that ships with the IDE.

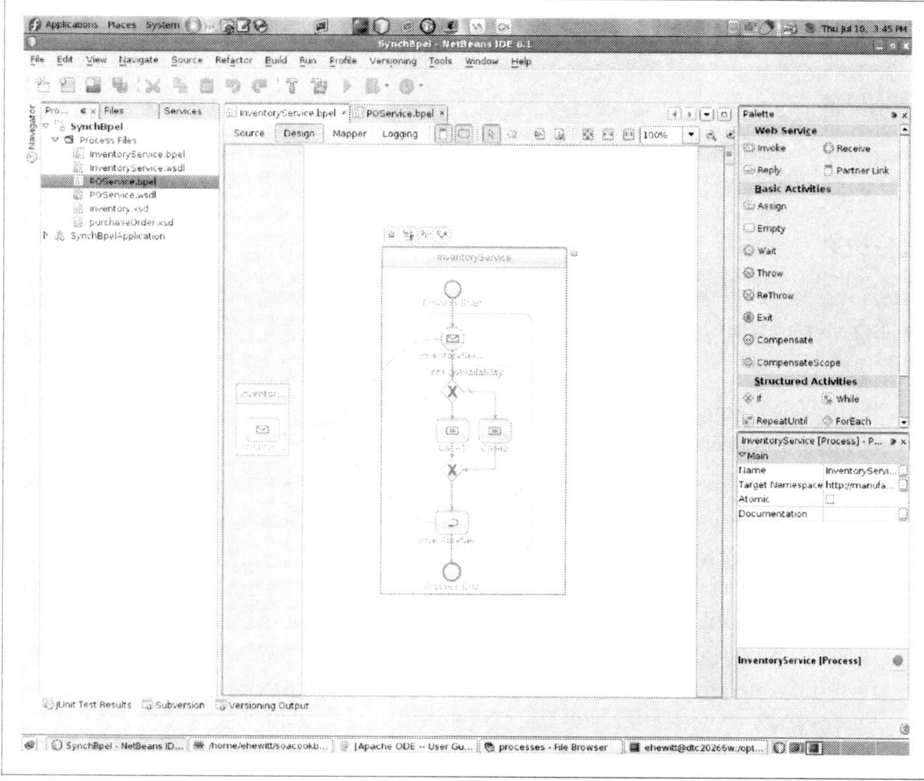

Figure 9-2. The NetBeans BPEL graphical editor is representative of the tools that allow you to create orchestrations without coding

This very simple process defines a partner that accepts a purchase order and checks availability. If the inventory check passes (is true), then case 1 is executed; otherwise, case 2 is executed. Either way, the `<reply>` activity is invoked in order to send a response back to the invoker.

Using the editor, it is easy to drag and drop items from the palette on the righthand side. Switch to the source code view to check your work and see what's being generated. From the source view, you can right-click and make sure that your BPEL is valid. The visual editor will also alert you when you need to add something to your process.

Overall, the BPEL editor is a full-featured plug-in. It offers an intuitive and simple approach that makes BPEL designing easy, without robbing you of any control.

9.7 Creating a BPEL Process That Invokes a Partner

Problem

You want to create a complete, real-world type process that accepts input from a client, does some BPEL work, and invokes a partner web service along the way.

Solution

Even creating a "Hello World" process in BPEL is somewhat labor-intensive. The following steps create a basic orchestration that only invokes one service to return a response:

1. If you don't already have a web service or a set of services to invoke as part of the application, create one.
2. Create a BPEL project in your IDE. Add the WSDL of the web service your orchestration will invoke and any schemas it uses to your project. Create a *.bpel* file.
3. Build the orchestration. There are several basic activities to perform to do this. You need to create a partner link that represents the client-facing aspect of the orchestration. Then create a partner link for the services you're going to invoke. Then start building the process a container such as a `<sequence>` and add activities to it. At minimum, you will need to `<receive>` incoming messages, `<assign>` the incoming message to a variable you can pass to the service you're going to invoke, then `<invoke>` the service, and `<assign>` its response to an outbound message that can be used in a `<reply>` back out of the orchestration to the client.

Creating such a process is a very good way to start with BPEL. It covers all of the basic functions of an orchestration, and it gives you a simple and flexible base where you can experiment with more elaborate capabilities such as fault handling, correlation sets, and so forth. However, from a design point of view, the orchestration just shown is a pretty bad example. There is little point in creating a BPEL that just invokes another service. If you want a layer of indirection between your client and your service, that's what ESBs and other mediators are for—it is not the purpose of orchestrations. Orchestrations are intended to represent business processes that have a variety of steps requiring decision points and that may be long-running. So the example outlined in this recipe is a great way to start learning BPEL, but a not a great example of how to use orchestrations.

Discussion

Let's now walk through creating an orchestration. Once you're familiar with the concepts, it is not hard to create a BPEL process by hand. But because in the real world you're likely to use an IDE of some kind to create orchestrations, and because doing so will give you some validation and guidance as you're creating them, it's worthwhile to try out the one that ships with NetBeans 6.1. It has robust support for BPEL constructs, is easy and intuitive to use, and doesn't add any proprietary extensions, so your code stays as portable as possible. Let's build your process.

As we go through the many steps required to create, deploy, and test an orchestration, be assured that I will reference the code that is being created under the hood as much as possible. I don't like being tied to an IDE, and I don't expect that you do either. So I will do my best to clearly reflect the XML snippets that are being added to the process as you create it. That way, you'll be able to navigate the XML source easily in any IDE, and because the process will be portable (compliant with the spec), you should be able to move it into another designer and deploy it to a different BPEL runtime.

Creating a simple partner web service

First create a simple web service (Example 9-2) so that the orchestration has something to invoke during execution of the business process. This method will retrieve a customer's name based on an ID. You'll build the customer data business process around this service.

Example 9-2. Customer lookup service implementation, CustomerWS.java

```
package com.soacookbook;

import javax.jws.WebParam;
import javax.jws.WebResult;
import javax.jws.WebService;

package com.soacookbook;

import javax.jws.WebParam;
import javax.jws.WebResult;
import javax.jws.WebService;
import javax.jws.soap.SOAPBinding;

/**
 * This is a dumb service that returns the zip code
 * for a given customer.
 */
@WebService(name="CustomerLookupService",
    serviceName="CustomerLookupService",
    targetNamespace="urn:com:soacookbook",
    portName="customerLookupPort")
public class CustomerWS {

   @SOAPBinding(
       style=SOAPBinding.Style.DOCUMENT,
       use=SOAPBinding.Use.LITERAL,
       parameterStyle=SOAPBinding.ParameterStyle.WRAPPED)
```

```
    public @WebResult(name="customerFullName") String
            getCustomerFullName(
            @WebParam(name="customerID",
            mode=WebParam.Mode.IN) int id) {

        System.out.println("Getting name for customer with ID: " + id);

        //go to database here, etc...
        if (id == 888) return "Homer Jay Simpson";
        if (id == 999) return "Henry Walton Jones";
        return "???";
    }
}
```

The `CustomerWS` class implements a web service with a single method. It retrieves the string representing a customer's full name when passed an integer representing his ID.

Now verify that you can access the WSDL of your deployed service because the BPEL will need to reference it. To do this, log into your Glassfish web administration console, go to Web Services→CustomerLookupService and click the View WSDL link.

Here is the WSDL file that represents the service:

```
<?xml version="1.0" encoding="UTF-8"?>
<!-- Published by JAX-WS RI at http://jax-ws.dev.java.net.
RI's version is JAX-WS RI 2.1.3.1-hudson-417-SNAPSHOT. -->
<!-- Generated by JAX-WS RI at http://jax-ws.dev.java.net.
RI's version is JAX-WS RI 2.1.3.1-hudson-417-SNAPSHOT. -->

<definitions xmlns:wsu="http://docs.oasis-open.org/wss/2004/01/
  oasis-200401-wss-wssecurity-utility-1.0.xsd"
  xmlns:soap="http://schemas.xmlsoap.org/wsdl/soap/"
  xmlns:tns="urn:com:soacookbook"
  xmlns:xsd="http://www.w3.org/2001/XMLSchema"
  xmlns="http://schemas.xmlsoap.org/wsdl/"
  targetNamespace="urn:com:soacookbook"
  name="CustomerLookupService">

<ns1:Policy
    xmlns:ns1="http://schemas.xmlsoap.org/ws/2004/09/policy"
    wsu:Id="doWorkBindingPolicy">
  <ns1:ExactlyOne>
  <ns1:All>
  <ns2:RMAssertion
    xmlns:ns2="http://schemas.xmlsoap.org/ws/2005/02/rm/policy">
  </ns2:RMAssertion>
  <ns3:UsingAddressing
    xmlns:ns3="http://www.w3.org/2006/05/addressing/wsdl">
  </ns3:UsingAddressing>
  </ns1:All>
  </ns1:ExactlyOne>
</ns1:Policy>

<types>
  <xsd:schema>
```

```
      <xsd:import namespace="urn:com:soacookbook"
        schemaLocation="http://localhost:8080/TestXslWSWebApp/
        CustomerLookupService?xsd=1">
      </xsd:import>
    </xsd:schema>
  </types>

  <message name="getCustomerFullName">
    <part name="parameters"
      element="tns:getCustomerFullName"></part>
  </message>

  <message name="getCustomerFullNameResponse">
    <part name="parameters"
      element="tns:getCustomerFullNameResponse"></part>
  </message>

  <portType name="CustomerLookupService">
    <operation name="getCustomerFullName">
      <input message="tns:getCustomerFullName"></input>
      <output message="tns:getCustomerFullNameResponse"></output>
    </operation>
  </portType>

  <binding name="customerLookupPortBinding"
      type="tns:CustomerLookupService">
    <soap:binding transport="http://schemas.xmlsoap.org/soap/http"
        style="document"></soap:binding>
    <operation name="getCustomerFullName">
      <soap:operation soapAction=""></soap:operation>
      <input>
        <soap:body use="literal"></soap:body>
      </input>
      <output>
        <soap:body use="literal"></soap:body>
      </output>
    </operation>
  </binding>

  <service name="CustomerLookupService">
    <port name="customerLookupPort" binding="tns:customerLookupPortBinding">
        <soap:address
          location="http://localhost:8080/TestXslWSWebApp/CustomerLookupService">
        </soap:address>
      </port>
    </service>
  </definitions>
```

The service as defined by this WSDL will use the document/literal wrapped style, which is compliant with the Basic Profile 1.1. It defines a single method that accepts an integer (wrapped in the "parameters" element in the message) and returns the corresponding name.

The schema that the service references is very simple:

```
<?xml version="1.0" encoding="UTF-8"?>

<xs:schema xmlns:tns="urn:com:soacookbook"
  xmlns:xs="http://www.w3.org/2001/XMLSchema"
  version="1.0"
  targetNamespace="urn:com:soacookbook">

<xs:element name="getCustomerFullName"
  type="tns:getCustomerFullName"></xs:element>

<xs:element name="getCustomerFullNameResponse"
  type="tns:getCustomerFullNameResponse"></xs:element>

<xs:complexType name="getCustomerFullName">
  <xs:sequence>
    <xs:element name="customerID" type="xs:int"></xs:element>
  </xs:sequence>
</xs:complexType>

<xs:complexType name="getCustomerFullNameResponse">
  <xs:sequence>
    <xs:element name="customerFullName" type="xs:string"
      minOccurs="0"></xs:element>
  </xs:sequence>
</xs:complexType>

</xs:schema>
```

Later in the orchestration, you will need to map the variables that the web service expects (which are defined in this schema) to global variables within the process to enable interaction between the client and the orchestration.

Here is the SOAP message used to invoke this web method:

```
<?xml version="1.0" encoding="UTF-8"?>
<S:Envelope xmlns:S="http://schemas.xmlsoap.org/soap/envelope/">
    <S:Header/>
    <S:Body>
        <ns2:getCustomerFullName xmlns:ns2="urn:com:soacookbook">
            <customerID>888</customerID>
        </ns2:getCustomerFullName>
    </S:Body>
</S:Envelope>
```

And here is the corresponding SOAP response message:

```
<?xml version="1.0" encoding="UTF-8"?>
<S:Envelope xmlns:S="http://schemas.xmlsoap.org/soap/envelope/">
    <S:Body>
        <ns2:getCustomerFullNameResponse xmlns:ns2="urn:com:soacookbook">
            <customerFullName>Homer Jay Simpson</customerFullName>
        </ns2:getCustomerFullNameResponse>
    </S:Body>
</S:Envelope>
```

Now that you have a WSDL defined, you're ready to create a new BPEL process project and add your service to it.

Creating a new BPEL process project

Through the SOA pack, NetBeans 6.1 allows you to visually create, build, and deploy BPEL processes. You can download it from *http://download.netbeans.org/netbeans/6.1/final/*. Choose the "All" bundle, which contains the SOA pack. If you already have NetBeans installed but don't have the SOA pack, you can install it from Tools→Plugins→Available Plugins within the IDE. Choose the SOA and BPEL plug-ins.

Once you've got the IDE support, choose File→New Project...→SOA→BPEL Module. The Ant scripts within NetBeans will allow you to build your project just by clicking the hammer icon. This button is tied to an Ant build target, and will put your process XML files into a JAR so that they are ready for consumption by a composite application project.

Glassfish v2 includes a JBI implementation, and a BPEL Service Engine (SE) should be installed with that. This is the runtime environment for your process. You can verify that your BPEL SE is installed by opening your Glassfish web administration console, clicking JBI→Components, and finding the "sun-bpel-engine" in the list of installed components. Also make sure that it's running: the list of components should show it in a "Started" state.

Importing the web service WSDL

You've created a BPEL project, but haven't yet created a process. You'll do that in a moment. In this step, you'll import the WSDL from the web service you created earlier. In order to avoid making costly network connections to the file at runtime (which also requires an Internet connection), you can import an externally defined WSDL into your project. This way, the resulting deployable BPEL JAR artifact will store a copy and avoid this overhead. Here's how to do it.

Right-click on the Process Files folder under your project. Choose New→Other→XML→External WSDL Document. In the "From URL" field, point to your WSDL and save your work. This creates a local copy of the external WSDL and any referenced XML schemas in the BPEL project. If you make changes to your web service in the future that impact the interface, you will need to delete these locally created copies and import them again.

Now that you have imported the WSDL, you have a port type that can be invoked as a partner in the business process. But in order to do that, you need to create a partner link to reference the service as a partner of the process.

Creating a partner link for the web service

Now you're ready to create the partner link for the local WSDL because one wasn't defined in the remote WSDL. Find the *CustomerLookupService.wsdl* file. This is the WSDL you just imported, and it is located under a Process Files folder that is named after the remote host from which you retrieved it.

Once the WSDL is open, click the Partner label near the tool bar. This takes you to the view where you can define partner links on your WSDL; your WSDL as defined earlier does not contain any partner link information. Click the Autocreate button, and change the name of the CustomerLookupService role from "role1" to "lookupRole". Doing this is a convenience for writing the following text in your local WSDL file copy:

```
<plnk:partnerLinkType name="CustomerLookupService">
  <plnk:role name="lookupRole" portType="tns:CustomerLookupService"/>
</plnk:partnerLinkType>
```

Now you're done creating the partner, and you can start creating the process that will invoke it.

Creating the process

Now you're ready to create the business process that will invoke this partner service. In the Project view, right-click on the project name and choose New→BPEL Process. In the filename field, enter `CustomerProcess`. For the target namespace, change the default value to `http://soacookbook.com/bpel/CustomerProcess`.

This will create a file with a *.bpel* extension that will contain your executable business process. Now you're ready to add BPEL activities to orchestrate your business process.

You can't import an existing BPEL process into a BPEL project directly from within NetBeans. If you want to start a new BPEL project from an existing *.bpel* file, go to the filesystem and copy it directly into the *<project-name>/src* folder.

Adding a partner to the process

Back in the Process Design view, in the Web Services palette, click the Partner Link label and drag it onto the righthand side of the canvas. An orange circle will illuminate near the middle, indicating where you can drop the partner link. A dialog box will then pop up, containing the name of your newly added WSDL file and some other default values.

Leave "Use an Existing Partner Link Type" as it is. It should have your `PartnerLink Type` selected. Click the Swap Roles button to move the "lookupRole" from the My Role field into the Partner Role field, and click OK to save your changes. This will create a representation of the invokable partner web service on the righthand side of the canvas.

Now that you have made the web service available for the process to invoke, you need a way for clients to invoke the process.

Creating a process WSDL

You'll now create the partner link that represents the process itself so that you can invoke it from a client. That means wrapping the process in a WSDL.

Right-click on the Process Files folder of your BPEL project and select New WSDL Document. In the Name field, type `CustomerProcessEsb`. Change the target namespace field to `http://soacookbook.com/wsdl/CustomerProcessEsb`.

You need to make the schema element types available to this WSDL so that you can map them to the service on their way in and out from the client. So check the Import XML Schema File(s) box and browse to the file that contains the schema your partner process uses.

Check the box in the Import column next to the *CustomerLookupService.xsd_1.xsd* file. In the Prefix column value, change "ns0" to "csl". Doing this in the IDE generates the following:

```
//...
<types>
  <xsd:schema
    targetNamespace="http://soacookbook.com/wsdl/CustomerProcessEsb">
    <xsd:import namespace="urn:com:soacookbook"
      schemaLocation="localhost_8080/TestXslWSWebApp/
        CustomerLookupService.xsd_1.xsd"/>
  </xsd:schema>
</types>
```

Hit Enter and click OK. Now you'll specify elements of the Abstract WSDL (which means the port type and its operations along with their required messages) This is shown in Figure 9-3. Create the inputs and outputs that match what your process requires. Here you'll specify a customer ID and return a name for that customer that differentiates these variable names from the ones the web service expects. This will become clearer when you map them.

Because in this example your orchestration simply invokes the backend web service, your input and output will just reflect what that service requires. However, it is important to keep in mind that that is not usually what happens within an orchestration. Typically, they will invoke a variety of services, perform transformations, and generally have a client-facing facade that is quite different from what the composing services themselves provide.

To complete this step, you need to specify the elements from the available schema you're going to use for the input and output. To choose them from a list, click the button with ellipses to bring up a dialog box. Navigate down the tree in the pop-up to the input element `getCustomerFullName`. Do the corresponding work to select the

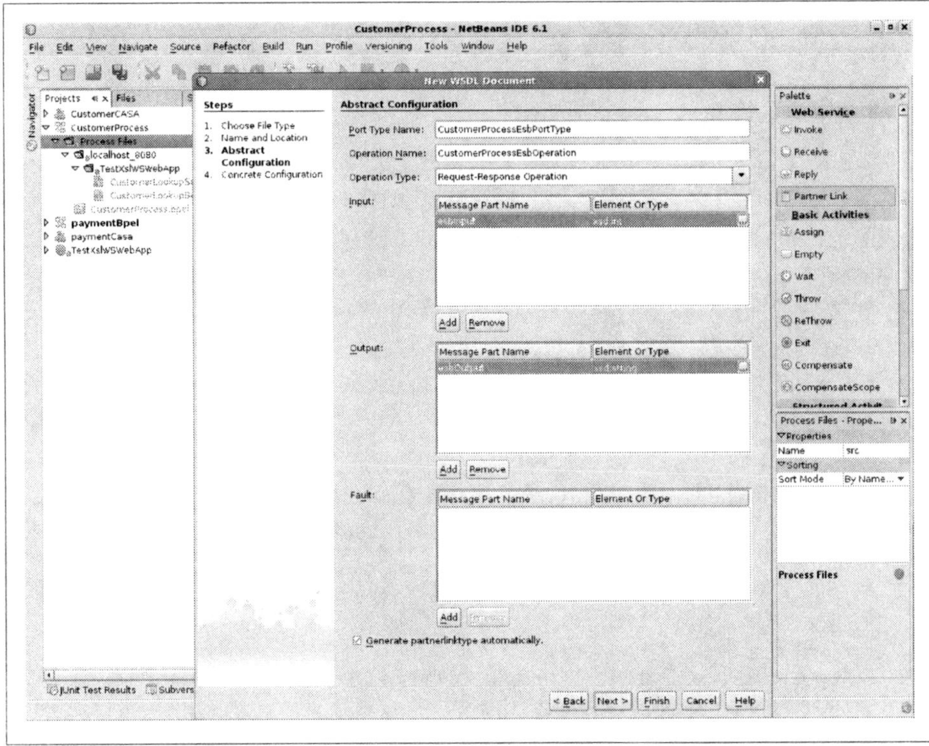

Figure 9-3. New document for BPEL WSDL

`getCustomerFullNameResponse` for the output. Doing this in the IDE generates the following in your WSDL:

```
//...
<message name="CustomerProcessEsbOperationRequest">
  <part name="getCustomerFullNameEsb"
    element="ns:getCustomerFullName"/>
</message>
<message name="CustomerProcessEsbOperationResponse">
  <part name="getCustomerFullNameResponseEsb"
    element="ns:getCustomerFullNameResponse"/>
</message>
```

You can see in Figure 9-4 that you are selecting the elements from the available schema that match the types required by the service.

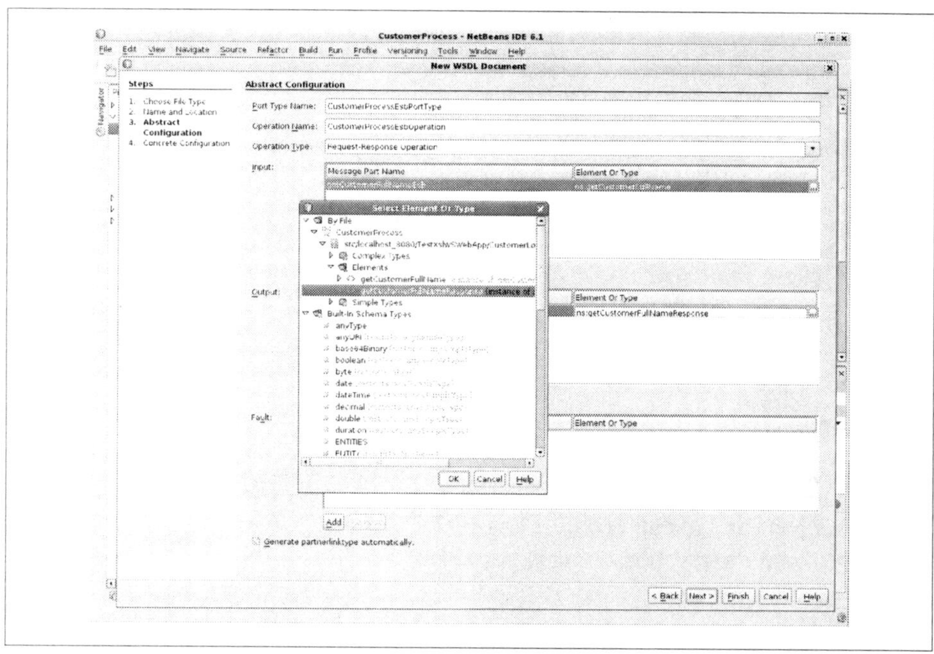

Figure 9-4. Selecting elements

Click Next. This next step, shown in Figure 9-5, allows you to indicate values for the concrete aspect of the WSDL. Choose a binding subtype of document/literal.

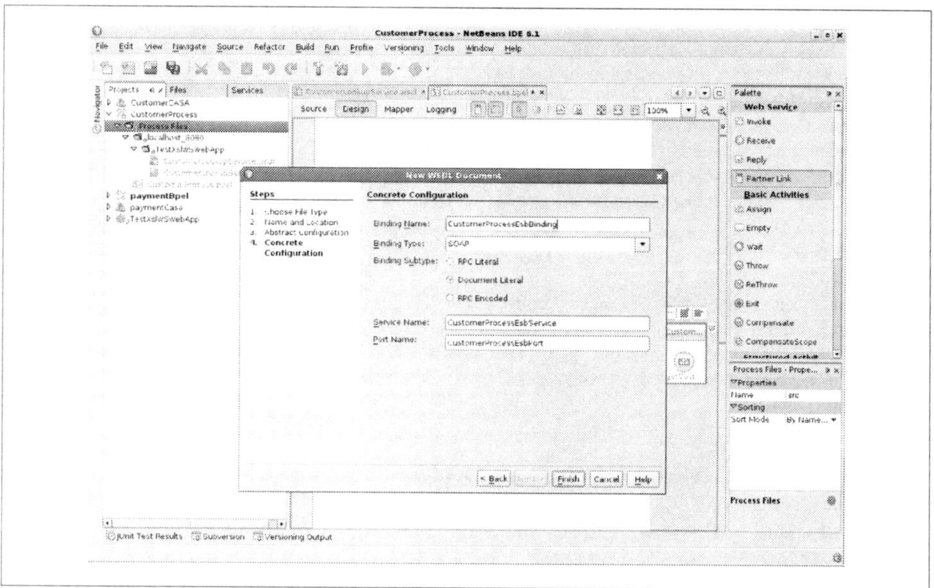

Figure 9-5. Specifying concrete asspects of the WSDL

Using this screen in the IDE generates the following:

```
<binding name="CustomerProcessEsbBinding"
    type="tns:CustomerProcessEsbPortType">

  <soap:binding style="document"
    transport="http://schemas.xmlsoap.org/soap/http"/>

  <operation name="CustomerProcessEsbOperation">
    <soap:operation/>
      <input name="input1">
        <soap:body use="literal"/>
      </input>
      <output name="output1">
        <soap:body use="literal"/>
      </output>
    </operation>

</binding>
```

Of course, you can type all of this if you prefer to learn that way or if you don't like NetBeans. Everything you're doing is portable.

Completed WSDL

You should now have a WSDL file that looks like the one in Example 9-3.

Example 9-3. Completed WSDL representing the process, CustomerProcessEsb.wsdl

```
<?xml version="1.0" encoding="UTF-8"?>
<definitions name="CustomerProcessEsb"
  targetNamespace="http://soacookbook.com/wsdl/CustomerProcessEsb"
  xmlns="http://schemas.xmlsoap.org/wsdl/"
  xmlns:wsdl="http://schemas.xmlsoap.org/wsdl/"
  xmlns:xsd="http://www.w3.org/2001/XMLSchema"
  xmlns:tns="http://soacookbook.com/wsdl/CustomerProcessEsb"
  xmlns:plnk="http://docs.oasis-open.org/wsbpel/2.0/plnktype"
  xmlns:ns="urn:com:soacookbook"
  xmlns:soap="http://schemas.xmlsoap.org/wsdl/soap/">

  <types>
    <xsd:schema
      targetNamespace="http://soacookbook.com/wsdl/CustomerProcessEsb">
      <xsd:import namespace="urn:com:soacookbook"
        schemaLocation="localhost_8080/TestXslWSWebApp/
          CustomerLookupService.xsd_1.xsd"/>
    </xsd:schema>
  </types>

  <message name="CustomerProcessEsbOperationRequest">
    <part name="getCustomerFullNameEsb"
      element="ns:getCustomerFullName"/>
  </message>
  <message name="CustomerProcessEsbOperationResponse">
    <part name="getCustomerFullNameResponseEsb"
```

```
    element="ns:getCustomerFullNameResponse"/>
  </message>

  <portType name="CustomerProcessEsbPortType">
    <operation name="CustomerProcessEsbOperation">
      <input name="input1"
        message="tns:CustomerProcessEsbOperationRequest"/>
      <output name="output1"
        message="tns:CustomerProcessEsbOperationResponse"/>
    </operation>
  </portType>

  <binding name="CustomerProcessEsbBinding"
      type="tns:CustomerProcessEsbPortType">
    <soap:binding style="document"
      transport="http://schemas.xmlsoap.org/soap/http"/>
      <operation name="CustomerProcessEsbOperation">
        <soap:operation/>
          <input name="input1">
            <soap:body use="literal"/>
          </input>
          <output name="output1">
            <soap:body use="literal"/>
          </output>
      </operation>
  </binding>

  <service name="CustomerProcessEsbService">
    <port name="CustomerProcessEsbPort"
      binding="tns:CustomerProcessEsbBinding">
      <soap:address location="http://localhost:${HttpDefaultPort}/
        CustomerProcessEsbService/CustomerProcessEsbPort"/>
    </port>
  </service>

  <plnk:partnerLinkType name="CustomerProcessEsb">
    <plnk:role name="CustomerProcessEsbPortTypeRole"
      portType="tns:CustomerProcessEsbPortType"/>
  </plnk:partnerLinkType>
</definitions>
```

So as you can see in the source that you just created with the wizard (as noted you're also free to write it by hand), the `<message>` values match what you specified by selecting them from the imported schema, which defines the namespace `urn:com:soacookbook`. The rest of the WSDL is pretty straightforward, but check out Recipe 9.14 on BPEL partner links if you want a clearer picture of their role in the process. This step in the wizard is shown in Figure 9-6.

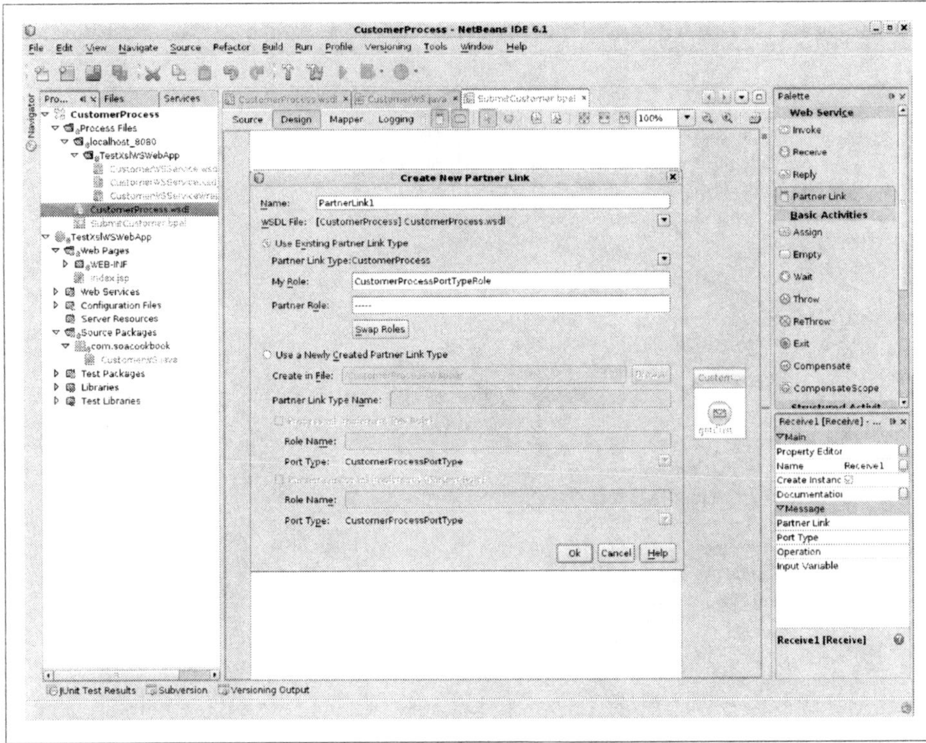

Figure 9-6. Creating a partner link

Now that your WSDL is ready, you can begin building the process.

Adding external WSDL to the process

To add the WSDL to the process definition, click the Partner Link label and drag it onto the lefthand side of the canvas. The orange circle will illuminate, indicating that you can drop it there. This will cause a dialog box to pop up that helps you define the "My Role" partner, that is, the role representing the process itself. The dialog is quite good about anticipating what you want here. Note that it points to the *CustomerProcessEsb.wsdl* file that you just created.

Call the partner link "CustomerProcessPartnerLink" by replacing the default value in the Name field. Leave the name "CustomerProcessEsbPortTypeRole" in the MyRole field, and click OK. Now your Process WSDL partner link is created on the lefthand side of the canvas, representing the entry point through which partners can contact the process.

Note that the two partner types look different. Partner links on the left indicate receivers of incoming messages and have a rectangle around the message icon. Partner links on the right are enclosed in a circle and represent services the process will invoke.

By this point, you should have a bare process that looks like the one shown in Figure 9-7.

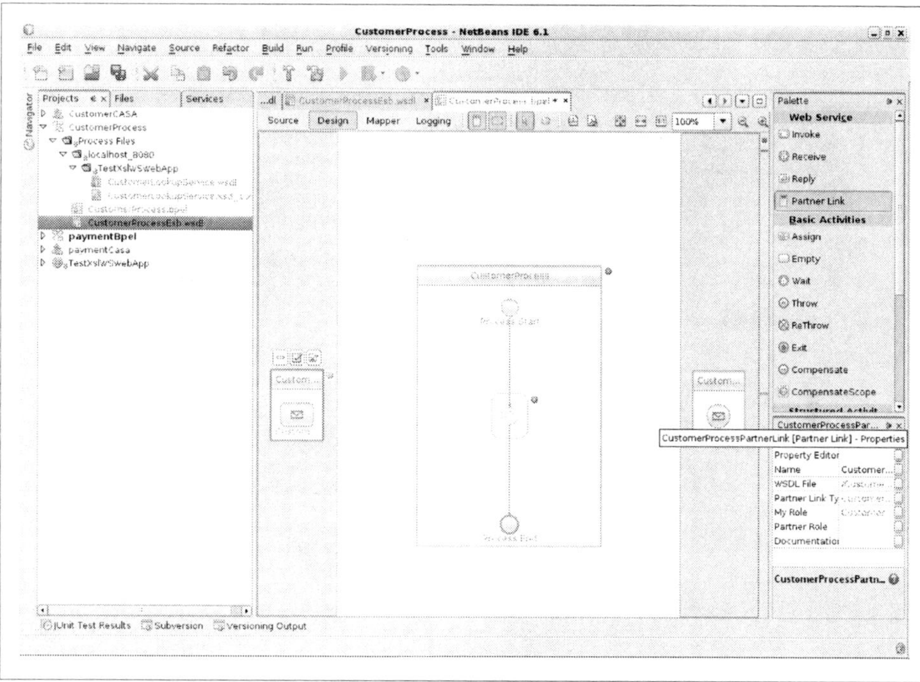

Figure 9-7. Process with partner links defined

Basically what you're saying here is: the process will receive messages from clients that invoke operations on the interface exposed through the WSDL you created as *CustomerProcessEsb.wsdl*. It will call operations on the CustomerProcess web service to get the work of the process done. You haven't actually connected any of those dots yet. Let's start to build the process.

Creating the <receive> activity

From the Web Service palette, click on the Receive label and drag it onto the canvas to create a `<receive>` activity. Click the edit icon above the activity to edit it and change the value in the Name field to "ReceiveLookupRequest". Choose your `CustomerProcessPartnerLink`, and it should select the `CustomerProcessEsbOperation` for you.

Click the edit pencil icon to edit the properties of an element anywhere on the canvas.

Now you have to create a variable that represents the input, so click the Create... button and then click OK. Completing this step will add an arrow to your diagram pointing from the `CustomerProcessPartnerLink` to the receive activity. At this point, your process should look like Figure 9-8.

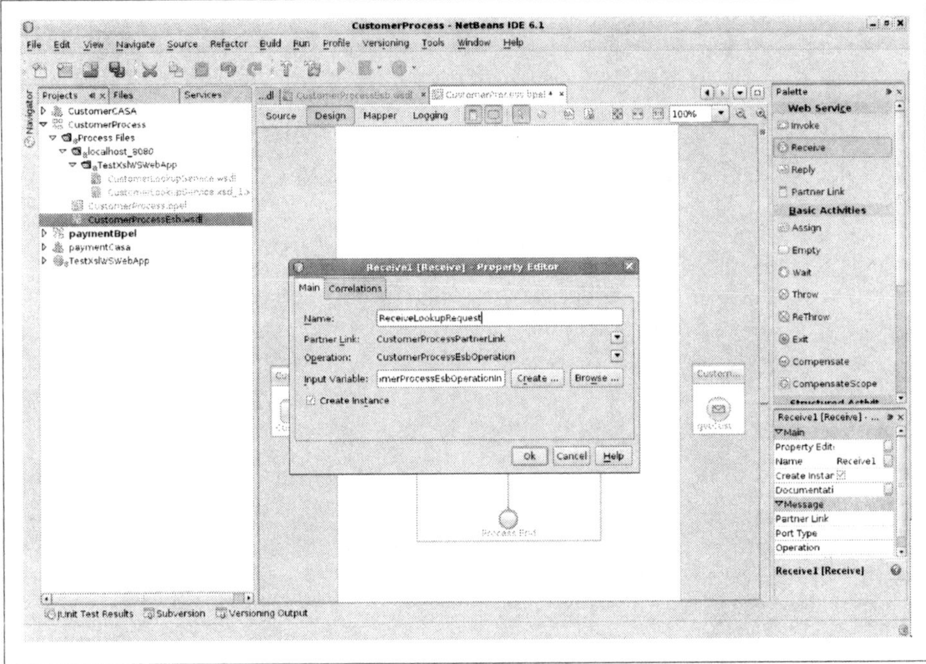

Figure 9-8. Process including <receive> activity

Of course, completing this step in the wizard is just a convenience for writing the `<receive>` activity into your BPEL source XML. The snippet created looks like this:

```
//...
<sequence>
  <receive name="ReceiveLookupRequest"
    createInstance="yes"
    partnerLink="CustomerProcessPartnerLink"
    operation="CustomerProcessEsbOperation"
    xmlns:tns="http://soacookbook.com/wsdl/CustomerProcessEsb"
    portType="tns:CustomerProcessEsbPortType"
    variable="CustomerProcessEsbOperationIn" />
```

Creating the <invoke> activity

In this step, you'll add the invocation of the `CustomerLookupService` to the process. Click the edit icon to change the values in the `<invoke>` activity. Change the Name field to

"InvokeCustomerLookup". Select the `CustomerProcessPLink` for the Partner Link value and the `getCustomerFullName` for the Operation field.

Then you need to create two variables, one to receive the input, and the other to hold the output that some other part of the process can consume. Do this by clicking the Create... button next to the Input and Output Variable fields and naming them "GetCustomerFullNameIn" and "GetCustomerFullNameOut", respectively.

This step is reflected in Figure 9-9, and the code for the `<invoke>` activity that is generated in the process in that step is as follows:

```
<invoke name="InvokeCustomerLookup"
  partnerLink="CustomerProcessPLink"
  operation="getCustomerFullName"
  xmlns:tns="urn:com:soacookbook"
  portType="tns:CustomerLookupService"
  inputVariable="GetCustomerFullNameIn"
  outputVariable="GetCustomerFullNameOut"/>
```

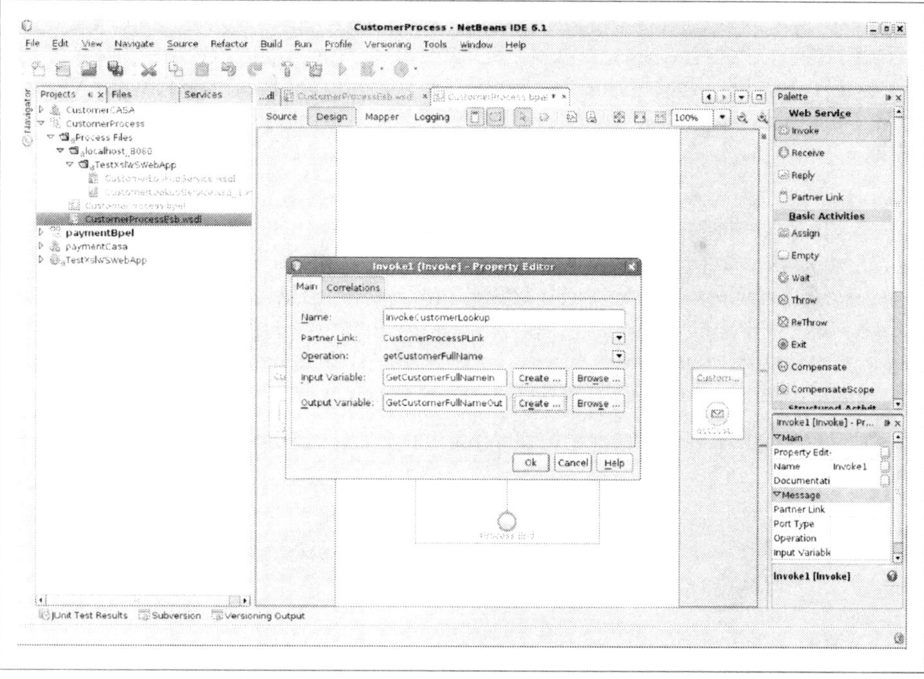

Figure 9-9. Creating the <invoke> Activity

So at this point in your process, you need to define what happens after you invoke the web service that does the actual work of looking up the customer. For this simple process, you will just return the result of the service back to the client.

Creating the <reply> activity

At this point, the NetBeans 6.1 BPEL designer should be showing two additional items: an arrow pointing from the `CustomerProcessPLink` (the WSDL representing the process), and a red X icon, indicating that you have an error in the process. That's because you have specified a two-way operation, but haven't yet specified a reply. So let's do that now.

There are a lot of attributes of a BPEL document that can be statically validated. The writers of the specification took special care to indicate throughout the spec the process violations that can be detected at design time or compile time. For example, any implementation should be able to statically enforce that a partner link is correctly constructed. So any designer tool should be able to find the predominant number of errors in your process before it gets to a runtime engine, which is great.

From the palette, click the Reply label and drag it into the sequence after the Receive. Click the edit icon to edit the attributes of the `<reply>` activity and enter the name "ReplyToClient". In the selector, choose "CustomerProcessPartnerLink" because that represents the client-facing output that you're replying to. Near the Output Variable field, click the Create... button to create a variable that will hold the contents of your reply.

Note that you are not specifying a Fault Response. Your web service does not declare any checked exceptions, and you're choosing to ignore runtime exceptions. In the real world, this wouldn't be a great idea, and you'd normally want to specify a Fault Response and do more robust error handling. I am avoiding the topic now to focus on the bare bones of creating a running process. But if you do this in the real world and anything goes wrong in your web service code, a SOAP fault with precious little helpful information will be thrown all the way back to your client.

As shown in Figure 9-10, accept the default name of `CustomerProcessEsbOperationOut` and click OK.

The `<reply>` will actually be the last step in the process, as it sends the response back to the client. But you're not quite done yet. Now you need to go back and fill in two assignment activities to make the process complete.

Creating the inbound assignment

You need to add two `<assign>` activities: the first assignment follows your `<receive>`, and the second follows your `<invoke>`. You cannot just accept a message in the receive activity and then immediately invoke your partner service. You need to indicate what element of the received message you want to pass into the service as a parameter.

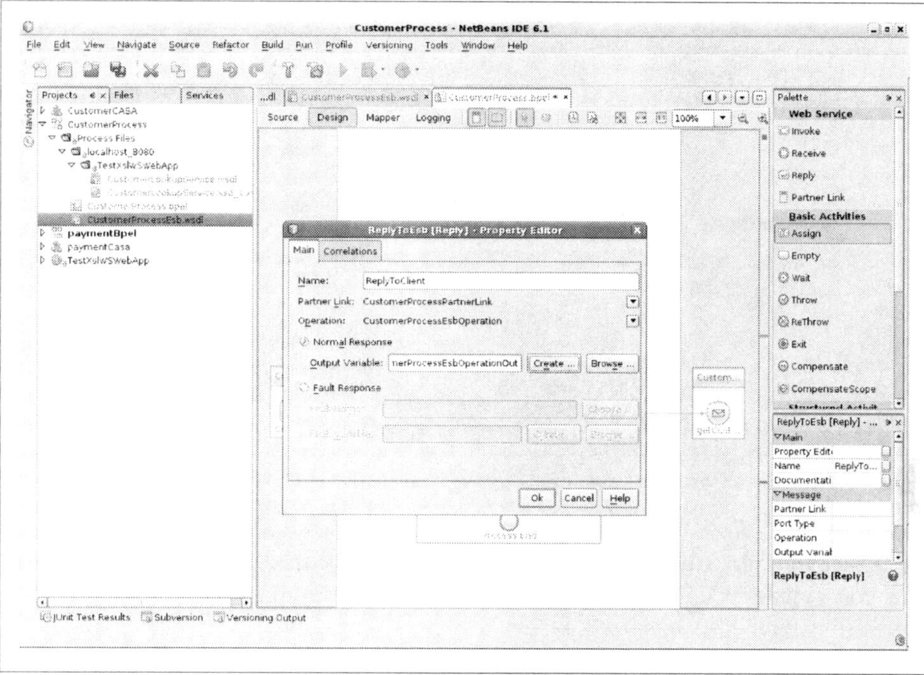

Figure 9-10. Specifying attributes of the <reply> activity

To create an `<assign>` activity, click the Assign label in the Basic Activities section of the palette and drag it onto the sequence between the `<receive>` and `<invoke>` activities.

Now you have to map the data from the available variables you've defined into the available partner links. To do this, click the Mapper button on the toolbar and drill down to the CustomerProcessEsbOperationIn→getCustomerFullNameEsb→customerID variable. The mapper screen is shown in Figure 9-11. Drag that variable across the canvas to Variables→GetCustomerFullNameIn→parameters→customerID. This will create an arrow linking the two, effectively creating the assignment from the data that comes in from the client given the BPEL's client-facing WSDL types into a form that the web service expects given its WSDL definition.

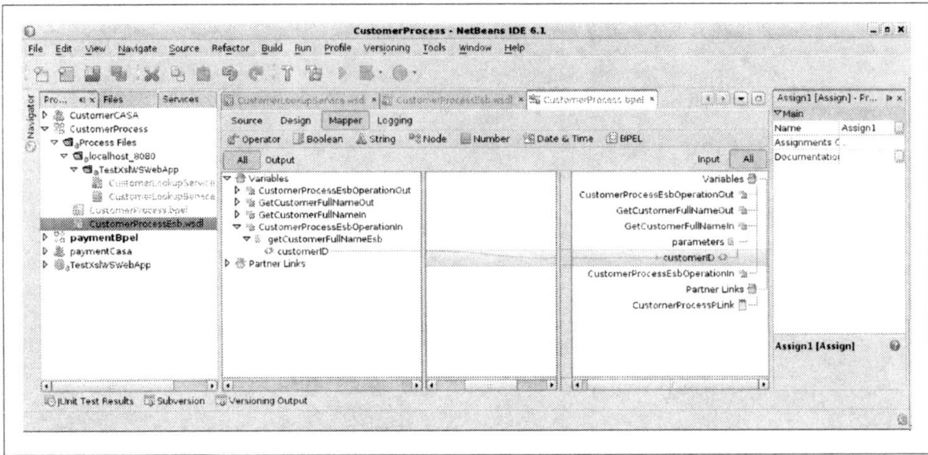

Figure 9-11. Assigning incoming data elements from a message

Note that your types need to match here, or you'll get a warning. If that happens, check that you've mapped directly to the proper type. Ultimately, the underlying source code for your assignment looks like this:

```
<variables>
  <variable name="CustomerProcessEsbOperationIn"
      xmlns:tns="http://soacookbook.com/wsdl/CustomerProcessEsb"
      messageType="tns:CustomerProcessEsbOperationRequest"/>
  <variable name="GetCustomerFullNameIn"
      xmlns:tns="urn:com:soacookbook"
      messageType="tns:getCustomerFullName"/>
  //...
</variables>

<receive .... partnerLink="CustomerProcessPartnerLink"
    operation="CustomerProcessEsbOperation"
    xmlns:tns="http://soacookbook.com/wsdl/CustomerProcessEsb"
    portType="tns:CustomerProcessEsbPortType"
    variable="CustomerProcessEsbOperationIn"/>

<assign name="Assign1">
  <copy>
    <from>$CustomerProcessEsbOperationIn.getCustomerFullNameEsb/customerID</from>
    <to>$GetCustomerFullNameIn.parameters/customerID</to>
  </copy>
</assign>
```

So to make your assignment work, first declare a global variable called `CustomerProcessEsbOperationIn`. This variable is empty when the process starts, and then once the `<receive>` activity is invoked, it gets is filled with the data coming into the `CustomerProcessPartnerLink`. The operation and port type indicate the data types expected in the incoming operation. In this example, that matches the incoming data that the Customer Lookup web service requires, so just pass it straight through. If you wanted to do some massaging of the data, say, with an XSL transformation, or using another standard function, this is a good opportunity to do that.

The assignment just uses a basic expression to drill down to the `customerID` node of the incoming data element, and assigns it to the `customerID` node in the `GetCustomerFullNameIn` variable. These are different message types, but they share this element, and that's why you do the assignment. Note that you have to drill down through the parameters element of the `GetCustomerFullNameIn` variable because its type corresponds to the `getCustomerFullName`, which was defined as document/literal/wrapped, and the default name for the wrapper element is `parameters`.

Creating the outbound assignment

Now you're going to basically repeat the same process you just completed for the inbound assignment to create the outbound assignment.

To create a new `<assign>` activity, click the Assign label in the Basic Activities section of the palette and drag it onto the sequence between the invoke and reply activities. You can double-click on the assign activity to bring up the Mapper. Click the arrows next to Variables→GetCustomerFullNameOut→parameters→customerFullName (recall that this is what is returned by your web service), and then on the right side of the canvas, click to open Variables→CustomerProcessEsbOperationOut→getCustomerFullNameResponseEsb→customerFullName. This is the value that will be returned by your process service and out through the client-facing WSDL.

Just as before, the `$` is used to indicate that you're referencing a variable.

The following code snippet shows what you're generating when you do this in the IDE:

```
<variables>
  <variable name="GetCustomerFullNameOut"
      xmlns:tns="urn:com:soacookbook"
      messageType="tns:getCustomerFullNameResponse"/>
  <variable name="CustomerProcessEsbOperationOut"
      xmlns:tns="http://soacookbook.com/wsdl/CustomerProcessEsb"
      messageType="tns:CustomerProcessEsbOperationResponse"/>
  //...
</variables>

  //...
<invoke ... outputVariable="GetCustomerFullNameOut"/>
<assign name="Assign2">
  <copy>
    <from>$GetCustomerFullNameOut.parameters/customerFullName</from>
    <to>$CustomerProcessEsbOperationOut.getCustomerFullNameResponseEsb/
        customerFullName</to>
  </copy>
</assign>
```

Just as with the first `<assign>`, you're copying data out of the response that the web service returned (packaged in the variable called `GetCustomerFullNameOut`) and putting it into the global process variable called `CustomerProcessEsbOperationOut`.

You have to do these assignments because you are mapping between what your client sees and how the service is exposed. With an orchestration, these aren't the same thing! The client never sees your internal WSDL here, as it is not invoked directly, but through the process, which has a slightly different WSDL interface. However, you know that in this case, they wrap the same data types.

Check the source code

You now have a completed BPEL process that you are ready to package. Example 9-4 shows the complete *CustomerProcess.bpel* file.

You can view the source code of your BPEL file by clicking the Source tab at the top of the designer.

Example 9-4. CustomerProcess.bpel

```
<?xml version="1.0" encoding="UTF-8"?>
<process
    name="CustomerProcess"
    targetNamespace="http://soacookbook.com/bpel/CustomerProcess"
    xmlns="http://docs.oasis-open.org/wsbpel/2.0/process/executable"
    xmlns:xsd="http://www.w3.org/2001/XMLSchema"
    xmlns:tns="http://soacookbook.com/bpel/CustomerProcess">

  <import namespace="urn:com:soacookbook"
    location="localhost_8080/TestXslWSWebApp/CustomerLookupService.wsdl"
    importType="http://schemas.xmlsoap.org/wsdl/"/>
  <import namespace="http://soacookbook.com/wsdl/CustomerProcessEsb"
    location="CustomerProcessEsb.wsdl"
    importType="http://schemas.xmlsoap.org/wsdl/"/>

  <partnerLinks>
    <partnerLink name="CustomerProcessPartnerLink"
        xmlns:tns="http://soacookbook.com/wsdl/CustomerProcessEsb"
        partnerLinkType="tns:CustomerProcessEsb"
        myRole="CustomerProcessEsbPortTypeRole"/>
    <partnerLink name="CustomerProcessPLink"
        xmlns:tns="urn:com:soacookbook"
        partnerLinkType="tns:CustomerLookupService"
        partnerRole="lookupRole"/>
  </partnerLinks>

  <variables>
```

```
    <variable name="CustomerProcessEsbOperationOut"
      xmlns:tns="http://soacookbook.com/wsdl/CustomerProcessEsb"
      messageType="tns:CustomerProcessEsbOperationResponse"/>
    <variable name="GetCustomerFullNameOut"
      xmlns:tns="urn:com:soacookbook"
      messageType="tns:getCustomerFullNameResponse"/>
    <variable name="GetCustomerFullNameIn"
      xmlns:tns="urn:com:soacookbook"
      messageType="tns:getCustomerFullName"/>
    <variable name="CustomerProcessEsbOperationIn"
      xmlns:tns="http://soacookbook.com/wsdl/CustomerProcessEsb"
      messageType="tns:CustomerProcessEsbOperationRequest"/>
    </variables>

  <sequence>
    <receive name="ReceiveLookupRequest" createInstance="yes"
      partnerLink="CustomerProcessPartnerLink"
      operation="CustomerProcessEsbOperation"
      xmlns:tns="http://soacookbook.com/wsdl/CustomerProcessEsb"
      portType="tns:CustomerProcessEsbPortType"
      variable="CustomerProcessEsbOperationIn"/>

    <assign name="Assign1">
      <copy>
        <from>$CustomerProcessEsbOperationIn.getCustomerFullNameEsb/
                 customerID</from>
        <to>$GetCustomerFullNameIn.parameters/customerID</to>
      </copy>
    </assign>

    <invoke name="InvokeCustomerLookup"
      partnerLink="CustomerProcessPLink"
      operation="getCustomerFullName"
      xmlns:tns="urn:com:soacookbook"
      portType="tns:CustomerLookupService"
      inputVariable="GetCustomerFullNameIn"
      outputVariable="GetCustomerFullNameOut"/>

    <assign name="Assign2">
      <copy>
        <from>$GetCustomerFullNameOut.parameters/customerFullName</from>
        <to>$CustomerProcessEsbOperationOut.getCustomerFullNameResponseEsb/
            customerFullName</to>
      </copy>
    </assign>

    <reply name="ReplyToClient"
      partnerLink="CustomerProcessPartnerLink"
      operation="CustomerProcessEsbOperation"
      xmlns:tns="http://soacookbook.com/wsdl/CustomerProcessEsb"
      portType="tns:CustomerProcessEsbPortType"
      variable="CustomerProcessEsbOperationOut"/>

  </sequence>
</process>
```

You can also switch back to the design view to check out the completed process. You should have no red error marks on your canvas, and your process should look like Figure 9-12.

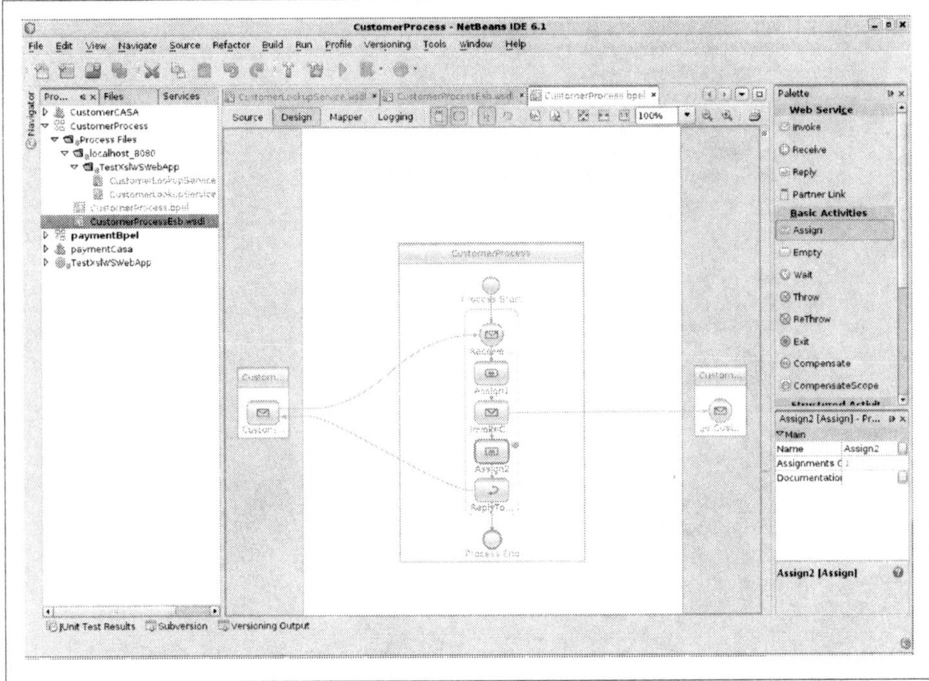

Figure 9-12. Complete CustomerProcess.bpel in design vew

Remember that the purpose of this exercise is to give you a solid foundation for using any of the wide variety of BPEL Basic and Structured activities, and that while this will execute properly, it does not represent a good use of an orchestration from a design standpoint. This is the standard structure you'll follow to create a process, but your real-world process will typically be far more complex, as they generally need to include more than one partner to constitute a reasonable candidate for a workflow.

Notwithstanding that, you now have a completed process, and you're ready to build and deploy it.

Build the BPEL project

Before you can deploy the process, you need to build it. The BPEL source must be packaged into a JAR file for deployment within the BPEL Service Engine that will act as the runtime environment for your process. The BPEL Service Engine is a JBI component that executes as part of the OpenESB add-on to Glassfish.

To build your BPEL project, just click the Build icon in NetBeans, which will copy the schemas, WSDLs, and process file into the JAR. Again, if you don't want to use

NetBeans, you can easily set up a Maven or Ant project that will add these files to a JAR. Here is the output of building the BPEL process through NetBeans:

```
Deleting directory /home/ehewitt/soacookbook/repository/code/chapters/
  CustomerProcess/build
Created dir: /home/ehewitt/soacookbook/repository/code/chapters/CustomerProcess/build
Copying 5 files to /home/ehewitt/soacookbook/repository/code/chapters/
  CustomerProcess/build
Building jar: /home/ehewitt/soacookbook/repository/code/chapters/
  CustomerProcess/build/SEDeployment.jar
BUILD SUCCESSFUL (total time: 0 seconds)
```

This makes your process available to the JBI Service Engine as a JAR file called *SEDeployment.jar*.

See Also

Recipe 9.8 discusses how to deploy your new BPEL process.

9.8 Deploying a BPEL Process to OpenESB's BPEL Service Engine

Problem

You have a complete BPEL process built-in to a JAR, and you want to deploy it to OpenESB v2's BPEL Service Engine to execute it.

Solution

Create a CASA (Composite Application Service Assembly) project using NetBeans. This will combine the BPEL process bundle with the JBI deployment files required by OpenESB, and deploy it to the runtime engine.

Discussion

While the definition of a BPEL process itself is standardized through the specification, the manner in which you deploy that process is left undefined. That means that it's up to each vendor to figure out its own way of installing a process into its engine so that it can be executed. This is not great news for developers, but tools do make it easier.

Here you will deploy the process that you defined in Recipe 9.7 through NetBeans 6.X. So let's start from there. You should have the partner web service that you created in that recipe deployed already.

It doesn't take long to deploy the process, part of which is shown in Figure 9-13. Here is an overview of the basic steps:

1. Build the BPEL module into its JAR.
2. Create a Composite Application Service Assemby (CASA), which you'll wrap the BPEL process JAR in so that it can be deployed in the JBI container.

3. Add the BPEL JAR to the CASA project.
4. Build and deploy the CASA.

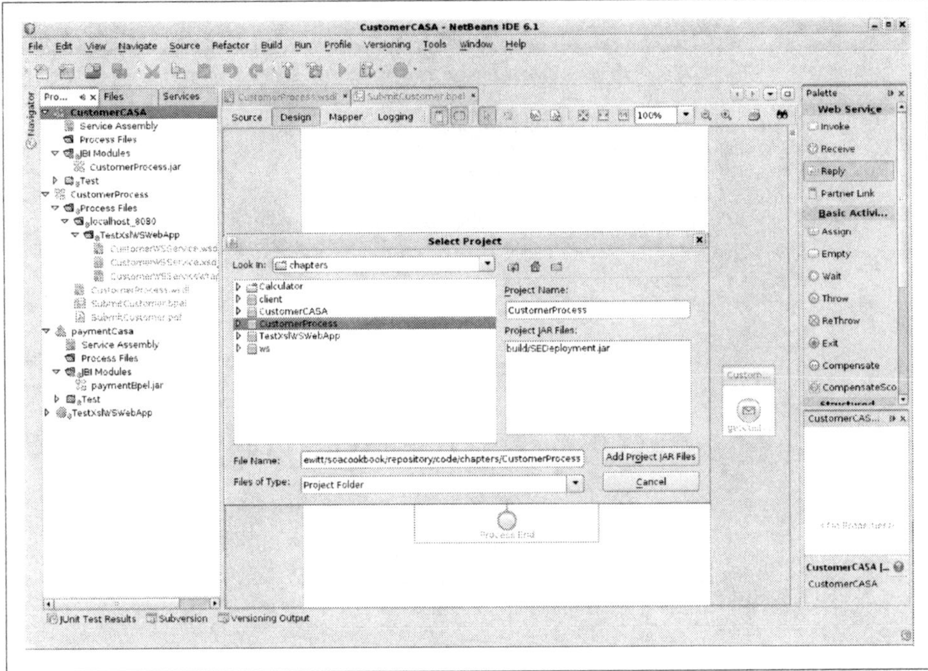

Figure 9-13. Adding the BPEL JAR to the CASA

Creating a new CASA project

Click the New Project button, select SOA→Composite Application, and click Next. Select a name and location for the project and click Finish. Call your project "CustomerCASA".

CASA represents a deployable JBI unit. You will import your recently created BPEL process into the JBI assembly and make it available through OpenESB, which you can then contact as a client.

Adding the BPEL project to the assembly

Now right-click on the project name and choose Add JBI Module... from the menu. Select the project folder containing the BPEL process (in your case, "CustomerProcess"). If it is a BPEL process, the window should show the name of the project's JAR files in the text field. Click Add Project JAR Files.

Right-click on the Service Assembly file under the CustomerCASA project in the project view, and choose Edit. This will show you a partitioned canvas that is used to lay out the components in the assembly in a graphical view of the JBI file.

Building the assembly

Click the hammer icon (Build Project) to build the project. This will reveal the partner links available on the process WSDL. NetBeans will automatically wire up your inputs and outputs appropriately to indicate that the message will come in from the BPEL Service Engine, do its work, and come back out again.

If the build is successful, you should see output indicating that it successfully created a *CustomerCASA.zip* file. In an unusual format for Java projects, it is this ZIP file that represents the deployable artifact.

Deploying the assembly to the BPEL service engine

This is where you can have validation problems, so despite the fact that you've built your BPEL and CASA successfully, you might not be out of the woods quite yet. Click the wrench and paper icon to deploy the project. If successful, you should see output like this:

```
//...
[deploy-service-assembly]
    Deploying a service assembly...
        host=localhost
        port=4848
        file=/home/ehewitt/soacookbook/repository/code/chapters/
             CustomerCASA/dist/CustomerCASA.zip
[start-service-assembly]
    Starting a service assembly...
        host=localhost
        port=4848
        name=CustomerCASA
BUILD SUCCESSFUL (total time: 1 second)
```

To verify your installation, open the Glassfish web administration console and expand the JBI→Service Assemblies node. This is illustrated in Figure 9-14.

You need to have the BPEL Service Engine installed and running in your OpenESB installation with Glassfish for this example to work. Expand the JBI→Components node to verify that it is present and running.

See Also

Recipe 9.9 to see how to test your process now that it's deployed.

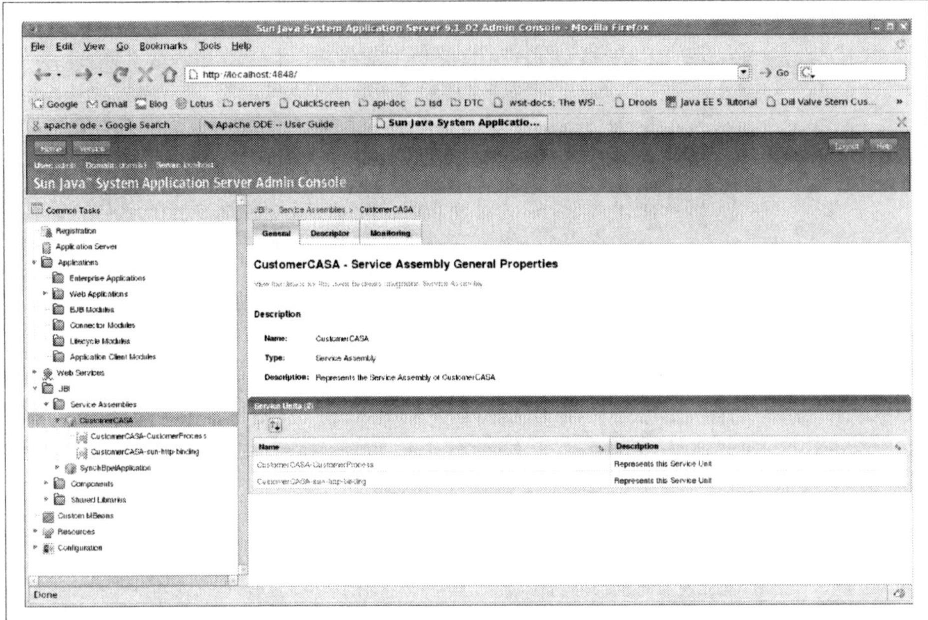

Figure 9-14. Verifying that the assembly deployed to Glassfish

9.9 Testing a Deployed BPEL Process

Problem

You want to create and run tests against the BPEL process that you deployed using a CASA project in NetBeans.

Solution

Create a new test case and point to the process WSDL. You'll be asked what operation you want to test, and the IDE will generate a SOAP message that will serve as input to the operation.

Discussion

Unlike unit tests, these test cases generate SOAP messages that match your WSDL, and just know how to invoke your service behind the scenes. Following are step-by-step instructions for creating a new SOAP test for your BPEL process.

This recipe expects that you have created the process from Recipe 9.7 and deployed it as shown in Recipe 9.8. However, the general idea is the same for any deployed BPEL process.

Creating the test

Within your CustomerCASA project, right-click on the Test folder and choose New Test Case. Enter a name of "TestHomer" for the test case and click Next. Homer is the name of the customer you expect to get back given the ID you'll supply.

You should now see the WSDL Document Selection screen, showing a selection of possible WSDL documents based on your project. Drill down to Customer Process→Source Packages and select the *CustomerProcessEsb.wsdl* file. This is the file that represents the client-facing BPEL process, and that's what you want to invoke. Click Next.

The wizard will read the WSDL file and present you with a selection of possible operations that you could invoke with the test you are creating. You only have one operation in this example, so choose it: CustomerProcessEsbOperation. Click Finish.

A new folder named after your test will appear. It contains a new test case called *input.xml*. This is not a JUnit test case, but rather a complete SOAP envelope representing a valid input based on your WSDL file. Here is the generated SOAP message that matches the input required by your WSDL operation:

```
<soapenv:Envelope
  xsi:schemaLocation="http://schemas.xmlsoap.org/soap/envelope/
    http://schemas.xmlsoap.org/soap/envelope/"
  xmlns:xsi="http://www.w3.org/2001/XMLSchema-instance"
  xmlns:xsd="http://www.w3.org/2001/XMLSchema"
  xmlns:soapenv="http://schemas.xmlsoap.org/soap/envelope/"
  xmlns:urn="urn:com:soacookbook">

  <soapenv:Body>
    <urn:getCustomerFullName>
      <customerID>?3?</customerID>
    </urn:getCustomerFullName>
  </soapenv:Body>

</soapenv:Envelope>
```

The SOAP message is created according to the WSDL, with question marks inserted in the `customerID` element as place holders to indicate that you should supply meaningful values that will produce the expected result. So enter "888" as the `customerID` element value because that's Homer Simpson's customer ID as defined by the massively complex business logic in your web service.

Executing the test

Now that you have a SOAP message ready to pass to the customer process, you need to invoke it. Right-click on the test case and choose Run. This will invoke the service using your generated SOAP message, and will write the response to the *Output.xml* file in the same test folder along with the input.

Here are the contents of the *Output.xml* file as returned by the BPEL orchestration, through the service:

```
<SOAP-ENV:Envelope
  xmlns:SOAP-ENV="http://schemas.xmlsoap.org/soap/envelope/"
  xmlns:xsd="http://www.w3.org/2001/XMLSchema"
  xmlns:xsi="http://www.w3.org/2001/XMLSchema-instance"
  xsi:schemaLocation="http://schemas.xmlsoap.org/soap/envelope/
    http://schemas.xmlsoap.org/soap/envelope/">

  <SOAP-ENV:Body>
    <ns1:getCustomerFullNameResponse
      xmlns:msgns="http://soacookbook.com/wsdl/CustomerProcessEsb"
      xmlns:ns1="urn:com:soacookbook">
      <customerFullName xmlns="">Homer Jay Simpson</customerFullName>
    </ns1:getCustomerFullNameResponse>
  </SOAP-ENV:Body>

</SOAP-ENV:Envelope>
```

The first time the test is invoked, you may be in for a shock. The testing tool won't know what to expect as a response, so your first execution will fail. Once you get a response that you expect and that you want to compare future invocations against to determine if they've passed, right-click on the Output node and select "Use Recent Result as Output". The next time you invoke the same service with the same parameters, the response will be compared against this result; if they match, the tool assumes that your test has passed.

This output represents the desired result. Therefore, you want to save it so that future invocations will check against this SOAP response to determine if they passed or not. To save this output, right-click on the file (the name should be the date and time at which you executed it) and click "Use as Output".

Now if you run the test again, you should see the more favorable output in the console:

```
Test TestHomer
Threads count Success: <1> Error: <0> Not completed: <0>
------------- ---------------- ---------------
BUILD SUCCESSFUL (total time: 1 second)
```

Load testing

NetBeans 6.X makes it easy for you to do some light load testing as a developer. If you click on the name of the test in your project view, you should notice a palette on the righthand side of the IDE that contains properties for the test. Tweak these values to add a number of concurrent threads and a number of invocations of the service that each thread should perform.

For example, on my core duo Linux workstation that is running both the server and the client, I set the number of concurrent threads to 4 and the number of invocations per thread to 10. That will run the test 40 times with the click of a button. And because I also checked the "Calculate Throughput" property, the tool will tell me how long it is taking to go from the test through the orchestration, to the web service, and back. Here's my result:

```
Threads count Success: <4> Error: <0> Not completed: <0>
Throughput: <40> invocations in <11.129>s = <3.594213316560338> invokes/s
```

Adjusting the test timeout setting allows you to prevent runaway invocations from bringing down your entire test battery.

9.10 Installing Active Endpoints BPEL Designer

Problem

You want to create your BPEL processes more quickly and present them in a way that process analysts can understand.

Solution

Use a graphical BPEL designer, such as Active Endpoints Community Edition. This designer is available for Linux and Windows. It can be installed as a standalone Eclipse-based product, or as a plug-in to your existing Eclipse environment.

Discussion

To download an evaluation edition of Active Endpoints Designer, which gives you a 30-day trial, go to *http://www.activevos.com/download-trial.php*. You will be asked for your email address and you'll be emailed an evaluation license key good for 30 days.

As of this writing, the current version of Active Endpoints Server is 5.0.2. After downloading, follow these steps to install it on Windows:

1. Run the executable file *ActiveVOS_Designer_windows_<version>.exe*.
2. A wizard will launch, and you'll be asked to browse to the location of your license file. The URL of the file should have been given to you in the email you received after registering. You can use your browser's File→Save As feature to download the file locally. Make sure to save it as a text file, or the browser may try to save it as HTML, which will corrupt the key.
3. Active Endpoints Designer will use an in-memory Tomcat server, and you'll be asked to choose ports.
4. You'll then be asked for the location where Designer should be installed. Once the installer is complete, you'll be ready to go.

Installing on Linux is even easier:

1. Untar *activeVOS_designer_<version>.tar.gz* directly into the directory from which you want to run it.
2. To start the Designer IDE, double-click on *{install-dir}/designer/designer*.

See Also

You will want to install Active Endpoints Server before going too much further. See Recipe 9.11.

9.11 Installing Active Endpoints BPEL Engine

Problem

Instead of using an open source project such as Apache ODE to execute your BPEL processes, you want to try an established BPEL engine that has a commercial license and support available, as well as the ability to incorporate human tasks.

Solution

Install Active Endpoints VOS Server. Commercial versions of the designer and the BPEL runtime engine are available from *http://www.activevos.com*, but there is also a free community edition available, licensed under the GNU GPL and downloadable from *http://www.activevos.com/community-open-source.php*.

Discussion

Here's how to install the server:

1. Run the Active Endpoints Server on Windows, which allows you to execute BPEL processes, and run the installer executable.
2. A wizard will launch, and you'll be asked to browse to the location of your license file. The URL of the file should have been given to you in the email you received after registering. You can use your browser's File→Save As feature to download the file locally. Make sure to save it as a text file, or the browser may try to save it as HTML, which will corrupt the key.
3. Active Endpoints Designer will use a Tomcat server to run on, and you'll be asked to choose ports.
4. You'll then be asked for the location into which Active Endpoints Server should be installed.
5. Once the installation is complete, you can start the server from the final step of the wizard.

As the Active VOS server starts on its internal Tomcat server, you will see information indicating that the BpelAdmin WAR has deployed. This is the web-based console that you can use to interact with the server. If you're using an evaluation edition, you will see the number of days you have remaining in your evaluation period. You will also see that some sample WARs are deployed that can help you get started.

Like ODE, the ActiveVOS server includes an embedded Apache Derby database that it uses to keep track of runtime variables within executing processes. It also includes deployed tutorial processes, URN mapping for endpoint reference resolution, and Identity Service data.

Once your installation is complete, user you browser to navigate to *http://localhost:8080/BpelAdmin/*. This is the address of the web-based administration console you can use to work with ActiveVOS. You should see a screen similar to the one shown in Figure 9-15.

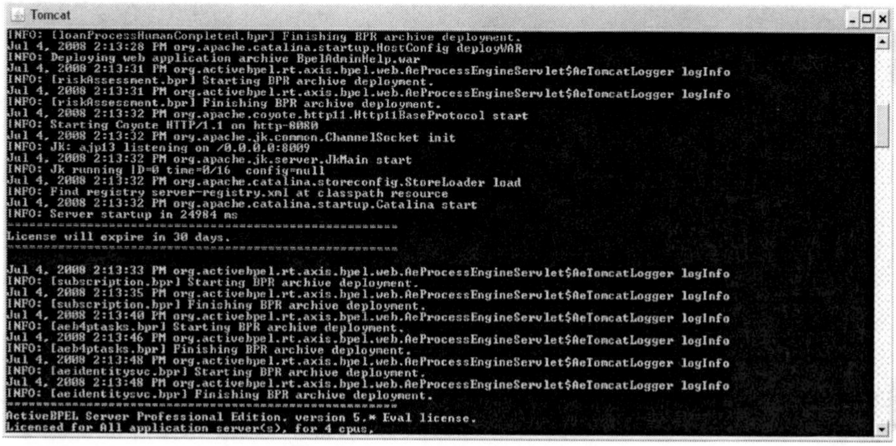

Figure 9-15. The Active Endpoints Server startup

You can see from a quick look at the console that your BPEL server is running. During development, you may want to set the logging level to Full on the Configuration page. The web console with links to Configuration and other items is accessible from `http://localhost:8080/BpelAdmin`, as shown in Figure 9-16.

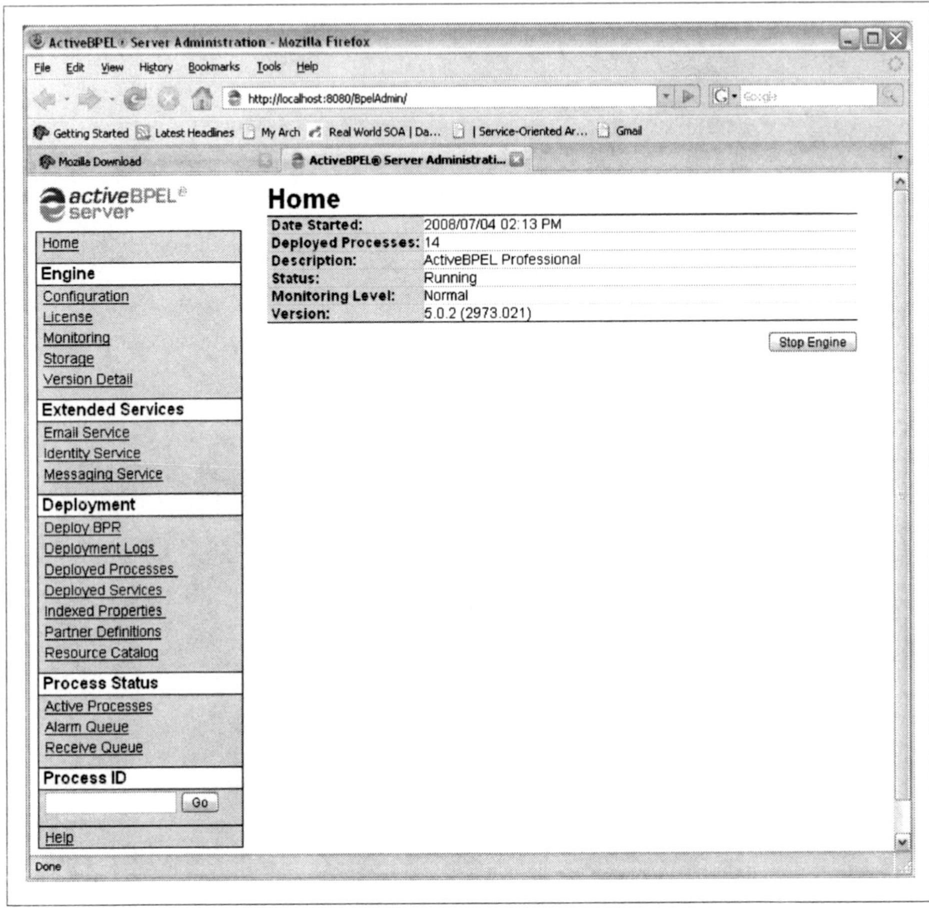

Figure 9-16. ActiveVOS administration console

Now you're ready to create a process with the designer tool and deploy it to ActiveVOS Server.

See Also

Recipe 9.10, where we saw how to install Active Endpoints Designer.

9.12 Creating a BPEL Process in Active Endpoints Designer

Problem

You want to create a simple BPEL process within a graphical designer.

Solution

Run Active Endpoints Designer and drag and drop some basic activities into it so that you can test deployment. This will give you a feel for the round-trip working cycle.

Discussion

Navigate to the location where you installed the designer and run the *designer* executable. It is based on Eclipse, so dealing with a workspace and general navigation should be familiar.

To get started, create a new orchestration project by selecting File→New→Orchestration Project. This will create a set of folders that you can use to store your orchestration designs, as shown in Figure 9-17.

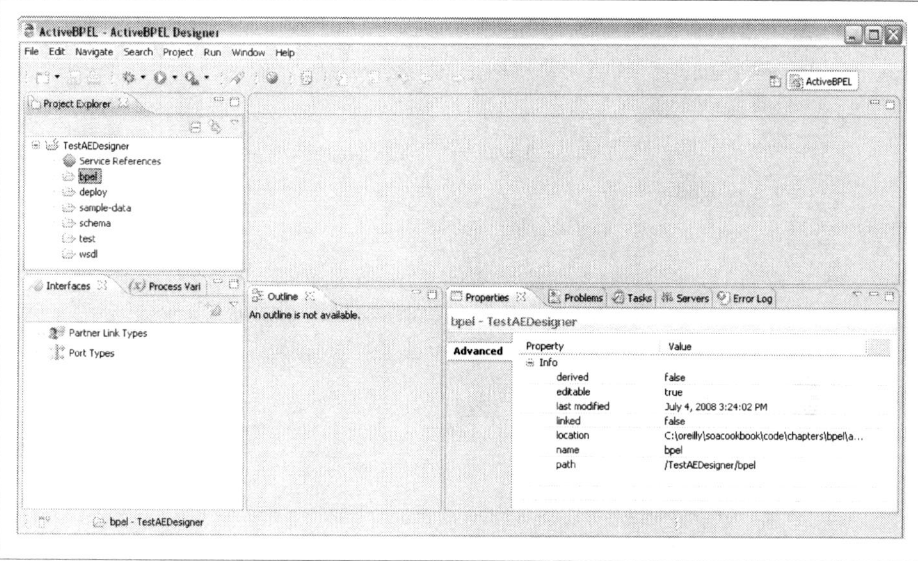

Figure 9-17. New orchestration project in Active Endpoints Designer

Now you're ready to create a process.

Creating a new process

Right-click on the "bpel" folder and choose New→BPEL Process from the context menu. Give a meaningful name to your process if you simply use the defaults, the same name will be used for your orchestration's namespace. Note that you don't need to include the *.bpel* extension, as it is automatically appended for you—to choose a different one, click the Advanced button. Now you have an empty process that you can start designing. An error icon will appear on your BPEL file because it's not yet valid. So add some activities to the process to correct that.

To add BPEL activities to your orchestration, you can either right-click on the blank page and choose Add, or click the Palette label on the righthand side of the workspace to expand the Palette view. This lets you drag and drop the items you want into the workspace.

Figure 9-18 shows one of the sample orchestrations that comes with the designer.

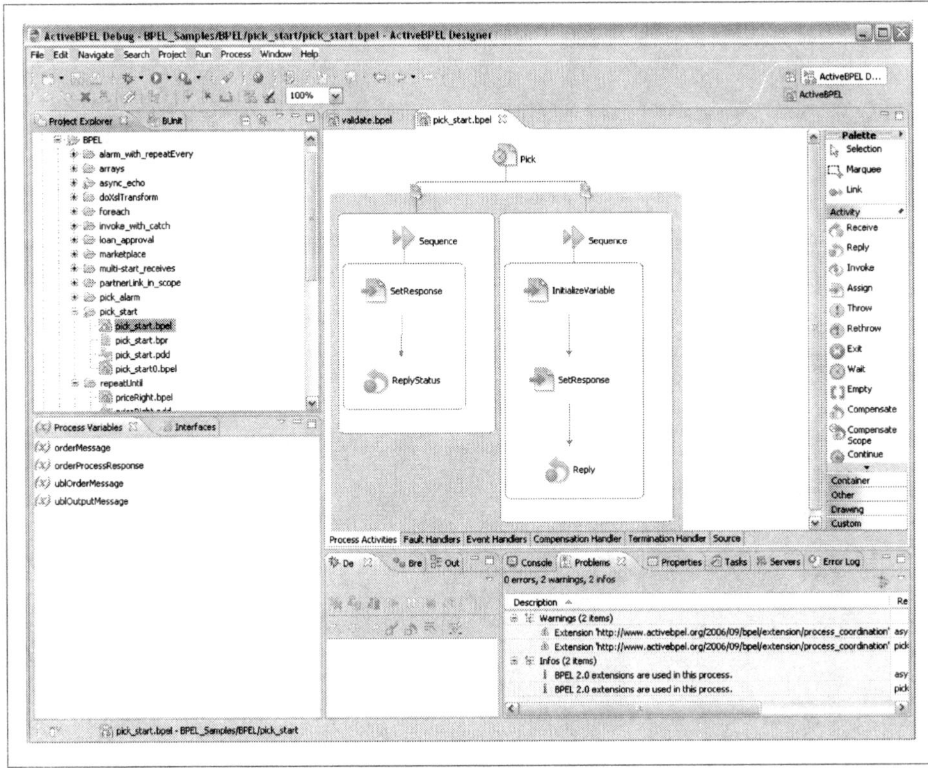

Figure 9-18. Sample orchestration in Active Endpoints Designer

For more on using the Active Endpoints BPEL designer, consult its extensive Help section. One thing to keep in mind when using this designer is that it is not friendly about allowing you to edit the BPEL XML source directly, which you will frequently need to do. The NetBeans 6.X BPEL designer does allow this.

9.13 Deploying a Process to Active Endpoints Server

Problem

You want to deploy a process to your Active Endpoints Server.

Solution

Doing this entails a few simple steps that may not be absolutely intuitive:

1. Create the orchestration project and populate your BPEL as necessary.
2. When you are ready to deploy your project, right-click on the project name in the designer and choose Export.... Then go to Orchestration→Business Process Archive File.
3. Point to the folder you want to export the *.bpr* file to. I usually choose the *deploy* folder under the orchestration project.
4. Under the Type selector, choose Web Service. This will point to your Active Endpoints Server installation. Replace the pre-populated value with *http://localhost:8080/active-bpel/services/hello* and type a username and password as applicable.
5. Make sure your Active Endpoints Server is up and running, and click Finish in the wizard to install your archive.

9.14 Using Web Service Partners

Problem

You want to define a business process that uses external web services as partners in performing the work of the process. These partners represent services that this process will invoke.

Solution

Define a `<partnerLink>` and `<partnerLinkType>` for the web service you want to invoke.

Discussion

Partner links and partner link types are important in BPEL. If you want your orchestration to be able to invoke other web services—and you surely do—you need to define the relationship between the web services involved. So a partner link represents a possible interaction between two services by indicating the port types used in the relationship. Partner links represent an extension to WSDL definitions, and because the relationship is defined using port types, it quickly becomes obvious that possible invocations from within a BPEL are restricted to services exposing a WSDL. The latest version of ActiveVOS Professional does allow you to invoke RESTful services by translating the XML to standard WSDL messages.

Each partner link is characterized by a partner link type. The BPEL 2.0 specification defines partner link types as follows: "A `<partnerLinkType>` characterizes the conversational relationship between two services by defining the roles played by each of the services in the conversation and specifying the `portType` provided by each service to receive messages withing the context of the conversation."

Every partner link in a BPEL has an associated partner link type that indicates how two services will interact. Partner links are made available within a BPEL document by adding the namespace of `xmlns:plnk="http://docs.oasis-open.org/wsbpel/2.0/plnktype"`.

Partner link types frequently define two roles: `myRole`, which indicates the role of the process itself in the relationship, and `partnerRole`, which indicates the role of the partner.

It is also common for a partner link type to define only a single role. Creating the partner link type in this way indicates that the partner is able to link with any other partner, without additional requirements.

Though they are frequently defined globally, at the process level, you can also specify partner links within a certain scope, in which case their life cycle matches that of their enclosing scope.

Say you wanted to create a relationship with a partner service that the process itself will always initiate. You can use a single `<role>` element within your `<partnerLinkType>` as in this example, borrowed from the WSDL defined in Example 9-3:

```
//...

<xmlns:plnk="http://docs.oasis-open.org/wsbpel/2.0/plnktype"

<plnk:partnerLinkType name="CustomerProcessEsb">
    <plnk:role name="CustomerProcessEsbPortTypeRole"
        portType="tns:CustomerProcessEsbPortType"/>
</plnk:partnerLinkType>
```

Defining partner links allows you to manage the conversation between partners, and essentially is a matter of deciding which side of the conversation each participant is on. A partner link is just a variable that lets you indicate the role of the process, or the role of the partner service.

In some cases (for example, when using a callback), you need to specify two roles. If you specify two roles in the partner link type, you can indicate both roles at once.

9.15 Invoking a Partner Service from a BPEL Process

Problem

The whole point of defining a service orchestration is to invoke the web services that do the actual work during the execution of the process. So, you now want to invoke a service from within your BPEL.

Solution

Use the `<invoke>` activity.

Discussion

You can think of the `<invoke>` activity as being roughly analogous to calling a method on another object from within a Java class. You have determined a flow that represents an overarching business process, such as Provision New Employee. You might have a web service that sends a message to facilities to get the employee's physical workspace set up, and another service that initiates some scripts within your IT infrastructure department to provision a new workstation and create an LDAP account for her. Both of these services would be defined as partner links in the process, and then invoked at the appropriate point using the `<invoke>` activity.

You can perform partner invocations either synchronously or asynchronously.

Here is the basic construct of an invoke, and how you might often see it used:

```
<invoke name="InvokeNewHire"
    partnerLink="hr"
    portType="employeePT"
    operation="provisionNewHire"
    inputVariable="newHire"
    outputVariable="employee"
</invoke>
```

Let's break this up a bit:

- `name` simply gives an identifier to this invocation element. This is key to keeping track of what exactly is happening when. You may want to adopt a standard naming convention for different constructs within your organization.
- `partnerLink` is required, and indicates which partner link construct to use in identifying the process to be invoked.
- `portType` indicates the port type on the partner to use. Note that while this is typically explicitly named within the `<invoke>` activity, it is optional here. That's because the port type can be derived from the combination of the partner link and its partner role. It is repeated for clarity at design time, which is a good thing. The downside is that in the event that the port type changes, the code will become outdated and need to be changed.
- `operation` is required, and specifies the operation to invoke on the service.

- `inputVariable` points to a variable containing the message or message part data that is used as a parameter to the service. This is the data going into the service during invocation.
- `outputVariable` indicates the variable that will hold the data as returned by the service. Defining this indicates that your invocation is request/response. One-way operations cannot include this attribute.

You can leave out the `outputVariable` if the service you're invoking is one-way. In such a case, processing will just continue normally without waiting for the partner.

The following list contains all of the optional child elements you can use within an invoke:

- `<correlations>`
- `<catch>`
- `<catchAll>`
- `<compensationHandler>`
- `<toParts>`
- `<fromParts>`

We'll examine all of these elsewhere in this book except for `<toParts>` and `<fromParts>` constructs. According to the spec, `<toParts>` is "used as an alternative to explicitly creating multi-part WSDL messages from the contents of WS-BPEL variables" [10.3.1], and `<fromParts>` is used to get data from an inbound message and use it to set BPEL variables. They have the following structure:

```
<toParts>?
     <toPart part="NCName" fromVariable="BPELVariableName" />+
</toParts>
<fromParts>?
     <fromPart part="NCName" toVariable="BPELVariableName" />+
</fromParts>
```

9.16 Manipulating Data with BPEL Variables

Problem

You want to reference incoming XML data within a message, or define a new variable.

Solution

Use the `<variable>` construct.

Discussion

The following sections describe the different ways you can use the `<variable>` construct to manipulate data.

Creating variables

The variables section of the process defines local variables that will be used during process execution. It looks like this:

```
<variables>
   <variable name="myVar" messageType="test:HelloMessage"/>
   <variable name="tmpVar" type="xsd:string"/>
</variables>
```

When the execution starts, following the `<sequence>` element, a message coming into the process will need to be assigned a name and some memory space so that the process can refer to it. Once defined, these variables can be assigned to other variables, queried using XPath expressions, transformed, and used as input to service invocations (partner links).

Variables must be WSDL message types or XML Schema types or elements. Using variables, a process can keep state between activities, much like fields in a Java object.

In this example, there are two variables created, "myVar" and "tmpVar". The "myVar" variable has a type of `HelloMessage` in the test namespace. That type is defined as a WSDL message type in *HelloWorld2.wsdl*. It looks like this:

```
<wsdl:message name="HelloMessage">
    <wsdl:part name="TestPart" type="xsd:string"/>
</wsdl:message>
```

So a `HelloMessage` has a `TestPart` that is a string. This is used by the `<receive>` activity, which we'll look at shortly.

Referencing variables

Once a variable has been created, you can reference it using XPath expressions. Prefix the variable name with a dollar sign to access its data. Perhaps the best way to understand the path referencing of data within a variable is to see an example. Say that you have the following type defined:

```
<xsd:complexType name="Book">
    <xsd:sequence>
        <xsd:attribute name="title" type="xsd:string" minOccurs="1"/>
        <xsd:element name="author" type="my:Author" minOccurs="1"/>
    </xsd:sequence>
</xsd:complextType>
<xsd:complexType name="Author">
    <xsd:sequence>
        <xsd:element name="firstName" type="xsd:string"/>
        <xsd:element name="lastName" type="xsd:string"/>
```

```
    </xsd:sequence>
</xsd:complexType>
```

Given a BPEL variable like this:

```
<variables>
   <variable name="aCookbook" messageType="my:Book"/>
</variables>
```

You could find out the last name of the author using an expression like this, skipping the element name:

```
$aCookbook/author/lastName
```

An alternative syntax that you'll sometimes see is the more verbose built-in function `bpel:getVariableProperty("variableName", "propertyQName")`. This is a BPEL XPath extension that can be used to get data from a global property.

You can use full XPath expressions to reference variables. For example, rather than pointing directly to a physical path down the tree, you can use indexes within your expressions to find matching elements.

Say that you have a schema that defines a **`Books`** complex type that in turn holds a collection of `Book` complex types. Each `Book` (as in the schema example above) has a `title` attribute. You could reference the third title in the collection of `Books` like this:

```
//your bpel variable:
<bpel:variable name="Books" type="soa:Books" />

//this expression gets the third title:

$Books/soa:Books[3]/@Title
```

Please refer to Recipe 3.4 if you need a refresher on using XPath expressions.

In-scope namespaces

This is straightforward enough, but what if you add the difficulty of dealing with in-scope namespaces? You must use the prefix of the in-scope namespace when referencing variables. An example makes this clear. Say you have a BPEL variable that you'd like to copy data from. If its namespace prefix is different, you can still work with the data, but you must indicate that in your expression:

```
<o:author xmlns:o="http://oreilly.com">
  <o:firstName>Tim</o:firstName>
</o:author>
```

In order to reach the value of the first author here (despite hiding the namespace prefix), you could use the following expression within your copy/from to return the value `Tim`:

```
<from xmlns:orm="http://oreilly.com">
  $AuthorVar/orm:firstName/text()
</from>
```

Here the namespace prefixed has changed, and you reference the enclosing prefix within the expression.

Comparing variables

You can compare the values extracted from variables using some standard comparison features. For example, to see if a variable value for certain inventory is less than 10 (perhaps so you could order more stock), you could write this:

```
bpel:getVariableProperty('stockResponse', 'inv:stockLevel') < 10
```

Validating variables

During the execution of a process, data can be validated easily—as long as your vendor supports it. You can do it using the validate activity:

```
<validate variables="var1 var2">
</validate>
```

Separate the variable names you want to validate with spaces.

Apache ODE 1.2 (current as of this writing) does not support variable validation.

Vendors may also optionally implement validation within other related activities that handle message values, such as `<receive>`, `<invoke>`, `<reply>`, `<pick>`, and `<onEvent>`.

9.17 Using Literals

Problem

You want a fast and easy way to add data to your process using string literal values. For example, you'd like to take parts of the variable data within a received message and construct an email from it. You might want to have some boilerplate text that is always the same, and then populate the dynamic parts of the email body using data extracted with XPath from a SOAP message at runtime.

Solution

Use the `<literal>` construct and specify the value for the literal between the start and closing tags.

Discussion

Here's an example that illustrates using a literal to populate part of an email variable type. Hypothetically, this can be used by a partner process to send the email message over SMTP:

```
<variables>
  <variable name="SendEmailIn"
     messageType="emailws:sendEmail"/>
//...

<sequence name="CreateEmailSequence">
  <assign name="CreateEmailMessage">
    <copy>
      <from>
        <literal>myProcess@example.com</literal>
      </from>
      <to>$SendEmailIn.emailMsg/fromAddress</to>
    </copy>
//...
```

This is very simple. All you have to do to create a literal string value that you want to assign in some useful way is to wrap it with the `<literal>` element. In this example, you have a variable called `SendEmailIn` that is of a type defined in a schema associated with this process. The `emailMsg` element has a `fromAddress` element, and here you assign your literal email address string as its value. Other literals or values from message data can be used to populate the remainder of the email.

9.18 Concatenating Values

Problem

You want to merge two values together within a BPEL variable. Perhaps you want your result to be a combination of runtime values and literals.

Solution

Use the `concat()` function, and comma-separate the values you want to concatenate.

Discussion

This function is very straightforward. This example highlights how to combine a literal value with a runtime value that is extracted using XPath expressions:

```
<copy>
      <from>
concat('The application received an error message:',
' AUTH-NUMBER=', $ProcessAppIn.app/authNumber,
' STATUS-MESSAGE=', $ProcessAppOut.appResponse/status/statusName,
' STATUS-CODE=', $ProcessAppOut.appResponse/status/statusCode)
</from>
```

```
        <to>$SendEmailIn.emailMsg/body</to>
    </copy>
```

Here you are creating the body of an email message using literal values, as represented inside the tick marks, combined with values extracted from variables at runtime. The `$` represents the variable of some schema type, and the `.` represents the path to its element. The / represents the path down the XML data tree to the value you're interested in extracting.

At the end of the execution of this `<copy>` block, the body of the email will look something like this, depending on runtime values (and without the line breaks):

```
The application received an error message:
AUTH-NUMBER=605516
STATUS-MESSAGE=OUT OF STOCK
STATUS-CODE=SC404
```

9.19 Choosing an Activity to Execute Based on Runtime Conditions

Problem

You want to perform conditional logic within your process, for example, by testing values within messages.

Solution

Use the `<if>` activity. Specify the primary condition you're testing for using a nested `<condition>` element. The `<if>` can be followed by a series of `<elseif>`s and a single `<else>`.

Discussion

This operates just as you would expect from using conditional logic in any language. While the basic ideas are the same (unlimited "else-if" statements and a single "else" statement), the syntactical structure is what's unusual.

Here's a basic example:

```
<if name="IfInsufficientQty">
  <condition>
      ( ($ProcessAppOut.appResponse/status/statusName='INSUFF_QTY' )
    or
      ($ProcessAppOut.appResponse/status/statusName='OUT_OF_STOCK') )
  </condition>

  <sequence name="EmailErrorSequence">

    //make email message here using assign, etc...
```

```
        <invoke name="InvokeSendEmail" partnerLink="EmailPartner"
              operation="sendEmail" portType="emailws:Email"
              inputVariable="SendEmailIn"/>

      </sequence>
    </if>
```

This example supposes that a service has been previously invoked that returns a type with an element of `appResponse` that holds, among other things, status information. So create an `<if>` block that will only be executed if the expression specified inside the `<condition>` block returns true. Give your conditional check a name to help any visual editor you might be using, and to help you keep it straight within the XML source.

The expression specified will be true if the response `statusName` element contains one of two literal values about how much merchandise is on hand, and the sequence of activities inside the `<if>` block will be activated. You want to do more than one thing if the expression is true (create an email, and then invoke the partner service that will send it), and you want to execute the activities in a specific order, so you need to use a `<sequence>` to demarcate the activities as a single unit.

<elseif> and <else>

These function just as you would expect: if the initial `<if>` activity they're partnered with does not evaluate to true, each `<elseif>` condition is evaluated until one of them returns true. If `<elseif>` returns true, an associated `<else>` condition is evaluated (if one is present). If none return true, no nested activity is executed. Once one of the `<elseif>`s returns true, the remaining possibilities are never evaluated. Of course, the XPath 1.0 expressions used in the conditions must evaluate to a Boolean value.

Some BPEL engines extend the possibilities for expression languages you can use. Active Endpoints, for example, allows you to use JavaScript 1.5 or XQuery 1.0 as expression languages.

Here is the basic structure of a set of if/elseif/else branches:

```
<if standard-attributes>
   standard-elements

   <condition expressionLanguage="someURI"?>
       boolean-expression
   </condition>
   activity

   <elseif>*
       <condition expressionLanguage="someURI"?>
            boolean-expression
       </condition>
       activity
   </elseif>
```

```
        <else>?
            activity
        </else>
    </if>
```

The * indicates that zero or more `<elseif>` constructs are allowed; the ? indicates that zero or one `<else>` constructs is allowed.

Here is a complete example:

```
<if name="checkAvailability">
  <condition>
    starts-with($purchaseOrder.purchaseOrder/po:orderDescription,
               'Product 123')
  </condition>

  <assign name="InventoryAvailable">
    <copy>
      <from>true()</from>
        <to>$inventoryStatus.inventoryPart/i:inventoryAvail</to>
      </copy>
      <copy>
        <from>'This item is available'</from>
        <to>$inventoryStatus.inventoryPart/i:inventoryStatusMessage</to>
      </copy>
    </assign>
<else>
    <assign name="InsufficientQty">
        <copy>
          <from>false()</from>
          <to>$inventoryStatus.inventoryPart/i:inventoryAvail</to>
        </copy>
        <copy>
          <from>'Out of stock'</from>
          <to>$inventoryStatus.inventoryPart/i:inventoryStatusMessage</to>
        <copy>
      </assign>
    </else>
</if>
```

Here you're using a starts-with expression to determine whether you are dealing with a certain product. If so, you indicate that inventory is available; otherwise, put a value in the status message indicating that you're out.

9.20 Executing Multiple Activities in a Sequence

Problem

You want to execute two or more activities sequentially.

Solution

Use a <sequence> container structure to encapsulate the activities. They will be executed in the order in which they appear.

Discussion

Sequences do no work themselves, but rather define a structure around other activities. A sequence uses only the standard attributes that are allowed for any activity (name and suppressJoinFailure), and those are optional. A sequence must define one or more child activities. Apart from that, there's nothing more to it:

```
<sequence name="CheckInventory">
  <receive name="InventoryServiceReceive"
    partnerLink="inventorySevicePL"
    portType="i:inventoryPortType"
    operation="inventoryService"
    variable="purchaseOrder"
    createInstance="yes">
  </receive>
  <if name="ifQty">
    <condition>...</condition>
      //...
    <else>
      //...
    </else>
  </if>
  <reply name="InventoryServiceReply"
     partnerLink="inventorySevicePL"
     portType="i:inventoryPortType"
     operation="inventoryService"
     variable="status"/>
</sequence>
```

This sequence will ensure that the receive, the conditional logic, and the reply all happen in the specified order.

If you want to execute activities in parallel, you cannot use a sequence, and instead should use a <flow>.

See Also

Recipe 10.1 to see how to execute activities all at once instead of one after another.

9.21 Using Logical Divisions to Group Activities

Problem

You have defined variables or activities whose scope you want to limit to only a certain subset of the process.

Solution

Use a `<scope>`. These are frequently used, and in a way constitute the building blocks of processes. They are simple elements to use, but their usage can be subtle, so check out the discussion below.

Discussion

In Java, variables and other language constructs have *scope*, meaning they have a defined range within the code in which they are visible or usable. A method-local variable is not visible outside of that method; a private method is not usable from another class. Scope is useful to logically divide code to ensure that some given functionality is available only within certain parameters. BPEL provides a similar capability to organize activities within subsets of a process.

BPEL scopes are actually closer to the HTML `<div>` tag than they are to the implicit scopes in Java. Not only do they encapsulate what can obtain within a given context, they are explicitly stated, and do no actual work of their own.

A BPEL scope provides a context for the behavior surrounding one or more units of work. Using scopes, you can associate various constructs such as event handlers, fault handlers, compensations, variables, and more.

A BPEL process can include one or more scopes. Each scope can also include other scopes, nested to any depth. A process can also define peer-level scopes that set off different areas of code.

Certain commonsense rules apply regarding the visibility of activities and variables within a scope:

- Variables declared at the topmost level of a process are global, meaning they are available from any aspect of the process.
- Variables declared within a certain scope are visible only within that scope or any scopes nested inside that scope. Nested scopes are also called child or descendant scopes. If a variable is declared inside a scope, it is not visible to any parent scopes (also called "ancestor scopes").

- Variable hiding obtains within nested scopes, just as in Java, where a method-local variable can hide a field of the same name.

Scopes are merely a logical division used to offset functionality that should be in effect only if a given circumstance is true, for example, if a SOAP fault is thrown. They can include a variety of activities, such as variable assignments, correlation sets, event handlers, or fault handlers.

Two activities in BPEL require the use of scopes: `<forEach>` and `<onEvent>`. With `<forEach>`, the scope defines the event handler variable. For `<onEvent>`, the scope owns the definition of the loop counter variable.

You define a scope using the `<scope>` element. A scope can declare variables, partner links, message exchanges, and correlation sets. Here is its structure:

```
<scope isolated="yes|no"? exitOnStandardFault="yes|no"?
       standard-attributes>
   standard-elements
   <variables />?
   <partnerLinks />?
   <messageExchanges />?
   <correlationSets />?
   <eventHandlers />?
   <faultHandlers />?
   <compensationHandler />?
   <terminationHandler />?

   activity

</scope>
```

Any of the above constructs (variables, partner links, fault handlers, etc.) defined within a scope are usable within that scope. A scope is actually similar to a process tag too. The only thing that you can do at the process level that you cannot do at the scope level is import anything or declare any extensions to use. But there are also two things that you *can* do in scopes that you can't do at the process level: termination handlers and compensations.

Scopes actually get their own chapter in the BPEL 2.0 specification, and it's more than 30 pages long. So while they are a very simple concept to understand, are usable throughout most of the BPEL constructs, and generally behave just as one hopes they would according to common sense, they can have subtle side effects depending on how you use them. If you're puzzling about your scopes, you might consult the spec.

Here is an example that highlights a standard use of a scope:

```
<scope>
   <faultHandlers>
      <catch>
         <terminate/>
      </catch>
   </faultHandlers>


   <!-- The "primary activity"-->
   <sequence>
      <invoke .../>
      <assign .../>
   </sequence>
</scope>
```

The primary activity of the scope is to execute the sequence that contains an invoke followed by an assign. If anything goes wrong during one of those activities, processing will be handed over to the fault handlers in this containing scope. Constructs not defined in this scope will force any side effects of the primary activities to be escalated to the next enclosing scope. Scopes can be arbitrarily nested, so this continues until the process level itself is reached.

Summary

BPEL 2.0 allows you to represent business processes in a standard orchestration language. With BPEL, you can wire together existing web services to create new composite applications. This helps you to streamline and automate processes.

But BPEL 2.0 is a long and complex specification, so we've only scratched the surface. There are many more advanced features of BPEL, and those are really what make it worthwhile. We'll examine these advanced features in the next chapter.

CHAPTER 10

Advanced Orchestrations with BPEL

10.0 Introduction

This chapter picks up right where we left off. Chapter 9 got you going on BPEL basics. You saw how to install a variety of BPEL engines and how to write and deploy basic BPEL orchestrations. But BPEL is a large and complex subject, and in this chapter, we'll look at some of the more advanced topics, including include parallel execution, timers, correlation, looping, faults, and more. Let's jump right in.

10.1 Executing Activities in Parallel

Problem

You want to execute a set of related activities concurrently.

Solution

Use the BPEL `<flow>` structured activity.

Discussion

In its simplest form, the `<flow>` appears much like a `<sequence>`, in that it is merely a container for other activities that do actual work. The difference is that all of the items specified within the `<flow>` are executed at roughly the same time. In other words, one does not wait for another to finish, and therefore you cannot treat the result of one operation within a flow as the input to another. Here is an example:

```
<else>
  <sequence name="Purchase">

    <flow name="SaleCompletedNotifyFlow">

      <invoke name="NotifySeller"
        partnerLink="contactPLink"
        operation="contactService"
```

```
            portType="ct:contactPortType"
            inputVariable="ContactServiceIn"
            outputVariable="ContactServiceOut"/>

          <invoke name="NotifyShipper"
            partnerLink="requestShippingPLink"
            operation="shippingService"
            portType="shp:shippingPortType"
            inputVariable="ShippingServiceIn"
            outputVariable="ShippingerviceOut"/>

        </flow>

        <assign name="AssignValues">
    //...
```

In this example, the <flow> activity is kicked off when a customer makes a purchase. The invocations of the customer contact service and the shipping service both need to happen right after a sale is made. They don't require input from one another, and executing one doesn't have to wait until the other is complete. The flow itself completes when all of its child activities have completed.

You can also add a <documentation> element as a direct child of a <flow>, which allows you to enter arbitrary text data to indicate how the flow works.

This is useful in many situations, particularly in distributed service environments where the services do not rely on shared processing resources.

See Also

It is frequently the case that you will need to synchronize the execution of certain activities within a flow; that is, you may want to run some activities concurrently, but then force one to wait for another to complete. Check out Recipe 10.2.

10.2 Synchronizing Activities Executing in Parallel

Problem

You're using a <flow> to allow parallel activities to execute, but you want to synchronize some of the executing tasks.

Solution

Define a set of <links> within the <flow>. Use their names as values for <source> and <target> structures that will synchronize the flow based on a <joinCondition>.

Discussion

Say that you have two activities, such as invoking two separate services, that both need to complete before some next step can begin. If you don't know which of the invocations will complete first, you can use a link within a `<flow>` to express this dependency.

The elements `<sources>` and `<targets>` respectively contain `<source>` and `<target>` elements, which are used to establish a relationship for synchronizing their encapsulating activities. The relationship is defined using a `<link>`. Here's an example of the chiefly relevant elements:

```
//...
<flow>
   <links>
      <link name="airplaneBooked" />
      <link name="hotelBooked" />
   </links>

   <receive name="receiveAirReservation" ...>
      <sources>
         <source linkName="airplaneBooked" />
      </sources>
   </receive>

   <receive name="receiveHotelReservation" ...>
      <sources>
         <source linkName="hotelBooked" />
      </sources>
   </receive>

   <scope name="submitExpenseScope">
      <targets>
         <joinCondition>
            $airplaneBooked and $hotelBooked
         </joinCondition>

         <target linkName="airplaneBooked" />
         <target linkName="hotelBooked" />
      </targets>

      <compensationHandler>
         <invoke name="handleReservationIssue" ... />
      </compensationHandler>

      <invoke name="submitExpenseReport" ... />
   </scope>
</flow>
```

In this example, you have a process for creating a trip reservation that defines an operation for booking air travel and another for booking a hotel. The flight and the hotel are handled by your business partners, and your company policy dictates that the complete trip must be booked before you can submit an expense report for the travel.

Therefore, you can't invoke the `submitExpenseReport` action until you know that both dependent operations are complete. So you create two links, one for each action. Inside the activity that defines the action, specify each as a `<source>` to indicate that it is an object of interest to be synchronized later.

The names of links must be unique throughout the enclosing flow. So while technically you could define the same link name twice in a process as long as they're in different flows, this is considered bad form.

The two source activities (book airline ticket and book hotel reservation) are referred to as targets in the `submitExpenseScope` scope. That is, you specify a `joinCondition` that indicates an expression combining the two link sources: once both are done, then the separate threads of activity can join back into one, and execution can continue. The compensation handler will be invoked if anything goes wrong, and the process will exit. If everything goes all right and the travel is booked, and then you finally submit the expense report and the flow will end. The `joinCondition` is a Boolean expression, in which a result of true will allow the flow to continue.

There are a considerable number of fairly detailed rules regarding `<link>` semantics. If you wish to do anything more complicated than what is shown here, check out the BPEL 2.0 standard, published by OASIS Open at *http://docs.oasis-open.org/wsbpel/2.0/wsbpel-v2.0.html*.

See Also

Recipe 10.1.

10.3 Doing Nothing

Problem

You want to use a BPEL construct that requires an activity, but you don't have any actual functionality to execute there. Or perhaps you want to specify a point of synchronization within a flow, or you want to suppress a fault you've caught.

Solution

Use an `<empty>` activity.

Discussion

The empty activity exists as a placeholder, allowing you to create a point in your BPEL diagram that does not actually do anything. Other related activities, however, can take advantage of this. Depending on how you structure your process, your process may sometimes need to have an activity to join two structures. You can use `<empty>` to do this.

The example given in the specification for when to use an empty activity is this: there is a fault that you must catch, but you'd like to suppress that fact. Of course, this is usually not a brilliant idea.

10.4 Executing an Activity at a Specific Point in Time

Problem

You want your business process to wait until a specific point in time before it executes the next block of code, such as an `invoke` activity.

Solution

Use the `<wait until="...">` activity to make the process wait until a specific deadline is reached. Supply a value to the `until` attribute using the XPath expression syntax for a deadline.

Discussion

The complete expression syntax for deadlines is shown in Table 10-1.

Table 10-1. XPath deadline expression values

Value	Meaning
T	Time designator, indicating that the following values represent the time of day.
C	Centuries.
Y	Years.
M	Months.
D	Days.
h	Hours.
m	Minutes.
s	Seconds. You can use `ss.sss` to represent greater precision with milliseconds.
Z	UTC time (Coordinated Universal Time). This element should immediately follow the time of day element (`T`).

There are a few ways to represent deadlines with more or less precision, as shown in the following example.

This timer will expire on New Year's Eve, 2010, a second before midnight:

```
<wait until="2010-12-31T23:59:59+01:100"/>
```

10.5 Executing an Activity After a Specific Delay

Problem

You want your business process to wait for a set amount of time before it executes a given activity.

Solution

Use the `<wait for="...">` activity. Supply a value to the `for` attribute using XPath expression syntax after a "P" (durations always start with "P").

Discussion

The complete expression syntax for durations is represented in Table 10-2.

Table 10-2. XPath Duration Expression Values

Value	Meaning
P	Duration designator, indicating that the following values represent a period of time.
Y	Years.
M	Months or Minutes, depending on relation to the T.
D	Days.
H	Hours.
S	Seconds.

There are a few ways to represent durations with more or less precision, as shown in the following examples.

Remember that all durations start with a "P", and the time must be demarcated by prepending a "T".

The following timer will expire in three hours, five minutes:

```
<wait for="PT3H05M" />
```

The following timer will expire in one year, two months, three days, four hours, and five minutes:

```
<wait for="P1Y2M3DT4H5M" />
```

10.6 Selective Event Processing

Problem

You want your process to wait for a given event to occur from within a set of possible events, and then execute the activity associated with that event.

Solution

Use the standard `<pick>` construct.

Discussion

There are two "start" activities in BPEL. The first, and perhaps most common, is `<receive>`, and the other is `<pick>`.

A `<pick>` is similar to a switch/case construct in programming languages; it allows you to define a set of events you are interested in getting notice for, typically when a message from a certain operation is received. When the process detects that this event has occurred, it will execute the activities associated with that event. In its most common form, this "event" is an `<onMessage>` construct that indicates the `portType` and `operation` that it is waiting to get messages from.

When you use the attribute value of `createInstance="yes"`, an `<onMessage>` activity is equivalent to a `<receive>`, in that it waits to get a message incoming to the process. Once an `<onMessage>` is activated, it can perform any kind of process work, which typically is to invoke a web service operation exposed by the business process using a variable containing the received message. Further, once an event has been selected, none of the other event possibilities can be accepted by that `<pick>`.

Here is the basic outline of this activity:

```
<pick name="Pick1">
  <onMessage partnerLink="SupplyServicePLink"
    operation="addItem"
    portType="sp:purchaseOrderPT"
    variable="LineItemIn">
    <correlations .../> <!--do work to accept a new order line item-->
  </onMessage>

  <onMessage partnerLink="SupplyServicePLink"
    operation="submitOrder"
    portType="sp:purchaseOrderPT"
    variable="SendPurchaseOrderIn">
    <correlations .../> <!--do work for when order is complete -->
  </onMessage>

  <onAlarm>
    <for>'PODT2H'</for>
    <empty/><!-- notify timeout on order completion -->
```

```
        </onAlarm>
    </pick>
```

In this example, you define two branches, one as a business partner that sends supplies they're ordering, and in the other branch you complete the order. Once the order is complete, you will do some work such as notifying shipping.

Using alarms

In the example just shown, an alarm will go off after two hours of waiting. Many of the attributes used in the `<onMessage>` activity are the same as those used in `<receive>`. The `<onAlarm>` behavior within a `<pick>` is similar to that of a `<wait>`, in which the countdown begins right when the `<pick>` activity starts. It links a deadline to the execution of the activities. In the previous example, you used a `<for>` to express a duration, but you could also use `<until>`.

If your `<pick>` has an attribute value of `createInstance="yes"` indicating that it is the starting activity for the process, all of the `<pick>`'s children must be `<onMessage>` activities; that is, it cannot have an `<onAlarm>` child in that case.

One usage for alarms in a `<pick>` is following an `<invoke>`. Your process could define a sequence wherein an invoke is followed by a pick that contains one `<onMessage>` and one `<onAlarm>` with a certain timeout. The alarm would time out after waiting a certain duration for the message to be received. This allows you to keep your process from getting hung up by a runaway service. It works well because, as you'll recall, other activities are disabled after one has been selected.

10.7 Handling Faults

Problem

You want to gracefully handle exceptions that are thrown during the execution of a partner web service within your process.

Solution

Use a `<faultHandlers>` container and its associated `<catch>` or `<catchAll>` constructs.

Discussion

You can't always assume that everything will go according to plan with a composite service process. Just as you would use exception handling within Java, BPEL makes available certain constructs that allow you do to cleanup work when an exception is thrown during the execution of your process. Using fault handlers is intuitive and simple. Catching faults is very similar to catching exceptions in Java except that you needn't define an associated `try`. Fault handlers can be declared globally across an entire process, within a scope, or directly on an `<invoke>` activity.

Fault handlers are made available immediately upon initialization of the scope to which they are attached. If a fault occurs during processing of the attached scope (even if there is no formal scope declared and the implicit global scope is used), the error will be propagated to the associated fault handler. Faults are initialized within a BPEL process if the associated WSDL operation returns a fault message. Faults can also be thrown by the BPEL process itself, such as in the event that some complex construct (such as a `<join>`) fails, or a network failure occurs.

Here is the basic construct to define a global fault handler (that is, one that is not associated with a more specific, explicitly defined scope):

```
<variables>
    <variable name="CartFault" messageType="pos:cartFaultType"></variable>
</variables>

<faultHandlers>
    <catch faultName="CartFault"
        faultVariable="CartFault">
    //...handle with an activity, such as <reply> to caller
    </catch>
</faultHandlers>
```

The `faultName` attribute refers to the name of the SOAP fault that you want to catch. Note that your WSDL must include fault information for the variable's `messageType` attribute value. For example, because here you have decided that the `CartFault` variable will be of type `<cartFaultType>`, you need that message defined in a WSDL referred to by this process. Here's a snippet from an example WSDL that represents the shopping cart service acting as a process partner:

```
<message name="cartFaultType">
  <part name="faultInfo" type="xsd:string"></part>
</message>

<portType name="CartPort">
  <operation name="placeOrder">
    <input name="submitOrderRequest" message="tns:OrderMsg"></input>
    <output name="orderResponse" message="tns:OrderMsg"></output>
    <fault name="cannotCompleteOrder" message="tns:cartFaultType"></fault>
  </operation>
</portType>

<binding name="cartBinding" type="tns:cartPort">
  <soap:binding style="document"
    transport="http://schemas.xmlsoap.org/soap/http"/>
  <operation name="placeOrder">
      <soap:operation style="rpc"/>
      <input name="submitOrderRequest">
          <soap:body parts="purchaseOrder" use="literal"/>
      </input>
      <output name="orderResponse">
          <soap:body parts="purchaseOrder" use="literal"/>
      </output>
      <fault name="cannotCompleteOrder">
```

```
            <soap:fault name="cannotCompleteOrder" use="literal"/>
        </fault>
    </operation>
</binding>
```

Here the WSDL represents the <fault> as a first-class citizen along with the inputs and outputs. You declare a message type that holds the fault detail information, and that information is associated with the placeOrder operation in the abstract portion of the WSDL. Finally, in the binding section, that fault is made concrete in the form of a SOAP fault.

The <catch> activity can contain a variety of other constructs; for example, a <sequence> allows you to do more than one thing inside the handler.

Each <catch> is intended to handle a single fault. There are three ways to associate a <catch> with a fault type:

- Match the faultName and faultVariable type.
- Match a global variable by its faultName only (which must be a unique QName).
- Match a global variable by its faultVariable type. In this case, it must refer to a WSDL faultMessage type, or an XML schema element (faultElement type).

It is best to match both the name and variable type, as this is the clearer and most specific option. The BPEL engine will attempt to find the best match it can for a fault that has been thrown in the current scope. If it can't find any match, the engine looks for a <catchAll>; if none is defined, the fault gets thrown to the default handler. You don't want to rely on the default handler any more than you would in a Java program. Doing so is a lot like writing this:

```
public static void main(String... arg) throws Exception { ... }
```

Default fault handling

A fault handler is allowed two different types of children: <catch> and <catchAll>. The <catchAll> construct is defined as a default handler for exceptions that you do not explicitly name. You use the <catchAll> construct as a child of a <faultHandler>. You define this construct at the end of a fault handler, usually after you have defined specific faults that you explicitly want to catch.

Often a fault handler is defined within an <invoke> activity to catch any faults thrown during the invocation of a given service. Such a construct looks like this:

```
<bpel:invoke inputVariable="aRequest"
    operation="checkStock" outputVariable="aResponse"
    partnerLink="myCartPartner" portType="cart:CartPortType">
    <bpel:catchAll>
      //...
    </bpel:catchAll>
</bpel:invoke>
```

You can combine the two as well:

```
<bpel:invoke inputVariable="aRequest"
    operation="checkStock" outputVariable="aResponse"
    partnerLink="myCartPartner" portType="cart:CartPortType">
    <catch faultName="CartFault"
        faultVariable="CartFault">
    //...handle with an activity, such as <reply> to caller
    </catch>
    <bpel:catchAll>
      //...
    </bpel:catchAll>
</bpel:invoke>
```

This is roughly analogous to the following Java code:

```
try {
  //...some work
} catch (IOException ioe) {
  //handle
} catch (Exception e) {
  //handle
}
```

10.8 Explicitly Throwing a Fault

Problem

You want to signal a fault within the process itself, rather than using only those available in a partner WSDL.

Solution

Use the `<throw>` construct.

Discussion

If a WSDL used as a partner in a process declares a SOAP fault, your business process should deal with it (though it is not required to). If your orchestration is largely composed of invocations of a series of other services in a sequence, you may have nothing further to say on the subject of errors in your process itself; you may choose just to propagate the faults signaled by the partners.

But in more sophisticated or complex BPELs that perform more decision logic, branching, waiting, and so forth, it can be very useful to declare a fault within the process itself. You can then signal that fault according to the demands of your process. For example, say you're `<wait>`-ing on a partner that isn't responding. It's obviously not going to throw a fault, so you can decide on a reasonable timeout and do it yourself.

Throwing a fault is a way of transferring control within a process. As in Java and other languages with structured exception handling, you're signaling that you want to halt the normal flow of processing, and start the work defined in the fault handler.

The <throw> activity provides a name for the fault and, if you like, can also carry detail information.

Here's an example of using this construct:

```
<if name="Decision">
  <condition>
    starts-with($cartRequest.cartData/po:userDomain, 'WEST')
  </condition>
  <sequence name="MySequence">
     <assign name="MyAssign">
       <copy>
         <from>'User must order from a different region.'</from>
         <to part="faultInfo" variable="wrongDomainFault"/>
       </copy>
     </assign>
     <throw name="ThrowAddToCart" faultName="pos:wrongDomain"
        faultVariable="wrongDomainFault" />
   </sequence>
</if>
```

Here, the <throw> is inside an <if> condition. You use an XPath function to determine the value of a node, and decide based on that value to explicitly throw a fault. The fault will then get picked up by the most suitable handler in the nearest containing scope.

In this example, you use an XPath expression to compare a constant value against data in the current message, and decide to throw a fault if the condition is met. You start a sequence in order to add detail information to the fault from a literal value.

The <throw> activity does not require you to define a fault name elsewhere. The fault can also be provided by a WSDL or be a standard BPEL fault. Here is a list of standard BPEL faults (of these, `joinFailures` are probably the most common):

ambiguousReceive	completionConditionFailure
conflictingReceive	conflictingRequest
correlationViolation	invalidBranchCondition
invalidExpressionValue	invalidVariables
joinFailure	mismatchedAssignmentFailure
missingReply	missingRequest
scopeInitializationFailure	selectionFailure
subLanguageExecutionFault	uninitializedParterRole
uninitializedVariable	unsupportedReference
xsltInvalidSource	xlstStylesheetNotFound

10.9 Stopping a Process

Problem

You want to immediately end the execution of a process.

Solution

Use the `<exit>` activity.

Discussion

In general, you should have good fault handling defined in your process. There are many problematic situations that we as process developers can anticipate and handle gracefully. This is no different from how we would work in any programming language with structured exception handling.

But there are times when something severe, something so outrageous happens that you want to shut down the process immediately, ending all current activities, without compensating or rolling back in-flight transactions, without performing error handling, and without notifying any other process. To do this, you use the `<exit>` activity. It looks like this:

```
<if>
    <condition>...
  <else>
    <condition>...
  </else>
  <elseif>
    <exit />
  </elseif>
</if>
```

There certainly are times when you are simply unable to handle a severe error on the server, and may have few other options than to just stop the process. But keep in mind that this is considered a serious, if not brutal, way to handle a flow. If you're thinking of using `<exit>`, put your Java programmer hat back on for a moment and consider how frequently you actually resort to `Thread.stop` or `System.exit`. (Hopefully not very often!)

10.10 Performing an XSL Transformation on BPEL Message Data

Problem

You want to transform the data in an incoming message before routing its contents to a partner service.

Solution

Use BPEL's built-in XSLT transformation function, `doXslTransform()`.

Discussion

Combined with XPath 1.0, BPEL assignment is handy. But when you add the ability to transform in-flight XML data with XSLT, you've got something very powerful. BPEL 2.0 implementations are required to support the `doXslTransform()` function.

The function takes the following form:

```
bpel:doXslTransform(xslStyleSheetPath, sourceDocument,
                    [paramName, paramValue]*)
```

Let's break this down to look at the required variables.

The `xslStyleSheetPath` must be a string literal value that points to the URI of the imported XSL stylesheet, and it must be available to the compiler at design time. The `sourceDocument` refers to the node-set that you want to transform. This is an XML document or fragment available within a message or variable part.

Finally, you have a pair of optional parameters (demarcated here by square brackets) that may be used to pass name/value pairs into your XSLT stylesheet if it uses them. The name must be qualified. Note that the * indicates that you can pass a variable-length list of these name/value pairs. Passing an odd number of parameters is invalid, and your BPEL compiler will tell you so.

The result of the transformation is returned by the function so that it can be assigned to another local variable, or passed into a web service call.

The `doXslTransform` function is terrific if you need to maintain different versions of messages that route to the same service. For example, say that you have defined a service that accepts customer address information, but industry restrictions or some new business partner now requires you to send them additional information that your source service does not provide. A cardinal virtue of a profitable SOA is interface stability. You don't have the time or ability to change every client of your service to provide this additional data, or data in the newly required format. This is where XSLT may offer a good solution. Using the `doXslTransform` function allows you to provide your business partners with the right data (say, in the form of defaults) in the right format, but in a way that doesn't force you to change your client-facing interface.

Here is a quick example of how to use the `doXslTransform` function:

```
<invoke partnerLink="Warehouse"
   outputVariable="inventoryItems" ...>
</invoke>
```

```
<!-- Reformat the items coming from the warehouse
     for another system in the process -->
<assign>
  <copy>
    <from>
      bpel:doXslTransform("orderItems.xsl", $inventoryItems)
    </from>
    <to>
      $orderItems
    </to>
  </copy>
</assign>

...
```

The XSL stylesheet will be applied to the items that are returned by the invocation of the warehouse partner service, massaging them into a format that is consumable by another part of the process. This could be a different partner operation you're going to invoke, or some other activity. The point is that you copy from the transformation to a variable (here, `$orderItems`) that will hold the result of the transformation.

10.11 Validating Inbound Message Data

Problem

You want to validate the data in an inbound message against its XML schema definition.

Solution

Use the `<validate>` activity, and specify the name of the variables to validate. If validation fails, the standard BPEL fault `invalidVariables` is thrown.

Discussion

The `<validate>` activity validates a list of variables against the schema that defines them. Here is an example:

```
<sequence>
    <receive name="sendPurchaseOrder"
         partnerLink="POServicePLink"
         portType="pos:purchaseOrderPT"
         operation="sendPurchaseOrder"
         variable="purchaseOrderRequest"
         createInstance="yes">
    </receive>
    <validate name="validatePO" variables="purchaseOrderRequest" />
<assign name="Assign_2">
```

This activity is fairly straightforward, defining only the two attributes just shown, and one other: `suppressJoinFailure`. If more than one variable is intended to be validated, separate them with spaces in the `variables` attribute. If the engine discovers a violation of the schema in the variables listed, it will throw an `invalidVariables` fault. You can catch this fault and deal with it as you would any other. Not all engines support this feature. For example, Sun's BPEL SE that runs in the OpenESB JBI container does not implement this activity.

Validation baked into your process in this manner can be a hindrance to performance.

10.12 Correlation Sets

Problem

You want to specify a unique identifier that is common to a set of messages to ensure that they are all served by the same instance of your process.

Solution

Use a `<correlationSet>`.

Discussion

The basic premise of a correlation set is as follows:

- A single process instance typically requires sending a message through a series of service invocations as a conversation.
- You typically have many unique instances of a process executing at once.
- Messages typically carry information that can be used to uniquely identify them.
- This uniquely identifying information in messages can be used to ensure that all of the inputs and outputs during a conversation participate only in the process instance they're meant to.
- The correlation set is the definition of a process conversation: it defines which participants use what identifying data to make sure that the intended instance of the process is the only one that receives this instance of a message.

If this sounds a little tricky, it is. An analogy is useful here. A BPEL process is to a Java class what a BPEL process instance is to a Java object. In Java it's easy to correlate messages. You just pass around the object instance you're interested in and call methods on it. You can do that in Java because you can work directly with both a class (defining a class in the first place or calling static methods) and an object instance (inside a method, for example). When you write a BPEL process, it's as if you're working just at the class level. That is, you're defining the blueprint for creating any given process instance, but you never have access to the actual instances; they just run in the engine.

So you need a way to tell the process how to route messages that belong together in the same conversational instance. Enter the `<correlationSet>`.

Once multiple instances of a process are running, you use identifying data, such as `customerNumber` and `orderNumber`, within the messages to create a unique combination that identifies messages that belong together within each instance. Figure 10-1 shows what can go wrong in the absence of correlation sets.

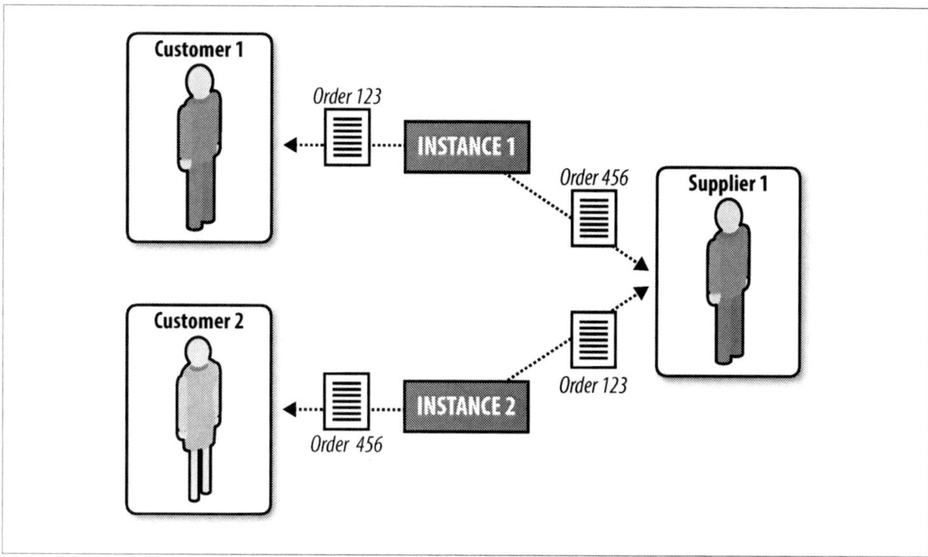

Figure 10-1. Mismatched messages in a fulfillment process without correlations

In this case, multiple customer orders are received, creating different process instances. The supplier partner, without a correlation set, cannot find the already running process instance that the fulfillment notices are intended for. Customers may have multiple orders submitted at once.

Here are the basic steps for correlating your process:

1. Create message properties and aliases for them.
2. Create a correlation set.
3. Find the activity that you want to initiate the conversation.
4. Correlate the messages to their instances.

We'll look at each of these steps in order now.

Creating message properties and aliases

Properties must be globally unique names that are bound to a simple XML schema type. You define properties using the `property` element. Here's a sketch of how they're defined:

```
<wsdl:definitions...>
  ...
<wsdl:message name="sendPurchaseResponse">
  <wsdl:part name="Confirm" element="po:purchaseResponse" />
</wsdl:message>

<!-- Correlation properties here -->
<vprop:property name="customerId" type="xs:string"/>
<vprop:property name="orderId" type="xs:string"/>

<vprop:propertyAlias propertyName="tns:customerId"
    messageType="tns:sendPurchaseResponse" part="Confirm">
  <vprop:query>/purchaseOrder/cust/email</vprop:query>
</vprop:propertyAlias>
```

As you can see from this example, properties are defined in WSDLs, *not* in *.bpel* files. They take advantage of the same extensibility mechanism that allowed you to create partner links earlier. In effect, they are simply names for data that already exist in your messages. Property aliases associate a `vprop:property` and a `wsdl:message` part.

In the example just shown, you've identified the `customerId` and `orderId` as the correlates. The `propertyAlias` is used to map the properties to fields within the message data. Aliases use queries in the form of a `query` child element, whose result type must match the type defined in the property. They tell you how to extract the property data from the message.

The writers of the specification went out of their way to create correlation sets to avoid having to require that every message include some sort of specific token when you want to correlate within a BPEL process. Doing so would have undermined the loosely coupled nature of services by tying them, however subtly, to an implementation. Basically, correlation sets allow you to define your messages however you want, and not have to include any additional out-of-band mechanism for matching messages to process instances.

Properties can be created using XML Schema simple types, as well as derived simple types. A derived simple type is usually a string whose content is restricted by a pattern.

Creating correlation sets

BPEL uses correlation sets to associate messages with their proper running instances. They can be defined globally (at the process level), or within a scope. Correlations can be used on all types of message activities: `<receive>`, `<reply>`, `<onMessage>`, `<onEvent>`, and `<invoke>`.

You may need to specify more than one correlation set. This could happen for a single partner if the process invokes more than one operation on a port for that partner, and if they use different message parts to represent the data you need to correlate. However, it could also be necessary if you're invoking operations from a variety of partners.

You define the correlation sets that will be used in your process with a `<correlationSets>` construct that contains `<correlationSet>` child elements, as shown here:

```
<process>
<correlationSets>
  <correlationSet name="PurchaseOrder"
     properties="po:customerId po:orderId">
  </correlationSet>
</correlationSets>
```

Here you define a global correlation set that uses properties to identify the data that constitutes a composite key. This may be necessary depending on the nature of your conversation. The point is that you have to ensure that your correlation key/value pair is unique. Think of this as you would primary and composite keys in a relational database. And, just like in a relational database, all of the data in a key must match for the correlation to work; in the preceding example, getting a new message from the same customer with a different order ID will not correlate.

The `<pick>` and `<onEvent>` activities are specialized versions of the `<receive>` activity. As such, you can specify a correlations element within them; this will contain the correlation set that they participate in.

The `<correlations>` element looks like this:

```
<correlations>?
   <correlation set="NCName" initiate="yes|join|no"?
      pattern="request|response|request-response"? />+
</correlations>
```

The `pattern` attribute is only used in the event that the correlation is used with an `<invoke>` activity. You use this attribute to limit when a correlation should be used. For example, specifying a value of "request" would make the correlation apply only during the outbound invocation, so only the request would have its data validated according to the correlation.

Initiating the conversation

Partners in a correlation can act as conversation initiators or conversation followers. To initiate a conversation, set `<correlation initiate="yes">`. The initiator of a conversation sends the first message by invoking an operation; doing so defines the values in the correlation set's properties that "tag" the conversation. Followers use `<correlation initiate="no">`. They receive data from an incoming message and mine it for values to bind within their correlation set.

Use the initiate attribute to specify whether this correlation set will start the conversation, or use "join" if you want to allow whichever participant who gets there first to start the conversation. That is, using "join" means that the related activity will start the conversation if it hasn't been started yet, or follow it if someone else has already started it. Using `<correlation initiate="join">` means that you have a "multi-start" activity, wherein multiple receive blocks can initiate a conversation.

If something goes wrong during conversation initialization, the standard fault `bpel:correlationViolation` is thrown.

Correlating the messages

To complete the correlation definition, you need to specify how messages will be correlated once received within a flow.

The `<invoke>` activity defines the `pattern` attribute, which allows you to specify when a correlation set should be used. Its possible values are shown in Table 10-3. If the operation is one-way, the `pattern` attribute need not be used.

Table 10-3. Values for invoke's pattern attribute

Value	Purpose
`request`	Applies the correlation on the outbound message
`response`	Applies the correlation on the inbound message
`request-response`	Applies the correlation on both inbound and outbound messages

A correlation set can only be initiated once within the scope it belongs to during a conversation. Once it is initiated, the values become constants for the process instance to ensure that subsequent requests can be correlated against a determined identical value.

Here is an example snippet of using a correlation from section 9 of the specification:

```
<invoke partnerLink="Seller" portType="SP:PurchasingPortType"
  operation="Purchase" inputVariable="sendPO"
  outputVariable="getResponse">
  <correlations>
    <correlation set="PurchaseOrder" initiate="yes" pattern="request"/>
    <correlation set="Invoice" initiate="yes" pattern="response" />
  </correlations>
  <catch faultName="SP:RejectPO" faultVariable="smsg:POReject">
    <!-- handle fault -->
  </catch>
</invoke>
```

In this case, the `<invoke>` consists of an outbound request and an inbound reply. The `pattern` attribute is used to specify which correlation should be used in which case. Here the `PurchaseOrder` correlation will apply to the outbound request that initiates it, making the purchaser the leader or initiator of that correlation. The purchaser is also a follower of the `Invoice` correlation, based on the properties of the `Invoice` instance used in the reply from the seller.

10.13 Looping

Problem

You need to repeat the execution of some activity until a condition fails, as in a loop.

Solution

Select from one of the available BPEL constructs for this purpose: `<while>`, `<repeatUntil>`, or `<forEach>`.

Discussion

These constructs are rather straightforward, so we'll just take a quick tour.

while loop

As in Java, the `<while>` activity allows you to repeat a block of code (or, more specifically, the BPEL activity you're enclosing) until a certain `<condition>` no longer evaluates to true.

Here is the basic structure:

```
<while>
  <condition>$lineItems < 10</condition>
  <scope>...</scope>
</while>
```

A slightly more ambitious example illustrates how you can increment a variable counter within a loop:

```
<while>
   <condition>$counter < $lineItems</condition>

   <sequence>
      <invoke partnerLink="CheckInventory" ... />
      <!-- Here we increment the condition's counter-->
      <assign>
         <copy>
            <from expression="$counter + 1" />
            <to variable="counter" />
         </copy>
      </assign>
   </sequence>
</while>
```

This all behaves just as you would expect. If the condition is not true the first time it is evaluated, the activity it contains will never be executed.

repeatUntil loop

The `repeatUntil` loop acts like a do/while loop in Java. That is, its primary distinguishing feature is that it always executes at least once, as the condition is evaluated after the enclosed activity has been run. Its structure looks like this:

```
<repeatUntil>
   <some activity />
   <condition>
       boolean expression
   </condition>
</repeatUntil>
```

Here is the previous example reformatted to execute at least once:

```
<repeatUntil>
   <sequence>
      <invoke partnerLink="CheckInventory" ... />
      <!-- Here we increment the condition's counter-->
      <assign>
         <copy>
            <from expression="$counter + 1" />
            <to variable="counter" />
         </copy>
      </assign>
   </sequence>

  <!-- Now the condition is down here -->
  <condition>$counter < $lineItems</condition>
</repeatUntil>
```

Note that with any of the looping activities, you can specify the `expressionLanguage` attribute on the `<condition>`, which allows you to use alternate languages for your Boolean expression. The default is XPath 1.0.

forEach loop

The third iterator BPEL makes available is the `<forEach>` activity. The primary distinguishing characteristic of this loop style is that you can execute activities either sequentially or in parallel.

It executes its enclosing activities according to a counter. The counter is specified with `start` and `final` values, and the loop runs the number of times equal to `final` minus `start` plus one; this value gets assigned to the attribute `counterName` on each iteration. Here's how that looks:

```
<forEach counterName="i">
   <startCounterValue>1</startCounterValue>
   <finalCounterValue>
      count($order.document/items/lineItem)
   </finalCounterValue>
```

```
   ...
</forEach>
```

The counter is important because it allows you to reference nodes in lexical order using the variable value in an XPath expression. For example, you can use the following query to drill down to the current line item given a set of line items in an order:

```
<forEach counterName="i">
   <startCounterValue>1</startCounterValue>
   <finalCounterValue>
      count($order.document/items/lineItem)
   </finalCounterValue>

   <scope>
      <sequence>
         <assign>
            <copy>
               <from variable="order"
                 part="document"
                 query="/items/lineItem[$i]/partNumber"/>
               <to variable="part" />
            </copy>
         </assign>
         <invoke partnerLink="Supply" ... />
      </sequence>
   </scope>

</forEach>
```

An important thing to note about <forEach> is that it is only allowed to have a <scope> activity as its child, in contrast to the other structured activities, which are allowed any activities as their children.

Preventing some children from executing

Sometimes you want to prevent some of the child activities in a loop from executing. To specify this, you can optionally use a <completionCondition> child in your <forEach>. A <completionCondition> lets you indicate that you only need to perform N number of branches of a number of M possible branches. The process will ignore any remaining branches after N is reached. That is how <completionCondition> is used in the sequential version of the loop. We'll look at what it means for parallel executions in a moment. Here's the basic construct:

```
<forEach parallel="yes|no">
  ....
  <completionCondition>
    <branches>...
  </completionCondition>
<scope>...
```

The completion condition is evaluated before the loop starts. Once the condition is met, processing breaks out of the loop. It evaluates to an `xs:unsignedInt` that represents the value for N.

If you want to count only the iterations that have completed normally, you can set the `<branches successfulBranchesOnly="yes">` attribute.

To make your branches run in parallel, simply set the parallel attribute of the loop to "yes".

The `<completionCondition>` can be used in the parallel version of the loop to indicate that you want to terminate some of the child activities early.

Let's look at an example that runs in parallel and supplies a `<completionCondition>` that limits the number of successful executions that need to be completed before the loop is allowed to quit. In this example, you are processing invitations to a seminar. You will go ahead and book a room if a requisite number of people are going to come; otherwise, you might just cancel. So in this scenario, you've sent out 300 invitations, and once you receive 50 confirmations, you'll break out of the loop and go on with the process:

```
<forEach counterName="i" parallel="yes">
   <startCounterValue>1</startCounterValue>
   <finalCounterValue>300</finalCounterValue>

   <completionCondition>
      <branches successfulBranchesOnly="yes">50</branches>
   </completionCondition>

   <scope>
        <invoke partnerLink="Confirm" ... />
        <receive partnerLink="Confirm" ... />
   </scope>
</forEach>
```

10.14 Adding Human Tasks to a Business Process

Problem

Your workflow cannot be completed by machines alone; your business process includes human beings who need to complete one or more of the steps.

Solution

Extend your orchestration work with one of the tools that implement the WS-HumanTask specification.

Discussion

The WS-HumanTask specification was first released in June of 2007, making it among the newer WS-* specifications. This spec, published by OASIS, was written as a joint effort between Adobe, Active Endpoints, BEA, IBM, Oracle, and SAP. Its purpose is to define a standard way to include the fact that many business processes require people to do one or more of the tasks. You can't always automate all of your processes—some things require human input or decision-making. Some things can be automated but haven't been yet. Using WS-HumanTask allows you this flexibility.

WS-HumanTask offers a way to do roles-based work, and a way to define interactions with a running process. For example, let's go back to the business process that provisions new employees. Perhaps there are a number of steps that can be performed by computers, such as ordering business cards, provisioning a workstation, and so forth. But maybe once these steps are complete, someone in HR needs to meet with the employee and have him sign certain forms on paper for filing on a physical shelf. This is obviously not automated, and happens outside the world of computers altogether. WS-HumanTask allows you to capture this idea.

In this scenario, once the executing process arrived at the point where the person in HR needs to do her part, the process would notify her and then tap its fingers, waiting for her to perform the work. Once she is done, she can notify the process of that (typically in a web-based form running on a portlet), and then the process can continue going about its automated work.

Implementations

If you want to open up your business processes to incorporate people, there are a few vendors that offer implementations for you to try.

The first is Active Endpoints. It was a leader in the specification and one of the first to market with an implementation. If you are using Active Endpoints designer and server, you should be ready to use the extensions for humans.

Another vendor with a full-blown production-quality product is IBM. It actually originated this idea with SAP in a whitepaper it published in July 2005 called "BPEL4People." Originally envisioned as a set of extensions to the BPEL 1.0 specification, the WS-HumanTask specification grew out of that 18-page kernel.

You can read the "BPEL4People" whitepaper at *http://download.boulder.ibm.com/ibmdl/pub/software/dw/specs/ws-bpel4people/BPEL4People_white_paper.pdf*. Note that many practitioners now conflate the terms "BPEL4People" and "HumanTask" in conversation.

Because of SAP's early involvement authoring the specification, its NetWeaver product also provides an implementation. Companies that offer SOA suites, such as Oracle,

SoftwareAG, and TIBCO, all offer commercial BPM engines that support workflows with human tasks. These BPM engines also provide advanced functionality, such as automatic generation of Ajax-based user-interaction screens.

However, if you're looking to try it out, you might start with Intalio, a company that makes an Eclipse-based designer and a server that supports BPEL, BPMN, and BPEL4People, both of which are free to get started with. Check out the free Intalio-based BPMN modeler at *http://www.eclipse.org/bpmn*.

10.15 Invoking a RESTful Web Service from BPEL

Problem

You have an orchestration that needs to use a service that doesn't have a WSDL, such as a RESTful service, or an EJB.

Solution

Create an adapter service.

Discussion

BPEL requires a WSDL in order to communicate with a partner service. That can make it difficult to orchestrate services that are written using REST, EJB, or some other technology that does not produce a WSDL. However, it can be done.

One way is to create an adapter service. To do this, create a WSDL and schema based on your REST interactions. Then create a service implementation of that WSDL that simply forwards its operation calls to the RESTful service. The `doXslTransform` function can be very helpful here.

Some BPEL engine vendors provide proprietary tools to do this conversion automatically for you. The advantage to this is that it's convenient and easy, and doesn't require that you maintain a separate adapter. The disadvantage, of course, is that it locks you into their server and designer tools. The vendors that allow you to natively interact with a REST resource include Cape Clear and Active Endpoints. The feature is soon to be added to Apache ODE, but it is not yet implemented as of ODE 1.2.

Summary

BPEL 2.0 allows you to represent business processes in a standard orchestration language. With BPEL, you can wire together existing web services to create new composite applications, which will help you streamline and automate processes and realize a return on investment in your SOA.

CHAPTER 11
SOA Governance

11.0 Introduction

While this book is predominantly technical, it is also essential to address some non-technical items in order to highlight SOA as a unifying concept. Without considering the non-technical work within the framework of SOA, we are doomed to wind up over-engineering a bunch of software components that could have been written less expensively, more efficiently, and in a more easily maintainable manner. To focus solely on building web services is to miss the point of SOA entirely.

We have been creating web services in the industry for several years, and while the term "SOA" may already be 10 years old, many organizations are still only at the evaluation stage. Gartner research shows that only a small percentage of organizations that self-identify as those doing SOA are actually in a mature stage, meaning that they utilize a wide catalog of reused services in a repository; activity monitoring and automated alerts; brokered ESBs executing under governance domains; rules-based services; solid change management; federated partnering and security; advanced process automation that includes dynamic discovery, binding, and composition; and a complete governance board. Governance can act as perhaps the primary caretaker that helps nurture a fledgling SOA into a mature SOA.

Some of the discussions in this chapter, such as those on return on investment, may seem out of place in a technical cookbook. But SOA brings to the forefront the alignment of software with business strategy.

SOA attempts to undermine the traditional dichotomy between business and IT, an exaggerated view of which casts admins and engineers as feared and loathsome Quasimodo-like creatures, madly toiling nerdy beasts who work on their exotic art projects for vending-machine treats. They secretly ridicule their executive and marketing overlords for having all the flash, polish, and witless bravado of a hopped-up surfer dude with nothing on his mind but the next chance to hang ten on some sick Aussie waves. SOA recognizes that this dichotomy is part of the problem in modern software development, and seeks to define strategic ways of overcoming it. The architectural, design, and management principles that SOA makes available help support the alignment of business and IT, recognizing that a little more harmony is key to realizing the greatest benefit.

Many of the topics in this chapter will address practical matters that developers and architects must face, such as service versioning and retirement processes. But to really make this an SOA book, and not a "Let's Tape a Bunch of Web Services Together and Call It a SOA" book, we need to examine some of the more business-oriented topics as well. We won't get into too much detail, but at this stage a dose of awareness is probably all we need.

11.1 Assigning Roles

Problem

There are a variety of roles specific to SOA development, maintenance, and governance, and these do not necessarily map to your existing human resources. You need to map current developers, analysts, executives, and infrastructure team members to support your SOA work, and you're not sure who you'll need.

Solution

As appropriate given the skills, backgrounds, and flexibility of the people you have or can hire, consider filling the following roles:

- Enterprise architect
- Solutions architect
- Technical architect
- Service developer
- Service custodian

These are discussed in detail in the next section.

Discussion

You may already have people in place for some of these roles, such as enterprise architect. In that case, making a slight adjustment to keep the special needs of SOA on their radar might be all the updating for that role that's required. But let's take a moment to discuss each of these roles in turn, to see what value they might add to your organization:

Enterprise architect
: The custodian and ultimate decision maker of the overall architecture, enterprise architects take a 50,000-foot view of general activities. This is a business role, and its primary function is interacting with other business executives. It is his responsibility to ensure that the broad SOA efforts are in step with business goals, and

that the SOA is helping increase business agility. He will translate business goals into broad SOA objectives, set the overall direction of the SOA, and ensure that the work progresses within the established architecture for the organization.

There is often only one enterprise architect, and he is usually most visible at the incipient stages of a project.

Large corporations may have many enterprise architects, following Lines of Business. This is the case, for example, at a company like Dell.

Solutions architect

Solutions architects generally report to the enterprise architect or CTO, and may have more or less of a hands-on role, depending on the size of the organization. Solutions architects works with software architects, network specialists, and developers to come up with a technical plan for implementing business goals. To do so, they typically also work with Lines of Business managers or domain owners.

Solutions architects are really translators between business objectives and designs that can fulfill those objectives, and they consult with both the management and technical sides of the house to architect a solution. They may assist in vendor selection and focus on business integration, making sure that their solutions are aligned with all impacted business domains.

Depending on the size of the organization, there may be one or more solutions architects.

Technical architect

Technical architects fall right in the middle of the SOA, as they work closely with the solutions architect, business analysts, service infrastructure administrators, and service developers to identify viable technical specifications that conform to the needs of all of these different areas. This is a technical role, deepening the contours suggested by the solutions architect's work product. They must be sharply aware of SOA technology options, as well as fundamentals like network technology, infrastructure support technology, and so on.

Technical architects should have deep knowledge of the products in use. Just as the solutions architect is the translator between the business and the architecture, technical architects are the translators between everyone at the technology level in order to determine an appropriate architecture that's ready to be implemented by the service developers. They can also serve in a consulting capacity, when project managers and others in standard IT roles need assistance determining budgets, timelines, etc. Technical architects typically come with a specialty, such as service implementation, network infrastructure, or business processes.

Achieving the real promise of SOA ultimately means analyzing current and future business processes in order to streamline them and discover service candidates.

Architects who focus on business processes will use business process modeling tools to create standard representations of business processes. These models typically can be exported to a form such as BPEL. The output of this work can be used by service developers.

There are generally a number of technical architects.

Service developer
: Service developers work with technical architects to implement services using an IDE. They work with the network administrators to ensure the safe arrival of the services into production. They may also support and maintain services after they are developed.

Service custodian
: Service custodians' primary tools are the registry and repository. They ensure that services are available and documentation is correct. They may serve with architects on a change control or governance board, and they keep on top of versioning and availability.

11.2 Creating a SOA Roadmap

Problem

You want to build out your SOA in an organized, thoughtful manner, and be ready to address the wide variety of concerns that come into play as you embark on your SOA journey.

Solution

Create an SOA roadmap.

Discussion

SOA is a kind of architecture, or, rather, an approach to systems integration that represents a long-term strategy to realize an architecture. It takes a long time to build: as the SOA cliché goes, you can't boil the ocean. Between figuring out services, security, registries, and repositories; performing vendor selection; getting an ESB running; and advancing to technologies such as business process management, rules, and service virtualization, there is a lot to do in one lifetime. To get a picture of everything you need to do and the order in which you need to do it that makes the most sense for your business, you need a roadmap.

A roadmap in general terms defines checkpoints along the path of a journey. So the first thing you need to know is what you want out of SOA. Where are you going? Why are you employing SOA in your organization? What benefits, in concrete terms, do you hope to realize? What is your target state? What is the dream architecture that you hope to have in place? Frequently cited reasons for implementing SOA in an organization include the following:

Business agility
: IT needs to be in step with the business, so that it can respond more quickly to changing markets and business demands. Services can help you realize this by promoting reuse, a clean and manageable infrastructure, and interoperability with a wide variety of systems.

Legacy modernization
: Companies that have been around for a long time may have lots of code that is 20 or 25 years old. In order to scale or take advantage of developer skills and new productivity and automation tools, you may feel the need to modernize certain applications. Ripping out and replacing lots of working technology, especially in business-critical systems, is often a very costly and time-consuming proposition. This is aggravated by the fact that businesses don't often see the value (and indeed, sometimes there may not be enough value) in simply rewriting working systems just for the sake of using the language of the moment. But wrapping legacy systems with services is a good first step that allows you to gradually create platform-independent facades for your key systems. In this way, you can eventually reach a point where it is less expensive and time-consuming to achieve the kind of flexibility you want within your enterprise.

Process improvement and automation
: Organizations may want to improve their business processes using business management strategies such as Six Sigma or Lean. Six Sigma, for example, is a management strategy created by Motorola in 1986 that defines five basic steps: define, measure, analyze, improve, and control. Process management allows organizations to run at optimal efficiency. While these ideas have been around for more than two decades now, we have only recently gotten to the point where SOA can assist in management improvement efforts. The SOA tools give us a high degree of flexibility, transparency, tracking, and analytics.

  Business process management (BPM) is an approach that enables organizations to map out their business processes, including the interactions of systems and humans, to determine how their processes actually work and to allow selective process automation with services. This is often done with business process modeling (also BPM) tools. BPM in conjunction with BAM (Business Activity Monitoring) is the chief means of realizing process improvements within a SOA.

Business Activity Monitoring Tools

Business activity monitoring will be a crucial aspect of SOA going forward. BAM allows companies to define key performance indicators (KPIs) around various aspects of their services, at the business and operational levels. A BAM-enabled SOA allows you to siphon off data as it flows across your service invocations (in near-time or real-time) in order to help make business decisions. For example, imagine that your company offers a New Hire service that allows people to apply for jobs, and then takes the job applications through the process of review by the hiring manager and HR, interviewing, hiring, and on-boarding. You define metrics around various data points in the process, and allow the tools to generate executive dashboards, typically represented as portlets.

Presenting and understanding the data culled from BAM tools is a terrific way to make process efficiency improvements. For the New Hire process, such metrics might include a ratio of interviews to actual hires, or the average time it takes to provision an employee workstation once they are hired, or the number of times a given hiring manager took too long to review an application, causing that point in the process to be escalated up the organizational chain.

To get this kind of functionality, you'll need to get BAM tools and a Business Process Management Suite from a vendor such as Oracle, TIBCO, IBM, or SoftwareAG, sometimes in conjunction with rules engines and analytics engines such as Cognos.

This is considered an advanced stage for a SOA, and some organizations that are heavily invested in such strategies and supporting tools have even termed their architectures POAs, or process-oriented architectures.

The basic idea here is that there are a variety of reasons that organizations might want to adopt SOA. And SOA doesn't happen overnight. So understanding why you want to invest in this long-term architectural strategy in general terms can help you refine your general goals into smaller, more workable, and more concrete goals.

Building on the principles of agile development methodologies such as Scrum, we can create a roadmap that allows us to do a little work and deliver value to the business incrementally. We generally don't use a waterfall method to develop our software, and likewise we shouldn't create a roadmap that front-loads lots of research and development with no proposed pay-off for a long time to come. Such a "big bang" approach is very dangerous in SOA.

As support for the idea that SOA represents a real change not just in technology but in organizational approach, it is useful to recall Conway's Law: "organizations which design systems...are constrained to produce designs which are copies of the communication structures of these organizations." You can't do SOA without examining how your project teams and organizational attitudes need to change.

There are a few general steps that every SOA roadmap is likely to define. These steps can (and should) be performed in an iterative fashion, as you reach each new milestone:

1. Starting a SOA, especially if you have not done much web services development before, can be very difficult. The market is overwhelmed with hype and noise. Figuring out what you need for your particular enterprise can be tricky, especially when you don't know what you don't know about SOA. You therefore need to start with a research and planning stage that will probably involve a lot of reading. Attend industry conferences and talks. Read whitepapers. Engage vendors in conversations with a clear statement that you're in a discovery stage and don't plan on buying anything just yet. If you have relationships with analysts such as Gartner or Burton Group or Forrester, engage them. Figure out first what you don't know. Remember that SOA is not just about getting an implementation of the WS-* specifications. The business must be involved. And while you can start top-down, and indeed you will need support up the organizational chain, your SOA will ultimately be realized bottom-up.
2. Now that you know what you don't know, use this knowledge to create a set of flexible checkpoints. To borrow from Six Sigma, this is a kind of measuring stage. Determine what needs to be worked on. Establish a set of tools that you will need for the current iteration. Establish organizational boundaries within IT. SOA represents a significant change in how a business operates. It's not the case that, in the manner of Internet startup accounting departments circa 1997, the SOA team should decide that all of the old rules don't apply to them. But an enterprise that is used to operating with traditional project teams may find the cross-cutting concerns of SOA very difficult to work with. Expect some resistance from teams who may feel threatened by SOA. Expect resistance from a potentially large set of tools that you may have in place to manage projects. SOA requires some organizational change, and you need to be prepared to address this. While this step may gradually become easier with each iteration of the architecture, each iteration will bring new concerns, and it will likely remain an important a challenge.
3. Do the work. Get the tools, write the code, automate the processes, build out infrastructure, update build processes, flesh out the governance scheme, do whatever it is that needs to be done to fulfill your concrete objectives. This is the execution step. Recall that SOA is not merely a technological endeavor, so part of the execution is also to engage the business to ensure that you have sponsorship and support. They must understand to some degree what SOA is, why you're doing it, the organizational changes that are typically necessary, and the new kind of input and involvement you'll require from them. At each iteration, re-engage the business to ensure that you're still on the same page, and highlight the ways in which future business initiatives will be supported by new SOA increments.
4. The final step is to optimize and adapt. Some of the choices that you made earlier might need to be revisited. Determine how you can improve efficiency, interoperability, processes, or other items within your SOA.

Create a set of roadmaps, each with a different scope. One might be a five-year plan for SOA that contains general goals. Another could zoom in on a more confined scope, perhaps a year or a quarter, and define tasks very concretely. It should indicate how you plan to address each aspect of SOA:

- Governance
- Business agility and organizational shift
- Tools
- WS-* specs or other related supporting items to learn and use
- RESTful or WOA concepts
- Monitoring, KPIs, BAM
- Rules engines/rules as a service
- Security enforcement points/security as a service
- Policies
- Registry
- Repository
- Interoperability
- Service identification and creation
- Infrastructure such as hardware and networking software

You don't need to address each of these items fully in every iteration. For example, you might choose to make your first services for internal use only, behind the firewall, therefore taking certain security measures out of scope so that you can focus initially on the core service creation and management.

11.3 Keeping Track of Your Services

Problem

You have developed several web services and want to keep track of them. They need to be visible to potential consumers, and your architecture team needs a central place to define their SLAs (service-level agreements) and policies and keep documentation and other metadata. Generally, you need to manage the entire service life cycle.

Solution

Use an enterprise repository. The repository will support your governance efforts. A good repository is a network-enabled data store that will serve as the location of record for all of the design-time and runtime artifacts your operating SOA requires. This includes XML schemas, WSDLs, service policies, and so forth.

There are many tools for this sort of thing, each with a different user interface and slightly different feature set. Software AG and Fujitsu have jointly developed a popular repository product called CentraSite, and offer a Community Edition license with limited functionality for free. The client is Eclipse-based, which is likely familiar to you, so this might be a good way to get started. Download CentraSite Community Edition 3.1.7 from *http://www.centrasite.org*.

Vendors such as IBM, Oracle, TIBCO, and others have robust enterprise repository tools that integrate with Eclipse-based development tools. Repositories are much more than regular databases, and are frequently combined with UDDI registries to allow dynamic discovery of services at runtime. They also can support migration of services between environments, and at design time can offer governance support. Such support often includes things like the ability to limit who can add a service to the repository (to prevent the Bunny Services and Rogue Services anti-patterns), and who can use which services.

Discussion

The enterprise repository is a cornerstone of your governance program. It is one of the chief tools employed by your architecture team or Center of Excellence. Repositories can also be very expensive. And while you can definitely get started without one, doing so will require careful maintenance of your meta-model. Still, using a model cannot prevent developers from putting their own services into production, and after a time you could end up with six slightly different services that you will need to maintain, version, decommission, and migrate clients for.

Ideally, your repository product should be standards-based and offer both a visual client browser and an API that you can use to invoke it programmatically. Repositories are typically integrated with the developer IDE so that during application development, programmers can simply browse the list of available services just as they would see classes in a selected package.

Many of the better enterprise repositories also make available a view for business users, or at least business analysts who work at the process level. As your SOA matures, and your service catalog is built out, you may find that you want to connect your services using executable business processes. Such business processes will be sewn together using services available in your repository. So a business analyst using something like BPMN within the IDE or studio tool will be presented a different view from that of the developer based on LDAP credentials, and see documentation and high-level details of each service. The analyst can then drag and drop items from the repository catalog to build the executable process.

Once the process is complete, the analyst can typically make a change to it and immediately see the impact across schemas and other artifacts participating in the composite service. Frequently, the impact analysis is presented in a graphical interface that shows the interconnected web of resources. This can be very handy in helping to ensure that your business runs smoothly.

11.4 Determining a Data Ownership Scheme for Services

Problem

SOA presents a particular difficulty for determining ownership of data. A service must be able to not only manage but to truly own the data that it represents, or chaos will ensue. But an enterprise will frequently define services that must share common data such as customers, products, and so forth. How can this be managed?

Solution

As you define your architecture, differentiate between services that *own* objects, and services that *reference* objects owned by other services. Depending on the context, you may need to use caching techniques or subscription patterns to handle updates to the data.

Every service must be self-sufficient and must be defined as being totally in control of its own data. It is clearly preferable to never use data across business domains, as doing so can destroy the loose coupling SOA attempts to achieve. In the real world, however, our business domains sometimes do not match our data definitions as purely as we might like, especially when we're dealing with large companies with lots of opportunities for legacy modernization. You must make sure that a service only *references* data from other domains so that only one single domain is ever in control of a given business object.

Discussion

In your SOA, you have a `CustomerDataService`. This service represents the data for a fundamental aspect of your enterprise, and it can participate in many business processes or composite services. It will be used in a variety of contexts, including your Invoice service. Similarly, an Employee data management service could be used within an HR process and a Payroll process. Because service reuse is a chief aim of SOA and the reason it can realize significant ROI (return on investment), it would appear that you are on the right track.

But the way you handle the referencing of data across these services presents a problem, one that can become quite serious if not addressed clearly and decisively. The problem lies in data ownership. Services must own the data that they manage. It is perfectly sensible that the Customer service should be the ultimate decision maker and system-of-record or "gold copy" for all customer data. But the Invoice service must refer to customer data as well. What if a customer record needs to be updated, such as in the case of an address or phone number change? If the Invoice service maintains a copy of the customer data, it must duplicate the update efforts of the Customer service, effectively undermining the point of your SOA.

So you cannot have the customer data stored in 2 or 3 or 17 places, as the Customer service would lose its credibility as the owner of that data. It cannot manage what it does not have a view into. Moreover, inventing a clever way to have the Customer service reach into each of the local data stores of the referencing services to manage the customer data they have "borrowed" is brittle, unmaintainable, and clearly does not support the agility concerns that SOA aims to address.

The naive solution would appear to be this: simply have the Invoice service go out to the Customer service every time it needs any information regarding customers. The Invoice service stores only an identifier, and not a full copy, reducing the record management problem. In this case, you don't have two competing services that both own the customer record; instead, you have the Invoice service only referencing the data that the Customer service owns. This is a common solution in a number of environments, but it does not cleanly and wholly address the problem at hand within a SOA. For example, what happens to the Invoice pointer if a customer is deleted? This creates instability and invalidates the Invoice service without anyone being aware of it.

Moreover, this introduces an altogether different kind of problem: accumulated network latency. Having a variety of composite services reference such core services as Customer Information can create undue or unanticipated load. This can have a ripple effect that slows down services across domains.

So the crux of the problem is this: the Invoice service (which does not own but only references the data managed by the Customer service) must be able to use customer data flexibly and must have up-to-date information, but not be allowed to sink beneath the weight of the considerable latency involved in constantly invoking the Customer service every time it needs a small slice of information.

Happily, there are some reasonable ways of dealing with this issue.

Timed caches and distributed caches

An obvious but perfectly reasonable solution to this problem is to have the referencing service obtain a copy of the data from the owned service and treat the records as it would any other cached data. So the data is not a first-class citizen within the referencing application.

One way to handle this is to use a distributed caching mechanism. In Java, you can try EHCache, which is available from *http://ehcache.sourceforge.net* under an Apache license. The current version as of this writing is 1.5.0.

As a distributed cache, EHCache maintains stores on disk and in memory and can replicate data to listeners, as well as invalidate stale data. It has a number of extensions that allow it to support advanced performance improvement facilities such as ZIP compression and caching of JSPs and servlets. EHCache allows you to programmatically create a cache manager object that is responsible for conducting the CRUD business of the cache and for coordinating work among its constituent caches.

In its upcoming version, EHCache supports both SOAP and RESTful web services, as well as SOAP security specifications and the WS-I Basic Profile. Under the hood, the EHCache server edition uses Glassfish.

When you push updates to the cache, interested services (such as Invoice) can reference the distributed cache. There are a couple of trade-offs though. First, you will need to have a lot of storage capacity, and you could waste processing cycles and consume network resources pushing updates that may never be read.

You might also use a timer (such as the EJB `TimedObject` interface) to perform a cache update in the middle of the night. The update could be pushed from the service of record (in this example, the Customer service) out to a distributed cache that referring services use. Or, if each referring service maintains its own cache, it can pull the data into its local database or cache structure. The advantage to this approach is that it's simple. The disadvantages are many, and include the inability to get updates outside the pre-set schedule. It might work for some brick-and-mortar retailers, but it is not effective for global organizations operating 24/7.

It's important to keep in mind that the cached copy is nothing more than that, and that the real service of record must always remain the true manager of its data. Perhaps more importantly, you must not undermine the authority of the service of record by going in any back doors. This issue is a reality in modern organizations. A developer who knows the location of the "real" data (and has been accessing it that way for years) may be reluctant to go through the front door of your web service interface and incur the attendant overhead. This is dangerous, and you must take steps to lock down your data store or record set to ensure that your service of record is the only custodian of that data.

As a general architectural principle, you can also consider data partitioning within your caches to improve speed. Partition data across date ranges, alphabetic keys, by function, group, or whatever makes sense for your dataset.

Messaging

Some of the problems introduced by caches and their maintenance can be addressed with messaging. Actually, used together, this is a one-two punch combination that can really improve the robustness, dependability, and performance of your service-based systems.

Synchronous communications (such as the request/response-based system of the Web) are frequently required. They are simple from a user standpoint and from an architectural standpoint. But they can also tie up resources under heavy load, and forego a degree of reliability.

Standards-based messaging systems, such as JMS, can scale very, very well. Because they are asynchronous as opposed to synchronous, they do not send a request and wait for an immediate response. Email is a form of asynchronous communication, whereas a telephone call is synchronous. Because the two sides of the line are not tied up concurrently, in asynchronous communication the system is free to perform the work with the highest priority and provide a timely response. Generally, of course, this happens very fast.

Your service can post to a messaging system, or be directly invoked over JMS, and if a reply is required, there are a few different ways clients can receive their reply. You can employ the JMS Reply-To mechanism, and set up a second queue as the destination for the initial queue to deliver its reply messages.

Clients can then poll the queue to check for messages. You can also use the message selector feature of JMS to narrow down the list of potential messages a client will receive.

11.5 Handling Legacy Programs and Heterogeneity Within Your SOA

Problem

Your evolving SOA defines services in different ways: you have some services that use WSDL and SOAP over HTTP, you have some standard JMS messaging services that use mediators, you have a couple of services defined using RESTful services implemented in PHP and need to unify them all.

Solution

In fact, you don't need to unify them all. This is not a problem, and may be a sign that you're doing some things right. Of course, it would be convenient if there were only one way to do everything in the world, but there isn't. So just make sure that you know exactly what services you actually have (a registry/repository product helps with this) and know the consumers of your services. As your SOA grows, make sure that you have products in place to identify "rogue" services.

Discussion

There is not one single way to create a SOA, and an enterprise large enough to bother with creating an SOA will have services defined in different languages. Programs that have been running for 15 or 20 years on a mainframe should not be ripped out and replaced just because they are not written in the language du jour. They have stood the test of time, and more importantly, they do what they are supposed to in a reliable way. There may be considerable knowledge within your enterprise about how those programs work and what they do (even if most of that is stored in an old-timer's head). In fact, this situation is exactly what SOA is intended to address.

There are many options (which are generally vendor-specific) for wrapping legacy programs to expose them over a network so that they are accessible within a SOA. If a legacy program or some generated "modernization" wrapper code does not present an interface that you want to carry over into the future, consider using the Facade pattern to present to the world the interface that you want it to see, at the level of granularity that you like. Under the hood, use adapter code to connect with the legacy program.

With respect to having a variety of platforms implementing your services, such as SOAP/WSDL, REST, or straight Java components, that is OK. You want to have your services visible to the enterprise, and using a variety of formats may make representing your service catalog in a uniform matter slightly more difficult. But that is certainly not a show-stopper, and most enterprise repository products will handle this just fine. Do not attempt to wrap everything in the single services style you've selected. Allow services to be defined in the format that best suits them, assuming that considerable work has already been put into creating, testing, and documenting these existing systems.

11.6 Documenting Services

Problem

You want to document your web services appropriately so that developers can find them, and understand what they provide and how they provide it.

Solution

Use your enterprise repository. If you don't have one, there is no single way to do this, but there are some questions that you should make sure to ask yourself as you document your services. We'll examine these now.

Discussion

Given the wide variety of implementations and platforms for services and governance within any given organization, there is not one single way to do this. You might be running REST services with PHP clients, with OpenLDAP as a service repository. Or you could have services implemented with JAX-WS using a vendor platform for your registry/repository such as Software AG's CentraSite, or IBM WebSphere Service Registry and Repository, or you may be using Apache Scout for UDDI. The capabilities provided by these different products and platforms obviates any discussion of a single way to document services. But there are some things to keep in mind as general rules, which you can then adapt for your organization.

Here is a list of things you should include in your documentation:

- The name of the service.
- The general type of service: a business process, a data service representing a business entity, a functional service, and so on.
- A succinct statement (one sentence) indicating the purpose of the service.
- A descriptive overview that acts as an executive summary. This makes browsing services easier for project managers and analysts.
- A specification that is a business analyst could understand. It should be detailed enough for the analyst to be able to decide if a service is appropriate for use within a given solution.
- A technical specification. This is written for an audience of developers who need to know how to use your service. Keep this discussion client-facing; they should be able to figure out what they need to do to consume this with only this section. It should indicate operation signatures and actions (if present).
- Any special items for consumers, such as whether using the service requires an account, how to authenticate, what headers might be required, if attachments are expected, and so forth.
- The major and minor versions of the service. If this service is deprecated in favor of a newer version, indicate that along with an end-of-life date (assuming that you know all of the consumers or are ready to do that). If there are other versions in use, you might link to them as well.
- Optionally, an example of how to consume the service in different languages, if that's appropriate in your organization.
- Any related services that may also be of interest, or that might be what the user is really looking for.
- Service-level agreements, including QoS response times, responsible parties, etc.
- Any standards or conventions that have been used. Indicate if you are using WS-Addressing, MTOM, etc. These might include in-house conventions if that's your audience.

Here are some special considerations to take into account if the service is being developed for internal consumption, within your organization:

- Indicate which compositions may use this service. Often, tools will do this for you, showing graphically what other items in the repository refer to this service and even its attendant documents such as schemas.
- Include data resulting from tests that you've executed against the service, so that architects and administrators can make informed decisions regarding usage levels.
- Describe network-related data for the service, such as throughput, response time, availability, scheduled maintenance windows, etc.
- Optionally, include dates the service entered production and dates for each version.

Sophisticated commercial repository tools will handle all of this for you automatically. This should give you a reasonable start as you consider how to document your services. If you do not have a vendor tool available for this purpose, consider adding this information as a part of your build process. If you've used Maven to create your project, this is very easy to add to the site template and send to an internally available web server. Alternatively, you could consider using a doclet, Docbook, or other markup to generate this structure for you. Docbook is a good idea if you want your documentation in a variety of formats, such as HTML, PDF, or Office documents. If you have little in the way of automated technical documentation tools, you might use an XML grammar and XSLT to generate a site.

11.7 Setting Up a Service Registry

Problem

You want a centralized location in which to store your web services so that they can be dynamically discovered.

Solution

Try using an implementation of the Java UDDI (Universal Description, Discovery, and Integration) specification, such as the free and open source Apache jUDDI project.

Discussion

A UDDI registry provides a standard way of storing information about web services and the organizations that provide them. Registries allow you to store, query, and update the information surrounding your SOAP-based web services. They support models for two basic items: information about organizations, including government bodies, corporations, and business units; and these organizations' requirements for accessing their services.

UDDI

jUDDI (pronouned "Judy") is an Apache project implementing UDDI v2 (many commercial products now support UDDI v3). The most recent release of Apache jUDDI is from December 2007, and it supports JDK 1.5 and Servlet 2.3. The registry is deployable as a WAR, and acts as a frontend to a relational database.

Originally the idea with UDDI was this: businesses would create services and add them to a registry, and then make the registry available to the public. The conglomeration of registries in the world would act as a sort of Yellow Pages, in which software agents could be set up to query service registries, discover services that matched their needs, and establish a business relationship on the fly. Runtimes would use these agents to select and invoke services at runtime, using a Java API called JAX-R.

Things never quite happened like this. To begin with, businesses don't (and probably shouldn't) trust software to establish business relationships on the fly for them. Businesses establish relationships on the golf course, and with careful consideration. Developers still had to integrate the services on which their software depended using the grizzly JAX-R API.

As a consequence, UDDI has waned significantly in popularity in recent years. That having been said, there is some potential value in setting up a private, internal registery for your company that you do not intend for public consumption. As your organization grows its SOA, you need to have a single location that catalogs your services. The process of service enablement in your organization is likely to graph like a hockey stick. That is, it can take a while for people to understand SOA, see the value, get the infrastructure set up, and deliver some services. But once it takes seed in an organization, SOA can blossom fairly quickly. You need a way to manage service proliferation so that developers do not create redundant services.

If you are looking at repository products, many of them will fold a registry into the repository, so you may not require separate installations. You might look into products that combine a registry with an ebXML repository, as ebXML offers a more robust set of features.

Getting jUDDI

The current releases of jUDDI are available for download from *http://ws.apache.org/juddi/releases.html*. As of this writing, the current release is 2.0rc5, available as a WAR for installation in a container such as Tomcat, and as a standalone JAR. jUDDI is a frontend to a relational database, accessed with JDBC. So aside from the jUDDI bundle, you need to connect to one of the supported databases as well.

Deploying jUDDI on Tomcat

Let's look at how to set up jUDDI on Tomcat. These instructions work with jUDDI WAR 2.0rc5 and Tomcat 6.0.16. Once you have downloaded jUDDI and have Tomcat running, here are the steps to set it up:

1. Rename the file "juddi", as this will make configuring the datasource and other items easier. There are a number of properties that expect your installation to be at *<host>/juddi*. Of course, you can change all of those if you prefer. They can be found under the root of the WAR in *juddi.properties*.
2. Copy *juddi.war* into the *tomcat-home/webapps* directory. It will deploy automatically.
3. Visit the jUDDI homepage in your new installation at *http://localhost:8080/juddi-web-2.0rc5*.

4. Click the "validate" link. You will see the "happy jUDDI" page indicating whether jUDDI was able to find all of the components necessary to run.

If your database is not set up or is set up incorrectly, you may see an error such as this one on the "happy jUDDI" page:

```
DB connection was not acquired.
(Cannot create JDBC driver of class '' for connect URL 'null')
- SELECT COUNT(*) FROM PUBLISHER failed (null)
```

In this case, you'll have to set up the jUDDI database and a Tomcat datasource for it.

Setting up the jUDDI JDBC connection

For this example, you'll use MySQL as the jUDDI database. To complete the installation, you'll have to get the MySQL driver installed, get the datasource set up, and create the jUDDI database.

Setting up Log4J. First, some minor housekeeping. To log jUDDI correctly, create a file called *log4j.properties* under the *WEB-INF/classes* folder of your jUDDI WAR. You may have to create the classes directory:

```
/opt/tomcat-6.0.16/webapps/juddi/WEB-INF/classes/log4j.properties
```

Edit the file so it has the following contents (according to the location of your Tomcat installation):

```
log4j.appender.LOGFILE.File=/opt/tomcat-6.0.16/logs/juddi.log
```

The next step is to set up the database.

Setting up MySQL database. There are a number of steps involved in setting up the database. Navigate to your expanded jUDDI WAR and find *WEB-INF/juddi.properties*. Uncomment all of these lines:

```
juddi.jdbcDriver=com.mysql.jdbc.Driver
juddi.jdbcUrl=jdbc:mysql://localhost/juddiDB
juddi.jdbcUsername=juddi
juddi.jdbcPassword=juddi
```

This will allow you to connect using JDBC directly.

Now you need to create the database that will store the registry entries. It will be called juddiDB, with a username of "juddi" and a password of "juddi".

jUDDI comes with a bunch of scripts specific to different database platforms that will create the database it needs for you. Supported platforms include:

- db2
- derby
- hsqldb
- mysql
- oracle

- postgresql
- informix
- daffodildb

However, you should be able to use jUDDi with any ANSI-compliant server. The only trick here is that the scripts are not in the WAR you downloaded. You have to download *juddi-2.0rc5.jar* from the ws.apache.org/juddi releases page to get the necessary scripts. Navigate to the directory to which you downloaded the JAR and extract the scripts:

```
$ jar -xvf juddi-2.0rc5.jar juddi-sql
```

This creates a directory called *juddi-sql* that contains the scripts you need to execute to create the database. Navigate into the *mysql* directory and open the README file, which contains instructions on how to proceed.

Now you'll set up the database on the command line with the MySQL client. First, make sure that MySQL is started. I'll use this command:

```
$ /etc/rc.d/init.d/mysqld restart
```

Then make sure that you have a user named "juddi" with a password of "juddi".

Now copy the *create_database.sql* script in the *mysql* directory to a file named *create-juddi-db.sql*. This is to ensure that you retain a pristine copy in case you make a mistake when modifying the file. Add an insert statement to the bottom that will create a publisher—someone who can add services to the registry:

```
INSERT INTO PUBLISHER (PUBLISHER_ID,PUBLISHER_NAME,
  EMAIL_ADDRESS,IS_ENABLED,IS_ADMIN)
VALUES ('eben','Eben Hewitt','eben@example.com',
  'true','true');
```

Now open the file using a text editor. You'll see a number of `${prefix}` variables. Remove those using a search-and-replace with an empty string. Then add the following code to the top of the file to create the database and allow `juddi` to access it:

```
DROP DATABASE IF EXISTS juddiDB;
CREATE DATABASE juddiDB;

GRANT ALL ON juddiDB.* TO juddi@'%' IDENTIFIED BY 'juddi';
GRANT ALL ON juddiDB.* TO juddi@'localhost' IDENTIFIED BY 'juddi';

USE juddiDB;
```

Here you are going to use MySQL in batch mode to process this collection of SQL statements all at once. Using the < sign indicates this to the server:

```
$ mysql -h localhost
 -u root -p < /home/ehewitt/mysql/create-juddi-db.sql
```

This will create the database, add the tables, and put a publisher in it. You can now run a simple query to make sure your publisher exists:

```
$ mysql -u juddi -p
Enter password:
Welcome to the MySQL monitor.  Commands end with ; or \g.
Your MySQL connection id is 50
Server version: 5.0.22

Type 'help;' or '\h' for help. Type '\c' to clear the buffer.

mysql> use juddiDB; select * from PUBLISHER;
```

If you see the data you inserted into the database before, you're in business.

Setting up a Tomcat datasource. Now that the database is set up, let's create a Tomcat datasource for it so that the web application can use it.

Get the MySQL JDBC driver (Connector/J) from *http://dev.mysql.com/downloads/connector*. I am using *mysql-connector-java-5.0.6-bin.jar*. Install the *.jar* file containing the JDBC driver in Tomcat's *<tomcat-home>/lib* folder.

There is already a `<resource-ref>` element set up in the *web.xml* file for jUDDI, so you don't need to add that.

You'll now create a datasource called `jdbc/juddiDB`. Navigate to the *<tomcat-home>/juddi/META-INF* directory in the exploded WAR. Create a file called *context.xml*. This will hold your datasource information for connecting with Tomcat. If you're using a different container, just set up the datasource as you normally would using the same properties here. In the file, type the following:

```
<?xml version="1.0" encoding="UTF-8"?>
<Context>
<Resource name="jdbc/juddiDB" auth="Container"
  type="javax.sql.DataSource"
  username="juddi" password="juddi"
  driverClassName="com.mysql.jdbc.Driver"
  url="jdbc:mysql://localhost:3306/juddiDB?autoReconnect=true"
  maxActive="100" maxIdle="30" maxWait="10000"
  />
</Context>
```

If you want to use a different database, just install its driver and put the appropriate URL in the `url` field.

Note that you will have to restart Tomcat to pick up the changes in the context. To do so, navigate to your Tomcat *bin* directory and issue these commands:

```
$ ./shutdown.sh
$ ./startup.sh
$ tail -n1000 -f ../logs/catalina.out
```

The `tail` command allows you to see the end of the logs file, and the `-f`(force) switch keeps it scrolling as entries are added. (Of course, that's optional.) Now that the server is running again, go to the home page at *http://localhost:8080/juddi/* and click the "Validate" link to make sure that everything went well.

If the Happy jUDDI page has no red in it, as shown in Figure 11-1, you're all set to start publishing to your repository using the JAX-R API.

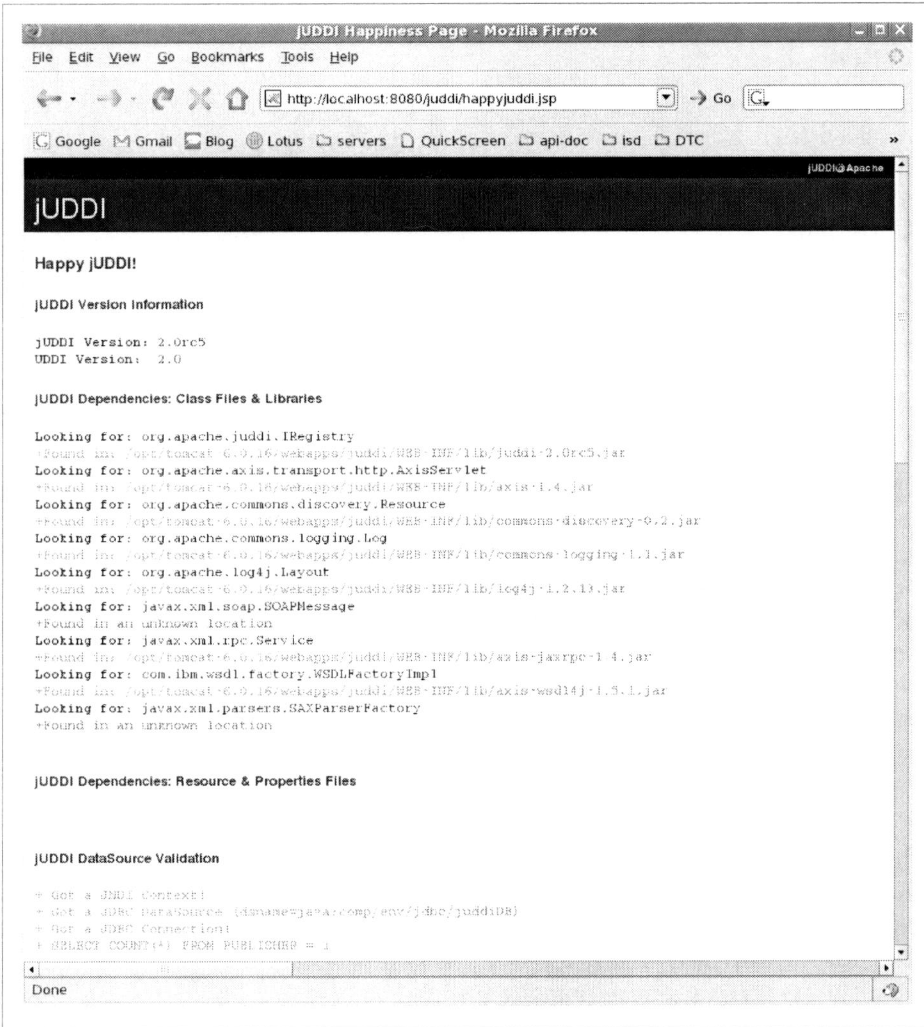

Figure 11-1. Happy jUDDI page showing complete installation

See Also

Recipe 11.11.

11.8 Packaging Related Services

Problem

You want to create a set of web services that are related conceptually and package them appropriately.

Solution

Require a separate source project and deployable artifact for each individual service implementation. Never allow more than one service implementation per WAR or EAR, even though it may initially seem more convenient.

Discussion

We're used to creating web applications that require us to put dozens of servlets in a single WAR. We're used to creating EAR and EJB-JAR archives that allow us to put multiple EJBs in a single deployable artifact. Do not allow this habit to permeate into your source projects when creating services. If you know that for a given solution you need to create a set of services, resist the urge to put more than one servlet or EJB that implements a service endpoint into a single deployable artifact.

For example, you might be charged with creating some data services for internal use in your organization. One will retrieve customer information, and another will retrieve store information. These services may appear related for a variety of reasons: because they are not intended for external use, because you're going to encapsulate them behind the same domain's ESB, because they are read-only, because they wrap legacy code on the same iSeries mid-range box, or because they both must use the same third-party adapter to communicate with a backend. However, to package these two services together is a category mistake. If two services are so designed that it appears incontrovertible that they be deployed together, they are poorly designed. A service should have a single purpose (high cohesion). If it is composable within a larger service, that's terrific. But that's yet another deployable artifact because it, too, is just a service.

The obvious drawback to lumping multiple services together is that you cannot truly version them separately, and you cannot fix bugs in one without recompiling and redeploying the lot of them. Because, like regular servlets, they have separate URLs (and separate WSDLs), it may seem that you can package them together to save development time. This may seem especially important when you have to include some third-party API, such as a JAR that allows your related services. Do not allow the idea of saving a few development steps to seduce you into defeating the whole point of SOA.

Always allow only one service implementation per deployment. If your service is implemented as a servlet, put that single servlet in your WAR, along with any supporting classes. If you have another web service that seems related, create a separate project, and put the second implementation in it. If it, too, requires some of the same supporting classes as your first service did, then you have a shared dependency that must be treated as a first-class citizen. JAR those classes up, put them in a versioned repository somewhere (such as Archiva if you're using Maven), and declare the dependency in both service implementation projects. The extra time you take here is absolutely negligible in comparison with the flexibility you gain down the road. There's no point in doing SOA to create business agility, just to tie everything together on a fundamental and practical level. This will strangle your future efforts.

11.9 Retiring a Service

Problem

You need to retire a service from use.

Solution

As with so many items in the world of SOA, some of these activities will be dependent on your environment. But here are the basic steps for retiring a service:

1. In the repository, discover any compositions or partners that are using this service. Update them to the new version, or, if you are removing the functionality entirely, make sure that you compensate within the partner services so that they don't break once this service is gone.
2. The service is still deployed, and rogue consumers in your organization can discover the WSDL and start invoking it. So undeploy the service entirely from its container so that it can't possibly do any more work.
3. If you are using a Business Activity Monitoring solution, remove the service entry in that tool to minimize skewed numbers and unnecessary alerts. You do this after undeploying the service so that you can catch any continued activity and take necessary precautions.
4. Remove the service from the registry/repository. This takes down the "advertisement" for the service so that no new consumers begin using it.

11.10 Browsing a UDDI Registry

Problem

You want a quick and easy way to view the contents of a UDDI registry without having to write loads of JAX-R code.

Solution

Try UDDI Browser, available from *http://uddibrowser.org*.

11.11 Querying a UDDI Registry Programmatically

Problem

You want a way to query your UDDI-compliant registry in Java code.

Solution

Add the *<glassfish-home>/lib/javaee.jar* to your classpath, and use the JAX-R API to publish and query your registry.

Discussion

If you have set up a UDDI registry, you may want a way to query it from within Java code. The API for doing this is called JAX-R, or Java API for XML Registries. You can check out the JavaDoc for JAX-R online at *http://java.sun.com/j2ee/1.4/docs/api/*.

The UDDI spec is enormous and very complicated, and would require a whole book to cover it. Here you're just going to get a feel for using the registry, and I'll point to some useful tools for you to explore on your own. You can read the spec at *http://www.uddi.org/pubs/uddi_v3.htm*.

Overview

There are two basic interactions with a JAX-R registry: publish and inquiry. Publish adds information about organizations and services, while inquiry runs query statements against it that allow you to find information.

There are a few steps to get set up. First, put the *javaee.jar* on your classpath. That gives you the JAX-R API. You also need an implementation of things like the Connection Factory.

Testing the client

Example 11-1 shows a Java client that accesses your jUDDI registry and queries it for a little information.

Example 11-1. Querying a jUDDI registry with JAX-R

```
package com.soacookbook.scout;

import java.util.ArrayList;
import java.util.Collection;
import java.util.List;
import java.util.Properties;
import javax.xml.registry.*;
import javax.xml.registry.infomodel.*;
```

```
public class Query {

    private static String INQURY_URI =
            "http://localhost:8080/juddi/inquiry";
    private static String PUBLISH_URI =
            "http://localhost:8080/juddi/publish";

    private static String OREILLY = "O'Reilly Media";

    public static void main(String[] args) throws Exception {
        getVersion();

        queryOrgs();
    }

    public static void queryOrgs() throws Exception {
        Connection conn = createConnection();
        RegistryService registry = conn.getRegistryService();
        BusinessQueryManager query =
                registry.getBusinessQueryManager();

        List<String> orgs = new ArrayList<String>();
        orgs.add("O'Reilly Media");

        BulkResponse response =
            query.findOrganizations(null,
                orgs, null, null, null, null);

        @SuppressWarnings("unchecked")
        Collection<Organization> data = response.getCollection();

        System.out.print("Response Size: " + data.size());
        for (Organization org : data) {
            System.out.print("Org: " + org.getName());
        }
    }

    public static void getVersion() throws Exception {
        Connection conn = createConnection();
        RegistryService registry = conn.getRegistryService();
        CapabilityProfile profile = registry.getCapabilityProfile();
        String version = profile.getVersion();

        System.out.print("Version: " + version);
    }

    public static Connection createConnection() {
        Connection connection = null;
        try {
            Properties props = new Properties();
            props.setProperty("javax.xml.registry.queryManagerURL",
                    INQURY_URI);
            props.setProperty("javax.xml.registry.lifeCycleManagerURL",
                    PUBLISH_URI);
```

```
            System.setProperty("javax.xml.registry.ConnectionFactoryClass",
                    "com.sun.xml.registry.uddi.ConnectionFactoryImpl");

            ConnectionFactory factory = ConnectionFactory.newInstance();
            factory.setProperties(props);
            connection = factory.createConnection();

        } catch (JAXRException ex) {
            ex.printStackTrace();
        }

        return connection;
    }
}
```

You get the properties for connecting to the UDDI registry just as you might for connecting to a JMS or EJB service, and once your connection is created, you use the `BusinessQueryManager` class to execute JAX-R queries. You execute a `findOrganizations` query, which returns a `BulkResponse`, and then loop over it to print the results.

See Also

Recipe 11.7.

You can also try the free and open source Apache Scout project, available at *http://ws.apache.org/scout*. There are precious few examples of using Scout, and continued activity on the project is unclear. But if you're willing to slog through the JavaDoc for the API, it's available. Scout is packaged with some popular open source containers, including Apache Geronimo and JBoss 4.0.2 and better.

To use Scout, you'll also need XMLBeans. The latest release as of this writing is 2.4, which you can download from *http://xmlbeans.apache.org*.

11.12 Understanding SOA ROI

Problem

Determining ROI for a traditional software project is different from determining ROI within a SOA. You need to understand these differences.

Solution

The guidelines below may help you to find operational money from the general principles of SOA. Or, you may determine that there is *not* significant ROI in SOA, and that it is rather a cost of doing business.

Discussion

As SOAs wind their way into more and more enterprises, the question of ROI becomes unavoidable. Many industry analysts and stack vendors (who, surprise! have a bunch of SOA software they're happy to equip you with) imply that the ROI in SOA is significant, but also suggest that the value is deferred until the benefits of reuse can be assessed. This recipe explores the reasons for this.

At the end of this recipe, we'll examine the contrarian view that suggests that you can't determine the ROI associated directly with SOA because the question itself is inappropriate.

ROI in traditional software projects

The return on investment for a traditional software project is simpler to calculate than that for SOA projects. Traditional projects tend to focus on the following factors:

- Structure or design that will reduce maintenance and overhead costs. These factors include developer time as well as environmental factors such as how much electricity or cooling is required.
- Features that will win new customers and streamline business processes.
- Features that will reduce time to market.
- Cost reduction. This could occur through licensing arrangements, reduced hardware requirements, consolidation of equipment and function, etc.
- Compliance with regulations such as Payment Card Industry or Sarbanes-Oxley. Indemnification is a form of relief that can be monetized.
- Enabling features that do not directly generate cash themselves but aid in creating the business intelligence can drive more profitable decisions.

The traditional pillars of calculating ROI include the following:

Cost-benefit analysis
: Determining the real value of a proposed solution by examining the monetary benefits against the costs of deriving those benefits. This requires measurement of a variety of factors throughout the business, not just the development process.

Net-present value
: A method of capital budgeting that focuses on figuring the time-value of money against present-day terms. This is used to determine the benefit of long-term projects.

Opportunity cost
: This represents the amount of money it costs you to obtain the new product as compared to the money you would have made, if you had instead invested in a competing product. A common example of opportunity cost is that just leaving your money in the bank allows it to collect interest. But if you choose to invest that

money in order to make more than you can in interest, that interest is still money lost if you withdraw it to invest.

This all gets very complex rather quickly, and goes far beyond the scope of this book. The important thing to realize is that it's difficult enough to determine an ROI for a standard software project, despite the fact the constraints and structure of doing so are fairly well understood at this point. In general, managers focus on a fairly limited data set, regarding the proposed project in terms of costs and future expected benefits derived from features, consolidation, time to market, and other factors just shown.

Frequently, cost-benefit analyses are calculated with careful, perhaps even fanciful precision. I was part of a software project where a small portion of the ROI (a couple hundred thousand dollars) was attributed to its new user interface, in which users would have to make only three clicks instead of five to perform a certain use case. This portion of the ROI was determined thusly:

- T = Total amount of time in seconds it currently takes to perform the use case with the existing "five-click" user interface, averaged over a small sampling with a stopwatch.
- S = Time in seconds it would take to complete the use case with the "three-click" user interface, or roughly 3/5 T.
- U = Projected total number of users performing the use case.
- W = Average hourly wages of said users, divided by 360 to determine wages per second.
- N = Number of times each user was projected to perform that use case in the next five years.

That gave something like the following equation: R = (T * .6) * W * N * U.

Everything gets rather more slippery in an SOA environment. Let's examine why now.

ROI in SOA

While SOA as a concept has been around for a number of years, it remains relatively new as a widespread practice. Determining a long-term ROI therefore has little precedent. But remembering what the goals of SOA are in the first place can help you establish some clear guidelines for ROI.

Primary business drivers for SOA are agility and flexibility. But these concepts are too general to be monetized and must be unpacked in operational terms. Because the advantages inherent in the idea of software reuse are well understood through their roots in traditional software projects and components, reuse makes a good starting point.

There are different kinds of reuse that SOA affords, however. In "application modernization," SOA architects and developers find meaningful ways to service-enable legacy code. There are millions upon millions of lines of COBOL code in operation in the business world. These applications may be viewed as dinosaurs, and developers and business users alike might love to replace them with slick new applications. But these legacy applications are frequently the foundation of the enterprise, and represent decades of stability, testing, and proven ability in the field. Rather than ripping and replacing, SOA seeks to leverage these significant investments by wrapping them with modern web services that can increase the agility and responsiveness of the enterprise. At the same time, there is a diminishing return on any system as it becomes more costly to contrive ways to manipulate and adapt these older applications natively into use within a modern application. SOA recognizes the benefit of tried-and-true applications in the enterprise, and attempts to walk this line by extending established value once compositions enter the picture. Which is where the next aspect of reuse enters the picture: after a service catalog is established.

Reusing existing services from a variety of clients through orchestrations and automated business processes makes a compelling cost benefit. Once your enterprise is service-enabled, the ability to quickly deploy new products on new platforms that build on the existing infrastructure can be quite valuable. The "network effect" (wherein the value grows exponentially as the number of nodes on the network increases) really blossoms at this point.

But it also seems clear that SOA as an integrative technology is going to be more expensive up front. Developers need education, the organization needs infrastructure to support it, and it can take some time to get used to and really learn to leverage the depth and breadth of the tools. Creating a service is far more complex than writing a series of classes or a component. You must put more careful consideration into how the service will be used, and by whom. The runtime environment for a service can be more volatile, particularly as you grow the number of service compositions.

A primary benefit of SOA is agility through reuse, and therefore you see the greatest return the more times a service gets reused, often over a period of many years. There is a little bit of art and a lot of educated guessing in the work of calculating an ROI. We can't lay out an entire ROI plan here, but there are some general points to look for:

Improved quality
: Because services are vetted through the governance process, and because of their more manageable level of granularity, services can be developed in a straightforward manner, monitored closely, and improved without changes to clients. Often services show greater quality than their application predecessors, which translates into real money.

Increased return on legacy applications
: By service-enabling or modernizing legacy applications, you extend their functional life, which increases the value gained by the original legacy applications.

Reduced integration costs
: Integrating with purchased systems such as Peoplesoft, SAP, or Oracle Financials can be expensive, and you typically need to purchase adapters for working directly with their proprietary interfaces. Products that expose a service interface can be

much less expensive to integrate with. Providing a service interface to business partners on unknown systems can make on-ramping easier, less labor-intensive and error-prone, and more cost-effective.

Reduced traditional application development costs
: While this book focuses on developing services, one key driver of SOA is that it is easier to put together traditional applications by leveraging services. Within a standard development project, introducing an existing service (perhaps created by a third party) to handle specific functional aspects can reduce costs as well. Moreover, your developers can be more effectively used if they are orchestrating composite services from existing services rather than writing custom code for everything. If you have made an investment in SOA tools offered by the suite vendors (such as Software AG, IBM, TIBCO, etc.), you may find a drastic reduction in the amount of time it takes to create and deploy service-based applications. Their tools can require little or no coding to wrap legacy services and build sophisticated workflows. The time saved can make a good argument for real ROI in SOA.

In order to realize these benefits, you must make a sustained investment in SOA. The return happens over time—specifically, the amount of time it takes for your organization to have some significant number of services and a significant number of consumers. You must track, so that you can later show, the cost avoidance benefits due to your SOA efforts.

ROI implications of building out services within traditional projects

As you are building out your SOA, it is unlikely that you will be given a blank check and a well-appointed private room and told to write services until it's done. Most of your services will be developed alongside or as part of traditional application development projects. The way that these projects are budgeted, and the way that their ROI is determined, will not take into account the potential ROI locked inside the services that you will develop. That ROI will only be realized across a long time frame, as it obtains stature within a vibrant SOA.

So that presents a challenge. Specifically, you need to create a separate business case and a separate ROI prospect for the services themselves, taking their role within SOA into account. That is, the business case for creating the application that will use a service that you're about to develop will not be the same as the business case for the service itself.

Project managers and business managers will often want to conflate the service and the initial application that consumes it. This is tempting because it's easy to do, it's what we're used to, and we spent a long time learning our existing IT tools for project management. However, that doesn't mean it's the right thing to do.

You must protect the long-term life of the SOA by showing the benefits with which it rewards the business for its patience. You won't be able to do that if the ROI is baked together with applications. Baking them together is a kind of category mistake. The use of the application project will generally be well known, clearly understood, and fairly succinct. An application that allows business users to change the prices of their products is probably not going to be used in any other way.

Just as you govern and monitor the life cycle of the services themselves, be prepared to govern their ROI life cycle as well. This will require a separate set of criteria than in traditional project-based software applications. For example, consider an item such as Time Value. Services can allow you to reduce batch processing cycles. Typical data warehouses perform ETL (extract, transform, and load) operations that can take significant time to process. This results in "data latency," postponing the ability to make business decisions. Rather than saving data in staging areas and moving it around the enterprise, SOA may allow you to get to your data more quickly through data-based services.

There's no ROI in SOA

The contrarian view suggests that there may *not* be significant ROI that can be readily and clearly associated with SOA. This view says:

- SOA is an architecture. It is a particular strategy for building software. It is not a business venture (unless you live in the Bay Area). It gives you certain benefits, and the reason that it has become popular in recent years is that it is an architecture that includes the business within its scope. It can generate real business value, but it's not clear how an architectural approach translates readily and directly into a return on investment.
- SOA is a way to make the software you really care about. Let me make the point this way. If it's fair to ask what the ROI on SOA is, then it is presupposed that SOA *is* something: that is, that it's a product in its own right that the business is interested in. But I suspect that this would be greeted with considerable skepticism. The great Irish playwright Samuel Beckett once wrote, "Art isn't *about* something, it *is* something." With SOA, it's the opposite: SOA is *about* something, it *isn't* anything. SOA helps you make the products that your business needs. SOA is not what you want; it helps you get what you want. It's just another cost of doing business. In the same way, businesses may not want to spend $25 million on a building for their corporate headquarters. But you can't have very productive executive meetings in a tent in the backyard.
- SOA is a software strategy that has certain aims, including better support of business initiatives. Within the context of a pilot project, in which you build a service and perhaps a project around it in order to show value quickly and support your fledgling SOA, it may be easy to see how avoiding services altogether and writing the application using a traditional, baked-in approach would be far less expensive. Detractors from the idea of SOA ROI suggest that there are other reasons for creating a SOA: that as an approach to software, the better able SOA is to support your business initiatives, the more return you can realize in the context of your

business initiatives. However, they would contend that there is little way to precisely map real dollars to SOA.

- SOA has certain benefits, not every conceivable benefit, including ready-bake ROI. Businesses do things all the time that don't show tangible returns. For example, many companies send 2, 3, 6, or 10 employees to the JavaOne conference each year, or have large, lavish corporate parties. Such items, frequently contextualized as "team building" and related matters, are difficult to map directly to a return. But these companies believe that such events and others like them help create a desirable workplace. While desirability cannot be quantified, it seems reasonable to believe that such benefits can allow companies to hire and retain better employees and to have a more productive workforce. Intangible benefits, such as "increased customer satisfaction" and "improved customer service" are no less real simply because they are difficult or impossible to quantify.

So it may be that SOA is a good idea for some businesses in some contexts, and just because you can't map an ROI precisely doesn't mean you shouldn't do it. It may also be the case that there is ROI in SOA, but that attempts to show it will only subject you to the fallacy of False Precision. One example of False Precision is to suggest that the normal human body temperature is 98.6 degrees. This is simply a traditionally used value, and there is no actual "normal" temperature that can be identified to a precision of a tenth of a degree. Instead, there is a basic range of perhaps 97–99 degrees in which different people normally operate.

The point of this recipe is to get you thinking about all of these factors in your organization. You may have to do some work to "sell" SOA within your organization, and only you can decide on the best way to determine the ROI for SOA. But consider if you're asking the right question, or even a fair question.

Finally, just because SOA is an architecture that includes the business within its scope in a variety of ways (including governance, BPM, and so forth), consider carefully if you are asking SOA to be responsible for more than it can reasonably be. Consider the well-publicized fringe benefits Google offers, including onsite dry cleaning and a gourmet chef. What's the ROI for gourmet food? Could you specify, with anything other than wild speculation, a return on investment in Kobe beef instead of ground chuck?

I have tried to give reasonable voice to both sides of the argument here. But sometimes, if solving a certain problem is really, really hard, it's because we're trying to solve the wrong problem.

One simple and perfectly reasonable way of looking at SOA ROI is to present SOA as a solution, and compare it with the cost of not getting a solution.

PART IV

Interoperability and Quality of Service

CHAPTER 12

Web Service Interoperability

12.0 Introduction

A primary purpose of web services is to interoperate with other services, regardless of the platform on which they are running or the language in which they are implemented. While the WS-* specifications go a long way toward describing platform-independent mechanisms for message exchange, the devil is in the details. As with any specification, there are many areas of the WS-* specifications that are open to interpretation, and there are a numbers of questions to which vendor platforms must determine the answers themselves. The specifications for XML, SOAP, and WSDL were written independently of one another, and therefore have minor gaps and overlaps between them. Moreover, developers are free to implement services in a variety of ways given the choices that the specifications make available, and that makes interoperability more challenging. Between different transport layers, policy and security implementations, message encoding mechanisms, platform-specific character encodings, and differences in implementation details, interoperability can become a daunting task.

Let's look at this concretely. A WSDL describes a web service in general terms. It allows for customizations, exposing implementation details (such as Java customizations), and a number of combinations of transport and encoding mechanisms. It is perfectly acceptable to implement your service as RPC/encoded, which defines the format of messages over the wire. As a developer starting from Java, you're not going to see any difference between an encoded or a literally formatted message. However, some platforms have difficulty working with SOAP encoding, and some elements of SOAP encoding are handled differently from one platform to another. That makes RPC encoding a poor choice if you want to make sure as many people as possible can use your service.

The challenge then becomes finding a suitable middle ground for service implementation so that the greatest variety of platforms can consume your services. Enter the Web Services Interoperability Organization, or WS-I. The WS-I consists of representatives from a large number of vendors, whose basic mission is to define standards to which web service implementations should conform in order to ensure the widest possible audience for their services. The chief product of the WS-I is the Basic Profile (BP), currently in version 1.2. At the time of this writing, however, version 1.1 of the Basic Profile probably still enjoys the widest support amongst vendors.

The Basic Profile is a document that indicates the specific choices that you as a developer should make when implementing a service to ensure interoperability with other service implementations that conform to the BP. Services that make the implementation choices indicated in the BP are said to conform to some particular version of the BP.

You can download and read the Basic Profile guidelines at *http://www.ws-i.org/deliverables/workinggroup.aspx?wg=basicprofile*.

It is not necessary to make your services conform to the BP, but Sun's specification for J2EE 1.4 and Java EE 5 require vendors to support it. If you do make your services conform to the BP, you can rest assured that they'll work with services written in any language (C#, Perl, Python, Ruby, or C wrapper code around a COBOL program), running on any OS (Windows, Linux, Mac), with any vendor platform (IBM WebSphere, Oracle WebLogic, Glassfish, and so forth). Because a primary purpose of web services is to interoperate with others, and because it isn't any harder for you to do so, there is really no defensible reason not to conform to the BP.

It is the case, however, that not every platform implements the same version of every specification that WSIT (Web Services Interoperability Technology) supports. The clear focus of WSIT has been to get Java-based clients and services to interoperate with those written for the Windows Communication Foundation in .NET 3.0 and 3.5.

The recipes in this chapter contain little discussion. We already covered the material that comprises different aspects of SOAP-based web services in earlier chapters; this chapter is intended to serve as a quick lookup guide to assist in your decision-making. It will perhaps be most useful if you have already made an implementation choice and want to do a quick check to make sure that the BP supports your decision.

You can read more about the WS-I at *http://www.ws-i.org*.

In this chapter, I make the assumption that you want to follow the Basic Profile 1.1.

12.1 Dealing with Arrays

Problem

You need to define an array data type in a schema that your service will use, but the BP disallows using arrays.

Solution

Define a complex type, and give its `maxOccurs` attribute a value of greater than 0. If you want to replicate a true Java array, give the attribute an actual value to bound the number of cells it holds. If you want to replicate a Java list, specify `unbounded`.

Discussion

Section 4.3.3 of the BP 1.1 disallows using SOAP-encoded array types because of the number of interoperability problems that arrays present. You are not allowed to use the `soapenc:Array` type or the `wsdl:arrayType`.

You use the array encoding type like this:

```
...
<xsd:restriction base="soapenc:Array">
   <xsd:sequence>
     <xsd:element name="x" type="xsd:string"
       minOccurs="0" maxOccurs="unbounded"/>
   </xsd:sequence>
   <xsd:attribute ref="soapenc:arrayType"
     wsdl:arrayType="tns:MyArrayType[]"/>
...
```

This type would serialize in a SOAP message as something like the following code:

```
<MyArray soapenc:arrayType="tns:MyArrayType[]">
  <x>123</x>
  <x>456</x>
</MyArray>
```

Luckily, it's easy to address this problem. All you have to do to overcome this issue is avoid use of the array type altogether, and define a complex type whose `maxOccurs` attribute value is `unbounded`, as shown in the following:

```
<xsd:element name="Books" type="tns:Books"/>
<xsd:complexType name="Books">
  <xsd:sequence>
   <xsd:element name="title" type="xsd:string"
    minOccurs="0" maxOccurs="unbounded"/>
  </xsd:sequence>
</xsd:complexType>
```

This schema code produces the following serialized message:

```
<Books>
  <title>Hamlet</title>
  <title>King Lear</title>
</Books>
```

Also, section 4.2.3 of the Basic Profile 1.2 indicates that you should not use the `ArrayOf Something` naming convention. This was suggested in section 4.2.3 of the Basic Profile 1.2. If you are using a "Start from Java" approach, use a `java.util.List`. For example, `public List<Book> getBooks()`.

12.2 Abstracting Addressing

Problem

You are developing a service starting from Java, and want to abstract the addressing mechanism for message exchanges in your services away from the transport specified in your binding to make your services more interoperable.

Solution

Use an implementation of the WS-Addressing specification, such as is included with JAX-WS 2.1.

Discussion

The WS-Addressing specification exists to provide a way to address web services and messages without directly referencing their transport mechanism. It allows your web service to use HTTP, SMTP, JMS, XMPP, or any other protocol as a transport layer, and to address your messages independently without identifying protocol-specific characteristics. What this means in practice is that a service can be consumed by a client with the same semantics, even across protocols.

This is particularly useful in sending messages through networks that include processing nodes such as firewalls and gateways. As a result, WS-Addressing offers another method of achieving greater interoperability.

Toward this aim, WS-Addressing indicates two constructs: a service endpoint and message information headers. The endpoint is the target for messages, the service to which they are addressed. Message information headers include addressing information for message sources and endpoints, as well as message identity.

You can use Addressing with Apache Axis2 1.1.0, CXF, Glassfish/Metro v2, WebLogic 10gR3, and others. It is also implemented in .NET 3.0 and 3.5. Members of the Microsoft and Sun web services teams regularly get together for what are called "plugfests." These events invite developers of various spec implementations to bring their laptops and run a defined test suite against other implementations to ensure that they actually work together. The results of these plugfests are typically posted online, sometimes in developer blogs.

Like WS-Policy, WS-Addressing is a "foundational" spec, used by a number of other WS-* specs, as its concerns cut across use cases. It is therefore very useful to understand the basic idea behind it.

Endpoint references

The data in an endpoint reference is mapped to the message. The mapping is dependent on the particular protocol in use (SOAP is the default, and what is defined in the spec), and the representation of the data used to send the message. The specification only requires the mapping to SOAP semantics. So despite the fact that others could be used, sticking to SOAP is a good idea if you want to make sure that your addresses are interoperable.

The SOAP binding for addresses will copy the `address` property into the destination header field in the SOAP request. The specification also includes the idea of reference properties and reference parameters. A reference property is used to make sure that the dispatch of messages to endpoints happens correctly; they are not something of interest to clients. A reference parameter is similar, but it serves to facilitate particular interactions that the endpoint requires.

Message information headers

The specification defines a set of elements that are inserted into the headers of your SOAP messages when Addressing is enabled. These headers define the semantics that allow addressing to work, primarily by enabling the identification of messages and the location of endpoints.

The most common message information headers used in WS-Addressing for a SOAP request are shown in Table 12-1.

Table 12-1. Message information headers

Header	Description
`wsa:MessageID`	Uniquely identifies a message in an exchange. It is optional unless `wsa:ReplyTo` or `wsa:FaultTo` is used.
`wsa:RelatesTo`	Indicates a relationship type using the message ID. If the message is a response, this property indicates the ID of the request message that this response relates to. Optional unless this message is a response.
`wsa:ReplyTo`	The endpoint that a reply should be sent to. Must use message ID. If not specified, implementations generally reply to the originating endpoint.
`wsa:From`	The source endpoint reference where this message came from.
`wsa:FaultTo`	The endpoint reference to which fault responses should be sent. If not specified, implementations will generally send the fault response to the originating endpoint.
`wsa:To`	The destination for this message.
`wsa:Action`	A URI that uniquely identifies the semantics for this message, indicating, for example, what operation should be invoked on each request. In addition to the SOAP header, this will commonly add an HTTP header indicating the `SOAP Action` value.

Anonymous addressing

While most of the elements in Addressing are devoted to finding the proper endpoint and defining it carefully and uniquely, the spec also defines something called an anonymous endpoint. Within a SOAP interaction, this basically is used to indicate that no specific endpoint with a stable, resolvable URI, has been set. The Addressing runtime will then take over and insert this anonymous address, which is stable and well known, into the headers.

It looks like this:

```
<To xmlns="http://www.w3.org/2005/08/addressing">
  http://www.w3.org/2005/08/addressing/anonymous
</To>
```

This is not something that you write yourself, but rather something you are likely to see in your messages as the result of using a regular Java client to access your service, and the client does not define an endpoint address of its own. In more complex exchanges, the anonymous address is useful given the range of network appliances that may receive your message as intermediary nodes and need to forward it on. Items such as firewalls or DHCP have no mechanism by which to process a meaningful endpoint address. The anonymous address satisfies both of these cases.

12.3 Using Addressing in a Java Service

Problem

You want to specify that your web service uses WS-Addressing.

Solution

In your Java web service class, use the `javax.xml.ws.soap.Addressing` annotation along with the `Action` annotation:

```
import javax.xml.ws.Action;
import javax.xml.ws.soap.Addressing;

@WebService
@Addressing
public class HelloAddressingWS {
```

This enables Addressing generally in your service; you must then apply the `Action` annotation to your operations, like this:

```
@WebMethod
@Action(
  input = "http://soacookbook.com/name",
  output = "http://soacookbook.com/greeting")
public String sayHello(String name) { ...
```

Discussion

The Addressing specification is wrapped into the JAX-WS 2.1 specification, so any vendor implementing JAX-WS 2.1 will make the Addressing feature available.

The Addressing annotation is used only on an endpoint implementation class. This was implemented as a feature type (`AddressingFeature`) in previous versions of JAX-WS. The new annotation simplifies usage, but under the hood it all works the same, and the feature instance is still required in some cases (see Recipe 12.5).

Let's unpack the code a little bit to see how this works. Adding addressing to your simple Hello service as you did earlier makes the following changes to the resulting WSDL:

```
<portType name="HelloAddressingWS">
  <operation name="sayHello">
    <input wsaw:Action="http://soacookbook.com/name"
      message="tns:sayHello"/>
    <output wsaw:Action="http://soacookbook.com/greeting"
      message="tns:sayHelloResponse"/>
  </operation>
</portType>
...
<binding name="HelloAddressingWSPortBinding"
  type="tns:HelloAddressingWS">
  <wsaw:UsingAddressing/>
```

First, the annotation's attributes map clearly to the input and output of the operation they modify. The values specified in the Java file are added to the addressing `Action` attribute. Then, in the binding, the WSDL now indicates that it is set up for WS-Addressing so that clients are free to use Addressing if they would like to, via the `<wsaw:UsingAddressing/>` element. This element also has a required attribute that indicates if you want the service to force clients to use addressing. By default, it is set to false. But you could just write `<wsaw:UsingAddressing required="true"/>` to force clients to use Addressing, if you had started from WSDL. To generate that from Java, use the following code:

```
@Addressing(required=true)
```

The current version of JAX-WS is what the spec calls "incomplete" with respect to addressing. That's because there is no standard way to indicate within a WSDL that you want to use WS-Addressing, and there is no standard default value for the `Action` headers that WS-Addressing uses. Once the W3C (the sponsor of the working group defining the addressing spec) defines these items, JAX-WS will be updated to enforce them.

To make sure that your endpoint and its client are portable, the endpoint must use the `Action` annotation to indicate their WS-Addressing actions, and it should use the `FaultAction` annotation for creating WS-Addressing-compliant SOAP faults.

If you wish to set up addressing in Apache CXF, see *http://cwiki.apache.org/CXF20DOC/ws-addressing.html*.

See Also

Recipe 12.4.

12.4 Explicitly Enabling Addressing on the Client

Problem

You want to invoke a service that declares it uses addressing.

Solution

You don't need to do anything, as the JAX-WS runtime can determine that the WSDL advertises that it uses addressing based on the presence of the `<wsaw:UsingAddressing/>` element in the binding section of the `wsdl:definitions`.

Create an instance of `javax.xml.ws.AddressingFeature`, using `true` as a constructor parameter. Then pass this feature instance to the port accessor method on the service stub you got from `wsimport` (or its equivalent). The code to do so looks like this:

```
new MyImplService().getMyImplPort(
  new javax.xml.ws.AddressingFeature(true)
);
```

Discussion

The JAX-WS 2.1 specification indicates that clients must explicitly enable addressing in order to use addressing in a web service that declares support for it. For each invocation, the client must also explicitly set `BindingProvider.SOAPACTION_URI_PROPERTY`.

If you attempt to invoke a service that specifies that addressing is required and you have not enabled addressing on the client, you'll get an error message such as this in the SOAP response's Fault `<faultstring>` element: "A required header representing a Message Addressing Property is not present." You may also get an error that you can read off of a response header that looks like this:

```
<S:Header>
  <FaultDetail xmlns="http://www.w3.org/2005/08/addressing">
    <ProblemHeaderQName>
      {http://www.w3.org/2005/08/addressing}Action
    </ProblemHeaderQName>
  </FaultDetail>
</S:Header>
```

The client in Example 12-1 can be built to invoke the simple Hello service from Recipe 12.3. This class assumes that you have performed a `wsimport` (or equivalent) and added the generated artifacts to your classpath. Example 12-4 in Recipe 12.7 shows how to use the `AddressingFeature` class with a service port object to enable WS-Addressing on the client.

Example 12-1. AddressingClient.java

```
import javax.xml.ws.soap.AddressingFeature;

/**
 * Calls the WebService with WS-Addressing enabled.
 */
public class AddressingClient {
public static void main(String...args) {
    try { // Call Web Service Operation
       HelloAddressingWSService service = new HelloAddressingWSService();

       //enable WS-Addressing
       HelloAddressingWS port =
               service.getHelloAddressingWSPort(
                new AddressingFeature());

       String result = port.sayHello("Eben");
       System.out.println("Result = "+result);
    } catch (Exception ex) {
       ex.printStackTrace();
    }
  }
}
```

So all you have to do is create a new `AddressingFeature` using the default constructor. There are two Boolean arguments that you can optionally pass to the constructor as well, indicating preferences for "required" and "enabled."

Running this client produces a SOAP request that looks like this, including the HTTP headers:

```
SOAPAction: "http://soacookbook.com/name"
Content-Type: text/xml;charset="utf-8"
<?xml version="1.0" ?>
<S:Envelope xmlns:S="http://schemas.xmlsoap.org/soap/envelope/">
<S:Header>
<To xmlns="http://www.w3.org/2005/08/addressing">
  http://localhost:7777/TestWS/HelloAddressingWSService
</To>
<Action xmlns="http://www.w3.org/2005/08/addressing">
  http://soacookbook.com/name
</Action>
<ReplyTo xmlns="http://www.w3.org/2005/08/addressing">
    <Address>
      http://www.w3.org/2005/08/addressing/anonymous
    </Address>
</ReplyTo>
<MessageID xmlns="http://www.w3.org/2005/08/addressing">
  uuid:8c5ff38d-6a7b-477e-8558-2b6572f7ba84
</MessageID>
</S:Header>

<S:Body>
<ns2:sayHello xmlns:ns2="http://soacookbook.com/">
  <arg0>Eben</arg0>
</ns2:sayHello>
</S:Body>
</S:Envelope>
```

Recall that if you want to view the SOAP messages as they are being sent on the wire, put the WSIT *webservices-rt.jar* on your classpath and add the following code to your invocation. In your IDE, you can specify this as a "run" argument. I mention it again here because addressing adds so many headers that it becomes particularly useful.

```
-Dcom.sun.xml.ws.transport.http.client.HttpTransportPipe.dump=true
```

As you can see from the dump of this SOAP message, using the `AddressingFeature` message adds considerable length to your messages.

Invoking the service with this request will give you the desired output. The SOAP response message comes in the following form (the HTTP headers have been omitted because there's nothing in them that's specific to Addressing):

```
<S:Envelope xmlns:S="http://schemas.xmlsoap.org/soap/envelope/">
<S:Header>
<To xmlns="http://www.w3.org/2005/08/addressing">
  http://www.w3.org/2005/08/addressing/anonymous
</To>
<Action xmlns="http://www.w3.org/2005/08/addressing">
  http://soacookbook.com/greeting
</Action>
<MessageID xmlns="http://www.w3.org/2005/08/addressing">
  uuid:5ea13011-8163-4c03-9d86-dd54159d2165
```

```
</MessageID>
<RelatesTo xmlns="http://www.w3.org/2005/08/addressing">
  uuid:8c5ff38d-6a7b-477e-8558-2b6572f7ba84
</RelatesTo>
</S:Header>

<S:Body>
  <ns2:sayHelloResponse xmlns:ns2="http://soacookbook.com/">
    <return>Hello, Eben</return>
  </ns2:sayHelloResponse>
</S:Body></S:Envelope>
```

The SOAP header also includes an addressing `Action` element. This element has the value that was indicated by the `Action` attribute on the web service, like this:

```
@Action(output = "http://soacookbook.com/greeting")
```

But of course the client is not reading the Java class; it's examining the WSDL created by that class, which has the following form:

```
<portType name="HelloAddressingWS">
<operation name="sayHello">
  <input wsaw:Action="http://soacookbook.com/name"
    message="tns:sayHello"/>
  <output wsaw:Action="http://soacookbook.com/greeting"
    message="tns:sayHelloResponse"/>
</operation>
</portType>
```

You can also see in the response that it includes a `<RelatesTo>` SOAP header. This header indicates the value of the universally unique ID that was specified as the value of the `<MessageID>` element in the request to which this message is a response.

12.5 Explicitly Disabling Addressing on the Client

Problem

You want to invoke a service that declares it uses addressing, but you want to disable this in your client.

Solution

Create an instance of the `javax.xml.ws.AddressingFeature`, using `false` as a constructor parameter. Then pass this feature instance to the port accessor method on the service stub. The code to do so looks like this:

```
new MyImplService().getMyImplPort(
  new javax.xml.ws.AddressingFeature(false)
);
```

Discussion

You might want to disable the processing of addressing instructions in certain cases. For example, a client that uses a SAAJ `Dispatch` with a mode of `MESSAGE` (instead of `PAYLOAD`) can indicate that it wants to process `ReplyTo` or `FaultTo` constructs in its own way, in the absence of anonymous addressing.

See Also

Recipe 12.4.

12.6 Abstracting Addressing in the Transport Layer from WSDL

Problem

You are developing a service starting from WSDL, and want to abstract the addressing mechanism for message exchanges in your services away from the transport specified in your binding in order to make your services more interoperable.

Solution

In your WSDL, import the addressing namespace, add addressing to the binding section, and add the `wsaw:Action` attribute to your operations. The code to do so looks like this:

```
<definitions name="AddNumbers"...
  xmlns:wsaw="http://www.w3.org/2006/05/addressing/wsdl">
...
<operation name="doWork">
  <input message="tns:doWork" wsaw:Action="workIn"/>
  <output message="tns:doWorkResponse" wsaw:Action="workOut"/>
  <fault name="doWorkFault" message="tns:workFault"
    wsaw:Action="doWorkFault"/>
</operation>

<binding name="MyServiceBinding" type="tns:MyPortType">
  <wsaw:UsingAddressing wsdl:required="false" />
  <soap:binding transport="http://schemas.xmlsoap.org/soap/http" style="document" />
```

12.7 Addressing Faults

Problem

You want your declared faults (exceptions), and not just your operation inputs and outputs, to participate in Addressing.

Solution

Use the WS-Addressing `@Action` annotation's fault attribute. It accepts a `@FaultAction` annotation for each exception your method throws.

Discussion

Most of the work is handled for you in the annotations. All you have to do is declare the fault action above the method that throws the exception you want to map with WS-Addressing. It accepts a `Class` instance indicating the exception you're mapping, along with the URI you want to give as the address of the exception. The complete solution is shown in Examples 12-2 and 12-3.

Example 12-2. The web service that uses addressing on faults

```
package com.soacookbook;

import javax.jws.*;
import javax.xml.ws.Action;
import javax.xml.ws.FaultAction;
import javax.xml.ws.soap.Addressing;

/**
 * Shows a class that uses WS-Addressing, including
 * a Fault that is Addressing enabled.
 */
@WebService
@Addressing(required=true)
public class HelloAddressingFaultsWS {

  @WebMethod
  @Action(
    input="http://soacookbook.com/name",
    output="http://soacookbook.com/greeting",
    fault={
      @FaultAction(className=HelloException.class,
        value="http://soacookbook.com/myFault")})
  public String sayHello(String name) throws HelloException {

    if (name == null || "".equals(name)) {
      throw new HelloException("The name was null or empty.");
    }
    return "Hello, " + name;
  }
}
```

That's all there is to it. Because the fault attribute of the `Action` annotation accepts an array, you can specify multiple `FaultActions`, one for each exception your method throws. For this example, I created a new exception called `HelloException`, which is shown in Example 12-3.

Example 12-3. Exception that is addressed using FaultAction in web service

```
package com.soacookbook;

public class HelloException extends Exception {
  public HelloException(String msg){
    super("Could not say hello: " + msg);
  }
}
```

This class just extends `Exception` as a checked exception, and because it's not the focus of this recipe, I haven't added lots of other methods to it. It only exists to show how you could map to a custom exception.

Deploying this service endpoint implementation code generates the WSDL shown in Example 12-4.

Example 12-4. The WSDL using WS-Addressing for faults

```
<definitions xmlns:wsaw="http://www.w3.org/2006/05/addressing/wsdl"
targetNamespace="http://soacookbook.com/"...>
<types>
<xsd:schema>
<xsd:import namespace="http://soacookbook.com/"
schemaLocation="http://localhost:7777/TestWS/HelloAddressingFaultsWSService?xsd=1" />
</xsd:schema>
</types>

<message name="sayHello">
<part name="parameters" element="tns:sayHello" />
</message>
<message name="sayHelloResponse">
<part name="parameters" element="tns:sayHelloResponse" />
</message>
<message name="HelloException">
<part name="fault" element="tns:HelloException" />
</message>

<portType name="HelloAddressingFaultsWS">
<operation name="sayHello">
<input wsaw:Action="http://soacookbook.com/name"
message="tns:sayHello" />
<output wsaw:Action="http://soacookbook.com/greeting"
message="tns:sayHelloResponse" />
<fault message="tns:HelloException" name="HelloException"
  wsaw:Action="http://soacookbook.com/myFault" />
</operation>
</portType>

<binding name="HelloAddressingFaultsWSPortBinding"
type="tns:HelloAddressingFaultsWS">

<wsaw:UsingAddressing />

<soap:binding transport="http://schemas.xmlsoap.org/soap/http"
```

```
style="document" />
<operation name="sayHello">
<soap:operation soapAction="" />
<input>
<soap:body use="literal" />
</input>
<output>
<soap:body use="literal" />
</output>
<fault name="HelloException">
  <soap:fault name="HelloException" use="literal" />
</fault>
</operation>
</binding>
<service name="HelloAddressingFaultsWSService">
<port name="HelloAddressingFaultsWSPort"
binding="tns:HelloAddressingFaultsWSPortBinding">
<soap:address
location="http://localhost:7777/TestWS/HelloAddressingFaultsWSService" />
</port>
</service>
</definitions>
```

To begin with, the WS-Addressing element `<wsaw:UsingAddressing />` is added to the WSDL to indicate that clients should use addressing to interact with this service. You can see that, in general, the exception is treated as a normal SOAP fault would be in a WSDL, with one addition: the `wsaw:Action` attribute has been added to the `<fault>` element associated with the `sayHello` operation. Faults will be addressed, using WS-Addressing, to this URI.

The code listing in Example 12-5 represents a client that will invoke that service using WS-Addressing, including setting the addressing on the fault in the service WSDL.

Example 12-5. Addressing client that gets a fault

```
package com.soacookbook;

import javax.xml.ws.soap.AddressingFeature;

/**
 * Calls the WebService with WS-Addressing enabled,
 * with the service declaring addressing for an
 * exception that can be thrown.
 */
public class AddressingFaultClient {

    public static void main(String[] args) {
        //do something we know will cause a fault
        sayHello(null);
    }

    private static void sayHello(String name) {
        try {
            //call Web Service Operation
```

```
            HelloAddressingFaultsWSService service =
                    new HelloAddressingFaultsWSService();

            //enable WS-Addressing
            HelloAddressingFaultsWS port =
                    service.getHelloAddressingFaultsWSPort(
                    new AddressingFeature());

            String result = port.sayHello(name);
            System.out.println("Result = " + result);
        } catch (Exception ex) {
            ex.printStackTrace();
        }
    }
}
```

Here you simply invoke the service using a null parameter, which you know will generate the fault for the `sayHello` operation. Recall that when getting the port stub in the client, you must add the `AddressingFeature`.

This produces the following output, shown in a fragment:

```
---[HTTP response 500]---
<S:Header>
  <To xmlns="http://www.w3.org/2005/08/addressing">
    http://www.w3.org/2005/08/addressing/anonymous
  </To>
  <Action xmlns="http://www.w3.org/2005/08/addressing">
    http://soacookbook.com/myFault
  </Action>

//other WS-Addressing headers...

<S:Body>
<S:Fault xmlns:ns4="http://www.w3.org/2003/05/soap-envelope">
<faultcode>S:Server</faultcode>
<faultstring>
  Could not say hello: The name was null or empty.
</faultstring>
<detail>
<ns2:HelloException xmlns:ns2="http://soacookbook.com/">
  <message>
    Could not say hello: The name was null or empty.
  </message>
</ns2:HelloException>
```

First, you get an HTTP 500 response code, which is in accordance with section 3.4.7 of the Basic Profile 1.1.

Next, you see that the value of the `Action` element is the WS-Addressing address specified in your `FaultAction` annotation in the service endpoint operation, which looks like this:

```
@Action(..., fault= {
  @FaultAction(className=HelloException.class,
    value="http://soacookbook.com/myFault")})
```

12.8 Creating a .NET Web Service Client in Visual Studio

Problem

You want to create a client in Visual Studio to invoke a Java-based web service.

Solution

In Visual Studio, you can add a web reference to your project and provide a WSDL URL, and it will create the proxy code for you. Then you can reference the service based on the server name.

Discussion

In this example, you'll walk through the steps associated with creating a .NET client for a web service written in Java. Using Visual Studio 2005, you can easily add a reference to an existing web service. First, you'll create a regular console project in C# with a `Main` method. Then you'll go to Project→Add Web Reference and give it the URL of a local calculator web service written in Java. This will generate a set of proxy classes (as `wsimport` would in the solution), which are now available to invoke.

This is slightly different from how you do it in Java: the proxy is in the namespace (similar to a Java package) of the server name that hosts the WSDL. In your case, that's `localhost`, so you can access your service proxy by referencing it from that namespace. The complete class is shown in Example 12-6.

Example 12-6. SimpleCalcClient.cs

```
using System;
using System.Collections.Generic;
using System.Text;

namespace ConsoleApplication1
{
    class Program
    {
        static void Main(string[] args)
        {
            InvokeCalculator();
        }

        private static void InvokeCalculator()
        {
            localhost.CalculatorWSService service =
                 new localhost.CalculatorWSService();
            int result = service.add(6, 9);
```

```
            Console.WriteLine("The result is " + result);
        }
    }
}
```

This entire process takes under a minute. If you don't have Visual Studio, you can try the Sharp Develop product, a free and open source IDE for .NET that is hosted at Source Forge. You can get it from *http://sourceforge.net/projects/sharpdevelop*. Alternatively, just download the .NET framework for free from Microsoft and use the console, as shown in Recipe 12.9.

12.9 Creating a .NET Web Service Client in C#

Problem

You want to create a service proxy in C# with more control over the generation than Visual Studio web references give you.

Solution

Use `wsdl.exe` from the command line and supply the parameters you want.

Discussion

Adding a web reference doesn't afford any customizations on how the WSDL is handled during proxy generation. You may want to change the name of the service as your client application will use it, or you may want to output the proxy in a language other than C# (such as VB.NET). Let's first walk through a simple example of invoking a Java-based web service.

This example will work with any WSDL, but the specifics are addressed as if you have deployed a calculator web service that adds two numbers together and returns a sum. There's a similar example in the NetBeans 6.1 samples that you can easily deploy locally.

Example 12-7 shows basic WSDL from the NetBeans 6.1 sample that represents the adding service you're going to call (I've modified it slightly to keep it small).

Example 12-7. Calculator.wsdl

```
<?xml version="1.0" encoding="UTF-8"?>
<definitions ...
targetNamespace="http://calculator.me.org/"
name="CalculatorWSService">

<types>
<xsd:schema>
```

```
<xsd:import namespace="http://calculator.me.org/"
  schemaLocation="http://localhost:8080/CalculatorApp/CalculatorWSService?xsd=1">
</xsd:import>
</xsd:schema>
</types>

<message name="add">
<part name="parameters" element="tns:add" />
</message>
<message name="addResponse">
<part name="parameters" element="tns:addResponse" />
</message>
<portType name="CalculatorWS">
<operation name="add">
<input message="tns:add" />
<output message="tns:addResponse" />
</operation>
</portType>

<binding name="CalculatorWSPortBinding" type="tns:CalculatorWS">
<soap:binding transport="http://schemas.xmlsoap.org/soap/http"
  style="document" />
<operation name="add">
<soap:operation soapAction="" />
<input><soap:body use="literal" /></input>
<output><soap:body use="literal" /></output>
</operation>
</binding>

<service name="CalculatorWSService">
<port name="CalculatorWSPort" binding="tns:CalculatorWSPortBinding">
<soap:address location="http://localhost:8080/CalculatorApp/CalculatorWSService" />
</port>
</service>
</definitions>
```

The service just defines an add operation that takes two integers and returns a sum. Here's the associated schema:

```
<?xml version="1.0" encoding="UTF-8"?>
<xs:schema xmlns:tns="http://calculator.me.org/"
  xmlns:xs="http://www.w3.org/2001/XMLSchema"
  version="1.0"
  targetNamespace="http://calculator.me.org/">

  <xs:element name="add" type="tns:add" />

  <xs:element name="addResponse" type="tns:addResponse" />

  <xs:complexType name="add">
    <xs:sequence>
      <xs:element name="i" type="xs:int" />
      <xs:element name="j" type="xs:int" />
    </xs:sequence>
  </xs:complexType>
```

```
    <xs:complexType name="addResponse">
      <xs:sequence>
        <xs:element name="return" type="xs:int" />
      </xs:sequence>
    </xs:complexType>
  </xs:schema>
```

The schema defines two elements: `add`, which takes two integers, and `addResponse`, which has an element named `return` that holds the sum.

Let's get started making a full-blown GUI app that will frontend this calculator service. Open the .NET framework console, and execute the following command, supplying the location of your WSDL:

```
C:\Program Files\Microsoft Visual Studio 8\VC>wsdl
/out:C:/oreilly/soacookbook/code/chapters/interop/dotNetClient/Calcul
atorProxy.cs  http://localhost:8080/CalculatorApp/CalculatorWSService?wsdl
```

Here you just indicate that you want the `wsdl` utility to write the C# file to the specified location on the filesystem, using the provided WSDL URL. The utility options always come first, each indicated by a / character, followed by the option name, a colon, and the value. The WSDL location always comes last, after the options list.

The code the WSDL tool generates looks like that shown in Example 12-8, though I've cut some unnecessary parts to keep it short and added a little formatting for readability.

Example 12-8. CalculatorProxy.cs

```
using System;
using System.ComponentModel;
using System.Diagnostics;
using System.Web.Services;
using System.Web.Services.Protocols;
using System.Xml.Serialization;

[System.CodeDom.Compiler.GeneratedCodeAttribute("wsdl", "2.0.50727.42")]
[System.Diagnostics.DebuggerStepThroughAttribute()]
[System.ComponentModel.DesignerCategoryAttribute("code")]
[System.Web.Services.WebServiceBindingAttribute(
  Name="CalculatorWSPortBinding", Namespace="http://calculator.me.org/")]
public partial class CalculatorWSService :
    System.Web.Services.Protocols.SoapHttpClientProtocol {

    private System.Threading.SendOrPostCallback addOperationCompleted;

    public CalculatorWSService() {
        this.Url = "http://localhost:8080/CalculatorApp/CalculatorWSService";
    }

    public event addCompletedEventHandler addCompleted;

    [System.Web.Services.Protocols.SoapDocumentMethodAttribute("",
RequestNamespace="http://calculator.me.org/",
ResponseNamespace="http://calculator.me.org/",
```

```
Use=System.Web.Services.Description.SoapBindingUse.Literal,
ParameterStyle=System.Web.Services.Protocols.SoapParameterStyle.Wrapped)]

    [return: System.Xml.Serialization.XmlElementAttribute("return",
Form=System.Xml.Schema.XmlSchemaForm.Unqualified)]

    public int add(
[System.Xml.Serialization.XmlElementAttribute(
  Form=System.Xml.Schema.XmlSchemaForm.Unqualified)] int i,
[System.Xml.Serialization.XmlElementAttribute(
  Form=System.Xml.Schema.XmlSchemaForm.Unqualified)] int j) {
        object[] results = this.Invoke("add", new object[] {
                    i, j});
        return ((int)(results[0]));
    }

    public System.IAsyncResult Beginadd(int i, int j,
System.AsyncCallback callback, object asyncState) {
        return this.BeginInvoke("add", new object[] {
                    i, j}, callback, asyncState);
    }

    public int Endadd(System.IAsyncResult asyncResult) {
        object[] results = this.EndInvoke(asyncResult);
        return ((int)(results[0]));
    }

    public void addAsync(int i, int j) {
        this.addAsync(i, j, null);
    }

    public void addAsync(int i, int j, object userState) {
        if ((this.addOperationCompleted == null)) {
            this.addOperationCompleted =
              new System.Threading.SendOrPostCallback(
                        this.OnaddOperationCompleted);
        }
        this.InvokeAsync("add", new object[] {
                    i,
                    j}, this.addOperationCompleted, userState);
    }

    private void OnaddOperationCompleted(object arg) {
        if ((this.addCompleted != null)) {
            System.Web.Services.Protocols.InvokeCompletedEventArgs invokeArgs =
((System.Web.Services.Protocols.InvokeCompletedEventArgs)(arg));
            this.addCompleted(this, new addCompletedEventArgs(invokeArgs.Results,
invokeArgs.Error, invokeArgs.Cancelled, invokeArgs.UserState));
        }
    }

    public new void CancelAsync(object userState) {
        base.CancelAsync(userState);
    }
}
```

```
[System.CodeDom.Compiler.GeneratedCodeAttribute("wsdl", "2.0.50727.42")]
public delegate void addCompletedEventHandler(object sender,
  addCompletedEventArgs e);

[System.CodeDom.Compiler.GeneratedCodeAttribute("wsdl", "2.0.50727.42")]
[System.Diagnostics.DebuggerStepThroughAttribute()]
[System.ComponentModel.DesignerCategoryAttribute("code")]
public partial class addCompletedEventArgs :
    System.ComponentModel.AsyncCompletedEventArgs {

    private object[] results;

    internal addCompletedEventArgs(object[] results,
      System.Exception exception, bool cancelled, object userState) :
            base(exception, cancelled, userState) {
        this.results = results;
    }

    public int Result {
        get {
            this.RaiseExceptionIfNecessary();
            return ((int)(this.results[0]));
        }
    }
}
```

There are a number of things to note in this file. Let's compare and contrast this proxy with one generated in Java EE 5:

- The Java version provides multiple constructors: an empty one that uses the WSDL location you passed the tool, and another one that allows client classes to pass in a different URL. This is really important during the development life cycle. But in this C# class, there is only one constructor, and the class is declared `partial`. This is a .NET idiom that allows you to split the construction of classes across two files. It is an extensibility mechanism that potentially allows you to override the location of the WSDL URL by using a different class that sort of appends a constructor to this one.
- By default, asynchronous methods are generated invoking the `add` operation. You didn't tell the tool to do that, and the WSDL doesn't specify it. The asynchronous work is implemented using event handler methods.
- A C# property is generated for the response type. The schema for the `add` result looks like this:

```
<xs:complexType name="addResponse">
  <xs:sequence>
    <xs:element name="return" type="xs:int" />
  </xs:sequence>
</xs:complexType>
```

That XML schema type generates in a read-only C# property called `Result` on the proxy. You can use this property in a caller to get the sum of the `add` operation.

- The Java EE 5 proxy mechanism is modeled after .NET. In .NET the metacodes between the square brackets are called attributes. In Java, of course, you use the `@` sign and call them annotations. But the idea is the same, and you can see how similar they are. Consider the `SOAPDocumentMethodAttribute`, which allows you to specify the namespace and the parameter style and use.

Now that you have generated a proxy and understand what it's doing, let's put it to work in an application:

1. Create a new project called `CalcGUI`, of type Windows Application. This will start you off with a class called `Form1.cs` (*.cs* is the file extension for C#). Change its name to `GUICalc.cs` by right-clicking on it in the Solution Explorer.
2. Change the Text property of the form name to Calculator.
3. Add a label with the text "Enter numbers to add:". You can add components to the form by dragging them from the toolbox.
4. Users will need a place to enter the values the service will calculate, so add two text fields.
5. Add a button. Change the button text to "Get Result". In the button's event handler, you'll read the values from the text field and send them to the web service through your proxy.
6. Now you need a place to show the sum returned by the web service. Create another label, make its text empty, and change its name to "labelResult". Change its visibility to false because when the GUI starts, you won't have a sum yet.

Now you should have a decent shell to start filling in your business logic.

In the Project dialog, click Add Existing Item, and then navigate to the location where you saved your web service proxy. This will make your proxy class available to use in your GUI class.

Before you can use the service, you need to tell the .NET project that you're going to invoke a service proxy. Go to Project→Add Reference and add an assembly reference for the `System.Web.Services` namespace. This is similar to putting a JAR on your classpath, except with a *.dll*.

Now switch to the source code view of `GUICalc.cs`, and add code so it looks like Example 12-9.

Example 12-9. GUICalc.cs

```
using System;
using System.Collections.Generic;
using System.ComponentModel;
using System.Data;
using System.Drawing;
```

```
using System.Text;
using System.Windows.Forms;

//GUI that lets user add two integers
//by invoking web service
namespace CalcGUI
{
    public partial class GUICalc : Form
    {
        public GUICalc()
        {
            InitializeComponent();
        }

        private void Form1_Load(object sender, EventArgs e){ }

        //button click handler
        private void button1_Click(object sender, EventArgs e)
        {
            //get user input
            int x = Convert.ToInt32(textBox1.Text);
            int y = Convert.ToInt32(textBox2.Text);

            //call the service
            int result = calculate(x, y);
            labelResult.Text = Convert.ToString(result);

            //show on form
            labelResult.Visible = true;
        }

        //call the service
        private int calculate(int x, int y)
        {
            CalculatorWSService service =
                new CalculatorWSService();
            return service.add(x, y);
        }
    }
}
```

This code is pretty straightforward. By double-clicking the Get Result button, your `button1_Click` method is added to the class. Then you can fill in code that handles the user input from the text fields and converts them to integers. You then pass those two numbers into your calculate method, which just hides the web service invocation from the rest of the program. The calculate method instantiates the proxy that you generated with the WSDL tool and then calls the add method.

Figure 12-1 shows the result of executing the program.

By passing the numbers 3 and 4, you get back from the service just the answer you wanted: lucky 7.

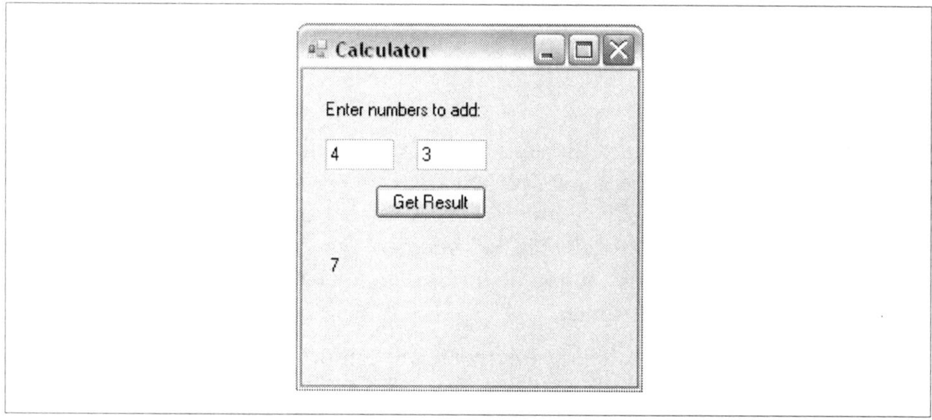

Figure 12-1. The result of executing the GUI calculator that invokes the add web service

12.10 Creating a .NET Web Service

Problem

You want to create a web service in ASP.NET.

Solution

In Visual Studio, go to New→Web Site→ASP.NET Web Service. Then enter the implementation code in the generated template.

Discussion

This quick recipe highlights the similarities between a Java EE 5 web service and one written in .NET using C#. Example 12-10 shows the boilerplate code Visual Studio generates when you create a new web service.

Example 12-10. C# web service template for ASP.NET

```
using System;
using System.Web;
using System.Web.Services;
using System.Web.Services.Protocols;

[WebService(Namespace = "http://tempuri.org/")]
[WebServiceBinding(ConformsTo = WsiProfiles.BasicProfile1_1)]
public class Service : System.Web.Services.WebService
{
    public Service () {
        //Uncomment the following line if using designed components
        //InitializeComponent();
    }

    [WebMethod]
```

```
    public string HelloWorld() {
        return "Hello World";
    }
}
```

If you substitute in your mind the annotations you use in Java EE 5 with the square brackets used in C# (or the angle brackets used in VB.NET), it's pretty easy to get around. Much of the Java EE 5 annotations are based on this way of creating web services in .NET, as this is basically the API Microsoft has provided since 2002. Instead of calling them "annotations" as you do in Java, in .NET the meta-code above classes and methods are called "attributes."

You can see that the code itself indicates that it will conform to the Basic Profile version 1.1. Let's add a few other attributes to see how you can control the web service with a few parameters. Example 12-11 is your simple update of the boilerplate file.

Example 12-11. Greeting web service, Service.asmx

```
using System;
using System.Web;
using System.Web.Services;
using System.Web.Services.Protocols;

[WebService(
    Namespace = "http://soacookbook.com/dotnet",
    Name="GreetingService",
    Description="Returns greetings.")]
[WebServiceBinding(ConformsTo = WsiProfiles.BasicProfile1_1,
    EmitConformanceClaims=true)]
public class Service : System.Web.Services.WebService
{
    public Service () { }

    [WebMethod(MessageName="HelloMsg",
        Description="Returns a nice greeting.",
        CacheDuration=100)]
    public string niceGreeting(string name) {
        return "Hello " + name + " from " +
            Server.MachineName;
    }
}
```

We've modified the attributes a bit, and added an implementation for the operation.

Web services in .NET have a *.asmx* file extension. This file is called *Service.asmx*, so you can access it through your browser at *http://localhost:3416/WebSite1/Service.asmx* after publishing the site to your local IIS.

If you access the service page directly, IIS returns a service home page, shown in Figure 12-2, similar to what you would see if you deployed a web service to Apache Axis. It gives you a link directly to the WSDL via the "Service Description" link (or you can

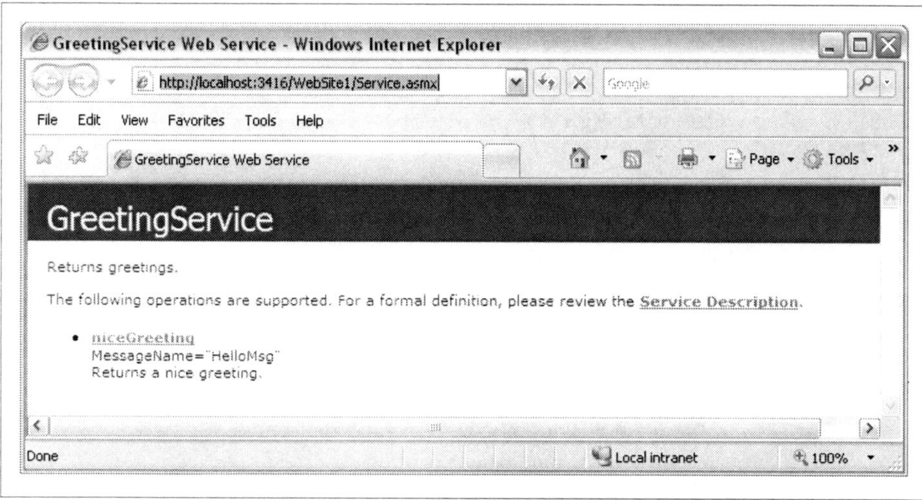

Figure 12-2. The .NET GreetingService home page

just append `?WSDL` to the URL as usual). This home page also prints the description you entered in the `WebMethod` attribute.

As with WebLogic 10, you can click the name of the operation, and .NET will give you a testing page that prints an acceptable XML document that you can pass to the service, replacing the boilerplate parameters with your own values.

Here is the WSDL representing this service:

```
<?xml version="1.0" encoding="utf-8"?>
<wsdl:definitions xmlns:soap="http://schemas.xmlsoap.org/wsdl/soap/"
xmlns:tm="http://microsoft.com/wsdl/mime/textMatching/"
xmlns:soapenc="http://schemas.xmlsoap.org/soap/encoding/"
xmlns:mime="http://schemas.xmlsoap.org/wsdl/mime/"
xmlns:tns="http://soacookbook.com/dotnet"
xmlns:s="http://www.w3.org/2001/XMLSchema"
xmlns:soap12="http://schemas.xmlsoap.org/wsdl/soap12/"
xmlns:http="http://schemas.xmlsoap.org/wsdl/http/"
targetNamespace="http://soacookbook.com/dotnet"
xmlns:wsdl="http://schemas.xmlsoap.org/wsdl/">
<wsdl:documentation
  xmlns:wsdl="http://schemas.xmlsoap.org/wsdl/">Returns greetings.
</wsdl:documentation>

  <wsdl:types>
    <s:schema elementFormDefault="qualified"
targetNamespace="http://soacookbook.com/dotnet">
      <s:element name="HelloMsg">
        <s:complexType>
          <s:sequence>
            <s:element minOccurs="0" maxOccurs="1"
name="name" type="s:string" />
          </s:sequence>
        </s:complexType>
```

```
      </s:element>
      <s:element name="HelloMsgResponse">
        <s:complexType>
          <s:sequence>
            <s:element minOccurs="0" maxOccurs="1"
name="HelloMsgResult" type="s:string" />
          </s:sequence>
        </s:complexType>
      </s:element>
    </s:schema>
  </wsdl:types>

  <wsdl:message name="HelloMsgSoapIn">
    <wsdl:part name="parameters" element="tns:HelloMsg" />
  </wsdl:message>
  <wsdl:message name="HelloMsgSoapOut">
    <wsdl:part name="parameters" element="tns:HelloMsgResponse" />
  </wsdl:message>

  <wsdl:portType name="GreetingServiceSoap">
    <wsdl:operation name="niceGreeting">
      <wsdl:documentation
xmlns:wsdl="http://schemas.xmlsoap.org/wsdl/">Returns a nice greeting.
</wsdl:documentation>
      <wsdl:input name="HelloMsg" message="tns:HelloMsgSoapIn" />
      <wsdl:output name="HelloMsg" message="tns:HelloMsgSoapOut" />
    </wsdl:operation>
  </wsdl:portType>

  <wsdl:binding name="GreetingServiceSoap" type="tns:GreetingServiceSoap">
    <wsdl:documentation>
      <wsi:Claim conformsTo="http://ws-i.org/profiles/basic/1.1"
xmlns:wsi="http://ws-i.org/schemas/conformanceClaim/" />
    </wsdl:documentation>
    <soap:binding transport="http://schemas.xmlsoap.org/soap/http" />
    <wsdl:operation name="niceGreeting">
      <soap:operation soapAction="http://soacookbook.com/dotnet/HelloMsg"
style="document" />
      <wsdl:input name="HelloMsg">
        <soap:body use="literal" />
      </wsdl:input>
      <wsdl:output name="HelloMsg">
        <soap:body use="literal" />
      </wsdl:output>
    </wsdl:operation>
  </wsdl:binding>

  <wsdl:binding name="GreetingServiceSoap12" type="tns:GreetingServiceSoap">
    <soap12:binding transport="http://schemas.xmlsoap.org/soap/http" />
    <wsdl:operation name="niceGreeting">
      <soap12:operation soapAction="http://soacookbook.com/dotnet/HelloMsg"
style="document" />
      <wsdl:input name="HelloMsg">
        <soap12:body use="literal" />
      </wsdl:input>
```

```
      <wsdl:output name="HelloMsg">
        <soap12:body use="literal" />
      </wsdl:output>
    </wsdl:operation>
  </wsdl:binding>

  <wsdl:service name="GreetingService">
    <wsdl:documentation xmlns:wsdl="http://schemas.xmlsoap.org/wsdl/">
     Returns greetings.
</wsdl:documentation>
    <wsdl:port name="GreetingServiceSoap" binding="tns:GreetingServiceSoap">
      <soap:address location="http://localhost:3416/WebSite1/Service.asmx" />
    </wsdl:port>
    <wsdl:port name="GreetingServiceSoap12" binding="tns:GreetingServiceSoap12">
      <soap12:address location="http://localhost:3416/WebSite1/Service.asmx" />
    </wsdl:port>
  </wsdl:service>
</wsdl:definitions>
```

You can see that the WSDL generated by .NET Framework 2.0 is very different from that generated by Java EE 5, but many strides have been made in recent years to ensure interoperability between the Java and .NET platforms. Some of the changes are little more than cosmetic, but some offer different features. To begin with, the ASP.NET-generated WSDL allows you to invoke the service over SOAP 1.1 or SOAP 1.2. There are two binding entries in the `wsdl:service` element, one for each `portType`, bound to the same address.

I've also highlighted the `<types>` element in the WSDL. You'll notice the difference here right away: the .NET-generated WSDL puts its types directly inline, without creating a separate external document the way that the Java EE 5 service does.

Also, check out the indication on the SOAP 1.1 binding to make sure that it conforms to the Basic Profile 1.1. This was added to the WSDL using the `WebServiceBinding` attribute on the service class itself, and by setting `EmitConformanceClaims=true`.

Also, the WSDLs generated by JAX-WS do not include any Sun- or Java-specific code. While you can ignore it here, and the service does in fact comply with the BP, you can see that there is a Microsoft namespace imported.

Here is a SOAP 1.1 message that represents a valid request for this service:

```
POST /WebSite1/Service.asmx HTTP/1.1
Host: localhost
Content-Type: text/xml; charset=utf-8
Content-Length: length
SOAPAction: "http://soacookbook.com/dotnet/HelloMsg"

<?xml version="1.0" encoding="utf-8"?>
<soap:Envelope xmlns:xsi="http://www.w3.org/2001/XMLSchema-instance"
  xmlns:xsd="http://www.w3.org/2001/XMLSchema"
  xmlns:soap="http://schemas.xmlsoap.org/soap/envelope/">
  <soap:Body>
    <HelloMsg xmlns="http://soacookbook.com/dotnet">
```

```
        <name>string</name>
      </HelloMsg>
    </soap:Body>
  </soap:Envelope>
```

If you just use the tester web page to check your service, the page will use the HTTP method to invoke it. This method expects you to make an HTTP POST using the following content:

```
POST /WebSite1/Service.asmx/HelloMsg HTTP/1.1
Host: localhost
Content-Type: application/x-www-form-urlencoded
Content-Length: 9

name=Eben
```

The HTTP headers indicate the destination, and other items that allow you to invoke the service without SOAP altogether, though the response will be a standard HTTP response, and not a more structured XML document.

Here is a JSP that invokes the service with an HTTP POST:

```
<%@page contentType="text/html" pageEncoding="UTF-8"%>
<!DOCTYPE HTML PUBLIC "-//W3C//DTD HTML 4.01 Transitional//EN"
   "http://www.w3.org/TR/html4/loose.dtd">
<html>
    <head>
        <meta http-equiv="Content-Type"
        content="application/x-www-form-urlencoded; charset=UTF-8">
        <title>.NET HTTP Client</title>
    </head>
    <body>
        <form method="POST" target="_blank"
            action="http://localhost:3416/WebSite1/Service.asmx/HelloMsg">
            <input name="name" value="Eben" type="text"/>
            <input type="submit"  />
        </form>
    </body>
</html>
```

This will call the web service you've deployed and give you back a non-SOAP response, like this:

```
<?xml version="1.0" encoding="utf-8"?>
<string xmlns="http://soacookbook.com/dotnet">string</string>
```

Now you can write a JSP using a proxy, as you've done before. First generate the proxy using `wsimport` or an equivalent tool. Then you can create a JSP like the one in Example 12-12.

Example 12-12. soap12.jsp

```
<%@page contentType="text/html" pageEncoding="UTF-8"%>
<%@ page import="com.soacookbook.dotnet.*" %>
<!DOCTYPE HTML PUBLIC "-//W3C//DTD HTML 4.01 Transitional//EN"
   "http://www.w3.org/TR/html4/loose.dtd">
```

```
<html>
    <head>
        <meta http-equiv="Content-Type" content="text/html; charset=UTF-8">
        <title>SOAP 1.2 Invoker</title>
    </head>
    <body>
    <%
    try {
        GreetingService service = new GreetingService();
        GreetingServiceSoap port = service.getGreetingServiceSoap12();

        HelloMsg parameters = new HelloMsg();
        parameters.setName("Eben SOAP 1.2");
        HelloMsgResponse result = port.niceGreeting(parameters);
        out.println("Result = "+result.getHelloMsgResult());
    } catch (Exception ex) {
        ex.printStackTrace();
    }
    %>
    </body>
</html>
```

This is standard stuff by now, and the Java toolkit has no problem working with the compliant web service. Here is the response printed to the browser:

```
Result = Hello Eben SOAP 1.2 from LUCKY
```

12.11 Creating a Ruby Client for a Web Service

Problem

You want to create a Ruby program that consumes a web service written in Java.

Solution

Use the `wsdl2ruby` program or, preferably, the `SOAP::WSDLDriverFactory` class.

Discussion

The `wsdl2ruby` program is similar to `wsdl.exe` in .NET or `wsdl2java` in Apache Axis, or `wsimport`. The `WSDLDriverFactory` class dynamically generates code for you at runtime based on a WSDL, which hides the complexity of dealing with services.

Let's make a client that invokes a Java web service calculator. Here's the most relevant part from the schema for this example:

```
<xs:complexType name="add">
  <xs:sequence>
    <xs:element name="i" type="xs:int"/>
    <xs:element name="j" type="xs:int"/>
  </xs:sequence>
</xs:complexType>
```

This WSDL defines an add operation, with two parameters, i and j, which are integers to be added. It's a document/literal wrapped service. Now you can make a Ruby program that will invoke this service, which I've written in Java (see Example 12-13).

Example 12-13. JavaWsdlDriverClient.rb

```
require 'soap/wsdlDriver'
wsdl = 'http://localhost:8080/CalculatorApp/CalculatorWSService?wsdl'
service = SOAP::WSDLDriverFactory.new(wsdl).create_rpc_driver
service.wiredump_dev = STDOUT

result = service.add(:i=>'6', :j=>'9')
puts "Result is %s!" % "#{result.return}"
```

Here the `require` statement indicates the library that you want to use. You create a variable called `wsdl`, and because Ruby is not strongly typed like Java is, you don't need to give the variable a reference type; Ruby can determine it from context. Then create a proxy instance using the `WSDLDriverFactory` class, pointing to the calculator service WSDL. You then indicate that you want to dump to the standard error output stream the contents of the SOAP messages destined for the service.

Next, invoke the service. The add operation is defined on the calculator WSDL. You set the values of i and j, also defined as the parameter names on the WSDL, to 6 and 9 respectively. The value returned by the service is stored in the result variable. You call `puts` to print the string containing the message and the result to the console. The string in this case is similar to how you would use the `String.format` feature added in Java SE 5. To get the sum, you need to drill down to the value of the `return` element in the SOAP response.

Running this in the Ruby interpreter prints the complete SOAP request and response to the console (as a result of the wire dump), and then shows the result:

```
Result is 15!
```

Despite the fact that this is a document/literal wrapped web service, the call to `create_rpc_driver` works just fine. The interesting line of code is this one:

```
"#{result.return}"
```

Java web services, if left to their default mapping (with no `@WebResult` annotation), will enclose their wrapped results in an element called `<return>`, which is a keyword in Ruby. You need to inspect the returned XML document to get to the value that you're interested in here. But you don't need to do extensive XPath-type drilling down through each element as you might with the SAAJ library. You can just indicate which element's value you want from the SOAP response using that syntax.

So you have to use a Ruby feature called *interpolation*, which inserts a string into a literal and evaluates the call. If you just tried to print the result directly, you'd see something like this:

```
Result is #<SOAP::Mapping::Object:0x2802094>!
```

That's because while you're getting a SOAP mapping object returned, it's printing something similar to what you get in Java if you don't override the `toString` method. So the wire dump would still show the contents of the entire SOAP response, but if you want to do some actual work with the values buried within the response, you need to do this.

The result is printed to the console using a C-style formatter that is similar to the functionality added to Java SE 5.

12.12 Creating a Ruby Client for a .NET Service

Problem

You have a web service written in .NET that you want to consume from a Ruby application.

Solution

Require the `soap/rpc/driver` library, and then use the `SOAP::RPC::Driver` class to reference the WSDL and the `SOAP::EncodingStyle::ASPDotNetHandler` class to invoke the service.

Discussion

First, make sure that Ruby is installed. You can download the latest version available at *http://www.ruby-lang.org/en/downloads/*. On Windows, you can download the "one-click installer," which includes a number of additional libraries and is the easiest way to get started.

The installer will install a program called SciTE, which is a lightweight code assistant/highlighter. To test your installation, create a new file in Notepad or SciTE, with the following text:

```
puts "Hello, World"
```

Save the file as *Hello.rb*. Now open a console and type `ruby Hello.rb` to run your program in the interpreter, and you should see the venerable output. Now you'll use Ruby to create a SOAP client at *http://www.WebServiceX.net*. The service itself, shown in Example 12-14, simply converts the monetary exchange rates between two countries.

Example 12-14. Ruby client for .NET currency conversion service

```
require 'soap/rpc/driver'

#create a connection to the service
Converter = SOAP::RPC::Driver.new(
  "http://www.webservicex.net/CurrencyConvertor.asmx",
  "http://www.webserviceX.net/")
```

```
#set the encoding style
Converter.default_encodingstyle =
  SOAP::EncodingStyle::ASPDotNetHandler::Namespace

#add the SOAP Action HTTP header
Converter.add_method_with_soapaction(
  "ConversionRate",
  "http://www.webserviceX.net/ConversionRate",
  "FromCurrency", "ToCurrency")

#send the SOAP messages to the console
Converter.wiredump_dev = STDERR

#call the operation and print result
puts Converter.ConversionRate("USD","CAD")
```

If you examine the WSDL for this service, you'll see that it accepts two strings indicating the currencies to convert from and to. I won't show the entire SOAP messages, but the headers are interesting:

```
POST /CurrencyConvertor.asmx HTTP/1.1
Accept: */*
Content-Type: text/xml; charset=utf-8
User-Agent: SOAP4R/1.5.5
Soapaction: \"http://www.webserviceX.NET/ConversionRate\"
Content-Length: 432
Host: www.webservicex.net
```

You can see here that the SOAP4R library is doing the heavy lifting for you, and it identifies itself in the request as the user agent. This library is an implementation of SOAP 1.1 for Ruby.

Using Ruby in Eclipse

You can use Ruby from within Eclipse for a somewhat easier time of working with projects. To do so, get the Ruby plug-in from *http://rubyeclipse.sourceforge.net/*. Then you just need to point to the Ruby interpreter executable so that Eclipse can use the version you want to run your code. This is very similar to setting up multiple JDKs in Eclipse, so I won't dwell on the details.

If you create a new project, choose the Ruby Project type. If this is your first one, you'll have an error indicating that you need to tell Eclipse where to find Ruby; can remedy this by pointing to the *ruby.exe* file that is included with the download. You should see Eclipse add a number of libraries to its list when you add this file to the wizard, and you should be all set.

Now add a source folder. I'll call mine *src*. Eclipse should open the Ruby Perspective to assist you. Type a "Hello, world" program to make sure you're set up. In your source folder, create a file called *Hello.rb*. Then add the following code to it, which is a slightly more exciting an example of Hello World than you used earlier:

```
def hello() return "Hello, World!"
end
puts hello()
```

Run the program using the regular Run button, and you should see the venerable text printed to the console.

To get back to this configuration screen later, choose Window→Preferences→Ruby→Interpreters.

12.13 Conforming to the Basic Profile

Problem

You want to make all of the choices you can to help ensure that your services are interoperable across the greatest number of platforms.

Solution

Follow the guidelines of the WS Basic Profile 1.1. The most prominent of these are highlighted in the following discussion.

Discussion

The Web Services Interoperability Organization, or WS-I, consists of representatives from a large number of vendors. It was created as a vendor consortium charged with establishing best practices for the interoperability of web services. The working groups of WS-I create profiles that highlight ways in which web services developers can promote interoperability in their services. The WS-I Basic Profile covers standards, such as SOAP, WS-Addressing, MTOM, XOP, and so forth, and indicates the kinds of choices developers should make in implementing services. It indicates information about faults, messages, descriptions, discovery, and more.

Services that make the implementation choices indicated in the BP are said to conform to some particular version of the BP—the most popular of which at this point is 1.1.

You can read the BP at *http://www.ws-i.org*.

BP 1.1 is around 60 pages long, and I encourage you to read it if you're interested. But there is a lot in the profile that vendor implementations of web services plumbing take care of for you, so it's really not necessary for you to wade through the entire thing.

This recipe attempts to summarize the key points from a developer's point of view; it's not an exhaustive list, but it's a good start:

SOAP envelopes have one body and cannot use DTD
: The body of a SOAP envelope must have exactly zero or one child element, and it must be namespace qualified. It must not contain processing instructions or a DTD.

Use literal message encoding
: You must use literal message encoding, not SOAP encoding.

Use 0 or 1 in the `mustUnderstand` *attribute*
: If you use the `soap:mustUnderstand` attribute, use 0 to indicate "no" or "false" and 1 to indicate "yes" or "true".

Do not use dot notation in SOAP fault codes
: Do not use dot notation to refine the meaning of a `faultcode` element, as allowed in SOAP 1.1. For example, some implementations allow the following:

```
<soap:Fault...>
  <faultcode>soap:Server.ProcessingError</faultcode>
</soap:Fault>
```

In this case, the `ProcessingError` it narrows the meaning of the error. The profile urges you to instead leave all such detail information to the `<faultstring>` element.

Use HTTP 1.0 or 1.1
: SOAP 1.1 indicates a binding for HTTP only, and the profile follows suit. You must use HTTP POST, and not the HTTP Extension Framework, which the SOAP 1.1 spec allows.

Do not rely on SOAP Action
: While SOAP Action is intended to help indicate what operation to route messages to, it must be used only as a hint. The service disallows use of SOAP Action, so that all pertinent information is carried in the SOAP envelope, and not HTTP headers.

Use quoted strings for SOAP Action
: All SOAP actions must be specified in the WSDL using a quoted string. But even if you do *not* specify a SOAP action for an operation, you must use an empty string for its value, like this:

```
<soap:operation soapAction="" />
```

Use HTTP status codes
: If the service processed a request properly and does not contain a fault, the 200 OK HTTP status code should be used in the response.

Services should return the 307 Temporary Redirect HTTP status code to indicate to the user agent whether to use the original method or HTTP GET. It is optional for service consumers to automatically redirect based on receipt of this status, however, as many services could be participating in automated processes.

SOAP fault messages should indicate HTTP 500 Internal Server Error. You probably won't have to deal with the HTTP return types directly, unless you are using SAAJ to create responses from scratch.

Cookies
: Cookies may be used, but this is not encouraged, and services should not break for consumers who don't understand cookies. Because cookies are out of band for SOAP, they probably aren't a great idea. I can't think of a really strong case for using them in a service, especially if you are still conforming with the Basic Profile's mandate that your clients don't break if they don't support cookies.

Use XML 1.0
: XML 1.0 is the only version that the BP supports for XML Schema and WSDL.

Use UTF-8 or UTF-16 encoding
: This should be self-explanatory.

No namespace coercion
: This means that the `targetNamespace` indicated by the WSDL definitions element that is being imported must be the same as the namespace of the WSDL you're importing.

Do not require support for WSDL extensions
: This means that indicating "required=true" for WSDL elements is discouraged:

```
<wsaw:UsingAddressing required="true"/>
```

It's best to define requirements in policies where possible. If you decide to require certain items, then consumers that don't support those items must fail processing.

Beware of arrays
: Usage of the array types in WSDL 1.1, section 2.2 has left proper usage somewhat unclear, leading to a variety of interpretations regarding how they should be used. WSDLs must not extend or restrict the `soapenc:Array` type, or use a `wsdl:ArrayType` in their types section. Likewise, SOAP envelopes must not include the `soapenc:arrayType` attribute. See Recipe 12.1 for a workaround.

Do not use encoding
: The BP does not allow use of the RPC/encoded or document/encoded style, as they are not interoperable. You should only use document/Literal or RPC/literal in the `wsdl:binding` element.

The SOAP body element should only contain a single child, and RPC/encoded allows for multiple children. Also, it does not allow for message validation, and children are not namespace-qualified.

Modular WSDLs
: The WSDL spec and the WS-I recommend separating WSDL files into modular components such as external schema definitions, and creating separate physical files for the concrete and abstract WSDLs. This is illustrated in Recipe 12.16.

Use SOAP binding
: Though web services are often touted as having the ability to abstract message and operation content away from the underlying transport layer, only SOAP is supported by the BP in `wsdl:binding` elements.

Beware of SOAP Actor
: The SOAP Actor attribute represents a private agreement between the service consumer and the service provider, unless you're using `http://schemas.xmlsoap.org/soap/actor/next` as a pass-through.

There are all sorts of common-sense directives in the BP, including things like "your WSDL has to be valid according to the WSDL schema" (section 4.2). Hopefully this overview has saved you some time by covering the less obvious points.

JAX-WS 2.x does a great job of conforming with BP 1.1, so in general a lot of interoperability issues are solved for us. The .NET 3.5 framework does a good job of generating compliant WSDLs as well.

12.14 Automating Testing for Basic Profile Conformance

Problem

You want to test your service for Basic Profile 1.1 and SOAP binding profile conformance.

Solution

If you're using JAX-WS 2.0 or 2.1 (or .NET 3.5), your services should be compliant unless you've done lots of customization. If you aren't sure, try the testing tools available from the WS-I website.

Discussion

The WS-I published compliance testing tools for both C# and Java. Let's look at how to use the Java version of the Interoperability Testing Tools 1.1.

First, download the tools from *http://www.ws-i.org/deliverables/workinggroup.aspx?wg=testingtools*. Extract the archive and navigate to the *wsi-test-tools/java/bin* directory. Run the Analyzer program with a `-config <file_path>` option that points to the XML configuration file describing the service you want to analyze for compliance. The samples folder includes sample XML configuration files that you can copy and change the values for to invoke your own web service.

Some tools, such as IBM's WebSphere Developer Studio, will warn you if a service for which you are generating a client is not compliant with BP 1.1.

12.15 Interoperability Best Practices

Problem

It's easy enough to get web services to interoperate between different platforms such as .NET and Java when the messages are straightforward, but you want to know the general best practices for interoperability.

Solution

The following list describes a few interoperability best practices that should help you steer clear of the basic issues developers can run into:

- Use document/literal wrapped. This is the default on both the .NET and Java platforms. .NET clients can have the services appear to be RPC style when they invoke .NET services. This is conceptually similar to how WebLogic allows you to set a remote EJB to appear local to clients in the same JVM.

  If you are writing a .NET web service, you can use the `SoapRpcService` attribute to indicate whether you want to use `SOAPAction` (the default) or the first child of the SOAP body element. You can manipulate this as shown here:

  ```
  [SoapRpcService(
    RoutingStyle = SoapServiceRoutingStyle.RequestElement)]
  [WebService(...
  ```

- Use MTOM instead of DIME (Direct Internet Message Encapsulation) for attachments. DIME is considered deprecated. It was an efficient mechanism for handling MIME attachments by reading the message headers to determine attached file lengths. This allowed it to forego scanning the entire file, so it was able to work quickly. However, this also meant that it didn't have a sufficient understanding of the attachments to provide an infoset model for the message and the attachment. Without an XML infoset, there are no namespace constraints, and well-formedness can't be determined.

  In .NET 3.0 and higher, you can set the following value in your *web.config* file (it's equivalent to the *web.xml* file) to ensure the use of MTOM on all inbound and outbound messages:

  ```
  <microsoft.web.services3>
    <messaging>
      <mtom serverMode="always" />
    </messaging>
  </microsoft.web.services3>
  ```

- Beware of generated WSDLs. It is very easy to produce a web service quickly when you write a simple Java or .NET class and toss a couple of annotations on it. But you must not forget that the WSDL represents the clearest aspect of the contract between consumer and producer. If you are in a business-to-business scenario, discuss the WSDL to make sure that you can curtail any difficult discussions about interoperability problems later. But the WSDL is meant to be produced by machines and read by machines, and can be very tedious to write. What I usually do is write a class, generate the WSDL only the first time, and then save a copy within my service. I modify the WSDL so that it's clearer and doesn't contain any extraneous or vendor-specific code, and I can then make small tweaks to it without too much effort. This of course leads to the problem of ensuring that your implementation and your WSDL are in sync, but unit tests should allow you to handle this quickly.

12.16 Using Modular WSDLs

Problem

You want to physically separate the concrete from the abstract WSDL in order to provide a more modular and flexible interface.

Solution

Create a set of files: one or more schema files that you import into the WSDL in place of the `<types>` section, and then create two WSDLs that import an abstract WSDL via the `<wsdl:import>` or `<wsdl:include>` directive.

Discussion

The ideas in this solution are simple, but let's see how they works in code. Here's an example of using the schema import, which is how most of the examples in this book work:

```
<wsdl:types>
<xsd:schema>
<xsd:import namespace="http://soacookbook.com/email"
  schemaLocation="http://localhost:8080/EmailService/Email.xsd" />
</xsd:schema>
</wsdl:types>
```

That's the preferred alternative to specifying types inline within the WSDL `<types>` section like this:

```
<wsdl:types>
    <s:schema elementFormDefault="qualified"
       targetNamespace="http://soacookbook.com">
     <s:element name="SomeElement">...
```

Besides specifying an external schema, you can also break up the WSDL itself. The abstract WSDL document contains the namespace definitions, the messages, and the port type. The concrete WSDL imports the abstract WSDL and contains the `<binding>` and `<service>` elements because these provide actual values for transport mechanism, encoding, and service URI.

The WSDL in Example 12-15 is based on the specification example of an abstract WSDL in its own document.

Example 12-15. StockQuoteAbstract.wsdl

```
<definitions name="StockQuote"
  targetNamespace="http://soacookbook.com/stockquote/defs"
  xmlns:tns="http://soacookbook.com/quote/defs"
  xmlns:xsd1="http://soacookbook.com/quote/schemas"
  xmlns:soap="http://schemas.xmlsoap.org/wsdl/soap/"
  xmlns="http://schemas.xmlsoap.org/wsdl/">

   <import namespace="http://soacookbook.com/quote/schemas"
     location="http://soacookbook.com/quote/stockquote.xsd"/>

    <message name="GetLastTradePriceInput">
        <part name="body" element="xsd1:TradePriceRequest"/>
    </message>

    <message name="GetLastTradePriceOutput">
        <part name="body" element="xsd1:TradePrice"/>
    </message>

    <portType name="StockQuotePortType">
        <operation name="GetLastTradePrice">
           <input message="tns:GetLastTradePriceInput"/>
           <output message="tns:GetLastTradePriceOutput"/>
        </operation>
    </portType>
</definitions>
```

On its own, this can't be presented as the service WSDL because no bindings or service location is specified. Clients would be pointed to the concrete WSDL, which is shown in Example 12-16 as *StockQuoteConcrete.wsdl*.

Example 12-16. StockQuoteConcrete.wsdl

```
<definitions name="StockQuote"
  targetNamespace="http://soacookbook.com/quote/service"
  xmlns:tns="http://soacookbook.com/quote/service"
  xmlns:soap="http://schemas.xmlsoap.org/wsdl/soap/"
  xmlns:defs="http://soacookbook.com/quote/defs"
  xmlns="http://schemas.xmlsoap.org/wsdl/">

  <import namespace="http://soacookbook.com/quote/defs"
    location="http://soacookbook.com/quote/StockQuoteAbstract.wsdl"/>

    <binding name="StockQuoteSoapBinding"
        type="defs:StockQuotePortType">
        <soap:binding style="document"
          transport="http://schemas.xmlsoap.org/soap/http"/>
        <operation name="GetLastTradePrice">
           <soap:operation
             soapAction="http://soacookbook.com/GetLastTradePrice"/>
           <input><soap:body use="literal"/></input>
```

```
            <output><soap:body use="literal"/></output>
        </operation>
    </binding>

    <service name="StockQuoteService">
        <documentation>Returns the current price for a given ticker.
        </documentation>
        <port name="StockQuotePort" binding="tns:StockQuoteBinding">
           <soap:address location="http://soacookbook.com/quote"/>
        </port>
    </service>
</definitions>
```

Here the concrete WSDL imports the abstract WSDL defined in a separate document. The concrete WSDL indicates how and where to consume a service ("use SOAP and go to this URI"). The abstract WSDL indicates what the service does by showing the operations it performs, as well as the data types required to use those operations.

To perform a WSDL import in this way, the import needs to be the first statement following the `<wsdl:definitions>` element.

This modularity of design allows you to provide different binding possibilities or service URIs, and still maintain the basic interface definition. It can be easier to use and maintain WSDLs that are specified this way. It also can aid with interoperability because it allows you to give clients on other platforms a SOAP interface, for example, and other clients a different transport. You might also define a service that uses both MIME and DIME types for attachments. If that case, you could indicate support in two different concrete WSDLs that both import the same abstract WSDL.

You can read the WSDL 1.1 specification at *http://www.w3.org/TR/wsdl*.

CHAPTER 13
Quality of Service

13.0 Introduction

"Quality of Service" is a general term that refers to a number of topics in different fields within computing. For web services, it means simply the set of supporting infrastructure that enhances the reliability, security, performance, and overall ability of your system to do its job in accordance with its contract. In web services, these ideas are supported by a set of specifications that complement each other and rely on each other to support message reliability and delivery guarantees, metadata, transactions, and security.

These concepts are likely familiar to you through EJB. Indeed, this list is very similar to the enhancements that a container provides around an EJB to make it operate as a full-blown component.

While there are more than 100 WS-* specifications, they are not all used, and some are more central to our work than others. This chapter will examine a small set of specifications that address quality-of-service issues, including those for transactions, reliability, and policy metadata. Given the breadth and scope of these specifications, and the wide array of vendors that incorporate them into their products, it would be impossible to cover everything about these specifications in one chapter, or even one book. Here I attempt to hit some of the primary use cases you'll encounter.

Quality-of-Service Specifications

The web service features that we examine in this chapter are reliability, transactions, and metadata. These are expressed in the specifications discussed in the following sections.

Reliability

The two specifications surrounding message reliability and delivery guarantee mechanisms are WS-ReliableMessaging and WS-ReliableMessaging Policy.

WS-ReliableMessaging defines a messaging protocol to identify, track, and manage the reliable message delivery between two parties, termed a source and a destination.

Apache Sandesha is one open source project that implements this specification. It is also implemented in .NET WCF, Glassfish, and WebLogic 10gR3.

WS-ReliableMessaging Policy enables a web service endpoint to indicate that a reliable message delivery is required.

You can read the WS-ReliableMessaging specification available at *http://docs.oasis-open.org/ws-rx/wsrm/200702/wsrm-1.1-spec-os-01.pdf*.

Metadata

WS-Policy defines a general-purpose framework to express the capabilities of an endpoint.

WS-MetadataExchange and WS-Transfer are used by the client to retrieve the information about the endpoint.

Transactions

The WS-Transaction specification set by OASIS-Open comprises three different specifications: WS-AtomicTransaction, WS-Coordination, and WS-BusinessActivity. These specifications are implemented separately by vendors. The Apache project Kandula is working on an implementation of all three specs, and while Axis 1 and 2 incorporate WS-Coordination and WS-AtomicTransaction, WS-BusinessActivity has been in the works since 2005, with nothing published from that project since 2006. An implementation of WS-BusinesssActivity is actually very rare to see.

WS-Transaction provides a distributed transaction capability to a set of web services.

You can read the WS-Transaction specification at *http://www.oasis-open.org/specs/index.php#wstransactionv1.1*.

WS-Coordination 1.1 provides an extensible framework for defining coordination context and types for protocols that coordinate distributed actions.

You can read the WS-Coordination specification at *http://docs.oasis-open.org/ws-tx/wscoor/2006/06*.

WS-AtomicTransaction provides the definition of transaction context and the atomic transaction coordination type that is to be used with the framework defined by WS-Coordination. This enables transactions flowing across a set of web services.

WS-* Specifications and Vendor Implementations

Vendor tools frequently make it so that you do not have to work with or even see the XML that makes all of this go at runtime. In general, vendors will create some GUI as part of their environment that allows you to check a box indicating that you want your service to be "reliable." Behind the scenes, this will add 50 lines of XML to your WSDL and some other configuration files. Indeed, some products, such as the Active Endpoints BPEL engine, do not allow you to edit the XML directly at all. Vendors tell you what their products do: they'll say, "our product allows your service clients to dynamically determine what policies a service requires at runtime so you don't have to redeploy." That sounds like a neat feature, and it is. But it's often the WS-MetadataExchange specification that they're implementing behind the scenes to make it happen.

This means that it's a good idea to read specifications so that whatever tools you're using don't do too much "magic" for you, and so that you know when they're locking you into something proprietary. You want to know what specs there are and what they do. But as a web services developer, you often won't be using the spec directly, typing loads of XML to make a WS-Security Policy work. Instead, you'll be using a tool that uses the spec for you. Clearly, we can't cover every vendor tool in this book, so I'm going to stick with a couple of the basic implementations of what I'm calling a subset of quality-of-service specifications. The WSIT implementation, now folded into Project Metro, provides an implementation of several specifications that we'll look at in this chapter. Metro is available as a separate download and within Glassfish, and is in turn used under the hood by Oracle's WebLogic 10gR3 product. This is what we'll be using for the examples in this chapter.

13.1 Understanding Reliable Messaging

Problem

You think you might want to use reliable messaging (RM) in your applications.

Solution

Before jumping in, check out this introduction.

Messages get lost all the time. The sticky note falls off the fridge. The network has a slight hiccup. As a result, messages can be delivered out of order, or not at all. HTTP is an "unreliable" protocol, meaning that it does not guarantee that data will be delivered completely, or at all. HTTP is popular for many reasons, but when you're sending

SOAP messages over it in business transactions with dramatic financial implications, you need something to improve the reliability of your client/service interactions.

WS-ReliableMessaging (WS-RM) attempts to make up for the fact that the networks on which service technologies are based cannot guarantee that messages are properly delivered to their destinations. WS-RM gives us the idea of delivery assurance, which can take one of four forms:

`AtMostOnce`
: Messages are delivered at most once, without duplication. Some messages can potentially get lost.

`AtLeastOnce`
: Messages are guaranteed to be delivered, but it's possible that some messages are delivered more than one time.

`ExactlyOnce`
: No message will be duplicated.

`InOrder`
: Messages will arrive at the service for processing in the order they were sent.

The last assurance, `InOrder`, can be combined with one of the other three to indicate your WS-RM policy regarding how many times messages can be delivered and whether they must be in order. If you don't care if they're in order, you can just leave that element out of the policy.

Policies are implemented in XML files that are then associated with the WSDL. You either have to manually associate them with the WSDL by writing them inline, or you can sometimes use a vendor's proprietary convenience mechanism to get them attached to the service without having to muck about in the WSDL.

Source and destination

WS-ReliableMessaging defines a way to keep track of and manage the reliable message delivery between two parties, the source and the destination. A source is an application endpoint that sends a message (a client), and the destination is the endpoint to which messages are delivered. Messages in WS-RM are not sent directly to the endpoint, but are submitted to the WS-RM implementation for handling, which starts the reliability guarantee.

> The manner in which WS-RM implementations handle the persistence of messages at the source in order to retry unacknowledged messages is out of scope for the specification. It's handled differently by different vendors; WebLogic, for example, builds on its JMS Store-And-Forward framework.

The WS-ReliableMessaging protocol

WS-RM follows this basic order of events in the lifetime of a reliable message exchange:

1. Preconditions are established between the source and destination to ensure policies are understood.
2. When a message is submitted to the runtime, the WS-RM source requests that the destination create a new sequence.
3. The WS-RM destination creates a sequence, assigns it a unique ID, and establishes memory allocation for temporary persistence of the sequence.
4. The WS-RM source sends its first message in the sequence, assigning it an ordinal position (message number).
5. The WS-RM source sends additional messages as it likes, incrementing each message number by 1. Each additional message contains the sequence ID so that the destination can correlate the message properly.
6. The last message in the sequence indicates in a header that it is the last message.
7. The WS-RM destination acknowledges receipt of all of the messages that it has.
8. If any messages were lost in transit, this is indicated in the acknowledgment.
9. Missing messages are re-sent by the source. They include the same message number and sequence ID as the original messages so that the destination can recognize them.
10. The WS-RM destination receives any re-sent messages and acknowledges this.
11. The WS-RM source asks for acknowledgment that the messages were all received properly using an `<AckRequested>` header.
12. The WS-RM source receives the acknowledgment from the WS-RM destination, and sends a `<TerminateSequence>` header to indicate that it's done sending messages for this sequence. The WS-RM source cleans up any resources associated with the sequence.
13. The WS-RM destination receives the terminate sequence message and reclaims the resources associated with managing the sequence.

WS-ReliableMessaging and WS-Addressing exchange

Beware that WS-RM adds considerable bloat to your messages. To illustrate the various parts of the WS-RM infrastructure at work, Example 13-1 is a request that is generated to accommodate the need for WS-ReliableMessaging and WS-Addressing.

Example 13-1. WS-RM request message

```
---[HTTP request]---
SOAPAction: "http://soacookbook.com/sigcap/get"
Accept: text/xml, multipart/related,
text/html, image/gif, image/jpeg, *; q=.2, */*; q=.2
Content-Type: multipart/related;
```

```
start="<rootpart*c19f6849-27ee-473a-b02c-5e7b1130818a@example.jaxws.sun.com>";
type="application/xop+xml";boundary="uuid:c19f6849-27ee-473a-b02c-5e7b1130818a";
start-info="text/xml"
--uuid:c19f6849-27ee-473a-b02c-5e7b1130818a
Content-Id: <rootpart*c19f6849-27ee-473a-b02c-5e7b1130818a@example.jaxws.sun.com>
Content-Type: application/xop+xml;charset=utf-8;type="text/xml"
Content-Transfer-Encoding: binary

<?xml version='1.0' encoding='UTF-8'?>
<S:Envelope xmlns:S="http://schemas.xmlsoap.org/soap/envelope/">
<S:Header>
  <To xmlns="http://www.w3.org/2005/08/addressing">
    http://localhost:8080/sigcap-ws-1.1.0/SigCapService
  </To>
  <Action xmlns="http://www.w3.org/2005/08/addressing">
    http://soacookbook.com/sigcap/get
  </Action>
  <ReplyTo xmlns="http://www.w3.org/2005/08/addressing">
    <Address>http://www.w3.org/2005/08/addressing/anonymous</Address>
  </ReplyTo>

  <MessageID xmlns="http://www.w3.org/2005/08/addressing">
    uuid:1ab08d0b-b919-479c-b0f6-9a843b4c8b28
  </MessageID>
  <ns3:Sequence xmlns:ns2="http://www.w3.org/2005/08/addressing"
    xmlns:ns3="http://schemas.xmlsoap.org/ws/2005/02/rm"
    xmlns:ns4="http://docs.oasis-open.org/wss/2004/01/oasis-200401
      -wss-wssecurity-secext-1.0.xsd"
      xmlns:ns5="http://docs.oasis-open.org/wss/2004/01/oasis-200401
      -wss-wssecurity-utility-1.0.xsd"
      xmlns:ns6="http://schemas.microsoft.com/ws/2006/05/rm">
    <ns3:Identifier>uuid:8ce634c6-7b0f-4e7c-9e21-77eac4491944
  </ns3:Identifier>
  <ns3:MessageNumber>1</ns3:MessageNumber>
  </ns3:Sequence>
</S:Header>

<S:Body>
  <ns2:get xmlns:ns2="http://soacookbook.com/sigcap">
    <ns2:getRequest>
      60990aff-1c1f-45a7-b35c-cf0410908e36
    </ns2:getRequest>
  </ns2:get>
</S:Body>
</S:Envelope>
--uuid:c19f6849-27ee-473a-b02c-5e7b1130818a--
```

There's a SOAPAction attached to the message in the HTTP header, and the SOAP envelope headers contain all of the WS-Addressing information. The <To>, <Action>, and <ReplyTo> elements are all in the WS-Addressing namespace. In a way, addressing represents an attempt to provide a URI in a manner similar to how RESTful services do. The <ReplyTo> address is for the "anonymous" user because the client was not identified as having a URI of its own.

The WS-RM information is also included in the SOAP envelope headers. The message in this case is given an ID that conforms to the structure of a universally unique ID (UUID, usually generated based on an intersection of a timestamp and information from the NIC). The specification does not require that this ID be in the UUID structure, however, as long as it is unique. The runtime uses this message ID to keep track of whether the request has been acknowledged as received, and in what sequence.

The `<Sequence>` header is used to indicate an identity for this specific set of message exchanges, and the ordinal position of this message within that sequence. This ordinal is 1-based, not 0-based, and increments by 1 for each message in the same sequence.

Looks complicated, huh? You might think that this code was sending a rocket to the moon given its length. But this is a lot of text to represent a single message in a single SOAP request matching an operation called `get` that takes a single parameter, defined like this in the schema:

```
<xs:schema xmlns:tns="http://soacookbook.com/sigcap"...>
 <xs:complexType name="get">
  <xs:sequence>
    <xs:element name="getRequest" type="xs:string"
      form="qualified" minOccurs="0" />
  </xs:sequence>
```

In other words, it's one element that wraps a string. Wow, that's a big package for such a tiny present. Reliable messaging and addressing really add to the size of every single message. And reliable messaging sends additional messages to indicate to the destination that the sequence is complete.

Let's look at the reliable messaging response to the request just shown. The first pertinent things that we see in the response are the HTTP headers, which indicate that the response is multipart. The content type is `application/xop+xml`, and it uses binary content encoding. This is due to the fact that this service returns binary data with an image as its content, based on the unique identifier passed into the request. The service does a lookup for that ID and returns the corresponding image, which is the `<signatureData>` element, specified as `xs:base64Binary` in the schema.

But the binary content is not inlined within the message; instead, it is replaced with an XOP `<Include>` element. The image data itself is then exported to an attachment and assigned the same ID. Runtime processes can then reconstruct the binary data using the include ID as a reference. The HTTP headers indicate the multipart content using UUIDs. This is shown in Example 13-2, which contains the response message.

XOP stands for XML-binary Optimized Packaging. This is a W3C standard that describes a means to efficiently serialize XML infosets that have binary content. It's not directly part of WS-A or WS-RM, but because it's part of this example, it seemed useful to make the distinction. You can read the XOP spec at *http://www.w3.org/TR/xop10*.

Example 13-2. WS-RM response message

```
---[HTTP response 200]---
Transfer-encoding: chunked
null: HTTP/1.1 200 OK
Content-type: multipart/related;
start="<rootpart*23d59158-64d6-4555-89d3-5ccbfaa187f3>";
type="application/xop+xml";
boundary="uuid:23d59158-64d6-4555-89d3-5ccbfaa187f3";
start-info="text/xml"
Server: Sun Java System Application Server 9.1_02
X-powered-by: Servlet/2.5
Date: Tue, 09 Sep 2008 00:22:45 GMT
--uuid:23d59158-64d6-4555-89d3-5ccbfaa187f3
Content-Id: <rootpart*23d59158-64d6-4555-89d3-5ccbfaa187f3>
Content-Type: application/xop+xml;charset=utf-8;type="text/xml"
Content-Transfer-Encoding: binary

<?xml version="1.0" ?>
<S:Envelope xmlns:S="http://schemas.xmlsoap.org/soap/envelope/">
<S:Header>
  <To xmlns="http://www.w3.org/2005/08/addressing">
    http://www.w3.org/2005/08/addressing/anonymous
  </To>
  <Action xmlns="http://www.w3.org/2005/08/addressing">
    http://ns.dte.com/dtc/sigcap/getResponse
  </Action>
  <MessageID xmlns="http://www.w3.org/2005/08/addressing">
    uuid:f31721de-af5b-470d-9f22-1bab02383130
  </MessageID>
  <RelatesTo xmlns="http://www.w3.org/2005/08/addressing">
    uuid:1ab08d0b-b919-479c-b0f6-9a843b4c8b28
  </RelatesTo>

  <ns2:Sequence
    xmlns:ns6="http://schemas.microsoft.com/ws/2006/05/rm"
    xmlns:ns5="http://docs.oasis-open.org/wss/2004/01/oasis-200401
      -wss-wssecurity-utility-1.0.xsd"
    xmlns:ns4="http://docs.oasis-open.org/wss/2004/01/oasis-200401
      -wss-wssecurity-secext-1.0.xsd"
    xmlns:ns3="http://www.w3.org/2005/08/addressing"
    xmlns:ns2="http://schemas.xmlsoap.org/ws/2005/02/rm">

    <ns2:Identifier>
      uuid:0ffa7ef6-bcea-4d63-ba2c-1a5c3d1a4832
    </ns2:Identifier>
    <ns2:MessageNumber>1</ns2:MessageNumber>
  </ns2:Sequence>

  <ns2:AckRequested
    xmlns:ns6="http://schemas.microsoft.com/ws/2006/05/rm"
    xmlns:ns5="http://docs.oasis-open.org/wss/2004/01/oasis-200401
      -wss-wssecurity-utility-1.0.xsd"
    xmlns:ns4="http://docs.oasis-open.org/wss/2004/01/oasis-200401
      -wss-wssecurity-secext-1.0.xsd"
    xmlns:ns3="http://www.w3.org/2005/08/addressing"
```

```
    xmlns:ns2="http://schemas.xmlsoap.org/ws/2005/02/rm">

    <ns2:Identifier>
      uuid:0ffa7ef6-bcea-4d63-ba2c-1a5c3d1a4832
    </ns2:Identifier>
  </ns2:AckRequested>

  <ns2:SequenceAcknowledgement
    xmlns:ns6="http://schemas.microsoft.com/ws/2006/05/rm"
    xmlns:ns5="http://docs.oasis-open.org/wss/2004/01/oasis-200401
      -wss-wssecurity-utility-1.0.xsd"
    xmlns:ns4="http://docs.oasis-open.org/wss/2004/01/oasis-200401
      -wss-wssecurity-secext-1.0.xsd"
    xmlns:ns3="http://www.w3.org/2005/08/addressing"
    xmlns:ns2="http://schemas.xmlsoap.org/ws/2005/02/rm">
    <ns2:Identifier>
      uuid:8ce634c6-7b0f-4e7c-9e21-77eac4491944
    </ns2:Identifier>

    <ns2:AcknowledgementRange Upper="1" Lower="1" />
  </ns2:SequenceAcknowledgement>
</S:Header>

<S:Body>
  <ns2:getResponse xmlns:ns2="http://ns.dte.com/dtc/sigcap">
    <ns2:getResponse>
      <fileFormat>TIFF</fileFormat>
      <signatureData>
        <Include xmlns="http://www.w3.org/2004/08/xop/include"
          href="cid:2b048436-7fcb-4166-b142-65121d32008f"/>
      </signatureData>
      <signatureId>60990aff-1c1f-45a7-b35c-cf0410908e36
      </signatureId>
    </ns2:getResponse>
  </ns2:getResponse>
</S:Body>

</S:Envelope>
--uuid:23d59158-64d6-4555-89d3-5ccbfaa187f3
Content-Id: <2b048436-7fcb-4166-b142-65121d32008f>
Content-Type: application/octet-stream
Content-Transfer-Encoding: binary

[binary data]
--uuid:23d59158-64d6-4555-89d3-5ccbfaa187f3--
```

Let's examine the parts of this SOAP response to see how it correlates the message. The first part of the SOAP header is related to WS-A. The first interesting WS-RM element is the `<Sequence>` element. The sequence contains an identifier and a message number to indicate the ordinal position of this message in the flow.

The `<SequenceAcknowledgement>` header indicates the successful receipt of a message and can be returned with an application message, or the WS-RM destination can send one independently.

The sequence must include a <LastMessage> element to signal that this is the last message to expect. In this case, the runtime must respond with a <SequenceAcknowledgment> header (if there is an application message to be sent; if not, it can choose to send a message with an empty body containing only the <LastMessage> header). Generally, after you get the response to your request, the client runtime *will* originate a new request containing the <LastMessage> header, and the WS-RM destination (the service provider) will send a response containing a <SequenceAcknowledgement> header and a <TerminateSequence> message in the SOAP body. This is the case in the Glassfish/Metro implementation of WS-RM, for example. A snippet of such a response is shown here:

```
<S:Body>
  <ns2:TerminateSequence
    xmlns:ns2="http://schemas.xmlsoap.org/ws/2005/02/rm" ...>
  <ns2:Identifier>
    uuid:0ffa7ef6-bcea-4d63-ba2c-1a5c3d1a4832
  </ns2:Identifier>
</ns2:TerminateSequence>
</S:Body>
```

The <TerminateSequence> element holds an <Identifier> that corresponds to the UUID for the sequence as presented in the previous response, so that the runtime knows which sequence to end and free up its resources.

Next in the response message are the <AckRequested> and <AcknowledgementRange> elements. These elements indicate to the runtime the scope of what's being acknowledged as successfully handled. <AcknowledgementRange> contains a set of message numbers indicating the inclusive range of messages it is acknowledging. In this example, the <MessageNumber> in the request was 1, so the acknowledgment corresponds to that value.

While in this case we're just acknowledging a single message, acknowledgments can indicate what messages from a sequence have not yet been received by the destination. For example, the following valid acknowledgment range indicates that something is missing:

```
<wsrm:SequenceAcknowledgement>
   <wsrm:Identifier>http://soacookbook/123</wsrm:Identifier>
   <wsrm:AcknowledgementRange Upper="2" Lower="1"/>
   <wsrm:AcknowledgementRange Upper="6" Lower="4"/>
   <wsrm:AcknowledgementRange Upper="10" Lower="8"/>
</wsrm:SequenceAcknowledgement>
```

This shows that the destination has lost or not yet received messages 3 and 5 in the sequence. That should be a signal to the source to resend those messages.

The addition of sequence acknowledgment messages creates considerable extra overhead for the runtime. A single request becomes several requests when WS-RM is included.

Because of this, be sure you have a good reason for putting this stuff into play. Don't put it on everything just because you can, and make sure that you load test. Note that too many of the leading SOA stack vendors, including TIBCO and Software AG, do not yet (as of this writing) implement WS-RM. TIBCO, for example, uses its Rendezvous messaging infrastructure to make its communication reliable; it just isn't implementing WS-RM to do it.

13.2 Configuring a Java Web Service with Reliable Messaging

Problem

You have a web service endpoint, and you want it to guarantee delivery of messages.

Solution

As of this writing, there is no annotation to make your life easier, so you have to write it into the WSDL. If you have been generating your WSDL, you can save it locally in your project in the *WEB-INF/wsdl* folder, point the service to the WSDL, and add the following code:

```
<definitions
 xmlns:wsu="http://docs.oasis-open.org/wss/2004/
   01/oasis-200401-wss-wssecurity-utility-1.0.xsd"
 xmlns:wsp="http://www.w3.org/ns/ws-policy"
 xmlns:wsrm="http://schemas.xmlsoap.org/ws/2005/02/rm/policy"
 ...>
<wsp:UsingPolicy required="true" />

<wsp:Policy wsu:Id="MyPortBinding_ReliableMessaging_Policy">
    <wsp:ExactlyOne>
         <wsp:All>
           <wsrm:RMAssertion>
                <!-- 2.5 minutes -->
                <wsrm:InactivityTimeout Milliseconds="150000"/>
                <!-- Retry after 5 seconds unacknowledged -->
                <wsrm:BaseRetransmissionInterval Milliseconds="5000" />
            </wsrm:RMAssertion>
        </wsp:All>
    </wsp:ExactlyOne>
</wsp:Policy>

//....

<binding name="MyPortBinding" type="tns:MyPort">
  <wsaw:UsingAddressing required="true"/>
  <wsp:PolicyReference URI="#MyPortBinding_ReliableMessaging_Policy"/>
```

Basically what you're doing here is adding the reliable messaging assertion to the policy in the WSDL. You're defining a policy that you have to use reliable messaging in this particular way (timing out after 2.5 minutes and retrying requests after 5 seconds if they aren't yet acknowledged). The value given in the `wsu:id` must be unique within the WSDL. You can write several different policies and then hook them to a port binding. So you could write a few different port bindings and allow clients to choose their terms.

If you examine the `wsdl:binding` element, you'll see that the binding has a name that represents the `MyPort` type. It's the binding, and not the port itself, that contains the reference to the RM policy.

Policies are conventionally defined at the top of the WSDL, though the WSDL will validate wherever you put them.

Now when you deploy your service on a container that supports reliable messaging, your service will use it.

Discussion

Recall that WS-Policy is a general extension point specification that allows WSDL to extend its capabilities to include functionality afforded by other specifications concerned with some particular aspect of Quality of Service. These might include reliable messaging, atomic transactions, or security.

One problem with WS-ReliableMessaging is the difficulty presented in clustering the reliable service. The sequence ID needs to be shared between the nodes in the cluster. The scalability of services using RM is also jeopardized because the client and server must participate in a stateful conversation.

See Also

Recipe 13.3 To see how to set up a client for use with the reliable service.

13.3 Configuring a Java Client with Reliable Messaging

Problem

You have a web service endpoint that declares it uses reliable messaging, and you want your client to be able to participate.

Solution

If you're using Ant to build your project, you need to put Metro 1.3 on your classpath or unjar its contents into your client JAR.

If you're using Maven, include the following in your client project's POM:

```
<dependency>
  <groupId>com.sun.xml.ws</groupId>
  <artifactId>webservices-rt</artifactId>
  <version>1.3</version>
  <scope>compile</scope>
</dependency>

<dependency>
  <groupId>javax.xml</groupId>
  <artifactId>webservices-api</artifactId>
  <version>1.3</version>
  <scope>compile</scope>
</dependency>
```

The client of a Glassfish RM service doesn't have to do anything special otherwise. With WS-Addressing, for example, you need to pass an `AddressingFeature` instance to the proxy when you create it. There's no corresponding construct for WS-ReliableMessaging. The policy negotiation is handled by the runtime, and messages are stored in memory.

For WebLogic, you need to do a little more. In the Administration Console, follow these general steps:

1. Create some kind of persistent store (either JDBC or file based). WebLogic server will use this store to track the WS-RM sequences and messages. You can create a new store, or use an existing one if you prefer.
2. Create a JMS Server or use an existing one.
3. Create a Store-And-Forward agent or use an existing one, and set its Agent Type field to `Both` to allow the agent to handle both sending and receiving of messages.

See Also

Recipe 13.2 to see how to set up a service endpoint for use with the reliable service.

13.4 Configuring a Java Web Service with Reliable Messaging on WebLogic

Problem

You want to deploy your service with reliable messaging support to WebLogic 10, and you don't want to write WSDL code by hand.

Solution

Use one of the pre-packaged policy files that comes with WebLogic 10. You can use the proprietary `@Policy` annotation to associate one of their policy files with the class. Then set up a JMS queue and store-and-forward agent to hold the messages.

Discussion

Example 13-3 is a class that runs only in WebLogic that handles WS-RM for you without forcing you to write WSDL code by hand.

Example 13-3. HelloRM.java, a reliable messaging web service

```
package com.soacookbook;

import javax.jws.WebService;

import weblogic.jws.Policy;
import weblogic.jws.ReliabilityBuffer;

@WebService
@Policy(attachToWsdl=true,
  direction=Policy.Direction.both,
  uri="DefaultReliability.xml")
public class ReliableWS {

  @ReliabilityBuffer(retryCount=10,
    retryDelay="10 seconds")
  public void sayHello(String input) {
    System.out.println("Hello from RM, " + input);

  }
}
```

This class features the `@Policy` annotation and points to the *DefaultReliability.xml* file, which is one of the two that ships with WebLogic (the other value you could put there is "LongRunningReliability.xml"). If you just wanted to write the policy section, you could do that and substitute the value of the `uri` attribute with the name of your file.

The file does not have to be relative within the deployment; it can be specified from an absolute URI, like this: `@Policy(uri="http://soacookbook.com/policies/myPolicy.xml"`.

The `@ReliabilityBuffer` annotation indicates that the runtime should try to deliver reliable messages to the service a maximum of 10 times, at 5-second intervals.

There are two RM policies included with WebLogic 10. The default file has the following contents:

```
<?xml version="1.0"?>
<wsp:Policy
   xmlns:wsrm="http://schemas.xmlsoap.org/ws/2005/02/rm/policy"
   xmlns:wsp="http://schemas.xmlsoap.org/ws/2004/09/policy"
   xmlns:beapolicy="http://www.bea.com/wsrm/policy">

  <wsrm:RMAssertion >
```

```
    <wsrm:InactivityTimeout
        Milliseconds="600000" />
    <wsrm:BaseRetransmissionInterval
        Milliseconds="3000" />
    <wsrm:ExponentialBackoff />
    <wsrm:AcknowledgementInterval
        Milliseconds="200" />
    <beapolicy:Expires Expires="P1D" optional="true"/>
  </wsrm:RMAssertion>

</wsp:Policy>
```

This is much easier to write than a whole WSDL, and it's far more modular. Defining policies in this form allows you to reuse policies across multiple services, and to store them in a central repository. This is just the sort of scenario that makes SOA, and the WS-* set of specifications, so compelling.

But as with so many things, using this method of offering support for RM trades convenience for portability. Notice that in the pre-prepared policy file you get a BEA namespace and an assertion that is vendor-specific. This is in addition to the proprietary annotation used to associate the policy with the service. If you aren't worried about breaking your service interface in this way if you ever want to port your deployment to another platform, knock yourself out. But it's not for everyone.

13.5 Using a WebLogic Reliable Messaging Error Handler

Problem

You want to invoke a reliable messaging-enabled service in WebLogic 10 from another service.

Solution

Use the proprietary classes that ship with WebLogic for just such a purpose. You don't have to do anything special to inject a port type reference. Just call the method you want to call, as you normally would. But you can configure an error handler that receives the timeout event if the RM runtime determines that the operation won't return as planned:

```
import weblogic.jws.ReliabilityErrorHandler;
import weblogic.wsee.reliability.ReliabilityErrorContext;
import weblogic.wsee.reliability.ReliableDeliveryException;
//...

@ReliabilityErrorHandler(target="port")
public void onReliableMessageDeliveryError(ReliabilityErrorContext ctx) {
  ReliableDeliveryException fault = ctx.getFault();
  String msg = "";
  if (fault != null) {
    msg = ctx.getFault().getMessage();
```

```
    }
    String op = ctx.getOperationName();
    System.out.println("Reliable operation " + op +
      " was probably lost. Message=" + message);
}
```

The event will get received by a handler method that fulfills two requirements: it is annotated with @ReliabilityErrorHandler, and it accepts a ReliabilityErrorContext parameter. The code above accepts the context, which you can use to retrieve the fault and process further as you wish. Note that the error context also allows you to get the name of the operation that the runtime was trying to invoke when it failed. This entire solution is, of course, specific to WebLogic 10.

CHAPTER 14
Enterprise Service Bus

14.0 Introduction

In this chapter, we'll diverge from the problem/solution format used in the rest of this book in order to present an overview of an enterprise service bus (ESB). We'll look at what an ESB is and what problems it solves. We'll also examine some of the popular ESBs in the commercial and open source arenas to give you a solid foundation for selecting one that best suits your environment.

We'll take a tour of the JBI specification, design patterns that form the foundation of ESB, and some key features of any implementation. We'll also look at what some of the important players in the ESB space (including free and open source projects) are doing with their products.

Focus of This Chapter

Throughout most of this book, we have focused on standards published by the W3C, OASIS-Open, OAGI, Sun, and other organizations. They allow vendors to implement the specifications or recommendations. Vendors can then add their own proprietary extensions to be more competitive in the marketplace. In some cases, functionality of any specific implementation (such as the deployment of a component) is left entirely to vendors because the specifications are silent on certain matters viewed as beyond its scope. The standards for Java APIs, XML-related technologies, BPEL, and especially WS-* have allowed us to create solutions that, for the most part, are portable across such implementations. A JAX-WS web service will work in roughly the same way in any container that implements JAX-WS.

However, there is no specification for ESB. There is no standard that supports the creation of an ESB, or even a precise definition of what an ESB is. While by now the industry generally agrees on what features should be present in a product calling itself an ESB, vendors offer a wide variety of products with features that differ dramatically from one ESB to the next.

Because there is no standard for ESBs, and you will have a variety of constraints at work as you select your SOA tools, it seemed to me that a low-level, detailed, and very specific chapter on ESB would be inappropriate for this book. Showing how to create a route in Oracle Service Bus is completely different from creating a route in TIBCO ActiveMatrix or a delivery channel in Apache ServiceMix. They don't all have the same features, and the common features they do have are implemented in very different ways. So the knowledge you would gain about the specifics of one ESB would not be transferable to any other. A deep dive on Mule would offer very little insight for developers who aren't using Mule, and there are so many ESBs to choose from. Therefore, my aim in this chapter is to arm you with the most transferable and portable knowledge no matter what ESB you chose.

In some cases, vendors, such as Oracle, Software AG, IBM, TIBCO, and others, offer "SOA suites" that comprise a collection of products such as an ESB, an orchestration engine, a SOAP engine, an enterprise registry/repository, a BPEL engine and design-time tools, Business Activity Monitoring and related tools, and more. The features present in these products from vendor to vendor are not consistent. For example, you might have an ESB from one vendor that handles transformations for you, and another ESB product that delegates transformations to an orchestration engine.

It can all get very confusing. You can get a standalone orchestration engine, such as Apache ODE or Active Endpoints VOS, as well as standalone ESBs. Some ESBs run on an application server. Some vendors, such as Oracle, include a "light" subset of orchestration functions directly in their ESB but also sell an orchestration product.

For all of these reasons, I abandon the problem/solution format for this chapter. You might even wonder why this chapter is included at all. In my view, an ESB is the backbone of SOA, and I hope this chapter will illustrate its benefits.

14.1 What Is ESB?

SOA is a kind of architecture, an approach to building an integrated IT landscape. Enterprise service bus, like the definitions of "service" and "SOA" themselves, can mean different things depending on whom you talk to. But one clear distinction is that an ESB is generally considered a piece of infrastructure. You can't buy SOA, but you can buy an ESB.

Some would argue that you needn't buy an ESB either and you could instead implement basic routing patterns by following *Enterprise Integration Patterns* by Gregor Hohpe and Bobby Woolf (Addison-Wesley Professional). The only problem with this approach is that you could end up replicating a lot of already available features that could have gotten you up and running very quickly and losing the advantage of the product having been tested and optimized. In fact, the MuleSource open source ESB is an explicit implementation of the patterns recorded in Hohpe and Woolf's book.

There are many architects who view ESB as a set of patterns, and not a product at all. This view is discussed in Recipe 14.2.

That having been said, let's look at what really constitutes an ESB. The term ESB is derived from the idea of a hardware bus, which transfers messages from one subsystem to another, using the same set of wires to logically connect several hardware peripheral components such as PCI cards. We're all familiar with the Universal Serial Bus, which allows us to connect a wide variety of hardware components to our PCs, and has the advantage of plug-and-play and hot-swapping.

In a sense, an enterprise service bus builds on these ideas that have been present in computing for decades, and attempts to perform the same logical function for the vast set of software applications within an enterprise that the USB and other bus technologies have done for hardware.

The ESB is capable of connecting a variety of messaging systems without forcing you to create point-to-point channels that are visible to application clients. Clients connect to the bus, which serves as a mediation layer that shields clients from the disparate messaging formats and protocols used in the backend systems. The bus choreographs message interactions with a variety of related SOA technologies, such as rules engines (external or embedded), an orchestration engine (employing BPEL or XPDL), adapters for legacy and packaged applications, and internal routing and transformation mechanisms. This allows all of the nodes of the bus to interact without having to create specific routes to each application, thereby reducing the maintenance overhead. Because the bus abstracts and mediates connected nodes, some flexibility is achieved; if you want to swap out one application for another one, you can do so with minimal disruption to the overall solution. This is illustrated in Figure 14-1.

Features of an ESB

ESBs are the backbone of SOA. They provide the opportunity to really make your entire IT landscape visible, integrated, and ready to participate in new composite applications across EAI, supply chain, B2B, portals, and more. They allow you the flexibility to not rip and replace existing systems that are functioning properly and represent a considerable investment of intellectual capital. One colleague of mine is fond of this definition of "legacy applications": they're the stuff that works. To protect this investment, and yet still allow you to modernize as necessary and integrate with newer applications, the ESB does not require that you install software at each node that you want to integrate. An ESB is often lightweight, and offers a centralized system for deploying components that can scale independently.

An ESB allows you to send messages between multiple services in a distributed environment, offering a layer of indirection that provides a rich set of mediating features

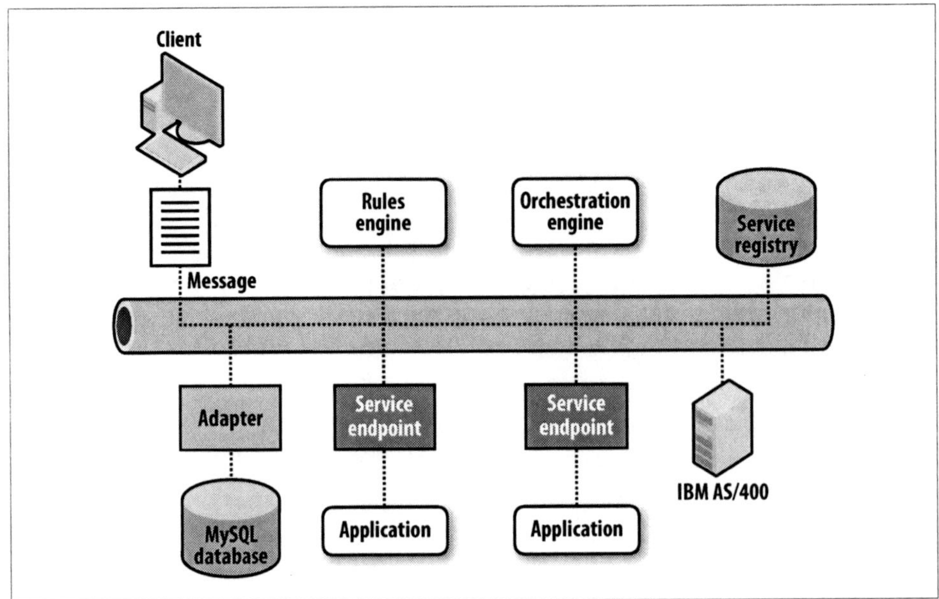

Figure 14-1. The role of the ESB in SOA

for those messages. An ESB is typically platform-independent in the sense that it will run on a range of operating systems and is often neutral with respect to application server and programming language. The bus allows you to connect native Java applications, .NET applications, object request brokers, and legacy platforms.

To achieve this end, most ESBs offer support for invoking web services and other network-ready application nodes, employ adapters to connect with packaged and legacy applications, offer robust routing support for messages, allow orchestration and transformation of message content, and more.

As mentioned previously, any given product calling itself an ESB may not have all of these features. However, many ESBs have all of them and may also include additional capabilities.

Let's look more closely at each of these features.

Web services support

ESBs offer the ability to invoke SOAP- and WSDL-based web services, as well as POX (Plain Old XML) services over HTTP. In general, you use a design-time tool to create a proxy WSDL to a web service that you want to expose on the ESB. Instead of connecting directly to your web service WSDL, clients connect to the WSDL exposed by the bus. This allows you to create a small connector that executes within the bus that includes your routing or transformation logic. Different ESBs handle this connector portion very differently, which is one reason this chapter is structured the way it is. For example, OpenESB (soon to be renamed GlassfishESB) handles this entirely through BPEL. The Oracle Service Bus has you create a "route" in their Eclipse-based tool, and you can add rules and message enhancements within the route. You can then publish the route to your enterprise repository.

In general, ESBs indicate support for REST simply as the ability to invoke an endpoint URI with an XML message.

Adapters

For applications that do not directly have a SOAP or XML interface, many vendors will provide adapters (often at additional cost) that allow you to integrate specifically with different third-party ERP, databases, or other packaged systems, such as PeopleSoft, SAP R/3, and Siebel. Adapters typically exist for relational databases, file interfaces, and so forth.

Many packaged applications, such as PeopleSoft, expose lots of their functionality as web services. But you may have customized certain aspects of the application, or want to connect with it in a way not provided by their XML services. Adapters also allow you to avoid paying for runtime translation to and from XML if the system supports direct object serialization. So adapters can be a good option even in these cases.

Invocation

As a standard feature, ESBs support synchronous and asynchronous calls to services, and sometimes callbacks. You can map one service to another if necessary. Some ESBs allow runtime policy negotiation through WS-MetadataExchange, allowing services to be invoked on behalf of clients according to what the client's capabilities are for security or other features.

Mediation and protocol independence

Mediation within a bus means that a variety of protocols can be reconciled for complex routes across a variety of platforms. This allows you to integrate your enterprise but maintain loose coupling between indirectly connected components. For example, an incoming SOAP message over HTTP may need to be formatted for JMS if a backend system on the route requires this; the bus is capable of handling such mediation.

Buses typically will allow you to plot many different protocols on a message path, including not only HTTP and JMS but HTTPS, SMTP, XMPP, FTP, and so forth. Many buses feature the ability to seamlessly connect a variety of other formats such as Electronic Data Interchange (EDI), JDBC, COBOL copy books, and flat files. This is a powerful feature that allows you to maintain the independent components within your enterprise as you like, and yet connect them all with minimal intrusion.

Routing

Many buses support addressing and allow you to perform service lookup in conjunction with a registry/repository to perform dynamic routing. You can perform routing based on a variety of possible connection methods, including content-based routing, routing based on a rules service, and routing based on policies. Perhaps the most popular of these is content-based routing, in which, for example, you use XPath to select data from a SOAP envelope and, based on the content, select a new service destination for the current message.

Some buses offer advanced features such as service pooling, in which the bus can determine that a particular service endpoint is unavailable (say, due to a crash) and can dynamically route messages to another service instance in the pool.

Transformation

Data represented as XML can be transformed using XSLT, and queried using XQuery and XPath. These technologies together allow you to enhance the content of messages to prepare it for downstream invocation of other systems. If you are using a canonical data model, this feature is important.

Orchestration

Many ESBs offer the ability to coordinate multiple services to expose them as a single proxy service. This can be done with a lightweight internal orchestration engine that offers basic orchestration features such as conditions, waits, and parallel flows. Some buses delegate most or all of this functionality to a full-blown BPEL or XPDL engine.

Security

We have seen many examples in this book of security-related functions in individual service components. A service bus will typically provide additional security capabilities, enforcing the use of security policies in conjunction with policy enforcement points, security as a service, SSL, and SAML (Security Assertion Markup Language).

SOA Without an ESB

It is worth mentioning that not every SOA practitioner thinks that an ESB is essential to SOA. However, I do not know any architects who are using mostly SOAP-based services who do not recommend an ESB. In my view, SOA without the ESB repeats the past complexities of Enterprise Application Integration efforts, wherein each integrated node requires an adapter for every other node it is connected to, and interfaces for these components are tightly coupled to the other connected nodes.

Most of this book has focused on creating SOAP-based web services as a means to abstract the underlying platform of these connected nodes. This is a positive evolution over integration attempts of the past because when you define a web services endpoint, it is represented by a WSDL with the message format defined in XML Schema. These XML-based formats do not reveal the underlying platform in a way that is necessary with other distributed technologies.

For example, if you were to use EJBs to connect remote systems, not only would they have to be written in Java, they would expose interfaces written in Java and require the distribution of an EJB client JAR. Imagine that you have the following interface defined:

```
public interface CRM {
    public Customer getCustomer(int id);
}
```

If your company acquires another company whose customer IDs are defined with strings because they contain alphabetic characters, you would need to either create a different interface for that system and disburse the integration logic into client systems (thereby creating tighter coupling), or change the interface that you expose to clients, redistribute the client JAR, and redeploy the clients. While this may work fine for departmental applications, it may not scale as a good maintenance solution for larger or geographically dispersed enterprise-level integration efforts.

Consider the WSDL interface that might expose this same customer relationship management function:

```
<service name="CRM">
  <port binding="sc:CrmPortBinding" name="CrmPort">
    <s:address location="http://soacookbook.com:8080/CustomerService"/>
  </port>
</service>
```

A WSDL and XML Schema wrapper around such a system aids in this effort somewhat, as you do not reveal the underlying implementation platform, and your services can be maintained more independently of the client systems that rely on them. However, the protocol (HTTP) and the endpoint location of the service are still revealed. Moreover, the message format is defined by XML Schema, but if it declares that a customer ID is represented as an integer, you still have some of the same problems of the previous EJB-based solution.

An ESB is one important way that you truly achieve the promise of SOA. Because the ESB provides a layer of abstraction, clients can talk only to the bus, and not actually ever know the location of the service endpoint itself. Once the XML message is received on the bus, as the central integration point, it can perform necessary transformations to ensure that the legacy CRM system integrates smoothly with the newly acquired system. This is where a canonical data model gains real importance, as the client systems can still talk in the way they want to, and the bus can serve to translate the message format as needed.

To take this example further, the bus can aggregate services into a service composition, exposing the desired simple interface to clients, though behind the scenes it is managing the invocation of a set of services working in conjunction to fulfill the request.

Depending on the size of your organization and your proposed SOA buildout, you may want to consider introducing ESB after the initial phase. In order to minimize initial complexity and realize ROI more quickly, many SOA practitioners will defer putting an ESB in place until after several services are developed and the basic building block is understood. This view makes a lot of sense. The only concern is that you will have to re-point clients to a new WSDL (the ESB proxy representation of the service).

By the end of this chapter, you should be in a position to decide for yourself whether an ESB has a place in your SOA.

Benefits of ESB

As we have seen, there are many benefits to using an ESB, both for IT and for the business, including the following:

- Reduced time to integrate new and existing applications.
- Increased flexibility because system dependencies are reduced. Applications don't have to "know" as much about each other, making it easier for you to change system interfaces or switch them out altogether.
- Simultaneous centralized management of the service catalog while services themselves are distributed.
- Because of the centralized management ability, many buses can collect service metrics. In conjunction with Business Activity Monitoring (BAM) tools, you can get the benefits of centralized logging and create your own service-level agreements (SLAs) that can be monitored. You can collect statistics against these SLAs and feed them into your reporting platform. An ESB provides this to the business and IT without them having to instrument the services themselves (for example, using a technology such as JMX).
- Encourages use of industry standard interfaces, reducing total cost of ownership.
- Greater agility and responsiveness to change.
- More accurate and up-to-date information via logical centralization of data management, or a "single version of the truth."

In a modern SOA, which consists of automated Business Process Management tools, BAM tools, monitoring SLAs and metrics with KPIs, a registry, a repository, perhaps a rules engine, and federated security with policy enforcement points, it seems imperative to have a solid ESB in place, given the many benefits. It is the foundation that ties these many SOA features together and ensures that they will be visible and usable.

14.2 ESB As a Set of Patterns

There are many SOA practitioners who contend that an ESB is not a product that you buy, but is rather the implementation of a set of key integration patterns. I have respect for this position, and in my view, it was this idea that helped modern ESBs rise up from their origins as merely re-packaged EAI products. Once vendors determined that there was a real roadmap for ESB and that people were starting to do it themselves, they kicked into high gear a bit.

The patterns typically referenced in this view are those found in Hohpe and Woolf's book, *Enterprise Integration Patterns* (Addison-Wesley Professional) (the patterns are also available at *http://www.eaipatterns.com*). This view may have been more relevant several years ago, before any mature ESBs were on the market. But a number of products (including open source products such as Mule) now exist, and their founders indicate that they started these projects specifically in order to encapsulate a wide number of these well-known integration patterns.

Consider just a few of the relevant patterns Hohpe and Woolf define: Message Bus, Content-Based Router, Pipes and Filters, Point-to-Point Channel, Normalizer, Canonical Data Model. These patterns are indeed the core of any modern ESB, which will implement many of the key EAI patterns, tie into a larger SOA stack in ways that make development far easier, and offer crucial performance and reliability features.

So you could get their book (good idea anyway!) and implement the patterns yourself. But many of these are not Gang of Four type stuff where you write 10 lines of code and you have a singleton. Some of these patterns require lots of work. And it is likely that if you start down the path of implementing a few of the key integration patterns, you will eventually find that you really have to finish what you've started to have a complete system that does what you need as the backbone of your SOA. As there are a number of viable commercial and open source alternatives available, you should make a very careful assessment of your IT landscape and SOA roadmap before you talk yourself into implementing a few patterns on your own so that you don't have to bother with a full-blown ESB.

14.3 JBI

Java Business Integration 1.0 (JBI) is a specification published by the Sun JSR process as JSR 208. It was released in August 2005, and it defines a standards-based architecture for integration built on the idea of a meta-container. As Java developers and architects, we're used to talking about servlet containers (which serve as an execution environment for servlets and JSPs) and EJB containers (which serve as an execution environment for Enterprise JavaBeans). Developers write an EJB, and they execute inside an EJB container. But JBI defines a meta-container, or a container of containers. This meta-container does not execute anything itself. It serves as a life cycle management point for a collection of engines that are each capable of executing a specific kind of integration technology. That means that as long as you conform to the interface required by JBI, you can write an engine that executes some arbitrary specific code, instead of the specification dictating to you what you will be allowed to execute (as is the case with EJB).

The idea is this: someone implements the JBI spec and then they (or other vendors) can in turn implement engines that are pluggable within that container. Just as a servlet written to run in Tomcat can port to WebSphere and run there with little or no modification, so too can JBI service engines port from one JBI implementation to another. Each engine plugged into the JBI environment is capable of executing one specific integration technology, such as BPEL for orchestration, JDBC connectors, file connectors, and so forth.

JBI is intended for SOAs, with an aim toward avoiding vendor lock-in. In fact, JBI is actually a little SOA itself, with this architecture supporting very loose coupling between components.

The overall goal of JBI is to help you avoid creating an SOA in order to free yourself from the underlying legacy platforms in your enterprise, only to find that you have tied yourself to a proprietary underlying ESB technology right at the heart of your enterprise. This is a laudable goal indeed.

The JBI Architecture

JBI is a message-based, pluggable meta-container. As mentioned earlier, a meta-container acts as a host of hosts. It allows arbitrary container environments, each specific to a certain technology, such as JDBC, XSLT, BPEL, Java, and so forth, to execute inside it. It doesn't define the components that will be plugged into JBI; it only defines the framework, the interfaces, and the abstract life cycle that allows plugged-in components to execute together in harmony and be leveraged by developers writing components deployable to one of those single environments.

To accomplish this goal, the JBI architecture defines four primary elements: service engines, binding components, normalized message router, and the runtime environment. These are shown in Figure 14-2.

Service engines

Service engines (SEs) are JBI components that enable pluggable business logic. An SE is a standard container for hosting WSDL-defined service providers as well as service consumers used internally by JBI. For example, the OpenESB project, which implements JBI, offers a BPEL SE. You install the BPEL SE into OpenESB and then you can write a BPEL orchestration; create a JBI Service Unit project that contains XML descriptors (such as *jbi.xml*), the BPEL XML file, the WSDL, and the XML schemas; bundle this into a *.zip* file; and deploy it to the JBI container. Once that's done, your BPEL SE is installed and you are able to accept requests bound to a WSDL that ultimately will be routed to the BPEL engine, and execute the *.bpel* file inside that SE.

The JBI runtime hosts SEs, which in turn host service units to provide business logic, processing, and transformation. There are a number of SEs available for download that

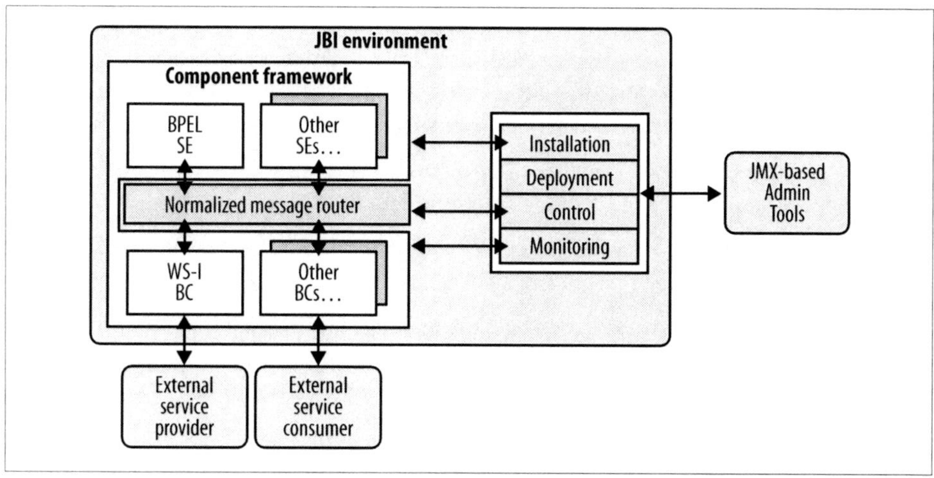

Figure 14-2. The JBI high-level architecture, as shown in the JBI 1.0 specification

you can plug into your JBI-compliant bus. These include SEs for XSLT, scheduling, SQL, and Camel.

Binding components

Binding components (BCs) offer protocol independence, which represents the power of JBI to help SOA-enable your enterprise. They provide transport protocols (and other communication-based protocols such as those for talking to flat files) for external services to use. They act as a proxy for services deployed in the JBI runtime that require a particular protocol.

A binding component converts a message that is bound to a specific protocol or transport into the normalized form. Both BCs and SEs create a "delivery channel" to the normalized message router. A BC is generally used to enable the pluggability of an external protocol or format. For example, you use a BPEL SE to execute a BPEL engine because the message format BPEL requires is XML. The JBI runtime doesn't have to do anything special to convert an XML instance message coming into the bus as SOAP/HTTP because that's what a BPEL process instance expects.

But if you need to do some conversion based on the protocol or transport of the message, you may need to employ a BC. BCs exist for File, LDAP, JMS, HTTP, JDBC, CICS, DCOM, CORBA, XMPP, and more. These protocols require specific message formats, and that's why there are BCs for them. You can download these BCs for free from either the OpenESB or ServiceMix websites and then plug them into your bus to enable your message exchange using one of these protocols.

Normalized message router

The normalized message router (NMR) mediates the message exchange between SEs and BCs within the framework. The NMR is at the heart of the bus and allows services to interoperate by passing messages between all of the components in the system. The message route is determined by the NMR, and the normalized message is translated into the format for the specific BC that is being invoked. SEs and BCs all communicate with the NMR via a pipe called a *delivery channel*.

A normalized message itself consists of two parts: the abstract XML message and the message metadata, also called message context data.

The abstract message defines the structure and constraints for valid messages, written in XML schema, as represented in the abstract message type in a WSDL.

The second part of a normalized message, the message context data, allows plug-in and system components to provide additional information about a message during its processing. This information might include the following kinds of items:

- Security tokens provided by SAML or another mechanism
- Context information provided by a given protocol, such as a path
- Transaction management information
- Data from other components

The NMR is bidirectional, so it is used to send requests and responses.

JBI runtime environment

The JBI runtime encompasses all of the above—it includes SEs, BCs, the NMR, and a framework allowing for deployment, management, monitoring, and installation.

The Case Against JBI

As Java developers, we're used to vendors implementing Sun specifications for Java-based technologies, and for this reason, it's easy to be inclined to look for an ESB that implements JBI. In fact, the Expert Group contributing to the specification includes a long list of organizations, including:

- Members of the Apache Software Foundation
- Borland
- Cap Gemini
- Fujitsu
- IONA
- JBoss
- Intalio
- Novell
- Nokia
- Oracle
- SAP AG

- Sonic Software
- Sun Microsystems
- Sybase
- TIBCO
- Vignette
- WebMethods

And this is only a partial list. Such a broad and diverse set of companies coming together in 2004 and 2005 to support the creation of JBI might suggest that JBI would go on to become the primary means of representing an enterprise service bus. Things did not quite turn out that way, however.

In reality, by 2009, few commercial vendors support the JBI spec as the centerpiece of their ESBs. There are a variety of reasons for this. One is that some vendors realized that they could spruce up and re-package EAI offerings that they already had implemented. By tying together a set of connectors and adapters they had previously developed, they could breathe new life (and new sales) into existing products.

But in contrast to something like Java application servers, the industry was not just waiting for Sun to come out with a specification for ESB. They had their own ideas about what ESB could and should mean, and they were free to implement it however they saw fit. This has led, in part, to less support for JBI than a Java developer might imagine. In addition to this, the benefit of being able to port a service engine or binding component as a pluggable object from one JBI container to another is not entirely clear. Presumably, the vendor that develops the engine will see the best return on investment by optimizing performance and adding features that rely on intimate knowledge of the underlying container. That has played out in the market, where each vendor that implements JBI actually does all of the work of implementing their own SEs and BCs for HTTP, FTP, JMS, File, BPEL, and so on. Because of this, the barrier for developing an ESB based on the JBI specification is set rather high for vendors, and given the lack of clarity as to what benefit they receive from making their SEs and BCs portable, vendors have been reluctant to implement JBI.

In addition, there is a practical limitation in that JBI expects all service contracts to be WSDLs. This does not account for WADL contracts, which may become popular for POX/HTTP, or for straight Java.

The complete list of BCs and SEs for OpenESB is available at *https://open-esb.dev.java.net/Components.html*.

JBI also has some problems with its classloader and packaging architecture, such that the ServiceMix project is adding support for OSGi in order to make it easier to work with. Deploying to a JBI meta-container can require lots of files that are rather opaque.

Finally, because the normalized message router in a JBI container specifies that the message format must be XML, some have objected to the fact that this transformation produces unnecessary overhead for non-XML based messages. JBI also does not allow for streaming data within the NMR, adding further to the processing overhead in certain cases. It's worth noting, however, that XML is used as the basis for many commercial normalized messages internal to the bus, including products such as TIBCO's ActiveMatrix.

That having been said, there are good implementations of JBI out there. However, these do not always turn out to be the most popular ESBs in production use today, regardless of whether they are open source or commercial products.

JBI is definitely something worth looking at in an ESB and something you'll benefit from knowing about. It can be a smart strategy to start building your SOA with free and open source tools during your investigation period and then graduate to a more robust, performant, and stable ESB once SOA gains traction in your organization. That means that you'll have at least one migration effort moving from the pilot to the new platform, and this will be an easier task if you've stuck with standards.

Time will tell if JBI comes to be viewed as making important enough distinctions that it gains popularity. Perhaps JBI 2.0 will help it make more inroads.

14.4 Commercial ESBs

In this section, we'll examine a variety of ESB products. These products do much of what the open source products do and generally add features around ease of use, integration with other products on their platforms (such as IDEs or repositories), and of course performance and reliability claims. In many cases, they are not cheap; some of the ESBs in Gartner's magic quadrant can run more than $75,000 per processor.

Some of the leading ESBs on the market include the following:

- IBM WebSphere ESB and DataPower.
- Sonic ESB. They were one of the first in the business, and their chief technology evangelist is David Chappell, author of *Enterprise Service Bus* (O'Reilly) (*http://oreilly.com/catalog/9780596006754*).
- TIBCO BusinessWorks and ActiveMatrix Grid.
- Cape Clear. They offer two versions of their ESB, one that is standalone and another that can be integrated with IBM WebSphere.

- iWay Software. This New York-based software company offers an adapter-based ESB that is capable of wrapping IBM CICS, Tuxedo, and .NET applications natively.

At this point, because ESBs can differ in functionality and features more than, say, the application servers we might be used to, let's look at a few of the large stack vendor's ESB products to see what differentiates them.

Oracle Service Bus

BEA released AquaLogic Service Bus 3.0 in late 2007. After Oracle bought BEA in the middle of 2008, the bus was rebranded to Oracle Service Bus (OSB) 10.3. Before Oracle purchased BEA, it sold an ESB of its own called Oracle Enterprise Service Bus. The current statements from Oracle indicate that product will continue to be supported, but will not be the "strategic" ESB that Oracle will promote going forward.

OSB differentiating features

Oracle Service Bus is available as a free 875 MB download from Oracle's website (*http://www.oracle.com*). It has a number of features that differentiate it from other service buses on the market, including open source ESBs. Let's briefly look at them here:

WorkSpace Studio
: Along with the bus itself, you can get a development environment based on Eclipse called Oracle Service Bus WorkSpace Studio. OSB has a number of features that differentiate it from other ESBs on the market. The Studio allows you to view resources on the OSB through the navigator window. This supports the creation of composite service development and design-time transparency, as well as Service Component Architecture. Using this feature requires the Oracle Enterprise Repository to store your SOA artifacts.

  Many free and open source ESBs require that you write XML descriptors or Java classes by hand to create your integration logic. Using a graphical interface to create your routes and save them to the central repository with a click is a real time saver and reduces maintenance overhead.

Endpoint failover
: Just as WebLogic and other containers pool EJBs, the OSB can pool service instances. If a particular service endpoint is unavailable due to a network or component failure, the bus can reroute requests for a given URI to another instance. The bus will take the endpoint URI offline while it is having problems, and then automatically resume sending it requests once it is back online. This has the net effect of service endpoint failover, supported by the service pool.

Transport optimization
: If you are familiar with the WebLogic application server, you may recall that there is an option to allow the container to treat remote EJBs that are collocated in the same JVM as the invoker as if they were local EJBs. This performance optimization

avoids expensive RMI calls. The OSB builds on this technology so that invocations made within the same machine can use a transport optimization mechanism to forego expensive serialization that isn't required in such cases.

WS-ReliableMessaging support

The OASIS WS-RM specification, covered earlier in this book, is supported within the OSB. The technology used to support WS-RM in WebLogic 10gR3 is reused here. In the case of WebLogic and OSB, the WS-RM support is robust. It supports not only replay of messages that are not acknowledged due to transport failure (which is all the Glassfish implementation supports) but also replay following a client or server crash.

OSB divides the world into two types of services: proxy services and business services. A proxy service is exposed to the client as a thin wrapper around your service implementation, which provides location transparency and an opportunity to inject various abilities such as security, transformation, and so forth. A business service is metadata around an existing service external to the bus. The design tool performs introspection of the external service for you, so that you can quickly start working with it to create a pipeline. Figure 14-3 shows an "Any XML" proxy service with an error handler being created in the WorkSpace Studio.

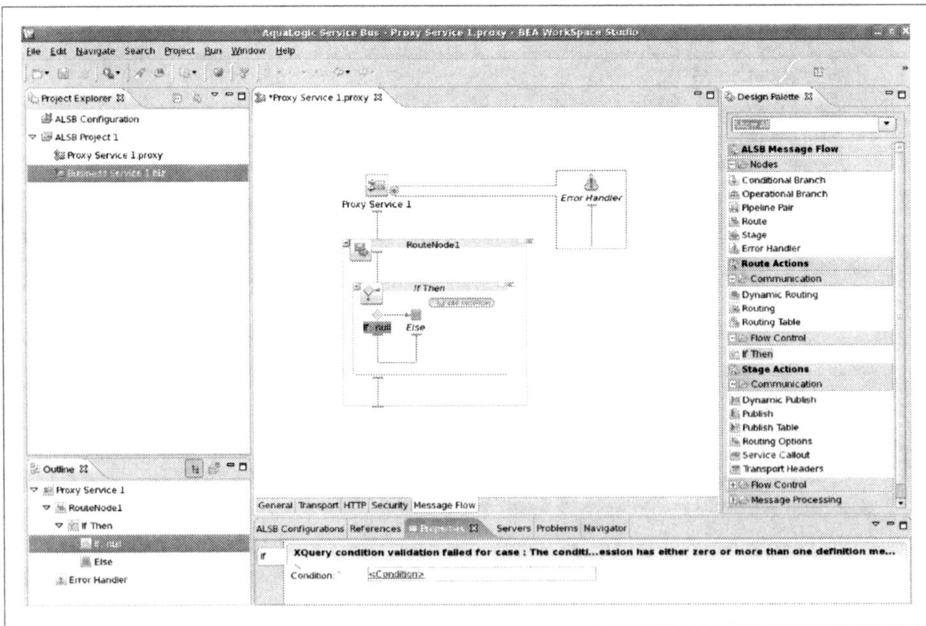

Figure 14-3. Building a route in Oracle WorkSpace Studio

The Oracle Service Bus uses SOAP as its internal canonical message format, so even when you send a non-SOAP message to the bus, it will be transformed into SOAP so that you can use XQuery and XPath in a standardized way through the interface.

Monitoring and service-level agreements

OSB also allows you to define SLAs and apply them at runtime to the messages flowing through the bus. For example, you might define an SLA to indicate that Gold Members must receive a response within 0.7 seconds, whereas Silver Members must receive a response within 1.5 seconds. Another SLA can indicate that a response of greater than 3 seconds represents a failure, and should be routed to what is called the Alert Destination (which could be an email address, JMS queue, SNMP trap, and so forth).

To create an SLA, you create an alert rule (indicating the conditions under which the bus should signal an SLA violation for a message flow) and a destination.

This feature not only alerts you of failures, but it also allows you to prevent failures by identifying when the system is starting to reach a performance limitation. Alerts can be specific to a single operation within a service or to the entire service. OSB ships with a set of alerts to get you started out of the box, and you can create your own custom alerts.

Reporting

OSB also allows you to generate graphical reports based on the status of SLAs within your system. These reports are based on near-time data collected by the bus, and allow you to search, sort, and filter based on service name, date ranges, and error codes, as you would expect.

Security

While the security available in OSB is robust, it is tightly integrated with the WebLogic application server. It allows for message- and transport-level security. One nice feature of OSB is that you are provided with a set of commonly used WS-Policy XML files that you can link with your service using a single line of code. You can also link your security policy using an arbitrary HTTP URL within your service bus project.

OSB steers you toward its proprietary security mechanisms. The Web Services Security Policy (WSSP) specification is relatively new and is supported by WebLogic 10. However, OSB supports features from WSSP 1.2 only at the transport level, not at the message level.

Supported specifications

The Oracle SOA stack supports a variety of specifications and other standards, including the following:

- WS-Policy
- WS-ReliableMessaging
- XACML
- WS-Addressing
- SCA

- XPDL
- SAML
- PKI

It does not implement JBI, BPEL4People, or WS-HumanTask. If you want to create business processes that allow both automation of service calls as well as human tasks, take a look at its BPM suite.

Software AG/webMethods ESB

In 2007 the German company Software AG bought webMethods. It offers a BPMS (Business Process Management Suite) that represents its SOA stack, and at the center of it is its ESB, the webMethods Enterprise Service Bus.

Differentiating features

The webMethods ESB does not require an application server, but it does extend the Java EE capabilities of the platform by running on top of the JBoss container. Its differentiating features are as follows:

Bidirectional Java invocation
: The webMethods platform includes functionality that allows you to directly invoke EJB methods running in another application server, but it also allows application servers to invoke logic running within the webMethods integration platform. The platform supports the same bidirectional functionality for JMS.

JCA-based adapters
: The Java Connector Architecture (JCA) has been popular for several years as a standard mechanism for using Java to connect to legacy systems and packaged apps. JCA is to such apps what JDBC is to relational databases. The webMethods implementation uses JCA, and you can take advantage of this fact if you have existing JCA-based adapters.

Reliability
: The ESB and integration server supports clustering and failover. The bus maintains session information so that a request can be failed over to another node and continue processing transparently.

Robust rules support
: The business rules implementations in some ESBs are fairly limited. The webMethods strategy is to incorporate the Fair Isaac (creators of FICA scores everywhere) Blaze Advisor Rules Engine (see Figure 14-4).

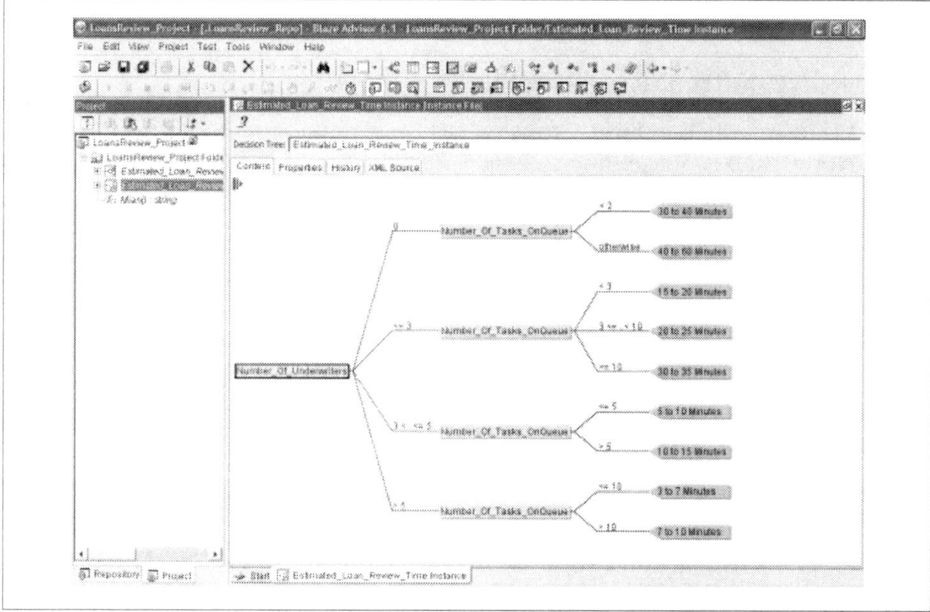

Figure 14-4. The Fair Isaac Blaze Advisor Rules Engine showing the standard Loan Application decision tree in Software AG's design tool

Supported specifications

Software AG's SOA suite (ESB and BPM runtimes) claims support for a wide array of WS-* specifications among commercial vendors. The following are supported in the current general release version of webMethods ESB and CentraSite registry/repository:

- WS-MetadataExchange (Software AG coauthored the specification)
- WS-Transaction (a collection of three specifications: WS-Coordination, WS-AtomicTransaction, and WS-BusinessActivity)
- WS-Security
- WS-SecurityPolicy
- WS-SecureConversation
- WS-Policy
- WS-PolicyAttachment
- WS-Federation (which allows different security realms to federate by brokering trust of identities, attributes, and authentication between participating services)
- SCA
- BPEL, BPEL4People, and WS-HumanTask
- SAML and XACML

- PKI

TIBCO ActiveMatrix and BusinessWorks

TIBCO (The Information Bus COmpany) has been around for more than 20 years in various forms, and its integration story goes back for most of this time. Its integration products are well known and popular, and companies such as Delta, Lockheed Marin, Lufthansa, MLB, Qualcomm, Reuters, Seagate, and more use them.

TIBCO's ESB is ActiveMatrix Service Bus, which allows you to develop, manage, and monitor web services in Java and .NET. BusinessWorks is a related product that handles orchestration of web services, employing SOAP/HTTP or SOAP/JMS.

ActiveMatrix ESB uses a grid-based architecture, which allows you to scale both up and out dynamically at runtime and on commodity hardware.

Event framework

The primary idea that distinguishes TIBCO's ESB from other implementations is that it is built on an eventing framework. In JBI-based ESBs, messages enter the bus and are sent via a delivery channel to the normalized message router for immediate delivery to one of the other components defined in the service unit.

But in TIBCO's ESB (which does not implement JBI), messages instead enter an "event cloud," which is essentially a database that stores message state, allowing for message fragments to be used within an event framework. This allows for a very loosely coupled runtime.

Grid-based architecture

The grid-based architecture featured in TIBCO's ESB means that you can use commodity hardware but still enjoy reliability, recoverability, and self-healing via other nodes on the grid.

The ESB can also be clustered and load-balanced, and it does not require an application server to run.

Supported specifications

TIBCO sits on the committees for many WS-* specifications. They have coauthored or cosponsored a sizeable number of the specs, and this is reflected in their products:

- WS-ReliableMessaging (TIBCO is a coauthor of the standard, with BEA, Microsoft, and IBM)
- WS-Eventing
- WS-Addressing
- WS-Transfer

- WS-Enumeration
- WS-Security (supported through TIBCO Policy Manager)
- WS-Policy
- X.509
- UDDI v3
- SAML
- PKI
- BPEL (full support for 1.1, some 2.0 support in their BusinessWorks product)
- SCA

TIBCO's ESB does not support BPEL4People or WS-HumanTask for workflows that involve people and not just automated systems processes. For that, you need its BPM product.

14.5 Open Source ESBs

There are a number of open source ESBs available now, including OpenESB from Sun, Mule ESB from MuleSource, and Apache ServiceMix. These have some key differences, which we'll explore in the following sections.

Mule

Mule is one of the most popular open source ESBs, in use at organizations such as Wal-Mart and MLB, and with more than 2,000 users in production. It was started as a project in 2001 by Ross Mason, and is now available from *http://www.mulesource.org*. The ESB is free and open source, but the company MuleSource, started in 2006, also offers a commercial version called Mule Enterprise. In a business model similar to that of JBoss, the company offers subscriptions, educational services, and consulting around its product.

The implementation of Mule is based on the book *Enterprise Integration Patterns* by Gregor Hohpe and Bobby Woolf. The patterns in that book form the basis for the Mule framework and capabilities. As such, the bus provides the standard set of features that one would expect from an ESB, including routing, transformation, and message management.

Basic usage

In the Mule documentation, you may see reference to the term UMO, which stands for Universal Message Object. This term is deprecated in favor of the more recent Service Object (though you will still see UMO classes in the code base). A Service Object manages component events as well as pooled resources. It is carried between components over a transport, which is one of the available mechanisms for data exchange. A wide variety of popular transports are available.

Transports are made available via transport providers, which implement a message receiver or dispatcher. This connects to a protocol and offers an opportunity for the developer to also implement an optional Transformer. A Transformer converts a Service Object from one protocol format to another (for example, an inbound SOAP message can be transformed to a Java object for a subsequent RMI invocation).

In Mule, one application connects to another by implementing a set of related components. An application makes uses of a channel within a connector. The connector sends the message to an inbound router that is known to the Service Object, which then manages the route bound out of the bus to the backend application using another router and another connector over an appropriate channel. As with many other ESBs, this setup does not require the developer to modify any of the application resources used from the bus.

Message transformation can also be accomplished with the recent addition of the Smooks transformation engine. It is a Java framework for performing a wide range of data transformations, including XML to EDI, CSV, Java, and more. You can process large messages and can split, transform, and route message fragments to JMS, File, or database destinations.

Mule is nonintrusive, meaning that classes that you implement to perform some function don't have to import any Mule-specific libraries. Once you have written a component that does some work for you, you need to tell Mule about it. Similar to Spring, Mule configuration is done using XML files that describe the inbound and outbound routes for components. The Mule configuration file is shown in Example 14-1.

Example 14-1. mule-config.xml

```
<mule xmlns="http://www.mulesource.org/schema/mule/core/2.0"
  xmlns:xsi="http://www.w3.org/2001/XMLSchema-instance"
  xmlns:stdio="http://www.mulesource.org/schema/mule/stdio/2.0"
  xsi:schemaLocation="http://www.mulesource.org/schema/mule/core/2.0
      http://www.mulesource.org/schema/mule/core/2.0/mule.xsd
    http://www.mulesource.org/schema/mule/stdio/2.0
      http://www.mulesource.org/schema/mule/stdio/2.0/mule-stdio.xsd">

  <stdio:connector name="inConnector" promptMessage="Your Message: "/>

  <model name="HelloWorld">
    <service name="HelloComponent">

      <inbound>
        <stdio:inbound-endpoint system="IN" connector-ref="inConnector"/>
      </inbound>

      <component class="com.soacookbook.HelloComponent"/>

    </service>
```

```
  </model>
</mule>
```

This is about as simple as a Mule configuration file can get. The standard I/O connector (`stdio`) is used here to accept input from a console, as indicated by the `<connector>` element. The connector declares that it uses System In, and that will be used as a router for the inbound message. `HelloComponent` is a class that you could write to log or echo the statement made by the end user; that class is indicated with the `<component>` element. The `<service>` element combines the inbound message with the component class that does something with it. Mule can attempt to determine the appropriate method to call using reflection based on the payload of the message.

To execute this new service, you would create a JAR file that contains the component class and this configuration file and then put that JAR in Mule's *lib/user* directory so that it's available on the classpath when Mule starts.

If you want to create a transformer for a message flow, you would write a class that extends `org.mule.transformer.AbstractTransformer`, and then point to this class in the `<inbound>` or `<outbound>` route of the `<service>` in *mule-config.xml*.

Obviously, the point here is not to give you a Mule tutorial; I'm only trying to illustrate what the programming model is like so that you'll have an idea of how your days will be spent if you use Mule. In short, you'll be writing Java code and XML to do the hookups, and you'll need to code directly against the Mule API.

MuleForge

Mule is popular and has many of the basic features of a commercial ESB, but it doesn't come in a slick package or have a particularly friendly interface. Instead of dragging and dropping to create a new route, developers must write against the API directly. The website's documentation is slight, but developers are encouraged to check out the MuleForge community site at *http://www.muleforge.org*.

MuleForge hosts a wide array of developer projects that support different transports (including Hibernate, Hl7, JIRA, JXTA, TIBCO Rendezvous, and others). Developers contribute visualizers, dashboards, and other items to enhance the Mule development experience. At this point, many of these projects are simply proposals, or are in an alpha or pre-alpha stage.

Supported transports

Mule also supports a wide variety of transports, including the following:

- JMS
- File
- FTP
- HTTP/S

- IMAP
- JDBC
- SOAP
- POP3
- Remote EJB
- RMI
- SMTP
- UDP
- XMPP
- AS400 Data Queues

In general, Mule is intended as a framework that takes advantage of and integrates with popular open source products, in a manner similar to Spring. That is, instead of reinventing the timer wheel, for example, Mule just lets you point to Quartz for job scheduling.

Deployment options

Mule can be deployed as a standalone Java application, or it can be executed within a web container or application server. Mule supports a variety of application servers such as Tomcat, WebLogic, WebSphere, JBoss, and Jetty.

Mule IDE

Like commercial vendors, MuleSource offers an IDE to assist with building its connectors.

SOA governance and management with Mule

In addition to its ESB, the company offers a product called Mule Galaxy, which it touts as its SOA governance platform. Galaxy offers the following features:

- Policy enforcement
- User-defineable life cycle and workflow
- Metadata storage (schemas, WSDLs, JARs, Mule configuration files, etc.)
- Version management and control
- Publishing, indexing, and discovery services (publishing is supported with Atom Publishing Protocol, and queries are supported with XQuery, XPath, OpenSearch, Groovy, and their web console)
- Centralized application management and reporting

The Galaxy product is relatively new, and it provides a basic set of functions for managing the life cycle of your services. But it doesn't come close to commercial offerings in terms of supporting real-time graphical dependency maps between service resources, and design-time contract violation detection. In addition, its reporting capabilities are limited. However, this product is likely to grow more robust in the months to come, and it's worth watching.

Apache ServiceMix

Apache ServiceMix is the most popular open source implementation of the JBI 1.0 specification. Because it implements JBI, all messages within ServiceMix are serialized to XML, following the normal form defined by the container. Classes that you write to represent your integration logic in ServiceMix have a variety of dependencies on the ServiceMix framework.

The ServiceMix project is very active, and as of this writing, the project team is working to deliver ServiceMix 4, which will incorporate many of the features that are charted for the JBI 2.0 specification (even before it is released).

Extensibility

Like Mule, ServiceMix can be readily integrated with Spring. ServiceMix also uses OSGi, which offers another clear and simple way that the bus can provide extensibility to developers.

OSGi represents a framework that defines an application life cycle management model, a runtime environment, a service registry, and the idea of bundles and modules. A module represents a collection of declared dependencies, which hides its internals behind well-defined interfaces to encourage reuse and freedom to change.

OSGi is a specification of the OSGi Alliance, a nonprofit organization, which you can visit at *http://www.osgi.org*.

Deployment in ServiceMix

ServiceMix is somewhat less lightweight than Mule at deploy time. In order to deploy a simple class that represents some functionality you want to make available on the ESB, you need to create a service assembly (SA) that contains service units, following the JBI specification. You can use either Ant or Maven 2 to create the SAs for you. If you're using Maven 2, there are a great number of pre-existing project archetypes written specifically for ServiceMix that you can take advantage of. NetBeans 6 makes these readily available via the New Project wizard, as shown in Figure 14-5.

To deploy in a JBI environment such as ServiceMix, you need to create the *jbi.xml* file to represent your deployment. Visual development environments with JBI support will do this for you, generating the JBI XML file as you drag and drop components. As we're used to with Sun specifications, the *jbi.xml* file is the standard descriptor that every

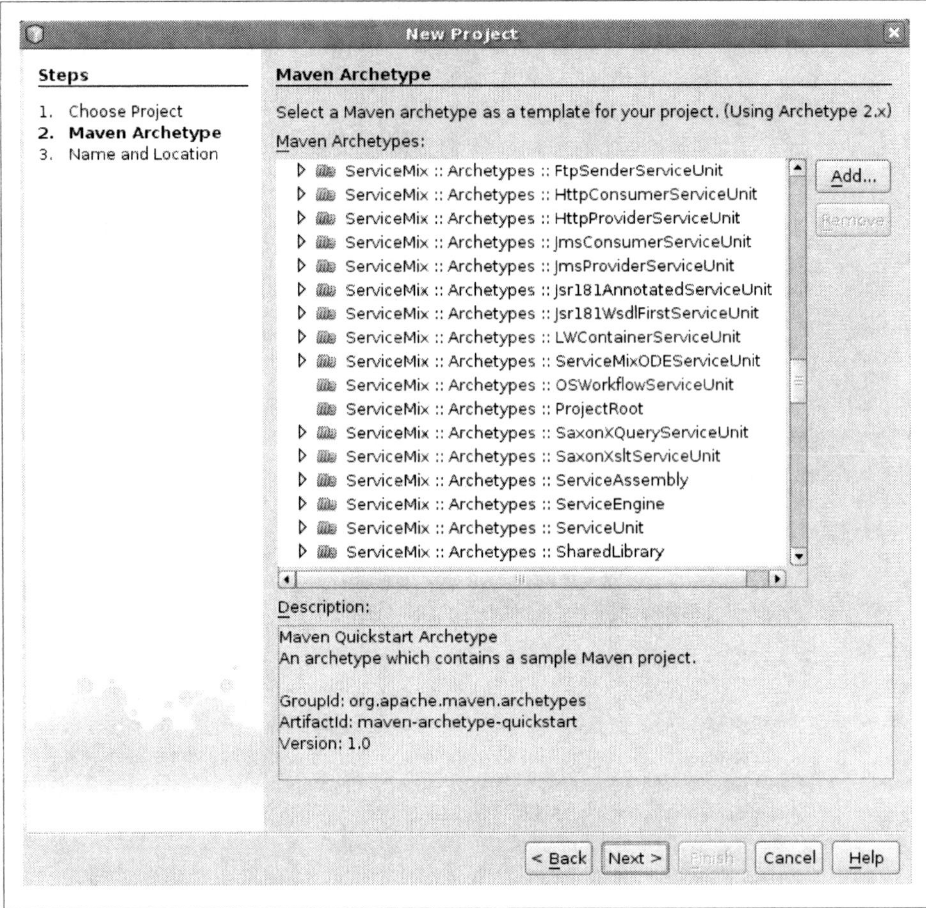

Figure 14-5. The NetBeans 6 New Project wizard makes available lots of different ServiceMix projects to jumpstart your development and deployment

container must support, and vendors can then present their own specific files to support deployment. In the case of ServiceMix, you create *xbean.xml* files.

A very short *jbi.xml* looks like this:

```
<?xml version="1.0" encoding="UTF-8" standalone="no"?>

<jbi xmlns="http://java.sun.com/xml/ns/jbi" version="1.0"
  xmlns:ns0="http://soacookbook/lookup"
  xmlns:esb="http://soacookbook/esb/customerScreen"
  xmlns:ws="http://soacookbook/ws/customerScreen">

<services binding-component="false">
  <provides endpoint-name="LookupEsbPortTypeRole_myRole"
    interface-name="esb:LookupPreApprovePortType"
    service-name="ns0:LookupEsb"/>
```

```
    <consumes endpoint-name="LookupRole_partnerRole"
      interface-name="ws:Lookup"
      service-name="ns0:LookupPartner"/>
  </services>

  </jbi>
```

That's about as simple a standard deployment file as you can have with JBI.

OpenESB

OpenESB v2 was released in late 2007 and implements JBI 1.0 as its reference implementation. It was a written by members of the Sun technical staff and contributed to by members of the larger development community. It is actually somewhat rare to find OpenESB in production in organizations of any size.

But if you use NetBeans as your development environment and want to check out an ESB, OpenESB is by far the easiest way to go. NetBeans has very robust graphical support for OpenESB. You can drag and drop service definitions to create service compositions, generating the JBI XML and other deployment descriptors behind the scenes. No other ESB has integration like this for NetBeans.

GlassfishESB is a binary distribution of a subset of OpenESB that packages OpenESB into a commercially supported product. It combines NetBeans, Glassfish Application Server, and OpenESB into a single download.

However, if you use the more popular Eclipse IDE, you are going to find working with OpenESB arduous, and you'll have to write all of that tedious XML by hand. At the time of this writing, I'm not aware of any OpenESB Maven 2 archetypes.

Though it is tightly integrated with Glassfish 9.1, OpenESB will run on JBoss, on WebSphere, or as a standalone application on a bare JVM. The bus running in standalone mode has a very small footprint, and starts up very quickly.

Monitoring OpenESB

As with many other open source ESBs, there is no graphical monitoring console for OpenESB. For visibility into the SOA backbone where all of your messages are exchanged, it is important to have that sense of closeness and control over the bus as it is running. This is one obvious place where many commercial products really excel over their open source counterparts.

However, there is a new project forming alongside OpenESB called ESB Console, which wil offer a pluggable web-based management console for OpenESB. It is available at *https://esb-console.dev.java.net*.

Project Fuji

The roadmap for OpenESB is called Project Fuji. This is essentially OpenESB version 3. Like ServiceMix version 4, Fuji is based on both JBI and OSGi. Fuji itself will be packaged as an OSGi bundle and installed as a micro-kernel into any OSGi-compliant runtime. That means you'll be able to run the container within Apache Felix, Knopflerfish, or Eclipse Equinox without an application server.

Fuji also introduces a new rapid development language called IFL (Integration Flow Language). IFL is essentially a domain-specific language for creating the routes and integration points necessary within an ESB. This could turn out to be a smart choice, as it addresses the disadvantages in current ESB development models: ESBs all seem to require lots of boilerplate code written against their API. If the Fuji development model is successful, and the convention and configuration model is as easy to use as it is in a tool like Maven 2, it could lead to a more developer-friendly product that meets with some success.

Summary

An ESB is an important part of a balanced SOA breakfast. I really encourage you to take a look at what's available and strongly consider incorporating an ESB into your SOA strategy. Not only will this help you avoid service-to-service integration issues in the future, but the ESB will serve as a central point of management for your entire SOA infrastructure, including registry/repository, rules engines, Business Activity Monitoring, connectors and adapters to legacy systems and packaged applications, orchestration engines, and Business Process Management solutions.

If you're working on web services in a strategic rather than a purely tactical manner, developing applications that invoke remote systems in diverse languages, and need to integrate a variety of systems to present a single unified interface, taking a close look at the ESBs on the market and in the rich world of open source will help you realize a world of benefits.

Creating web services is only the beginning of implementing a SOA. The second step is to incorporate an ESB, which will give you the foundation to grow in other important directions.

Index

A

We'd like to hear your suggestions for improving our indexes. Send email to *index@oreilly.com*.

B

C

D

E

F

G

H

I

K

L

M

N

O

P

Q

R

S

W

X

Z

X

Z

About the Author

Eben Hewitt is a technical architect at a multibillion dollar national retail company, where he has been focused on designing and building its SOA. He has 10 years of experience in IT and holds several industry certifications, including Sun Certified Java Web Services Developer for EE 5. Eben has been a popular speaker on SOA at JavaOne and is the author of four previous programming books and several industry articles. Most recently, he contributed to O'Reilly's *97 Things Every Software Architect Should Know*, edited by Richard Monson-Haefel (*http://oreilly.com/catalog/9780596522698*).

Colophon

The animal on the cover of *Java SOA Cookbook* is a harlequin longhorn beetle (*Macrodontia cervicornis*). Ranging from Mexico to South America, harlequin longhorn beetles are one of the world's longest beetles. They belong to the long-horned beetle family, *Cerambycidae*. There are various members of this family, with over 20,000 species, slightly more than half from the Eastern Hemisphere. This beautiful beetle is a popular pet for Amazon children.

They are characterized by extremely long antennae and legs, which are often as long as or longer than their bodies. A male's forelegs can measure nearly 3 inches. The beetle itself can be as long as 8 inches—bigger than a man's hand! In addition to serving as a sexual enticement to females, the long legs help the males fly and crawl from branch to branch. Despite their conspicuous colors, they are able to hide themselves effectively among the lichen- and fungus-covered trunks of tropical woods such as fig trees.

Harlequin beetles are active during the day but can be attracted to lights at night. Females prefer to lay their eggs on trunks and logs with bracket fungus, which provides excellent camouflage. Before laying, the female gnaws an incision about 0.8 inch wide and 0.3 inch deep in the bark. She will lay 15 to 20 eggs over the course of two to three days. When the larvae hatch, they bore into the wood. When they mature at seven to eight months, the 5-inch larvae tunnel further, where they dig a cell in which to mature. The adult beetle emerges four months later, gnawing its way out of the wood. The life cycle is annual.

The beetle's body often hosts a species of tiny arachnids known as pseudoscorpions, which live beneath the harlequin's colorful wing covers. These tiny scorpions use the beetle for transport to new food sources and as a way to meet potential mates. To keep from falling off when the beetle flies, they attach themselves to the harlequin's abdomen with silken threads spun from pincher-like glands in their claws. When they arrive at a suitable new site, they anchor to their destination with a new strand of silk and slide off the beetle.

The cover image is from Dover Pictorial Archive. The cover font is Adobe ITC Garamond. The text font is Linotype Birka; the heading font is Adobe Myriad Condensed; and the code font is LucasFont's TheSansMonoCondensed.

CPSIA information can be obtained at www.ICGtesting.com
Printed in the USA
BVOW060323200911

271677BV00005B/87-102/P